FOREIGN POLICY IN WORLD POLITICS

FOREIGN

AUTHORS

VERNON V. ASPATURIAN, Pennsylvania State University

GEORGE I. BLANKSTEN, Northwestern University

KARL W. DEUTSCH, Yale University

LEWIS J. EDINGER, Michigan State University

LEON D. EPSTEIN, University of Wisconsin

ROY C. MACRIDIS, Washington University

HANS J. MORGENTHAU, University of Chicago

RICHARD L. PARK, The University of Michigan

ROBERT A. SCALAPINO, University of California, Berkeley

KENNETH W. THOMPSON, Rockefeller Foundation, New York

P. J. VATIKIOTIS, Indiana University

ALLEN S. WHITING, The Rand Corporation

POLICY IN WORLD POLITICS

. . . ROY C. MACRIDIS, editor

SECOND EDITION • 1962

PRENTICE-HALL, INC., Englewood Cliffs, N. J.

First Edition

First printing ....April, 1958
Second printing ....May, 1959

Second Edition

Third printing ....January, 1962

Printed in the United States of America
32640–C

Preface to the Second Edition

When the first edition of this volume appeared in the spring of 1958, we had no way of knowing that it would be received as well as it was. We knew that we were involved in subject matter that was new, and all that we could hope for was to give to the student and the teacher supplementary material for courses in comparative government and international relations.

This second, revised, edition is now being presented with the assurance that at the level of research and at the level of college instruction there is a deep concern with the comparative study of foreign policy. We feel more than gratified, and we hope that other volumes will appear to supplement and improve our efforts.

This second edition is richer than the first in coverage and more systematic in its approach. The student will find a comprehensive introductory chapter, new chapters on India and Egypt, and a drastically overhauled and updated chapter on French foreign policy. He will also find a new chapter on the processes and objectives of American foreign policy.

Again, as with our first edition, it is our hope that the volume will serve as an introduction to the recently developed courses in comparative foreign policy and that it will continue to be a useful supplement to the study of comparative government and international relations. My deepest thanks for help and cooperation again go to all the contributors and to Al Goodyear and his staff at Prentice-Hall.

R. C. M.

St. Louis

Preface to the First Edition

The study of comparative government has dealt traditionally with the parallel descriptive analysis of the political institutions and processes of individual countries, with particular reference to domestic politics. At the same time, the study of international relations has been primarily concerned with relations between states—power relations, ideological conflicts, and the resolution of conflicts through treaties, various international organizations, and, ultimately, war. Thus the study of one of the most significant aspects of policy— foreign policy— has remained in something like a no man's land. Comparative government texts usually ignore it and international relations texts assume a knowledge both of the processes through which foreign policy is made in various countries and of its substance, that the student rarely possesses. It is the purpose of this volume, at a somewhat modest level, to attempt to fill this gap in our approach to both comparative government and international relations and to provide the missing link that should logically connect the two fields of our discipline. This link is the comparative study of foreign policy-making and of the foreign policies of various countries.

It was not our purpose to develop a general theory in which the complexity of our material could be conveniently "fitted in." Given the state of political science today many of the recent efforts made to develop comprehensive theories and conceptual schemes have become Procrustean beds, and the subject treated emerges sometimes without any feet to stand on and more often without a head and sense. Our purpose is simply to study the foreign policy of a number of political systems and thus to supplement our existing knowledge, and to show the characteristics of foreign policy both in terms of the contextual elements of a given political system and in terms of the existing balance of international relations. The one naturally affects the other.

It is regretted that a projected section on the foreign policy of India by Professor Richard L. Park of the University of California could not be included in this edition because of its author's illness. The omission will be rectified in a future edition.

Much of the credit for this publication goes to Mr. Donald Hammonds of Prentice-Hall. It was in part his idea and he followed the project with interest and patience and gave to it his full support whenever any difficulties emerged. Professor Almond provided the outline that suggested a common approach and he and Dr. Kenneth Thompson of the Rockefeller Foundation read most of the chapters and made many helpful suggestions. I wish to thank both of them. But above all I wish to thank all the contributors for the good will and cooperation they showed every time I called upon them for modifications, reductions, additions, bibliographical references, and the like. The very fact that a symposium of this kind reached the stage of publication within a relatively short time is a tribute to their kindness and understanding.

Roy C. Macridis

Contents

vii

1

THE COMPARATIVE

STUDY

OF

FOREIGN

POLICY

TWO BASIC APPROACHES TO FOREIGN POLICY

Two approaches to foreign policy have vied with one another in Western thought at least since the days of the French Revolution. One is the *ideological* approach, according to which the policies of states vis-à-vis the rest of the world are merely expressions of prevailing political, social, and religious beliefs. In this approach, foreign policies are classified as democratic or totalitarian, libertarian or socialist, and peace-loving or aggressive. The second approach to foreign policy is *analytical*. At the heart of this viewpoint is the proposition that policy rests on multiple determinants, including the state's historic tradition, geographical location, national interest, and purposes and security needs. To understand foreign policy, the observer must take into account and analyze a host of factors.

The ideological approach

In the twentieth century it has been commonplace for critics to proclaim that the United States or Britain or France has no foreign policy or has been unfaithful to liberal or socialist or conservative principles, as the case may be. This is one way to think about foreign policy; to the present day it is perhaps the prevailing approach. Periodically the domestic

KENNETH W.

THOMPSON

and

ROY C. MACRIDIS

1

political arena rings with angry charges that a set of political leaders, a political party, or an administration is opportunistic and morally derelict to its political creed or ideology in foreign affairs. Governments are condemned for not supporting democracy or free enterprise or a particular social class everywhere around the world. This dominant approach views the conduct of foreign relations primarily in psychological terms; it looks to the motives or ideologies of leaders or governments as the essential if not the sole determinant of policy. It maintains that a democratic regime pursues one type of foreign policy, an autocratic government another, a communist government a third, and a democratic-socialist administration still another. There is a fairyland-like simplicity about this that makes it widely acceptable and easily understood. Foreign policy is considered a function of a political system in action or of the preferences or convictions of political leaders who carry out its programs.

The analytical approach

There is a second approach to foreign policy, however, which has at least as respectable a heritage. It was a ruling point of view throughout much of the eighteenth and nineteenth centuries, whether in doctrines of *raison d'état* or in broader historical interpretations, and it is being revived in our day by a handful of analysts and scholars.

Its renaissance is partly an outcome of the apparent shortcomings of the psychological or ideological approach, especially in accounting for present-day international developments. This approach has been shaken and discredited by inner contradictions and has faltered and failed in describing the continuities of objective and purpose in the policies of states. Regardless of the party in power or the leaders and their private or public philosophies, British and American and French and Russian foreign policies display unities that transcend individual beliefs or ideologies. In the early postwar period the Labor government in England, despite long-standing protests against Tory imperialism and power politics, turned inevitably to the protection—in Western Europe, in the countries of the British Commonwealth, in the Iberian Peninsula, and in the Near and Middle East—of substantially the selfsame interests that Tories and Whigs had considered vital for several centuries. In the United States, the Dulles-Eisenhower and the Kennedy-Rusk foreign policies have looked to the central goals with which the administrations of Roosevelt and Truman were concerned. The means or methods or techniques may have changed, but the interests and objectives have been relatively constant.

Therefore in a period of a little more than a decade the study of international relations has witnessed a reaction against the ideological approach. It should perhaps have been obvious that a conception in which foreign policy is nothing more than a by-product of domestic politics could hardly do justice to the elements of continuity in national policy. At some point recognition was needed that objective requirements of the national interest place certain irremovable limits upon any statesman seeking to formulate foreign policy. Regardless of the intentions, social philosophy, or religious outlook of individuals, there are broad strategic interests intimately bound up with a nation's geographic position and international role that must be safeguarded if its independence is to be preserved. Not only are these interests permanent for Bolsheviks as well as Tsars, but continuity also appears in the approach of a nation's statesmen, who stand guard over their country's security and whose conception of that security has been formed and molded by the same institutions and traditions. However intangible, the "national mind," which interprets the national interest, is itself a factor in the permanence of foreign policy. Out of the interplay of a durable international position with permanent traditions and institutions the larger nation-states have fashioned foreign policies which, in broadest outline, have been consistently maintained over long periods, even in the face of drastic changes on the domestic political scene.

According to this second approach, foreign policy demands of policy-makers choices and discriminations of a basic order. Not only are the interests of a nation permanent in character, but they range themselves in a hierarchy of greater and lesser interests. In a classic statement intended as a guide in the formulation of Belgium's foreign policy but with relevance for all foreign policy, Monsieur Paul-Henri Spaak observed:

There must be a hierarchy in international obligations. The nations of a continent cannot reasonably be asked to consider with the same realism and sincerity of judgment affairs which directly concern them and events which are taking place thousands of kilometres away in regions where they have neither interests nor influence.

Certain interests must be defended at all costs; others should be safeguarded under particular circumstances; and certain others, although desirable, can almost never be defended. It is the task of foreign policy, in the first instance, to determine its own hierarchy of interests and, next, to examine the scale of interests revealed in the principles or practice of other nations' foreign policies. Even when national leaders forswear the formulation of hierarchies of interests, the hard tests of practice often evoke underlying conceptions of vital interests. The United States' decision in World War II to bring the fighting to a successful conclusion in Europe and the North Atlantic before turning to destroy the enemy in the Pacific, or Britain's waiting, at the turn of the nineteenth century, until Poland was attacked and other nations were invaded before forming coalitions against Napoleon—these are examples of action in terms of a basic perception of interests.

The interests of states and their power to pursue their claims are of course immutable for any given historical period only in the sense that they set broad limits within which choices in foreign policy are made. They set the framework within which the domestic political contest over external policies must be waged. In the same way that no German political party today can afford to ignore the sometimes latent but ever-present demands for German reunification, no American government can take steps that would compromise the security of the Western Hemisphere. It is obvious that both power and interests can be made responsive to the forces of change. For example, a so-called "peace-loving" nation faced by emergent threats to its security can translate its resources into military power, its influence into foreign bases and real estate, and its industrial and military potential into forces in being. This has in effect been the trend of postwar American foreign policy. Or a state may suffer a loss in power as Britain did in World War II with the consequent need for revising its estimates of national interest. Technology can demand continuing reappraisals of national security and of the means of preserving it and may lead to changes in the ranking of the great powers. Britain may fall in the hierarchy of powers as other nations belatedly experience the industrial revolution, but it may recapture at least some of its vaunted supremacy in an era of atomic energy and hydrogen bombs. The existence of continuities in the foreign policies of states is admittedly more subject to debate in an era when one of the few certainties is the continual unrelenting pace of technological change.

Yet most students of international politics are persuaded that those recurrent patterns of the foreign policies of nations which most diplomatists appear to take for granted are amenable to study and analysis by the modern scholar. These patterns have been approached along several distinct if parallel lines. Scholars have engaged in more general studies of the geographical, industrial, and physical position of nations; the peculiar historical circumstances in which these conditions have operated; the actual adjustment of nations on the basis of their objective position to successive historical circumstances; and the claims and declarations made by statesmen engaged in pursuing a certain historic foreign policy. Obviously the intent of the studies in this volume is not to do basic research in any or all of these areas, but significantly and almost without exception each separate inquiry starts with an examination of some aspect of the objective patterns and conditions of foreign policy in the respective countries. At the same time, successive chapters go on to consider the role of ideology, of those changing institutions and domestic political factors which give to the policies of states that endless subtlety and richness that throws in question every simple generalization about the conduct of states. In effect, the theme of the book is one of continuity and change, of unities and coherences alongside the unique and particular in foreign relations. The authors, although wary of what Burckhardt described as "grand simplifications," are nevertheless compelled by their interests as political scientists to examine what can be said in general about foreign policy. This provides a unifying theme or central core of intellectual interests not everywhere made explicit but unquestionably at hand for those who seek understanding in this complex and fascinating realm.

THE ELEMENTS OF FOREIGN POLICY

The study of foreign policy, despite the two major approaches described above, provides no ready-made taxonomy or set of categories that can be applied to every nation. Perhaps even in the physical sciences the effort to uncover total systems, at least in these terms, is less fruitful than is sometimes imagined. In any event, there is marked diversity in the categories of analysis by which foreign policy has been studied in the present volume. To a considerable extent this results from differences in national context. For example, social stratification has implications for the making of foreign policy in Britain that it seems not to have in the Soviet Union, and the policy-making process in Britain has greater continuity and tradition even than the American system. A fortiori the newer states cannot point to the same political experience and diplomatic tradition in which the older nations can take pardonable pride. Despite these individual variations in the species, the nation-states whose policies are described have much in common. Their foreign policies are susceptible of analysis in terms of a check list of elements that exist and can be identified and that merge and comprise the bases of foreign policy.

The elements of foreign policy may be thought of in terms of concentric circles. At the center are certain elements that are more or less material in character. Some of these are relatively permanent, such as geography and natural resources. Others, like the economic, industrial, and military establishments, are more responsive to change and human manipulation. Then there are human factors, largely quantitative in the case of population, and qualitative as regards national character, social structure, national morale, political institutions and experience, and an effective tradition of diplomacy. From these elements and the instrumentalities of the policy-making process, the substance of foreign policy derives and major historic policies and the vital interests of countries emerge.

It may be worth at least passing mention that students of international politics have for the most part concentrated their attention on the elements of foreign policy. By contrast, writers on comparative politics have dealt more particularly with the policy-making process, including the influence of political parties, interest groups, effective political ideologies, and the peculiar executive-legislative relations in a country. The attempt has been made in the present volume to marry these two approaches and to combine the study of objective factors in foreign policy and the study of processes by which decisions are reached and policies implemented.

SIGNIFICANT FACTORS IN THE STUDY OF FOREIGN POLICY

THE ELEMENTS OF FOREIGN POLICY

A. The relatively permanent material elements
  1. Geography
  2. Natural resources
    a) Minerals
    b) Food production
    c) Energy and power
B. Less permanent material elements
  1. Industrial establishment
  2. Military establishment
  3. Changes in industrial and military capacity
C. The human elements: quantitative and qualitative
  1. Quantitative: population
  2. Qualitative
    a) Policy-makers and leaders
    b) The role of ideology
    c) The role of information

THE FOREIGN POLICY-MAKING PROCESS

A. The governmental agencies
  1. Executive (e.g., prime minister, relevant ministries, and inter-ministerial or interdepartmental organizations)
  2. Legislature (including relevant committees)
B. The nongovernmental agencies
  1. Political parties
  2. Interest groups
  3. Media of communication
  4. Characteristics of public opinion

TRENDS AND ISSUES

A. National purposes
  1. Peace as national purpose
  2. Security as national purpose
  3. Power as national purpose
  4. Prosperity and economic development as national purpose
B. Diplomacy
  1. Diplomatic practices
  2. The transformation of diplomatic practices
  3. The rediscovery of diplomacy
C. Democratic and totalitarian systems
D. The impact of the Cold War

The relatively permanent material elements

Geography. The more or less permanent elements of foreign policy obviously include geography, perhaps the most stable factor undergirding a nation's policies. It is not without significance that "except for Japan . . . Britain is the only major power of modern times to be based on an island rather than a sizeable continental area."[1] Its separation from the European continent by a narrow but strategic body of water, the English Channel, proved as decisive in frustrating the designs of Hitler and Napoleon as it had those of Julius Caesar or Philip II. No less an authority than Sir Eyre Crowe observed: "The general character of England's foreign policy is determined by the immutable conditions of her geographical situation on the ocean flank of Europe as an island State with vast oversea colonies and dependencies, whose existence and survival as an independent community are inseparably bound up with the possession of preponderant sea power."[2] This passage gives a clue to an important source of one of the most successful foreign policies in history. Going back to the fifteenth and sixteenth centuries, England, with but two exceptions, has neither been invaded nor defeated; and the exceptions—the American Revolution and the Afghan Wars—are hardly impressive evidence to challenge the importance of its geographic position. Even today England remains an island with what Winston S. Churchill described as three-fold commitments to Europe, the British Commonwealth, and the "New World." Historically and down to the present, it has striven to retain for itself sufficient freedom of action to harmonize its commitments

in each of these orbits, and only at points where they overlapped have new undertakings been possible. It is true that technology, through inventions like the airplane and submarine, has transformed the character of Britain's location, and there are signs that its interests today are drawing it ever closer to Europe. In part political factors have prompted this trend, including the British failure to pursue a successful independent foreign policy when its interests were in conflict with those of the super-powers, as in the autumn of 1956 with the Suez crisis. But in Arnold Toynbee's apt phrase, "in this postwar age, the English Channel is no broader—in the subjective human terms of measurement which have to be applied in this context—than a Dutch dyke in the age of Alva and William the Silent; and the Atlantic itself is no broader than the Channel at the time when Napoleon's army of invasion was encamped at Boulogne."[3] Nonetheless, there are reasons for treating with some reserve claims about the annihilation of distance, for this statement dates back to 1934—only a few short years before the backbone of Nazi strategy was broken by an island state whose geography continued to make a difference.

No one would doubt that communications and modern warfare have shifted the emphasis that can properly be laid on geographic location, but its influence continues in various ways, not least in the case of the great powers. The territorial expanse of the Soviet Union with its land mass extending over one-seventh of the land area of the earth, or the vast reaches of the Chinese empire—both make military conquest and control problematical even with absolute weapons. The policies that the

[1] See Chapter 2.
[2] Sir Eyre Crowe, "Memorandum on the Present State of British Relations with France and Germany, January 1, 1907," *British Documents on the Origins of the war 1898–1914*, ed. G. P. Gooch and H. Temperley (London: 1938), III, 402–403.

[3] Arnold J. Toynbee, *A Study of History* (London: Oxford University Press, 1934), III, 353.

United Nations was able to pursue in Korea were circumscribed by the magnitude of the military effort of fighting a successful war on the seemingly endless terrain of the mainland of China. At the same time the difficulties of maintaining communication networks in these vast areas can be a source of weakness in defense. For Russia the lack of natural frontiers in the west or of natural obstacles to invasion across the plains of Poland and Eastern Germany has been a source of conflict and weakness from the fourteenth century up to the present day. This condition must be considered at least partly responsible for Soviet policies toward the satellites and for the insistence of the late Premier Stalin that "Poland is a matter of life and death."

Consequently, experienced diplomats like Ambassadors Charles E. Bohlen and Llewelyn Thompson warn that the most probable *casus belli* for the Russians could be a sudden change in the status of Eastern Europe. Short of a general settlement, they would fight to preserve their position in this area.

Natural resources. The crisis in the Middle East provides a reminder that natural resources continue to be a vital element in foreign policy. The decisive importance of the countries in the Arabian peninsula rests largely in the control they exert over oil. In practice modern technology has made Middle Eastern oil production an increasingly vital necessity, especially for regions like Western Europe. Instruments of production, transportation, and war require oil as a source of energy—Clemenceau once observed that "one drop of oil is worth one drop of blood of our soldiers"—and its importance has led to a shift in the relative power of major regions of the world (as in the rise to importance of the Middle East) and of some of the major na-

tions. Self-sufficiency in this natural resource has enhanced the power of Russia and the United States while Britain and other European nations have been made weaker by their want of oil. The Middle East furnishes about 80 per cent of Western Europe's oil supplies; and barring major conflicts, this figure was expected to increase to 90 per cent by the 1960's. Other estimates suggest that with the expansion of industrial production and national income and in the face of the flagging output of Europe's coal industry, Western European oil consumption may be trebled in twenty years. Hence control of oil becomes a crucial stake in world politics, and oil diplomacy has emerged as a term of art among policy-makers.

Other natural resources influence foreign policy; the most basic has tended to be food production. Germany's military and political strategy in two World Wars was influenced by the need to gain a comparatively early victory before its limited food reserves were exhausted. For much the same reason Britain, which before World War II produced only 30 per cent of its food, ran the risk of destruction when its lines of communication with other regions were threatened by submarines and air power. In the degree that Britain's economic enterprise extended its influence until by the 1930's there was no part of the world not linked in some way with London, its security became more precarious in proportion to its dependence on tenuous and extended lines of communication. Liberals prompted by their zeal for international trade frequently decry a nation's quest for autonomy and self-sufficiency, yet in wartime this becomes a decisive source of strength. Food and energy are the lifeblood of a nation; its leaders must find ways, whether domestically or internationally, to satisfy these needs.

Less permanent material elements

Industrial establishment. The twin forces of the industrial revolution and the contemporary political revolution, symbolized by approximately 40 new nations gaining recognition since World War II, underscore the vital importance of another element of foreign policy. In the nineteenth and twentieth centuries, the industrial establishment of countries has been the most basic index of world power. So long as Britain had no equal as an industrial power, its weight in the balance of power was bound to be decisive. With the increase in industrial strength of Germany and the Soviet Union or of Italy and Japan, to say nothing of the United States, Britain's capacity to influence the course of world politics was substantially reduced. Britain, having lost its industrial supremacy, also lost its capacity to serve as a balancer. France's industrial decline in relation to Germany meant that it was no longer able to resist German expansionism. Industrial capacity in both World Wars, even more than peacetime military preparedness, proved to be the *ultima ratio*. It was the latent power of the United States reflected in its industrial resources that tipped the scales and gave the victory to the allied powers. "In any comparison of the potential resources of the Great Powers the United States, even before Hitler's war, far outstripped every other nation in the world in material strength, in scale of industrialization, in weight of resources, in standards of living, by every index of output and consumption. And the war, which all but doubled the American national income while it either ruined or severely weakened every other Great Power, has enormously increased the scale upon which the United States now towers above its fellows." [4]

[4] *The Economist* (London), May 24, 1947, p. 785.

The realities of industrial capacity can therefore be ascertained and measured, at least in approximate terms. India, for example, seems to have been lacking in the industrial resources essential to a great power. Although it has substantial deposits of coal and iron and ranks high in manganese production, it has in the past lagged far behind the first-rate powers in the level of its industrial establishment. Only a tiny percentage of its total population has been engaged in industry, and its industrial plants have been severely limited. India is but one of a number of new nations whose rising political expectations carry with them demands for expanded industrial capacity. Its Five Year Plans are in part the expression of the drive for economic development and industrialization. Most of the nations that only recently have attained independence regardless of their natural resources seek economic growth as the indispensable prerequisite of status in the international society. For some, the quest for rapid industrialization cannot be other than abortive. The "objective observer" can suggest that they might play a more significant role if they held to a more modest view of their destiny and cast their lot with neighboring states in a regional development program. In so doing, however, they would accept a permanently inferior position in which their freedom of action would be hedged about, and this they are unwilling to do.

Military establishment. The military establishments of nations comprise another and possibly the most explicit element of foreign policy. Diplomacy and military strength go hand in hand. In an earlier day, the great powers sent gunboats up the rivers of states they were seeking to influence; today a show of strength involves air forces, fleets, and satellites. The postwar distribution of power was an outcome of the position of the Red Army at strategic points in the heart of Europe. Germany's demoniacally successful diplomacy in the interwar period was clearly the direct outgrowth of superior military preparedness. The explosion and testing of atomic weapons by the Soviet Union has been joined with strategic moves in the Cold War. The frontiers separating the spheres of influence of warring states often demarcate the limits of their effective military forces, as, for example, in Korea. As long as force remains the final arbiter of rivalries among nations, the comparative strengths of military establishments will set boundaries to actions in foreign affairs.

Military strength quite obviously lacks the permanence of the elements of geography or natural resources. Throughout history it has been subject to the compulsions of technological changes that have brought far-reaching shifts in power. The phalanx was the key to Sparta's victory over Athens in the Peloponnesian War of 431–404 B.C. Its effectiveness lay in the use of heavy infantry in close-order formation and in reliance upon shock techniques. The Athenians recovered from their defeat and 33 years later employed swarms of light infantry to conquer the Spartans. Somewhat later, the Thebans improved the phalanx by distributing its power in depth, thus introducing an element of surprise which had been missing. The Macedonians revamped the Spartan phalanx, made use of Greek mercenaries, and put their stress on a war of movement. But Macedonia was succeeded by the military genius and mobile legions of Rome. Hardened in civil and border wars, the Roman army proved versatile enough to fight as skirmishers or heavy armed infantrymen in open country and in villages and towns. However, the battle of Adrianople against heavy armed cavalrymen from the east brought the challenge Roman military

leaders had foreseen but for which they were unprepared. In modern times, technology has given dramatic opportunities to those military leaders who proved capable of adaptation and innovation. By contrast, failure to respond to change has usually meant failure even for those whose traditional military resources appeared to be adequate. The Germans were defeated in World War I by using the strategy of 1870 against their opponents' order of battle of trench warfare and economic blockade. The French in the 1930's, expecting another costly and brutal war of attrition, built the Maginot Line to fight the kind of struggle that military technology had already rendered obsolete. Short of warfare itself, the failure of military establishments to keep pace with fast-moving technological changes can also reduce nations' influence in the chancelleries of the world. This was the tragedy of France before World War II.

The difficulties inherent in maintaining military establishments that will not suffer defeat are more complex than mere responses to technological change. A nation may recognize the need for military organs capable of supporting the foreign policies it pursues but be limited in the margin of its economic resources that can be turned to military use. Some countries exhaust their resources in attaining a viable economy; others, like the United States, have a surplus with which to meet foreign military and political commitments. Belgium cannot afford to devote the same part of its gross national product to military ends as can the Soviet Union or the United States. Thus, both in absolute and relative terms, the military establishment of smaller powers must lag behind.

Three errors are commonly made in appraising the military component of foreign policy. First, military power is often confused with national power, and a nation's capacity to impose its will is equated with its military establishment. Military power is like the fist whose force depends on the health and vitality of the body politic and the whole society. Troops are an important determinant of a successful foreign policy, but without other foundations they will not suffice. Second, the military element is often viewed in more static terms than is appropriate. The democracies in two World Wars, although the last to arm, rallied their forces to gain the victory in the end. Third, it is difficult to analyze and foresee in advance of a particular war the most effective distribution of the components of military force. For example, what comprises a strong military force today? Is it large ground forces, hydrogen bombs, or intensive research? Is a small, highly specialized army more desirable than a large number of ground forces, or are both essential for a nation that seeks to be strong? The answers to these questions will probably be decisive in determining a state's future influence in the world, yet it is sobering that estimates must be made on the basis of contingencies that cannot now be foreseen. We know in a general way that an effective foreign policy must be supported by a military program that can safeguard national security. But this leaves those who make decisions with the painful task of distributing resources among alternative means of defense without any certainty of the kind of war they may have to fight.

Changes in industrial and military capacity. Beyond this, the weapons of today may not be used in future wars because technology has rendered them obsolete. It is said that conventional weapons are fast being supplanted by new and more deadly weapons and therefore traditional armaments fail to provide an adequate basis for foreign policy. On the other hand, there are military experts who question whether atomic and hydrogen weapons will ever be used, given the prospect of mutual annihilation. Is it not fair then to ask whether the stockpiling of an unlimited supply of weapons that no nation would dare to use furnishes a state with the requisite military support? A military establishment grounded in conventional weapons may fall short of providing a defensible military posture, but so may a military program aimed at superior atomic capacities. These are the horns of the dilemma on which defense strategists could be impaled.

The human elements: quantitative and qualitative

Quantitative: population. Students of foreign policy have stressed another set of elements that make up a third concentric circle of factors of policy. They constitute the human forces—both quantitative and qualitative. Population is a quantitative factor that obviously must be considered in every calculation of the capacity of states. The Middle East provides an example of the weight that policy-makers give to numbers of people and to the fact that Arabs are more numerous than Jews. The importance of China and India at the end of the second World War rests partly in the size of their populations, which exceed 400 million people. Both the Soviet Union and the United States, numbering less than half the populations of these countries, have shown respect for their potential. Conversely, nations with falling birth rates have lost influence among the society of nations, as France did after World War I. In the past, the wide diversity in technological skills for instance between an Englishman and a Chinese, meant that population was not a factor. In recent years this situation has been undergoing change—especially in the last decade. The 50 million people now living in the United Kingdom enjoy a high degree of scientific skill, but there is no longer any certainty that the peoples of underdeveloped areas may not eventually approach them or that the combined skills of so large a population may not compensate for a persistent technological lag.

The use of population statistics and of the forecasting of trends suggests that the science of estimating and predicting the numbers in states relative to one another is simple and precise. Yet demography is subject to many of the vicissitudes to which scientific research is exposed in other social spheres. For example, World War I had the effect of virtually wiping out a whole generation of Frenchmen. France's casualties from 1914 to 1918 numbered 1,400,000 young men. By 1938 the French birth rate no longer compensated for the death rate; and in World War II France lost 625,000 men, almost three times America's losses in a country one-fourth America's size. Yet since World War II the French birth rate has reversed itself, and since 1946 the surplus of births over deaths has been about 300,000 a year—a surplus greater than that of Italy or West Germany. France, which had been static and immobile between the wars, has witnessed a renewal of its rate of growth. In more general terms, then, population as an element of foreign policy is lacking in absolute predictability and certainty and depends on other related elements. It may enable or prevent a state from achieving its national purposes, but in either role it is also subject to change and fluctuation.

Qualitative: policy-makers and leaders. Another crucial element of policy is the role of policy-makers within a political system. The study of the methods, style and quality of the process by which policies are implemented is the concern of students of both international and comparative politics. Moreover, capacities vary greatly from state to state for rational and responsible actions in this sphere.

From a formal point of view, a policy-maker is the official empowered with making the relevant decisions in foreign policy. In some political systems, the officials are the effective decision-makers, as is the case with stable democratic systems and well-established authoritarian systems. In other cases, the officials are not the effective decision-makers. The matter is one for empirical observation. knowledge of existing domestic systems, and study of historical patterns of foreign policy action. In most cases, observation will disclose the effective wielders of power and the real centers of decision-making. Doubts will always be present, especially when competing groups and elites have different foreign policy aspirations, or when there is conflict on foreign policy goals or on means of achieving these goals. In societies where the officials are not the true wielders of power, the search for the centers of power may lead us to the party, the military, the trade unions, the tribal chiefs, or the intellectuals. No prediction about foreign policy trends can be made for many countries without a careful assessment of the relative strength of the students, the trade unions, the military, the church, and the business groups.

Formal or informal decision-makers reflect the existing balance of forces in any given political society, from the most consensual to the most divided and fragmented. There are some long-range trends, however, that are very relevant to the study of foreign policy. These include the growing managerialism of advanced industrialized societies; the growing influence of the natural scientist, both as a policy-maker and as an important "group"; and the relative independence of the "military." Industrialization and technological improvement, together with rising material expectations and their satisfaction, create similar societies in which ideologies progressively give place to pragmatic and technical considerations. Ideological conflicts become secondary. Such a trend inevitably leads to emphasis upon peace, since material satisfaction and the utilization of technology for this purpose are possible only if there is peace. Although there are qualifications to be made, one might well hypothesize that present industrial and technical developments put primacy upon fulfillment of material goals and satisfaction of material expectations, rather than upon international conflict. However, the growing importance of the military in all contemporary societies is prima-facie evidence of the reverse trend.

Political leaderships in most societies act in order to maintain the security of their national state. An indispensable ingredient of security is power. The "realist" theory in international relations claims that power considerations are of primary significance in the behavior of the ruling groups of any nation-state, and that ideology and all other considerations are subordinate. This is undoubtedly true, and power objectives often come in conflict with welfare or even internal status considerations; groups in power, in order to increase the power of the nation-state, may sometimes undermine their own position. The extent to which considerations of power will come into conflict with considerations of internal status, wealth, and leadership position of certain elites is a matter for empirical and historical study. In order to study comparative foreign policy, we ought

to know how well entrenched are the effective wielders of power and how likely is it that their decisions will be obeyed. On the basis of the existing constellation of the various groups in a society, international conflict will strengthen or weaken leadership. Systems such as the Soviet Union need conflict for the continuation of the leadership in power. In other cases, the reverse may be true. It is important to discover the circumstances under which an external threat leads to the consolidation of the power of an existing leadership group, and, conversely, those circumstances under which leadership is undermined in case of conflict.

It is also important to define the relations between the various decision-makers and/or the effective wielders of power. The question applies with equal relevance to the "Soviet world" and the so-called "free world."

The role of ideology. What is the role of "ideology" within the international system? The term ideology applies not only to the manner in which objectives are shaped, but also to how the given objectives will be pursued. There is a range of means extending from outright violence to attachment to the established procedures. As long as international rules for the adjustment and the accommodation of conflict have a very low degree of legitimacy, conflict will always involve a threat of violence. At what point is conflict likely to lead to war? It is difficult to make an accurate prediction, but certain obvious alternatives can be envisaged.

Some nation-states and their political leadership are likely to resort to violence more readily than others.

The available instruments of violence are an important consideration in assessing the likelihood of war. The more destructive the weapons available, the less likely their use, and hence the effort will be to accommodate conflict. "Total" destructive power in the hands of only two powers may lead to a number of alternatives—progressive disarmament of all other political systems, progressive bipolarizations in the form of alliances under the leadership of the two states, effort to redress the balance by the manufacturing of weapons by a third power, or bloc, as in de Gaulle's France. A situation of bipolarization may be stable if it brings about either complete disarmament of the rest of the world with the express or tacit agreement of the two states involved, or the physical division of the world into two clearly demarcated and integrated spheres. All other situations are bound to be highly unstable.

Barring disarmament, the likelihood of conflict persists because, curiously, the more absolute the weapons in the hands of two powers, the more likely for smaller powers to use violence as long as the two powers are in disagreement. Neither power can interfere actively in the conflict for fear that the other might be engaged, with the possibility that ultimate weapons may be used.

Consideration of surprise attack and retaliation obey essentially simple rules if there are only two nuclear powers. The moment ultimate weapons are available and held by many states—a threat implicit in the so-called n^{th} country problem—there can be no stabilizing force such as the one implicit in the balance of power theory. The situation is one in which there is no possible balancer—each nation-state, once it possesses a given number of ultimate weapons, is just as powerful as the other. At this point, the instability is so high that it is safe to predict that conflict inevitably will lead to violence on an unprecedented scale. Our world will approximate Hobbes' model, and we will be compelled to lay down our arms to avoid "sudden death," with no assurance that "natural law" will be followed this time!

The role of information. What importance does *information* have in shaping policy? The problem of available information, which forms the basis of the policy-makers' decision, is very complex. Game theory postulates its free flow, much as the liberal economics assumed perfect mobility and price competition. The "liberal model" is useful because, on its basis, we can infer about events and developments even when empirical reality does not fit the model. The game theory does not have this advantage, because it assumes a game without telling us what the game is about: war, peace, accommodation, maintenance of the *status quo,* surprise attack and annihilation. Despite the theory's emphasis upon the "rules," we cannot understand what they are unless we assume that the participants have similar objectives, norms, and leadership characteristics, a situation that obviously never obtains. If the participants all play different games with different rules, we have no game amenable to rational observation. Therefore, where and how reality differs from the model cannot be shown in any terms. The game theory, useful in military analysis when we consider the use of weapons and force, is not relevant to the study of foreign policy.

To undertake a discussion of the relationship between "information" and policy-making or formulation of objectives, we would have to consider *a*) information available to decision-making and governing elites; *b*) information as a source of conflict among elites; *c*) possession of information as a source of power and influence among certain of the political elites or decision-makers; *d*) the manner in which information is perceived; and *e*) the serious problem of the disparity between the information available to the "public" and that available to various public policy-making and leadership groups. A subsidiary problem is that of "information-manufacturing" in different degrees in all political systems.

It is hard to relate the above meaningfully and arrive at certain hypothetical generalizations. The Wilsonian theory that the free flow of information would keep opinion alert, and pave the way to the resolutions of all conflicts without resort to war, was based on the notion that decision-makers and governing elites are more prone to conflict and war than the people. It was further based on the assumption that the public, when given all the facts, would make "rational" judgments, and that "rational" judgment excludes war. There are reasonable doubts, however, that public opinion exhibits any greater traits of rationality, or shows a great propensity to modify beliefs held in the light of information received. There is also less evidence than had been assumed that withholding of information by the decision-makers, or limiting its access to only a small group of persons with leadership positions, is more likely to lead to war.

Diplomacy: national purposes

Another element of foreign policy is the quality of a nation's diplomacy. At one level, this involves a clear conception of national purposes; at another, it involves prudence and skill in the use of the tools of statecraft. For purposes of analysis, both can be examined in the context of American foreign policy.

It is well to remind ourselves that issues confronting the makers of American foreign policy compete for attention, crowding out and succeeding one another in headlines of the daily press.

Korea, Indochina, Formosa, Israel, Laos, Berlin, and Cuba flash kaleidoscopically across each of our horizons as we seek to understand international affairs. Sensing this process, it is tempting to second-guess the future. When one is asked what will be the most compelling and troublesome problems of the next six months or a year, he can prophesy the threat of war in the Middle East, orderly transition to independence or self-government in former colonial areas, or agreement on atomic controls. But behind these issues and affecting their resolution are deep-seated, underlying questions relating to this country's basic goals and national purposes. What do Americans seek in the world? Is it peace? Power? Prosperity? Each of these goals is often set forth as a national fundamental aim. Sometimes peace, especially in this atomic age, is made an absolute purpose; prosperity sometimes seems to emerge as the one end Americans seek above all others in the conduct of their affairs in the world. We shall look in turn at each of these goals, seeking to ascertain its relevance to the real issues in America's foreign affairs.

Peace as national purpose. It is sometimes considered a mark of bad judgment to recite a succession of "great generalities" at the outset of any discussion. However, the present crisis imposes upon us responsibilities of perceiving more clearly the ebb and flow of certitude and truth with respect to the root principles of world affairs. Recent events have shaped and molded the dimensions of the international problem in a manner that few anticipated. Take as an example the issue of peace. For the first time in centuries, rational men have been claiming—apparently with some accord—that war has become obsolete as an instrument of national policy. President Eisenhower reiterated this view, and he maintained again at the First Geneva Conference that victor and vanquished alike would be casualties in any nuclear or hydrogen war. His successor, President Kennedy, has continued nuclear test negotiations at Geneva because of an awareness of this peril. At the end of such a war they would look out upon the charred ruins of civilization itself. If Geneva settled anything, we are told, it registered a tacit agreement—founded on the stalemate in atomic production—outlawing this form of warfare. But does this mean that peace is inevitable and atomic warfare impossible? Apparently not, if we consider recent policy statements, the informed opinions of experienced leaders, or events in Hungary, Suez, Syria, and the growing Chinese and Russian threats in Asia and at the heart of Europe.

Power as national purpose. The most celebrated and controversial policy statements in the mid-Fifties were those attributed by *Life* writer James Shepley to Secretary of State John Foster Dulles. In discussing the policy of "massive retaliation," Mr. Dulles observed: "The ability to get to the verge without getting into the war is the necessary art. If you cannot master it, you inevitably get into war. If you try to run away from it, if you are scared to go to the brink, you are lost." Earlier he had said that a potential aggressor must know that his acts would be met by such retaliation and that he would lose more than he could gain. Specific targets for retaliation had to be selected and agreed upon in advance. "The way to deter aggression is for the free community to be willing and able to respond vigorously at places and with means of its own choosing." Its response should be massive and overwhelming.

If we separate the chaff from the wheat, the political from the inescapable truth in this contested statement, it seems clear that the possibility of resort to military measures has not been cast out from the armory of American foreign policy. Since the Eisenhower administration stressed wherever possible the replacement of manpower with decisive weapons, the risk of warfare with ultimate weapons can hardly be said to have passed. Nor is this possibility made any less ominous by the boasts of Soviet leaders that they too have developed a strategy of retaliation. The Soviet resistance to a neutral administrator of a disarmament agreement and their refusal to accept other reasonable procedures are further evidence. In this situation an accident, a miscalculation, or an act of desperation could easily set off the conflict that Geneva was said to have made impossible.

Prosperity and development of national purpose. Turning to the issue of prosperity, we enter the presence of the most appealing of the current trends of informed thinking on our foreign affairs. This trend of though maintains, with varying reservations, that most of the tensions between the West and the non-Soviet but uncommitted countries of the world are the result of mutual suspicions, and that these can be composed through economic cooperation and aid. Put in the proper perspective, a policy of contributing modestly and consistently to prosperity and the raising of standards of living in the world is a viable if not an utterly essential goal for American foreign policy. Its emphasis is all the more crucial because of the neglect of this facet of American thinking in the past. However, prosperity, like peace, is at best a proximate guide to action. It offers no panacea to all the ills that engulf the world. Tensions may be eased when the fruits of economic development and growth are more widely shared at home and abroad. Yet American experiences of intense strife and division nationally during the past decade should caution against excessive optimism. The wounds of the worst bitterness and rancor in the lifetime of some Americans are a sobering reminder that 60,-000,000 employed is scant guarantee of peace and tranquillity among peoples and parties.

On a world scale, the limits of a form of inverted Marxism that looks to economic development as a miraculous device for purging tensions and strife are even more graphic. India and the United States have not been deterred from misunderstandings by India's phenomenal economic growth. The fact that India has literally raised herself by her own bootstraps, that she increased real income 15 per cent in the period from 1949 to 1954 and attained in 1953–54 the highest rate of economic growth in the world, has if anything prompted her to press claims more vigorously, even when they conflicted with those of the West.

Furthermore, those who would lay the disparities in standards of living throughout the world on the conscience of the West sometimes seek to exact a heavier tribute than any nation or civilization can fulfill. These developments in other countries are intimately bound up with cultural traditions, with political order and stability, with resources and attitudes and population pressures and a thousand local conditions that Western powers can only slightly shape or affect. If Western efforts can assist others to inch their way to a happier and more promising state of economic well-being and political justice, this will be enough, and it may even stem the advance of hostile forces. However, it can lead at best to public disillusionment and perhaps a deep and festering embitterment with the West's role in the world if public justification of these programs claims more than is warranted.

That the West should be left to find its way gropingly, painfully, and with uncertainty can come as a shock only to those who forever seek simple absolutes and the easy pathway. Peace more than ever before in America's history is a paramount goal of American foreign policy. However, it is a goal that knows its limits. Power throws a spotlight on those dark corners of American action which were but dimly lighted throughout the era of intellectual pacifism and political neutralism. Prosperity—especially in Asia, Africa, and the Middle East—must be as much America's aim as military security, particularly since the foe becomes ever more cunning and resourceful in his pursuit of this enterprise. Yet prosperity is a means and not an end. The interests of progressive no less than oppressed states clash and must be accommodated. Diplomats and not the experts in technical assistance must be called to this task.

We will be on surer ground if we recognize that peace, power, and prosperity are rough guide lines to action. They show us the perimeters within which to work, but in no way remove the demands placed on leaders for political judgment and practical wisdom.

Diplomacy and democracy

Democratic theory rests on the supposition that the very broad goals of foreign policy must be decided by the people, but the concrete decisions and implementation within these goals is the function of the political leadership, primarily the executive branch of the government. Bryce argued, in the heyday of the Wilsonian "populism" in matters of foreign policy, that broad ends of foreign policy should be decided by the people, and he produced evidence to show why democracies had displayed more "wisdom" than despotisms in the formulation of such broad objectives. Most democratic theorists tempered their remarks with a realization that popular awareness and popular infallibility were more restricted in matters of foreign policy than in domestic matters. Bryce himself put this in the following terms: ". . . one of the strongest arguments for democratic government is that the masses of the people, whatever else they may not know, do know where the shoe pinches, and are best entitled to specify the reforms they need. In foreign policy this does not apply . . ." [5]

These basic presuppositions about the role of public opinion and the relationship between leadership and public opinion require comparative analysis and study. To begin with, the rationalist assumptions about public opinion have been subjected to careful criticism and reconsideration ever since the publication of Walter Lippmann's *Public Opinion* and the *Phantom Public*. Secondly, the apathy of public opinion in matters of foreign policy in contemporary systems calls for the reconsideration of those presuppositions. When the European Defense Community sharply divided the French Parliament and stalemated any legislative action in the second legislature of the Fourth Republic, ". . . four-fifths of the public (in France) had heard about the project but (were) uncertain as to whether the plan had been voted or not . . ." [6] The surveys carried on by the Institute of Public Opinion in France reveal the colossal ignorance of foreign policy matters of an electorate that has been traditionally considered alert and sophisticated. In the United States, 75 per cent of the electorate have been considered as unaware of, or uninformed on, foreign policy questions.[7] Strangely enough, if public opinion polls have any relevance, the postwar German public opinion has been consistently more alert and informed than that of the traditionally democratic and enlightened nations. Thirdly, Professor Almond's careful study of opinion, curiously enough, has not brought forth parallel studies for other countries, although his analysis of the structure and organization of public opinion could probably be widely applied. A recent study indicates the same general division between an informed active minority and a large mass of uninformed and passive public. It may be warranted, therefore, to raise this fundamental question as an invitation to comparative study of foreign policy. Are the democratic presuppositions valid? If not, why? If so, under what conditions do they obtain?

Diplomatic practices and diplomacy. In diplomacy, the choice of methods and techniques is no less vital than clarity about objectives. Democracies sometimes assume that the demands of coherence and consistency in diplomacy fall less heavily upon them than upon other states. In part this goes back to a prevailing outlook about democracy and foreign policy.

The first two decades of the twentieth century witnessed the flowering of a philosophy of international politics that was unambiguously simple, straightforward, and capable of engendering widespread popular appeal. This philosophy looked in a spirit of buoyant optimism to democracy and

---

[5] James Bryce, *Modern Democracies,* II (New York: The Macmillan Co., 1921), 370.

[6] Pierre Gerbet, "L'influence de l'opinion publique et des partis sur la politique entrangere en France," *La Politique Etrangere et ses Fomdaments* (Paris: Armand Colin, 1954).

[7] Lester Markel, ed., *Public Opinion and Foreign Policy,* Martin Kriesberg, *Dark Areas of Ignorance.* When Secretary of State Dean Acheson was under severe attack for the Truman-Acheson foreign policies, only 23 per cent of those polled could identify the Secretary of State.

national self-determination as the twin sources of international peace and order. The creation of popular regimes on the Anglo-American model everywhere throughout the world was heralded as a sure corrective to the harsh conflicts that for centuries had wracked international life. New nations brought into existence at the will of a self-conscious community of peoples would dissolve the rivalries and frictions that had always led to conflict among contiguous social groups. The faith of modern Western *homo sapiens* in man's potentialities for unending progress found its expression on the international scene in the assurance that a brave new world merely awaited the fulfillment of these goals.

It is ironic that this illusion based on an excess of faith in essentially divine-right *vox populi* has in the recent past been rudely shaken on numerous fronts. The phenomenon of totalitarian democracy, unknown in the nineteenth century, has not only left political rivalries and conflict intact but has heightened and made virtually irreconcilable the disputes among the new collectivities. Inflamed public passions playing on statesmen have made moderation and compromise more difficult of attainment. National leaders, by pandering to popular passions, have often reduced the alternatives open to responsible makers of foreign policy. Nationalism has led not to more peaceful relations among peoples who rested content with their political status, but instead has bred the most embittered antagonisms between new nations and their former colonial masters or between non-Western states and their erstwhile exemplars in the West. National self-determination and democracy can hardly be said to have ushered in a new era; our more serious observers find deep anguish in the steep and sudden decline of influ-

ence and self-confidence of the Western democracies. The West succeeds in engendering resentment and suspicion more often than it earns respect. Yet many students and statesmen insist on talking in bated breath about the causes and conditions of our decline. The bulk of those who assume leadership in intellectual and political life are singularly inhibited when it comes to diagnosing the source of our ills. It is commonplace to respond to a critical evaluation of the conduct of foreign policy in a democracy by pointing the finger of scorn at non-democratic societies that are still more obviously the authors of our most recent historic catastrophes. The key to this difficult problem is surely not loss of faith in democracy. It is rather a deeper awareness of the methods of diplomacy.

Democratic diplomacy, like all diplomacy, must adhere to certain sound principles and rules. It must prove its consistency with the diplomatic tradition and the imperatives of effective negotiation. Majority votes in multilateral conference, dialectics, invective, or propaganda may hold a certain fascination for the spectators of world affairs. But more often than not their effect is to sow international distrust and increase rather than alleviate world conflicts. The first principle worth noting is that, historically, diplomacy and foreign policy have not been considered identical. Foreign policy has been viewed as the legislative aspect and diplomacy as the executive aspect of managing foreign relations. Diplomacy has called for experts with freedom of action; policy is a matter for the most responsible branches of government, including at some point the legislature. Diplomacy is not the framing of policy but rather its execution. It is no more a point of focus for public attention than is the execution of the national budget as distinct from its authorization.

The Oxford English Dictionary states: "Diplomacy is the management of international relations by negotiation; the method by which these relations are adjusted and managed by ambassadors and envoys; the business or art of the diplomatist." This definition suggests a second principle. The test of diplomacy is not the vindication of some abstract moral principle or the rewarding or punishment of virtuous or evil forces. It is rather the most effective accommodation of state relations that are sometimes in harmony, but other times in conflict.

Third, diplomacy calls for an intimate knowledge of the mechanics of negotiation, for endless patience in the use of numberless expedients in working out agreements, and for consummate skill in adjusting national proposals and making them acceptable at home and abroad without sacrificing vital objectives.

In recent years many serious writers have questioned whether or not diplomacy has measured up to the standards inherent in these principles. Hugh Gibson, who has few peers among twentieth-century American diplomatists, wrote:

What we have come to call diplomacy in the course of the past twenty years has failed to achieve results and has led into all sorts of disasters. But it wasn't really diplomacy. It was the usurpation of diplomatic functions by politicians and inept amateurs; it was the new method of having the negotiation of infinitely complicated world problems handled by politicians, amateurs, and adventurers; the forcing on the world in critical times of new and untried methods; publicity stunts and hurried personal discussions between the political leaders, who should stay at home and be the heavy artillery in reserve rather than trying to direct operations on hurried visits to the front-line trenches.[8]

These words have even greater relevance today than they had a little more than a decade and a half ago.

The transformation of diplomatic practices. For nearly four centuries the statecraft of Europe had certain salient features. It sought, in theory at least, to mitigate and reduce conflicts by means of persuasion, compromise, and adjustment. It was rooted in the community of interests of a small group of leaders who spoke the same language, catered to one another as often as to their own people, and played to one another's strengths and weaknesses. When warfare broke out, they drew a ring around the combatants and sought to neutralize the struggle. The old diplomacy carried on its tasks in a world made up of states that were small, separated, limited in power, and blessed, ironically enough, by half-hearted political loyalties. Patience was a watchword; negotiations were often as protracted during war as in peace. It was taken for granted that talks would be initiated, broken off, resumed, discontinued temporarily, and reopened again by professionals in whose lexicon there was no substitute for "diplomacy."

Today not one of these conditions any longer prevails, and the search for new formulas in diplomacy has gone on apace. The first and most novel pattern to crystallize after World War II found expression in the United Nations and in what is called "popular diplomacy." It looked to international forums and to majority votes in the General Assembly as a substitute for

[8] Hugh Gibson, *The Road to Foreign Policy* (Garden City, N. Y.: Doubleday and Company, Inc., 1944), p. 63.

the tortuous paths of traditional diplomacy. It must be said that this choice was expressed more rigorously in practice than in the United Nations Charter, which emphasized talks among the parties to a dispute before placing an issue on the agenda. Popular diplomacy reflects the faith in parliamentary procedures, in the rule of the people, and in straightforward, rational, and open discussion. It is jointly the product of an age of rationalism and an age of popular government. It translates into global terms supreme political attainments of free people within the democratic state. Popular diplomacy, despite the role of the Great Powers in the Security Council, marks a swing of the pendulum to diplomacy by all the peoples of most of the nations. It is the antithesis of secret diplomacy by a concert of leaders of the pre-eminent countries.

Because popular diplomacy has been the basis of much of our postwar diplomacy, we are able to make a modest estimate of its success. To use Lester Pearson's phrase, we find that the problems of "diplomacy in a gold fish bowl" are more intractable than we had supposed. Publicity has been both a virtue and a vice. It has kept the spotlight of public opinion on world affairs, but it has encouraged the actor in world politics to take inflexible positions from which it is difficult to retreat. Majority votes on Korea have demonstrated who controlled greater support; they have left conflicts of interest unaffected or have actually contributed to their increase. When this new pattern of diplomacy has worked, it has been savored with more ancient techniques, as with the private diplomacy of Mr. Ralph Bunche in Palestine and of Mr. Jessup on Berlin, and the "quiet diplomacy" of the Secretary General on Suez and the Belgian Congo.

These successes, however noteworthy, have failed to arrest the sharp swing of the pendulum to another type of international diplomacy. The Eisenhower administration has espoused personal diplomacy as a means of correcting the excesses of public negotiations. The first Geneva Conference, the United States-Canadian-Mexican Conference at White Sulphur Springs, and the meeting with India's Prime Minister Nehru and with Prime Minister MacMillan of England illustrate a new and emerging pattern. It is a pattern based upon the President's partiality "for talking things out rather than negotiating things out" in an atmosphere of genial informality. It reflects the view that some of the roots of conflict will dissolve when leaders from other nations, sitting across a table from Mr. Eisenhower, become persuaded of his good intentions. The personal touch of a famous personality has been placed on the scales of world diplomacy.

The rediscovery of diplomacy. The two novel approaches—personal and parliamentary diplomacy—are at opposite poles of the spectrum. One emphasizes public speeches, mass assemblies, and resolutions emerging from open forums; the other stresses informality and man-to-man conferences free of protocol, agendas, and advance preparation. (At White Sulphur Springs the Canadians on the eve of the so-called "Little Summit Conference" didn't know the topics to be discussed.) Yet these new patterns, so divergent in conception and design, share one thing in common. They constitute a revolt against traditional diplomacy.

For diplomatists, the first rule has always been that negotiations are essential when national interests are in conflict. Since such conflicts arise from causes more basic than personal hostility, personal amiability can hardly resolve them. Sir Harold Nicolson has argued:

Diplomacy is the art of negotiating documents in a ratifiable and dependable form. It is by no means the art of conversation. The affability inseparable from any conversation . . . produces illusiveness, compromises, and high intentions. Diplomacy if it is ever to be effective, should be a disagreeable business, and one recorded in hard print.

The trouble with approaches that set aside the lessons of the past is that history has a way of returning to haunt us. Both popular and personal diplomacy have their place, especially if we safeguard them against their excesses. The best way of doing this is to remember that foreign policy has a memorable tradition, not all of which is folly in the present.

REFLECTIONS ON THE STUDY OF FOREIGN POLICY IN THE CONTEXT OF THE COLD WAR

Theory in the social sciences runs the risk of departing too sharply from social reality. By contrast, advances in the medical sciences are often accounted for by the phrase, "the scientist is never too far from the patient in the sickbed." The scientist is close to nature so long as he poses relevant and researchable questions. The focus of his interest must be "operationally relevant." Economics, particularly since Walras and more notably since Keynes, has become at once more scientific and more useful. Practitioners of foreign policy are often critical of the unfortunate irrelevance of much theorizing in approaches such as decision-making and behaviorism. They charge that theories remain on the drawing board without being tested or applied against reality.

At the same time, policy-makers are the first to signal the need for principles of wider application or a manage-able body of doctrine on foreign policy. Public leaders need help not merely from efficiency experts, but also political and constitutional theorists, on problems involved in the organization of the government for the conduct of foreign policy. How should foreign policy be carried on in a democracy? Who takes responsibility and who should be the coordinator of policies and programs? What aspects of foreign policy are the appropriate concern of appointed or elected officials? What part is the responsibility of the whole of the body politic? What are the objectives of foreign policy and how should they be ranged in what hierarchical order? For example, how should statesmen order and relate the goals of most Western countries, which include national security, avoidance of thermonuclear war, the preservation of western values, and support for the rising expectations of newly independent peoples?

These issues are clearly amenable to study, to the ordering of facts and data, to trial and error in testing alternative hypotheses, and to building a body of more generalized theory with relevance for practice. Propositions put forward by one observer will invariably be challenged by others. This is the story of evolving knowledge. If scholars and writers with commitments to rigorous and systematic analysis leave this rich field to others, understanding will suffer. Yet it is disheartening to note how many serious scholars prefer the simpler if tidier tasks of abstracting from reality those problems on which great masses of data are at hand, regardless of their significance.

The elements of foreign policy and the forces of international politics may seem abstract, remote, and distant when conceived of in principle or viewed in the light of an historical past. However, the present conflict between the Soviet Union and the United States is approached more meaningfully if seen in terms of the scheme of the basic factors that lie at the roots of foreign policy. The cold war is more than a decade old by now, and is plainly visible as a conflict with at least two dimensions. At one level, the struggle is for men's minds; the vitality and universality of communism and democracy are at stake. At the other level, the struggle engages two great configurations of power who by reason either of necessity or of design reach out to influence others. A treatise on foreign policy is perhaps not the most appropriate place to analyze the comparative strengths and weaknesses of democracy and communism, for in one sense this is chiefly an issue in political theory, albeit theory in action. Soviet-American rivalry, however, is more clearly a problem in foreign relations.

Both the Soviet Union and the United States have been blessed with the most favorable of geographic situations. The United States is surrounded in the north and south by friendly and weaker states and bounded and safeguarded in the east and west by two great ocean moats. The geographic area of the Soviet Union, constituting about one-seventh of the earth's surface, has historically swallowed up any would-be invader, although its western boundaries are exposed by the open terrain of the European plains. The natural resources of both powers are immense, and their technology is far advanced. In conventional military weapons Russian strength probably exceeds American, but in the production of new weapons—first of an offensive type but more recently of a defensive kind—the Russians despite their progress with satellites have lagged behind. Russia's population is slightly greater than America's, although their per capita technical skill is probably less. Ameri-

can political institutions should in the long run prove superior, but the Russians may temporarily enjoy the advantages that flow from a system in which instantaneous decision-making and kaleidoscopic initiative are possible. National morale, particularly in the hydrogen age, is difficult to measure before a crisis. The quality of diplomacy on both sides is subject to the broader tendencies and problems that have been described.

Americans live by the faith that other peoples will come to embrace a political creed involving a decent respect for the dignity of mankind, and that an international order may be founded on respect for the rights and interests of other sovereign states. However, there are three obstacles that confound American policy-makers and that must at least be mitigated if the struggle is to be won.

Policy and public opinion. The first obstacle is inherent in the problem of marshalling support domestically for American policies while at the same time putting America's best foot forward in the eyes of the rest of the world. To mobilize support for policies, Americans say things to themselves that, from the standpoint of other peoples, might better be left unsaid. (In this the United States is of course not unique.) America is a vast sprawling continent of great diversity of political and religious beliefs; in its constitutional system power and responsibility are broadly diffused, although less so in foreign affairs than in the conduct of domestic affairs. Thus Americans speak in many voices, some raucous and strident, as they seek to persuade one another of the right course to follow. The language of domestic politics is not the language of political theory. It aims to unite as many as will join to support policies or programs. It looks to a common denominator that can more often be found in broad principles and moral generalities than in specific directives of strategy, which, like military policies, must be cast in practical alternatives to meet circumstances. It prefers militant slogans to qualified truths and a crusade to public conversations on a problem.

Above all, it is a permanent part of the landscape of international relations that American foreign policy must draw its support from a union of the experts, the public, and friends and allies abroad. History demonstrates that no American statesman can ignore any point on the triangle without courting disaster. Before World War II, the public ostensibly lagged behind the thinking on foreign affairs of experts and allies. Following World War II and up to 1950, American policy—especially for Europe—was acceptable alike to the authoritative views of the experts, to the public, and to the members of the postwar grand alliance. This day has passed, and demands of the three groups have tended increasingly to go their separate ways. America's allies have more and more viewed their national interests as not necessarily identical with the United States', and ironically, at a time when American policies are vulnerable to criticism by experts at home and abroad, they enjoy broad endorsement at all levels of American life to the point of becoming virtually untouchable. By stressing one side of the triangle and striving above all for harmonious domestic political relations, the Eisenhower administration created difficulties for itself at the other points on the triangle. In this way it illustrated a perennial problem in the conduct of foreign relations. Although the Kennedy administration has the support of most experts, its sources of public support remain to be tested.

Colonialism. Another obstacle stems from the colonial dilemma, which reaches beyond America's national life and touches conflicting interests at work throughout the rest of the world. We know that the colonial problem stands at the top of every agenda for discussion of American foreign policy. Responsible officials are encouraged to issue proclamations and to throw America's weight behind popular revolutions. In this setting it is tempting to take general and sweeping positions and to express an American doctrine on the rights of peoples everywhere to independence and self-government. This is particularly true because Americans' own experience is so rich in its lessons and apparently pregnant with meaning. The fruits of attempts thus far made to propound a dogma should serve, however, to give us pause, for the record of America's efforts to align itself squarely with either colonial or anticolonial powers is sprinkled with as many failures as successes.

Nevertheless, Americans face new situations today and demands crowd in upon them for new and more vigorous policies. We are reminded that Senator Vandenburg with his emphasis on Europe and Western unity never disparaged the rights of colonial or former colonial peoples. Nationalism is on the march in Asia, the Middle East, and Africa, and Americans implore one another to identify their country with these movements rather than appearing to stand in their pathway. Unhappily, the colonial problem is less tractable than those exhortations suggest. For at the same time as the fight is waged to end old imperialisms, a new and more demoniac expansionism threatens. To meet it, some feel that America must cleave to its trusted friends and allies with whom it has interests and military bases in common, striving to preserve a more stable world balance of power. Yet, in itself, this is not likely to be enough. The present equilibrium of power will be upset unless America can join with new forces in the so-called underdeveloped areas. We may say, therefore, that the United States faces the triple challenge of stemming the tide of Russian imperialism and world Communism, uniting the other Western states, and drawing closer to non-Western peoples only recently emerging as independent states. In a manner of speaking, policy-makers must keep three balls in the air. This is the unenviable task of American statesmanship.

The pathos of our present position may be illustrated briefly from recent events. First there was the statement on Goa recognizing Portugal's authority in the tiny enclave in India, prompted doubtless by the zeal of European officers in the State Department to display a sense of community with Portugal. This provoked deep resentment in India and perhaps throughout much of Asia. Next came the expression of "sympathy" for Greek feelings in the Cyprus dispute by the United States Ambassador to Greece, Cavendish W. Cannon, which loosed a torrent of British protest. Then the Dutch voiced dismay at Mr. Dulles' warm and friendly comments during a visit to the Indonesian Republic. More recently the United States aroused its European friends by appearing to take sides with Egypt, and Middle Eastern friends by reassuring Turkey against Syria and Russia. Taken together, American efforts to cement ties of community and good will with one side in the colonial struggle threatened or ruptured the bonds of unity with the other. Possibly the one exception was Ambassador Dillon's speech supporting France's search for "liberal solutions" of her problems in North Africa, and even this was challenged by the moderate Tunisian nationalist leader Bourguiba. The United States' position on the Angola dispute before the United Nations illustrates the margins of choice that may be open to Western policy-makers. Here the abuses were flagrant, and the political position of a minor ally was sufficiently weak, so that a less ambiguous American position was possible.

Perceiving these problems, can we say anything about this perplexing picture that will offer some guidance to the juggler or policy-maker of whom we have spoken? Perhaps there are guidelines or principles we can enunciate to spotlight a few of the darker corners of this colonial problem. First, we must start with the presumption that the colonial problem is fraught with dilemmas with which America must learn to live. Nor will dogmas for or against colonialism waft them away. Solutions must be worked out case by case; and as, for example, Tunisia is not identical with Algeria, policies must be shaped to meet individual needs. Second, timing is of the essence. The statement supporting Indonesia stirred up a hornets' nest because of Dutch-Indonesian tensions at that time over the trial of a former Chief of Dutch Military Intelligence charged with plotting to overthrow the Indonesian government, the conflict over Netherlands New Guinea, and the unilateral abridgment by Indonesia of certain financial and economic treaties. Third, if any general solution can be found it rests in the coordinating or mutual interests, not in the wholesale sacrifice of one set of interests to another. In North Africa, French, American, and African interests appear to coincide as respects "liberal solutions." Likewise in other regions the goal should be the harmonizing of interests. This calls for a judicious balancing of claims. Fourth, it is one of the ironies of history that force may be necessary to preserve colonial arrangements, not in order to perpetuate them, but that their orderly liquidation may be achieved. Fifth, it will not do to call every conflict of view between America and its European allies a colonial issue. On October 2, 1956, in what one commentator called a Freudian slip that betrayed the main lines of American thinking, Mr. Dulles noted that Britain and America were at odds over Suez on the question of the "shift from colonialism to independence." He treated Suez as an issue between the "colonial powers" and "the powers which are primarily and uniquely concerned with the problem of getting their independence as rapidly as possible." Walter Lippmann was prompt to point out that Egypt could hardly be considered a colony, especially as it sought to expand its national power. A British journal observed: "The American desire to keep the goodwill of the Arab states is good sense . . . but it will defeat itself in the end if, in pursuing it, the Americans think in anti-colonial conventions which are current. . . . In that way they will merely seek to please everybody, committing their strength to the support of local weak men, and overlooking that the conflicts which trouble the region, being real conflicts, require solutions of substance which are bound to give offense to some." [9] Finally, conflicts of interest— as in the past between Britain and India or the Dutch and the Indonesians— may be swept along by powerful historical movements until one side emerges supreme. Here it may be necessary for American policy-makers to choose sides, and in this way inevitably give offense. These facts need not preclude prudence and restraint, but the

[9] *The Economist* (London), December 8, 1956, p. 853.

end of the colonial era has changed the form, if not the substance, of choices Western leaders must make.

The moral problem. A final obstacle has roots in the moral problem. The question of right and wrong is continuously raised in international relations, as in all the other social orders. Nations as individuals either seek to do, or claim to have done, what is right. The nature of Western values as embodied in American culture assures that, far from being an exception, America persistently aspires to justice and to the goal of international order. We are pained when some aspect of national conduct cannot be justified in broader international terms, yet we can take comfort from the fact that historically this has been among the most baffling philosophical problems. The question is whether an action shall be called good if it serves the group of primary loyalty or whether it must serve a more inclusive purpose. Political morality as distinct from pure law or justice answers this question in terms that give it a unique flavor. It looks for the point of concurrence between the particular and the general value or interest, rather than calling for the sacrifice of the part to the whole. Politics can count on a residual egotism or self-interest which represents the creative potential of individuals and groups. The nascent international community must guard against extreme forms of parochial loyalty that claim too much and reserve to themselves the right to suppress and overwhelm weaker neighbors. Short of this, however, the larger community is able to harness, beguile, and deflect the more limited national purposes even though it cannot easily transcend them. In Reinhold Niebuhr's words: "The individual or the group may feel called upon to sacrifice an immediate value for the sake of the more ultimate or general interest. But the community cannot demand this sacrifice as its right." Nor, one might add, can another sovereign state.

The American credo of political morality, especially in recent years, has been more pretentious and less modest than this. It has often called upon others to sacrifice local advantage to some nobler and higher cause. Some of the statements we have had from French, Israeli, Egyptian, and British leaders on the Suez crisis have thrown a dash of political realism on the standards that the United States sought to impose. Justice and international order are properly considered the broad framework of political morality, but their relative emphasis in any decision and the particular content they should receive can never be determined in advance. The values of community and order are frequently in tension with the principles of justice, which are liberty and equality. In the fall of 1956, the international order suffered a threat to the peace. At the same time three of the nations invoked the principle of justice, which in equality calls for giving each man his due, including his right to survival. If the national community cannot assure a tolerable measure of justice, even though as a despotism it maintains order, in the long run its authority tends to erode. Similarly, if the international order lacks the power and prestige to safeguard all its members, they will be tempted to seek justice in other ways. There is an indefiniteness in political morality resulting because "various and frequently contradictory values are involved in political decisions and the preference which is given one value and end over another, must be determined by historical contingencies rather than fixed principles. There are fixed principles and norms in the political realm, but

there is no fixed principle for relating the norms to each other. It is possible to define as 'bad' only those situations in which one or more norms are completely wanting. . . ." [10]

America's policy-makers look for shortcuts to the moral problem. They talk a great deal more about promoting the impact of morality than about determining its content. They seize on the most readily available expressions congenial to their tastes and interests, like "majority rule" and "the will of the United Nations." The workings of political machinery are invested with all the trappings of a religious exercise, and political pronouncements are equated with the glorification of God. Repelled by all the talk of "missions" and "crusades," one of our most sensitive critics has said: "I would rather *be* moral than claim to be it; and to the extent we succeed in lending moral destruction to the conduct of our affairs, I would rather let others discover it for themselves." The deep pathos of the moral problem calls more for Christian humility than for a moralistic self-righteousness, which can win few friends abroad and serves only to lower the currency of moral principles.

CONCLUSION

When it comes to studying foreign policy in its various manifestations, and most particularly international conflict including war, the social scientist is in a difficult position. He is asked to explain and predict attitudes whose complexity makes a mockery of the few "scientific" tools we have. The layman presses us to predict American or Chinese foreign policy; to unwrap the famous riddle of the Soviet foreign

[10] Reinhold Niebuhr, unpublished manuscript on "Theory of International Politics," p. 11.

policy; or to explain the nature and conditions of conflict in our contemporary world.

The more stubborn and complex the material, the greater the temptation to move into the realm of abstraction. The canons of science call for simplicity and economy in the formulation of hypotheses that are to be tested. It is only when simple hypotheses are tested that the scientist moves into the more complex, slowly relating and checking his findings with the outside world. We, in contrast, find that we cannot test. As a result, many of us today find it easier *not* to relate our speculations to the outside world at all, and to create "propositions," "conceptual schemes," and "models" that have logical coherence, but fail to pass the test of empirical relevance. There is much futility in this.

The way out, in our opinion, is to assume from the start that the range of indeterminancy in our social and political world is great. This is even more applicable to the behavior of states that goes under the name of foreign policy. To attempt generalizations and construction of models that will give us a rigorous scientific understanding and prediction of foreign policy is a hopeless task.

As we move more into the realm of abstraction in the name of "science," we become more likely to evade—and perhaps evasion is the basic reason for the "scientific" trend involving a high degree of abstraction and conceptualization—our responsibilities in advancing an understanding of politics, notably in international relations and conflict. We would, for instance, suggest a better understanding and study of the existing laboratory conditions of conflict, i.e., history. (We cannot understand why simulated war games are more important to devise and study than actual or historical conflict situations from which all degree of simulation is eliminated by the stark and brutal necessity of real choice and decisions.) Secondly, we believe that case studies of the individual foreign policy-making process, including conflict of various states in terms of the descriptive categories suggested, would give us considerable food for thought and might lead us to more fruitful hypotheses.

One of our aims should be to find regularities in the behavior of nations and to develop general propositions by setting forth carefully the conditioning factors that account for types of behavior. Thus we may hope to reduce the range and degree of indeterminacy. But ours is also a world where exercise of will and choice calls for more than a scientific knowledge of man and nations.

The analytical approach to foreign policy, as distinct from the ideological approach, is no miracle-working device for understanding the complex problems of international affairs. It gives no clue to the specific decisions that must be reached daily in the cold war. It is not a cookbook with recipes for action to fit every contingency. It does, however, provide a way of thinking about the foreign policy of any country and ordering the factors that contribute to the conduct of foreign relations. If prediction is still beyond the reach of scholars, analysis in the face of varying contingencies may be attainable. In some form or another, this method is useful in studying the acts of great and small powers. With all the variation of individual scholars writing about unique national policies, the present book serves to demonstrate the role and the limits of the systematic analysis of foreign policy.

SELECTED BIBLIOGRAPHY

Almond, Gabriel A., *The American People and Foreign Policy* (New York: Frederick A. Praeger, Inc., 1960).

Aron, Raymond, *A Century of Total War* (New York: Doubleday & Company, Inc., 1954).

Beloff, Max, *Foreign Policy and the Democratic Process* (Baltimore: Johns Hopkins Press, 1955).

Buchanan, William, *How Nations See Each Other: A Study in Public Opinion* (Urbana: University of Illinois Press, 1953).

Duroselle, Jean-Baptiste, *La Politique Étrangère et ses Fondements* (Paris: Armand Colin, 1954).

Gross, Feliks, *Foreign Policy Analysis* (New York: Philosophical Library, 1954).

Haas, Ernest B. and Allen S. Whiting, *Dynamics of International Relations* (New York: McGraw Hill Book Company, Inc., 1956).

Halle, Louis J., *Civilization and Foreign Policy* (New York: Harper & Brothers, 1955).

Kennan, George F., *Realities of American Foreign Policy* (Princeton: Princeton University Press, 1954).

————, *American Diplomacy, 1900–1950* (Chicago: University of Chicago Press, 1951).

Marshall, C. B., *The Limits of Foreign Policy* (New York: Holt, Rinehart & Winston, Inc., 1955).

Morgenthau, Hans J., *Politics Among Nations* (New York: Alfred A. Knopf., 1954).

————, *The Purpose of America* (New York: Alfred Knopf, 1960).

————, and Kenneth W. Thompson, *Principles and Problems of International Politics* (New York: Alfred A. Knopf, 1951).

Nicolson, Harold, *Diplomacy* (New York: Harcourt, Brace & World, Inc., 1933).

————, *The Evolution of Diplomatic Methods* (New York: Harper & Brothers, 1955).

Thayer, Charles W., *Diplomat* (New York: Harper & Brothers, 1959).

Thompson, Kenneth W., *Christian Ethics and the Dilemmas of Foreign Policy* (Durham, North Carolina: Duke University Press, 1959).

————, *Political Realism and the Crisis of World Politics* (Princeton: Princeton University Press, 1960).

de Visscher, Charles, *Theory and Reality in Public International Law* (Princeton: Princeton University Press, 1956).

2

BRITISH

FOREIGN POLICY

The formation and execution of British foreign policy has often been regarded as a model for other countries, particularly for the United States. Much of the world has been willing to admire the method, if not always the substance, of British policy, assuming that Britain's policy-making process was calculated to serve the national interest, and that the wisdom and shrewdness of diplomacy prevailed over political emotions and parochial concerns. This diplomatic prestige was probably inevitable in light of so small an island kingdom's existing as a world power for several centuries. The reputation of the process by which British foreign policy was made and executed was enhanced by its success. It may be more difficult to sustain this reputation during the contemporary period of decline in Britain's status among the great powers. Neither the adjustment to second place in a military alliance nor the accommodation to massive imperial withdrawal, even if graciously accomplished, can appear as impressive as the policies that previously established Britain's leadership and empire. No nation has ever surrendered so much in so short a time as

LEON

D.

EPSTEIN

Britain has since 1945, but the world is not awed in the way that it was by the original accumulation of territory and power.

THE NATIONAL BACKGROUND

Economic geography

Except for Japan, whose days of glory were few, Britain is the only major power of modern times to be based on an island rather than a large continental area. It is easy to forget how small the British island home is. The whole of the United Kingdom, including the six counties of Northern Ireland, plus England, Wales, and Scotland, comes to just over 94,000 square miles—an area smaller than Oregon and only slightly larger than Minnesota. Over 50 million people now live in the United Kingdom, and about 44 million of this total are in England and Wales, which together have one of the highest population densities of any white community of comparable size. Ten million persons live in London and its immediate environs, and almost every Englishman is within a

29

day's rail journey of London.[1] This densely populated island is separated from the northwest coast of Europe by only 21 miles of open water, but even this distance has been sufficient for British life to develop its own distinctive pattern. Although isolation from European power struggles (in the nineteenth-century American manner) has never been feasible, the British have avoided identification as a purely European power.

Britain's island location and the absence of a nearby frontier, either in Britain or on the continent, made it natural for Englishmen to seek their fortunes in faraway places. This meant sea trade as well as colonial settlement, and both ventures were highly developed before the industrial revolution. Thus almost from the start British factories supplied an established overseas trade in addition to a domestic market. By the mid-nineteenth century, the large-scale exchange of domestic manufactures for overseas raw materials and foodstuffs became the cardinal feature of the British economy. Abundant coal, only recently expensive to mine, provided an important base for the early British industrial supremacy. Not until 1870 did this supremacy begin to fade in relation to the more rapid industrial growth of Germany and the United States.[2]

Nineteenth-century industrialization made the British almost entirely an urban people, and reduced agriculture to a decidedly secondary status. Now less than 5 per cent of the nation's gainfully employed workers are engaged in agriculture—a lower proportion than that of any other country in

the world.[3] Despite recent successful efforts to increase agricultural production, the British must remain predominantly a manufacturing people and also a people largely dependent on outside sources of food and raw materials. Well over half of the nation's food is now imported, and in order to pay for the food Britain must export a very high percentage of its manufactured products. British per capita real income does stand relatively high in the world, comparing favorably with that of continental Europe, but this standard rests heavily and uneasily on the vicissitudes of international economic relations.

Social structure

Class differentiation, on various bases, is treated more openly as a fact of life in Britain than in the United States, and this may lead to an exaggeration of the relative importance of class in British politics. It is true, however, that working-class consciousness has, at least until very recently, been definite and substantial. Despite the occupational rise of many Englishmen in each generation,[4] resembling American mobility patterns, the working class long retained a distinctive status resting on the assumption that most children of workers would themselves become workers. Except when this sense of status lead to a deferential attitude toward a traditional ruling class, it was associated with the solidarity of manual laborers, both in industrial unions and in political movements. Class consciousness of this kind may have been stronger in Britain than in the United

[1] Demographic and economic data are published by the Central Statistical Office, *Annual Abstract of Statistics* (London: H.M. Stationery Office).
[2] W. Stanford Reid, *Economic History of Great Britain* (New York: Ronald Press, 1954), pp. 337, 377.

[3] P. Sargent Florence, *The Logic of British and American Industry* (London: Routledge and Kegan Paul, 1953), p. 5.
[4] D. V. Glass, ed., *Social Mobility in Britain* (London: Routledge and Kegan Paul, 1954), p. 20.

States because of the residues of a feudal past and because of the uneven distribution of more limited benefits of early industrialization. But after the prosperous 1950's, there are signs of a less distinctive working class as the result of its exposure to material advantages previously reserved for the middle class. The egalitarian policies of government during and after World War II also played a part in blurring the strictly economic distinctions between workers and others.[5] Status has come to be identified more clearly with occupation than with income, and also with intangibles like style of life or manner of speech.[6]

An important role in the preservation of social class distinctions is played by the British educational system. This is obviously true of the famous "public schools," which are really private boarding or day institutions attracting at the secondary level almost all children whose parents can afford the fees. These fee-paying schools remain the most prestigious, and the best of them provide an education of extremely high quality. Government grammar schools also provide secondary education of quality, but only for a minority who display sufficient academic promise in examinations given at about age 11. The remaining students of secondary age go to other less academic government schools, most of them created since World War II. Comprehensive schools designed, like American high schools, to give courses under one roof for students of different abilities are still exceptional. The basic pattern, in publicly-supported secondary education, is to separate students sharply on the basis of ability. The best students are given the kind of education that fits

them, along with the products of the private fee-paying schools, to compete for the very limited number of places available in British universities, and to compete also for the scholarships that subsidize a large percentage of university students. It is clear that this system produces an able intellectual elite, selected largely on the basis of merit.[7] Now that ability counts heavily, along with wealth and family background, the child of the working class is able to secure both a grammar school and a university education. In doing so, however, he enters for most purposes an elite of the middle and upper classes, distinguished in educational experience and attainment from the bulk of the population. The tradition of class status is thus maintained even though opportunity to rise is modernized. It may be observed in the wide gulf between the newspapers of the elite, notably the *Times* and the *Guardian,* and those of the mass, still characterized by an extremely low quality popular press.

On the other hand, there are many ways in which the British population is markedly homogeneous. The population, despite a recent immigration from the West Indies, is still almost entirely white. It is also overwhelmingly of a "British stock," formed by successive invasions of long ago. The Scots and the Welsh preserve some distinctions, but their national background is assuredly British. Irish immigrants must be noted separately, but they, along with smaller numbers of continental refugees, are decidedly exceptional minorities. The great bulk of Britain's inhabitants, unlike Americans, have no national background save their present one. The British also have a considerable religious homogeneity. The nation is largely Protestant, with fewer than

[5] Dudley Seers, *The Levelling of Incomes Since 1938* (Oxford: Basil Blackwell, n.d.).

[6] T. H. Pear, *English Social Differences* (London: Allen and Unwin, 1955).

[7] Michael Young, *The Rise of the Meritocracy* (London: Thames and Hudson, 1958).

four million Roman Catholics and a half-million Jews.

Political experience

Not only are the British old as a people, but they are also old as a nation. The unity of England and Wales goes back to the Middle Ages, and even the union with Scotland dates from the beginning of the eighteenth century. The island was small enough to be dominated early by a single political authority, representing the numerically superior English population. National political institutions are of such long standing that loyalty to them can be taken for granted in a way that would be difficult for a people of a more recently created nation. Furthermore the supremacy of Parliament, in relation to the monarch, has been constitutionally established since 1688. Traditionally, the parliamentary regime was liberal and aristocratic: it was liberal in the sense of standing for the liberty of individuals and of property, and it was aristocratic in that relatively few were eligible to choose parliamentary representatives. Like British society in general, the political system was non-egalitarian until late in the nineteenth century, when the vote was extended to the mass of the population. That the political institutions, managed over centuries by a special ruling class, should thus have been democratized without revolution distinguishes British history from so much of the European continent's. But that history is also distinguished from America's by the fact that Britain had a long predemocratic political experience, and adapted universal suffrage to an old institutional pattern.

The liberalism of the British tradition has been associated particularly with the toleration of dissenting and unpopular opinions. Although there have been exceptions, respect for individual liberty of expression has been characteristic of modern British history. To some degree this reflects the heritage of Protestant religious differences which, since the seventeenth century, have been tolerated for the sake of internal peace. Whatever the source, there is no doubt about the vitality of the tradition in political as in religious matters. Sometimes it has meant toleration of eccentrics and even of those regarded as subversive elsewhere in the democratic world.

Persistent external concerns

Historically, Britain has had two major international concerns. The first has been to maintain ocean access to the Empire, the second to prevent any one power from dominating the continent of Europe. Both concerns have been vital to the national interest. Without overseas connections, Britain would be cut off not only from imperial possessions or Commonwealth partners, but also from the world trade sustaining British life. Even more directly would Britain be adversely affected if any single nation controlled Europe and so threatened to dominate Britain as well.

In the days when the British Empire was at its zenith, and when most of the now equal partners in the Commonwealth were imperial colonies, the simplest way to maintain overseas access was for Britain itself to command the seas. This is just what Britain did on its own until about the time of World War I. As long as "Britannia ruled the waves," the nation's trade routes were secure and so were military communications with the Empire. The growth of American naval power ended exclusive British control of the seas, but the advantages of that control remained because the United States became an ally and not an enemy. The first direct threat came from a German navy, and especially from German submarines in both world wars. For the first time in modern history an enemy was equipped with a force that could just possibly cut the British lifeline to the outside world. The airplane and the rocket bomb threatened the island even more dramatically during World War II. Ruling the waves, even if still within the power of Britain joined by the United States, was no longer enough to provide security for the island and its people.

The classic British concern with the European balance of power has sometimes been explained as a corollary of the nation's general position in the world. In his famous Foreign Office memorandum of 1907, Eyre Crowe assumed that Britain's capacity to command the seas, which he regarded as essential, would inspire fear and jealousy among other countries. To avert an anti-British combination based on such fear and jealousy, Crowe thought that Britain needed to make special efforts to develop a policy that harmonized with the interests of other nations. First among these interests, Crowe said, was independence, and therefore Britain had rightly championed (and should continue to champion) the independence of nations against any single powerful and ambitious state. In practice, this policy meant a grouping of forces against first one strong European power and then another, "but ever on the side opposed to the political dictatorship of the strongest single State or group at a given time."[8] So explained, Britain's

policy in Europe is a striking instance of high-mindedness coinciding with national self-interest.

THE POLICY-MAKING PROCESS

In discussing the conduct of British foreign affairs, observers sometimes hold that there has been a sharp change from control by a nineteenth-century executive elite to control by a twentieth-century legislative democracy.[9] This seems to overstate what has happened. Now as before the initiative remains in the hands of the executive branch. It may be granted that the contemporary executive, in exercising initiative, responds to a broader public than did nineteenth-century statesmen, whose concern was limited to an upper- and middle-class electorate. But the concern to secure support for a given foreign policy was no less real for a popular and successful nineteenth-century Foreign Secretary like Lord Palmerston, just because his public was smaller, than it is in present-day democratic Britain.[10] Moreover, the informed public, regularly concerned with foreign affairs, is by no means overwhelmingly large in our own time.

Governmental agencies

The executive authority. The basic constitutional principle is that the Crown is responsible for British policy. In modern times this means that responsibility is exercised by ministers of the Crown—the Government. Although

[8] Memorandum by Mr. Eyre Crowe in *British Documents on the Origins of the War 1898–1914*, Vol. III, ed. by G. P. Gooch and Harold Temperley (London: H.M. Stationery Office, 1928), p. 403. On the balance of power, see also Harold Nicolson, *Diplomacy* (London: Oxford University Press, 1950), p. 135.

[9] The belief that such a change has taken place is accepted, admiringly, by many left-wing writers, but it is also accepted as a fact, though an unfortunate one, by a conservative critic like Walter Lippmann, *The Public Philosophy* (Boston: Little, Brown & Co., 1955), p. 24.

[10] Sir Charles Webster, *The Foreign Policy of Palmerston*, Vol. I (London: G. Bell and Sons, 1951), pp. 44–51.

ministers hold office only by having the confidence of a majority in the House of Commons, the conduct of foreign policy is firmly in their hands and rarely subject to concessions necessary to retain that parliamentary confidence. Policy is not conceived as the product of legislative deliberation, but only as matter for debate after it has been submitted by the government. Practically speaking, the government usually consists of a Cabinet of fifteen to twenty ministers, chosen by the Prime Minister from among his party's most important political leaders. The members of the Cabinet share executive responsibility in a way that an American administration does not. The Prime Minister is not so dominant as is a President in relation to his Cabinet.

Nevertheless, the Prime Minister himself assumes a special responsibility in all major foreign policy matters even though ordinarily—and always since 1924—the foreign secretaryship is entrusted to another member of the Cabinet. The Foreign Secretary is much more than the Prime Minister's agent, but he is not free to make policies without the approval of his chief, and, more generally, of the Cabinet. Contrary to general impressions, the foreign secretaryship has not always, especially in recent years, gone to a man greatly experienced in international affairs. Sir Anthony Eden did have such an orientation even before he first became Foreign Secretary, but Labour's two postwar appointees, Ernest Bevin and Herbert Morrison, had both been concerned almost exclusively with domestic matters before assuming the Foreign Secretary's duties. Considerations other than experience in foreign affairs evidently guide the selection. It may be just as important to find a man—like the trade unionist Ernest Bevin—who is fully equipped to lead party members, or a man in whom the Prime Minister can have great personal confidence. The latter is illustrated by the combination of Prime Minister Churchill and Foreign Secretary Eden, by Eden and Selwyn Lloyd in 1956, and by Macmillan and Lord Home in 1960.

The Prime Minister and the Foreign Secretary are not the only members of the political executive (that is, of the government) who deal with foreign affairs. Since World War II, with the Foreign Secretary in the Commons, there have been four additional ministerial, non-cabinet appointees in the Foreign Office: two ministers of state and two joint under-secretaries of state, distributed between the two houses of Parliament. This arrangement was modified in 1960 when Lord Home became the first foreign secretary since 1940 to be in the House of Lords; it was then found suitable to have a foreign affairs spokesman in the Commons who would carry the authority of a cabinet member, and accordingly an important M.P., Edward Heath, was made Privy Seal for this purpose and one of the ministers of state was dropped. Beyond these Foreign Office appointees, there are other ministers whose work relates closely to foreign affairs. This is especially true of the Chancellor of the Exchequer and the Minister of Defense, and of the secretaries for Commonwealth Relations and for Colonial Affairs. What must be said of all ministers dealing with foreign affairs, whether or not they are directly assigned to that sphere, is that they are primarily politicians and only secondarily specialists in the subject-matter of their ministries. The Foreign Secretary, like any minister, exercises executive authority as a member of his government, and the government represents the political leadership of the nation.

The foreign service. Deliberately and carefully differentiated from the political level in the conduct of foreign affairs is the career service. As a distinguished retired career officer explained, "The Foreign Service is an instrument of Government; it does not formulate policy." However, it is granted that the Foreign Service, by presenting all the material facts, "advises the Secretary of State on what his policy should be." [11] Obviously the giving of advice in this manner contains an element of influence. Even though the power to make policy remains in the hands of the political authority, and that authority has been known to act against the advice of career officials, the description of the Foreign Service's role as limited to carrying out policy must be qualified in view of the inevitable indefiniteness of any line between formulation and execution.

A sense of profession is highly developed and of long standing in the Foreign Service. Admission to the Foreign Office itself as well as to the diplomatic service has been firmly based on open competitive examinations since the 1870's, when a similar procedure was adopted in the British civil service generally. Recruitment, then as now, was separate from recruitment of members of the home service, and the development of special standards of competition gave the Foreign Service a prestige of its own. Until after World War I there was even a separation between diplomatic personnel and Foreign Office (or headquaters) personnel. Not only has this separation disappeared, but since the large-scale reorganization of 1943 the Foreign Service now includes the formerly distinct Consular and Commercial-Diplomatic Services plus some auxiliary services. The whole of this enlarged Foreign Service, however, remains distinct from the bulk of civil service employees.

The traditionally prestigious elements of the Foreign Service have been the diplomats and the top-level personnel of the Foreign Office. It is they who occupy the positions for which independent means and social status were once requisites, and for which the intellectual and personal standards have been so high as to favor those with the very best educational backgrounds. Ordinarily this meant high-ranking graduates of Oxford and Cambridge, but recently the class bias which this implies has been mitigated by the greatly enlarged state scholarship program at British universities. Intellectually the method of selection has remained as rigorous as ever, and possibly become more elaborate through the postwar use of an interview conducted during a candidate's 48 hours of residence in a town or country house.[12]

Real career opportunities have been afforded by the Foreign Service because the very top positions, with rare exceptions, have been reserved for members of the Service. With respect to diplomatic assignments, British practice has differed notably from the once-prevalent and still practiced American custom of giving the best foreign posts to politicians and businessmen as rewards for their contributions to successful presidential campaigns. It is equally important to appreciate that the British promotional ladder also includes the extremely important positions involving administrative direction of the Foreign Office, particularly the post of Permanent Under-Secretary for Foreign Affairs. The word "Permanent" in this context distinguishes the civil service position from those secretaries and

[11] Frank T. Ashton-Gwatkin, *The British Foreign Service* (Syracuse: Syracuse University Press, 1950), p. 49.

[12] *Ibid.,* pp. 85–88. Also on recruitment see Lord Strang, *The Foreign Office* (New York: Oxford University Press, 1955), chaps. 4–5.

under-secretaries who are political appointees of the Government of the day. Among career officers, the Permanent Under-Secretary is the main official adviser to the Foreign Secretary, and he is also the administrative head of the Foreign Service. His advice on policy matters may be ignored or overridden, as it was by the Chamberlain Government of the 1930's, but this is hardly regarded as normal or desirable in the British system.

Members of the Foreign Service have vigorously defended their position as *the* British specialists in international matters. For example, there have been strong protests against the Treasury's effort during the interwar years to maintain the same control over Foreign Office personnel procedure as was exercised by the Treasury over the domestic civil service. Such control by outsiders, it has been argued, was so serious as to contribute to the ineffectiveness of British foreign policy during the 1930's.[13] Since World War II, the independence of the Foreign Office has been secure, at least in the sense that the authority of the Secretary of the Treasury, as Head of the Civil Service, does not extend to Foreign Service personnel. No doubt much can be said for the spirit with which the Service guards its standards, but this very spirit has caused outsiders to suspect that the Foreign Service might have too much confidence in its own members. In particular, it has been suggested that the Service was slow in recognizing serious faults in the records of two subsequently notorious members, Maclean and Burgess, who defected to the Communists.[14]

One last point about the Foreign Service deserves notice. Its members, even the Permanent Under-Secretary, do not assume public responsibility for governmental policy even if their advice has helped to formulate it. The responsibility is the minister's and the government's. So well established is this principle, in custom as in law, that career officials remain entirely outside the arena of political debate over policy. Any attack on the government's policy is directed to political ministers, not to Foreign Service officers. Mistakes, if there are any, have to be accepted by politicians.

Parliament. To say that the British legislative authority does not make foreign policy is not to say that in this area it has no influence at all. As the most significant focal point for British debate and controversy, Parliament exerts a great influence, but the whole context of the British political system limits Parliament to an indirect role. The principle that the Cabinet holds office only as long as its policies are supported by the votes of a majority in the Commons must be understood in light of the fact that the Commons does not exercise its power to reject government policy. Plainly the Commons contains a majority of a given party which regularly supports the government and its policy. Although not all members of a parliamentary party always like all of their leaders' policies, only rarely does any one of them vote against the leadership on a parliamentary question involving confidence in the government. If individual members of the majority do directly influence their government's policies, it is through intraparty discussion and pressure. Regular occasions are provided for internal party communication between backbench members and their party leaders in the government. The parliamentary party meets as a whole from time to

[13] Ashton-Gwatkin, pp. 26–27.
[14] Ernest Davies, "The Foreign and Commonwealth Services," *The Civil Service in Britain and France,* ed. by William A. Robson (New York: Macmillan, 1956), p. 67.

time, and also in the form of subject-matter committees. Thus there is, within each parliamentary party, a foreign affairs committee for particularly interested M.P.'s. In the case of the majority party's committee, the appropriate ministers do meet with its members on request. Whatever the arguments here between backbencher and minister, the policy that emerges, whether or not it is influenced by the arguments, will regularly be supported in parliamentary voting by a cohesive and disciplined party.[15] The minority party, or parties, provides the opposition vote in the Commons, but by definition it always loses.

Since the Parliament is not an independent center of authority, there is nothing comparable to the loci of power represented by American congressional committees and their chairmen. Individual M.P.'s do not share in policy-making in foreign affairs, or ordinarily in any other area, unless they are also members of the Government, and particularly of the Cabinet, which is *the* significant committee of the House of Commons. Nor with respect to the administrative conduct of policy can M.P.'s outside the responsible executive authority exert the direct influence that is within the capacity of American legislators.[16]

Freed from independent decision-making, Parliament exists to debate the policies of the government. It does so vigorously and significantly. The popularly elected Commons is the main forum, but occasionally there are important foreign affairs debates in the House of Lords as well. Always, however, it is in the Commons that the

government is expected to make the principal defense of its policies against the Opposition. Although each parliamentary party contains a variety of individual views, which find expression in debate if not in voting, major attention is ordinarily focused on the give-and-take between party leaders. On an important occasion the government's policy will be presented and defended by the Foreign Secretary (if an M.P. and not a Lord), one or two of his political aides, and the Prime Minister; the Opposition will then be represented by appropriate members of its "shadow cabinet"—that is, particularly by its prospective foreign secretary and its prospective prime minister (the Opposition leader). Thus a Commons debate is mainly between those responsible for policy and those who would like to be and might well become responsible. It is a discussion between a government and its alternative.[17]

The question may be raised about how much a debate really matters. Although a bad governmental showing does not modify majority approval in the immediate circumstances, it can weaken the position of the cabinet leaders within their own party and so possibly lead to future changes in personnel or policy. And it can strengthen the Opposition before the country, thus influencing future elections. Similarly, a weak Opposition case can damage the leadership of the minority party. There is not much doubt that British politicians place great store by performance in debate, and no minister is likely to survive if his own supporters find him a poor spokesman for the government and the party.

Foreign policy debates in the Com-

[15] This subject is treated at some length in the author's "Cohesion of British Parliamentary Parties," *American Political Science Review*, Vol. L, pp. 360–77 (June 1956).

[16] Max Beloff, *Foreign Policy and the Democratic Process* (Baltimore: Johns Hopkins Press, 1955), pp. 25–26.

[17] The most dramatic example was the prolonged debate between the Labour opposition and the Conservative government over Britain's Suez intervention. 558–560 *H.C. Deb.* passim (30 Oct.–8 Nov. 1956).

mons occur, in one form or another, with considerable frequency. Usually they are scheduled in order to discuss a currently controversial policy or subject, and accordingly the interval between debates varies with the number of international crises. However, there is at least one foreign affairs debate every three or four weeks. The politically conscious members of the community may follow the proceedings in the full reports of the nation's quality newspapers, and also in the columns of critical comment carried by the serious intellectual weeklies. Although little parliamentary news is carried in the popular dailies for the benefit of the mass of the population, the serious press does very well in keeping the sizable educated minority informed as to the course of parliamentary discussion.

In addition to full-fledged debates on foreign affairs, the government is subject to attack during the regularly scheduled Commons question period—the first hour of each of the first four meeting days of the week. During this period questions are addressed to ministers concerning their various policies. Foreign affairs receives its share of questions, both from Opposition members and from the majority party's own followers. Sometimes the questions are directed to the Prime Minister instead of the Foreign Secretary or his political aides. More often than is possible for other subjects, foreign affairs questions can be turned away on the ground that to answer would violate national security. However, there are many questions, sometimes difficult and embarrassing, that government spokesmen do attempt to handle. Politically it is unwise for ministers to dodge too many questions. The question period as well as the general debate serves to exemplify the usefulness of Parliament's role with respect to policy-

making: to question and criticize, but not to defeat the government.

Apart from strictly party criticism, designed to embarrass the Government for the Opposition's benefit, there are some parliamentary remarks that, although not unrelated to party considerations, reflect an individual M.P.'s concern with a particular aspect of world affairs. The leading case in point is the parliamentary performance of Winston Churchill in the 1930's. As a nonministerial member of the governing Conservative party, Churchill used the Commons as the principal forum for his views on the dangers of British military weakness in relation to Hitler's Germany. Much less famously, the left-wing Labour critics of Britain's postwar anti-Soviet alliance with the United States tried to employ parliamentary speeches as a way of gaining attention and support for their protests against the policies first of their own Labour government and later of the Conservative government. A number of imperialist Conservative M.P.'s used their parliamentary opportunities in the late 1950's to protest what they regarded as the scuttling of the Empire—illustrated in their minds especially by British withdrawal from the Suez Canal Zone.

Nongovernmental Agencies

Political parties. Although there are wide areas of agreement on some critical occasions, as illustrated by wartime coalitions, it is normal and legitimate for the party out of power to attack either the substance or the execution of the foreign policy of the party in office. Outside of Parliament, both major parties (and the recently revived Liberal party as well) maintain large mass organizations with rather loosely defined relations to the respective parliamentary parties and their leaders.

These extraparliamentary organizations are not simply cadres of office-holders and prospective office-holders.[18] Nor are they skeletonized structures to be filled out only during election campaigns. They contain large numbers of regular dues-paying members. On this score, the Conservative structure is simpler than Labour's. Conservative membership is entirely individual and direct. The member joins a Conservative constituency association, which is affiliated to the National Union of Conservative and Unionist Associations. Total membership has risen to about three million in the postwar years. Labour's more complicated structure allows both direct and indirect memberships. In addition to about one million who belong to constituency Labour associations, over five million are counted as members because they belong to trade unions that are affiliated to the Labour party and pay dues to the party out of the union dues of their members.

From the viewpoint of each party's parliamentary leadership, the principal purpose of the mass membership is undoubtedly to help win elections. Advice, let alone direction, on policy questions is hardly desired, but this does not prevent the organized membership from offering and even urging such advice. Regular dues-paying members have often become active in the first place in order to have a role affecting policy. There are two levels at which rank-and-file members can try to influence decisions. The first is through the constituency organization, which in each case, Conservative or Labour, selects its parliamentary candidate, and would therefore appear to have the means to influence decisively the position of an M.P. How much and how often this channel of influence is used cannot readily be discovered. Certainly there are very few instances of sitting M.P.'s being locally rejected for subsequent candidacy because of policy disagreements, and in such cases (as those occurring after the Suez crisis of 1956) the M.P.'s have been rejected because they violated national party positions. Indeed, the constituency associations seem to reinforce national party leadership by using their candidate-selection power to make it unlikely that any M.P.'s would move toward the parliamentary opposition. This is understandable, since members of a constituency association are recruited on the basis of loyalty to the national party cause. They may tolerate M.P.'s who occasionally deviate toward a position more extreme than that of party leaders—that is, a position farther removed from that of the other party— but they do not want M.P.'s whose deviation tends to help the opposition. This means, among other things, that a constituency association is unlikely to press an M.P. to adopt a policy at variance with that of the national party leaders. That an association would have such a policy is itself unlikely in the highly centralized system of British politics.

The second level for rank-and-file influence is the national conference held annually by each major party. The conference seems designed for this purpose, and avowedly so in the Labour case. Delegates to each conference are chosen by the various units of the national party, and they have the opportunity to present, discuss, and vote on policy resolutions. On foreign affairs as on other matters the mass membership of each party has had distinctive views which it has sought, via conference resolutions, to persuade or pressure party leaders to adopt. The Conservative conference has done so

[18] The fullest account of the relationship of mass to parliamentary parties is by R. T. McKenzie, *British Political Parties* (London: William Heinemann, Ltd., 1955).

without claiming the power to fix the parliamentary leadership's policy, but the Labour conference has often acted as though it and the executive committee elected by the conference did have such power. The Labour party constitution gives the external mass organization the power to decide general policy, presumably for the parliamentary Labour party. This is at odds with the usual British conception of policy-making by parliamentary representatives individually and collectively responsible to the electorate. It is also at odds with much of Labour's own practice, especially in the really significant circumstances when the party formed the Government, 1945–1951. Then Labour government leaders succeeded in getting the party conference to support foreign policy positions already adopted by the Government. Parliamentary party leaders continued, during most of the subsequent decade after Labour went into opposition, to have the initiative and to be successful in persuading delegates to accept official policy, occasionally in compromised form. Only in 1960 did the Labour conference adopt foreign policy resolutions, advocating unilateral nuclear disarmament, which were opposed by the parliamentary leadership. At least for the time being, however, the leadership refused to accept these resolutions as policy to be adopted by the parliamentary party. Thus the issue of whether the external party could force its policy on a reluctant parliamentary party was left unanswered. The leadership, instead of resigning or shifting its own position, could still try to change the conference's resolution in another year.

Regardless of their disputed role in determining policy, organized parties do serve, much more regularly than in the United States, as media for the expression of public opinion and thus as agencies of popular pressure if not of popular control. Although the international view of neither party has been monolithic, it is fair to say that the tendency of activist pressure, Labour or Conservative, has been ideologically more doctrinaire than that of actual British policy as supported by moderate opinion. This is plainer and more significant in the Labour party, largely because of the already-noted role of the annual conference. Left-wing critics of official policy were numerous and persistent whether defeated, as they were on a variety of resolutions in the 1950's, or successful, as they were on unilateral nuclear disarmament in 1960. They represented a strong tendency among party activists; in fact, it is probable that their views represented a majority of such activists even in the 1950's when they failed as followers of Aneurin Bevan and of Bevanism to move the party to the left. Their failure then was the result of fairly solid support (until 1960) for the official leadership by the major trade unions and their bloc vote. Sources of this persistent left-wing advocacy in foreign affairs have been both socialist and pacifist. Opposition to "power politics" and "imperialism" is traditional in party ideology. So is a commitment to a distinctively "socialist foreign policy." In this perspective, zealots have opposed German rearmament, suspected the Anglo-American alliance itself, and rejected nuclear weapons.[19]

Among Conservatives there has been a contrary ideological tendency in the foreign policy that derives from party tradition. Generally the tendency is right-wing, but it is more accurately

[19] For examples, see the *53rd Annual Report of the Labour Conference* (1954), pp. 69–89, the *54th Annual Report of the Labour Conference* (1955), pp. 137–51, and the *59th Annual Report of the Labour Conference* (1960).

called imperial. "Empire" has been the emotive word for zealous Conservatives as "socialist" has been for Labour. Without so openly challenging established party leadership as has the Labour Left, the Conservative imperialists have used the annual conference to urge various measures to preserve the Empire—a term that Conservatives often prefer to Commonwealth even when they mean the latter. Speeches and resolutions have ordinarily been general and exhortative, but occasionally the party has been asked to take a specific stand. A case in point is past opposition to the General Agreement on Trade and Tariffs (GATT) on the ground that free trade would sacrifice the Imperial Preference system. Also, in one way or another, delegates to fairly recent Conservative conferences have demonstrated their uneasiness about how well the Empire was being protected, and a desire that the Conservative leadership adopt a tougher line against Britain's enemies than has been typical of postwar governmental policy, Conservative or Labour.[20] In particular, there has been a rank-and-file Conservative element, though not always a dominant one, that preferred the use of military force to the surrender of British interests, and so rallied readily to support the kind of action taken by Eden's government in Suez in 1956. Of course, the whole imperialist movement is now finally receding along with the Empire itself. Suez may have been a last fling. What seems to remain important within the Conservative party is a lingering identification with British settlers in east and central Africa, and consequently a possible internal party pressure against the prevailing governmental policy of yielding power to native African majorities.

Rank-and-file pressures in constituencies and in party conferences are often closely related to differences of opinion within the parliamentary parties. It is really the M.P.'s composing these parties who are the direct objects of whatever influence the external organizations can bring to bear. Despite the advantages, already described, of the party's leadership in maintaining parliamentary cohesion—especially when holding governmental office—the fact remains that the few hundred M.P.'s composing a majority party do have a final authority. Their backing for a policy has to be secured by a government. And when a party is out of power there is even room for some initiative by the parliamentary party membership. Labour formally gives control of its Opposition policy to the parliamentary party as a whole, and the Conservative party maintains an equivalent though less clear-cut means for backbench M.P.'s to express their opinions, which may also be the opinions of their constituency followers.

In discussing the role of parties it should be pointed out that, despite opposing extremists within each party, the moderate Conservative and the moderate Labour leaders have occupied a good deal of common ground with respect to Britain's postwar foreign policy. Rearmament and the American alliance, to take two leading examples, have not been at issue between the two parties. It has been unusual for there to be so significant an interparty division as was reflected by Labour's virtually united opposition to the Conservative government's Egyptian campaign of 1956. Generally the Liberals, the chief minor party, have also shared the common foreign policy of the Conservative and Labour moderates.

[20] See the *74th Annual Report of the Conservative Conference* (1954), p. 51, and the *75th Annual Report of the Conservative Conference* (1955), pp. 27, 33.

Liberal strength in parliament, however, has been so limited during the last few decades that the party, despite recent signs of revival, cannot yet be treated as an important channel of influence on policy-making. The Liberal party has not been an alternative government in the same way as the Labour party has during its last decade of opposition. Only the bare possibility exists that the Liberals will succeed in displacing Labour as the principal alternative to the Conservatives.

Interest groups. Lately the standard view of the unimportance of interest groups in the British political process has been subject to question, and the beginning of the study of such groups has disclosed a large influence, at least in domestic matters. Nor does anyone doubt that, on such questions as tariffs, British manufacturers, unions, and farmers have means of effectively conveying their preferences to governmental authority. However, it is evident that British interest groups, though as multifarious as those anywhere else, operate differently from their American counterparts. The very fact that political parties are national in character and cohesive in parliamentary organization limits the usefulness of pressuring legislators, directly or through constituents, for individual votes. To affect the main lines of governmental policy, certainly in foreign affairs, a British interest group would have to influence a party's leadership, or more remotely the bulk of a parliamentary party. Neither of these avenues seems feasible except for the biggest interest groups, although on lesser matters, particularly those involving administrative decisions, it may be assumed that smaller groups exert influence. Certainly it is established governmental practice to consult representatives of interest groups likely to be affected by con-templated policies. This practice is institutionalized and accepted in Britain.

Major British interest groups tend to have direct connections with a political party. The outstanding example is that of the trade unions, most of which are affiliated to the Labour party and thus share directly, often dominantly, in that party's policy-making. The unions also have a general organization, the Trades Union Congress, which is not affiliated to the Labour party and which does confer with Governments of either party in behalf of union interests. Somewhat similarly the cooperative movement works both within and outside the Labour party. The Conservatives have no precise organizational counterparts, but industrial leaders maintain close connections with the party. This they do both personally, as important Conservatives themselves, and through the usual business organizations, the most notable of which is the Federation of British Industries. More particularized trade associations, like individual trade unions, may also maintain communication with party leaders on policy matters of direct concern. A distinctive feature of this political communication, at least from an American point of view, is that often individual backbench M.P.'s openly serve as agents for interest groups—business, union, farm, and others. M.P.'s are even subsidized for this purpose by the groups they represent.

Generally the most substantial interest groups concerned with foreign policy decisions are not organized primarily to influence such decisions. This holds for the important domestic economic groups noted above, and also for other types of organizations. Churches would plainly be in this category. Through their official representatives, they do express opinions bearing on British foreign policy, although the expression of such opinions is only incidental to their main role. Veterans' groups are another case in point, although their efforts to influence general policy are less prominent in Britain than those of comparable groups in the United States. The same can be said, for a different reason, of the activities of ethnic groups. Such groups are simply less significant in Britain because of the absence of large ethnic minorities of the sort that compose so much of the American population. Although there are, and almost always have been, continental European refugees in Britain, their numbers have not been sufficient to constitute serious pressure on British foreign policy-making. Even the Jewish population of half a million cannot be said to be an electoral factor in determining British policy toward Israel, despite a vigorous Zionist movement—represented particularly in the Labour party. Similarly the Irish minority, largely in a few seaports and manufacturing centers, is not a major influence. It does, like the Zionists, have parliamentary spokesmen.

In addition to all of the groups, of varying influence, impinging on foreign affairs incidental to their other purposes, there are also many British groups organized entirely around foreign policy issues. These may be less substantial, but they are often most active propagandistically. Some organizations are devoted to particular causes, such as justice or freedom for certain people in a certain place, and they wax and wane with the excitement of the issue. Others are broader in scope and more durable. Examples are provided by the interwar League of Nations and the more recent United Nations. Another, operating at a scholarly and almost official level to influence opinion-makers, is the Royal Institute of International Affairs. Similar in its limited public is the newer Institute of Strategic Studies. At an altogether different level of activity, and also with a very different point of view, is the mass-membership organization, the Campaign for Nuclear Disarmament. Developed in the late 1950's to oppose Britain's retention of nuclear weapons, the CND undoubtedly mobilized the residual pacifism and neutralism of socialists, students, intellectuals, and miscellaneous middle-class citizens. Their most spectacular demonstration has been a well-publicized protest march each spring from a nuclear weapons center to a Trafalgar Square rally. The Nuclear Disarmers became active not only in this way and through a flood of speeches and literature, but also in the Labour party, where their position came to be accepted by important trade-union leaders as well as by many constituency party workers. To a high degree, the decision of the Labour party conference in 1960 to support unilateral nuclear disarmament was a victory for the campaign of the previous few years.

Mass media of communication. The basic point about British mass media is their national character. Strictly local and regional newspapers are minor in relation to the media centered in London. The British audience is essentially national for newspapers, magazines, radio, and television. Opinion concerning foreign policy, as that concerning most domestic policy, is formed nationally and not regionally.

British communication has also been given a special character by the continued monopoly of radio broadcasting by the government-owned British Broadcasting Corporation, and by a similar television monopoly until 1955, when closely supervised commercial television was allowed to compete with the B.B.C. The government-owned service has avoided the editorializing news commentary typical of American radio and television. The news is reported straight and without dramatization by the B.B.C., and a similar standard is expected of the new commercial television. However, B.B.C. facilities are used by Government spokesmen, particularly the Prime Minister and the Foreign Secretary, for official expositions of foreign policy. The importance of this means of communication with the nation was firmly established by the successful wartime speeches of Winston Churchill. Some radio and television time is divided, according to an agreed-upon formula, between political parties for a presentation of their views on international as well as other issues. Occasionally, too, there are discussion programs involving foreign policy. Television, as in the United States, is the growingly important means of reaching a mass public, but in no case is there any purchase of time for the presentation of opinions.

Neutrality in British radio and television contrasts with sharply partisan attachments on the part of the press. Except for Labour's London *Daily Herald,* whose policies have been affected by its trade-union connections, this partisanship is solely a matter of choice by ordinary private publishers. Most papers lean to the Conservatives, but the largest London paper, the *Daily Mirror,* is pro-Labour. Although none of the mass-circulation dailies, like the *Mirror* and its several pro-Conservative counterparts, give much serious editorial or news attention to international affairs, it is through their headlines, often slanted by partisan considerations, that a large share of the British population forms its perspective with respect to international policies. Nevertheless the quality press, even with its small circulation, deserves more attention as a molder of opinions.[21] A few papers reach most Englishmen who have opinion-making roles. Except in Scotland, where there are equivalent newspapers, almost every person seriously concerned with national and international affairs reads either the quasi-official *Times* of London or the liberal *Guardian.* If "seriously concerned" is defined more broadly, the category should include the readers of the Conservative *Daily Telegraph,* which is unusual in that its news presentation stands between the popular press and the quality press. Just as striking as this daily newspaper situation is the fact that either one of two Sunday papers, the *Observer* or the *Sunday Times,* is read by virtually the whole of the serious English public. In addition, the special importance of the weekly *Economist* should be noted; more than other intellectually oriented weeklies, like the *Spectator* and the left-wing *New Statesman,* the *Economist* reaches the influential. Although these various papers and periodicals often present divergent views, there is an intimacy about the English circle of discussion that is absent in a larger and less centralized political community.

Less highly organized media of communication also play an important role in Britain. Pamphlets, for instance, are still widely used by party and party-affiliated groups to reach the public. A good example was the Bevanite circulation in 1951 of a series of pamphlets outlining the left-wing's opposition to Britain's foreign policy. Furthermore, in a nation that does more book-reading than is usual in Amer-

[21] An excellent study emphasizing the role of the quality press in opinion formation is R. Bassett, *Democracy and Foreign Policy, A Case History: The Sino-Japanese Dispute, 1931–1933* (London: Longmans, Green & Co., 1952).

ica, it is worth mentioning that both scholarly and popular volumes on foreign policy reach the public. Nor should speeches at public meetings, even though declining in popularity as a result of television competition, be neglected as a means of influencing political audiences. A speech by a major public figure remains an important occasion at least for the membership of a political party.

General role of public opinion

Many of the agencies just discussed under the heading of "nongovernmental" are often conceived as representing public opinion in contrast to the official agencies of governmental policy-making. For analytical purposes it has been useful to adhere to this distinction, but there is another approach employed by English critics. The term "Establishment" is used to refer loosely to an inner circle of important ministers, top civil servants, editors of the serious press, and a miscellany of persons, many academic, who informally consult with the others. Based on common social and intellectual backgrounds, the members of this Establishment overlap governmental and nongovernmental agencies. They not only make policy; they also expound it through the quality papers and in university halls.

No doubt there is more divergence among the British influential than the concept of an Establishment conveys. But with or without the term, the British community frankly recognizes the leadership groups that, in Gabriel Almond's phrase, "carry on the specific work of policy formulation and policy advocacy." As Almond has also pointed out, though in reference to the United States, an elite of this sort does not operate independently of "certain policy criteria in the form of widely held values and expectations." [22] The British public, like publics elsewhere, sets such criteria, and the policy-makers are limited thereby—as, for instance, by the public's manifest desire for peace. The subtlety of these relations was well described by Kenneth Younger, a former Minister of State for Foreign Affairs. Control of foreign policy, he said, was more oligarchic than control of domestic policy, and on first reflection he thought of no occasion when he or his superiors "had been greatly affected by public opinion in reaching important decisions." But this first impression he realized was misleading, because public opinion did affect ministers in a general way. "The Government," he wrote, "tends to identify itself almost unconsciously with a vaguely sensed general will, and no clear formulation of the pressure of public opinion upon Government policy ever occurs." [23] Younger believed that a Government identified itself especially with its own supporters.

THE SUBSTANCE OF FOREIGN POLICY

Ordinarily it is assumed, whatever respective party positions happen to be, that major elements in British foreign policy are not subject to drastic change.[24] No such change was evident,

[22] Gabriel Almond, *The American People and Foreign Policy* (New York: Harcourt, Brace & World, Inc., 1950), pp. 5, 6.

[23] Kenneth Younger, "Public Opinion and Foreign Policy," *British Journal of Sociology* (VI) June 1955, pp. 169, 171.

[24] Basic material on British policy of the recent past may be found in *Documents on British Foreign Policy* 1919–1939, ed. by E. L. Woodward and Rohan Butler (London: H.M. Stationery Office, 1947–1954), and a general historical account in *The Cambridge History of British Foreign Policy 1783–1919*, ed. by A. W. Ward and G. P. Gooch (London: Cambridge University Press, 1922–1923).

for example, in the transfer of office from Conservative to Labour in 1945, or from Labour to Conservative in 1951. The definition of the national interest remains fairly stable, and the world situation allows a government only limited choices, often confined to methods, tone, and timing.

Commonwealth relations

Properly speaking, Britain's imperial policy may not belong in the sphere of foreign affairs, and the details of that policy cannot be specified here. However, in international matters the British themselves view the Commonwealth (or Empire as it has, at least until recently, been called by its oldest champions) as an overseas extension of the British nation and thus as an entity through which Britain can play a larger role in the world than it could as an island kingdom standing alone. As a recent British ambassador to the United States has declared: "It would be misleading to talk about the British contribution to the free world solely in terms of the efforts and the economy of the fifty million people in the British Isles. Britain lies at the heart of the Commonwealth, and the Commonwealth contains over six hundred million people, more than a third of the population of the free world." [25]

The Commonwealth is a unique institution. Its members in 1960 were 11 sovereign states without fixed political obligations. They regularly consult each other, and often reach agreement even though there is no legal need to do so. Each of the 11 states has some kind of British heritage, if not from immigration at least from a period of years under British rule. Each finds it convenient, economically at any rate, to maintain the Commonwealth tie. The symbol of free association is the Queen, acknowledged by all as Head of the Commonwealth and by some member nations as their own crowned head. In the latter category are Britain itself and those other Commonwealth members closest to Britain in ethnic origin, language, and customs: Australia, New Zealand, Canada, and, until 1960, the Union of South Africa. Significantly, the first new postwar members, India, Pakistan and Ceylon, became republics, and in their different view of the Queen as in other more substantial ways these nations, containing two-thirds of the Commonwealth's 600 million people, cause the whole structure to appear less united than the British would prefer. However, to hold the Asian members within the Commonwealth, Britain has been willing to make the structure even more flexible and informal than it was when originally developed in the inter-war period. Similar accommodation was possible for Ghana, Malaya, and Nigeria as they became member nations, 1957–1960.

In addition to its 11 present members the Commonwealth contains other countries that are not fully self-governing and are not therefore "members." [26] These remaining British dependencies contained only about 50 million people in 1960, many, such as the West Indies Federation and Sierra Leone, already on the verge of self-government and so of likely member-nation status as well. An exceptional instance is Southern Rhodesia, whose white settlers have long been self-governing in domestic affairs and whose government has been treated for some purposes as though Southern Rhodesia was a member na-

[25] Sir Roger Makins, "The Commonwealth in World Affairs," *Labor and Industry in Britain* (XIV), Sept. 1956, p. 116.

[26] K. C. Wheare, "The Nature and Structure of the Commonwealth," *American Political Science Review* (XLVII), Dec. 1953, p. 1025.

tion. This situation is further complicated by the inclusion of Southern Rhodesia in the presently shaky Central African Federation with Northern Rhodesia and Nyasaland, whose native African inhabitants object to the connection. This Federation as a whole, or if it collapses each of its three components (possibly joined to other territories), is a potential Commonwealth member-nation when the time arrives for choice as a self-governing country. The same choice is to be made eventually by every other substantial territory (like Tanganyika, Kenya, and Uganda) left as a British African dependency. In fact, the only exceptions, anywhere in the old Empire, to eventual full self-government, and so to choice about Commonwealth membership, are those territories too small to be viable nations and also, in an unusual case like Gibraltar, of primarily strategic significance. The future is by no means clear for the 29 British territories which now have a population of less than one million each. Otherwise what is envisioned for the Commonwealth is a multiracial body of self-governing nations largely coinciding with the world-wide expanse of the old British Empire. Within the new Commonwealth, substituting for power formerly exercised over colonial dependencies, the British would like to provide a leadership freely accepted as based on experience and mutual interest. On the intangibles of Commonwealth cooperation rests whatever aspiration Britain still has to play the role of a Great Power in the contemporary world.

British leadership in the new Commonwealth does indeed rest heavily on intangibles. Their significance may be questioned. The new Asian and African states have, it is true, a common heritage of former British rule and therefore of certain British governmental procedures and of an elite educated in the use of these procedures along with English language and culture. But this heritage may not be deep enough to withstand the rising nationalism of native masses. Moreover, there is hardly an identity of interest, even if anti-colonialism loses its relevance, between the newly developing but still impoverished Asian-African nations, and Britain as a white and relatively wealthy developed nation. The new Commonwealth nations simply look at the world in a different way from Britain as from the West generally. The difference has already been observed in Britain's relations with India, the largest member nation and the major contender for leadership of Asian-African countries, be they Commonwealth members or not. The Commonwealth front has surely been broken in the postwar world as Britain joined the American-led effort to contain Russian aggression, while India became persistently neutralist. Also on issues involving the remnants of Western imperial possessions, Britain, still a responsible imperial power, has taken a different position from the anti-colonialism fostered by India in the United Nations. This difference emerged most openly in the admittedly special circumstances posed by Britain's apparent reassertion of imperial policy at the time of the Suez crisis in 1956. Then India broke sharply with Britain in the United Nations. So, of course, did many Western nations, including the United States.

Generally, despite the difficulties raised by evident differences between Britain and the new Commonwealth nations, Britain seems determined, especially after the Suez affair, to try to accommodate many of its policies to those of its Asian and African partners. Some of the accommodation is simply part of Britain's adjustment to the mid-twentieth century world. Thus

the withdrawal from imperial possessions is not simply to please Asian and
African Commonwealth nations and to
create new ones; it is brought about by
the impracticality of Britain, or any
Western nation, any longer having the
will and the resources to resist native
nationalist movements. The problem
for Britain has been to withdraw at just
the right time: when a local population
was sufficiently prepared for self-government, so as to resist chaos and
Communists, and yet before a population was so aroused against British rule
as to make unlikely any peaceful
transition to Commonwealth membership. With the possible exception of
Burma, which chose a friendly relation
outside the Commonwealth, the British
did successfully meet this problem in
most areas during the first 15 years
after World War II. The British withdrawal was typically seemly, finally
even in Malaya where an expensive
battle against Communists had to be
waged before the transition to self-
government. Cyprus was more embarrassing since the British began by
regarding this eastern Mediterranean
island as so essential a military base
that its sovereignty could not be relinquished; partly for this reason and
partly because of Greek claims to
hegemony over both the Greek
majority and the Turkish minority on
the island, Britain sought through most
of the 1950's to repress a partly ter-
rorist revolt. In the end, however,
Britain settled for a self-governing
Cyprus, containing a modest British
military base.

More troublesome problems seem to
remain for Britain to deal with in
some of the African territories still in
states of dependency. Unlike the nations already established in West
Africa, notably Ghana and Nigeria,
those areas still under British rule in
East and Central Africa have the dis-

advantages of less advanced African
populations and, in some instances, of
substantial settlements by a white European minority (chiefly British). The
first disadvantage is only relative, and
it can be directly met (although with
problematic long-run success) by an
already accelerated educational program. But the disadvantage of having
substantial European settlements, particularly in Rhodesia and in Kenya,
is inherently more complicated. It
presents a complication which the
British have not had to meet on any
large scale in any of the Commonwealth nations so far established. On
the other hand, even in East and Central Africa the European settlements
do not pose so great a problem for the
British as such settlements in Algeria
have for the French. Yet the problem is
real enough, since the British settlers
are farmers, merchants, and urban
workers; and especially in Southern
Rhodesia they are accustomed to running their government's internal affairs much as a similar minority of
Europeans do in the Union of South
Africa. Britain is thus faced with two
conflicting sets of demands: self-
government by the educated white
minority, with at best a promised
gradual admission of the mass of
Africans to the governing process,
versus self-government very quickly for
all inhabitants, inevitably giving power
to the leaders of the African mass. Despite strong bonds of sympathy with
British settlers (and despite strong
political pressure particularly by their
friends in the Conservative party),
the British government has increasingly
moved to meet the demands of African
nationalists. Whether it can or will
move fast enough is not yet clear. Certainly no British authority will want
to yield altogether to African nationalism so that British settlers are completely abandoned. The hope, and it

may be unrealistic, is that adjustments within a multi-racial community can eventually be achieved. This is the way Britain would like to deal with what Prime Minister Macmillan has called Africa's "wind of change" when he specifically rejected the *apartheid* policy of the Union of South Africa.

Even with its occasional lapses and its remaining difficult imperial legacies, Britain takes an understandable pride in the whole postwar development of self-governing Commonwealth nations. Whatever guilt may be felt for Britain's earlier accumulation of imperial possessions, on which the community was and is divided, there can be little doubt that Englishmen now feel sadly misunderstood when their country is denounced as an oppressive colonial power. Such denunciations are resented not only because they come at a time when Britain is rapidly liquidating and transforming its empire, but also because the attacks often come from powers that have themselves expanded their territories over a continental land-mass. Criticism from such sources seems to be based on the salt-water fallacy: overseas expansion is evil in a way that continental expansion is not.

Cultural and ideological ties

Of a different sort but not necessarily less strong than the Commonwealth bond are Britain's noninstitutional ties based on culture and ideology. These ties cut across the line between Commonwealth and non-Commonwealth countries. Canada, Australia, New Zealand, and (to a lesser extent) South Africa would be regarded as kindred nations even without a Commonwealth structure. Their populations are heavily British in origin, their language is English (though with large exceptions in Canada and South Africa), and their political institutions are direct adapta-

tions of the British model. Together with Britain and the United States they constitute the nongovernmental entity that Englishmen, Sir Winston Churchill in particular, like to call the "English-speaking peoples." [27] The term is partly a euphemism for an inappropriate and offensively exclusionary phrase like "Anglo-Saxon world," and yet it conveys much of the feeling associated with a racial or ethnic bond.

Within the English-speaking world the British recognize the United States as a very special case. Although similarities in many matters, including a common (that is, an English) political heritage, are acknowledged and even overstated, relations are complicated by those differences which are found to exist between American and British customs. [28] Sometimes these differences are regarded as unfortunate deviations from a British norm, as in the case of American government preserving the separation-of-powers principle instead of adopting the parliamentary-cabinet system. More significantly, in postwar years the British have found it difficult to get accustomed to American predominance, militarily and economically, in relation to Britain and much of the Western World. The United States, as the newcomer in international affairs, sometimes appears to Englishmen as a brash usurper of Britain's former leading role, particularly in the Middle East. Irritation with American ways, however, has not prevented the broad central sector of British opinion from considering the postwar alliance with the United States to be natural and right. Ideologically, the Anglo-Ameri-

[27]As, for instance, in Churchill's famous Fulton speech. *The New York Times,* March 6, 1946, p. 4.

[28] The problems of the postwar Anglo-American relationship, as seen by Englishmen, are treated in the author's *Britain— Uneasy Ally* (Chicago: University of Chicago Press, 1954), chap. 2.

can alliance has been uncongenial only to left-wing socialists who objected to American capitalism, and to imperialist Conservatives who saw American criticism of the British Empire in terms of nationalist rivalry. Even many of these ideological critics objected mainly to the terms of the alliance, admitting, though bitterly, Britain's overriding need for American power.

Beyond the United States and the English-speaking members of the Commonwealth, Britain's cultural and ideological ties are less definite. A general attachment to political democracy causes Englishmen to identify more readily with some nations than others, and a minority in the Labour party sympathizes particularly with professedly socialist countries and with the ideological neutralism of Nehru's India. There is a cultural link with the nations of Western Europe, especially France, but its strength appears less than that of an English-speaking Atlantic community. This is in spite of the heavy volume of British travel to the continent, and in spite of the communion in an old and threatened culture which British intellectuals share with their continental counterparts. Apparently for most Englishmen the barriers of language and unstable continental politics outweigh geographic proximity. Germany presents a particular difficulty; its aggressive enmity is too recent for popular links to be easily established.

With respect to all of Britain's broad ties with other countries, the claim is often made that foreign policy has been developed apart from such considerations, particularly of ideology, and solely on the basis of a calculated national interest.[29] But even if it is true that policy is arrived at independently of ideological preferences, there can be no doubt that support for a given policy can be more readily obtained when that policy is in line with the attachments of the British community.

Foreign economic policy

Britain's dependence on overseas trade means that economic matters are always in the forefront among foreign policy issues. Since World War II the most constant national worry has been to maintain a sufficient volume of exports to pay for needed imports of food and raw materials. During much of the first postwar decade Britain required outside help in the form of loans and Marshall Aid in order to bridge the dollar gap. That is, Britain had to be given dollars, over and above those earned, so as to allow the purchase of goods from the United States and Canada. More recently American aid has been for military purposes, but this too involves a degree of dependency.

The general postwar economic policy of seeking to increase exports has been complicated by Britain's leading role among the nations associated in the sterling bloc. Within this bloc free exchange is encouraged, and earnings of gold and dollars are pooled for dealing with non-sterling countries. The sterling bloc consists of all parts of the Commonwealth except Canada, plus Burma, Iceland, Ireland, Jordan, and Libya. It is not Britain alone, but this bloc as a whole that seeks a balance of trade with the rest of the world. Britain serves as banker for the bloc. In this arrangement there are advantages for both British trade and British prestige. Besides helping to maintain London as a major center of international exchange, the sterling bloc facilitates the exchange of British manufactured goods for food and raw materials produced in Commonwealth countries.

---

[29] Note, for example, Churchill's rejection of the ideological case against Franco's Spain. *The Second World War*, Vol. 5 (Boston: Houghton Mifflin Co., 1951), p. 627.

To assist in the economic development of the bloc's non-Western sections, some of which, like Malaya, are large dollar-earners, Britain has sought to encourage investment of the relatively small amount of capital that the nation now has available for export. Investment on a larger scale within the sterling bloc has been envisioned and even projected in what is known as the Colombo Plan, but Britain itself now finds it difficult to produce the surplus needed to re-establish its prewar status as an overseas investor. That status was largely lost as a result of forced wartime sale of British assets. Re-establishing British overseas investments has also been complicated by the home market's increased attractiveness for capital during Britain's recently prosperous years.

Many of the marks of an economic policy geared to Britain's tenuous position in world trade were most obvious in the early postwar years, but some remained even through the 1950's. The government has closely controlled foreign exchange, limiting in particular the exchange of pounds for dollars and, thus, the purchase of American goods. In addition, Englishmen have been restricted from purchasing many of their own products, either by high sales taxes or by the establishment of quotas, so that such products might be exported in order to earn the foreign currency with which to buy necessities from abroad. For a similar reason, the British government has regulated the flow of industrial investment so as to secure the expansion of productive facilities most likely to manufacture goods saleable abroad and especially in the United States. These efforts to sell overseas in order to live have met with enough success to permit considerable relaxation of the immediate postwar policies of enforced austerity. Increases in the volume of British goods sold in the United States have been impressive, but their continuance is insecure and so therefore is Britain's whole economic situation.

Given the national need for external trade, it might be expected that Britain would have a low tariff policy. Of course, this was Britain's nineteenth-century position. Then Britain was able to compete in terms of price and quality of manufactures with almost any other country, and it was willing to encourage importing food from abroad because it was cheaper and because nations that sold Britain food could buy its manufactured products. Thus there was no high protective tariff for industry or agriculture. However, in the twentieth century this free-trade formula ceased to be so evidently to Britain's net advantage. British manufacturers now encountered difficulties in foreign markets from newer industries of other countries; some of these newer industries were more efficient, some employed cheaper labor, and some were protected in their own markets by tariffs. Additional cause for the British to re-examine their trade policy was provided by the difficulty of importing the usual food requirements under the siege conditions first evident during World War I. The result of all these circumstances, along with strongly nationalistic trends elsewhere, was a substantial British retreat from traditional free trade during the early decades of the twentieth century. Domestic agriculture came to be subsidized in various ways, including tariffs on foreign products. Selected manufacturing industries were now also protected by fairly high tariffs. Moreover the necessarily stringent postwar limitations on imports of foreign goods also served to protect British manufactures against competition in the home market; this was not the purpose of such limitations, which in any event were meant to be temporary during Britain's shortage of foreign exchange.

Closely linked to Britain's modest protective system is Imperial (now properly Commonwealth) Preference. Under this arrangement, like the tariff policy itself, a product largely of the interwar years, Britain and other Commonwealth nations negotiated reciprocal tariff advantages. The object was to encourage intra-Commonwealth trade, and from the British standpoint to have, in other Commonwealth nations, a protected market for manufactured goods in exchange for discrimination, by Britain, in favor of food and raw materials from the same other Commonwealth nations. Substantial mutual preferences of this nature were established in the 1930's, and their extension in the direction of a general Commonwealth free trade was advocated then and later by the heirs of the old turn-of-the-century belief in Joseph Chamberlain's imperial economic union. Commonwealth trade preference became, in fact, the last bastion of imperialist ambition. In the eyes of its champions, Imperial Preference, by establishing material advantages in Commonwealth relations, might be the beginning of a new and potent British-led economic and political unit. It represented an alternative to reliance on American trade and American power. Such hopes for the development of Imperial Preference failed, however, to be realized after World War II. Some of the other Commonwealth nations did not find it in their interests to extend preference on a broad front, and Britain's own need for more American trade was not compatible with enlarged discrimination in favor of Commonwealth producers. The alternative presented by the postwar American encouragement of a general free trade policy was simply more attractive. Consequently, the relative importance of Imperial Preference declined in the postwar years. Not only

were new preferences not negotiated, but the existing ones were not as significant, in terms of competitive advantage, as they had been in the 1930's.[30]

Imperial preference retained enough importance to play a part in molding opposition to British participation in the various European supranational economic arrangements of the 1950's. Britain's special economic relations with Commonwealth nations provided an argument for standing outside both the Schuman Plan, establishing a common Western European market for coal and steel, and the later European Economic Community, establishing a common market over a broad range of products. In the latter case especially, the British were reluctant to join in adopting a policy that would result in the elimination of preferences, in the British market, for food from Commonwealth nations. Nevertheless, it seems unlikely that Imperial Preference, with its significance already diminishing, was either an insurmountable or even a primary obstacle in the way of British membership with France, Germany, Italy, and the Benelux countries in common market arrangements. Reluctance to join these continental arrangements may also be explained by political and cultural, as well as economic, resistance to a strictly European identification. The continental common market conception has always implied some degree of political integration along with economic coordination.

Despite the general reasons for British resistance to European economic union, it was true that by the late 1950's such union had progressed sufficiently so that Britain was forced to

[30] Political and Economic Planning, *Commonwealth Preference in the United Kingdom* (London: Allen and Unwin, Ltd., 1960), p. 5.

reconsider its earlier aloofness. The fact was that the six continental nations, by mutually reducing their tariffs and by adopting a tariff common to the rest of the world, were threatening British sales within the common market countries. As an alternative policy, Britain sought to form a larger but looser free trade area, but this effort led only to the development of a more or less rival bloc called the European Free Trade Association, consisting of seven nations as against the six nations of the common market (European Economic Community). Negotiations continued between the seven, led by Britain, and the six, but no merger had been arranged by 1960. The European Free Trade Association, it should be noted, differed from the common market not only in being much less supranational in its political implications, but also in being without a common tariff toward the rest of the world. It was simply an association designed to reduce tariffs among the seven nations—Britain, Sweden, Denmark, Norway, Portugal, Austria, and Switzerland. Even this much participation by Britain, however, represents a significant degree of economic Europeanization. More seems likely to come, but compatibly with the maintenance of Britain's essential trade with the rest of the world. Like most of the rest of Europe, Britain is bound to remain dependent on overseas sources for a great range of supplies, notably oil.

Security policy

Britain assumes that it cannot protect itself against aggression without help. The island's location, vulnerability, and limited resources have dictated protection in the form of collective arrangements with other nations. Strictly speaking, it may be said that modern Britain never relied solely on its own military capacities. The traditional effort to maintain a European balance of power necessarily involved joining some nations against others. However, before World War I this policy, combined with command of the seas, allowed Britain considerable freedom of action and certainly a sense of having the national destiny in its own hands. The change in Britain's relative position may not have been fully appreciated until World War II, but in 1940 even the magnificent stand against Hitler could not conceal Britain's inability to protect its far-flung interests without the aid of a stronger power.

After World War II, and partly as its consequence, Britain appeared distinctly less imposing than either of the super powers, Russia and the United States. Britain's old problem of preventing an aggressive enemy from dominating the continent was made more difficult than ever. Against Russia after 1945, even more apparently than against Germany in the 1930's, no British-led combination of European states was strong enough to maintain a balance of power. Security against Russian domination of the continent required American participation. Accordingly, the cornerstone of Britain's postwar European policy was to obtain an American commitment, of a sort denied before World War II, to defend Western Europe, and by this means to deter aggression. American involvement in the North Atlantic Pact has thus been viewed as a prime diplomatic success. As a leading British diplomatic historian wrote of the treaty, "It is indeed in one sense the culmination of British policy during the last half century." [31] That is, Britain has at last,

[31] Sir Charles Webster in *United Kingdom Policy,* ed. by Sir Charles Webster (London: Royal Institute of International Affairs, 1950), p. 26.

through an outside ally, succeeded in righting the European balance of power which, in the twentieth century, she was unable to maintain. From this viewpoint, British participation in the military arrangements of the Western European Union, though a sharp departure in British policy, is decidedly subordinate to membership with America in the North Atlantic Treaty Organization.

Being a junior partner in an alliance has, however, been a new experience for Britain, and there have been British misgivings about the United States and its dominance. Since 1947, the British have tended to be fearful that American policies toward Russia would be too provocative, too zealously anti-Communist, and too uncompromising. These fears have gone up and down in response to particular acts and circumstances, but they have never disappeared. Regularly the British government, supported by its public, has urged conciliatory summit meetings of Western leaders with the Russians. Moreover Britain has been less completely hostile to Communist China, whose government the British recognized in accord with traditional diplomatic practice although they continued, at least through 1960, to go along with American opposition to Chinese Communist admission to the United Nations. Certainly Britain has made it clear that it is reluctant to be involved in any full-fledged war with China. For this reason, as well as because Britain has preferred American military efforts to be concentrated in Europe, there has been a dislike for any proposed American military action against China. Thus in late 1950, when the Korean War threatened to involve a major American commitment, Winston Churchill was surely expressing general British feelings when he said that the sooner "the Far Eastern

diversion" could be stabilized the better. It is in Europe, he said, that the world cause will be decided. "Perhaps," Churchill noted, "we are biased by the fact that we all live there or thereabouts. But none the less, one cannot conceive that our natural bias has in any way distorted the actual facts." [32] The subsequent American decision to strengthen the North Atlantic Treaty Organization met with a strongly positive British response. Britain's substantial contribution to European defense, as part of the price for greater American efforts, left no doubt about the primacy of British concern.

That concern, while it remained dominant, did appear to lose some of its urgency in British minds during the later 1950's. Participation in NATO was still the cornerstone of defense policy, but, instead of building a really large conventional military force, Britain, with its allies, accepted an increasing reliance on nuclear weapons as a deterrent against Russian aggression. Britain sharply reduced its total military force, particularly in 1957, and finally put an end to conscription in 1960. What remained by way of conventional forces were either in NATO's limited establishment or spread thinly over the reduced, but still widespread, imperial possessions. No large military reserve for conventional warfare was maintained. The potential power thus abandoned, largely because of expense, was supposed to be compensated by British development of nuclear weapons over and above those already in American hands. Britain did produce its own H-bomb in the late 1950's, and thus became the third nuclear power in the world. But before the decade ended this achievement was reduced in strategic significance by the realization that Britain was going to

[32] 481 *H.C. Deb.* 1336 (Nov. 30, 1950).

find it too expensive to develop its own missile delivery system. Even with a British H-bomb, the nation remained dependent on American retaliatory power in a vital respect. To that power, Britain continued to contribute by providing bases for American bombers, sites for intermediate range ballistic missiles, and anchorage for missile-carrying submarines. In these respects Britain was in the front line of American and allied deterrent strategy, and seemed likely to remain so until such time as the United States believed it could rely entirely on intercontinental missiles—or until, improbably, the British could be converted to the view that neutralism was less dangerous than the American alliance.

A special aspect of British security policy may be observed in the Middle East. Here Britain emerged from World War II temporarily re-established as the dominant power, but without the resources to maintain its traditional interests in the sea-routes to India and Australia or its newer interests in Persian Gulf oil. Arab nationalism became increasingly hostile to the indirect British imperial control, dating especially from the interwar years, and Britain retreated with less graciousness than anywhere else in the postwar world. British weakness in the whole Mediterranean area became apparent as early as 1947, when the defense of Turkey and Greece from Communist aggression was abandoned to the United States, and when Britain failed to solve the postwar Palestine problem to anyone's satisfaction. Yet Britain tried to hold what it still regarded as its strategic interest in the Middle East. This centered about the Suez Canal. As a distinguished British soldier wrote during the postwar years, "It has been an axiom of British policy that no hostile Power should be allowed to establish itself within striking distance

of Suez, and we have fought immense campaigns in support of this policy." [33] The same interest caused Britain to maintain troops on the canal until early 1956, and to attempt (with France) to return troops later the same year after the Suez Canal Company was seized by the Egyptian government and at the time of Israeli-Egyptian hostilities. It was the failure of this move, in the face of American and United Nations condemnation, that seemed to be the climactic event in Britain's decline as a Middle Eastern power. Loss of influence in Iraq followed in 1958, and only remnants of British tutelage subsequently remained in the Arab world. Leadership of the Western effort to court the growingly intransigent Arab nationalism and to counter Communist influence in the Middle East now passed to the United States. For Englishmen, particularly Conservative imperialists, this was ironic, since they had previously complained of American unwillingness to back British efforts in the Middle East.

The Suez misadventure of 1956 was a bench mark for British decline in a broader area than the Middle East. It was the one major British attempt, in the postwar world, to "go it alone"— that is, without the United States, even if with France. The ignominy of the forced withdrawal from Suez brought home the reality of Britain's new position in the world. Large-scale British action anywhere simply could not be carried out without the assurance of an American sympathy sufficient, at least, to provide economic assistance. Certainly no war against a major enemy could be risked in isolation from the United States. Manufacture of the H-bomb did not decisively change this British situation.

[33] Ian Jacob in *United Kingdom Policy, op. cit.,* p. 51.

A point that remains to be discussed is British membership in the United Nations. As one of the founding Big Five, Britain is a permanent member of the Security Council and a prominent participant in U.N. affairs generally. Except in the Suez altercation, Britain has tended to join in majority decisions of the organization. However, official British policy has never relied primarily on the United Nations as the agency for maintaining national security against aggression. Although many Englishmen, particularly liberals and Labour party members, display a considerable emotional attachment to U.N. ideals, British policy-makers have understandably found alliances like the North Atlantic Treaty Organization sturdier shields than the U.N. Charter. Britain has been anxious primarily to maintain the United Nations as a gathering place for all nations, including Communist nations, so that opportunities for discussion, negotiation, and compromise are available.

SUMMARY

The best way to summarize recent British foreign policy is to say that it has sought to meet immense responsibilities with severely limited resources. The diminution of British power, relative to the rest of the world, is a cardinal feature of the international situation in the twentieth century. It is only less noticeable than such other international phenomena as new superpowers or Asian nationalism because Britain has been going down and not up. The consequence for the rest of the world, as well as for the British themselves, may be just as serious even if not so obvious.

A drastic alternative, which the British have not accepted, is to drop out entirely as a world power and assume the "Little England" role that was advocated once before, in the mid-nineteenth century. The model might be the Netherlands, Switzerland, or Sweden. For the present, however, Britain's intentions do not involve an abdication of power and influence, and certainly not a surrender of the international policies enabling an island population of 50 million to survive. Even the accommodations that Britain has made to nationalist elements in the Commonwealth have been designed to retain British status in a revised form. Furthermore, the British have maintained a considerable share of the responsibility of defending themselves and others from Communist aggression. Neutralism as between East and West has so far been well in the background of British consciousness. Most Englishmen have been able to view the United States as a powerful ally brought in to help a common cause, and not as a nation using Britain for its separate purposes.

That Britain will continue to regard itself as an American ally is probable, but by no means certain. As was demonstrated by the popularity of unilateral nuclear disarmament within the Labour party in 1960, neutralism has begun to appeal to a substantial minority of the public. It would even have the virtue of bringing Britain in line with most of the Asian-African Commonwealth. Chiefly, however, it is presented as a means of eliminating the risk believed to flow from having American nuclear bases and thus inviting retaliatory attack against the especially vulnerable island. Conceivably the willingness to assume this particular risk, as well as to assume responsibility in general, might diminish as British consciousness, in a new generation, catches up with the nation's loss of status as a Great Power. Surrendering imperial possessions, while it removes a source of friction with anticolonialist America, may have the incidental effect of giving Englishmen less cause to participate in the defense of the world against aggression. They now appear to have less of their own to lose, and identification with American power and American interest is incomplete. All this, however, is highly speculative. The fact remains that Britain is not retreating from its active membership in the American-led alliance, and there is more reason to depend on the maintenance of this policy by Britain than on that of almost any other nation.

SELECTED BIBLIOGRAPHY

Churchill, Sir Winston, *The Second World War* (Boston: Houghton Mifflin Co., 1951).

Jennings, W. Ivor, *The Commonwealth in Asia* (London: Oxford University Press, 1951).

Miller, J. D. B., *The Commonwealth in the World* (London: Gerald Duckworth & Co., Ltd., 1959).

Nicolson, Harold, *Diplomacy* (London: Oxford University Press, 1950).

Strang, Lord, *The Foreign Office* (New York: Oxford University Press, 1955).

Thornton, A. P., *The Imperial Idea and Its Enemies* (New York: St. Martin's Press, Inc., 1959).

Ward, A. W., and G. P. Gooch, eds., *The Cambridge History of British Foreign Policy, 1783–1919* (London: Cambridge University Press, 1922–23).

Webster, Sir Charles, *United Kingdom Policy* (London: Royal Institute of International Affairs, 1950).

3

french foreign Policy

INTRODUCTION

The dilemma confronting French foreign policy may be stated in rather
simple terms. France, one of the great
powers of the nineteenth century, has
found her position in the world progressively declining, while the aspiration
and the illusion of greatness and
strength have persisted.

France emerged from
World War II militarily
weak, drained of man-
power, with her econ-
omy seriously undermined
after four years of oc-
cupation, facing urgent
problems of economic
and social reconstruction

ROY

C.

MACRIDIS

at home. Her situation was such that
she was dependent upon Britain and,
primarily, upon the United States. In
terms of Walter Lippmann's axiom that
commitments in foreign policy must
be commensurate with strength, it was
very clear that there were few commitments that France could undertake and
carry out successfully without Anglo-
American support. France's liberty of
action, therefore, was limited. Her
aspiration to remain a top-rank power
seemed to be at variance with her
capabilities.

Thus, the dilemma involved either the
acceptance of the realities of the post-
World War II situation, or a continuation of France's "vocation of greatness"
without the physical and economic resources to implement it. This problem
needed to be confronted throughout
the years after the Liberation. Neither
the political system nor the political
parties and the press
managed to present it
to the public in clear-
cut terms. There was no
"great debate" and no
"agonizing reappraisal"
for the purpose of re-
defining the French posi-
tion and status in the
world.

To explain the nature of the dilemma
will be the purpose of this chapter.
We shall discuss the background factors that have shaped French foreign
policy—geographic position, economic
and social development, cultural influence; the more persistent interests
pursued by France; and both the objectives and the institution of foreign
policy-making under the Fifth Republic.

BACKGROUND FACTORS

A number of interacting factors constitute the setting in which foreign

policy operates. Some of these factors are objective ones—they can be easily measured and compared; others are subjective and constitute a community's image of itself in the world. Among the objective factors, the most important are the nation's economic strength, its geographic position, its military potential and technological skill, its culture, and the diffusion of its culture in other parts of the world. The subjective factors are primarily ideological; they can be studied with reference to the various elites of the system and to the particular conception the elites have of their country's role in the world. Important among those elites is, of course, the political leadership.

Subjective and objective factors constantly interact to give to foreign policy a dynamic and ever-changing pattern; however, such interaction may be impeded for various reasons, so that "reality," i.e., the objective factor, may be at variance with "ideology," i.e., the subjective factor. As we pointed out, this might be a tenable hypothesis for the study of French foreign policy in the twentieth century.

The economic foundations

The most significant feature of the French economy has been, until the last decade, its gradual decline. While industrialization made rapid strides forward throughout the nineteenth century in England, Germany, Japan, and the United States, and also in the Soviet Union in the twentieth century, France's economy advanced at a snail's pace.

Yet France began with a marked head start over *all* other countries. During the Napoleonic era and until the middle of the nineteenth century France was one of the most economically developed nations of the world. From then on, despite a wealth of resources and skilled labor, her economy declined in comparison with almost all the countries of Western Europe. Her total national income between 1870 to 1940 rose by about 80 per cent; that of Germany increased five times; that of Great Britain three times and a half. In the years between the two World Wars (1918–1940), investment declined to a point below zero—that is, France was living on her capital, using her factories and equipment without replacing them in full. She was going through a period of disinvestment. The destruction of World War II, estimated at approximately $50 billion, was an additional setback. With her industrial equipment destroyed or dilapidated and her transportation network paralyzed, France's economy was in a state of collapse.

There were many long-range factors associated with this stagnation: notably, the very slow growth of population, a backward agriculture, the protectionist policies of the state, and finally the attitudes of the business groups.

Population. In 1800, France had the largest population of any country in Europe and the Americas, excepting only that of Russia. The Napoleonic armies were recruited from, and supported by, 26 million French men and women, when England had only 11 million inhabitants, the United States five and a half million, and the German states, including Austria, about 23 million. France maintained the population advantage until about 1860, when she had about 38 million. From then on, her population remained virtually static. In 1940, for instance, it was almost exactly 40 million, while that of the United States was close to 150 million, Great Britain 50 million, Germany (West and East, but without Austria) 65 million. In the years between 1930 and 1940 the French population actually declined—that is, there was an excess of deaths over births. Two wars had taken a heavy toll also of the young and active part of the population. The per cent of the aged (over 65 years) became disproportionately heavy, thereby contributing to economic stagnation.

Agriculture. The agricultural problem developed in the period between 1870 and 1940. The proportion of farmers—about 35–40 per cent of the active population—was the largest in Western Europe excepting Italy and Spain. Their productivity was one of the lowest in Europe. There were a great number of small marginal farms divided and subdivided into parcels to which new techniques and mechanization could not be applied. Until 1940, France used less fertilizer than any other Western European country, and the use of tractors remained insignificant.

Protectionism. That much of the population remained on relatively unproductive farms was due partly to the tariff policies of the state. Agricultural interests formed powerful lobbies which demanded and got a high protectionist tariff, sheltering French business and agriculture from foreign competition. They also received special subsidies and guaranteed price supports. Not only wheat producers and growers of beets (from which large quantities of alcohol are distilled) profited from these measures, but also wine growers, fruit growers, and dairy interests. High tariffs also sheltered manufacturing concerns. The state was perpetuating and supporting a situation that consecrated the weakness of the economic system.

Business attitudes. Industrialists and business groups did not show in France the initiative and willingness to take risks that we generally associate with a capitalistic system. Many business enterprises were family affairs. Production remained geared to a limited demand instead of seeking new markets. Profits were often "saved" instead of being re-invested.

A particularly vulnerable sector of the economy was made up of the distributors. Large chain stores were the exception. Small merchants and shopkeepers eked out a living through a limited volume of trade. As a result, efficient techniques to reduce costs and bring down prices did not develop. Retail prices kept far ahead of wholesale prices, with the many middlemen who handled the product making small profits. This inflated unduly the price the consumer paid. In addition to the agricultural population, the "middlemen" in France represented an oversized and relatively unproductive sector of the economy. They, too, organized in strong pressure groups and demanded subsidies and protection.

The end of World War II brought to light the weaknesses of the country and accentuated a number of them. The greater part of the foreign assets and investments of France had been wiped out; millions had lost their lives or health as a result of the war and the enemy occupation; the industrial equipment of the country had reached obsolescence. The tasks ahead were to stop inflation and put the currency back on a healthy basis; to rebuild the communication systems, the schools, factories, and homes; to improve the productive resources in order to bring production up to the prewar level and surpass it; and to rationalize and reorganize the agriculture.

Geographic position

France's geographic position created contradictory interests and commitments. On the one hand, she has been a continental power with frontiers that include to the east, Belgium, Germany,

Switzerland, and Italy, and to the south-west, Spain; on the other hand, she has had a colonial Empire with possessions throughout Africa and in the Pacific, Indian, and Atlantic oceans.

The French Empire had been developed and consolidated by the end of the nineteenth century. On the continent, the Spanish frontier, Belgium, and Switzerland presented no problems. The threat came from Germany —a Germany that after 1870 had been unified; and after 1930—despite its defeat in 1918—confronted France once more with a population of some 65 million and an economic and industrial system more productive than her own. At the same time, the Empire required everlasting vigilance against potential marauders, particularly England, and against nationalist independence movements. This required the maintenance of a strong army at home as well as a strong navy. The position of France, therefore, involved heavy economic sacrifices.

This situation accounted for the existence of two distinct mentalities within the French political leadership. One tended to favor a *rapprochement* with Germany. It was anti-British, since the traditional obstacle to French imperial ambitions and naval power had been Great Britain. The other mentality tended to emphasize the continental position of France, to plead for a strong army, and to underplay her imperial commitments. It tended to be pro-British and anti-German. Neither point of view could or did prevail. Germany was naturally in favor of encouraging France's imperial commitments, in exchange for a free hand in Europe—particularly in Eastern Europe and in the Middle East, which ultimately would endanger France's position in Europe. England, on the other hand, was anxious to encourage France in her continental policy, with

the full realization that a strong French army would be a deterrent against Germany and hence would allow England to concentrate on its naval strength and the development of its own Empire, ultimately at the expense of the interests of France in the world.

From whichever point of view one looks at the situation as it developed in the latter part of the nineteenth century, one cannot help but realize that the French predicament was a serious one. France, more than any other country of the world, had to assume the heavy burdens both of a continental power and of an Empire. The end of World War II and the subsequent developments indicate, as we shall see, that France stubbornly attempted to preserve both positions.

Cultural diffusion

It would hardly be an exaggeration to say that France was, in the nineteenth century, the cultural center of the world. In politics, art, literature, and education, French thought radiated everywhere. The French Revolution had given to the cause of freedom a clear-cut formulation which was carried to all parts of Europe by Napoleon's armies. The French Napoleonic code was plagiarized by almost every Latin-American and European nation. The French language was the medium of communication in international conferences and the second language of the educated classes of the world. France's philosophers, intellectuals, and scientists pioneered the cause of human and scientific knowledge.

Innumerable cultural ties linked France with most other countries. Such links constituted, without any doubt, a capital that, like the *Marseillaise,* was just as important as ships and soldiers, or the investment of the British merchants and storekeepers in the

British Empire. But it was the kind of capital whose logic calls for continuous reinvestment. It was also the kind of capital that tends to pervert the lender. With the relative decline of the French economy in the twentieth century, other nations began to attract scientists and intellectuals. The use of the French language in diplomacy and in other aspects of international relations began to be challenged. The French political system itself showed signs of strain, as her colonial policy revealed obvious incompatibilities with the universal ethical postulates that the French Revolution promulgated. The colonial elites who had studied in France and for whom French was a second language, chose to engage her in a dialogue in which the lessons they had learned became increasingly embarrassing for the teacher. But at the very moment the dialogue was engaged—particularly between the colonies and the metropolis—French cultural pre-eminence had become permanent and incontrovertible in the minds of the French elites. It became a myth, an *idée fixe,* which could allow no exception and permit no argument. French cultural supremacy was taken for granted. This produced innumerable reflexes which account for some of France's recent actions: her prolonged reluctance to change her policy with regard to the Empire; her extreme sensitivity to criticisms from abroad; a blind pride, considering her own system as superior to that of any other nation in the world; and finally a strong belief in the unique "mission" of France—to educate, to cultivate, to humanize.

Persistent patterns

A number of patterns underlie the French conception of foreign policy. In the nineteenth century they reflected France's strength, but they slowly crystallized into dogmas and myths that were ultimately separated from twentieth-century reality. It is nonetheless in terms of such myths that France's post-World War II foreign policy has been shaped rather in terms of the new factors that developed partly as a result of the war and partly as the result of a number of social, economic, and ideological forces that stirred the world.

The basic objectives of foreign policy remained: (1) the continuation of France's imperial position and (2) continental strength. The first meant, as we have seen, the maintenance of the far-flung Empire with all the financial difficulties and obligations it entailed. Not for a moment was the notion of federalism and self-government for its members seriously entertained. The Empire was conceived as a part of France's mission and as a continuous challenge to French culture and influence. The resurrection of France as a continental power was also an automatic reflex. No political leader doubted it. The end of World War II by the defeat of Germany was in a sense their revenge for the German occupation of France. Victory, it was thought, simply re-established the prewar balance. To implement France's continental position, the same alliances with the West and with the East were contemplated—all of them directed against a Germany that lay prostrate and divided. The fact that the Soviet Union had gained a foothold in the heart of Europe did not alter for a long time the traditional French reflexes. Germany was the enemy of France. A weak Germany and a Franco-Russian Alliance remained the condition of French security. When General de Gaulle visited Moscow and signed the Franco-Russian treaty in December 1944, he was preserving French security according to the best traditions of the nineteenth century.

Underlying his actions was the belief that France, with her Empire, secure from the resurrection of German might and German attack, was once more a great power ready to fill the power vacuum that lay in the heart of Europe and poised to throw her weight on one or the other side of the scale of the power conflict that emerged between the Soviet Union and the United States.

THE SUBSTANCE OF FOREIGN POLICY: TRENDS AND PROBLEMS

France has followed two basic foreign policy objectives ever since the eighteenth century. The first is the policy of *natural frontiers* and the second is the policy of what might be called *European status quo,* or *balance of power* in Europe.

According to the first objective, the natural frontiers of France have been on the Rhine and on the Alps. They include Belgium, Holland, Luxembourg, and the German territories that lie west of the Rhine. This was interpreted to mean that France's strategic and military interests extended to those areas and no other power could set foot there without jeopardizing her interests. The continuity of this policy is remarkable. Danton stated in 1793: "The frontiers (of the Republic) are marked *by nature.* . . . They are the Rhine, the Alps and the Pyrennean mountains." Clémenceau affirmed in 1919: "The move towards the Rhine was the tradition of our ancestors. . . . It was the tradition to create a frontier, a *true* frontier marking the French territory. . . ." General de Gaulle in 1944 demanded in the name of a weak and defeated country: "The Rhine *is* French security and I think the security of the whole world. But France is the principal interested party. . . . She wishes to be solidly established from one end to the other of her *natural frontier.*" [1]

The policy of *status quo,* on the other hand, was based upon three assumptions that became in turn three basic policy-objectives.

1. France was not interested in any European conquest.

2. No single power should gain preponderant strength in Europe. The *status-quo*—consisting of a number of competing political units, small if possible—should be maintained so as to give France the role of an arbitrator.

3. France became the protector of small states throughout Europe, since it was owing to the existence of many of them that she could effectively play the role of arbitrator and maintain her position of supremacy in Europe. "France, placed in the center of Europe, has the right to influence all the great developments. Her King, like a supreme judge, can consider his throne as a tribunal established by Providence to guarantee the respect for the rights and properties of the sovereigns," [2] wrote Vergennes in 1777. This providential role of France has been restated many times.

In 1919 the two policies converged. The theory of natural frontiers led to the demilitarization of the Rhine area, to the control of the Saar, and to the military hegemony of France over the Low Countries. The policy of the *status quo,* as redefined, led to an effort to divide Germany, the break-up of the Austro-Hungarian Empire, and the establishment of a number of new nations all over Eastern and South-Eastern Europe, with which France estab-

[1] *La Politique étrangère et ses fondements.* See the excellent article by J. Raoul Girardet, "L'Influence de la tradition sur la politique étrangère de la France," (Paris: Armand Colin, 1954), pp. 143–163.

[2] Quoted by J. Raoul Girardet, *op. cit,*

lished close political, economic, and military ties. Of course, a number of other factors entered into the picture. The Wilsonian idea of self-determination encouraged the establishment of small states which France was only too pleased to take under her protection, while the creation of a number of small states east of Germany formed a *cordon sanitaire* against the Soviet Union and at the same time prevented Germany from moving east.

By 1919, then, the two traditional French foreign policies had found a happy reconciliation. Despite a number of difficulties (the dismemberment of Germany did not take place, for instance) the general settlement gave France both a position of preponderance in Europe and a great degree of security and safety. If only the world had stood still, France might have maintained that position.

The policy of balance of power and security, in connection with Europe, also became France's world-wide policy. The Empire had been consolidated by the end of the nineteenth century and World War I. The imperial and with it the world vocation of France continued side by side with its continental vocation in the years after World War II—years that we intend to discuss now. We shall divide our discussion into three parts: (A) France and Europe, (B) France and the Empire, (C) France and the World.

France and Europe: the insoluble dilemma

The immediate reaction of France after the Liberation was to attempt to reestablish her traditional position of security in Europe and of independence as a world power. From 1944 until mid-1947, a policy was followed that for all practical purposes was

identical to that of 1919. France proposed the following:

1. The dismemberment of Germany and prolonged occupation of the country.
2. Heavy reparations and tight control of German industrial output.
3. The reestablishment of French control in the area west of the Rhine by the detachment of these territories from Germany.
4. A prolonged occupation, if not annexation, of the Saar.
5. The independence of the small nations of Europe.
6. An alliance with Russia directed against a threat to her security from Germany.
7. An alliance with Great Britain.

Under the government of General de Gaulle this policy was pursued with great tenacity. After the Liberation in December 1944, a Treaty of Mutual Assistance was signed with the Soviet Union. The two countries agreed to take "all the necessary measures in order to eliminate any new menace coming from Germany and to take the initative to make any new effort of aggression on her part impossible." (Art. 3). Immediately after the signature of the pact, General de Gaulle declared: "Because two of the principal powers of the world—free from any conflict of interest in any part of the world—decide to unite under specific conditions, it does not mean that either the one or the other envisages to organize the world and even its security without the help of other nations." [3]

But one might ask whether the haste with which General de Gaulle went to Moscow to sign the treaty was not motivated by considerations other than

[3] *Année Politique*, 1944–45, p. 89.

the security of France from an attack by Germany, which lay literally prostrate before the Anglo-American and Russian armies. By the treaty with Moscow, France was indeed serving notice to her former British and American allies that she intended to pursue an independent policy.

Throughout 1946 every effort was made by France to gain the support of *either* the Soviet Union *or* the United States and Great Britain in the implementation of her German policy. Neither of her two allies, however, responded favorably, since they both hoped to see ultimately an economically and politically unified Germany *on their side,* something that would have meant the end of French aspirations for European security and leadership. When the Soviet Foreign Minister, Molotov, in July 1946 declared himself in favor of a politically unified Germany, the author of the *Année Politique,* wrote: "There was reason for France, which could count on the support of her ally in the East *against* the Anglo-Americans, to be disappointed." [4]

There were more disappointments to come. The Soviet Union feared that France would ultimately become part of the Anglo-American camp and refused to support her aspirations to see the Ruhr and the Rhine provinces detached from Germany. The Soviet-American conflict at the time revolved around the control of the whole of Germany and the prize was to their eyes far more important than France. By the time it became quite clear that the conflict could not be resolved except by a partition of Germany, France discovered that her policy had failed. She had failed to gain the support of either the Soviet Union or the United States.

[4] *Année Politique,* 1946, p. 400.

She was faced with the dilemma of either accepting the division of Germany into two zones, a division that could confront France with a highly industrialized and powerful Western Germany, or of following an independent policy by maintaining her occupation of a small part of western Germany and the Saar.

The Cold War and the development of Western alliances. The Cold War, whose origin can be traced to Yalta and Potsdam, erupted in the middle of 1947. Two conferences, held in Moscow and in London, had failed to produce any kind of agreement on the problems of Germany. The lines were being drawn and the division of Germany into two zones—Soviet and British-American—became a certainty. The conflict implied the strengthening of both zones and hence the development of a strong Western German Republic with the support of the United States and England.

France managed to maintain control over the Saar, but failed in all her other claims. After June 1947 the whole of Western Europe and Great Britain received massive American aid to develop their economy. In 1948 the Brussels Pact brought together the Benelux countries, France, and Great Britain. It provided for a permanent consultative council, for negotiations to promote economic development of the countries concerned, and a military clause calling for immediate consultations to take common action against a German attack or aggression and to cope with a situation that constituted a menace to peace, no matter where it occurred or from where it came. In 1949 the creation of a large military umbrella was logically called for. Not only the Brussels signatories but also all the Western countries, including ultimately Greece and Turkey, participated. The United States became a permanent part of this alliance that continues in effect today under the name of North Atlantic Treaty Organization. Article 5 stipulated that an attack against any one of the signatories, either in Europe or in North America, would be considered to be an attack against all. It further provided (Art. 9) for a permanent deliberative organization and the establishment of a common military command. Western Germany was originally excluded from NATO.

These developments determined France's position. She became a member of NATO and of the various western alliances, under the over-all leadership and military direction of the United States. Such an alliance underwrote her security and, in general terms, the integrity of her Empire. The exclusion of Germany continued to give her a strategic position in Western Europe and the semblance, if not the reality, of national power and independence. But the question of Germany's future had been only postponed. A military Western alliance without Germany hardly represented a solution of the problems of military defense. Furthermore, as the struggle between the East and the West not only continued but was intensified with the Korean War, the prize of Germany became more important for the two major opponents. For the United States the rearmament of Western Germany seemed, rightly or wrongly, the logical step for the construction of a strong defensive wall in the West against a potential Soviet attack.

For France, however, such a rearmament was a threat. German economic development and the revival of German strength across the Rhine brought forth the traditional reflexes. Yet by 1950 or 1951, as we pointed out, there could be no imminent danger to France's security. The military alliance with Great Britain, the Brussels Pact, NATO, and the presence of American and British forces on the continent constituted adequate guarantees. Only France's notions of independence and European supremacy were really at stake. A Western Alliance in which an armed Western Germany participated might come under the domination of the strongest country —Western Germany.

The European Defense Community and its alternatives. The defensive arrangements of the Western world and the Atlantic powers did not include Western Germany. Yet Western German resources were considered indispensable by the United States. The problem, therefore, was to integrate Western Germany's power within the frame of a Western alliance without alienating France and the signatories of the Brussels Pact.

It was, strangely enough, the French who came forth with the answer: the creation of a Western European army —the European Defense Community —involving a genuine integration of national forces, a unified and, if possible, a supranational command. The United States became convinced that such a policy was preferable to the rearming of Western Germany within NATO. There were many tangible indications of a widespread movement in favor of European cooperation. The Council of Europe had been established in 1949, representing the Western European nations, with a European Assembly; the Organization of European Economic Cooperation was a European body studying the resources and needs of Western Europe and attempting to liberalize trade relations. The Western European Payments Union was functioning in order to control and regulate the deficits in the balance of payments of various European countries. Above all, the Coal and Steel Community, initiated by France, had become a reality that involved a supranational authority with power to make decisions on matters of investment, production, and transportation of coal and steel among the six signatory powers—Western Germany, France, the Benelux countries, and Italy. The establishment of a European army, ambitious though it appeared to be, was welcome in the context of these moves toward European cooperation and integration.

No sooner had the European Defense Community been announced and formulated than it provoked a storm of protest in France. The political parties were actively for or against it. Extreme right-wing and extreme left-wing parties joined hands against the Treaty, which was defended by a sharply divided center. To French public opinion the most controversial part of the Treaty was the envisaged German rearmament. A majority of the members of the National Assembly considered a German rearmament even within the EDC to be a direct challenge to French sovereignty, clearly spelling the end of France's aspirations to remain a leading European nation. The memory of Nazi Germany was too fresh in the minds of many; the possibility that Western Germany, once rearmed, might attempt to provoke a war with Russia in order to achieve its unification, and thus might drag the whole of Western Europe and France into a war, was pointed out; the assumption by Germany of a predominant role in Europe, at a time when France was heavily engaged in protecting her Empire, was also mentioned. Each party and each parliamentary group saw specific reasons for refusing to accept the Treaty, while its proponents defended it also for different reasons. Since there was no genuine majority[5] for or against the Treaty, it was on a procedural motion that, in August 1954, the EDC was rejected by the French National Assembly. In the meantime all its prospective members had honored the signature of their governments. Only the French Assembly used its constitutional prerogatives and refused to ratify the Treaty. The rejection climaxed four whole years of equivocation. It was only in December 1954 that the National Assembly, six months after defeating the EDC for fear of German rearmament, allowed Germany to become a member of NATO and to rearm herself within the context of the NATO alliance.

A Third Force? While the EDC was being debated and criticisms against it multiplied, the movement in favor of neutralism assumed great importance. It is hard to define or describe it briefly without doing injustice to its manifold aspects and characteristics. Essentially, it was a movement that answered the profound hopes of the French people that, in case of war, France would be allowed to remain out of it. Some 70 per cent of the French people answering a poll conducted by the French Institute of Public Opinion expressed this hope in 1951, when the Cold War was at its highest. At the same time, neutralism was a movement that tended to reassert the traditional French claims of independence and balance of power. Since the world was divided between two camps, France alone, or France at the head of Western Europe,

[5] The division of the political system in Parliament and in the various coalition cabinets reflected very closely the division of the public opinion. In July 1954, 36 per cent of those asked were "for" or "rather for" the EDC; 31 per cent were "against" or "rather against" and 33 per cent did not answer.

could afford to say "A plague o' both your houses!" and, if need be, to arbitrate between them.

The neutralist position, advanced by the Communist Party and by some left-wing intellectuals, had other motives. Essentially, they wanted to weaken American predominance over Western Europe. Many of the left-wing intellectuals were motivated by subtler considerations: the independence of the French nation to continue to develop her own way of life; the rejection of the realities of a bipolar world; an emphasis upon France's cultural and intellectual vocation. For some, it was mere anti-Americanism and a declaration of France's independence from American tutelage; for others, it was the belief that France had more to gain than to lose from a pro-Soviet orientation; for many others, it was a constructive step towards the building of a solid Western alliance with Great Britain as a partner, which would develop enough strength to play the role of Third Force that France could not play alone. Neutralism and nationalism were often linked.

But the German problem was again an obstacle. A Third Force in Europe without Western Germany and without wholehearted British commitment could not be strong enough. A Third Force with Germany, however, was one in which Germany, rather than France, might assume a preponderant role. The real tragedy was that France, weak alone, found that any form of European integration and alliance underscored her weakness and subordination—to the United States, to the Soviet Union, or possibly to England or Western Germany. By 1954, therefore, France found herself, after interminable zig-zags, equivocations, and soul-searching, in the Atlantic camp to which a fifteenth member had been added—Western Germany.

France and the Empire

France emerged from World War I as one of the three big powers. Russia lay in the throes of Revolution; the United States still was unwilling to assume international responsibilities that involved continuous commitments abroad; elsewhere in the world, the stirrings of nationalist awakening were making themselves heard, but not sufficiently to cause concern to the colonial powers, of whom, England and France were the most important.

The French Empire extended over every continent of the world. Its administration was a vestige of the Napoleonic conceptions of a highly centralized bureaucratic system—an administration in which Paris through the colonial officials made the ultimate decisions and legislated for the whole Empire. Its cementing ideology was that of "assimilation"—the notion that ultimately every inhabitant would become a French citizen and be represented in the French Parliament—a notion at marked variance with the Anglo-Saxon conception according to which political and cultural evolution of the colonial peoples would ultimately bring about political autonomy and self-government.

In 1944, the basic charter of colonial policy had been drafted at the Brazzaville conference. There it was decided that "the purpose of the civilizing work accomplished by France in the colonies excludes any idea of autonomy, any possibility of an evolution outside of the French Empire. The establishment, even in the remote future, of 'self-government' in the colonies must not be considered." [6] In 1945, when a Trusteeship Committee was appointed within the United Nations, the French made it quite clear that they

[6] *Année Politique*, 1944–45.

would not accept its jurisdiction. The Empire was French and hence a matter of domestic policy.

In almost every case, the French insisted upon assimilation and maintenance of French sovereignty. In 1945, France refused to withdraw her army from Syria and Lebanon. Within a year she had to give in. In 1947, she refused to enter into negotiations with Ho-Chin-Minh and engaged in a war that lasted until 1954. The war in Indochina cost France more than a billion dollars a year, drained her of resources, retarded her internal investment policy, paralyzed her alternate plans for an economic and social reconstruction of the North African territories. It was primarily responsible for France's inability to keep pace with German economic reconstruction in Western Europe.

But the Indochinese war brought other problems to a head. In Algeria, Tunis, and Morocco, the independence movements were gaining strength. These movements, however, envisaged continued cooperation with France. In every case, the French political leaders and representatives and the various military leaders in command of the French troops reiterated the philosophy of the French vocation. Time after time, the legitimate interests of France were evoked. Time after time, the representatives of the French government and the Army intervened. By 1956, both Morocco and Tunisia became independent. The refusal to grant self-government left only one alternative: secession.

This situation was most evident in Algeria, where there has been a very strong movement in favor of self-government since the period of the Liberation. It gained strength after the independence of Morocco and Tunisia. Yet there were many opportunities to cope with the Algerian situation, and progress had been made in 1947 when

special legislation granting considerable political autonomy to Algeria had been passed, although this legislation was never implemented. Claims of French sovereignty in Algeria and assertions that France "intends to stay there" made in the last years of the Fourth Republic sounded very similar to the assertions made for Syria, Lebanon, Indochina, Tunis, and Morocco.

France and the world: the vocation of greatness

The explanation of the predicament of the French Empire lies in the postwar vocation of France to maintain her top-rank power status in the world. The French Empire, a French commentator wrote in 1947, in an excellent but highly optimistic analysis of the prospects of the French Union, "corresponds without any doubt to the profound interest of France. . . . France cannot aspire to play an important international role except in terms of her ability to represent a powerful association of peoples." [7]

The fate of France was invariably presented in terms of the destiny of the nation in the world. The answer was given in terms of traditional historical reflexes—France's military power, her cultural superiority, her civilizing mission, and her Empire.

Over and above these misconceptions the assessment of national strength was also couched in terms of nineteenth century imperial perspectives. The equation, however, was no longer valid in view of the development of colonial nationalism. The British saw in it something the French refused to realize: that to maintain an Empire by force is far more expensive, far more

[7] *Année Politique,* 1947, "L'Union Française, Bilan Politique de l'Année 1947," p. 275.

debilitating to a nation's strength than to abandon it.

THE LEGACY OF THE FOURTH REPUBLIC (1946–1950)

Elements of stability

Despite the divisions of the political system under the Fourth Republic and the fact that they often spilled over into the area of foreign policy there was continuity in the pursuit of basic foreign policy objectives. The political elites, the political parties—with the exception of the Communists—and public opinion remained steadfast in their attachments to the traditional interests of France, in spite of rapidly changing world conditions. Discontinuities were occasionally introduced but only in the form of decisive choices. This was the case in 1954–55 with the termination of the Indochinese war, the granting of autonomy and later independence to Morocco and Tunisia, and the Paris agreements that consecrated Western German sovereignty and allowed for German participation in the NATO. The political system remained by and large committed to the following objectives: a) the maintenance of an Atlantic and world position that implied a weak Germany and a militarily independent France; b) a European rapprochement in terms of which France could gain strength at the head of Western Europe; c) the maintenance of a top-rank world position.

What has been called la politique du grandeur (the policy of greatness), according to which France's vocation is that of a world power and therefore a partner in the development of world strategy or—under propitious conditions—an independent force, are ever present. General de Gaulle's policy after his return to power on June 1,

1958 has been a faithful expression of the broad objectives pursued by the political leadership of the Fourth Republic.

The Empire: the foundation of a new policy. It was only in the last two years of the Republic, between 1956–58, that French leadership decided to move ahead of the irresistible trend of colonial emancipation rather than attempt to oppose it. In 1956 the French Parliament began consideration of new legislation to put an end to the theory and practice of assimilation. A *loi-cadre* (framework law) empowered the government to enact executive orders in order to give considerable autonomy to the African Republics and Madagascar. They became semi-independent Republics with their own parliaments and responsible executives. France retained jurisdiction over important areas of policy-making such as defense, foreign policy, trade and education. But the first path toward gradual political emancipation had been made. It proved to be irreversible.

Economic and military policy. The Fourth Republic also laid the groundwork of France's economic and military recovery. The Atomic Energy Commissariat founded in 1945 continued in operation throughout the years of cabinet instability and was endowed with adequate credits. The possession of an atom bomb in a world in which three powers had developed nuclear weapons became associated in the eyes of the French political leaders and public alike with France's national independence and security. Throughout the latter years of the Republic all governments favored the suspension of the fabrication of the bomb *and* the gradual destruction of nuclear weapons. Only if the latter condition were accepted would France be willing to abandon her effort to manufacture and test the bomb.

Although favoring the Atlantic alliance, the political leaders of the Fourth Republic never agreed to play a secondary role and acquiesce to American or British and American supremacy. They did not accept any genuine integration of military command within NATO and, alleging their colonial obligations, insisted on maintaining autonomy over their military forces. They remained reluctant to permit the establishment of United States nuclear stockpiles on French soil or the construction of launching sites. The same fear of integration of the military forces applied to a purely European Army, as we have seen.

Thus, while accepting participation in an Atlantic and European military alliance the French governments made sure that such alliances never took a form that undermined France's independence and freedom to use her own military forces at her discretion. By the same token they were unwilling to participate in any defense system with the British and the Americans unless it gave France full and equal power on all global decisions and strategy.

Public opinion. [8] Studies of opinion throughout the Fourth Republic indicate that there was a striking coincidence between the action of the political leaders and public opinion. French attitudes toward the Cold War, the Soviet Union or the United States, the problem of French military independence and Western Germany and toward European cooperation show stability and continuity.

The Cold War. Generally the attitude of the French with regard to the Cold War can be summed up as one

[8] I am indebted to the excellent summary of public opinion trends that appeared in the *Sondages* (Revue Française de l'opinion publique), Nos. 1 and 2, 1958, *La Politique étrangère de la France et l'opinion publique* (1954–1957).

of neutrality and considerable hostility to both protagonists. One out of every ten believed that the United States was to be blamed, two out of ten put the blame on the Soviet Union and four out of every ten on both. At the same time the French public thought that neither the United States nor the Soviet Union were doing all they could to avert the Cold War. Fifty-two and fifty-seven per cent of those interrogated in 1957 believed that the United States or the Soviet Union respectively were not doing as much as possible. From 1952 until 1957 the public, when asked to which camp France ought to belong, expressed itself as follows:

	The "West"	The "East"	Neither
Sept. 1952	42%	4%	43%
Nov. 1954	36	2	39
June 1955	18	3	57
Aug. 1955	23	4	51
Dec. 1955	35	5	45
May 1957	28	4	39
Dec. 1957	21	3	51

If there were a war between the United States and the Soviet Union, the preponderant choice would be for neutrality:

	With US	With USSR	Not take part
Sept. 1952	36%	4%	45%
Nov. 1954	22	2	45
June 1955	19	3	58
Aug. 1955	25	5	51
Sept. 1957	15	3	62

Europe. While the French continued to fear Western Germany and to be reluctant to see her rearm, there was a general resignation to Germany's participation in European cooperation schemes. From 1947 until December 1957 French public opinion favored a European Union. Fifty-five to seventy per cent were in favor and those opposed never exceeded 21 per cent. In only two polls, taken in 1955, did less than 50 per cent favor a European union. Support for the European Common Mark, for the Schuman Plan and for the European Atomic Cooperation program was equally strong. The rearmament of Western Germany, however, was considered until 1954 to be a "danger" and the general consensus favored a demilitarized Germany. In 1955, 53 per cent were against the participation of Western Germany in the defense of Western Europe.

Atomic weapons, NATO and the United States. Although opting for neutrality and condemning the manufacture and the potential use of atomic weapons, the French in December 1957 favored "giving more attention to atomic weapons" for the defense of their country. Forty per cent were in favor; 20 per cent opposed and 40 per cent declined to answer.

In December 1957 when the French were asked, "Under the present circumstances how can France best assure her security?" Sixteen per cent favored the maintenance of the existing alliances in western Europe, within NATO and with the USA; 5 per cent favored a military alliance limited to Western Europe only; 21 per cent favored a general security system including the United States, Western Europe and the Soviet Union; and 34 per cent favored withdrawal *from all alliances* and the assumption of an independent and neutral posture.

In the same context the general reaction of the French public with regard to NATO was one of indifference. Not more than 50 or 60 per cent prepared to answer on the basis of any knowledge of the organization. Of those answering only a small percentage favored the organization and considered it important for the security of France. Such a reaction was not caused by the intervention of the United States in the Suez expedition or

the delivery of arms to Tunisia—generally considered to be acts inimical to France. It stemmed primarily from the realization that the United States was exerting too much influence on French foreign policy. Forty to 42 per cent of the French interrogated between 1952 and December 1956 found that the United States had too much influence. In the same manner, more than 60 per cent believed in 1956 and 1957 that France was not treated by the United States as an equal in matters concerning the two countries. Some 27 to 40 per cent believed that Americans and French had common interests while some 25 per cent believed that the interests of the two countries were different. More than 33 per cent of those asked in December 1956 believed that a European union would diminish American influence and 35 per cent of them believed that such a diminution of American influence would be "a good thing."

Thus throughout the period of the Fourth Republic, the public, even if badly informed, reacted with a remarkable degree of unity in favor of neutrality and European cooperation; feared Germany; suspected NATO and in general agreed that independence and security can be based only on national strength and freedom of action. Despite an underlying realization of France's reduced world status the public continued to cling to the image of a strong and independent France. They deplored the reduction of French strength and accepted European unity as an instrument for the realization of national security vis-à-vis both the United States and the Soviet Union.

Foreign Service. An important factor in the continuity of the French foreign policy was the existence of a small but competent body of civil servants attached to the Ministry of Foreign Affairs. A hard core of some 4000 foreign service officers constitute the administrative network of the foreign service. About a thousand are in Paris and roughly three thousand scattered over the various embassies, legations, consulates and other foreign services. They are admitted into the foreign service on the basis of hard competitive examinations and since 1945 all candidates complete two or three years of study in the National School of Administration. Thus a greater percentage of candidates of modest fortune may enter the foreign service. Less than 5 per cent of the applicants pass the examination, thus maintaining a high level of intellectual competence.

The structure and the personnel of the Ministry of Foreign Affairs has not undergone serious modifications in the last century. The consular and the diplomatic corps have been combined, and a number of foreign service personnel were purged after the Liberation. The organization of the Ministry continues to be based on functional rather than geographic divisions: the General Office of Political and Economic Affairs, the General Office of Personnel and General Administration, the General Office of Cultural and Technical Affairs, the Office of Administrative and Social Affairs, the Office of Protocol, the Archives and the Legal Service section. However, there are certain broad geographic subdivisions: a) Europe and European organizations, b) Asia and Oceania, c) Africa and the Middle East, d) America.

The hard core of the foreign service has been a stable and an efficient body but has shared and in a way contributed to the perpetuation of many of the myths on which French diplomacy has been based, such as the supremacy of French culture and the top rank of France. What is more, it has remained for a long time, because of the educa-

tion of many of its officers, tradition-bound and excessively legalistic in its approach and mentality. Problems have been considered in legal terms, not in terms of the dynamics of the ever-changing power relations in our world.[9]

A "new" economic policy. There was a clear perception among most of the political leaders of the Fourth Republic that France could not recover its prewar position without drastic economic effort. A rapid modernization of the French economy and a gradual movement toward increasing European cooperation were required. A strong France in a well-integrated western European economy could be far stronger than if she acted alone. Therefore the Fourth Republic, after many equivocations, moved after 1956 in the direction of the European Economic Market, providing for liberalization of trade, lowering and ultimately elimination of all tariffs, and free movement of capital and labor among Western Germany, Italy, France, and the Benelux countries. The European Market Treaty was signed in Rome in 1957 and put into effect on January 1, 1959.

The beginning of economic modernization. The task facing the country immediately after World War II was thus twofold: Reconstruction and productive investment, to renew the industrial equipment of the nation and to expand its weak sectors. This was the objective of the first "Monnet Plan" (1947–50).

Programs for production and modernization for *six basic industries*— coal-mining, electric power, steel, ce-

[9] As Professor J. B. Duroselle points out, ". . . the service remains a caste ever prone to believe in its omniscience." Kertesz and Fitzsimons (ed.) *Diplomacy in a Changing World* (Notre Dame, Ind.: University of Notre Dame Press, 1959), p. 227.

ment, farm machinery, and internal transportation—were adopted for 1947, 1948, 1949, and 1950.

The following output targets were set for 1950: production of 65 million tons of coal; rapid increase in hydroelectric power to generate electricity— 25 billion kilowatt hours; production of about 12 million tons of steel; production of 50 thousand tractors a year; rapid increase in exports, and training of skilled workers.

Many of these targets were not achieved by 1950, partly because of lack of vigorous administration of the plan; partly because of the inflation that undermined economic progress; partly because of social unrest and strikes. Yet, despite the remarks of many critics, a beginning had been made. A second and third "plan" were developed and began to build upon healthier foundations. Their cumulative impact began to make itself felt by 1955–56. Whatever the weaknesses of the Fourth Republic; whatever the vacillations of the various governments, massive public investment was followed scrupulously, and expansion and growth became the commonly accepted policy. In 1956–57 the impact of the economic plans was clearly discernible. France was modernizing fast at a tempo that began to compare favorably with that of Germany in the years between 1952–56. By 1958 the gross national product had gone up by 65 per cent while the population also began to grow, registering a rise for the first time since 1870. It grew by about 10 per cent since the end of the war, and it should reach about 47 million by 1970.

Elements of instability

The governmental institutions of the Fourth Republic affected adversely the implementation of the long-range objectives, but only to a degree. Despite cabinet instability—there were twenty cabinets under the Fourth Republic— foreign policy was directed by only a very small number of Foreign Ministers. Under the Fourth Republic there were, in all, five Ministers of Foreign Affairs: Robert Schuman and Georges Bidault (from the MRP), Edgar Faure and Pierre Mendès-France (from the Radical Socialists), and Christian Pineau of the Socialist Party. Divisions, however, in domestic and colonial issues and growing parliamentary interference provided serious internal difficulties and a marked immobility in policy-making. This was the cause, for instance, of the equivocation on the European Defense Community. Cabinet instability undermined consistency in implementation.

The formulation of foreign policy, like the formulation of any other policy at the governmental level, involved the cooperation of the Prime Minister and his Cabinet with the Parliament. As a result, its formulation suffered because of certain inherent weaknesses of the governmental process in France. These weaknesses were (1) the coalition character of the Cabinet, and (2) Cabinet instability.

Coalition Cabinet. In France the Cabinet was and to a great extent continues to be composed of the leaders of a number of political parties. Ever since the establishment of the Third Republic hardly a party or a combination of two parties managed to provide a majority in the legislature. The Cabinet was a coalition of the leaders of many parties and groups. As a result, the desired homogeneity of views upon policy in general and upon foreign policy in particular was lacking. Very often the members of one and the same Cabinet held opposing views on matters of foreign policy. That happened, for instance, between 1952 and 1954 when members of the same Cabinet were in favor and against the European Defense Community.

Cabinet Instability. In France, the average life of a coalition Cabinet has been short. In the last two decades of the Third Republic the average life of a Cabinet hardly exceeded eight months. From the establishment of the Fourth Republic to the beginning of 1958 there were 18 Cabinets. The succession of Cabinets at this rate was responsible for the following consequences:

a) Lack of continuity in the implementation of foreign policy objectives.

b) Lack of planning on policy-goals.

Both these evils were to some degree alleviated as we have noted by the relative independence of the Minister of Foreign Affairs and by his continuity in office. However, this continuity in office of the Minister of Foreign Affairs could not compensate for the evils of Cabinet instability, since issues of foreign policy could not be dissociated from other issues of policy. They were part of a whole that engages the Cabinet and, as a result, called for a common Cabinet policy and planning.

The only two semipermanent coordinating cabinet committees were (1) the "general secretariat attached to the Organization of European Economic Cooperation (OEEC)," composed primarily of civil servants of the various economic Ministries, and (2) the "permanent secretariat of the National Defense," operating under the Ministry of the National Defense—a staff organization with rather limited functions and a turbulent history of continuous reorganizations. All the other existing coordinating organizations operated either at the administrative level and were composed of civil servants or were *ad hoc* organizations

formed to deal with a particular problem. As Professor Duroselle pointed out, "there were no coordinating agencies between the different bureaus of the *Quai d'Orsay* (the Ministry of Foreign Affairs) and the other Ministries." [10] There were some ministerial committees, but, because of the instability of the Cabinet, they were just as short-lived as the Cabinet itself. Furthermore, there was no permanent planning agency. To quote again Professor Duroselle, "the most striking fact is the complete absence of planning organisms. French policy was organized exactly as if decisions were to be taken on a day-to-day basis." [11]

The only planning agencies that existed, it may be argued, were the Ministry of Foreign Affairs and the Cabinet as a whole. But the first, as we have pointed out, was unable to cope with the volume and the complexity of the work involved, while the instability of the latter made planning in foreign policy impossible. It was generally admitted that since the Liberation France, despite the continuity of her objectives, had no foreign policy on many, grave matters that concerned her. There were many Algerian policies, a number of European policies, a great number of North African policies, succeeding each other, but never forming a whole and never followed in terms of a coherent plan.

Such a situation could not but invite growing parliamentary interference, which aggravated the situation. Disagreements on foreign policy inevitably reached the Parliament and became in turn matters over which political parties and parliamentary groups took sides, thus intensifying party warfare

[10] Jean-Baptiste Duroselle, "L'Élaboration de la politique étrangère française," *Revue Française de la Science Politique,* VI, No. 3 (Juillet–Septembre 1956), 418.

[11] *Ibid.,* p. 516.

in the National Assembly, causing frequent dislocations of the existing majorities, and accentuating Cabinet instability.

Conclusion

Tenacity and continuity in the perception of common goals; inability to implement these goals because of great disparity between aspiration and means —a disparity brought about by the influence of stronger powers, notably the United States—or inability created by the sharp internal divisions that produced discontinuities and vacillations in the over-all foreign policy tactics—this is perhaps the best way to summarize the foreign policy of France in the twelve-odd years of the Fourth Republic.

It was only at the very end that, after numerous setbacks, a new note of realism was injected into the relations between France and her western neighbors. The domestic economic efforts were beginning to pay off, and the French business elite became increasingly reconciled to the notions of decolonization and of European unity. The Schuman plan had functioned moderately well, and the prospect of an enlarged European Market began to appeal to many French manufacturers and to undermine the traditional protectionist mentality of business groups. By 1957 most political parties were willing to go along with the establishment of the European Common Market. For many, however, close economic and political European cooperation implied something else—the creation of a strong European bloc, possibly under the leadership of France, that would give her an opportunity to play a genuinely independent role in world affairs.

Colonial disengagement, economic modernization, the abandonment of a protectionist economic policy, the rapid development of resources including the discovery of rich deposits of oil and gas both on the soil of France and in Sahara, were beginning to provide for a sense of strength and recovery where in the past there had been only a feeling of weakness and frustration. The dismal way in which the Fourth Republic came to an end and the difficulty of finding a solution to the Algerian problem did not hide from the vast majority of French men and women the promise that lay ahead.

THE FIFTH REPUBLIC AND GENERAL DE GAULLE

The failure of the Fourth Republic to translate rapidly and effectively into action the commonly shared foreign policy objectives was one of the major reasons for its downfall. France's diminished status in the world, the successive defeats or withdrawals in the many and elusive colonial wars, the failure of France and Great Britain in Suez, the growing strength of Western Germany in NATO and in western Europe under a stable political leadership, were all factors in the growth of a spirit of nationalism in the country, contrasting sharply with governmental instability. Parliament and coalition cabinets continued to mirror the perennial and multiple divisions of the body politic at the very time when the public demanded unity and the realization of national objectives.

Whatever the factors and the immediate causes associated with the uprising of May 13, 1958 in Algeria, it was to General de Gaulle that most of the political groups and leaders turned. Army officers, veterans, the political parties from the Socialists to the Independents, a great number of intellectuals—some with considerable misgivings—turned to de Gaulle as the symbol and the person around whom this new spirit of French nationalism could find expression. The Fifth Republic is de Gaulle, and its policies and objectives are those of General de Gaulle.

The basic assumptions

De Gaulle's basic assumptions, what we may call his over-all philosophy, begin and end with the notion that there is one social force—the reality of the nation (*le fait national*)—that overshadows all others. No other force or forces, ideological, social, or economic, have succeeded in undermining the nation-state as the focal point of the ultimate loyalty of man.

From the postulate of national reality a number of inferences flow. They do not always have the logical consistency that an academician would desire; but consistency is not a necessary ingredient of statecraft. Situations change so fast in our world that the only consistency lies in the ability to adjust.[12] Consistency means in the last analysis realism. Yet the inferences that follow from the postulate on national reality constitute guides to action and must be spelled out.

The reality of the nation and the means of achieving independence. The reality of the nation requires power in order fully to manifest itself. Surveying the world situation before VE-day de Gaulle could not restrain his bitterness. "How dull is the sword of France at the time when the Allies are about to launch the assault of Europe." [13] Though not the only one, the basic

ingredient of power is the military. In the ruins of France after the Liberation de Gaulle set himself to recreate the French Army. He was haunted with the certainty that the allies were blocking his efforts because they were unwilling to allow France to develop the military strength that would enable her to become an equal. When the matter of Germany's occupation seemed in doubt he ordered his divisions into the German soil, suspecting, perhaps rightly, that the allies might prevent France from participating in settling the future of Germany and remembering also that in war possession is nine-tenths of the law. His vision remained the same throughout the months following the Liberation—to recreate the French Armed Forces. When there was not enough gas to heat the French stoves, he established a Commission for Atomic Energy.

But there are other important factors in the equation of power. De Gaulle recognizes many and has used them all: alliances, diplomacy and skill in negotiations, cultural relations, spiritual influence, economic resources, and population.

A strong ingredient of power, indeed the only valid expression of a nation, is the state and its political organization. Gaullist revisionism both before and throughout the Fourth Republic was predicated upon de Gaulle's ideas about world relations and the role of the French nation. To play the proper role France needed a strong state. In this state one man, the President of the Republic, should make foreign policy on behalf of the nation—the "real France"—incarnating the national interests over and above the welter of particular interests and ideological factions.

A third ingredient of power that de Gaulle has evoked very frequently since he returned to office has led him

[12] Almost always, for instance, de Gaulle in speaking on international issues will insert the phrase "given the present conditions in the world," or "in the actual state of developments," or "with things being what they are."

[13] *Mémoires*, Tome 2, p. 245

to follow policies to which he seemed firmly opposed only a decade ago. This is what he calls the imperative of the *grands ensembles*—of the "great wholes." Nations must establish co-operative "wholes" that provide the structural bases and the resources for the economic development and defense of each one and all. This is not contrary to his emphasis upon national unique-ness, nor does it lead him to the espousal of projects of military integration. The building of large wholes creates more than an alliance and less than a feder-ation. It is a close association and co-operation between nation-states which by pooling some of their resources find the strength to sustain a common pur-pose. Whether it stems from a profound realization on de Gaulle's part of con-temporary economic trends or is simply a tactical answer to the "two great empires" (the Soviet Union and the United States), whether it applies to Western Europe or to the French Community, he has been one of its most forceful advocates, reminding the African Republics time after time that independence nowadays is a fiction un-less sustained by strength and that strength can never be attained by small geographic political fragments that go under the name of sovereign states.

The idea of balance. De Gaulle's emphasis upon the reality of the na-tional phenomenon and its concomitant accessories—power, both military and political—leads him to a theory of international relations that is often re-ferred to as "realist." International rela-tions is an arena of conflict in which every participant nation-state attempts to maximize its strength at the expense of the other. Every political leader-ship, no matter what ideology inspires it, acts in terms of national considera-tion. *If so, it is only power that can check power—and the only possible international world is one in which an* *equilibrium of powers is reached.* This leads de Gaulle to follow conclusions that directly shape his actions.

The present balance is unnatural, precarious and unwise. Unnatural be-cause it involves a growing bipolariza-tion and satellization of the world which is inconsistent with the secular realities and interests of nations; pre-carious because it involves a continuous "brink" for the big and small nations; and, finally, unwise because, if allowed to continue, it gives to the two of the less qualified nation-states—the United States and the Soviet Union—full liberty to act: independence to decide their fate and with it the fate of the world.

Both the American and the Russian efforts are expressions of national power, in one form or another, and de Gaulle has no illusions about either. If they are allowed free sway they might enter upon armed conflict. If they find a temporary accommodation it will be in order to establish a joint hegemony over the world. *Either case will be to the detriment of the other nation-states* and, of course, of France and Europe. This can be avoided only by creating a balance of power consistent with the growing realities of the world, in which the economic and political development of Europe is bound to play a growing role.

General de Gaulle's conception of a "balance" has been a permanent trait of his thinking and action ever since he became a public figure. It has taken a number of forms.

In the third volume of his *Mémoires* de Gaulle pointed out that the only way to keep Russia out of the heart of Europe was to dismember Germany. By doing so the threat of a new Ger-many would be eliminated, alleviating the fears of the Soviet Union and the eastern European nations. More-over, a treaty with the Soviet Union directed against the revival of German power would free her to pursue her other world obligations. It was the failure of Yalta to revive the pre-World War II arrangement in Europe that also accounted for the bitter denunciations against the settlement. Though France received a number of compensations, perhaps far beyond what French leadership had a right to expect in terms of the reality of the power relations at the time, Yalta became slowly identified with a betrayal of Europe and France by the "Anglo-Saxons."

De Gaulle made an open offer to Churchill in November 1944 to combine forces so that the two countries with their far-flung Empires would be able to act independently of the Russians or the Americans. It is worth quoting his remarks to Churchill:

You can see, France is beginning to recover. But whatever my faith in her is, I know that she will not recover soon her former strength. You, English, will finish this war on the other hand with glory. But nonetheless your relative position may well be weakened in view of your losses and sacrifices, the centrifugal forces that undermine the Commonwealth and above all the ascendancy of America and Russia, and later on of China. Well then, our two ancient countries are both weakened at the time when they are to confront a new world. . . . But if England and France agree and act together in the future negotiations, they will have enough weight to prevent any decision that will not be acceptable to them. . . . It is this common will that must be the basis of the alliance that you are proposing to us. . . . The equilibrium of Europe . . . the guarantee of peace on the Rhine, the independence of the states on the Vistula, the Danube and the Balkans, the keeping on our side of the peoples to whom we opened up civilization in all parts of the

world, the organization of the nations in a manner that will provide something else than a battlefield for the quarrels of the Russians and the Americans, finally the primacy in our policy of a certain conception of man, despite the progressive mechanization of the societies, . . . is it not true that these are the great interests of the Universe? These interests, let us put them together and safeguard them together.[14]

A third scheme involved an alliance with the Soviet Union, directed against German recovery and guaranteeing the *status quo* of Europe. Speculating before his trip to the Soviet Union in December 1944, only a few weeks after he had made his offer to Churchill, de Gaulle writes wistfully, "Perhaps it might be possible to renew in some manner the Franco-Russian solidarity, which even if misunderstood and betrayed in the past, was nonetheless compatible with the nature of things *both with regard to the German danger and the Anglo-Saxon efforts to assert their hegemony.*"[15]

A fourth and perhaps more persistent effort to recreate a balance is the revival of Europe as a "Third Force." Definition of what "Europe" exactly means to de Gaulle is a difficult matter. In his *Mémoires* he spoke of an organization of the peoples of Europe from "Iceland to Istanbul and from Gibraltar to the Urals." Sometimes Russia is part and sometimes it is not, though emphasis is often put on the European destiny of Russia. Sometimes it is western Europe and sometimes the whole of Europe. Sometimes Europe implies the necessity of a dismembered Germany, sometimes a divided Germany and sometimes a

[14] *Mémoires,* Tome 3, p. 52 (author's translation).
[15] *Mémoires,* Tome 3, p. 54 (author's translation and italics).

Franco-German rapprochement without qualifications. Two things are certain: Europe, whatever it is, is distinct from the "Anglo-Saxon powers." It is also separate from Soviet Russia, without, however, excluding under certain conditions the European position of Russia and hence its participation.

With the economic recovery of Western Germany and the continuing division of this country into two blocs— de Gaulle's conception of Europe became clearer. A strong France in Western Europe can assume the leadership of the Western bloc and speak for it. But to be strong in Western Europe France must maintain good relations with a Western Germany that is never to be allowed, however, to match France's leadership. So underlying the new conception of balance in which Western Europe is perhaps to become for the first time a genuine Third Force, there is always an emphasis upon France's interest which means France's strength. A leader of Western Europe, France, can put all her weight, in the name of the new force, in world strategy and world leadership.

In the name of balance de Gaulle has in the course of less than twenty years envisaged the following alliances: (a) with the British in order to create an independent bloc *vis-à-vis* the Russians and the Americans; (b) with the Soviet Union in order to maintain French supremacy in Europe *vis-à-vis* Germany; (c) with all against the revival of a unified militarized and strong Germany; (d) with Western Germany and the West European states in order to create an independent bloc —a Third Force in Europe that might lead to drastic changes in the balance of power.

A new style

Harold Nicolson in his *The Evolution of Diplomacy* distinguishes between the "old" diplomacy and the "new." The distinction has both procedural and substantive traits. Substantively the old diplomacy assumed the primacy of Europe, the objective gradation of nations in terms of power and the responsibility of the big powers for the course of international events and, more particularly, for matters of peace and war. Procedurally the old diplomacy used diplomacy and negotiations and shied away from appeals to world opinion, large conferences, and ideologic confrontations. The "new" diplomacy is the work of secular forces that changed the balance of forces. Europe was progressively overshadowed. It was also the work of Wilson in introducing diplomacy by conference, in utilizing ideological slogans, and in stressing the equality of all nations.

All of de Gaulle's sympathies remain with the old diplomacy. While conceding basic alterations to the balance of forces that ought to be considered, he has no patience with the new procedures. The Old Concert of Europe, he is willing to concede, ought to become the new Concert of the World in which the United States has a permanent place—perhaps also with China and even India. But "Europe" is still in his mind a dominant, perhaps under the proper conditions *the* dominant, force. The powers that have global interests and global responsibilities are few; they must continue to play a leading role in all matters of international relations and particularly in matters of war and peace.

Negotiations and carefully prepared treaties must be once more the rule. Such negotiations must be conducted, as in the past, by experts, in secret, and communicated at the appropriate time to parliaments and the public. Neither the United Nations as organized today nor the various summit meetings past, present, or future have appealed to de Gaulle. In his press conference of November 10, 1959, he specifically criticized assemblies whose only purpose seemed to be the airing of grievances and the agitation of public opinion. Again, when France decided no longer to provide funds for the United Nations operations in the Congo, de Gaulle explained in his press conference of April 11, 1961 why support had been withdrawn. The Security Council, where decisions were to be made by five big powers, had lost virtually all power, he said. Power had shifted to the General Assembly. "It [the General Assembly]," he pointed out acidly, "has assumed all powers. It can deliberate on everything." This Assembly will soon consist of some 120 states "many of which are improvised states and believe it their duty to stress grievances or demands with regard to the older nations. . . ." The meetings of the United Nations "are no more than riotous sessions. . . ." "As the United Nations," he concluded, "becomes a scene of disturbance, confusion, and division, it acquires the ambition to intervene in all kinds of matters." France, he hinted, would maintain its aloofness toward "these United, or Disunited, Nations." [16] At the end of July 1961, France refused to acknowledge the competence of the United Nations in dealing with the France-Tunisian conflict in Bizerte.

The execution of treaties must be constantly in the hands of the Great Powers; their good faith must be taken for granted, and sanctions must follow any breach. Action, however, must be based in all events upon the free exchange of information by those concerned and must be taken in terms of

the global interests of all concerned. As in the years between the two wars, today the French position remains: that matters of war and peace are both global and indivisible. Regional alliances, like NATO, must be put in this context.

De Gaulle's actions ever since he assumed the Presidency—indeed, ever since he returned to power on June 1, 1958—exhibit all the traits associated with the "old" diplomacy: his firm commitment to European revival under the leadership of France; his emphasis upon global responsibilities and global strategy of the Great Powers; his underplaying of the United Nations and NATO (to the extent to which it consecrates the hegemony of the Anglo-Saxons and allows only them, especially the United States, freedom of action); and, above all, the exclusive jurisdiction he has assumed as President of the Republic for foreign affairs.

The new style is reflected in the constitutional arrangement and institutional development of the Fifth Republic.

The new Constitution. The Constitution of the Fifth Republic provides that the Cabinet "shall determine and direct the policy of the nation" and "it will be responsible to Parliament." "The Prime Minister is responsible for national defense." (Art. 20 and 21.) The President of the Republic, on the other hand, "shall be the guarantor of the national independence, of the integrity of the territory, and of the respect . . . of treaties." (Art. 5.) He "shall negotiate and ratify treaties" and "he shall be informed of all negotiations leading to the conclusion of an international agreement. . . ." (Art. 52.) All major treaties, however, must be "ratified by law." (Art. 53).

The contrasts with the constitutional arrangement of the Fourth Republic lie primarily in the conception of the role

---

[16] News conference of April 11, 1961, translated by the French Embassy, *Service de Presse et d'Information. Speeches and Press Conference, No. 162,* pp. 7–8.

of the President. He was given both implicitly and explicitly broader powers. The President is the guarantor of the national integrity, the commander-in-chief presiding over the meeting of the various defense councils, with large emergency powers. He is the "moderator"—*arbitre*—making presumably final decisions whenever there appears to be division and conflict in the country or his Cabinet. He has the power to dissolve the legislature and to appear to the public in a referendum asking the people to endorse or to reject his policy.

Under de Gaulle, the Presidency has become the coordinating office for the major decisions: military policy, foreign policy, and colonial policy including the Algerian problem. Cabinet meetings have been relegated to a simple role of execution and implementation of the decisions made by the President and his immediate advisers. De Gaulle is not simply "informed" of foreign policy negotiations. He negotiates directly with foreign representatives, Prime Ministers, and heads of State; he outlines the goals of the government—at times taking even the Cabinet and the Prime Minister by surprise. Matters pertaining to NATO, to the ties among the members of the Common Market, to negotiations concerning suspension of atomic tests, to the advisability of a Summit meeting—all are decided by General de Gaulle.

In order to implement the personal character of his foreign policy, de Gaulle has sought to strengthen the Ministry of Foreign Affairs and, at the same time, remove foreign policy issues from legislative interference. The new Minister of Foreign Affairs is a career diplomat (for the first time in many decades), a former Ambassador to Washington, London, and Bonn. Foreign policy matters are coordinated and handled through the Ministry and the Foreign Service under the over-all supervision of de Gaulle.

The role of Parliament is greatly diminished. Negotiations and policy formulation are kept secret in the best tradition of the old diplomacy. Only general developments and over-all policy issues have been discussed in Parliament. Since the establishment of the Fifth Republic, there have been at least five major foreign policy debates, lasting two or three days each. "Debate," however, is limited to the exposition of the Prime Minister's or the Minister's views and to foreign policy pronouncements by various party leaders. The government has not allowed, as a rule, a vote to follow the discussions.

The parliamentary committee on Foreign Affairs of the National Assembly has heard the Minister of Foreign Affairs frequently, and many questions on foreign policy have been addressed to the Prime Minister and the Minister. Answers and controversy have been perfunctory, however. Since the possibility of engaging the responsibility of the President of the Republic and the Cabinet is lacking in the first case and highly restricted in the second, debate is little more than academic.

Occasions for the expression of dissatisfaction have not been lacking. For instance, when the debate on the government's program on atomic weapons and the development of a retaliatory atomic force for France took place in connection with the voting of military credits, the Senate twice defeated the measure that had been passed in the National Assembly. The opposition in the National Assembly had the opportunity to introduce a motion of censure which was endorsed on the last two occasions by 215 and 217 votes—some 60 votes short of the required majority to bring the Cabinet down.

Dissatisfaction with the President's foreign policy also takes a covert form in the Cabinet, as in the case of the "dismissal" of the powerful Minister of Finance, Antoine Pinay, early in 1960. It was common knowledge that Pinay was in disagreement with de Gaulle's NATO policy.

Realism and the vocation of greatness

Without abandoning the basic objective of French independence and national power, de Gaulle has been able, since his return to power, to inject into France an element of realism that was lacking in the past. This is only too clear with regard to the colonial and economic policy he has pursued.

Algeria and the Empire—the end of Empire. In 1958 General de Gaulle pledged to all overseas territories a new political arrangement—the French Community—and if they wished it, their independence. All of the territories, with the exception of Guinea, entered the French Community. They became Republics federated with France. They were governed by the President of the French Republic, who was also President of the Community, with the assistance of an Executive Council which consisted of the President of the Republic, a number of French Ministers charged with common Community affairs, and the Prime Ministers, or their delegates, of the African Republics and Madagascar. A "Community Senate" with primarily consultative powers was also established, as well as a "Community arbitration court" for the purpose of hearing and passing on controversies among the member states.

In the course of 1959–60 the Community was abandoned. It still exists in name but its institutions have been set aside. Speaking in Dakar, Senegal, in December 1959 de Gaulle promised to grant "international sovereignty"— that is, complete independence to all the African territories. Special accords between France and the member states were passed and ratified by the French parliament, providing for diverse modes of cooperation between France and the individual Republics in the domain of economic, social, cultural, and military affairs. All provisions can be renegotiated and possibly cancelled by new accords in the future. All African Republics have become independent and all of them with the exception of Mauritania (because of a Soviet veto) have become members of the United Nations as independent individual states with the freedom to vote as they please at the United Nations Assembly and participate in its organs and specialized commissions.

Thus France under de Gaulle put an end to colonialism. In doing so she improved her position in Africa where she is assured of a reservoir of goodwill. Large subsidies to the African Republics and Madagascar guarantee a good rate of modernization and industrialization there which is bound to favor French trade and investments in Africa and improve the living standards of the Africans themselves. Thus politically and economically the road was paved for better relations.

Algeria. In Algeria, where a powerful French minority and a strong Army, acting both as a political force and a veto group, continue to be strongly entrenched, progress has been slow. The action of the government can be divided into two areas: *political* and *socio-economic.* Its first task was to reassert its authority over the Army and the French settlers. This entailed the dismantling of a number of paramilitary organizations among the settlers, transfers of generals and officers, and the elimination of the Psychological

Warfare Bureau of the Army responsible for propaganda and indoctrination of the Algerians. It was not until January 1960—and more particularly April 1961—when faced with open defiance by the settlers in the form of an armed uprising and later by a military putsch against his new policy of self-determination for Algeria that de Gaulle moved to take these steps. The leaders were arrested and brought to trial. The civil authority reasserted its claims over the military and the delegates of the government in Algeria began to assume responsibility in the name of de Gaulle and to issue orders to the Army.

Self-determination. Public opinion among the settlers became hostile to de Gaulle's policy, and the Army continued to be a threat to his authority. The reason was the policy of self-determination for Algeria announced in September 1959, in which he rejected the policy of "integration" of Algeria with France advocated by the overwhelming majority of settlers, and offered to let the Algerians (French settlers and Moslems alike) decide their own political future in a special referendum to be held after the cessation of hostilities. They could choose between integration, local autonomy, and independence.

But de Gaulle's policy of self-determination was associated with rigid conditions. He refused to recognize the rebel organization that had called itself since September 1958 the "Provisional Government of the Algerian Republic." He refused to negotiate directly with them or meet with any of their delegates; to consider negotiations on anything but the conditions of "a cease fire" which, he made clear, would entail the laying down of arms by the Algerian rebels. He dismissed the idea of Algerian elections under United Nations supervision and rejected the demand of the rebels that the French

Army be withdrawn. Even if Algeria were to opt for independence the French interests (including the oil wells, installations, and pipe lines) and the rights of French citizens—"who wished to remain French"—were to be safeguarded. In June 1960 delegates of the Provisional Government visited Paris but de Gaulle refused to see them. Only cease-fire talks would be considered by the French government. No political negotiations were to be undertaken. The Algerians withdrew their delegates and the rebellion went on.

In order to bolster his position and at the same time to indicate that those opposed to his policy were only a minority, a referendum on "self-determination" was held on January 8, 1961, in which his policy was overwhelmingly endorsed in metropolitan France. De Gaulle spoke of an "Algerian Algeria" and took his policy before the Algerians themselves in a trip that provoked wild demonstration, riots among the settlers, and a widespread indication that the Moslems favored independence.

The rebel "government" urged the Moslems to boycott the referendum—which they did in large proportions. The African Republics, Tunisia, and Morocco remained in sympathy with the cause of Algerian independence. In the United Nations there was increasing pressure in favor of a settlement. It became clear that de Gaulle's government had to negotiate with the rebels. The first genuine effort was made in the summer of 1961 but proved to be unsuccessful.

Despite the uncertainties and the slow progress made, de Gaulle's accomplishments should not be underestimated. The ideas of self-determination and of "Algerian Algeria" have irreversibly changed the situation and have paved the way to Algerian independence. This he admitted finally and unqualifiedly in his press conference of April 11, 1961. If the Algerians were anxious to have their "internal and external sovereignty." France would not oppose it. Echoing some of the anti-colonialism of the business groups, he pointed out that "Algeria costs us much more than she is worth to us." French policy and interests favor decolonization so that France can build her own resources at home and develop into a modern and strong nation. He pointed out that some people say that either "the Soviet Union or the United States—or both at once—would try to take France's place in the territories from which she withdrew." His answer: "I wish both of them a lot of fun." [17]

Socio-economic policies. The socio-economic policy of the government for Algeria was announced in de Gaulle's speech delivered in September 1958 that became the basis of the so-called Constantine Plan. It proposed an extensive transformation and modernization of the economy, more jobs for the ever-expanding Algerian population, and comprehensive social measures in the direction of equalization of the income of the Moslems with the French. The plan provided 1) an increase in the wages and salaries paid out in Algeria; 2) the distribution of some 670,000 acres of land to Moslem farmers; 3) a five year plan at the end of which the Sahara oil and gas would be made available to Algerian industries and factories; 4) the development of steel and iron production centers; 5) the building of housing for about one million people; 6) the construction of roads, ports and airports. It was hoped that these measures would provide employment for about 400,000 workers.

Longer-range plans were studied by the special commission of the Constantine Plan: to provide for one million new jobs within a period of ten years and to raise the average standard of living of Algerians by about 5 per cent every year. New villages were to be constructed to resettle the population that had been affected by the fighting or removed by the Army from certain regions for security and other reasons. Continued attention was paid to agricultural production and the training and education of civil servants and skilled workers.

Thus a major effort to "modernize" Algeria appears to have been on the way, which, again, barring a full-scale civil war, seems irreversible. The wealth of the Sahara in oil and gas will sooner or later make itself felt in the industrial and economic life of the region, and the economic effort made by the French will inevitably benefit the Algerian people. An independent Algeria will, without any doubt, prove to be one of the most powerful and modernized countries of Africa. This in turn only underlines the urgency and the significance of a political settlement. The uprising of powerful segments of the Army at the end of April 1961 indicated also that the military in Algeria had not been brought under control yet, thus endangering any political settlement with the Algerian Provisional Government that may be reached.

The national economy. For three years after de Gaulle's return to power the economic development of the country continued to improve. The improvement was partly due to the measures suggested by a "special" committee of experts appointed by General de Gaulle when he returned to power. It proposed an "austerity" program designed to eliminate inflationary tend-

[17] *Service de Presse et d'Information, Speeches and Press Conference, No. 162.*

encies and to restore monetary stability. As stated by General de Gaulle himself, this plan aimed "to restore to France its international status" in the economic field and "to establish the nation on a foundation of truth and severity, which alone can enable it to build its prosperity."

In order to achieve a sounder monetary position and a better competitive position of French goods in foreign markets, the franc was devalued again in December 1958 by 17.5 per cent. France restored convertibility of the franc, thus giving foreign companies all guarantees necessary to enable them freely to invest and remit profits. Foreign capital began to flow into the country, contributing appreciably to the improvement in the balance of payments.

The new price of the franc made it again possible to liberalize trade, and enabled France to fulfil its commitments towards its Common Market partners. On January 1, 1959, France implemented in full the European Common Market Treaty provisions for the reduction of customs duties and the liberalization of trade.

Moreover, as the devaluation had lowered prices of French goods, the country's foreign trade improved rapidly. In May 1959, for the first time in a very long period, France's foreign trade balance showed a surplus. Exports rose at a rapid rate. Industrial production, after a slight decline which lasted until the beginning of 1959, resumed its upward trend, and was followed by a steady rate of increase that averaged 6–7 per cent.

The vocation of greatness

The Memorandum of September 24, 1958. Immediately after his return to power, de Gaulle had asserted that it was not the purpose of France to limit her foreign policy "within the confines of NATO." Four days before the referendum on the Constitution of the Fifth Republic he addressed a memorandum, which is still technically secret, to Henri Spaak, Prime Minister Macmillan, and President Eisenhower *only*. It is, however, common knowledge that the memorandum was a diagnosis of the problems facing NATO and a statement of French policy. De Gaulle indicated the common responsibilities imposed upon the alliance in case of war but pointed to the inequality in armaments and, what is more, the inequality in the power to make decisions among the allies. Events in Egypt contrasted sharply with those in the Near East and Formosa. He proposed, therefore, the establishment within NATO of a *"directorate"* of three—England, France and the United States—with the responsibility of elaborating a common military and political strategy for the whole of the planet, the creation of allied commands for all theaters of operation, and joint strategy deliberations and decision for the use of atomic weapons. "The European states of the continent," he stated on April 11, 1961, ". . . must know exactly with which weapons and under what conditions their overseas allies would join them in battle." Thus he reminded President Kennedy, who was to visit him within a matter of weeks, that "the threats of war are no longer limited to Europe" and that NATO should accordingly revise its organization to meet joint non-European problems. There was also a threat in the memorandum: France would reconsider its NATO policy in the light of the response of England and the United States.

Though ostensibly addressing problems related to NATO, de Gaulle was actually attempting to place France at a level to which no other European power in NATO could aspire. NATO was to remain a regional organization, but with three of its members—France, England, and the United States—jointly in charge of global strategy. The three great powers were, in the best tradition of the "old" diplomacy, to be in charge at the NATO level of the Atlantic problems and jointly in charge of planetary strategy. De Gaulle has remained adamant. When his suggestions were rejected, France withdrew the Mediterranean Fleet from NATO command; she refused to integrate her air defense with NATO; she prevented the building of launching sites and the stockpiling of atomic warheads over which she could have no control. But this attitude against military "integration" was to bring France in conflict with West Germany. This became painfully evident during the visit of Adenauer in the first week of December 1959, and throughout 1960, when de Gaulle and his advisers talked freely about an "independent" Western European strategy and apparently foresaw even the possibility of the withdrawal of American forces.

The "Bomb." Since the allies seemed unwilling to subordinate use of atomic weapons to a "directorate," France proceeded with the explosion of her own atom bomb. A number of additional reasons were given: the uncertainty about the use of the bomb by the United States except in self-defense; the need of a French deterrent; the injection of a new pride and a higher morale in an army that had experienced one frustration after another, and finally the worldwide commitments of France.

As long as other powers have nuclear weapons the only policy consistent with French interests, according to de Gaulle, is to develop nuclear strength. The French position at the Geneva disarmament conference continues to favor the liquidation of stockpiles and delivery missiles *before* the suspension of manufacturing and testing of nuclear weapons.

The European Common Market. De Gaulle's enthusiasm for the Common Market was motivated in part by economic reasons and by considerations favoring the development of a European "whole." The crucial reason, however, was political. It gave him a bargaining position with the British in respect to the demands of the Memorandum of September 24 and a number of other issues, notably Berlin, atomic weapons, and the agenda of the ill-fated summit conference of June 1960. In repayment for Adenauer's participation in the Common Market and as a compromise to their disagreements about the extent and nature of military integration in NATO, de Gaulle became a staunch supporter of the Berlin *status quo.* However, he also accepted the existing frontier arrangements of Poland. Many still think, on the basis of his *Mémoires,* that he continues to consider the future of Germany to be the crucial problem of our times, and they believe that under no circumstances is he prepared to make any concessions to Germany other than on Berlin—which has only a symbolic value and does not alter the balance of forces.

Thus de Gaulle emerges today in control of an array of strong bargaining weapons in order to accomplish what he sought in the year after Liberation—the realization of a top rank for France. With England he appears as the leader of the Six in Western Europe with growing political ties, bent on what has haunted British policy-makers for so long—the creation of a Continental bloc whose attractiveness for other European nations may be great. Against Germany he holds the trump of Berlin, promising not to accede to the more flexible British policy and to remain the champion of the *status quo*. Vis-à-vis the United States, de Gaulle holds in his hands the fate of NATO, central in our Atlantic policy. Strategically, whatever the changing nature of warfare, France remains the cornerstone of a European shield against Soviet threats. Against the Soviet Union, finally, de Gaulle can threaten full integration in NATO or remain adamant on the Berlin question.

Each threat holds a promise: to England the broadening of the European Market to include other nations and England itself; to the United States and West Germany full military participation in NATO; to the Soviet Union a new agreement that will consecrate the *status quo* in Europe, undermine NATO, and give de Gaulle the uncontested leadership in Western Europe and the time to develop a constructive policy at home and in North Africa while continuing his close ties with the former Empire.

As André Fontaine wrote with justice in the influential *Le Monde*,[18] "Everything is aimed to accomplish an objective, however remote. A Europe to its full geographic limits, with African, Near Eastern and—who knows —South American extensions. . . . A Europe that will no longer be divided between American and Soviet zones of influence, a Europe which might even receive Russia the day it becomes 'Russian' as it is predestined by history, a Europe that will once more become the nerve center of the world and which might if it were necessary arbitrate between the great empires." De Gaulle,

like the other French political leaders, cannot envisage such a Europe except under French leadership, so that France in the name of Europe will have attained the rank of world power and full independence.

Thus the vocation of greatness continues to be the central part of French foreign policy. Relying upon national strength and nuclear weapons, counting upon the development of a modern economy which already begins to compare very favorably with that of Great Britain and Western Germany, de Gaulle believes that France is creating a Third European Force that will ultimately be able to arbitrate between the United States and the Soviet Union.

Ever since de Gaulle returned to power, he has pursued this objective with unrelenting effort, thus stretching the limits of French strength and accentuating, even with France's improved economic status, the disparity between objectives and capabilities. Despite his ability and great popularity —de Gaulle in foreign policy matters is truly a national spokesman—the difficulties ahead are many. The Algerian rebellion is not settled; an *intransigeant* attitude has led him to armed conflict with the Tunisian Prime Minister Bourguiba over the status of the French naval base of Bizerte, thus undermining beyond repair France's position in North Africa and threatening seriously France's relations with the African republics; the Army, the most important ingredient of national power, continues to be in a rebellious mood that neither atomic weapons nor his prestige have quelled; military expenditure continues to be inordinately high. But above all, de Gaulle's personal government cannot outlive de Gaulle! The vision of a strong France that he has symbolized may again haunt France in the future.

[18] *Le Monde*, March 10, 1960.

SELECTED BIBLIOGRAPHY

Année Politique. Annual volumes published since 1944. It constitutes one of the best sources of material on French foreign policy.

Aron, Raymond and Daniel Lerner, *France Defeats the EDC?* (New York: Frederick A. Praeger, Inc., 1957).

————, *France—Steadfast and Changing: The Fourth to the Fifth Republic* (Cambridge: Harvard University Press, 1960).

Brogan, D. W., *France Under the Republic, 1870–1939* (New York: Harper & Brothers, 1940).

de Gaulle, Charles, *War Mémoires,* Vol. I, *The Call to Honour* (New York: The Viking Press, 1955); Vol. II, *Unity* (New York: Simon & Schuster, 1959); Vol. III, *Salvation* (New York: Simon & Schuster, 1960).

Duroselle, J. B., *La Politique étrangère et ses fondements* (Paris: Armand Colin, 1954).

Furniss, Edgar, Jr., *France: Troubled Ally* (New York: Harper & Brothers, 1960).

Hoffmann, Stanley, *de Gaulle's Memoirs—The Hero in History, World Politics,* October 1960, No. 1, pp. 140–156.

Howard, J. E., *Parliament and Foreign Policy in France* (London: Cresset Press, 1948).

Luëthy, Herbert, *France Against Herself* (New York: Frederick A. Praeger, Inc., 1955).

Kertesz, Stephen D. and M. A. Fitzsimons, *Diplomacy in a Changing World* (South Bend, Ind.: University of Notre Dame, 1959). See the section by Professor J. B. Duroselle, *French Diplomacy in Post-World War,* pp. 204–250.

McKay, Donald C., *United States and France* (Cambridge, Mass.: Harvard University Press, 1951).

Macridis, Roy C., "De Gaulle: The Vision and the Record," *Yale Review,* Winter 1960.

————, "De Gaulle's Foreign Policy and the Fifth Republic," *Yale Review,* Winter 1961.

————, and Bernard E. Brown, *The De Gaulle Republic: Quest for Unity* (The Dorsey Press, 1960).

Sondages, Revue Francais de l'opinion Publique, La Politique étrangère de la France et l'opinion Publique, 1954–1957 (1958).

Williams, Philip, *Politics in Post-War France* (New York: Longmans, Green & Co., 1954).

De Gaulle's major pronouncements are indispensable. They are translated by the Press and Information Service of the French Embassy, 972 Fifth Avenue, New York 21, New York. The most important are: the press conferences of October 23, 1958; March 25, 1959; November 10, 1959; September 5, 1960; and April 11, 1961. The major addresses are those of September 16, 1959; December 13, 1959, pronounced at Dakar; and January 29, 1960.

4

Foreign Policy of the German Federal Republic

THE HISTORICAL SETTING AND BASIC ATTITUDES

In all countries the making of foreign policy is influenced by the *legacy of the past*. Among the small groups of influential persons as well as among the broad masses of the voters, memories of the past help to shape the images of what foreign policy is and what it could be. Such memories guide men's imagination as to what tasks any present or future foreign policy could accomplish, what persons and institutions should accomplish them, and by what methods. People turn to memories for answers to their basic questions: "Who are we?" "What do others expect of us?" and "What should we expect of ourselves?" In all countries, memories thus fashion expectations; everywhere they influence the interplay between foreign policy and the on-going process of national self-perception and self-definition. In Germany, however, these historical memories are in some respects more self-contradictory than in any other large country.

KARL W. DEUTSCH

and

LEWIS J. EDINGER

The heritage of memories

From the tenth to the thirteenth century the medieval German Empire was the leading power of Europe and claimed the symbolic and, at times, the actual leadership of Western Christendom. For another three centuries, from the thirteenth to the sixteenth century, German princes and cities, German knights and German merchants were predominant in Central and Eastern Europe without finding serious rivals. Generations of German school children have had impressed upon them those three centuries of universal greatness, and those six centuries of unchallenged German predominance in Central Europe; but they have been given a far less clear picture of the processes that were at work in the centuries of decline and catastrophe that followed.

By the sixteenth century, Germany had had no effective central government for almost three hundred years, without suffering until then any serious risk of foreign military invasions; but with the rise of more effectively organized states in Western Europe this

91

situation changed. France, at times allied with Sweden, fought the Spanish and Austrian empires on German soil for almost two centuries, leaving the country divided into innumerable independent states. The political fragmentation of Germany was made far deeper by the religious cleavages of the Reformation of the early sixteenth century, which left the German people approximately two-thirds Protestant and one-third Catholic. In the same period the routes of world trade shifted away from Central Europe to the Atlantic coast and to the ocean lanes to the countries overseas. These economic processes were subtle and anonymous, but their results were disastrous and conspicuous, like the decline of a patient who is weakened by a serious disease of which he remains ignorant. In any case, it seemed as if the world were turning cold and hostile toward Germany. Many of the prosperous German cities declined while French and English trade centers increased in size and influence. These unfavorable economic developments left the German middle class economically and culturally backward, as well as politically weak and lacking in self-reliance, during the time when the middle classes became more prosperous and more self-reliant in the West.

Throughout the sixteenth and seventeenth centuries German states, German cities, and German politics remained on the whole petty; no effective economic or political centers for the entire area developed. In spite and because of this situation a new concept —"Germany" (Deutschland)—came into use, and a vague notion spread that the Germans were a single people with some sort of common identity, some common destiny, and some common need for safety and prestige.

Early in the seventeenth century,

when economic decline and political frustration had become well established on the German scene, the full force of political catastrophe struck. In the Thirty Years War from 1618 to 1648 about one-third of the German people perished in a war waged essentially by foreign countries for reasons of European power politics, with no significant result for the German people other than sufferings and devastation. During the rest of the seventeenth and eighteenth centuries Germany remained a battlefield of foreign powers; in the course of these two centuries Germans acquired an image of Germany as the "land of the middle," helplessly exposed to attacks, surrounded by hostile powers, and condemned to be the perpetual victim of foreign aggressors because of her own lack of unity, organization, and concentrated military power.

By the end of the eighteenth century two major patterns of response to this situation had become widespread. One pattern consisted in accepting the political and religious division of the country, and the almost total absence of significant military power on the part of most of the petty states into which the country was divided. Resigned to view politics as hostile and evil—as already Martin Luther had pictured it—some Germans felt free to concentrate their energies on diligent productive work in trades and crafts, in economic activity, and perhaps most important of all, in the arts and sciences.

A contrasting but related pattern of response developed in the state of Brandenburg-Prussia: if politics was evil, force and cunning were its only realistic methods. This view stressed the strengthening of the state as the only organization that could safeguard the survival of the individual in a world of enemies. To make this state ever larger, stronger, more efficient, and more disciplined was believed the only way of ensuring a minimum of security and dignity for its population in a hostile world. The subjects of the King of Prussia might at least live in a state of law, with an orderly administration and some security against the arbitrary whim of foreign powers. Political passivity and military assertiveness—Potsdam, the town of the Prussian soldier-kings, and Weimar, the town of the German poets—these became two opposite and equally one-sided symbols of the Germans' response to their predicament.

In the course of the nineteenth century these two German traditions were in part fused under the impact of the German industrial revolution and of the German political unification movement, which culminated in 1871 in the establishment of a united German Empire under Prussian leadership. The new political and social system linked much of the German intellectual and literary heritage to the Prussian tradition of widespread public education and instruction. The German intellectuals of the generation that reached maturity after 1809 and experienced the closing phases of the Napoleonic Wars were receptive to nationalism and impressed with the need for national political power. It was not only the memories of the humiliating French occupation in the days of Napoleon that made national military power seem ever more important. The growth of German industry and commerce created a whole series of conflicts with the neighbors of Germany, such as disputes with the Netherlands about the shipping tolls on the lower Rhine, or with Denmark about the duchies of Schleswig and Holstein and, hence, about the territory of the future German Kiel Canal between the Baltic and the North seas. Only military power seemed likely to prevent endless frustrations in these conflicts and to resolve them in accordance with what were considered German needs.

In the course of the nineteenth century, and particularly after 1848, the German middle class and the German liberal parties turned increasingly to an alliance with their own princes, with the aristocracy and the military castes of Germany, and in particular to an alliance with the Prussian state. Bismarck's policy of "blood and iron," which accomplished the reunification of Germany in three wars between 1864 and 1871, found in the end the overwhelming support of the German intellectuals and the German middle class, as well as of most of the German people. The coming of the railroads and the triumph of industrialization and urbanization fell into the same decades as these triumphs of power politics, and Bismarck's empire was credited for all.

To this day, Bismarck's popularity has remained outstanding. In January 1955, 30 per cent of a cross-section of German adults said that among great men Bismarck had done most for Germany; five years earlier, in January 1950, 35 per cent of a similar cross-section of voters had given the same answer.[1] No other German historical figure even approaches this popularity. In popular memory, the empire that Bismarck founded, and that endured from 1871 to 1918, lives on as a golden age. Of a cross-section of German adults in October 1951, 45 per cent identified this empire as the period in

---

[1] Elizabeth Noelle and Erich Peter Neumann, *Jahrbuch der öffentlichen Meinung, 1947–1955* (Allensbach am Bodensee: Verlag für Demoskopie, 1956), p. 132. (All data are for samples of the adult population—*i.e.*, above 18 years—unless otherwise indicated.) Unless otherwise specified all data concerning opinions and attitudes come from this source.

which they felt Germany had been best off.

But the memories from the period of Bismarck's empire are by no means all idyllic. They include memories of the rivalries of international power politics in the age of imperialism, and images of the envy and resentment of foreign countries at German commercial and political successes. They include the beginning of the themes of a German bid for "living space," for a "place in the sun," and the double image of the empire-building and colony-owning Western powers, such as France and England: these countries were seen as models and reference groups whom the Germans should imitate and from whom they had to learn how to get on in the world, and at the same time they appeared as envious enemies ready to encircle Germany for her destruction. By 1914 a very large number of Germans saw themselves engaged at one and the same time in a bitterly competitive struggle for world power and a desperate defensive effort for national survival; and they welcomed the seemingly clear-cut state of open war as a long-awaited release from the tensions and frustrations of the pre-war years. The outbreak of World War I was thus accepted with enthusiasm; about three million poems celebrated the event within the first nine months after its outbreak in August 1914. At the beginning, volunteers for combat duty were numerous, and the fighting morale of front-line troups remained high until close to the end. Even after 1918 many Germans refused to accept the fact of defeat; about one-quarter of the German voters continued to support parties that insisted that with better home-front morale the war would have been won.

Some of these memories of an inevitable power struggle against foreign envy and hostility were revived and reinforced by the impact of the great economic depression that hit Germany in 1929, and which by early 1933 had produced six million unemployed, almost one-third of the industrial labor force. The image of a hostile international environment, the image of a German empire, similar to what the British Empire was considered to be like, as a solution to Germany's difficulties, the image of a desperate bid for "living space" and a place among the leading imperial nations of the world—all these played their part among the appeals by which Hitler rose to power. At the beginning of the Nazi terror, in the elections of March 1933, as many as 43 per cent of the German voters supported Hitler's National-Socialist party, and another 8 per cent supported Hitler's close allies in matters of foreign policy at that time, the German Nationalist party. Fifteen years later, in October 1948, 41 per cent of a cross-section of German voters recalled that they themselves had approved of the Nazi seizure of power in 1933. In the same month, 57 per cent agreed that National Socialism was a good idea that had been badly carried out.

The German defeat at the end of World War II, so much more shattering than that at the end of World War I, is vividly remembered. Four Germans out of every five in a cross-section of the adult population interviewed in October 1948, remembered aerial bombardments or fire at the front; almost one in four dreamed still of these experiences; about one out of every six reported these dreams as exciting, terrifying, frequent, or intense. By June 1954, almost two Germans out of every five expressed the belief that in the future Germany would be once again one of the most powerful states of the world. Another two-fifths of the same sample did not believe that this would ever again happen; the rest were undecided.

Compared to the glories and terrors of two world wars, the civilian interlude of the Weimar Republic between 1918 and 1932 is remembered as relatively colorless. Less than one-tenth of Germans interviewed in October 1951 remembered it as the best period for Germany in the twentieth century; one month later a somewhat smaller percentage named it as the worst.

The legacy of German history is thus profoundly ambiguous as a background for future German foreign policy decisions. It includes memories that counsel fear of remaining weak in a world of ruthless foreign interests, but it is also rich in memories of suffering and defeat following upon reckless bids for world power. It is rich in memories of success in fields requiring economic, technical, or scientific performance, but it lacks for much of a thousand-year period any impressive memories of sustained political successes following upon nonaggressive foreign policies and upon peaceful development of democratic and constitutional practice. Dictatorship and war are remembered by perhaps three-fifths of the German people as terrible failures; but democracy and peaceful international relations are not at all widely remembered as successes. This store of memories is likely to limit the number of German voters who will support a consistent and firm commitment to democracy and to wholehearted cooperation with the Western powers. But historical memories also influence German attitudes on foreign policy in other ways.

Images of foreign policy objectives

Perhaps more prominently than most other large peoples, Germans view their foreign policy in terms of their own collective status and prestige in the world at large. Its tasks include not only the procurement of material advantages, or the maintenance of peace, but it is also expected to contribute to the respect of the world for the Germans and thus to bolster indirectly German self-respect. One out of every three Germans interviewed in a survey in July, 1952, believed that the Germans were unpopular in the world at large; and one out of six believed that they were unpopular because of their good qualities, particularly their ability. On the other hand, one German in eight believed that their bad qualities, their loudness, lack of adaptability and their intolerance made the Germans unpopular abroad.

At present, the largest world power and one of the smallest—the United States and Switzerland—are among the countries most admired; 8 per cent of the persons asked in a survey in July 1954 said they would like most of all to live in the United States, another 7 per cent picked Switzerland, and another 8 per cent scattered their preferences over the rest of Europe. In November 1953 a cross-section of young people between 15 and 24 years old were asked whether the Germans could learn anything from other peoples, and if so, from what people. Almost two-thirds of the youngsters answered that Germany could indeed learn from others; 23 per cent then named as model the United States, 10 per cent named England, 7 per cent Switzerland, 5 per cent France, 3 per cent Sweden; the rest were scattered.[2]

Attitudes toward the United States. Germany today is a country in search of friends, just as she is a country in search of herself. Clearly, the political

[2] Karl-Georg von Stackelberg, ed., *Jugend zwischen 15 und 24: Eine Untersuchung zur Situation der Deutschen Jugend im Bundesgebiet* (Bielefeld: Emmid-Institut, 1954), p. 87.

friendship that is most popular is that with the United States. Large majorities in opinion surveys have consistently favored close association between the Federal Republic and the United States. In December 1958, 43 per cent of Germans questioned in such a poll desired an even more intimate relationship than existed already. During the last decade, when asked to choose between "East" and "West," a majority of Germans have consistently expressed overwhelming preference for the latter, while never more than 1 per cent declared themselves in favor of cooperation with the "East." [3]

The appeal of neutralism. Organized and overt expressions of neutralism have diminished drastically in recent years. However, poll results indicate that a sizable minority, between one fourth and one third of Germans willing to express a view on this problem between 1953 and 1958, continues to wish that the Federal Republic remain neutral in a conflict between "East" and "West." Confronted with the more specific problem of the withdrawal of Western troops from the Federal Republic in return for a withdrawal of Russian troops from Eastern Europe and Eastern Germany, 56 per cent of Germans favored such a development in a poll in March 1958, while only 16 per cent opposed it. When the same question was put to a cross-section of members of the West German parliament, however, 54 per cent opposed reciprocal troop withdrawal, while only 45 per cent favored it. In case of a Soviet attack on the United States, 52 per cent of respondents in a December 1958, poll wanted their country to remain neutral, 13 per cent favored giving merely non-military support to the United States in such a conflict and only 17 per cent were willing to live up to the Federal Republic's obligation under the NATO Treaty to give military aid to its American ally.[4] In general, while West Germans overwhelmingly reject Communism and favor the Western way of life and close cooperation with the United States, military neutrality appears to remain for quite a few of them a prudent policy for their country.

Popular images and expectations of the relative present and future strength of the United States and the Soviet Union no doubt play a part in these considerations. In December 1952, 66 per cent of Germans in a survey thought that the "West" would in the long run emerge victorious over the "East" in the competition for preeminence in the world. By December, 1958, this proportion had dropped to 43 per cent, while the percentage of those believing that both camps would emerge equally strong had risen from 7 to 21 per cent in these six years.[5] By February 1960, only 29 per cent of West Germans in an opinion survey expected the United States to be the stronger after 20 to 25 years, while just as large a proportion expected the Soviet Union to emerge on top. Nineteen per cent believed that the two superpowers would be equal in strength and 23 per cent expressed no opinion.[6] German faith in the military superiority of the United States has diminished drastically in recent years. While in a poll in June 1955, 39 per cent still thought the West stronger in atomic weapons than the Soviet Union, by December 1958 only 19 per cent of

---

[3] DIVO Institut, *Umfragen: Ereignisse und Probleme der Zeit im Urteil der Bevölkerung,* II (Frankfurt am Main: Europäische Verlagsanstalt, 1959), 36 f.

[4] DIVO, *op. cit.,* 21–23, 36.

[5] DIVO, *op. cit.,* 11.

[6] See poll results from a secret USIA survey, reported in "The United States in Foreign Eyes, 1960," *The New York Times,* November 2, 1960.

West Germans polled believed this to be the case and an equal proportion thought the West was actually weaker than the U.S.S.R.; 41 per cent thought both camps were equally strong in atomic weapons.[7]

Policy-makers thus can count on popular approval in their efforts to maintain a general climate of friendly relations with the United States, but they must be careful not to arouse fears of dangerous commitments, which could unite a majority of voters against them. At the same time, politicians who prefer a closer approach to neutrality in international affairs must be careful not to arouse fears of a loss of American friendship. As long as the Western Alliance appears to the German voters as primarily defensive and peaceful, these two attitudes can be reconciled. A considerable amount of agreement on basic foreign policy orientations has, in fact, developed among the major parties and among the great majority of the electorate. If, however, new and major tangible commitments should be demanded from Germany by her allies, or if the international situation should approach the brink of war, much of this consensus might disintegrate.

National reunification and the eastern territories. Other foreign policy aims on which there is a great deal of popular agreement stem directly from Germany's defeat and partition in World War II.

First of all, Germany after her defeat in 1945 was an exhausted, partly destroyed, and half-starved country, occupied by four foreign powers. Since no central government was set up for Western Germany until 1949, the tasks of procuring a minimum of food and shelter fell to the occupying powers and to new German local and pro-vincial governments that were set up under their supervision. When a federal government for Western Germany was established, its first and basic long-range task appeared to be the gradual regaining of national independence. This goal of independence had, up to a point, precedence over all others in the minds of voters. More than two-thirds of all respondents, and more than three-quarters of all men, said in August 1949 that they were "ready to commit all their strength to make Germany self-supporting and independent, politically and economically." This goal seemed to hold precedence even over the goals of maintaining friendship with the United States and regaining a respected position among the Western powers, equal eventually at least to that of France and the United Kingdom. The fact that the Adenauer government was able to pursue all these goals at the same time between 1949 and 1957 contributed much to its strength.

Other foreign policy goals also arose directly from the German post-war situation. First of these in the minds of most West German voters appears to be the reunification of Eastern and Western Germany, substantially on the basis of those political and social institutions that prevail in the German Federal Republic. While poll data of mass opinion has consistently indicated overwhelming desire for such reunification, qualitative measurement of such sentiment has not been available and it is not clear whether the strength of this sentiment has increased, decreased, or remained constant in terms of its quality. Next, there was the question of the German expellees from Eastern Europe and the former German territories east of the Oder and Neisse rivers. Over ten million persons of German language and sympathies were expelled from such East European

[7] DIVO, *op cit.*, 23.

countries as Poland, the Baltic countries, Czechoslovakia, Hungary, Rumania, Yugoslavia, and from those parts of prewar Germany east of the Oder and Neisse rivers which came under Polish or Russian administration after 1945. Many of these expellees wanted to regain their former lands, properties, and social positions; and their aspirations had the approval, mild or strong, of many German voters. Regaining particularly the former German Oder-Neisse territories, including coal-rich Silesia, thus became a long-range task expected from German foreign policy.

The fear of war. The fact seems to be, judging from many poll results, that a majority of Germans hold firmly to these foreign policy objectives in the abstract, but would be unwilling to fight for any of them. Asked in February, 1955, whether Germans should fight to defend Europe against an armed Soviet attack, only 38 per cent favored armed resistance; 34 per cent said that above all war should be avoided, and 28 per cent were undecided.

German public opinion seems thus largely united in disliking and distrusting Communism and Communist governments; in fearing and rejecting war; in seeking at least economic and political equality with other Western powers, such as France and the United Kingdom; and in desiring to remain friends with the United States. Subject to these overriding beliefs, large majorities wish for eventual national re-unification and, less urgently, for the recovery of former German territories in the East. In the third rank of possible foreign policy goals, smaller but still appreciable majorities desire German participation in some form of a United Europe.

The sympathies for Western European union. In September 1955, more than two-thirds of Germans polled said they would vote in favor of forming a United States of Europe; almost three-fifths in the same poll considered the formation of a United States of Europe a practical possibility; only 17 per cent thought it impossible. This favorable attitude seems to have persisted, albeit somewhat weakened. In September 1956, when asked to choose between two "solutions for the future: the rebuilding of Germany as a completely independent national state with its own customs-frontiers, or Germany as an equal member of a European union," a bare majority of 51 per cent chose membership in a European union, while 43 per cent preferred an independent national state.[8] In a September 1956 interview, 79 per cent of the adults favored "efforts toward uniting West Europe," but in another poll that year only 66 per cent of young people 16–24 years of age favored such action.[9]

The favorable attitude toward European integration is subject, however, to two qualifications: though not necessarily impractical, European union seems remote; and it must not take away from Germany the sovereign right of ultimate decision. Only 37 per cent of Germans questioned in January 1955 believed that they would live to see the Western European countries unite to form the United States of Europe; and of those polled in September 1955 only between 25 and 32 per cent, depending on the wording of the question, were willing to concede to a European Parliament the right of ultimate decision in questions touching important German interests, while between 42 and 46 per cent insisted that

[8] Emnid, *Ideologies,* p. 9.

[9] DIVO, *Basic Orientation and Political Thinking of West German Youth and Their Leaders 1956: Report on a Nation-wide Survey* (Frankfurt am Main: 1956), p. 200.

ultimate decisions must remain with the national Parliament or government of Germany. There the matter seems to have remained.

More specific institutions of European cooperation did not become popular foreign policy goals. The number of those endorsing the ratification of the European Coal and Steel Community (ECSC) declined from 39 per cent in June 1950 to 21 per cent in January 1952; a year later, in March 1953, only 19 per cent said it had "not been a mistake" for Germany to join in this arrangement, while 75 per cent were either undecided (15 per cent) or uninformed (60 per cent).

The project of a European Defense Community (EDC), which was to include German troops under a common European command, was endorsed by 33 per cent in March 1950, and 37 per cent in September 1954 expressed regret for the failure of the project. Throughout the period, however, polls always recorded more opponents than supporters of any German troop contribution to a West European defense force, but the levels of both support and opposition usually remained below those for or against an independent German army.

German membership in the North Atlantic Treaty Organization (NATO) has apparently increased in popularity in recent years. When Chancellor Adenauer succeeded in securing parliamentary ratification of the treaty, popular support was quite low. In April 1954, only 24 per cent of Germans in a survey could approximately identify NATO. By December 1958, of the Germans questioned in an opinion survey, 82 per cent had heard of NATO. Only 23 per cent of these, however, had great confidence in the organization's ability to provide security against a Soviet attack. Forty-five per cent had only "some," "a little" or "no confi-

dence" in NATO's ability to defend Western Europe. However, only 8 per cent wanted West Germany to leave the organization.[10] Evidently membership in NATO seemed worthwhile to Germans for reasons other than its ability to provide security for their country.

Among the popular images of major foreign policy goals one is conspicuous by its absence. This missing goal is national rearmament: no popular majority is pressing for it. In 13 polls from November 1950 to February 1955, opposition to an independent German army declined from 48 per cent to 43 per cent, but support only rose from 33 per cent to 39 per cent. By November 1956, after the Hungarian uprising, 46 per cent endorsed in principle the setting up of a German Federal Army, but another 46 per cent opposed it.[11]

What the German government does in the way of rearmament is thus a response to international considerations or conceivably to special interest groups; it is not being driven to rearmament by any domestic popular pressure.

Regardless of popular feelings on any matter of foreign policy, however, German foreign policy-makers have a great deal of leeway so far as domestic opinion is concerned. There is a long-standing German tradition of leaving such complicated matters to experts and persons of authority; and the German government may count on popular acquiescence even to relatively unpopular foreign policy moves. Thus the Adenauer government, without encountering serious domestic opposition, has been far more friendly to France on the issue of the Saar territory, and to Israel on the issue of German reparations, than public opinion would have liked it to be.

[10] DIVO, *Umfragen*, 45.
[11] Emnid, *Ideologies*, p. 5.

Ideologies and classes

The Germans of the Federal Republic are largely an urban and industrial people. By 1955, almost one-third (32 per cent) of Germans above 18 years of age lived in large cities of more than 100,000 population; another 14 per cent lived in middle-sized cities of between 20,000 and 100,000 inhabitants. This left 28 per cent for small towns (2,000–20,000 population) and 26 per cent in smaller, mostly rural communities. In part as a result of war losses, 55 per cent were women as against only 45 per cent men. As many as 20 per cent of the total were 60 years or older, while 24 per cent were under 30, and the rest were nearly evenly divided between those above and below 45 years of age.

In their occupations, almost one-half (48 per cent) were industrial workers, and another 4 per cent were rural laborers. There were also 18 per cent private white-collar employees, and 5 per cent public officials, bringing the total share of wage- or salary-earners up to 75 per cent, or three-quarters of the total. The remaining quarter were self-employed persons, made up of 12 per cent peasants or farmers, a little less than 12 per cent businessmen and artisans, and a little more than 1 per cent of persons in the free professions such as doctors, architects, or lawyers.

Educational levels are not high. Only 4 per cent of Germans above 18 years had the equivalent of a junior college education. Another 14 per cent had the equivalent (*Abitur*) of 10 grades in school (*Mittlere Reife*), while the remaining 82 per cent had no more than the equivalent of 8 school years (*Volksschule*).

No political group can win a majority in Germany without the support of at least part of these urban and industrial groups, but there are enough peasants, white-collar workers, and others of middle-class status or aspirations to permit a variety of political combinations and to reward political appeals designed to unite at least some wage- and salary-earners with some self-employed groups. This situation limits the effectiveness of class appeals and favors politicans who can present their views as serving the interests of the nation.

Other conditions likewise reduce the effectiveness of sectional or denominational politics and encourage the appeal to national interests. One-fifth of the Germans above 18 years are expellees or refugees who cannot be expected to support policies based on the interests of a single region or section.

Many among these expellees are of middle-class background, and whatever their present occupations may be, their memories and style of thinking are still at least partly middle-class. To the 47 per cent of persons who are now in middle-class or white-collar occupations there must thus be added an appreciable group of wage-earners with middle-class aspirations—all of which could lend themselves to expression in national terms. A similar consideration applies to the religious groupings. With the population above 18 almost evenly divided between 52 per cent Protestants and 44 per cent Roman Catholics (who are somewhat better organized), Germans could only expect deadlock from religious quarrels. Finally, the main ideological cleavages inherited from the days of the Empire, the First (Weimar) Republic, the Nazi dictatorship, and two world wars, all cut largely across regional, religious, and class boundaries.

The most important underlying cleavage in Germany is that between friends and enemies of the Republic—

supporters of democracy and adherents of dictatorship. In practical terms, this still means the latent but persistent difference between Nazi and anti-Nazi—between those who would like to see some equivalent of the Hitler dictatorship restored and those who wish to maintain democratic institutions.

The issue of Communism at present plays only a negligible role in Germany as a domestic issue. Only 8 per cent of West Germans indicated a favorable view of it in a poll in April 1950, and by March 1955 this had slipped to 2 per cent. The Communist Party is outlawed. In 1956, however, 38 per cent of a cross-section of German youth between 16 and 24 years of age expected the influence of Communism to increase in the world, while only 20 per cent believed it would decline. Confronted with the question whether "Communist Ideas" or "Western Ideas" had greater attraction for them, 38 per cent of the youths in this survey indicated that Western ideas had "much greater attraction" and 23 per cent thought that they had "somewhat greater attraction." Only 5 per cent found Communist ideas far more attractive, and 8 per cent found them somewhat more attractive.[12] The large majority of West Germans of all ages appear to be against Communism as they are against sin. Nazi sympathizers still are alternately vehement in denouncing Communism or particularly ready to play with the thought of making alliances with Communists against the West, in line with the old Stalin-Hitler pact of 1939, and with some more recent "national-bolshevist" propaganda themes. But it is in their appeal to the traditions of nationalism and authoritarianism that the potential strength of the Nazis must be sought;

[12] DIVO, *Basic Orientation . . . 1956*, p. 81.

it is here that the supporters of democratic institutions will have to resist them.

The consistent supporters of democracy seem to number about one-fourth of the adult population. On some issues they declined to one-fifth—which was the number of those polled in December 1952 who approved of resistance against Hitler even in wartime—but on the whole it has held remarkably steady. One German in four told interviewers in November 1953, " I would do everything I can" to prevent the return of a new Nazi party to power. Roughly the same proportions of 25 to 28 per cent reported themselves in October 1948 as having been "opposed to both the domestic and foreign policies" of the Hitler regime, and rejected National Socialism as an idea; the same fraction expressed in June 1952 unqualified condemnation of Adolf Hitler; favored in May 1954 the black-red-and-gold colors of the German Federal Republic as against the black-white-and-red of the Hohenzollern empire and the Nazis; said in October 1954 that men who had worked in Germany in the resistance movement against Hitler should be eligible for high governmental positions; and endorsed democracy in October 1956 in terms of implying an awareness of shared responsibility and duties as well as rights.

On the other side, there is a hard core of unreconstructed Nazis and a penumbra of their partial sympathizers. In Germany between 1950 and 1956 about one German in eight was for most political purposes a Nazi. That is, in poll after poll between 11 and 15 per cent said that they liked Hitler and Goebbels, professed race doctrines about Jews, and announced that they would welcome the return of a new National Socialist party to power. Among young people between 15 and 25 years, polls in November 1953, 1954, and 1955 showed about 10 per cent professing favorable opinions of Hitler and of National Socialism.[13] In a 1956 survey, only 25 per cent of German adults, but 41 per cent of youths between 16 and 24 wanted "again" to have a "single strong national party which merely represents the interests of all classes of all people." Only 16 per cent of the adults believed that "we should again have, as before, a national leader who rules Germany with a strong hand for the welfare of all," while 21 per cent of the young people supported this sentiment. Possibly, had the question not been phrased to point specifically to the Nazi regime of the past and its leader, the response might have even been more favorable. On the whole, women, younger people, the less educated and those living in small communities appeared to favor returning to a single strong national party and a powerful national leader more frequently than others in Germany. Despite efforts of governmental authorities to acquaint German youths with the activities of the Nazi regime, 62 per cent of German youth in the 1956 survey were unable to name any of the "chief aims" of Nazism.[14]

About one German in four was an emotional supporter of the Nazis in general, professing a predominantly favorable opinion of Hitler, his deputy Hess, and the Nazi Youth leader von Schirach. About the same proportion of Germans expressed an unfriendly attitude toward democracy and toward the black-red-and-gold flag of the Fed-

eral Republic. An equal number felt that the main responsibility for the outbreak of World War II lay with the Western powers; and that Germany had lost the war mainly because of domestic sabotage and treason. Not surprisingly, almost as many (24 per cent) wished to bar from high government positions any man who had taken part in the wartime resistance against Hitler.

On many specific issues, however, a much larger number of Germans held nationalistic views that made them potential allies or supporters of a revival of Nazi traditions or policies on these particular questions. Thus about one-third of Germans polled in 1952 expressed anti-Semitic views, while about two Germans out of five opposed the legal punishment of anti-Semitic propaganda and agreed that it was better for Germany not to have any Jews. Among youths between 15 and 24, 29 per cent had reservations in 1956 about Jews holding high positions in the federal government. Only slightly more, 33 per cent, had similar reservations about former leading Nazis holding such positions.[15]

A similar number opposed in 1954 the admission of former anti-Hitler refugees to high positions in the Federal Republic, and in the same year roughly the same proportion expected Germany to become once again one of the most powerful states in the world. Slightly more than one-half of Germans polled in 1951 favored the lifting of the ban on the wearing of Nazi World War II decorations with the swastika symbol (almost every second German man had at least one such decoration), and they opposed the idea of reissuing these decorations with the swastika omitted. A majority rejected the notion of German war crimes. More

[13] Rolf Fröhner, *Wie stark sind die Halbstarken? Dritte Emnid Untersuchung zur Situation der Deutschen Jugend* (Bielefeld: Stackelberg Verlag, 1956), pp. 119–121, 305–310.

[14] DIVO, *Basic Orientation . . . 1956*, pp. 36–39, 45.

[15] DIVO, *Basic Orientation . . . 1956*, p. 63.

than one-half (55 per cent) felt in 1953 that the German soldiers of World War II had nothing to reproach themselves for in their behavior in the countries they had occupied. As many as 70 per cent of the Germans polled said that they could not consider, or could not have considered, marrying a person of Jewish descent. Finally, we may recall what we noted earlier about the image of history that Germans hold today. More than four German adults out of every five polled have favorable memories of one or the other of the two authoritarian systems of government in Germany during the twentieth century: the Hohenzollern monarchy before 1918 and Hitler's Third Reich between 1933 and 1945.

Most of the large popular majorities on particular foreign policy issues thus seem to arise in those cases where many or all of the 25–30 per cent all-weather democrats and many or all of the 20–25 per cent antidemocratic Nazi sympathizers can agree. Where they all do so, a considerable part of the usually undecided or ambivalent persons may be likely to join in. We have surveyed the main issues that tend to produce this kind of agreement between pro- and anti-Nazis, adherents of nationalistic dictatorship and of democracy, friendly and hostile critics of the United States, France, and the United Kingdom. They are the familiar issues of opposition to Communism, preference for Western economic and political connections and living standards, desire for restoring and increasing national prosperity and German international prestige and bargaining power.

The nature of this consensus implies its limits: most voters will not follow nationalist goals to the brink of war; most democrats will not increase German international bargaining power to the point where extreme nationalists and militarists would actually regain

major power in domestic politics; most of the right-wing extremists do not wish to deepen their alliance with the West to the point where they would have to drop their anti-Semitism, admiration for much of the Nazi system, and contempt for democracy. Wherever those limits of consent are reached, democrats and Nazi sympathizers separate again; a considerable part of their countrymen withdraw into silence or indifference, and policy decisions though sometimes delayed or compromised are carried on by the government in line with the democratic sectors of opinion and in line with what is judged to be the relevant international opinion.

Wanted: a foreign policy of caution

Altogether, the structure of German public opinion in the mid-1950's favored a foreign policy of firm symbolic attachment to the West, coupled with caution and a preference for limiting the extent of actual commitment. There was a clearly accepted general goal—the prosperity and prestige of the German people on the level of the leading Western nations—and there were at least four specific goals which were agreed upon: (1) the exclusion of any major Communist influence from West Germany, (2) the preservation of peace, (3) the retention of United States friendship and support for German aspirations, and (4) the reunification of East and West Germany, substantially on West German terms. Two further goals were endorsed by majorities but were perceived as less urgent for the time being, and perhaps also as less important in the long run. These less salient goals were the recovery of former German territories east of the Oder and Neisse rivers, and Western European integration.

Above all, German opinion wanted

to avoid unpalatable choices. It rejected anti-Communism at the price of war, as well as peace at the price of Communist rule. It rejected national reunification at the price of either Communist penetration or the loss of Western friendship. It favored neutrality, provided it could be coupled with continuing close and friendly association with the West, but it would not favor any overt displays of neutralism that might alienate Germany's Western allies.

These preferences corresponded fairly well to the very limited range of opportunities offered to German foreign policy by the international situation of the time. The two great power blocs, led by the United States and the U.S.S.R. respectively, appeared in a position of near-stalemate. Neither side could count on a clear and certain shift of power in its favor in the immediate years ahead. At the same time, all major countries in Europe were committed to one of the two blocs. There was no effective bloc of neutral countries; only Sweden, Finland, Austria, and Switzerland were neutral in military terms, and Yugoslavia was not being firmly committed to either side. These countries could not form any effective combination that would offer any positive attractions or opportunities to Germany.

Under these conditions, some of the determinants of German foreign policy were likely to be negative: to avoid or delay any decisions that might make matters worse. As long as really attractive positive opportunities were lacking or, like Western European integration, seemed at best very slow in coming, German public opinion was most likely to favor a policy of cautious advance, designed to limit German risks and to increase quietly and steadily the extent of German bargaining power. But what any major political or economic shift, such as a major political crisis or a severe economic depression, would do to this alignment of opinion, no one could foretell.

This, then, was the popular image of the tasks of German foreign policy. What was the image of its makers? They should be experts, competent to make all necessary changes within the broad limits of the goals outlined. They should be cautious, but determined on essentials; persevering, persistent, resourceful; they should try every promising approach, but not make any major concessions or compromises at the expense of long-run goals. They did not have to be open or explicit; they should not bother the voters with the burden of decisions; above all, they should be united. If they could also be "crafty" or "foxy," so much the better; "prudence," "diplomacy," "smartness" and "foxiness" were all considered in January 1955 major traits of Chancellor Adenauer, at a time when his popularity was high.

There was less public concern about the constitutional, legal, and administrative details of the way in which foreign policy was supposed to be made. Nevertheless, these arrangements are important, and it is to them that we must now direct our attention.

THE ROLE OF GOVERNMENTAL AND NONGOVERNMENTAL INSTITUTIONS IN THE MAKING OF FOREIGN POLICY

Under the Constitution of the German Federal Republic foreign policy is the responsibility of the federal government. The ten constituent states of the Republic and their governments are bound by federal actions in the realm of foreign policy; if required, they are expected to pass enabling legislation to incorporate into state law commitments undertaken by the federal government toward foreign governments. To a limited extent, the states participate in the formation of foreign policy through the upper house of the federal legislature (*Bundesrat*); this house is composed of representatives of the ten state governments, and each state has from three to five votes according to the size of its population. This chamber has an absolute veto over all constitutional changes, but only a suspensive veto over ordinary legislation. Prior to the conclusion of treaties affecting the particular interest of one or more states, the state governments have the right to make their views known, but these opinions are not binding on the federal government and may formally be ignored by it, though political considerations may induce the federal government to take them into account in deciding a course of action. As under the constitution of the Soviet Union, and diverging from our own system, the states have the right to conclude treaties of their own with foreign nations—subject to the approval of the federal chancellor—when these deal with matters not specifically reserved for federal jurisdiction or with subjects of concurrent jurisdiction not yet pre-empted by the federal government. These, however, are minor matters; in the main, foreign policy is federal in theory and practice.

The key role of the chancellor

Within the federal government, the federal chancellor (*Bundeskanzler*) is constitutionally the principal decision-maker in the realm of foreign policy. His cabinet, the federal president, the two chambers of the federal legislature, and the federal constitutional court may under certain circumstances share in the decision-making process, but con-

stitutionally the final source of authority is the chancellor, who alone has the power and responsibility for determining public policy.

The framers of the "Basic Law" of 1948—the constitution of the federal republic—deliberately endowed the chancellor with considerable power in the hope of avoiding the sort of governmental instability that is common in many countries where an all-powerful legislature is divided into many bitterly antagonistic factions. At the same time, they wanted to prevent a recurrence of the sort of irresponsible executive absolutism that had prevailed in Germany before 1918 and in the early 1930's. Designed for the traditional German multi-party system, the Basic Law strives for executive responsibility by providing for a chief of government elected by and responsible to a majority of the popularly elected lower house of the federal legislature. It strives for governmental stability by providing that a chancellor remain in office until (1) a majority, or at least a plurality, of the lower house agree on a replacement, or (2) a new lower house is elected, or (3) the incumbent chancellor dies, resigns, or is convicted of certain criminal acts. The chancellor cannot be impeached. Thus, it was hoped by the fathers of the constitution, neither the disintegration of a coalition nor the opposition of a parliamentary majority unable to agree on a replacement should force the fall of a government. "Chancellor Government" (*"Kanzlerregierung"*) is intended to make the head of the government less dependent upon the legislature than under a pure parliamentary system, yet more so than under our own presidential form of executive leadership.

In accordance with these principles, the chancellor alone—and not the entire government—is supposed to determine government policy, see to its execution, and account for it to the legislature. There is no collective responsibility of the entire government. Accordingly, the chancellor in effect appoints and dismisses the members of his cabinet; his recommendations are binding on the federal president who has the formal power of appointment and dismissal. In turn, the ministers of the chancellor's government are solely responsible to him as his advisors and subordinate administrators, and their tenure ends automatically with his.

Constitutionally, neither the president nor the legislature can compel the chancellor either to include anyone in his government or to dismiss any minister. Chancellor Adenauer successfully maintained this point in 1955, when one of the parties in his coalition broke with him and sought to withdraw its representatives from the government. The ministers, Adenauer insisted, were his agents once they joined the government, and not those of their party. Subsequently, he dropped some cabinet members on his own because their presence in the government apparently no longer seemed politically advisable to him. Adenauer's actions underlined the fact that a strong chancellor who commands a majority in the lower house of the legislature can afford to defy suggestions concerning the composition and size of his government. On the other hand, a weak chancellor—that is, one who did not command such a majority or even a plurality—presumably would have to be far more considerate toward the leaders of parties whose support he sought in connection with the make-up of his cabinet. In order to gain such support he might be forced to accommodate them, to give ministerial portfolios to representatives of parties whose support he wanted, perhaps to create new portfolios or appoint ministers without portfolios. He might have to offer important ministries to powerful political leaders who were not necessarily qualified for these posts but would bring him the parliamentary support he needed.

Other offices and officials

Individually, the members of the chancellor's government are supposed to administer the affairs of their ministries in accordance with the general policy determined by their chief. As in the case of the chancellor himself, the personality, experience, and qualifications of the incumbent play an important part in determining the actual role he plays in the decision-making process and the extent to which he relies upon subordinate officials.

Chief among the ministries concerned with foreign policy is, of course, the Foreign Office (*Auswärtiges Amt*). It is officially charged with "attending to foreign affairs," and unless the chancellor makes special exceptions (as in the case of the Minister for Economic Cooperation in the second Adenauer Government), other ministries may deal with foreign governments and international organizations only with its approval. Jurisdictional conflicts are resolved either by the entire cabinet or by the chancellor alone. Other ministries directly or indirectly concerned with foreign policy decisions are those of Defense (*Bundesministerium für Verteidigung*); Finance (*Finanzen*); Economics (*Wirtschaft*); the Ministry for Expellees, Refugees, and Victims of War (*Vetriebene, Flüchtlinge und Kriegsbeschädigte*)—which was especially created to attend to the interests of some twelve million citizens who fled or were expelled from German and East European territories now dominated by the Soviet Union; and the

Ministry for All-German Affairs (*Gesamtdeutsche Fragen*)—whose special responsibility are matters pertaining to the reunification of divided Germany. The second Adenauer Government (1953–57), as previously mentioned, also included a Minister for Economic Cooperation (*Bundesminister für Wirtschaftliche Zusammenarbeit*) who dealt with questions pertaining to European economic operation.

Collectively, the ministers form the chancellor's cabinet and, as such, are supposed to advise him on matters of general policy decisions and to decide upon government proposals to be submitted to the legislature. The actual role of the cabinet and its individual members in decision-making would also appear to depend very largely upon the personalities and relative political power of the chancellor and of his minister. A strong chancellor, such as Adenauer, can largely dictate policy; a weaker chancellor would be more dependent upon the approval and support of at least the most powerful of his ministers.

A relatively recent creation is the Federal Defense Council (*Bundesverteidigungsrat*), a sort of inner cabinet, somewhat similar to the American National Security Council. Its members are selected by the chancellor. In 1956 it included, in addition to the chancellor, the vice-chancellor and the ministers for Atomic Questions (*Atomfragen*), Defense, Foreign Affairs, Interior (*Bundesministerium des Inneren*), Finance, and Economics. Other ministers and important officials may be invited to attend meetings at the chancellor's discretion.

Two other agencies of the executive branch of the federal government have in recent years played a considerable role in the making of German foreign policy, largely owing to the intimate relationships existing between their respective chiefs and Chancellor Adenauer. The first of these, the Chancellor's Office (*Bundeskanzleramt*), is formally charged with assisting the chancellor in his relations with other branches of the government and important nongovernmental agencies, with keeping him informed on political developments at home and abroad, and with preparing for the decisions that the chancellor may decide to take on the basis of this information. The second, the Press and Information Office of the Federal Government (*Presse und Informationsamt der Bundesregierung*), is supposed to assure close relations between the executive branch and the mass media—both foreign and domestic—, to gather and evaluate data on public opinion, and, generally, to interpret the policies, decisions, and actions of the government to the public at home and abroad. In terms of actual as well as potential influence over the foreign policy-making process, leading officials in both these offices are important members of the decision-making elite within the executive branch, the extent of their influence varying with the prevailing relationship between their incumbents and the chancellor.

The powers of the president

The role of the federal president in the foreign policy-making process is normally insignificant. Although he has the right to nominate a candidate for the chancellorship to the lower house of the legislature, he must appoint the choice of the majority of the deputies, whether he approves or not. The incumbent chancellor is supposed to keep the president informed and to consult with him on the policies of his government, but the president for his part is constitutionally bound to cooperate loyally with a man who has the support of a majority of the deputies. He must sign such treaties, bills, and decrees as are submitted to him by the chancellor or his ministers, appoint or dismiss officials on the chancellor's advice, and, in general, exercise his formal powers at the discretion of the chief of government, who bears ultimate responsibility for the actions of the executive branch. Some constitutional commentators would concede the president's limited influence over diplomatic negotiations, but even here a strong chancellor would appear to have the final word as principal decision-maker.

A few constitutional commentators have claimed that the powers of the president, particularly in foreign policy-making, might be used more decisively in the hands of a powerful incumbent. Such an interpretation may have led Chancellor Konrad Adenauer to consider exchanging the chancellorship for the presidency in 1959. His decision not to become a candidate for the presidency and his subsequent efforts to maneuver the popular Minister of Economics, Ludwig Erhard, into running for the office so he could not succeed Adenauer as Chancellor, seemed to indicate that the president has little or no influence in policy-making under present circumstances.

The president's role might become more important if the parliament should be so deeply divided that its members would neither support the incumbent chancellor nor agree upon a successor. Given the present division of parliament into two major parties more or less tightly organized and united, such a development is not likely to take place. Should a multi-party system re-emerge at some future date, as seems unlikely today, and should under such circumstances a deadlock develop between the incumbent chancellor and a majority of the deputies, the role of the president in the political process might temporarily become more significant.

The powers of parliament: the Bundestag

Of the two chambers of the federal legislature, the lower house (*Bundestag*) has by far the greater power in most matters, including foreign policy. Treaties that regulate the political relations of the Federation or that relate to matters of federal legislation can become the law of the land only with its consent. Similarly, the transfer of sovereign rights of the state to international institutions, such as the European Coal and Steel Community, require legislative action. Finally, all treaties and other legislation that conflict with the Basic Law require constitutional amendments, which must be approved by two-thirds of the membership of the lower house.

Apart from its legislative functions, the lower house is granted certain other powers which are designed to give the members a voice in the foreign policy-making process. A majority elects a chancellor and can dismiss him by choosing a successor. The deputies of the lower house provide half the votes in the Federal Assembly (*Bundesversammlung*), which every five years chooses a federal president, and which can initiate impeachment proceedings against him before the federal constitutional court.

In the lower house the deputies have the right to investigate and criticize the actions of the executive in plenary sessions or in committees. They may summon and question members of the government when they choose; the latter, for their part, have the right to demand to be heard by the deputies at any time, providing them with potential opportunities to influence important deliberations of the house at decisive moments.

Most of the important contacts between the executive branch and the deputies occur in the sessions of the standing and select committees of the lower house, rather than in plenary sessions. It is here that experts from the various parties examine the actions and requests of the government and question its members thoroughly. The vote in the committee is usually decisive and committee recommendations are usually approved in subsequent plenary sessions. With respect to foreign policy issues, the key committees are Foreign Affairs (*Auswärtige Angelegenheiten*), Defense (*Verteidigung*), Budget (*Haushalt*), Expellees (*Heimatsvertriebene*), All-German Affairs (*Gesamtdeutsche Fragen*), and Border Questions (*Grenzlandfragen*).

The role that the deputies of the lower house may play in the realm of German foreign policy appears to depend primarily on the authority that the chancellor exercises in the chamber. If he commands a stable majority— or better, two-thirds of the votes—his powers are fairly absolute and his position firm. However, if he lacks such strength, his freedom of action would seem to be more limited; he may be forced to rely on the cooperation of uncertain and demanding allies in order to see his program through the legislature and prevent the election of a successor.

In the case of constitutional disputes arising out of foreign policy issues the federal constitutional court may enter the picture. It may be called upon to adjudicate jurisdictional disputes between the federal government and the states or between the executive and the legislative branches of the national government. The court may also be asked to render advisory opinions on the constitutionality of certain pending actions, either upon the joint request of executive and legislature, or upon that of the federal president alone. The latter has the right to refuse to place his signature on treaties, acts of the legislature, or government decrees pending an advisory opinion from the court. Thus, in 1952, President Theodore Heuss tried to withhold his signature from the treaty providing for the arming of the Federal Republic until the constitutional court had advised him that it did not conflict with the Basic Law, but he finally signed the treaty on Chancellor Adenauer's advice.

To summarize what has been said about the formal role of various governmental institutions in making of foreign policy: foreign affairs are a federal matter and, within the federal government, the principal decision-maker is the chancellor, while lesser roles are assigned to the ministers, president, legislature, and constitutional court of the Republic. How this formal arrangement actually functions depends primarily on the prevailing relationship between a chancellor and the lower house of the legislature. A strong chancellor who commands a comfortable majority in the lower house will have a great deal of freedom in the conduct of foreign affairs; a chancellor who lacks such support is likely to be far more dependent on either or both the cooperation of the legislature and that of the president. Experience during the first twelve years of the Republic's existence indicates that the chancellor's position vis-à-vis both Parliament and legislature rests largely on his relationship to his party and on that party's strength and cohesion. A future chancellor might not necessarily be a party man at all—not even a member of the legislature—nonetheless, his power of making decisions would still depend primarily on his ability to gain the majority party or coalition of parties in the legislature.

The formal organization of the foreign policy-making process thus becomes a functioning party system, though it does provide the chancellor with some limited means of governing temporarily without parliamentary support should the parties fail to produce a stable majority behind him.

The role of the political parties

The Basic Law of the Federal Republic is unique in its specific recognition of the decisive role of political parties in the formulation of national policy. Through their representatives in the executive and legislative branches of the national government the parties are supposed to act as the responsible agents of the electorate in the conduct of government. The existing electoral law compels all aspirants for seats in the popularly-elected lower house to belong to a party and thus to identify themselves with and bear responsibility for its policies and actions. Referenda, plebiscites, and other devices for "direct democracy," by-passing parties and legislature, have been deliberately omitted from the constitution; its framers were all too aware of the anti-democratic uses to which such devices had been put in the past by demagogues who appealed to the "popular will" against the "selfish" interests of parties.

Anyone may organize a political party in the Republic, as long as its objectives and organization accord with the democratic principles of the constitution and do not aim at the overthrow of the present state. In fact, however, the electoral laws have made it almost impossible for any party receiving less than 5 per cent of the electoral votes to gain representation in the national legislature.

Contrary to the apparent expectations of the framers of the constitution,

recent years have seen the gradual elimination of the traditional German multi-party system and the emergence of two major parties as the principal representatives of the electorate. These are the Christian Democratic Union and Social Democratic Party. Between them, these parties received 60 per cent of the votes, 67 per cent of the seats in the 1949 election; 74 per cent of the votes, 83 per cent of the seats in 1953; 82 per cent of the votes, 88 per cent of the seats in 1957; 82 per cent of the votes, 87 per cent of the seats in the 1961 election.

The Christian Democratic Union (*Christlich Demokratische Union*), CDU—operating in Bavaria as the Christian Social Union (*Christlich Soziale Union*), CSU—represents a departure from the traditional German parties. Instead of following the traditional pattern of parties in Germany and becoming closely identified with some particular ideology, religious group, or economic interest, the CDU/CSU has managed to attract the support of rather heterogeneous elements among the voters in the name of its "Christian principles." Moderately conservative in its domestic economic and social program, the party has faithfully followed the lead of its chairman, Konrad Adenauer, in the realm of foreign policy. Its professed aims have been the reunification of Germany "in peace and freedom," the peaceful recovery of the German lands presently "administered" by Poland and the Soviet Union, permanent and intimate collaboration with the Western powers, and the economic, military and—ultimately—political integration of the states of Western Europe.

The Social Democratic Party (*Sozialdemokratische Partei Deutschlands*), SPD, is more strongly rooted in the past than the CDU/CSU—both in terms of its objectives and its supporters. The SPD is primarily a workers' party, as before the advent of Hitler and the prohibition of the party in 1933, many of whose supporters have been adherents for many decades. Heretofore far more homogeneous in both membership and electorate than the CDU/CSU, the SPD has lately made strenuous efforts to broaden its support among the voters. Most West Germans appear unwilling to cast their ballots for a "workers' party" and even many manual workers no longer want to be considered proletarians. Seeking to become a progressive "peoples' party" similar to the Scandinavian labor parties, the SPD has thrown overboard most of its traditional Marxist principles. In its domestic program, the party has gone far toward accepting the social and economic tenets of the Christian Democrats, while in foreign affairs it has abandoned its former neutralist inclinations and embraced rearmament and NATO membership.

None of the minor parties represented in the national legislature has played a very significant role in matters of foreign policy. The largest of them, the Free Democratic Party (*Freie Demokratische Partei*), FDP, aspires to hold the balance of power between the two major parties and has oscillated between opposing and supporting the CDU/CSU. Extremist parties have been conspicuous by their absence; the insignificant Communist party had had no representation in the national legislature even before it was outlawed in 1956; a small neo-Nazi party was also banned by the constitutional court; other extremist parties have been singularly unsuccessful in gaining support among the electorate.

The formulation of German foreign policy has thus been primarily in the hands of the two major parties. As the governing party since the establishment of the Federal Republic in 1949, the CDU/CSU has borne the prime responsibility for initiating and executing foreign policy decisions. The SPD has been compelled to play the role of a permanent opposition, endeavoring with mixed success to influence foreign policy through criticism of the government, through attempts to amend government bills in the national legislature, and through efforts to mobilize public opinion in order to compel the government to modify its position. Both parties have sought between elections to establish a clear distinction in the public mind between their respective policies in order to present the electorate with a decisive choice at election time. However, in foreign affairs the exigencies of the situation in which the Federal Republic has found itself have made it difficult for the Social Democratic opposition to formulate convincing alternative proposals for the conduct of West German foreign policy.

The role of the interest groups

The constitution grants all Germans the right to form organizations to represent their particular political, economic, or religious interests, as long as such groups are not directed against "the principle of international understanding." As in the United States, there exist in the Federal Republic numerous associations that in one way or another seek to influence the conduct of foreign affairs in accordance with their perceived interests. However, German interest groups are more inclusive, more tightly organized, and occupy a more privileged position in public life than do their counterparts in this country. On the other hand, public opinion in Germany tends to be more critical and suspicious of the influence of such interest groups than it is in the United States.

Economic and socio-political interests are organized into large national organizations (*Spitzenverbände*), all of which are ostensibly nonpartisan but by no means nonpolitical. Religious interests are primarily represented by the two major churches, the Roman Catholic and the Protestant, and their affiliated lay organizations. In general, the influence of interest groups in the conduct of foreign affairs has increased in direct proportion to the gradual restoration of German sovereignty and the recovery of independence of action by the government of the Federal Republic. Most of them have endeavored to exercise their influence over national policy through the political parties and, particularly, through party leaders in the executive and legislative branches of the federal government.

Economic interest groups in the Federal Republic fall roughly into two major categories: (1) employers' organizations, and (2) organizations representing employees, independent farmers, independent craftsmen, and the professions. The former groups have the greater financial resources, the latter the greater voting strength to offer to political leaders and parties. Reliable figures on financial support are lacking, but some of the potential voting power of different economic interests may be apparent from the 1955 percentage figures of gainfully occupied persons and their dependents, given earlier in this chapter under the heading "Ideologies and classes."

German employers are organized both regionally and by economic sectors. Every employer must belong to one of the 81 regional Chambers of Industry and Commerce, which are represented nationally by the Association of German Chambers of Industry and Commerce (*Deutscher Industrie- und Handelstag*), perhaps the most powerful of the employer groups. Next in importance is the Association of

German Industry (*Bundesverband der deutschen Industrie*), which represents the interests of the 38 branches of German industry. The Coordinating Committee of German Trade and Industry (*Gemeinschaftsausschuss der deutschen gewerblichen Wirtschaft*) includes all major employer groups and acts as a coordinating agency among the component interest groups. Other important employer interest groups concerned with foreign affairs are the Federal Association of Private Banking (*Bundesverband des privaten Bankgewerbes*), the Association of German Wholesalers and Exporters (*Gesamtverband des deutschen Gross- und Aussenhandels*), the Central Organization of German Retailers (*Hauptgemeinschaft des deutschen Einzelhandels*), the German Shipowners Association (*Verband der deutschen Reeder,* the German Section of the International Chamber of Commerce (*Deutsche Gruppe der internationalen Handelskammer*), and the Committee for Foreign Trade of German Business (*Arbeitsgemeinschaft Aussenhandel der deutschen Wirtschaft*). In addition to these permanent national organizations various business groups frequently will form temporary alliances for special ends, such as export drives or tariff reform.

Among employee groups, by far the largest and most important is the German Confederation of Trade Unions (*Deutscher Gewerkschaftsbund*). With 6.1 million members (1955) it not only includes all wage-earners' unions, but it is also the largest organization of salaried employees and civil servants. About 35 per cent of all wage-earners, 12 per cent of all salaried employees, and 41 per cent of all civil servants in the Federal Republic belong to the Confederation. Eighty-three per cent of its members are wage-earners (11 per cent salaried employees, 6 per cent civil servants), and the large industrial enterprises are the most thoroughly organized and represented within the Confederation. IG Metall, the largest industrial union, contributes 25 per cent of the total membership of the entire Confederation. The German Employees Union (*Deutsche Angestelltengewerkschaft*), with some 420,000 members (1955), includes about 8 per cent of all salaried employees, and the German Federation of Civil Servants (*Deutscher Beamtenbund*) with some 517,000 members (1955) about 43 per cent of all civil servants. Between them, these three groups thus include about 35 per cent of the wage-earners, 20 per cent of the salaried employees, and 84 per cent of the civil servants in the Republic. Individually or collectively, these organizations endeavor to influence the foreign policy-making process whenever they consider their special interests to be involved.[16]

The League of German Farmers (*Deutscher Bauernverband*) with 1.3 million members (1952) represents 77 per cent of all independent farmers. Perhaps its most important objective has been the protection of the high-cost, small German farm units against cheaper agricultural imports.

The League of German Artisans (*Zentralverband des deutschen Handwerks*) with 864,000 members includes practically all the independent craftsmen in the nation. Its interest in foreign affairs appears to be limited primarily to the protection of its members against cheaper imports and the promotion of the export of their products.

Organizations concerned with such matters as migration, trade, investment, tourism, and banking are obviously interested in asserting influence in the foreign policy-making process, but other groups, too, may take a strong interest when their particular economic sector is thought to be affected, as in the case of tariffs, international marketing arrangements, and wage-price agreements. Special issues may lead to temporary alliances between groups that may disagree on other subjects. Farm and industry groups may jointly seek tariff protection; employer and employee organizations in particular industries may temporarily unite to fight for or against proposed international agreements that affect them; or export industries may ally themselves to gain government support for trade expansion.

Only a few of the special socio-political interest groups play any significant role in the Federal Republic. The most important of these are the organizations of expellees—German citizens and ethnic Germans who fled or were expelled from German lands east of the Oder-Neisse line presently "administered" under the Potsdam Agreement of 1945 by Poland and the Soviet Union, and from other parts of Eastern and Southeastern Europe. There are about 9.3 million of these expellees living in the Federal Republic today, constituting about 18 per cent of the total population; about half of them are former residents of Silesia and the Sudetenland. Only a fraction of the expellees are organized into the various groups that claim to defend their common interests. The most important of these are the League of Expelled Germans (*Zentralverband Vertriebener Deutscher*) and the League of Regional Groups (*Verband der Landsmannschaften*), with its major affiliates of Silesians (*Landsmannschaft Schlesien*) and Sudeten Germans (*Sudetendeutsche Landsmannschaft*). There are also about 3.5 million refugees from the Soviet zone of Germany in the Federal Republic (6.8 per cent of the popu-

---

[16] Figures from the *Statistisches Jahrbuch für die Bundesrepublik Deutschland 1956*, pp. 111, 128; and from *Jahrbuch*, pp. 3–4.

lation), but although there are numerous organizations that would like to represent their interests, few of the refugees belong to them. Together, expellees and refugees number about 13 million persons or 25 per cent of the population, but most of them appear to have found adequate representation of their interests in the major political parties.

Mention should also be made of close to 1,200 veterans' organizations, though few, if any, of them appear at this time to exercise any major influence in German politics. The largest and potentially the most influential is the League of German Soldiers (*Verband deutscher Soldaten*), primarily an organization of present and former professional soldiers. Among its stated objectives are "loyalty to an undivided fatherland," the rehabilitation of all "defamed" former soldiers, and the liberation of still-imprisoned soldiers convicted of war crimes. The pre-Hitler, right-wing veterans' organization "Steel Helmet" (*Stahlhelm*) is a much smaller association with apparently little influence. The same is true for the Air Force Circle (*Luftwaffenring*) which is composed of former members of the German air force.

According to the 1950 census, 51.2 per cent of the population of the Federal Republic professed the Protestant and 45.2 per cent the Roman Catholic religion, compared to 60.6 and 33.3 per cent respectively in prewar Germany. In terms of relative strength the potential influence of the Roman Catholic Church in national affairs has thus increased considerably. However, no more than 11 million West Germans —about half of those professing the Roman Catholic faith—are thought to be active members of their church; in the case of the Protestants the proportion is about one-eighth. Of the two major churches the Roman Catholic

is probably politically the more active and influential.

The supreme organ of the Roman Catholic Church, the annual meeting of the hierarchy at the town of Fulda (*Fuldaer Bischofskonferenz*), also claims jurisdiction in the Soviet-controlled German Democratic Republic. Nonetheless, the influence of the Church is largely restricted to the Federal Republic, for not only are less than 20 per cent of the Germans living in the Soviet zone Roman Catholics, but the Communist government has greatly restricted contacts between the West German hierarchy and Roman Catholics living in the Democratic Republic. In the Federal Republic the Church maintains a liaison office at the capital to represent its interests. With the encouragement of the hierarchy, the members of numerous lay groups affiliated with the Church endeavor to translate Catholic interests into Catholic action by playing an active role in public life. Thus in a 1952 poll almost two-thirds of the Roman Catholics but only about one-half of the Protestants expressed approval of one of the two major parties: 35 per cent of the Catholics but only 22 per cent of the Protestants endorsed the CDU, while an equal proportion of 30 per cent in both denominations endorsed the SPD.

The German Evangelical Church (*Evangelische Kirche in Deutschland*), EKD, is a union of German Protestant Churches in both the Federal Republic and the Communist Democratic Republic. Since over 80 per cent of Germans living under Communist rule are Protestants and their church still exercises considerable influence over them, the EKD and its member churches have considerably stronger ties to and interest in the population of the Democratic Republic than the Roman Catholic Church. The Synod, Council, and Conference of the Evangelical Church used to be recognized representatives of the Protestants in both parts of the divided country, but in recent years the Protestants have found it increasingly difficult to maintain the religious unity of Germany. The Evangelical clergy in Eastern Germany has been hard pressed by the Communist government. Through its Office for Foreign Affairs (*Kirchliches Aussenamt*) the church maintains relations with other churches in both Communist and non-Communist countries.

The orthodox Lutherans among German Protestants have traditionally shunned political action on behalf of their church. Today, too, they exert only indirect influence in political affairs through their tacit support of the dominant liberal leadership of the Evangelical Church. The leaders of this liberal wing, although numerically in the minority, occupy most of the positions in the EKD and in this capacity endeavor to exercise some influence in both the Federal Republic and the Democratic Republic. In the Democratic Republic this has involved the church in many bitter clashes with the Communist rulers; in the Federal Republic its participation in public life is neither as extensive nor as intensive as that of the Roman Catholic Church. Although individual church leaders occasionally speak out on public issues, organized Protestant groups play a comparatively small role in the political process.

THE SYSTEM IN OPERATION: THE SUBSTANCE OF FOREIGN POLICY

The actual operation of German foreign policy-making is heavily influenced by three factors: the aims of German policy-makers, the pressure of various interest groups, and the massive involvement of the German economy with the United States, through various forms of United States aid and through private business relations. The intra-German factors will be discussed below, but the German stake in United States-German political and economic relations is so substantial that we must try to say something about its magnitude at the outset.

The economic influence of the United States

To indicate even the order of magnitude of the American dollar flow into the Federal Republic and West Berlin is not an easy task. The aid has been given in a large variety of ways, under a bewildering succession of alphabetical agencies: GARIOA, ECA, MSA, FOA, and others. Although these accounted publicly for their operations, data for other channels of dollar inputs into the German economy have not been so readily available. In the case of Germany, as in that of some other countries, many of these extraordinary dollar receipts, as a report of the U.N. Economic Commission for Europe points out, ". . . belong to the twilight zone of quasi-strategic information: at best, only general orders of magnitude are known. . . ." [17]

What is this general order of magnitude? The German Federal Ministry for Economic Cooperation acknowledged in 1956 that Germany had received almost $10 billion up to June 30, 1956, presumably for a period since early 1948.[18] Of the exact total of $9,935 million, $6,355 million was listed as aid to the Federal Republic

[17] United Nations, Department of Economic Affairs (Economic Commission for Europe), *Economic Survey of Europe in 1953* (Geneva, 1954), pp. 19–20.

[18] Bundesministerium für wirtschaftliche Zusammenarbeit, *Der europäische Wirtschaftsrat—OEEC: Handbuch, 1956* (Godesberg: Verlag für Publizistik), p. 70.

in general, and $3,580 million as aid to West Berlin.[19] Even if one assumes that this total includes all dollar aid since 1946, one would arrive at an average of $1 billion per year; or approximately $20 per year for every German man, woman, and child.

The effectiveness of these dollar inputs into the German economy was greatly increased by the manner in which they were employed and by the efficient response of German management and labor. Through counterpart funds and other devices a considerable part of these funds was used to increase capital investment and thus the technological equipment of German industry, without any of the sacrifices that German consumers otherwise would have had to make for an investment program of this magnitude. The result was an increase in both capital equipment and consumer goods. "To use a medical term," says a German government publication, "it was 'dollar therapy' and the tonic effect of an American blood transfusion. . . . Every Marshall Plan dollar spent in Germany has resulted in $10 to $20 worth of goods produced and services rendered." [20]

The economic influence of the United States is heavily reinforced by psychological, social, and military considerations that make American friendship appear as the most important basis of what security the members of the West German foreign policy elites can hope for in this uncertain world. The results of this relationship have been conspicuous. In every major German foreign policy decision the government of the United States has been an invisible—and sometimes not so invisible—partner. Nevertheless, there has been

a growing autonomous component in German foreign policy-making. The interplay of German aims and United States influence, and of the various domestic German interests, can be seen best by glancing briefly at a few actual cases of such policy decisions. The questions of German membership in the European Coal and Steel Community; of German rearmament; of German reparations to Israel; and of negotiations with the Soviet Union about German reunification—these are the cases in which we shall try to watch German foreign policy-making in operation.

Toward the recovery of German influence

A primary objective of German foreign policy since the creation of the Federal Republic in 1949 has been the recovery of German influence in international affairs. There have been differences between various elite groups and among the public at large over the means to be employed, but solid unanimity concerning the general objective. The man primarily responsible for the conduct of German foreign policy from 1949 to 1957, Chancellor Konrad Adenauer, was singularly successful in his efforts to regain for Germany independence of action in the conduct of foreign policy without losing the political, military, and economic support of the Western allies—particularly the United States. Adenauer's policy was to establish Germany as the leading power and the senior partner of the United States on the European continent by means of adroit and subtle moves, which gained for the Federal Republic full sovereignty and a leading position within the Western Alliance system in the course of a few years. In the face of frequently bitter opposition from some foreign policy elites, par-

19 *Ibid.* The latter sum may have included orders placed in West Berlin for work done elsewhere in the Federal Republic.

20 *Germany Reports,* 1953, pp. 239–243.

ticularly the Social Democratic leadership, and often without the specific support of public opinion, he gained his ends through close collaboration with the Western powers, particularly the United States. Adenauer gambled successfully that temporary concessions would eventually yield major gains for German foreign policy and that the voters would sustain him at election time. He owed his success to a combination of factors, including his unrivalled position as the leader of the governing political elite, his remarkable prestige inside and outside Germany, his ability to enlist the support of crucial German elites for specific foreign policy moves in spite of public opposition or indifference, his influence among leading policy-makers in Western countries, and last, but not least, the exigencies of the international situation. In general, Adenauer has exploited to the fullest his great formal and informal powers as chancellor and as leader of the largest German party —if necessary in the face of widespread public opposition at home and abroad —in order to gain his ends in foreign affairs.

The European Coal and Steel Community Treaty. The first step toward the recovery of German sovereignty and Germany's liberation from allied controls after the creation of the Federal Republic was taken with the creation of the European Coal and Steel Community (ECSC), popularly known as the Schuman Plan. Under the Occupation Statute of 1949, the new German state gained only limited independence from control over its affairs by the three Western occupation powers—the United States, Great Britain, and France. A tripartite Allied High Commission was established, endowed with broad powers designed to assure that the Federal Republic would conform to Western plans for a democratic and demilitarized Germany and would honor the political and economic obligations it had undertaken in return for Allied agreement to the establishment of the new state. The Allied High Commission controlled the organization and operation of German business, endeavoring to prevent its reconcentration in cartels and trusts and diverting a considerable share of the production of the Ruhr coal to foreign countries who had been victims of German aggression. It regulated political and economic relations between the new state and foreign countries; and, for all practical purposes, the Commission represented the interests of the Federal Republic and its citizens abroad.

The new German government, a coalition led by Adenauer, immediately sought ways and means to gain freedom from allied supervision. These efforts were helped immeasurably by the rapid economic recovery of the new German state—aided largely by generous financial assistance from the United States government—and by the intensification of the conflict between the Western allies and the Soviet Union. Failure to achieve agreement with the Soviet Union on the reunification of Germany and the belief that Russia might attack Western Europe through the territory of the Federal Republic led the Western occupation powers to yield to Adenauer's demands for complete sovereignty. Even before the outbreak of the Korean conflict in July 1950, Western policy had begun to change from treating the Federal Republic as a defeated enemy to seeking its inclusion in the Western Alliance system as a major bulwark against Soviet aggression. These developments played directly into the hands of the leaders of the Federal Republic, who offered intimate collaboration to the Western powers in return for independence and complete German equality in the councils of the Western Alliance. Their first opportunity to move toward their objective came almost as soon as the new state had come into being, in May 1950, when French Minister Robert Schuman called for the pooling of Franco-German coal and steel production in an economic union which he invited other interested European states to join.

The French foreign minister made his proposal for a variety of political, economic, and military reasons, including the desire to prevent the restoration of an independent German power on the continent that might once more become a threat to French security. Conscious of the rapid recovery of German power, Schuman sought to make a virtue of apparent necessity by proposing a close organic bond between the Federal Republic, France, and other states of Western and Eastern Europe which, he hoped, would permit resurgent German power to benefit, rather than threaten, the anti-Communist nations of Europe. Schuman advertised his proposal as the first step toward the economic and political unification of Europe which, he claimed, would put an end to past Franco-German conflicts and prove advantageous to all participating states.

Chancellor Adenauer immediately hailed Schuman's proposal as "epoch-making" and called for its speedy implementation in the form of a treaty. However, the spokesmen of the Federal Republic let it be known that their country would join the proposed community only if all existing restrictions on the Republic's sovereignty, imposed by the occupation powers, were removed. The Occupation Statute of 1949 was gradually revised in the course of the negotiations leading to the signing of the European Coal and Steel Community treaty in April, 1951. The Federal Republic was given partial control over its foreign relations and some of the most severe allied controls over its domestic affairs were gradually dropped. In January, 1952, the Bundestag approved the ECSC treaty by a vote of 232 to 143.

Bundestag approval of the ECSC treaty was not due to overwhelming public support. The "attentive public" in favor of the proposed coal and steel community declined steadily during negotiations, while opposition increased. The largest number of Germans, however, appear to have become increasingly indifferent toward the issue, leaving the final decision to the foreign policy-makers.

West German armament as an instrument of foreign policy. On the morning of May 9, 1955, the black, red, and gold flag of the German Federal Republic rose at the Supreme Headquarters, Allied Powers Europe (SHAPE), while the band played the old German national anthem, *Deutschland, Deutschland über alles, über alles in der Welt.* It signified the admission of a free and sovereign German state to the North Atlantic Treaty Organization (NATO)—almost ten years to the day since its new allies had dictated armistice terms to a vanquished Germany. After almost six years of determined efforts to throw off Western allied controls over German affairs, Chancellor Adenauer and his associates appeared at last to have obtained their goal. In exchange for the promise of a German military contribution to the defense of Western Europe they had gained for the Federal Republic "the full authority of a sovereign state over its internal and external affairs," a national military establishment, a major voice in the councils of the Western powers, assurances of Western military and political support against Soviet Russia, and, finally, Western recognition of the

Bonn government as "the only German Government . . . entitled to speak . . . as the representative of the [entire] German people in international affairs." [21]

As in the case of ECSC, the negotiations leading to the abolition of Western controls and the recognition of the Federal Republic as a sovereign and equal member of the NATO alliance demonstrated the far-reaching and generally uncontested independence of German foreign policy decision-makers from the influence of domestic public opinion. The price that the Adenauer government agreed to pay for sovereignty and NATO membership was the setting up of a national military establishment, a decision repeatedly opposed during the period of negotiations by more Germans than supported it.

Adenauer and his closest associates sought to achieve their objective—as in the case of the European Coal and Steel Community—in the name of European integration. In December of 1949 Adenauer launched a trial balloon by suggesting that Germans should contribute to the defense of Europe in a European Army. Apparently anticipating early Western demands for a German defense contribution, on the basis of formal and informal current suggestions along these lines from Western political and military leaders, he maintained his position in the following months despite violent opposition both in the Federal Republic and abroad. Adenauer sought to impress upon Western leaders the value of the Federal Republic as an ally and the

crucial role that it might play in a future conflict between the Soviet Union and the NATO powers. He claimed that the industrial and demographic resources of the Federal Republic might prove decisive in a future war; he stressed the danger of large-scale Soviet troop concentrations in Central Germany and the growing power of the so-called "People's Police" of the Communist-dominated German Democratic Republic, suggesting that short of a military contribution from the Federal Republic the Western powers lacked the forces to repel an attack from the East. For political as well as military reasons, Adenauer maintained, the Western powers needed the loyal support of the people of the German Federal Republic; he offered it in exchange for an end to allied controls and the termination of existing limitations on the sovereignty of the Federal Republic.

To gain his objective Adenauer was willing to risk Soviet threats against the Federal Republic and the possibility that the reunification of Germany might be deferred indefinitely; as in the case of ECSC, he was prepared to sacrifice *potential* sovereign rights in return for the surrender of *actual* sovereign powers by other nations participating in the creation of a European defense community. The same ideological motives that influenced the CDU elite, under Adenauer's leadership, to support the Schuman Plan of May 1950 also led it to support concurrent proposals for the creation of a European army, even though every one of ten opinion polls between 1950 and 1954 showed more opponents than supporters for the plan.

However, political considerations were every bit as important. Membership in a European integration scheme for a German state both wealthier and more populous than any other conti-

21 See U.S. Congress, Senate, *Protocol on the Termination of the Occupation Regime in the Federal Republic of Germany and Protocol to the North Atlantic Treaty on the Accession of the Federal Republic of Germany,* 83d Congress, 2d Session, Executives L and M, (Washington, D.C.: United States Government Printing Office, 1954).

nental state held out the prospect not only of equality for the Federal Republic in such a union, but of potential leadership of the democratic nations of continental Europe. Instead of remaining merely a rump German state, facing the prospect of indefinite occupation and control by foreign powers, the Federal Republic might at least become "first among equals," playing a leading role in international affairs as the leader of the continental nations, particularly toward the United States and the Soviet Union, the two super-powers of the world. Finally, such a role for Germany in a European military union promised to make it less dependent on foreign powers and to give its leaders a greater voice in matters affecting the defense of the Federal Republic against attack from the East. To gain these ends Adenauer was prepared to defy popular opposition to German rearmament. Sovereignty and equality for the Federal Republic through European integration were to him worth the price of a German military contribution, as Adenauer's official biographer was to note.[22]

Adenauer's arguments for a German military contribution to the defense of Western Europe against Communist attack seemed substantiated by the North Korean attack on South Korea in July of 1950. Particularly in the United States government, military and political leaders—some of whom had favored a German military contribution, at least since 1949—reportedly interpreted the unexpected invasion as a clear warning that either the Soviet Union herself, or her East German satellite, might invade the Federal Re-

public too. Western allied forces in Germany, never very strong and further weakened by the diversion of military resources to Korea, appeared inadequate to meet the threat. Simultaneously, the French government informed the United States that it was not interested in an allied strategy that depended primarily on U.S. air-atomic power, but wanted Western Europe to be defended by ground forces as far east as possible.

While United States leaders sought desperately to stem the North Korean sweep down the peninsula, Chancellor Adenauer pointed with increasing emphasis to the exposed situation of his country, and of Western Europe in general. In August 1950 he suggested to the Western allies the formation of a "special force of German volunteers" of the same size and strength as the "People's Police" in the Soviet Zone of Germany—estimated to consist of from 50,000 to 80,000 trained soldiers. He coupled this appeal with the renewed suggestion that the Federal Republic might make a sizable contribution to a European army in return for an end to allied controls and complete equality within a defense arrangement. Simultaneously, Adenauer appointed a former general to head a new office in the Federal government that was to lay plans for such a German military contribution.

The United States government, upon the urgings of its military leaders, replied to Adenauer's proposals by calling openly for the use of German productive resources and military manpower for the defense of Western Europe. Secretary of State Dean Acheson asked British and French government leaders to agree to the inclusion of about ten German divisions in the NATO forces in Europe. But, in the face of French opposition to the creation of an independent German army,

[22] See Paul Weymar, *Konrad Adenauer: Die autorisierte Biographie* (München: Kindler, 1955), pp. 500, 557. See also Fritz René Allemann, *Bonn ist nicht Weimar* (Köln-Berlin: Kiepenheuer and Witsch, 1956), pp. 187–212.

the three Western governments agreed that the German military contribution demanded "by democratic leaders in Germany" should become part of an integrated European army.

Urged on by United States leaders, the governments of the Federal Republic of Germany, France, Italy, Belgium, the Netherlands, and Luxembourg for over two years hammered out a scheme for a European Defense Community (EDC) that would more or less parallel the pattern agreed upon for the Coal and Steel Community. While French negotiators, led by Adenauer's friend, Foreign Minister Robert Schuman, sought to limit German influence in the proposed military arrangement, the representatives of the Federal Republic demanded complete equality and the termination of allied controls over German affairs. The German spokesmen were aided not only by strong United States support, but, paradoxically, by popular opposition to any rearmament in Germany itself. Pointing to gains for the opposition Social Democrats—strongly opposed to the scheme—in various local elections, Adenauer extracted major allied political concessions for the more "cooperative" German leaders.

When the EDC treaty was finally signed in May 1952, it provided for the creation of 12 German divisions, an air force, and a small navy, which were to become major components of a European military establishment. True, the German Federal Republic was not yet admitted to NATO, but Chancellor Adenauer had no doubts that membership would follow as soon as the German defense contribution had begun to take concrete form. Simultaneously with the signing of the EDC treaty the Federal Republic concluded a Contractual Agreement with the three Western occupation powers which was to replace the Occupation Statute of 1949. In effect, this agreement terminated the occupation and put an end to practically all allied controls. However, Western forces remaining in Germany as "allies" retained the right to intervene in case the democratic order in the Federal Republic should be threatened either from within or without.

In May 1953 the Bundestag approved the two agreements by a majority of 59 votes, a considerably smaller margin of victory for Adenauer's policies than in the case of the ECSC vote only a few months earlier. The treaties became the major issues of the campaign for the election of a new parliament, which followed ratification. The Christian Democratic elite, supported only diffidently by leaders of the smaller parties in the Adenauer coalition, claimed a major political victory for Germany. Opposition came largely from a peculiar alignment of militarists, pacifists, nationalist opponents of European integration, and "neutralists" who feared that military alignment with the West would prevent any Soviet agreement to the reunification of Germany. The Social Democratic and trade union elites, this time united, claimed that rearmament would restore the antidemocratic and bellicose German military leadership of the past and perpetuate the division of Germany. The Protestant elite was divided. Important members—like the Social Democratic leaders particularly sensitive to the needs of their silent "constituents" living under Soviet control in Central and Eastern Germany —claimed that membership in EDC would constitute a "betrayal" of their "oppressed brethren." The old military elite was also divided into proponents and opponents of EDC. Some supported Adenauer's claim that the political and military gains for Germany outweighed whatever disadvantages the agreements might include. Others maintained that the limitations imposed upon a new German military establishment were unacceptable and asked that rearmament be deferred until political conditions and popular opinion had become more favorable.[23] Strenuous Communist efforts, directed from the Soviet Zone, to draw the various opposition groups into a united "patriotic" front proved unsuccessful.

Despite widespread popular opposition to rearmament the promised restoration of German sovereignty and the gains in Germany's international position impressed many voters. Adenauer won a resounding personal victory in the election of 1953. His prestige and reputation as an effective representative of German interests gave the Christian Democrats for the first time an absolute majority in the Bundestag; the ruling coalition now commanded the two-thirds majority required for constitutional changes, which armament might require. Adenauer's policy of German political recovery in international affairs through European integration was dealt a setback in August 1954, when the French Chamber of Deputies rejected the EDC treaty and thus defeated the scheme. However, only 37 per cent of the respondents in a German poll following this defeat expressed regret for the failure of the project.

The German chancellor immediately demanded complete sovereignty for the Federal Republic, maintaining that it had fulfilled its part of the bargain and was not to blame for the failure of the armament scheme. However, the British and American governments insisted that a German military contribution agreed to by the French re-

[23] See, for example, excerpts from a memorandum by former Fleet Admiral Heinrich Gerlach, reprinted in *Der Spiegel,* April 3, 1957, p. 16.

main the *sine qua non* for political sovereignty. On British initiative, representatives of the United States, Britain, Canada, and the six continental countries that had signed the EDC treaty, formulated a hasty substitute. It provided for the creation of a national German military establishment and the admission of the Federal Republic to the North Atlantic Treaty Organization as a sovereign and equal partner, subject only to certain limitations on its future military power and the retention of a few formal rights on the part of the former occupation powers pertaining to West Berlin and German reunification. By May 1955 all the governments concerned had ratified these "Paris Agreements." A major goal of Adenauer's foreign policy since 1949 had been achieved, though not exactly in the manner the chancellor had intended. The immediate political gains for the Federal Republic were even greater than under the proposed EDC arrangement; however, many of the proponents of European integration among the German leaders paid the price only reluctantly. The immediate gains of sovereignty, NATO membership, and a national military establishment did not appear to them to be worth the sacrifice of the European army scheme and its apparent promise of German leadership of a European political union.

An unresolved foreign policy issue:
German reunification and relations
with the Soviet Union

The preceding analysis has suggested repeatedly that foreign policy-makers in the Federal Republic have tended to show a great deal of independence from the pressure of public opinion. To this, there has been one conspicuous exception. On the issue of German reunification no important leader has dared suggest that the Federal Republic is more than a provisional arrangement pending the "liberation" of the Soviet zone. During the years that German policy-makers concentrated on gaining sovereignty and freedom of action for the "rump" German state, reunification as a policy objective took second place to these more immediate foreign policy goals, leading many non-German observers to underestimate its potential importance once sovereignty had been achieved. Since 1955, however, it has become increasingly apparent that peaceful reunification through some sort of arrangement with the Soviet Union is one of the most crucial foreign policy issues confronting decision-makers in the Federal Republic, one that is likely to affect significantly the future relationship between the Republic and its Western allies.

Professions by official government spokesmen of support for European integration have tended to obscure the existence of considerable sentiment for Germany reunification, particularly among the refugees from the Soviet zone. As we said previously, while it is possible to get indications of mass support for reunification, the intensity of this support has not been measured. However, some indication may be gotten from comparing the attitude of the young Germans between 15 and 24 on the subject of European integration and German reunification. In 1956, 50 per cent of a cross-section of German youth expressed themselves as "very strongly" in favor of reunification at the present time and 30 per cent "strongly" in favor of it, compared respectively to only 34 per cent and 31 per cent of adults polled on the same issue. On the other hand, only 66 per cent of the young Germans were in favor of efforts toward uniting Western Europe, while 79 per cent of adults favored

such efforts.[24] Thus, among German youth sentiment for reunification appears to be a good deal stronger than sentiment for European unification, particularly when compared to the adult population. Not only do deep-rooted loyalties to the idea of a united German nation appear at the present time far stronger than support for the supranational ideal of European unification, but intimate personal bonds link a large number of citizens of the Federal Republic to German lands and peoples presently under Communist domination. Over 27 per cent of the foreign policy elites and 26 per cent of the population are natives of Central and Eastern Germany. In February 1953, 44 per cent of the respondents in a public opinion poll claimed either relatives or friends living in the Soviet zone of Germany; when one adds to these the number of West Germans with personal acquaintances, the share of West Germans with such personal contacts should be well above one-half the population of the Federal Republic. Many of these human contacts have remained active; in February 1953 almost two West Germans out of every five said they were sometimes writing letters to the East zone, and almost one in three had sent Christmas packages there. Every month several thousand refugees from the Soviet zone enter the Federal Republic, serving as a constant reminder that 17 million Germans remain outside the present "rump" German state.

In addition to national and personal sentiments, visions of potential political and economic gains motivate the demand for reunification. With a population of 81 million and the largest area by far of all European states, a united Germany would once more rank among the leading powers of the world—

[24] DIVO, *Basic Orientation . . . 1956*, pp. 123–139.

second only to the United States and the Soviet Union. Although presently trade between the Federal Republic and Communist countries is negligible —even trade with the Soviet zone amounted to only about 2 per cent of its total foreign trade—reunification might open up vast new markets.

The magnitude and intensity of popular pressure for German reunification is evidenced by the attitudes of the elites. Opinion leaders in the Federal Republic have sought to outdo each other in denouncing the division of Germany as intolerable and in labeling reunification the most important national duty confronting the government. General agreement exists that reunification must be achieved peacefully and by means of free elections of a national assembly throughout Germany, and not through negotiations with the "puppet" regime of the Soviet zone. Elite views diverge, however, on the strategy that should be employed by the government of the Federal Republic in achieving reunification.

Most German leaders acknowledge —however reluctantly—that the government is not a free agent in the matter of reunification. German unity, they admit, depends in the last analysis upon agreement between the United States and the Soviet Union. Chancellor Adenauer and his supporters have taken the position that the best means of obtaining such an agreement consists in inducing the Western leaders—and United States leaders in particular—to adopt this German national objective as their own, and to treat it as more important than any other United States interest that might conceivably be served by an American-Soviet settlement on other issues. Any general settlement of outstanding East-West differences, it is argued, would then have to include the unification of Germany on terms satisfactory to the gov-

ernment of the Federal Republic. To gain such support, however, the Republic and its leaders must convince Western leaders of their devotion and loyalty to the Western Alliance; above all, they must convince them that a reunified Germany would be no threat to the peace of the world. According to Adenauer, the most effective way to earn such confidence and support is for the Federal Republic to take the leadership in the movement for European Union. Therefore, the Chancellor has claimed, without the unification of Europe there can be no unification of Germany.

In recent years Germans appear to have become increasingly pessimistic regarding the chances for reunification of their country in the near future. While professing the desire for reunification with undiminished strength, both elite and mass opinion have reflected such pessimism. In September 1955, 18 per cent of Germans in a survey thought the chances for reunification were bad and 3 per cent thought they were very bad; by March 1958 this had risen to 33 per cent who thought the chances were bad and 7 per cent who thought they were very bad.[25] The new program of the Social Democratic Party, heretofore identified with efforts to seek reunification through neutralization, dropped all references to reunification and neutralization. Implied is the acceptance of the *status quo*. Leaders of the Protestant church, who in the past were often critical of Adenauer's pro-Western policies, have yielded in the face of Soviet intransigeance to a "more realistic" point of view. They, too, are no longer to be found in the forefront of the neutralist, pacifist, and nationalist elements who in the past believed that the cause of German unity would

[25] DIVO, *Umfragen*, 38.

be better served by loosening the ties that the Chancellor had forged between the Federal Republic and the West. Without enthusiasm, many West Germans have come to accept the present split of Germany. There appears to be a reluctant acceptance of a fact unacceptable to most West Germans in the past, that the *status quo* is likely to be perpetuated indefinitely by a tacit understanding between the leaders of the great powers to shelve the issue of German unification indefinitely for the sake of compromise on other issues, such as the state of Berlin, disarmament, and peaceful competition in the Afro-Asian area.

By 1961 Germany seemed further from reunification than in 1949. At best the foreign policy of the Adenauer government appeared to be preserving the *status quo;* at worst it seemed to be aggravating the division of the nation. However, Adenauer's failure to register any concrete gains by a supposedly dynamic drive for reunification seemed not to be counted against him by the electors. For this there was perhaps no greater evidence than the ceasing of opposition charges that he and his associates had merely paid lip service to the cause of reunification. Earlier claims that the predominantly Roman Catholic, West and South German conservative elites supporting Adenauer and influencing his foreign policy feared the political and economic effort of unification are no longer being heard. The elites, as well as mass opinion, appear to have fully awakened to the fact that, at present, reunification lies beyond the control of the German policy-makers.

These foreign policy-makers are faced with a deadlock between Soviet and Western leaders on a formula for German unity. Both sides conceive the potential status of a united Germany as a matter so vital to their respective interests that they have found it impossible to make the concessions that a compromise solution would require. Western leaders see the terms for reunification proposed by the Soviet leaders as designed to give control over this strategic area to the U.S.S.R., while the latter insist that a Germany united according to Western plans would constitute a menace to the Soviet Union and its allies in Eastern Europe. The resulting deadlock has aroused widespread suspicions in the Federal Republic that neither Western nor Soviet leaders are genuinely interested in resolving the issue—protestations by both sides to the contrary—while the German government seems unable to do anything about it. "The German people . . . [are merely] the subjects of negotiations between foreign powers which pursue only their own interests," observed the leading foreign affairs journal in the Federal Republic after ten years of inconclusive four-power negotiations on German unification. This sense of exasperation and frustration has repeatedly led to demands that the leaders of the Federal Republic take matters into their own hands and negotiate directly with the Soviet government. However, attempts in this direction have been singularly unsuccessful. This was illustrated by Adenauer's visit to Moscow in September 1955.

The termination of the occupation regime in May 1955 was taken by many influential leaders of the Federal Republic as the signal for the start of direct negotiations with the Soviet Union on reunification. Such sentiments were strengthened by the failure of the Geneva four-power talks on German unification the following July. Therefore, when Soviet leaders invited Adenauer to come to Moscow in September 1955, he accepted, evidently sharing the widespread German view that his bargaining position was strong enough to extract favorable terms from the Soviet government. It turned out, however, that he had overestimated his own position and underestimated that of the Russian leaders. The latter refused to discuss reunification, but suggested that he negotiate directly with the leaders of the German Democratic Republic—the satellite regime of the Soviet zone—which no political leader in the Federal Republic was then, or is now, willing to do. Adenauer refused, but agreed to the establishment of diplomatic relations between the Federal Republic and the Soviet Union in return for the release of several thousand German prisoners of war still in Soviet captivity. To many opinion-leaders in Germany it seemed that Adenauer had walked into a Soviet trap. By agreeing to the establishment of diplomatic relations he seemed to have accepted the Soviet claim that there were two German states, both represented in Moscow, and that unification could only come about by negotiations between their respective governments. However, Adenauer quickly sought to dispel the impression that he had abandoned the claim of the Federal Government to be the only German government and that he was moving toward recognition of the Soviet-zone regime. In fact, he had obtained the release of some prisoners, which his Western allies had failed to procure. The presence of a Russian ambassador in Bonn, and of a West German ambassador in Moscow, represented a relative increase in German independence and bargaining power vis-à-vis the West; and Adenauer had gained these points without injuring in any way his reputation for rock-solid reliability as an ally of the Western powers. However, it was evident that the Federal Republic could ill afford to go much further in the way of independent negotiations with the Soviet Union, and that it still depended upon the Western powers—and particularly upon the United States—to achieve the professed major foreign policy objective of its leaders: German unity.

Between 1949 and 1956 German foreign policy-makers were highly successful in obtaining their objectives in negotiations with the Western occupation powers, primarily because the latter were willing and able to pay the price demanded. To obtain the political, military, and economic participation of the Federal Republic in the Western Alliance against the Soviet Union, they agreed to Adenauer's demands for sovereignty and equality. Reunification is another matter. As long as international tensions remain acute, a united Germany may seem too dangerous to either side in the East-West contest. Small or unarmed countries can be neutral in the sense that neither side is forced to count them as enemies or allies, but a large, armed country would be not so much neutral as just uncommitted; it might keep everyone in fear as to what it might decide to do at any time with its concentrated power. In the case of Germany, now still divided, neither Eastern nor Western leaders seem overly eager to hasten the day when such fears might become real. Although German reunification often has been described—particularly by German leaders—as a major means to lessen tensions between East and West, it seems possible that a reduction of international tensions through compromises on some other issues might make German reunification more acceptable to the other powers.

Thus, the great threat confronting the German objective of a reunited nation is the possibility of a tacit agreement between the great power leaders to leave the issue indefinitely in abeyance—as in the case of divided Korea and Indochina. This possibility has become particularly acute with recent attempts to halt the armament race between the Soviet Union and the United States. Prodded by Chancellor Adenauer, Western leaders formerly insisted that agreement on German reunification must precede agreement on disarmament, but indications have been abundant that their position need not remain rigid: German unification, unlike disarmament, has little appeal among either foreign-policy elites or publics outside Germany.

German leaders could render the achievement of such East-West compromises on other issues more difficult. If they chose, they could exercise their influence to hamper or even block agreement on disarmament; they probably could intensify and dramatize the daily East-West frictions in divided Germany. But it is difficult to see how any such action would bring reunification closer. At most they could use their insistence on the priority of reunification as a bargaining technique, in order to exact concessions from both East and West to German interests on other and more manageable matters.

PROSPECTS FOR GERMAN FOREIGN POLICY

The study of the background of foreign policy-making in the German Federal Republic among the various policy-making institutions, interest groups, and sectors of public opinion, reveals a limited area of agreement, surrounded by substantial cleavages of attitudes and interests and by the possibility of stubborn deadlocks.

Government, interest groups, and the general public all desire, by and large, a peaceful return of Germany to leadership and power in Europe—and through Europe, perhaps in a larger area of the world. A substantial majority want peace, freedom from Communist control, and economic and political links to the United States—and they do not want to have to choose between these aims. Second to these primary goals comes German reunification as a long-range aim.

"The First Servant of Europe"

European integration comes only in third place; it is often seen as a road to German leadership or to the attainment of other German goals, rather than as an end in itself. Among German elite members, as well as among the electorate, there are many who are likely to show little enthusiasm for remaining in any close European community that would prove unresponsive to German leadership or major influence. Other groups—though perhaps less strong—might be willing to accept a more modest role for Germany in a united Europe. The cleavage between those who want Germany to lead a Western European community and those who want her merely to join it has been adroitly bridged for the time being by the formulation of a prominent CDU leader and former diplomat, the President of the Bundesrat, Kurt Sieveking:

England and France . . . will always . . . be preoccupied by extra-European tasks. . . . Italy is . . . not yet developed to its full strength. From this it is evident that Germany will become ever more the natural nucleus of crystallization for Europe. . . . Above all it must be made absolutely clear that this German foreign policy is far from any thought of any hegemony over Europe and that Germany, as one put it in a well-known saying, is "the first servant of Europe." [26]

The "well-known saying," so aptly recalled by Herr Sieveking, is indeed well known to almost every educated German: it is the classic eighteenth-century phrase in which the absolute ruler of Prussia, King Frederick the Great, called himself "the first servant" of the State, and thus pictured his enlightened despotism as a matter not only of right but of duty. Nationalists may take heart from what they may well read as a broad hint of future aspirations, whereas more liberal-minded "Europeans" may take comfort from the explicit rejection of any thought of German hegemony, which prefaces it in the same sentence. Like many a present-day political leader, Herr Sieveking is raising here two sets of overtones and expectations in the same statement, and thus appealing at the one and same time to different sections of his variegated audience.

How much stress on military power?

In practice, this policy of cautious advance toward greater power within the Western Alliance system may mean that German reunification will remain largely in the realm of rhetoric. The Soviet government has no motive, for the time being, to concede German reunion on Western terms, and the Western powers have no effective means of pressure to make the Soviets change their minds. Faced with a deadlocked international situation and a divided public opinion at home, some German statesmen in early 1957 again sought unity through ambiguity, by promising greater German power that would force concessions from other

countries, yet not endanger peace beyond the limits of tolerable risk. The implications for foreign policy have been put illuminatingly in an article by the Federal Minister of Defense, Franz-Josef Strauss: [27]

In the age of the *pax atomica* there are no military solutions. . . . The problem of reunification, too, must and can only be solved politically. . . . However one may regret it . . . the fact remains that the position and influence of a people depend as well upon the strength and dependability of its allies as upon its own military power. . . . Those who ask us —quite rightly—to accept Soviet power as a reality, should after all not deny their own people the right and the opportunity to become likewise a reality. In all negotiations about reunification, risks and chances must be weighed against each other. The risks will diminish, the chances will improve, the more Germany herself has to throw into the scales. . . . A policy of strength in the age of the hydrogen bomb means in no case that one wants to use military pressure, with the risk of a third world war, in order to bring about some territorial changes, if necessary even by force. A policy of strength means rather that one's own freedom of decision cannot be influenced by pressure from hostile or unfriendly quarters. . . . Germany . . . must become so indispensable to her Western friends, and so respectable for her potential adversary, that both will value her presence in the negotiations.

In another formulation of his views, Herr Strauss was quoted as adding: [28]

[26] Kurt Sieveking, "Die europäische Aufgabe der deutschen Aussenpolitik," *Aussenpolitik*, 6:3, March 1957, pp. 150–151.

[27] Franz-Josef Strauss, "Sicherheit und Wiedervereinigung," *Russenpolitik*, 6:3, March 1957, pp. 140–47.
[28] M.S. Handler, "Key Aide in Bonn Offers Unity Idea: Defense Minister Suggests Use of Military Potential to Attain Objective," *New York Times*, February 20, 1957.

... although there exists a preference ... for a reunited Germany to belong to a military alliance with the West, the hard political requirements of the German people might cause them to make a decision according to the Austrian pattern (of neutralization between East and West). . . . Such a decision would have to rest on very sober political and military considerations. . . . Without possessing potential power, Germany will never have a chance to be heard.

The game of juggling— and its limits

Some journalists took an exuberant view of German opportunities in the near future; thus a popular weekly wrote in April 1957: [29]

If all goes according to plan, German foreign policy . . . will at last be able to play the diplomatic game with two balls: on the one hand, one will be able to negotiate with the Western powers about an initiative in the German question, and on the other hand with the Soviets about an improvement in relations, which is—according to the concurrent views of Konrad Adenauer and Nikolai Bulganin—the precondition for reunification.

A respected review gave a more sober estimate: [30]

We have more of a bipartisan foreign policy than both (major) parties care to admit. . . . In foreign policy matters we are not independent, and it often smacks of phrase-making to call here for German initiatives. It is rather in regard to our internal affairs that we are really sovereign.

[29] Der Spiegel, April 3, 1957, p. 12.
[30] "Wo findet der Wahlkampf Statt?" Die Gegenwart, 12:5, March 9, 1957, p. 130.

The four views just cited—the hopes for German leadership in Europe, for German military power as a counter in diplomatic bargaining, the play with the "two balls" of possible negotiations with East and West, and the resigned acceptance of Germany's lack of real independence in international affairs—indicate some of the limits of the narrow space within which German policy-makers are confined for the decisions left to them. Thus confined and limited in its possibilities, German foreign policy might well promise stability for some years to come.

Much of this prospective stability, however, depends on outside limits and on outside props. If economic prosperity in the Western world should give way to a serious depression; if American interest and aid should be withdrawn; if a sharply increased risk of war should put much greater short-term strains and burdens upon Germany; if the Soviet Union should make some substantially more favorable offer on matters of German reunification; if a further deterioration of the French position at home or in her overseas territories should bring about a changed situation in Western Europe; or if some drastic change in some of the countries of the Soviet bloc should create new conditions among Germany's Eastern neighbors—in any of these events German foreign policy-makers might find themselves quickly face-to-face with the need for major new decisions.

Such decisions in response to major international changes might easily entail a broad revision of German foreign policy. What their outcome would be is hard to foresee. Here we encounter some of the limits of any political analysis based on the past and on the background conditions of the policy-making process. The past suggests that some German responses could be dramatic; but it does not tell us what they would be.

We can, however, look to some German policy choices that are currently being made—sometimes as specific moves, sometimes as mere shifts of emphasis—which may be tell-tale indicators of the possible ways in which larger decisions might be made if circumstances should demand them. Such a tell-tale indication are current German attitudes toward any efforts at reducing East-West tensions or at limiting the arms race, particularly in nuclear weapons. Will German policy leaders welcome such efforts as favoring later German reunification, or will they insist that reunification must come first? Related to this are changes in the emphasis on Germany's need for greater military power, in order to make the U.S.S.R. and other countries more receptive to the German point of view. Will such themes and hints diminish or increase as time goes on? What will happen in this respect when the German army becomes stronger, and when the question of nuclear weapons for Germany becomes acute?

What will be the next developments in German-Soviet relations? Some members of the German foreign policy elite are urging "genuine and fruitful" diplomatic relations with the U.S.S.R. "It makes no sense," wrote an SPD leader, Carlo Schmid, "to act as if the Soviet Union did not exist as a genuine business partner. For that, our direct and indirect business dealings with them are too large." In the same connection the question of German diplomatic relations to other Soviet-bloc countries has been raised, with both Social Democrats like Carlo Schmid and CDU leaders like Kurt Sieveking coming out publicly in favor of the opening of formal diplomatic relations with Poland.

Other indications of possible trends are found in German policies toward Western European integration, and in the development of German elite and popular attitudes toward the conflicts of West European powers with native independence movements in their colonies. German leaders have refused to become too closely identified with their European allies in the Afro-Asian countries which have lately gained their independence. German foreign policy leaders have not been eager to see their country join the United Nations, since membership might limit their present ability to be allied with former colonial powers in Europe without becoming identified with their policies in Afro-Asia. Economically and politically, the Federal Republic has been reaping the benefits of its relatively neutral position in the disputes between such of its European allies as France, Portugal, the Netherlands, and Belgium, and their present or former colonial possessions. When put to the test on such issues, German leaders have shown little of the "European" solidarity that has often been a general theme in official German foreign policy pronouncements. German press opinion has tended to stress the inevitability and strength of Asian and African independence movements and to rejoice in the favorable reception which German products and German businessmen have encountered in many newly independent countries. It is perhaps in this area, as friend and business partner of the so-called "uncommitted" nations of the world, that Western Germany may find its chief opportunities in the next decade.

What kind of Germany?

Perhaps the most important of all current decisions that may indicate possible German behavior in the event of a drastic international change or major crisis are those which bear on the official and unofficial attitudes toward the remnants of Nazism and old-line militarism inside Germany. Any major crisis in foreign policy is likely to strain the limited consensus of the different ideological and interest groups that have been held together by the conditions of the Adenauer era. Under such strains, any major decision about German foreign policy may well become involved in a decision as to what kind of country Germany is to become and what groups and ideas are to lead her. Some decisions of this kind—on the attitudes to the Nazi past, to the war criminals, to authoritarianism—have been made, while others have been largely or partly shelved thus far. If the rest of the world remains stable for the next ten years, Germany's moderate foreign policy and constitutional domestic evolution may well remain secure. The small current decisions about Germany's foreign policies, however, and even more those about her internal democracy and her domestic prestige and power structure, may give us some inkling of the conflicts that might erupt among different German foreign policy elites, and among different opinion groups, if times should become acutely critical or dangerous again.

On the surface, the German Federal Republic looks like a stable political community, whose leaders are pursuing a steadfast policy of national recovery within a Western Alliance, and who are backed in this enterprise by a wide measure of solid political consensus among their people. More closely considered, the same Republic resembles rather a political and psychological convalescent. The political unity of her population still is precarious, and it could easily break under strain. Any policy by other Western powers designed to make Germany bear the major burdens of maintaining Western power in Europe in a period of major stress might well prove hazardous in the extreme.

Under these conditions, time wisely used might well work for the West. Each additional year of peace, prosperity, and confidence might aid in the consolidation of German democracy and help Germany to become a full member of the Western community of nations by inner conviction and tradition, rather than only by strategic association and expediency. The great humanitarian and democratic traditions are alive in Germany today, and a constitutional system of government has had a few years to take root. Very much may depend on giving these traditions a chance to become stronger in the next few years in an international environment that is sufficiently peaceful to permit them to become more firmly and deeply established in the social fabric and the living memories of the German people.

SELECTED BIBLIOGRAPHY

Almond, Gabriel A., ed., *The Struggle for Democracy in Germany* (Chapel Hill: University of North Carolina Press, 1949).

Arntz, Helmut, *Facts About Germany* (Press and Information Office, Federal German Government, 1960).

Bathurst, M. E., and J. L. Simpson, *Germany and the North Atlantic Community: A Legal Survey* (London: Stevens and Sons, 1956).

Buchanan, William, and Hadley Cantrial, *How Nations See Each Other: A Study in Public Opinion* (Urbana: University of Illinois Press, 1953).

Commission on International Affairs, American Jewish Congress, *The German Dilemma* (1959).

Deutsch, Karl W., *Nationalism and Social Communication* (Cambridge: M.I.T. Press; New York: John Wiley & Sons, Inc., 1953).

Deutsch, Karl W., S. A. Burrell, R. A. Kann, M. Lee, Jr., M. Lichterman, R. E. Lindgren, F. L. Loewenheim, and R. W. Van Wagenen, *Political Community and the North Atlantic Area* (Princeton: Princeton University Press, 1957).

Deutsch, Karl W., and Lewis J. Edinger, *Germany Rejoins the Powers: A Study of Mass Opinion,*

Interest Groups, and Elites in Contemporary German Foreign Policy (Stanford: Stanford University Press, 1959).

————, "Germany Rejoins the Powers," *Yale Review*, Vol. 44, No. 1 (Autumn 1959), pp. 20–42.

Edinger, Lewis J., *German Exile Politics* (Berkeley: University of California Press, 1956).

————, *West German Armament* (Research Studies Institute, Air University, Maxwell Air Force Base, Ala., October 1955).

————, "Atomic Blackmail and German Democracy," *South Atlantic Quarterly*, Vol. 57 (1958), pp. 311–324.

————, "Post-Totalitarian Leadership," *American Political Science Review*, Vol. 54 (1960), pp. 58–82.

————, "Continuity and Change: Some Data on the Social Background of German Decision Makers," *Western Political Quarterly*, Vol. 14, No. 1 (March 1961), pp. 17–36.

————, "Electoral Politics and Voting Behavior in Western Germany," *World Politics*, Vol. xiii, No. 3 (April 1961), pp. 471–84.

Edinger, Lewis J. and D. Chalmers, "Overture or Swan Song?" *Antioch Review*, Vol. 20, No. 2 (Summer 1960) pp. 163–175.

Grosser, Alfred, *Die Bonner Demokratie* (Düsseldorf: Karl Rauch, 1960).

Grossman, Kurt R., *Germany's Moral Debt; The German-Israel Agreement* (Washington, D. C.: Public Affairs Press, 1954).

Haas, Ernst B., *The Uniting of Europe* (Stanford: Stanford University Press, 1958).

Hartmann, H., *Authority and Organization in German Management* (Princeton: Princeton University Press, 1959).

Hiscock, Richard, *Democracy in Western Germany* (London: Oxford University Press, 1957).

Janowitz, M., "Social Stratification and Mobility in West Germany," *American Journal of Sociology*, Vol. 64, No. 1, pp. 6–24.

Kecskemeti, Paul, and Nathan Leites, *Some Psychological Hypotheses on Nazi Germany* (Washington, D. C.: Experimental Division for the Study of Wartime Communications, Library of Congress, 1945). (Also in *Journal of Social Psychology*, November 1947–August 1948.)

Kitzinger, U. W., *German Electoral Politics* (Oxford: Clarendon Press, 1960).

Knight, Max E., *The German Executive 1890–1933* (Stanford: Stanford University Press, 1952).

Parsons, Talcott, "Democracy and Social Structure in Pre-Nazi Germany," in *Essays in Sociological Theory*, rev. ed. (Glencoe, Ill.: Free Press, 1954), pp. 104–123.

————, "The Problem of Controlled Institutional Change," *ibid.*, pp. 238–274.

Pollock, James Kerr, and Homer Thomas, *Germany in Power and Eclipse* (Princeton, N. J.: D. Van Nostrand and Co., 1952).

Price, Hoyt, and Carl E. Schorske, *The Problem of Germany* (New York: Council on Foreign Relations, 1947).

Robson, C. B. (ed.), *Berlin: Pivot of German Destiny* (Chapel Hill: University of North Carolina Press, 1960).

Speier, Hans, *German Rearmament and Atomic War: The Views of German Military and Political Leaders* (Evanston, Ill.: Row, Peterson and Co., 1957).

————, and W. P. Davison, eds., *West German Leadership and Foreign Policy* (Evanston, Ill.: Row, Peterson and Co., 1957).

United States Congress, Senate, *Protocol on the Termination of the Occupation Regime in the Federal Republic of Germany and Protocol to the North Atlantic Treaty on the Accession of the Federal Republic of Germany*, 83rd Congress, 2d Session, Executives L and M (Washington, D. C.: United States Government Printing Office, 1954).

Wallenberg, Hans, *Report on Democratic Institutions in Germany* (New York: American Council on Germany, 1956).

Wallich, Henry C., *Mainsprings of the German Revival* (New Haven: Yale University Press, 1955).

Wiskemann, Elisabeth, *Germany's Eastern Neighbors* (New York: Oxford University Press, 1956).

5

SOVIET
FOREIGN POLICY

CONTINUITY AND CHANGE IN RUSSIAN FOREIGN POLICY

One of the most baffling aspects of Soviet foreign policy is its remarkable capacity for evoking the most variegated and contradictory responses to its diplomacy. "In its distant objectives," writes Edward Crankshaw, "the foreign policy of the Soviet Union is less obscure and more coherent than that of any other country," yet its immediate intentions and the motivations behind its day-to-day diplomacy often appear incoherent, capricious, and almost always enigmatic.[1]

VERNON

V.

ASPATURIAN

The foreign policy of any country, the Soviet Union included, is not, however, simply the sum total of its avowed intentions, no matter how sincerely and devotedly they are adhered to, but must depend upon the capacity, in the present or in the future, to carry out its intentions. "In order to transform the world," Stalin told H. G. Wells in 1934, "it is necessary to have political power . . . as a lever of change."[2] Marxist ideology, reinforced by the early experiences of the Soviet regime, thus has persuaded the Kremlin that the capacity to transform intentions into reality is indistinguishable from power, a power which is objectively determined by the economic and social foundations of society, but which, in turn, can dictate the evolution of society towards particular ethical and political goals.

In order to draw a proper appraisal of Soviet diplomacy at any given time, the voluntaristic aspects of Soviet foreign policy must always be measured against its power to overcome the deterministic impediments of international reality. Thus, although the Soviet Union can plan the calculated growth of the economic and military foundations of its power, it cannot "plan" foreign policy. This fact was eloquently stated by Maxim Litvinov to the Central Executive Committee in 1929:

[1] *The New York Times Book Review,* July 3, 1949, p. 4.

[2] J. V. Stalin and H. G. Wells, *Marxism vs. Liberalism* (New York: 1934), p. 14.

133

Unlike other Commissariats, the Commissariat for Foreign Affairs cannot, unfortunately, put forward a five-year plan of work, a plan for the development of foreign policy. . . . In . . . drawing up the plan of economic development we start from our own aspirations and wishes, from a calculation of our own potentialities, and from the firm principles of our entire policy, but in examining the development of foreign policy we have to deal with a number of factors that are scarcely subject to calculation, with a number of elements outside our control and the scope of our action. International affairs are composed not only of our own aspirations and actions, but of those of a large number of countries . . . pursuing other aims than ours, and using other means to achieve those aims than we allow.[3]

The balance between the voluntaristic and deterministic components of Soviet foreign policy is neither fixed nor stable but is in a state of continual and deliberate flux. In the initial stages of the Bolshevik Republic, its foreign policy was virtually at the mercy of external forces over which it could exercise little control, and Soviet diplomacy assumed the characteristic contours of a weak power struggling for survival under onerous conditions. As its economic and military position enhanced, it gradually assumed the characteristics of a Great Power, and given its geographical and cultural context, it took on the distinctive features of its Tsarist predecessors and the impulse to subjugate its immediate neighbors.

The geographic and historical inheritance

"Marxism," writes a contemporary Soviet specialist on diplomacy, "teaches

that economic factors determine the foreign policy and diplomacy of a state only in the long run, and that politics and diplomacy are, in a certain sense, conditioned by the concrete historical period and by many other elements (not excluding even, for instance, the geographical situation of a given country)." [4] Although Soviet writers may still tend to agree with the observation of the hapless Karl Radek, that "it is silly to say that geography plays the part of fate, that it determines the foreign policy of a state," geography is nonetheless the most permanent conditioning factor in a country's foreign policy; for location, topography, and natural resources are significant—and often decisive—determinants of a country's economic and military power.[5] Geography's effects, however, are relative, rarely absolute, always dependent upon the more variable factors in a country's character, such as its cultural traditions, political institutions, size and diversity of its population, the exploitation of its natural resources, and the skill of its statesmen. A country's geography, with rare exceptions, cannot be remade; it can only be utilized more effectively. Thus, although Radek's contention that "the questions raised by geography are dealt with by each social formation in its own way . . . determined by its peculiar economic and political aims," remains incontestable, it was the blessing of Providence that this vast empire secreted all the basic ingredients for the erection of a powerful industrial and military state, given the necessary will and determination of its leadership. Had Russia been a wasteland with limited raw materials,

[3] *Protokoly Zasedani Tsentralnovo Ispolnitelnovo Komiteta Sovetov,* Bulletin 14, (Moscow: 1930), p. 1.

[4] F. I. Kozhevnikov, "Engels on 19th Century Russian Diplomacy," *Sovetskoye Gosudarstvo i Pravo* (No. 12), December, 1950, pp. 18–34.

[5] Karl Radek, "The Bases of Soviet Foreign Policy," in H. F. Armstrong, ed., *The Foreign Affairs Reader* (New York: Harper & Brothers, 1947), p. 173.

she would have been doomed as a permanent pre-industrial society, and the character of her foreign policy—her very existence—would have been vastly different, and her vaunted ideology would have long been relegated to the ash cans of history.

The Soviet Union, like Tsarist Russia before it, is the largest single continuous intercontinental empire in the world. Embracing fully one-half of two continents, the Soviet Union has the world's longest and most exposed frontier, which is both its greatest potential hazard and one of its prime assets in international politics. As a part of both Europe and Asia, and embracing more than 150 ethnic and linguistic groups ranging from the most sophisticated nations to the most primitive, the U.S.S.R. achieves a unique microcosmic character denied any other country, including the United States with its ethnically variegated but linguistically assimilated population. Russia's serpentine frontier is both a consequence of the indefensible character of the central Russian plain and at the same time an important conditioning factor in the further evolution and execution of its foreign policy. For a weak Russia, such a frontier affords maximum exposure to attack, but for a powerful Russian state, this extended frontier, bordering on nearly a dozen states, offers an enviable and limitless choice for the exertion of diplomatic pressure. Since 1939 the Soviet Union has annexed four of its former neighbors, seized territory from seven more, and has made territorial demands upon two others; most of this territory was previously lost by a weakened Russia. Of all her bordering states, only Afghanistan has not been imposed upon to cede territory to the Soviet Union.

In the past, Russia's geographical position has exposed her to continuous depredations and subjugation from all directions—an inevitable consequence of political disunity in a geographically indefensible community. If geography simplified the conquest of a divided Russia, it also facilitated the expansion of a united and powerful Russian state, which pushed out in all directions, until it was arrested by superior force.

In the absence of more obvious geographical obstacles to her enemies, Russia's physical security became irrevocably attached to landspace, while her psychological security became inseparable from political centralization. This conviction was confirmed by Stalin, himself, on the occasion of Moscow's 800th anniversary in 1947:

Moscow's service consists first and foremost in the fact that it became the foundation for the unification of a disunited Russia into a single state with a single government, a single leadership. No country in the world that has not been able to free itself of feudal disunity and wrangling among princes can hope to preserve its independence or score substantial economic and cultural progress. Only a country united in a single centralized state can count on being able to make substantial cultural-economic progress and assert its independence.[6]

It is a persisting fact of Russian history that this dual quest for physical and psychological security has produced a unique dynamic in Russian foreign policy: A divided Russia invites attack, but a united Russia stimulates expansion in all directions. The Revolutions in 1917 and the terrible purges of the Thirties—which Stalin undertook to enforce unity at home under his monolithic leadership—exposed Russia's internal schisms to the world and stimulated foreign intervention. In each crisis, after surviving the initial assault from without, she em-

[6] *Pravda*, September 11, 1947.

barked on a campaign designed to carry her beyond her self-declared national frontiers. The campaign failed in 1921 but succeeded after World War II in bringing all of Eastern Europe under her hegemony.

The Bolsheviks fell heir not only to Russia's geography and natural resources but also to the bulk of her population, her language, and the Russian historical and cultural legacy. Marxism gave Russia new goals and aspirations, but once the decision was taken to survive as a national state, even on a temporary and instrumental basis, the Soviet Union could not evade assuming the contours of a Russian State and falling heir to the assets and liabilities of its predecessors. Although Lenin thought that he had irrevocably severed the umbilical cord with Russia's past, the choice to unburden the new Soviet Republic of the disadvantages of Tsarist diplomacy was not exclusively his. Foreign attitudes remained remarkably constant; fears and suspicions, sympathies and attachments, wherever they existed, were reinforced more than erased. Designs on Soviet territory still came from the same quarter, exposure to attack remained in the same places, and the economic and commercial lifelines of the Tsars became no less indispensable to the new regime. In short, even if the Soviet Union refused to remain Russia, Japan remained Japan, Poland remained Poland, and the Straits remained the Straits.

The Russian language, permanently encrusted in its Cyrillic shell, became the official speech of Soviet diplomacy, and, as the vehicle of the Marxist dogma, it was pompously proclaimed the "language of the future." Russian cultural and scientific achievement became the basis for Soviet claims to cultural supremacy, of which Soviet science and culture were pronounced a

continuation; the symbolism of Holy Russia was revived. Although Moscow eagerly laid claim to all the advantages of historic Russia, the outside world just as assiduously refused to permit her to evade the liabilities and vulnerabilities of the Russian past. Thus, partly by choice and partly by necessity, the foreign policy of the Soviet Union could not but assume the contours of its predecessors.

The impact of a voluntaristic doctrine like Marxism on the geographical facts of Russia and her messianic traditions not only reinforced the psychological obsession for security, but provided an ideological rationale for assuming the implacable hostility of the outside world and sanctified Russian expansion with the ethical mission of liberating the downtrodden masses of the world from their oppressors. The hostile "West" of the Slavophils was transformed into the hostility of capitalism and imperialism; instead of the parochial messianism of the pan-Slav enthusiasts, Marxism provided Russia with a mission of universal transcendence—transforming the outside world into her own image in fulfillment of her historic destiny and as the only permanent guarantee of absolute security. Up until the 20th Party Congress in 1956, the Leninist-Stalinist thesis that "the destruction of capitalist encirclement and the destruction of the danger of capitalist intervention are possible only as a result of the victory of the proletarian revolution, at least in several large countries," [7] continued to be in force. Although "capitalist encirclement" was declared ended by Stalin's successors, the recent events in Poland and Hungary may have convinced the Kremlin that this proclamation was premature.

To assume, however, that Soviet for-

[7] *Kommunist* (No. 2), January 1953, p. 15.

eign policy is merely Russian imperialism in new garb would be a catastrophic mistake on both sides. Soviet foreign policy was bound to assume "Russian" characteristics during one phase of its metamorphosis, but now that the maximum, but still limited, aims of Tsarist imperialism have been virtually consummated, the aggressive (no longer necessarily expansionist) aspects of its foreign policy will assume a purely Marxist character, while only the defensive aspects (*i.e.,* the preservation of its present power position) of its diplomacy will retain distinctively "Russian" features. That these two aspects of current Soviet foreign policy are in flagrant contradiction is self-evident, even to the Kremlin and other Communist leaders. Chinese accusations of "Great Power chauvinism," the de-Stalinization campaign, and the uprisings in Poland and Hungary, are all manifestations of this fundamental schism in Soviet foreign policy. Whereas in the past, when the Soviet Union was weak, indiscriminate emphasis on the revolutionary aspects of its foreign policy tended to undermine its basic instinct to survive, now, its "defensive" reflexes tend to subvert not only its continuing leadership of world Communism, but the eventual success of the movement itself.

World revolution and national interest in Soviet diplomacy

Deciphering Soviet motives is an elusive and hazardous undertaking, yet it must be done systematically and with calculation, otherwise *ad hoc* and unconscious assumptions acquire priority by default. Miscalculation of motives can often be catastrophic since foreign policy expectations are built upon assumptions concerning the motives and capabilities of other powers, and diplomatic success or failure often depend on the

degree of accuracy with which these assumptions approach actuality. Much of the agony of postwar Western diplomacy can be traced directly to illusory expectations resulting from false calculations of Soviet motives by Western leaders. Diplomacy, however, is not an intellectual exercise, and motives are not always susceptible to rational and logical analysis. Assessment of motives, in any event, is rarely certain and in most cases calls not only for acute analytical intelligence, but for espionage, and above all for the intuitive wisdom of long experience in statecraft.

Information concerning Soviet motives is derived from three principal sources: (1) word, (2) conduct, and (3) personal contact with the Soviet leadership. In general, whenever there exists a discrepancy between publicly stated intention and conduct, the latter is a more reliable indicator of motives on a short-run basis. Actually there are three possible relations between speech and practice in Soviet diplomacy: (1) *identity;* (2) *approximation,* usually implying a temporary accommodation or modification of a preconceived intention, unless the latter itself receives explicit reformation; and (3) *divergence.* Cleavages between word and conduct may, in turn, result from faulty execution, misinformation, miscalculation, or deliberate confusion.

Analyzing Soviet diplomacy purely from documents, speeches, and ideological statements, gives undue weight to "rational" factors, since the irrational and accidental aspects of diplomacy can hardly be culled from documentary sources, and, although such a study may give a fairly lucid picture of the long-range outlines of Soviet policy, it is of limited validity as an investigation of Soviet diplomacy. On the other hand, calculating Soviet motives purely on the basis of day-to-day conduct and responses to particular situations can easily produce a distorted conception of Soviet foreign policy and lead to the erroneous conclusion that it is only slightly distinguishable from traditional Great Power diplomacy.

Diplomacy is neither impersonal nor automatic in its execution—although its working executors may often be both—but it is a human enterprise. Soviet motives cannot be separated from the character and personality traits of the principal decision-makers in the Kremlin. Any evaluation of the foreign policy of the Soviet Union, whose principal decision-makers are a well-defined oligarchy, without a prudent and careful examination and consideration of the various estimates and observations of the "human equations" in Soviet diplomacy is bound to be defective. The personal factor, particularly in the last fifteen years of Stalin's life, was of crucial significance in any evaluation of Soviet foreign policy. Personal observations of the Soviet leadership, however, are essentially subjective; they originate with observers who are free from neither ignorance, prejudice, nor gullibility, and the observations are apt to vary accordingly. Any attempt to distill the essence of Soviet diplomacy solely from personality considerations is in fact doomed to hopeless confusion and sterility. A sound analysis of Soviet motives must take into consideration ideology, conduct, and personalities, not as separate and independent entities, but as basic variables whose relative and relational significance is in a constant state of flux.

One question that inevitably arises is whether Soviet policy is actually motivated by ideological ends, such as world revolution, or by some other more mundane consideration, such as "power" or "national interest." Soviet ideology itself defines "national interest," "power," and "world revolution"

in such a way as to make them virtually as indistinguishable and inseparable as the three sides of an equilateral triangle. The transcendental goal of Soviet foreign policy, world revolution, was defined by Lenin even before the existence of the Soviet state, when he declared in 1915 that "the victorious proletariat of [one] country . . . would stand up against . . . the capitalist world . . . raising revolts in those countries against the capitalists, and in the event of necessity coming out even with armed force against the exploiting classes and their states." [8] " 'The fundamental question of revolution is the question of power,' " wrote Stalin quoting Lenin, and he went on to say that as the effectiveness of the Soviet Union as an instrument of world revolution is measured in terms of power, "the whole point is to retain power, to consolidate it, to make it invincible." [9] As a contrived and temporary nation-state, the Soviet Union assumed particular interests, but "the U.S.S.R. has no interests at variance with the interests of the world revolution, and the international proletariat naturally has no interests that are at variance with the Soviet Union." [10] Stalin's final fusion was to identify the consolidation and extension of his own power with the interests of the world revolution.

The abstraction of a Soviet national interest outside the context of Soviet ideology, no matter how superficially attractive it may appear to be as a useful analytical tool, ruptures the image of Soviet reality and results in the calculation of Soviet foreign policy on the basis of false assumptions. Soviet foreign policy is based upon the image

[8] V. I. Lenin, *Selected Words,* V (New York: International Publishers, n.d.), p. 141.
[9] J. V. Stalin, *Problems of Leninism* (Moscow: Universal Distributors, 1947), p. 39.
[10] W. K. Knorin, *Fascism, Social-Democracy and the Communists* (Moscow: 1933).

of reality provided by the Marxist-Leninist ideological prism, and whether this image be faulty or not is totally irrelevant in the calculation of Soviet motives, although such a foreign policy will eventually reap its toll in diplomatic failure. The Soviet conception of "interest" cannot be separated from class categories, and its determination is essentially horizontal rather than vertical. Although the legal expression of class interests is temporarily articulated through the nation-state, and assumes the character of a "national interest," nonetheless in the Soviet view there exist within each state not one but several parallel "national interests," corresponding to its socio-economic development. The "national interest" reflected by the state in its diplomacy, however, can only represent the interests of the "ruling class," and no other, regardless of its pretensions.

Soviet ideology recognizes the coexistence of three qualitatively distinct national interests in the modern world, owing to the uneven development of society: (1) the national interest of the feudal aristocracy, surviving only in extremely backward societies; (2) the national interest of the bourgeoisie, which allegedly is the dominant expression of most non-Communist states; and (3) the national interest of the proletariat, receiving diplomatic expression only in Communist states, which is presumed by the dialectic to be coterminous with that of society as a whole.

Marxism tenaciously holds to the view that the community of interests that binds identical classes of different nations is more fundamental and decisive than that which binds different classes within the same nation-state. Although division and disunity are inherently characteristic of the bourgeois classes of different states, whose conflicts of interest are periodically expressed in war, the interests of all proletarians (together with their peasant and colonial allies) are considered to be in total harmony, their basic identity being temporarily obscured by artificially stimulated national distinctions.

Given the premise of the total identity of interests on a class basis, the Soviet Union, as the only avowed proletarian state in existence and the self-proclaimed embryo of a universal proletarian state, pronounced its interests to be identical with those of the world proletariat:

The Communist Party of the Soviet Union has always proceeded from the fact that "national" and international problems of the proletariat of the U.S.S.R. amalgamate into one general problem of liberating the proletarians of all countries from capitalism, and the interests . . . in our country wholly and fully amalgamate with the interests of the revolutionary movement of all countries into one general interest of the victory of socialist revolution in all countries.[11]

Although this view is vigorously contested, is far from universally recognized, and does not correspond to actual facts, it is not thereby invalidated as a basis for diplomatic action or analysis.

The presence of one of two factors, both capable of objective verification, is sufficient to impart to the national interests of a particular state an authentic international quality. These factors are: (1) the creation of appropriate forms of political organization designed to articulate the national interests of one state as those of the world at large; and (2) mass recognition in other countries that the national inter-

[11] *Kommunist* (No. 2), January 1953, p. 15

ests of a foreign state are identical with a higher transcendental interest. Not one, but both of these desiderata characterize Soviet foreign policy. It is a cardinal aim of Soviet policy to replace the nation-state system with a world Communist state by shifting allegiance and loyalty from the nation-state to class, and this policy not only invites the nationals of other countries to recognize a higher class loyalty to the Soviet Union, but actively engages in fostering the appropriate political institutions, such as the Comintern, foreign Communist parties, front organizations, and the like, to implement this fusion.

The Soviet invitation to commit mass disloyalty has elicited wide response, and the formula identifying Soviet interests with the interests of the world proletariat has been accepted by millions of Communists throughout the world as a basis for political action. This gives to Soviet national interests an undeniable transcendental quality, denied to the national interests of any other state, no matter how persistently it may claim to be motivated by the interests of all mankind, for if such a claim neither is accompanied by a serious effort at implementation nor evokes a response in other countries, it remains an empty and pious pretension. Transcendental ethical ends in foreign policy, irrespective of their substantive nature, have relevance only if they function as effective instruments or stimulants for the limitation, preservation, or further accumulation of power, or as instruments for its focalization. Otherwise, they are meaningless slogans and utopias, devoid of anything but peripheral significance in the calculation of a country's foreign policy.

Expansionism is thus inherent in the Leninist-Stalinist ideology, since the Soviet state was conceived as an ideological state without fixed geographical

frontiers. Not only did this idea of the Soviet Union as the nucleus of a universal Communist state receive expression in the basic documents of the Comintern,[12] but the Soviet Constitution of 1924 itself proclaimed the new Union to be open to all future Soviet republics and a "decisive step towards the union of workers of all countries into one World Socialist Soviet Republic." [13] And at Lenin's bier Stalin personally vowed "to consolidate and extend the Union of Republics." [14] As the indispensable instrument and base of the World Revolution, the extension of Soviet power and territory, by any means, was equated with the exfoliation of the Revolution.

Stalin's attempt to preserve the dominant and privileged status of the Soviet proletariat in the postwar Communist fraternity of nations resulted in a specific form of Soviet imperialism that brought about Tito's defection and unleashed corrosive forces within the orbit as a whole. The failure of Stalin and his successors to calculate accurately the persistence and vitality of the community of interests based on national peculiarities is actually a reflection of the inadequacy of Marxist categories to deal with the conflicting interests of national communities, whether they be Communist or bourgeois.

Paradoxically, as long as the Soviet Union was the only Communist state, its universalistic pretensions were unchallenged by foreign Communist parties, but with the eclipse of the Soviet monopoly on the interests of the world

[12] Cf. W. H. Chamberlin, ed., Blueprint for World Conquest (Chicago: Human Events, Inc., 1946).

[13] Full text in M. W. Graham, New Governments of Eastern Europe (New York: Henry Holt & Company, 1927), p. 608.

[14] History of the Communist Party of the Soviet Union (New York: International Publishers, 1939), p. 269.

proletariat, occasioned by the emergence of a Communist China and national Communism in Eastern Europe, the universalistic pretensions of the Leninist doctrine have been blunted, while, at the same time, stimulating a more limited "regional interest" aimed at synthetizing the various national interests of the Communist orbit. The transmutation of several national interests into a single supranational interest remains an insuperable difficulty in the Communist world, so long as the incompatibility of individual Communist national interests, which the Marxist dogma fails to perceive accurately, prevails:

Marxism-Leninism has always strongly advocated that proletarian internationalism be combined with patriotism. . . . The Communist Parties of all countries must . . . become the spokesmen of the legitimate national interests and sentiments of their people [and] . . . effectively educate the masses in the spirit of internationalism and harmonize the national sentiments and interests of these countries.[15]

SOVIET IDEOLOGY AND FOREIGN POLICY

The exact relationship between Soviet ideology and foreign policy has been subject to great controversy, ranging from the view that it is substantially irrelevant to the conviction that foreign policy is rigidly dictated by ideology. Actually, aside from providing the transcendental objectives of Soviet diplomacy, Soviet ideology performs five additional and distinct functions in foreign policy: (1) As a system of

knowledge and as an analytical prism it reflects an image of the existing social order and the distinctive analytical instruments (dialectical laws, and categories like the "class struggle," "historical stages," and so on) for its diagnosis and prognosis. (2) It provides an action strategy whereby to accelerate the transformation of the existing social order into the Communist millenium. (3) It serves as a system of communication unifying and coordinating the activities of its adherents. (4) It functions as a system of higher rationalization to justify, obscure, or conceal the chasms that may develop between theory and practice. (5) It stands as a symbol of continuity and legitimacy.

This compartmentalization of Soviet ideology is frankly arbitrary and actually ruptures its basic unity, which is not necessarily to be found in its logic or reason but in the intuitive faith and active experience of its partisans—factors which often elude rational analysis. Elements of Soviet ideology that appear logically incompatible, in fact, are, but these rational contradictions can be unified only in the crucibles of revolutionary action, not in the intellectual processes of the mind. The true meaning of the Marxist-Leninist insistence on the "unity of theory and practice" is that contradictions cannot be resolved by logic, but by action, which is the final judge of "truth." Communist "truth" cannot be perceived without intuitive involvement, i.e., revolutionary action and experience, and to the outsider it remains as enigmatic as the mysteries of Zen.

The Soviet image of the world

The Soviet ideological prism reflects an image of the world that is virtually unrecognizable to a non-Communist, yet it is upon this image that Soviet foreign policy is based. It reflects a world of

[15] *Pravda,* December 31, 1956. Full text of the statement by the Chinese Communist Party, "Once More on the Historical Experience of the Dictatorship of the Proletariat."

incessant conflict and change, in which institutions, loyalties, and philosophies arise and decay in accordance with the convulsive rhythm of the dialectic, which implacably propels it upon a predetermined arc to a fore-ordained future—world Communism. This image is accepted as the real world by Soviet leaders. Their foreign policy rests upon the conviction that Marxism-Leninism is a scientific system that has uncovered and revealed the fundamental and implacable laws of social evolution and hence affords its adherents the unique advantage of prediction and partial control of events. This conviction imparts to Soviet diplomacy an air of supreme confidence and dogmatic self-righteousness:

Soviet diplomacy . . . wields a weapon possessed by none of its rivals or opponents. Soviet diplomacy is fortified by a scientific theory of Marxism-Leninism. This doctrine lays down the unshakeable laws of social development. By revealing these norms, it gives the possibility not only of understanding the current tendencies of international life, but also of permitting the desirable collaboration with the march of events. Such are the special advantages held by Soviet diplomacy. They give it a special position in international life and explain its outstanding successes.[16]

The history of Soviet diplomacy, however, is by no means a uniform record of successes, though "errors" in foreign policy are ascribed not to the doctrine but to the improper apprehension and application of these infallible laws. Failure to apply these laws, according to the Soviet view, divorces foreign policy from international realities, and although it is true

that "the record of Soviet diplomacy shows an inability to distinguish between the real and the imaginary, a series of false calculations about the capabilities and intentions of foreign countries, and a record of clumsy coordination between diplomacy and propaganda,"[17] it is fatuous to deny that Marxism-Leninism, on the whole, has furnished Soviet leadership with a system of analysis that, while frequently out of focus with reality, gives a sufficiently accurate comprehension of power, its calculation and distribution in the world, and the opportunities and limitations such calculations afford for Soviet foreign policy. The dogmatic reliance on techniques and methods that have proven successful under other conditions, the frequent refusal to jettison concepts that either have outlived their usefulness or consistently produce dismal results in terms of foreign policy aims, and the concentration of all decision-making authority in one man or in a tight oligarchy—these practices at times tend to convert Marxism-Leninism from a unique asset for Soviet diplomacy into a strait jacket.

The dialectical image of history. Soviet ideology exposes the forces and tendencies operating in international politics, but it is up to the leadership to calculate these forces properly, seek out the most decisive trends, and coordinate Soviet diplomacy with the inexorable march of history. The success of Soviet diplomacy, according to the Soviet view, is maximized as it is attuned to the rhythm of the historical dialectic, and its failures are multiplied as it falls out of harmony. Conversely, the occasional successes of bourgeois diplomacy are due to fortuitous and haphazard coordination with historical

---

[16] V. P. Potemkin, ed., *Istoriya Diplomatii,* III (Moscow: 1945), 763–764.

[17] Max Beloff, *Foreign Policy and the Democratic Process* (Baltimore: The Johns Hopkins Press, 1955), p. 98.

development, or to the equally accidental deviation of Soviet foreign policy from the implacable dictates of history. These accidental deviations are attributed to faulty application of historical laws by individual leaders.

Without attempting any extended discussion of Soviet dialectics, it can be said that in the Communist view, history progressively exfoliates as a series of qualitative stages, each with its own peculiar economic organization of society giving rise to corresponding social, political, and religious institutions. This inexorable movement from lower to higher forms of economic and social organization is propelled by means of a dialectical duel between perpetually developing economic forces of society and the social and political institutions that attempt to preserve the economic order in the interests of a particular ruling class, whose servants they are. As long as the institution of private property survives, class distinctions between property-holders and the propertyless, whose interests are irreconcilable, are perpetuated and eventuate in conflict, war, and revolution, only to be replaced by a new economic system that perpetuates class divisions and conflicts in new form. The class struggle, which is the principal motivating force of historical revolution, comes to an end only with the overthrow of the capitalist system by the proletariat, after which class distinctions, conflict, and war are finally eliminated. Once Communism achieves victory on a world scale, the state itself and its coercive institutions are supposed to "wither away." [18]

The Communists recognize five qual-

[18] For a more elaborate statement of the author's views on the nature of Soviet ideology, cf. Vernon V. Aspaturian, "The Contemporary Doctrine of the Soviet State and Its Philosophical Foundations," *American Political Science Review*, XLVIII, December 1954.

itative historical stages: primitive communism, slave-system, feudalism, capitalism, and socialism-communism, all of which, except for the first and last, are characterized by the institution of private property, two main contending classes (owners of the means of production and workers), and a state that represents the interests of the ruling class. Although the movement of history is from lower to higher stages, this movement is neither uniform nor without complications, and it does not pursue a uniform and rigid chronological evolution. This has been particularly true of the twentieth century. At the present time, Communists acknowledge the co-existence of all historical stages; and this recognition has had a profound influence on Soviet foreign policy. Furthermore, each historical stage is characterized by manifold sub-stages or "transitional forms."

The recognition of new or unforeseen historical stages or transitional forms in the dialectical movement of history is the most delicate and crucial problem of "creative Marxism," since Soviet policy must be based on a constantly changing historical reality and its strategy is subordinated to the dictates of each stage and varies geographically in accordance with different co-existing stages. Major doctrinal schisms arise whenever serious differences about the existence or nature of historical stages and their transitional forms cannot be reconciled. According to Stalin, Marxism is not

. . . a collection of dogmas that "never" change despite changes in the conditions of the development of society. . . . Marxism as a science cannot stand still, it develops and improves. In its development Marxism cannot but be enriched by new experience, new knowledge—consequently some of its formulae and conclusions cannot but change with the passage of time, cannot but be replaced by new formulae and conclusions, corresponding to new historical tasks. Marxism does not recognize invariable conclusions and formulae obligatory for all epochs and periods.[19]

Even seemingly unambiguous concepts like "inevitability" are neither absolute nor fatally deterministic, but must be understood within the context of a particular historical stage and under given conditions. Thus what may appear inevitable, viz., war, in one stage and under one set of conditions may no longer be inevitable if the conditions change or a new historical stage manifests itself. The single absolute is the abstraction of the dialectical movement itself; its content varies and hence is relativistic. Consequently, interpretation of Soviet dogma often assumes the character of tortured scholastic wrangling and frequently leads to tautological absurdities like "fatal inevitability," which presumably means inevitability in the absolute sense as differentiated from inevitability in the relative sense.

Soviet ideology is not self-executing; that is, it does not interpret itself automatically and does not reflect images of reality that can be unambiguously perceived, but rather it is based upon an authoritative interpretation of changing events by the Soviet leaders, who must choose from among a variety of possible interpretations, only one of which can be tested at a time for truth in the crucible of action. As long as Stalin was alive, interpretation of doctrine was a monopoly reserved for him alone, and it was his interpretation, whether it was concerned with the materialistic basis of the thought processes of the deaf and dumb or with the nature of the state, that became the basis for official policy. All other pos-

sible interpretations were consigned to heretical oblivion, to be resurrected later by him or by his successors who silently disputed his conception of reality.

The two-camp image. Stalin's image of the world after the Russian Revolution was one of forced "co-existence" between a single socialist state and a hostile capitalist world surrounding it —a co-existence imposed upon both antagonists by objective historical conditions. Neither side being sufficiently powerful to end the existence of the other, they were fated to exist together temporarily on the basis of an unstable and constantly shifting balance of power:

The fundamental and new, the decisive feature, which has affected all the events in the sphere of foreign relations during this period, is the fact that a certain temporary equilibrium of forces has been established between our country . . . and the countries of the capitalist world; an equilibrium which has determined the present period of "peaceful co-existence.[20]

The establishment in a capitalist world of a socialist bridgehead, which was inevitably destined to envelop the entire globe was, for Stalin, the supreme and ineluctable contradiction in the international scene. Although the capitalist world was infinitely stronger and could overwhelm the Soviet Republic if it could embark on a common enterprise, it was viewed as torn by internal divisions and conflicts that prevented the organization of an anti-Soviet crusade. Beside the over-riding contradiction between the Socialist camp and the capitalist camp, the bourgeois world was plagued with four additional inescapable contradictions: (1) the con-

[19] J. V. Stalin, *Concerning Marxism in Linguistics* (London: Soviet News, 1950), pp. 39–40.

[20] J. V. Stalin, *Political Report of the Central Committee to the 14th Congress of the C.P.S.U. (B)* (Moscow: 1950), p. 8.

tradiction between the proletariat and the bourgeoisie in each country; (2) the contradiction between the revisionist and *status quo* powers (Stalin referred to them as "victor" and "vanquished" capitalist states); (3) the contradiction between the victorious powers over the spoils of war; (4) the contradiction between the imperialist states and their colonial subjects.

The contradiction between the socialist and capitalist camps was considered by Stalin the most fundamental and decisive, but it was not to be aggravated so long as the Soviet Union was in a weakened condition. War between the two camps was viewed as inevitable; however, it could be temporarily avoided and delayed by astute maneuvering within the conflicts raging in the capitalist world:

England's attempts to form a united front against the U.S.S.R. have failed so far. The reasons for this failure are: the antagonisms of interests in the camp of the imperialists. . . . Hence the task of taking into account the antagonisms in the camp of the imperialists, of postponing war by "buying off" the capitalists. . . . We must not forget what Lenin said about very much in our work of construction depending upon whether we succeed in postponing war with the capitalist world, which is inevitable, but which can be postponed either until the moment when the proletarian revolution in Europe matures, or until the moment when the colonial revolutions have fully matured, or, lastly, until the moment when the capitalists fight among themselves over the division of the colonies.[21]

During Stalin's lifetime, despite his periodic strictures against "dogmatism," his image of the two-camp world remained remarkably fixed, although

[21] J. V. Stalin, *Political Report . . . to the 15th Congress* (Moscow, 1950), pp. 29–30.

the center of the developing anti-Soviet crusade passed first from England to Nazi Germany and finally to the United States, which he had predicted as early as 1925 would become the final bastion of world capitalism. Although this image of reality failed to apprise correctly the nature and motivations of Nazi Germany and incorrectly assumed the impossibility of a Soviet alliance with the Western Powers, Stalin's fixed vision of "two camps" poised in uneasy co-existence dominated Soviet diplomacy in the postwar period, becoming even more indelibly etched in Soviet ideology.

Stalin's postwar policy was predicted upon an inevitable conflict with the West, organized by the United States. The organization of the Cominform and the forced unity of the Communist orbit, the expulsion of Tito from the Communist fraternity, the extraction of public statements of loyalty from Communist leaders in all countries, the urgency with which Stalin sought to eliminate all possible power vacuums between the two blocs along the periphery of the Communist world, all were preparatory measures based on the false assumption that the American ruling class was betraying anxiety at the growth of Soviet power and was preparing the final Armageddon. At the founding convention of the Cominform the late Andrei Zhdanov revealed the authoritative Soviet interpretation of the emerging bipolarization of power:

The fundamental changes caused by the war on the international scene and in the position of individual countries have entirely changed the political landscape of the world. A new alignment of political forces has arisen. The more the war recedes into the past, the more distinct become two major trends in postwar international policy, corresponding to the division of the political forces operating on the international arena into two major camps; the imperialist and antidemocratic camp, on the one hand, and the anti-imperialist and democratic camp, on the other. The principal driving force of the imperialist camp is the U.S.A. . . . The cardinal purpose of the imperialist camp is to strengthen imperialism, to hatch a new imperialist war, to combat Socialism.[22]

Based on this grim image of the imminent expectation of violence, Soviet foreign policy assumed increasingly bellicose tendencies, which, in turn, evoked the natural response in the West that the Soviet Union, itself, was preparing to overrun Western Europe and all of Asia. Friction all along the periphery dividing the two worlds was frequent and finally erupted in the Korean war, when Stalin sanctioned the move into South Korea on the assumption that it had become a vacuum between the two blocs. This action accelerated defensive preparations in the West, and Stalin's policies, by predicting the increasing hostility of the West, actually forced its materialization.

During the Korean war and just prior to the 19th Party Congress in 1952, a "great debate" had apparently taken place in the Politburo concerning the validity of the expectation of imminent war between the two camps. Two essentially divergent views were petulantly discussed by Stalin in his *Economic Problems of Socialism:* (1) that wars between capitalist countries had ceased to be inevitable and hence war between the two camps was imminent, the view that was then current; and (2) that wars between capitalist states remained inevitable, but that war between the two camps was unlikely.

Although the first view was the basis of Soviet postwar policy, Stalin ascribed it to "mistaken comrades," and elevated the second to doctrinal significance:

Some comrades hold that, owing to the development of new international conditions since the Second World War, wars between the capitalist countries have ceased to be inevitable. They consider . . . that the U.S.A. has brought the other capitalist countries sufficiently under its sway to be able to prevent them going to war among themselves and . . . that the foremost capitalist minds have been sufficiently taught by the two world wars . . . not to involve the capitalist countries in war with one another again. . . . It is said that the contradictions between capitalism and socialism are stronger than the contradictions among the capitalist countries. Theoretically, of course that is true. It is not only true now, today; it was true before the Second World War. . . . Yet the Second World War began not as a war with the U.S.S.R., but as a war between capitalist countries. Why? . . . because war with the U.S.S.R., as a socialist land, is more dangerous to capitalism than war between capitalist countries; for whereas war between capitalist countries puts in question only the supremacy of certain capitalist countries over others, war with the U.S.S.R. must certainly put in question the existence of capitalism itself. . . . It is said that Lenin's thesis that imperialism inevitably generates war must now be regarded as obsolete. . . . That is not true. . . . To eliminate the inevitability of war, it is necessary to abolish imperialism.[23]

Stalin's only modification of his two-camp image was thus to concede that

[22] Full text reprinted in *Strategy and Tactics of World Communism* (Washington, D.C.: G.P.O., 1948), pp. 216–217.

[23] J. V. Stalin, *Economic Problems of Socialism* (New York: International Publishers, 1952), pp. 27–30.

imminent war between the two blocs was no longer inevitable, but would first be preceded by a series of inevitable wars among the capitalist powers themselves—between the United States and its satellite allies, France and Brittain, and its temporary vassals, Germany and Japan, whose ruling classes' resentment at American domination would provoke "national revolutions" and a renewed war over the ever-shrinking capitalist market, occasioned by the emergence of a "parallel" Communist market, which would remain outside the arena of capitalist exploitation. The Soviet Union would remain outside the conflict, which would automatically seal the doom of world capitalism. Stalin's policies actually accentuated the very conflict—that between the two camps—he wished to temporarily de-emphasize, while submerging those—among the capitalist states—which he wished to exacerbate. Soviet policy, by predicting war, was threatening to make a nuclear holocaust, which would destroy both worlds, inevitable.

The post-Stalin image. Stalin's image of reality was first challenged by Tito in 1948 and apparently later by his own colleagues on the Politburo. Khrushchev admitted that these differences were so serious that Stalin was plotting to liquidate all of his old associates for daring to question his ideological infallibility. Stalin's obstinate refusal to keep in step with changing conditions resulted in converting Soviet ideology from a prism that reflected reality into a prison that concealed it, resulting not only in a series of diplomatic blunders, but also in blinding Moscow to new diplomatic opportunities. As the man, next to Stalin, most closely associated with Soviet foreign policy, Molotov confessed on behalf of his departed chief:

We do not infrequently still remain prisoners of habits and patterns formed in the past, before World War II, and which now hinder the deployment of new, wider, and more active forms of struggle. . . . We not infrequently still suffer from underestimation of the new possibilities which have opened before us in the postwar period. . . . We must stop underestimating the immense possibilities which we have. . . . In the field of foreign policy our Party proceeds from the need for the most serious consideration of concrete conditions and from the need for understanding the given situation ad the prospects of historic development. The Leninist combination of adherence to principle and elasticity in pursuance of the foreign policy line is the factor which insures success for our Party in the solution of internal tasks.[24]

At the 20th Party Congress, Stalin's image of the world was considerably modified in an attempt to bring it into closer focus with the realities of international politics. These modifications were made to eliminate the threatening schisms in the Communist camp, to break up the unity of the non-Soviet world and dismantle anti-Soviet instruments like NATO, to head off the impending nuclear war that Stalin's doctrines and policies were unwittingly encouraging, and to enhance the flexibility of Soviet diplomacy in exploiting the contradictions of the capitalist world.

In place of Stalin's fatalistic image of a bipolarized world, the 20th Party Congress drew a more optimistic, and, in many respects, a mellower picture:

1. "Capitalist encirclement" was officially declared terminated as major speakers like Molotov echoed the Titoist

[24] Full text as broadcast by the Moscow Radio, February 20, 1956; *cf.* also *The New York Times,* February 21, 1956.

doctrine that "the period when the Soviet Union was . . . encircled by hostile capitalism now belongs to the past." [25] The permanent insecurity of the Soviet Union, pending the world-wide victory of Communism, as visualized by Stalin, was replaced with the image of a permanently secured Soviet Union, surrounded by friendly Communist states in Europe and Asia, embracing nearly one-third of the world, with imperialism in an irrevocable state of advanced decay.

2. In place of Stalin's fixed vision of "co-existence" between two irreconcilable camps poised in temporary balance, which was declared obsolete and inapplicable to the postwar world, his successors recognized a third "anti-imperialist" but nonsocialist group of powers carved out of decaying colonial empires, which had separated from the capitalist camp but had not yet joined the Communist. Stalin's inflexible two-camp image needlessly alienated these new states and tended to force them into the capitalist orbit. This belt of neutralist states—a concept which Stalin refused to recognize —insulated the entire Communist orbit from the capitalist world and, together with the socialist states, was viewed as constituting "an extensive 'zone of peace,' including both socialist and nonsocialist peace-loving states of Europe and Asia inhabited by nearly 1,500,000,000 people, or the majority of the population of our planet." [26]

3. Stalin's doctrine of the "fatal inevitability" of wars was pronounced antiquated, since its emphasis on coercive and violent instruments of diplomacy tended to render the Soviet peace campaign hypocritical, accelerated the formation of anti-Soviet coalitions, and, in an era of nuclear weapons, appeared to doom both worlds to a war of mutual annihilation. Soviet leaders, however, continue to go through the motions of insisting that war would result only in the unilateral extinction of capitalism, although it is unlikely that they really believe this.

4. Stalin's five main contradictions were retained as valid and persistent, but the radical shift in the equilibrium of class forces in the world dictated a change of emphasis and the reordering of priorities. Stalin stressed the conflicts among the major capitalist countries as the main object of Soviet diplomacy, relegating other contradictions to minor roles, but his successors see the main contradiction of the current historical stage to be that between the anticolonial and the imperialist forces. Just as "antifascism" was the key to the weakening of the prewar capitalist world, in the current phase, "anticolonialism" is viewed as promising the most successful possibilities for Soviet diplomacy. The sudden Soviet solicitude for Arab aspirations, the spectacular gestures to the countries of Southeast Asia, the conspicuous and indiscriminate support given to the anticolonial bloc in the United Nations, all are manifestations of the conviction that by harnessing the energies of the nationalistic anticolonial countries to the Soviet chariot, the capitalist world will be effectively isolated and more easily liquidated. In short, the world has moved out of the stage of the "capitalist encirclement" of the Soviet Union and during the current phase of "co-existence" is moving into the stage of the "socialist encirclement" of the United States as a prelude to the final victory of Communism.

The new image of the world drawn by Khrushchev at the 20th Party Congress was by no means the consequence of a unanimous decision, but was opposed by at least four and possibly five full members of the eleven-man Presid-

---

[25] *Ibid.*

[26] Full text as broadcast by Moscow Radio, February 18, 1956; *cf.* also *The New York Times,* February 19, 1956 (Mikoyan Report).

ium. Aside from his vigorous opposition to Krushchev's adventurist innovations in industry and agriculture, Foreign Minister Molotov and the so-called Stalinist faction bitterly resisted the demolition of the Stalin myth and the entire de-Stalinization program; and they systematically sabotaged the foreign policy decisions of the 20th Party Congress, which they publicly accepted.

Molotov's disagreement with the Khrushchev faction was not merely over the execution of foreign policy but over fundamental doctrinal propositions as well. Thus he disputed the thesis on the "fatal inevitability of wars" that was one of the key decisions of the Party Congress. "Comrade Molotov," according to the resolution of the Central Committee which expelled him from the Presidium on June 29, 1957, "opposed the fundamental proposition worked out by the party on the possibility of preventing wars in the present condition." Furthermore, he controverted the Titoist doctrine "on the possibility of different ways of transition to socialism in different countries," and resisted the decision "on the necessity of strengthening contacts between the CPSU and the progressive parties abroad [i.e. non-Communist socialist parties]." [27]

Molotov's doctrinal differences had practical consequences in the actual formulation and execution of foreign policy. His constant carping criticism of existing policies, together with the precarious nature of Khrushchev's majority in the Presidium, introduced an uncharacteristic hesitancy into Soviet diplomacy. The vacillations, abrupt reversals, hesitations, discrepancies between policy and administration, and other eccentricities of Soviet diplomacy after Stalin's death were due not only to the incapacitating incompatibilities in the Presidium, but also to Molotov's use of the Foreign Ministry and Soviet missions abroad as instruments to subvert the Government's policy in favor of his own.

Molotov strenuously objected to the decisions to seek a reconciliation with Marshal Tito and to meet President Eisenhower at Geneva. When Khrushchev and Bulganin returned from Geneva, Molotov was waiting with sarcastic and biting comments on their personal diplomacy. As a result of his persistent criticism and obstructionism, he was disciplined by the Central Committee in July 1955 and his "erroneous stand on the Yugoslav issue was unanimously condemned." This was followed shortly by his forced and pained confession of doctrinal error, which superficially appeared to have no connection with foreign policy but appeared designed to tarnish his ideological orthodoxy and was an unmistakeable sign that he was on his way out. His unrelenting sabotage through the Foreign Ministry, in particular his determination to poison relations with Tito, finally led to his ouster as foreign minister in favor of Shepilov on the eve of Tito's visit to Moscow in June 1956. Apparently Shepilov also fell out of sympathy with the foreign policy he was supposed to execute and for opportunistic reasons (Khrushchev scathingly characterized him as "the careerist Shepilov who . . . showed himself to be a most shameless double-dealer") cast his lot with the Stalinist faction. The Molotov group suddenly contrived a majority in the December 1956 Plenum of the Central Committee, but when Khrushchev regained it at the February 1957 Plenum, Shepilov was summarily dismissed as Foreign Minister in favor of Andrei Gromyko, who,

[27] Full text of the resolution reprinted in *The New York Times*, July 4, 1957. These and all subsequent references to this resolution are taken from this version.

as a professional diplomat, was neither able nor equipped to join the Kremlin power intrigues, and thus could be counted upon not to pursue a personal foreign policy.

In the bill of particulars against Molotov, who was supported most consistently by Kaganovich and sometimes by Malenkov, there was revealed an almost complete alternative foreign policy to the one currently adopted by the Soviet Government, one that in effect unwittingly constitutes the platform of a "disloyal opposition." "In the sphere of foreign policy," according to the indictment, "the group, in particular Comrade Molotov, showed narrow-mindedness and hampered in every way the implementation of the new pressing measures intended to ease international tension and promote universal peace." It was charged:

1. "For a long time, Comrade Molotov in his capacity as Foreign Minister, far from taking through the Ministry of Foreign Affairs measures to improve relations between the U.S.S.R. and Yugoslavia, repeatedly came out against the measures that the Presidium . . . was carrying out to improve relations with Yugoslavia.

2. "Comrade Molotov raised obstacles to the conclusion of the state Treaty with Austria and the improvement of relations with that country, which lies in the center of Europe. The conclusion of the Austrian Treaty was largely instrumental in lessening international tension in general.

3. "He was also against normalization of relations with Japan, while that normalization has played an important part in relaxing international tension in the Far East.

4. "Comrade Molotov repeatedly opposed the Soviet Government's indispensable new steps in defence of peace and security of nations. In particular he

denied the advisability of establishing personal contacts between the Soviet leaders and the statesmen of other countries, which is essential for the achievement of mutual understanding and better international relations [probably a reference not only to the Geneva Conference but also to the various junkets of Bulganin and Khrushchev throughout Asia and Europe, none of which included Foreign Minister Molotov]."

Beside these publicly stated charges against Molotov, it was reported from Warsaw that Khrushchev admitted in the Central Committee that Dulles was "practically right" when he accused Moscow of "trying for months to torpedo the disarmament talks," but he qualified this by saying that "it was not the Soviet Union that tried to torpedo the talks but Molotov, Kaganovich, and Shepilov." [28] He also accused Molotov of enflaming relations with other Communist parties, probably those of China, Poland, Japan, Italy, and the United States.

"Molotov," Khrushchev bluntly stated in a later speech, "found more convenient a policy of tightening all screws, which contradicts the wise Leninist policy of peaceful co-existence." [29] Thus, it can be assumed that Molotov advocated a continuation of the basic foreign policies of the Stalinist era, as modified during the Malenkov regime, based on a perpetuation of the two-camp image. It was Molotov's contention that Soviet policy could reap its greatest dividends by maintaining international tensions at a high pitch and running the risks of nuclear war on the assumption that an uncompromising, cold-blooded policy would force Western statesmen, through lack of nerve and under pressure of public opinion, to continually retreat in the

[28] *The New York Times,* July 6, 1957.
[29] *The New York Times,* July 7, 1957.

face of Soviet provocation for fear of triggering a war of mutual extinction. It appears that he considered as un-Marxist the idea that the ex-colonial countries could be regarded as having deserted the capitalist camp and as constituting an "extensive zone of peace" together with the Soviet bloc, but rather he considered their behavior in international politics to be motivated purely by considerations of opportunism and expediency. The main arena of rivalry for Molotov remained in Western Europe and the Atlantic area —the bastions of capitalism—and not in Asia or Africa, and he continued to view the new countries of Asia and Africa with hostility and suspicion as appendages to the capitalist camp.

Molotov's policy of "tightening all screws" was opposed by the Soviet Army and also by Peking, which seems to have played an influential role in reorienting Soviet policy eastwards. Speaking in Peking, Anastas Mikoyan, reputedly the principal Kremlin architect of the new Soviet diplomatic strategy, invoked Lenin in support of the current policy. Quoting Lenin's famous formula that "in the last analysis, the outcome of the struggle will be determined by the fact that Russia, India, China, etc. constitute the overwhelming majority of the world's population," he roundly condemned the Stalinist two-camp image to which Molotov still subscribed:

We must consider it harmful that all countries not belonging to the socialist system are sometimes put in the same category and then are mechanically included in the capitalist camp. . . . The paths which are now being followed and blazed by India, Burma, Indonesia, Egypt and other countries which have won their independence have a general international significance. . . . The development of these countries and their

policies weaken imperialism, deepen the crises in the capitalist system, destroy colonialism as one of the mainstays of this system and hasten the end of capitalism.[30]

Soviet diplomatic strategy in the underdeveloped countries of Asia, Africa and Latin-America appears to contradict the basic revolutionary strategy of Communism. Although Moscow's support of the so-called "bourgeois-nationalist" (roughly "neutralist" under existing conditions) independence or revolutionary movements in the underdeveloped regions (colonies and "semi-colonies") against Western colonialism, economic dependence upon the West and internal feudalism, is fully compatible with Leninist-Stalinist doctrine on revolution in the under-developed world, the Khrushchev pattern of political and economic assistance to local "bourgeois-nationalist" (roughly "neutralist" in foreign policy) regimes like those in India, Egypt, Iraq, Ghana and to a lesser extent, Cuba, does not fully conform to Communist doctrine. Red China has stepped into this breach and has challenged Moscow's refusal to encourage and support indigenous Communist parties in their efforts to overthrow native "bourgeois-nationalist" governments and establish authentic Communist controlled regimes. Instead, according to Peking, Moscow supports governments which persecute and imprison local Communists.

The Soviet position on this point is extraordinarily non-doctrinaire and pragmatic, for whereas China stresses the view that the Communist Party is the only reliable instrument of revolution, Khrushchev appears to be toying with the idea that under favorable circumstances, particularly when the balance of power has shifted decisively

[30] *Pravda,* September 18, 1956.

in favor of the Communist world, native bourgeois-nationalist leaders may be won over to Communism and the revolution could be consummated from above rather than below. As a practical diplomatic position, Moscow feels that any move to encourage Communist insurrection in these areas would simply stampede them all into the capitalist and anti-Communist camp, a developement which Peking considers—along with Molotov—as inevitable in any event. Peking's present strategy seems to be a conviction that the bourgeois nationalists will betray Khrushchev (as Chiang Kai-shek betrayed Stalin in 1928) and that by supporting the local Communist parties now, China can expect to earn their gratitude and support later on.

THE FORMULATION OF SOVIET FOREIGN POLICY

Introduction

Any attempt to describe the formulation of Soviet foreign policy in the crucibles of its decision-making organs is bound to be a hazardous and frustrating enterprise. The absence of periodic or systematic publication of documents, the inaccessibility of archives and officials, the virtual nonexistence of memoirs or diaries of retiring statesmen, the puzzling duplication of state and party institutions, the perplexing fluctuations in their relationships, the ambiguity of Soviet ideology and the wide discrepancy between theory and practice, the bewildering profusion of constitutional and institutional changes, the arbitrary tendency to ignore or short-circuit elaborately detailed institutional channels, and, finally, the capricious and convulsive turnover of personalities, are the more familiar impediments that must be contended with.

The decision-making process itself is a dynamic interaction between institutions and personalities, whose character varies with the effectiveness of institutions to impose limits on the acts of individuals. In constitutional states, characterized by relatively permanent institutions, the restraints upon officials are carefully defined, imposing ineluctable limits not only on the range of policy formulation but upon the choice of means as well. In a totalitarian system like the Soviet Union, where the impermanently rooted institutions are subordinated to relatively permanent personalities, the institutional aspects of the decision-making process are little more than ceremonial, in which case decision-making is essentially personal and bound to vary with the evolution of the ideological convictions, character, and judgment of the personalities in control of the levers of power, the nature of the rivalries between them, and, finally, their reaction to the internal and external political and social pressures that bear upon them.

The Soviet political superstructure, during most of its existence, was a complicated mosaic of shifting and interlocking institutions resting upon an entrenched foundation of one-man dictatorship, in which all powers were delegated from above. The institutions of both Party and State, as well as their relationship to one another, were essentially creatures of the late Joseph Stalin and were designed, not to limit his own power, but to limit that of his subordinates and rivals, and to facilitate the solidification of his own authority. As the instruments of his creation and manipulation, they could not, and did not, function as restraints upon his latitude of decision. Both institutions and subordinates were liquidated with remarkable dispatch when the occasion demanded.

The system of duplicating and overlapping political organs between the Party and State allegedly reflects a division of functions between the formulation and execution of policy, with policy formulation a monopoly reserved exclusively for the Party, while the function of the government was to be restricted to formalizing and legalizing the decisions of the Party into official acts of state. This dichotomy was never either rigid or absolute, but constantly varied in accordance with the degree of interlocking of personnel at the summits of the Party and State hierarchy.

The Party Congress

In theory the most exalted, but in practice the most degraded of the central Party institutions in the formulation of policy is the Party Congress. Traditionally the most important fundamental pronouncements on foreign policy have been made before the Party Congress, which is empowered to set the basic "line" of the Party and State, but in actual fact merely hears and rubber-stamps the decisions made elsewhere. All higher organs of the Party, including the Presidium and Secretariat, are responsible and accountable to the Party Congress which theoretically can remove and replace their membership.

The role of the Congress in foreign policy has actually varied throughout its existence. Under Lenin, and, in fact, as late as the 16th Party Congress (1930), serious debate on foreign policy and international revolutionary strategy frequently ensued, although never with the same intensity or wide range of diversity as on domestic policy. Because of its massive size (nearly 2,000 delegates), the Congress became increasingly unwieldy as an organ of debate and discussion, and it gradually

was converted into a forum which heard various sides and finally into a subdued sounding board for Stalin's deadly rhetoric. Discussion and debate first slipped behind the doors of the Central Committee and eventually vanished into the Politburo. All decisions were made in the Politburo, then reported to the Central Committee and, with increasing infrequency, to the Party Congress. The principal function of the Party Congress was reduced to the hearing of reports by the prominent figures of the Party.

The two most important reports to Party Congresses relating to foreign policy are the Main Political Report of the Central Committee, delivered in the past by Stalin (except at the 19th Congress), and a report on the activities of the World Communist Movement. At the 19th Congress, Malenkov delivered the Main Report, while Stalin restricted himself to a few enigmatic remarks to foreign Communist representatives at the close of the session. However, Stalin had ordered published his *Economic Problems of Socialism* on the eve of the Congress and this set the tone and dominated the entire proceedings of the Congress. At the 20th Congress, Khrushchev delivered the Main Report, incorporating radical doctrinal innovations affecting foreign policy, while Molotov confined himself to praising reluctantly the new policy and resentfully subjecting his own past conduct of foreign policy to self-criticism. The activities of foreign Communist parties were reported by their own representatives.

A close examination of the Main Political Reports betrays an almost rigid uniformity in organization. The entire first section is devoted to international affairs; an authoritative interpretation of the world situation; an appraisal of the Soviet position; trends, developments, and opportunities to watch for; warnings, threats, boasts, and invitations to bourgeois powers; congratulations and words of praise for friendly countries; and, finally, a summary of the immediate and long-range objectives of Soviet foreign policy. This report sets the line to guide Communists everywhere in their activities, and, thus, the Congress becomes not a forum for debate, but a unique medium of communication.

Debate and discussion vanished after 1930, and meetings of the Congress became less frequent until they threatened to vanish altogether. In his secret speech to the 20th Congress, Khrushchev gave this vivid description of the deterioration of the Party Congress.

During Lenin's life, party congresses were convened regularly; always when a radical turn in the development of the party and country took place, Lenin considered it absolutely necessary that the party discuss at length all basic matters pertaining to . . . foreign policy. . . . Whereas during the first years after Lenin's death, party congresses . . . took place more or less regularly, later . . . these principles were brutally violated. . . . Was it a normal situation when over 13 years [1939–1952] elapsed between the Eighteenth and Nineteenth Congresses? . . . Of 1,966 delegates [to the 17th Congress in 1934] with either voting or advisory rights, 1,108 persons were arrested on charges of revolutionary crimes.[31]

The Central Committee

As the body that "guides the entire work of the Party in the interval be-

tween Congresses . . . and . . . directs the work of the Central and Soviet public organizations [i.e., the government]," [32] the Central Committee became the principal arena of debate and discussion of foreign policy during the period preceding 1934. According to the Party rules at that time, the Politburo was obliged to report to this body at least three times a year, so that its decisions might be examined, criticized, and judged. The Central Committee elected the members of the Politburo, the Orgburo, and the Secretariat, and theoretically was empowered to appoint, remove, or replace its members. The Central Committee itself was elected by the Party Congress and was empowered to replace its members by a two-thirds vote, but this rule was rudely violated by Stalin who removed and appointed members of the Central Committee virtually at will.

On some occasions the Foreign Commissar—who invariably is at least a full member of the Central Committee—as well as high Soviet functionaries of the Comintern reported to the Central Committee on foreign policy and international Communist activities. More often, the Secretary-General (Stalin) would deliver a report on the nature and scope of the Politburo's work and explain the precise application of the "line" under changing international conditions. A fairly large body, composed of full members and alternate members (about equally divided), it was empowered to alter the policies of the Politburo and support the views of the minority. Only full members exercised the right of vote, while candidates had the right to participate in debate. Some of these reports, but not all, were made public, particularly if important modifications

---

[31] This extract and all subsequent references to Khrushchev's secret report to the 20th Congress are taken from the full text published in *The New York Times*, June 5, 1956. The speech has been widely reprinted elsewhere.

[32] *The Land of Socialism Today and Tomorrow* (Moscow: International Publishers, 1939), p. 473.

of the policies announced at the previous Party Congress were made. The records of the Committee's proceedings remain generally unpublished and inaccessible for examination.

The Central Committee too, in time, was reduced to little more than a sounding board; its meetings became increasingly infrequent, and there is little reason to believe that after 1934 its decisions were anything less than unanimous. According to Khrushchev:

> Even after the end of the war . . . Central Committee plenums were hardly ever called. It should be sufficient to mention that during the years of the Patriotic War [World War II] not a single Central Committee plenum took place. . . . Stalin did not even want to meet and talk with Central Committee members. . . . Of the 139 members and candidates of the Party's Central Committee who were elected at the Seventeenth Party Congress [1934], 98 persons, i.e. 70 per cent, were arrested and shot.

The Party Presidium (formerly the Politburo)

There is no question but that the most important organ of decision-making in the Soviet Union has been, and continues to be, the Presidium of the Party. In accordance with the principle of "democratic centralism," the ultimate power of the Party is entrusted to this organ. Its internal organization and recruiting procedures, the composition and convictions of its factions, and its voting practices remain essentially a mystery. No proceedings of its deliberations have been made public in decades, and, in the absence of any recent defections from this body, information concerning its procedures and activities can be derived only from the following sources: (1) fragmentary records of very early meetings; (2) public ex-

posure of its deliberations by Leon Trotsky and other rivals of Stalin during the period before 1930; (3) accounts by high-ranking diplomats or government and Party officials, whose activities brought them into close range of the Politburo, and who have defected from the Soviet Union; (4) personal accounts and memoirs of foreign statesmen who negotiated with members of the Politburo or with Stalin; (5) accounts of renegade officials of the Comintern and foreign Communist parties; (6) secrets spilled as a result of the Stalin-Tito feud; (7) Khrushchev's secret speech at the 20th Party Congress and its aftermath; (8) calculated leaks by the Polish Party and government since the rise of Gomulka; (9) examination of the decisions already taken; (10) rare public disputes between leading press organs of the Party and government; (11) shifts in Party and governmental officials; and (12) rare Central Committee Resolutions like that of June 29, 1957.

Under Stalin, all decisions of the Politburo on questions of foreign policy were in essence his, in one form or another. All rival and dissident views were quashed and their adherents liquidated. The membership of the body was hand-picked by him. In his relations with the Politburo, Stalin could either announce his decisions and expect unanimous approval, submit them for examination and ask for discussion with or without a vote, simply act without consulting his colleagues, or consult with various members on certain questions to the exclusion of others. According to a former Soviet diplomat, who was an eyewitness to some Politburo meetings in 1933:

> A thin appearance of collective work is still kept up at Politburo meetings. Stalin does not "command." He merely

"suggests" or "proposes." The fiction of voting is retained. But the vote never fails to uphold his "suggestions." The decision is signed by all ten members of the Politburo, with Stalin's signature among the rest. . . . The other members of the Politburo mumble their approval of Stalin's "proposal." . . . Stalin not only is generally called "the Boss" by the whole bureaucracy, but *is* the one and only boss.[33]

This general description of Stalin's style of work has been confirmed many times by diplomats and statesmen of many countries who observed that Stalin often made important decisions without consulting anyone, while Molotov and others would request time to consult with their "government." In the realm of decision-making, the role of the other members of the Politburo could best be described as consultative, although within the area of their own administrative responsibility they exercised the power of decision. Testimony concerning Stalin's intolerance of dissent is uniformly consistent. "Whoever opposed . . . his viewpoint," complained Khrushchev, "was doomed to be removed."

The relationship between the Foreign Ministry and the Presidium has always been unique. Since relations with other states are viewed in terms of a struggle for power among various "ruling classes," and thus directly involve the security and the very existence of the Soviet state, the Party center has always retained a tight supervision over the Foreign Ministry.

This supervision assumes different forms, depending upon the Party rank of the individuals who hold the posts of Foreign Minister and of Premier. The Premier has always been a Party figure of the highest rank, while the Foreign Minister may or may not be a member of the Party Presidium.

During the period when Maxim Litvinov was Foreign Commissar, his work was supervised by Molotov, the Premier of the government and his formal superior. Matters of routine interest, not involving questions of policy or fundamental maneuver, were decided by Litvinov himself in consultation with his collegium. More substantial questions were taken to Molotov, who, depending upon the nature of the question, would make a decision, or take it to the Politburo.[34]

The Politburo itself was broken down into various Commissions dealing with different aspects of policy. Questions of foreign policy were first considered by the Politburo Commission on Foreign Affairs, which included the Politburo specialists on the Comintern, Foreign Trade, and Defense. In matters involving exceptional or immediate importance, Molotov would deal directly with Stalin and get a decision.

The procedures of the Politburo were neither systematic nor rigid. Often Stalin would personally consult with the Foreign Commissar and his chief advisers; and Litvinov, on a few occasions, would be asked to make a report to the Politburo. The principle function of the Commission on Foreign Affairs was to act as a coordinating agency of all the departments concerned with foreign relations, to assemble and evaluate intelligence in-

[33] Alexander Barmine, *One Who Survived* (New York: Putnam, 1946), p. 213. "thousands of relatively unimportant, as well as all-important, problems," writes Barmine, "must pass through Stalin's hand for final decision. . . . Weeks are spent in waiting; Commissars wait in Stalin's office."

[34] *Cf.* Merle Fainsod, *How Russia Is Ruled* (Cambridge, Mass.: Harvard University Press, 1953), p. 282.

formation flowing from different channels, to devise strategy and policy, examine analyses, projects, and reports drawn up by specialists in the Foreign Commissariat, study reports of diplomats abroad, and then make a comprehensive report either to Stalin or to the Politburo as a whole.

Once the decisions were made, they would be transmitted in writing or verbally by Molotov to Litvinov for execution. These bureaucratic channels were often ignored and Stalin would act directly with Molotov, his principal agent, and they would personally give instructions to Litvinov. Deviation or improvisation from instructions by the Foreign Commissar or his subordinates in the Commissariat was neither permitted nor tolerated. According to Khrushchev, the system of Politburo Commissions was not primarily for organizational efficiency, but was a sinister device whereby Stalin weakened the authority of the collective body:

The importance of the . . . Political Bureau was reduced and its work disorganized by the creation within the Political Bureau of various commissions —the so-called "quintets," "sextets," "septets" and "novenaries."

When Molotov replaced Litvinov in May, 1939, this cumbersome procedure was simplified. The Nazi-Soviet Pact was worked out principally by Stalin and Molotov, with Zhdanov and Mikoyan the only other members of the Politburo apparently appraised of the crucial decisions contemplated. The Politburo Commission on Foreign Affairs gradually increased in size until, by 1945, it was large enough to be converted by Stalin from a "sextet" into a "septet." As it grew in size, so its importance diminished. During the war,

Stalin appeared to consult only Molotov on questions of foreign policy and frequently made decisions on the spot at the Big Three conferences.

Although Khrushchev reported that "during Stalin's leadership our peaceful relations with other nations were often threatened, because one-man decisions could cause and often did cause great complications," he failed to elaborate. He specifically accused Stalin of personally making the decision to break with Marshal Tito, while Walter Ulbricht, the German Communist leader, reported that Stalin's arbitrary policies almost drove Mao Tse-tung out of the Soviet orbit. After Stalin's death the Korean war was halted, the demands on Turkey withdrawn with appropriate apologies, Soviet interference in Manchuria arrested, the rift with Tito ended, the bases in Finland evacuated, and a number of other reversals of Stalinist policies undertaken. Molotov's complicity in these decisions remains obscure, but since he was in charge of foreign affairs during most of the period concerned, and in view of his expulsion from the Presidium, he probably played an important consultative role.

Khrushchev's description of how decisions were made by Stalin and the Politburo is probably exaggerated and self-serving, but accurate in its general outline:

After the war, Stalin became even more capricious, irritable, and brutal; in particular his suspicion grew. His persecution mania reached unbelievable dimensions. Everything was decided by him alone without any consideration for anyone or anything. . . . Sessions of the Political Bureau occurred only occasionally . . . many decisions were taken by one person or in a roundabout way, without collective discussion. . . . The importance of the Political Bureau was reduced and its work disorganized by the creation within the Political Bureau of various commissions. . . . The result of this was that some members of the Political Bureau were in this way kept away from participation in the decisions of the most important state matters.

Decision-making in the post-Stalin period: the agonies of collective leadership

The death of Stalin stimulated the expression of various opinions and unleashed a struggle for power among his successors. Six months before his death, at the 19th Party Congress, Stalin radically reorganized the Party summit, abolishing the Orgburo and replacing the 11-man Politburo with a Presidium of 25 full members and 11 candidate members as the key decision-making organ of the Soviet system. Since many of the new members of the Presidium were burdened with permanent administrative responsibilities far from Moscow, and since it was much too large to function as a decision-making body, there was secretly organized, in violation of the new Party charter, a smaller Bureau of the Presidium, whose membership has never been revealed. Whether expansion of the Presidium was designed by Stalin to widen the area of decision-making and prevent a struggle for power after his death—thus preparing the conditions for orderly transition from personal to institutional dictatorship—or whether it was a sinister device for liquidating his old associates in favor of a generation ignorant of his crimes, remains an intriguing enigma. According to Khrushchev:

Stalin evidently had plans to finish off the old members of the Political Bureau. . . . His proposal after the 19th Congress, concerning the selection of 25 persons to the Central Committee's Presidium, was aimed at the removal of the old Political Bureau members and the bringing in of less experienced persons so that they would extol him. . . . We can assume that this was a design for the future annihilation of the old Political Bureau members, and in this way, a cover for all the shameful acts of Stalin.

Immediately after Stalin's death, with utter contempt for the elaborate institutional rituals devised at the 19th Congress, the old members of Stalin's entourage repudiated his handiwork. As the principal aspirants to Stalin's power maneuvered against one another under the ideological umbrella of "collective leadership," the Presidium was summarily reduced to its former size. The removal of Beria and the dismantling of his secret police apparatus introduced an uneasy equilibrium among the various factions in the Presidium, none of which was powerful enough to overwhelm the others.

In the post-Stalin Presidium, decisions have been taken only after stormy controversies and agile maneuvering among the various factions, which have been posed in uneasy and rapidly fluctuating equilibrium. As a consequence, necessity was converted into ideology and conflicting opinions, within carefully circumscribed limits, were given official sanction:

Clash of opinions, on a foundation of Marxist-Leninist principles, must be thoroughly encouraged and developed . . . [but] within the framework of allegiance to the Party and Marxism—a clash in the course of which incorrect tenets and conclusions are rejected and a common viewpoint worked out.[35]

[35] *Kommunist* (No. 10), August 1956, pp. 3–13.

At the same time, the authoritative theoretical journal, *Kommunist,* warned that "views that are objectively directed toward dethroning the leadership elected by the Party masses," would not be tolerated. This danger is adumbrated in the Party Statutes, Article 28 of which reads:

A broad discussion, in particular on an all-Union scale concerning the Party policy, should be so organized that it would not result in the attempts of an insignificant minority to impose its will on the majority of the Party or in attempts to organize fractional groupings which would break down Party unity, or in attempts to create a schism that would undermine the strength and the firmness of the socialist regime.[36]

Diversity and clash of opinion have not been permitted to filter down below the level of the Central Committee (and even in this body they are carefully manipulated), for if the factional divisions in the Presidium should crack the Party pyramid down to its base, it would be impossible short of reestablishing one-man rule to prevent an eventual evolution towards a two or more party system operating within the framework of the Marxist-Leninist ideology. Already such an evolution has approached a crucial stage in the Polish Communist Party.

Decisions in the Presidium, whose proceedings remain unpublished, are reached by simple majority, with only full members entitled to vote, although alternate members participate in the debate and discussion. Meetings of the Presidium are regularly held at least once a week, and according to both Khrushchev and Mikoyan most decisions are unanimous. Mikoyan has further elaborated by stating that if a consensus were unobtainable, the Presidium would adjourn, sleep on the matter, and return for further discussion until unanimity was achieved. Since 5 full members out of 11 were expelled on June 29, 1957, for persistent opposition and obstruction to the Party line, the unanimity of the Presidium's deliberations appear to have been exaggerated.

In view of Khrushchev's bitter attack on the organization of Politburo Commissions under Stalin, the Presidium's internal compartmentalization may not be as rigidly demarcated as before, and foreign policy decisions, instead of being merely the concern of the Commission on Foreign Affairs, are discussed and made by the body as a whole. "Never in the past," Molotov sputtered regretfully at the 20th Party Congress, "has our Party Central Committee and its Presidium been engaged as actively with questions of foreign policy as during the present period." [37] The vitiating effects of Stalin's commission system, however, have been more than matched by the crystallization of factional groupings and cliques within the Party's highest body.

Under the Soviet one-party system, which does not permit the organization of an opposition with an alternative slate of leaders and policies, factional rivalry within the Party summit becomes a crude and primitive substitute for a two-party contest, while the relationship between the Central Committee and its Presidium constitutes the nearest approximation to a system of institutional responsibility and accountability.

The sharp and close divisions in the Presidium have revived the prominence and activity of the moribund Central

[36] *Pravda,* October 14, 1952.

[37] Molotov's speech at the 20th Congress; *cf.* footnote 24.

Committee. Factional differences have been displayed before Plenums of the Central Committee (at least twice a year) where the actions of the Presidium have been appealed by the opposition for reversal or revision. In this relatively large body of 133 full members and 122 alternates, discussion of the various views current in the Presidium is still more ritualized than free, with each faction in the Presidium supported by its own retinue of retainers in the Central Committee. Voting is conditioned not only by divisions in the Presidium but also by considerations of political survival and opportunism, with members being extremely sensitive to the course that the struggle assumes in the higher body. "At Plenums of the Central Committee," according to the revealing statement of one low-ranking member, "Comrade Khrushchev and other members of the Presidium . . . corrected errors in a fatherly way . . . regardless of post occupied or of record." [38]

It was in the Central Committee that Malenkov reputedly indicted Beria and where, in turn, he and Molotov were disciplined and attacked by the Khrushchev faction. Shifts in the balance of factions in the Presidium are almost always immediately registered in the Central Committee, whose proceedings inevitably sway with those of the higher body. The Central Committee, whose decisions are invariably reported as unanimous, is empowered to alter its own membership and that of its higher bodies by a two-thirds vote; and in the June 1957 Plenum it expelled three full members and one alternate from the Presidium and the Central Committee, demoted one to alternate status,

and cut off still another at full membership in the Central Committee. Correspondingly, the Presidium was expanded to 15 full members and nine alternates.

Since then it has met to expel Marshal Zhukov, Bulganin, Kirichenko and Belyayev (actually to confirm their expulsion) and to add Podgorny and Polyansky to membership in the Presidium. Now that factional groups have been eliminated, the Central Committee is no longer an arena of debate and maneuver, but simply a more selective organ for the confirmation of changes in personnel and policies, the announcement of new policies, and the coordination of administrative and executive action. It also serves as a meeting before which subordinates—those below Khrushchev—are subjected to criticism and where confessions of error, failure, or venality are heard. Khrushchev appears—in the published records—to be in complete control of the proceedings. He interrupts, chastizes, corrects, and admonishes speakers, who reply in varying degrees of fear or familiarity, but he never reciprocates. The Central Committee, however, secretes great potential power; and since it is in the nature of the Soviet system not to tolerate dissenting clusters or factions of opinion, if possible, it would be a mistake to assume that authentic collective decisions are possible only after parliamentary or quasi-parliamentary procedures. The Central Committee performs its most crucial and vital functions during periods of extreme crisis or succession, which inevitably yield differing opinions representing various factions, but these disappear once a single faction or combination of factions succeed in reasserting monolithic control. This is, in the evolving Soviet political process, a successful resolution of a divergence

38Moscow Radio broadcast, February 21, 1956. Speech of Z. I. Muratov, First Secretary of the Tatar Oblast Committee.

in policy positions, much as a majority vote represents a successful resolution in a parliamentary situation.

The precise relationship between the Central Committee and its Presidium remains in flux and is still evolving.

Factional rivalry and foreign policy. Differences in the Presidium arise as a result of both personal ambitions for power and fundamental conflict over doctrine and policy. Both factors are so intricately interwoven that attempts to draw fine distinctions between personal and policy conflicts are apt to be an idle exercise. Although Soviet ideology neither recognizes the legitimacy of factional groupings in the Party nor tolerates the doctrinal schisms that are their ideological expression, the Party throughout its history has been constantly threatened with the eruption of both. After Stalin's death the rival cliques he permitted—and may even have encouraged—to form among his subordinates developed into factions, each with its own aspirations and opinions. Since no single faction was sufficiently powerful to annihilate the others, necessity was converted into virtue and the balance of terror in the Presidium was ideologically sanctified as "collective leadership."

Even before the revelations of the resolution that hurled Molotov and his associates from their places of eminence, it was unmistakable that serious factional quarrels kept the Presidium in a continual state of turmoil. At least three factions appear to have existed in the Presidium before June 1957, although the members of each faction were not permanently committed to issues; and personality and tactical shifts, though not frivolous, were also not unusual. The Presidium was divided against itself on four major issues that had important foreign

policy repercussions: the Stalinist issue; the relations between the Soviet Union and other Communist states and parties; economic policy and reorganization; and relations with the ex-colonial states.

The so-called Stalinist faction had at its core the veteran Politburo members, Molotov and Kaganovich, and was frequently supported by Malenkov. The nucleus of the anti-Stalinist faction was made up of Khrushchev, Mikoyan, Voroshilov, Bulganin, Kirichenko, and the alternate members of the Presidium. This faction was in decisive control of the Party Apparatus and the Central Committee, and it found crucial support in the Army, in Peking, Warsaw, and Belgrade. Pervukhin and Saburov made up the so-called "Managerial-Technical" faction, which appeared to have close connections with Malenkov in the past but generally cast its vote with the Khrushchev group on questions of Stalinism. The group deserted Malenkov for Khrushchev when Malenkov appeared to be the apostle for increased emphasis on the production of consumer goods and Khrushchev continued to rely on heavy industry. These factions were bound together by bonds of common ideological and policy considerations, but personal ambitions and opportunism played a considerable role, allowing wide room for maneuver and re-alignment of positions as the main chance presented itself.

The events in Poland and Hungary together with the uncompromising attitude of Marshal Tito encouraged the Stalinists to believe that the Khrushchev group had fumbled, while Khrushchev's sudden interest in decentralizing the economic structure of the State stampeded Pervukhin and Saburov foolishly to join the Stalinist faction in an anti-Khrushchev coalition that made a desperate effort to thwart the proposed dismantling of their economic empires. At the December 1956 Plenum of the Central Committee, this combination was sufficiently powerful to arrest the de-Stalinization program temporarily and to guarantee the preservation of the centralized economic structure by installing Pervukhin as the virtual dictator of the economic system. Relations with Tito were once again inflamed, and Satellite policies appeared to harden. During this period, Malenkov—as representative of the new majority—accompanied Khrushchev to the Communist gathering held in Budapest, from which both Warsaw and Belgrade were deliberately excluded.

The inconclusive factional strife in the Kremlin and the ideological ferment in Eastern Europe provided an opportunity for Peking to intervene, and Chou En-lai embarked upon an emergency trip to Moscow and Eastern Europe to shore up the Khrushchev faction. Because of the unnatural and unstable amalgamation organized against him, Khrushchev's ouster was deferred; but once the crisis had subsided and it was clear that the Armed Forces and China preferred Khrushchev's policies in preference to those of his opposition, a re-alignment of forces in the Presidium enabled Khrushchev once again to reconstitute a majority at the February 1957 Plenum, and Pervukhin was toppled from his brief perch on the economic throne. The economic levers of power were wrenched from his hands, while Shepilov was ousted from the Foreign Ministry in favor of Gromyko.

With the Presidium so sharply and evenly divided, "collective leadership" threatened to abandon Soviet foreign policy to the mercies of an inconclusive see-saw struggle plunging the Kremlin into a condition of perpetual indecision. While key Khrushchev supporters were out of town, Stalinist forces, by engineering a rump meeting of the Presidium—ostensibly to discuss minor matters—regrouped and resolved to unseat Khrushchev through a parliamentary ruse. When the meeting took place on June 17–18, 1957, the First Secretary found himself momentarily outmaneuvered and apparently irrevocably outvoted. Saburov and Pervukhin once again voted with the Stalinist faction, as did Khrushchev's erstwhile protégé, Shepilov. But the key figure in the new re-alignment was Bulganin, who miscalculated the power of the anti-Khrushchev forces and underrated the First Secretary's political agility (leading Khrushchev to confide later that some of his colleagues knew more about arithmetic than politics); and in an opportunistic maneuver voted to oust Khrushchev from power in the meeting over which he presided. Refusing to resign, Khrushchev conducted a filibuster while his supporters quickly assembled a special meeting of the Central Committee and its Auditing Commission (a total of 319 members), which sat from June 22–29, 1957.

After a bitter ventilation of all the contentious issues of doctrines and policy, during which 60 members reportedly took part in the debate and 115 filed statements, the Molotov-Managerial coalition was overwhelmed by a unanimous vote tarnished only by a single obstinate abstention by Molotov—the first such publicly admitted dissonance in a Central Committee vote in almost thirty years. The Stalinist wing of the coalition was charged in the resolution which expelled them with engaging in illegal factional activity and cabalistic intrigue.

Entering into collusion on an anti-Party basis, they set out to change the policy of the Party, to drag the Party back to the erroneous methods of leadership condemned by the 20th Party Congress [i.e. Stalinism]. They resorted to methods of intrigue and formed a collusion against the Central Committee.

The others were not specifically condemned, but Saburov lost his seat on the Presidium and Pervukhin was demoted to alternate status. In their humiliating appearances before the 21st Party Congress, held in February 1959, both confessed their complicity in the plot against Khrushchev although they maintained that they later switched to Khrushchev on the vote to actually oust him as First Secretary. Saburov was eventually exiled to the obscurity of a factory manager in Syzran, while Pervukhin wound up with the less than exalted post of Ambassador to East Germany. Apparently for purposes of concealing the fact that a majority of the Presidium actually voted against him, Bulganin lingered on as Premier until March 1958 and as a member of the Presidium until the following September, although it was clear that his position had been compromised. He was formally charged with being part of the anti-Khrushchev conspiracy on November 14, 1958 and at the December 1958 Plenum, Bulganin made a grovelling confession in which he denounced himself as the "nominal leader" of the plot because of his position as chairman of the Council of Ministers. He made an abject plea for forgiveness, unleashed a vicious attack on Molotov and Kaganovich, and was consigned to the bemeaning post of Chairman of the Stavropol Economic Council.

Interest groups and foreign policy. It is at once obvious that factions could neither arise nor flourish unless they received constant sustenance from powerful social forces in Soviet society. Just as Party factions do not organize into separate political organizations competing with the Party for political power, so interest groups in Soviet society do not constitute separate organizations, but rather seek to make their influence felt as formless clusters of vested interests. Within the context of Marxist-Soviet ideology an interest group can only be a social class with economic interests that conflict with the interests of other classes. After the Revolution only the interests of the working class, as distorted by the Marxist prism, were given legitimate recognition—although the concrete political articulation of these interests was usurped by the Communist Party—and all other interests and parties were condemned to oblivion. In 1936 Stalin declared the eradication of class conflict in Soviet society, but he continued to recognize the existence of separate social classes, whose interests had merged into a single identity. The Communist Party was transformed from a party representing only the interests of the working class into one representing the transcendental interests of all Soviet social classes. Consequently, Soviet ideology neither recognizes the legitimacy of competing interest groups nor tolerates their autonomous existence. In Soviet jargon, an interest group that develops interests that deviate from the Party line is a hostile class; the faction that represents it in the Party is an attempt to form a party within a party; and its articulated views on policy and doctrine constitute an ideological deviation.

Separate interest groups, however, continue to flourish in Soviet society, but not in conformity with the doctrinaire and contrived premises of nineteenth-century Marxism, nor within the synthetic social divisions given official sanction. The collective-farm peasantry and the working class constitute the numerically preponderant classes in Soviet society, but the major interest groups with sufficient power and influence to apply political pressure do not follow the artificial constructions of Soviet ideology; in accordance with the unique dynamic of Soviet society the privileged elites find their social differentiation within a single recognized group, the intelligentsia, which is not recognized as a social class but is euphemistically called a *stratum*.

Although the Soviet intelligentsia (roughly identical with what Milovan Djilas labels the "New Class") is a variegated congeries of differentiated elites, they all have in common a desire to perpetuate the Soviet system from which they have sprung and from which they benefit as privileged groups. But each group is immediately concerned with its own vested stake in Soviet society and seeks to force doctrine and policy to assume the contours of its own special interests. Since these groups do not enjoy official recognition, they all seek to exert their influence through the Communist Party, not outside it, and political rivalry assumes the form of competing for control of the Party's decision-making organs and its symbols of legitimacy. Because Soviet ideology rigidly and inaccurately insists upon the existence of a single monolithic interest, representing that of society in its collective entity, conflicts between major groups are resolved not by political accommodation but by mutual elimination and by the attempt of one interest group to establish its supremacy and to impose its views as those of society as a whole. Thus the Communist Party, under the pressures of diverse groups seeking political articulation and accommodation, has become a conglomeration of interests whose basic incompatibilities are only partially obscured by a veneer of monolithic unity.

Not all interest groups in the Soviet Union are sufficiently powerful to exact representation for their views by factions in the Party hierarchy. There are six principal groups within Soviet society that have accumulated sufficient leverage, either through the acquisition of indispensable skills and talents or through the control of instruments of persuasion, terror, or destruction, to exert pressure upon the Party. These are: (1) the Party Apparatus, consisting of those who have made a career in the Party Bureaucracy; (2) the Government Bureaucracy; (3) the economic managers and technicians; (4) the cultural, professional, and scientific intelligentsia; (5) the Police; (6) the Armed Forces.

These major groups are by no means organized as cohesively united bodies, speaking with a single authoritative voice, but rather themselves are made up of rival personal and policy cliques, gripped by internal jealousies, and often in constant collision and friction with one another in combination or alliance with similarly oriented cliques in other social groups.

The Party Apparatus itself was thus divided into rival cliques, the two main contending groups being those led by Khrushchev and Malenkov. Since the denouement of Malenkov, his supporters in the Party Apparatus have been systematically rooted out and replaced with followers of Khrushchev. Although the function of the Party Bureaucracy is essentially administrative rather than policy-making, it has a tendency to feel that it "owns" the Party and thus seeks first to subordinate the Party to its control and then to force the other major groups to submit to the domination of the Party. After Stalin's death, the serious and imminent threat posed to the Party by Beria and his Secret Police caused Khrushchev and Malenkov to temporarily bury their rivalry in the apparatus of the Party in order to crush the Secret Police, which under Beria had developed into an independent center of power and threatened to subjugate the Party to its will. The Secret Police was dismembered with the aid of the Army, which then displaced the Police as the most important instrument of violence in the Soviet system.

After Beria was dispatched, the rivalry in the Party Apparatus entered its crucial phase. Malenkov was at a distinct disadvantage because he had given up his post in the Party Secretariat in favor of the premiership, and although he had built up a substantial following in the Government Bureaucracy, principally among the energetic and ambitious young corps of managers and technicans in Soviet society, he was outmaneuvered in the Party Secretariat as Khrushchev systematically replaced Malenkov's Party bureaucrats with his own. A close scrutiny of the convulsions that have taken place in the Party summit since Stalin's death reveals that Malenkov's followers in the Party Bureaucracy were essentially in the Central Apparatus, while Khrushchev's supporters were principally provincial Party leaders, most of whom had had some experience in the Ukrainian Party organization. By ousting Malenkov from the Secretariat, Khrushchev was able to destroy his organization in the Party Apparatus, and then by forcing his resignation as Premier, the groundwork was prepared for dispersing his adherents in the Government Bureaucracy, particularly in the economic sector.

The lines of rivalry and clique formation in the other major groups tend to follow the contours of those which develop within the Party Secretariat, with various cliques uniting their fortunes with contending forces in the Party Secretariat. Their representation in the Party is thus not functional, but fortuitous and opportunistic, and the views of their representatives in the Party's leading bodies often reflect only the views of the prevailing clique within each group. The fall from grace of a leading member of the Secretariat (Andrei Zhdanov, G. M. Malenkov) is registered throughout all the major social and functional forces in Soviet society and is accompanied by purges in the Party Apparatus, the Government, the Armed Forces, the Arts, Sciences, and Professions.

There appears to be no systematic attempt to select members of the Central Committee and its Presidium from among the major forces in Soviet society; and the composition of these bodies appears to depend upon the balance of forces at any given time. Ample evidence exists, however, that their composition reflects deliberate recognition of these major interest groups. Traditionally the Party Apparatus accounts for slightly less than half the total membership of the Central Committee, with the Government Bureaucracy (including the economic administrators) following close behind. The representation of the other groups is substantially less, although, because virtually all members of the Party's two highest bodies who are not career Party Bureaucrats are employed by the State, it is often difficult to distinguish the main line of work pursued by a particular member of the Central Committee. This is especially true in cases where an individual moves from one group to another. Consequently all distinctions are provisional and in some

cases arbitrary because of the ambiguous careers of many members of
the Party's highest bodies. With respect
to the composition of the Presidium,
differentiation is more precise and accurate, although even here, because of
the interlocking nature of the top
organs of State and Party, some ambiguity prevails.

Major Groups Represented in the Central Committee

	1952	1956
Party Apparatus	103	117
Government Bureaucracy	79	98
Professional Military	26	18
Police	9	3
Others	18	19
Totals	235	255

Major Groups Represented on the Presidium

	1952	1953	1956	1957	1961
Party Apparatus	13(5)	2(2)	4(3)	10(6)	10(3)
Government Bureaucracy					
Economic Sector	5(3)	4	4	1(2)	2(1)
Noneconomic	4(2)	3(1)	3(1)	3	2(2)
Professional Military	0	0	0(1)	1	0
Police	2	1(1)	0	0	0
Cultural Intelligentsia	1(1)	0	0(1)	0(1)	0(1)
Totals	25(11)	10(4)	11(6)	15(9)	14(7)

The Party Apparatus continues to dominate the composition of the Party's highest body, but whereas at the 19th Party Congress the Party Bureaucrats in the Presidium repre-sented two rival cliques led by Party Secretariat Malenkov and Khrushchev, in the current Presidium all the career Party officials, with the exception of Suslov and Kuusinen, are part of the Khrushchev machine. The Government Bureaucracy correspondingly has suf-fered a drastic decrease in representa-tion, with the economic sector being in a state of virtual eclipse. Pervukhin, dis-graced and demoted to lowest-ranking alternate, is the only representative of the hitherto powerful managers of heavy industry. Since the execution of Beria, the Police, Stalin's favorite in-strument of terror, has been deprived of its traditional seat on the Party's highest body, the seat being tem-porarily given to its principal competi-tor, the Army. The representatives of the Cultural Intelligentsia in the Pre-sidium appear barely distinguishable from those of the Party Apparatus, since they are normally professional ideologists and propagandists.

The informal recognition of groups with distinctive special interests of their own and the admission of their repre-sentatives to the decision-making bodies of the Party cannot but exercise fundamental influence on the country's foreign policy, although how this in-fluence is exerted and in what direction is difficult to determine. Although it is true that none of the major groups has publicly thwarted the decisions of the Party in foreign policy, it has been officially admitted that Party decisions have been administratively distorted by both a Minister of Internal Affairs and two Foreign Ministers. The removal of the Managerial bureaucrats from both the Presidium and high government posts was motivated at least in part by the fear that their control of the key economic levers of society could be used to frustrate the decisions of the Party.

Marshal Zhukov's leadership of the

Army posed an even grimmer potential threat to the supremacy of the Party Apparatus, had he been permitted to remain in the Presidium and the Defense Ministry where he could seriously question the basic decisions of the Party concerning military and foreign policy and frustrate their implementation. His removal in October 1957 from both strategic positions over the relatively trivial controversy concerning the political indoctrination of the military was essentially a preventative measure designed to remove a popular and commanding personality who might at some future date challenge even more crucial decisions of the Party and thus produce an internal crisis of incalculable magnitude. Zhukov's denouement was painlessly engineered by skillful exploitation of his own vanity and the intense personal jealousies and factional cleavages within the Army leadership itself as well as by adroit manipulation of the Middle-Eastern crisis. His replacement on the Presidium was not another representative from the military, but yet another worker in the Party Apparatus, promoted up from alternate membership.

By 1958, the Party Apparatus under Khrushchev's direction had dismembered the Police, domesticated the Managerial bureaucrats and decentralized their empire, exiled the leaders of factional groupings in the Party to Siberia, and subordinated the military to its will. As the chart indicates, neither major instrument of coercion in the Soviet system now has a representative in the Party Presidium, which is now overwhelmingly dominated by career Party *apparatchiki*.

As the Soviet system matures and becomes inextricably identified with the interests of its various privileged elites, the decision-makers must give greater consideration in the calculation of foreign policy to factors affecting the internal stability of the regime; and they will show greater sensitivity to the effects of decisions on the vested interests of the various elites in Soviet society. The rise of powerful social and economic elites in the Soviet Union and their insistent pressures for participation in the exercise of political power could only introduce stresses, strains, conflicts, and hence new restraints into Soviet diplomacy.

Within the context of an ideology that imposes a single interest representing society as a whole, each interest group will tend to distort ideology and policy in an endeavor to give it the contours of its own interests; the next step is to elevate these to transcendental significance. Under these conditions, Soviet ideology may be constantly threatened with a series of fundamental convulsions if one interest group displaces another in the struggle for the control of the Party machinery, unless a rational system of accommodating conflicting interests evolves to replace the custom of mutual obliteration. As the vested stake of each major group becomes rooted in the Soviet system, the contours of Soviet diplomacy and national interest will inexorably tend to be shaped more by the rapidly moving equilibrium or accommodation of interests that develop internally than by abstract ideological imperatives, which may conflict with the concrete interests of specific major elites in Soviet society.

Since 1958 the Party Apparatus under Khrushchev's control and direction has been the dominant voice in the Party and organs of the State. Factional disturbances within the hierarchy have been reduced, although the social and economic basis of factional rivalry remain and factionalism is likely to be revived when the question of succession once again demands resolution. Neither the outcome nor the precise process can be predicted, however, since the course of the future struggle for power will depend not only upon the nature of the personalities involved, the exact issues and conditions which will be pressing, but also upon the lessons which were learned as a result of the struggle for power during the Khrushchev era as well as the Stalin era. The permanent dominance of the Party priests over the Party itself is by no means assured, for given competent and skillful leadership within a favorable concatenation of circumstances, conditions and fortuity, the Party Apparatus itself can be wrenched from the control of the high priests, subdued by one of the other elite groups (or a combination of others), and reduced to a domesticated administrative instrumentality of the State, just as the princes established their primacy over the bishops in another era.

Khrushchev's assumption of the premiership in 1958 obviates the possibility of strife for the moment, but at the same time it is an eloquent tribute to the State as the most powerful and implacable rival of the Party as a legitimate constitution of power and authority as well as a symbol of stability and continuity. The Party Apparatus retains a vested interest in the ideological norm of the "withering away of the state" if only for the reason that the longer the State persists, the less it becomes simply a subordinate administrative instrument of the Party, the more it becomes an autonomous center of prestige and power, and the greater the vested stake of the State bureaucracy in its perpetuation. In this curious revival of the conflict between popes and emperors, priests and princes, the contest so far has been resolved within the context of the Caesaro-Papist tradition of Byzantium and Imperial Russia, but in inverted fashion, for up to now, the popes have become emperors rather than the other way around. It should be noted that Khrushchev's movement into the Council of Ministers has been accompanied by shifts of other career Party officials into organs of the State. Aside from the massive influx of Party officials into the diplomatic service (discussed below), F. R. Kozlov functioned for a brief period as a First Deputy Premier, the veteran Party functionary, L. Brezhnev, has succeeded Voroshilov as ceremonial Chief of State as Chairman of the Presidium of the Supreme Soviet, and A. N. Shelepin, a long-time leader in the *Komsomols,* has been made Chairman of the Committee for State Security, which supervises the Secret Police.

Virtually all expulsions and reorganizations of the Presidium of the Party since 1958 have been non-factional in character. They were simply reflections of Khrushchev's determination to root out ambitious, opportunistic and unreliable allies and protégés, like Kirichenko, or expulsions of otherwise faithful acolytes, like Belyayev, who were unable to meet the exacting and sometimes impossible standards of administrative and executive performance set by the First Secretary. Voroshilov, on the other hand, who was nearly 80 years old at the time of his withdrawal from the State and Party organs, seems to be an authentic case of retirement after long and harrowing years of successful political opportunism and public service.

THE ADMINISTRATION AND EXECUTION OF SOVIET FOREIGN POLICY

Party policy and state administration: conflict and harmony

Responsibility for the actual *execution* of foreign policy as distinct from its *formulation* rests with the Council of Ministers and its Presidium, which is nominally accountable to the Supreme Soviet and its Presidium but in fact is subordinate to the Party Presidium, with which it normally shares key personnel. The relationship between the Party's highest body and the Council of Ministers and its Presidium in the decision-making process, which is often ambiguous and is currently in a state of transition, depends more upon the degree of interlocking membership between the two organs than upon constitutional forms. Under Stalin, particularly after he became Premier in 1941, interlocking membership was virtually complete and was designed to ensure maximum harmony between Party policy and state administration. Distinctions between formulation and execution of policy were ambiguous to the point of complete irrelevance under these conditions. Before Stalin held any formal executive position in the government, the institutions of the Party were the chief decision-making bodies of the regime, but with Stalin's assumption of the premiership, Stalin, the Secretary-General of the Party, made policy, and in his capacity as premier he was also in charge of its execution and administration. As head of both Party and government he did not need to employ all the institutions of decision-making; and those of the Party virtually withered away. Since all diplomatic relations with the outside world are carried on through State institutions, the organs of the State had to retain sufficient vitality to legalize Stalin's decisions into formal acts of government.

The apparent rise of the State to a position superior to that of the Party was undoubtedly a major factor in Malenkov's decision to succeed Stalin as Premier rather than as First Secretary of the Party. Legally, as Premier, he had under his control the two principal instruments of violence, the Police and the Armed Forces; and thus he chose the State in preference to the Party Secretariat as his instrument with which to subdue his rivals in the Presidium. The Police and the Army, however, turned out to be virtually separate entities with their own informal lines of organization and loyalty which radically departed from constitutional and legal patterns. By relinquishing control of the Party Secretariat to Khrushchev in favor of the premiership, Malenkov abdicated the symbols of legitimacy in favor of the shell of power, since within the context of the Party rules and institutional controls bequeathed by Stalin, the Premier and the Government were mere creatures of the Party's will. As long as the Secretariat and the premiership are united in a single personality, relationships of control and subordination are irrelevant, but once they are separated, custom and precedent, as well as ideology, favor the Secretariat in any rivalry for supremacy.

With the eruption of factional rivalry in the Presidium and the separation of the Party Secretariat from the Government, interlocking membership between the Council of Ministers and the Party's highest body, instead of ensuring harmony between policy and administration, in fact guaranteed conflict and friction, as the Party Presidium came under the control of one faction while key administrative organs of State were in the hands of members of rival factions.

The first overt instance of conflict between Party policy and state administration was Beria's attempt to thwart the decisions of the Party through his control of the Ministry and Internal Affairs. Since then, both major and minor discrepancies between policy administration have taken place. Thus, while Khrushchev could muster narrow majorities in the Presidium, members of the opposition were in strategic administrative positions where they could subvert the implementation of Party decisions. One of the major accusations against Foreign Minister Molotov, and also against Shepilov, was that he was using the Foreign Ministry and Soviet missions abroad to subvert and sabotage, rather than to carry out, the policies formulated by the Party. Similarly, Khrushchev's plan for breaking up the concentration of economic power in Moscow was probably opposed by the Managerial bureaucrats like Kaganovich, Pervukhin, and Saburov, who controlled key economic levers in the nation's industrial system and could effectively frustrate the dismantling of their own source of power and influence. Thus, before the reorganization of the Presidium in June 1957, of the nine members of the Presidium of the Council of Ministers, four first deputy chairmen and one deputy chairman were members of the opposition minority in the Party Presidium. It was untenable that the minority faction in the Party Presidium should enjoy a majority in the Presidium of the Council of Ministers, whose function it was to implement the very policies rejected by a majority of its members.

The power of the Council of Ministers as a policy-making and executive institution was severely curtailed during the brief period of Bulganin's continued incumbency after the 1957 reorganization. Before June 29, 1957, the nine-man Presidium of the Council of Ministers included seven full members of the Party Presidium, but after the reorganization only Bulganin and Mikoyan remained members of both bodies. The displacement of Bulganin by Khrushchev in March 1958 marked a revival in overlapping membership in the two organs, whereby career Party workers moved into top government positions. By 1961, four

of the seven-man Presidium of the Council of Ministers were also members of the Party Presidium. The situation remains highly fluid for the degree of overlapping membership depends more upon the course of internal political maneuvering than anything else.

The constitutional basis of Soviet foreign relations

Under the Soviet Constitution of 1936, as amended, foreign policy is administered and executed at four different institutional levels: (1) the Presidium of the Supreme Soviet; (2) the Supreme Soviet; (3) the Council of Ministers; and (4) the Union Republics, of which there are now 15. Although the Soviet constitutional system is based on the principle of complete fusion of executive, legislative, and administrative power, each institutional level is invested with certain foreign policy functions, which may be permissive, exclusive, or concurrent. These legal relationships, however, do not function in any way as limitations on Soviet diplomacy.

The Presidium of the Supreme Soviet. The Presidium of the Supreme Soviet is vested under the Constitution with a wide range of ceremonial, executive, and legislative functions. Juridically a creature of the Supreme Soviet, for which it acts as legal agent, it is, in fact, its institutional superior and surrogate, since it is empowered with virtually the entire spectrum of authority granted to the Supreme Soviet during the long and frequent intervals between sessions of the Soviet legislature. Technically, all of its actions are subject to later confirmation by the Supreme Soviet, but, in practice, this is an empty ritual.

According to *Istoriya Diplomatii*, in the area of foreign affairs, the Presidium, in the person of its chairman, functions as the ceremonial chief of state, much like the American president and the British monarch:

In accordance with the universally recognized doctrine of international law, the supreme representation of the modern state is vested in the chief of state, whether he be an actual person (monarch, president of the republic) or a collective body (Presidium of the Supreme Soviet of the U.S.S.R., Federal Council of Switzerland). . . . As a general rule, the competence of the chief of state includes the declaration of war and conclusion of peace, nomination and reception of diplomatic agents, granting powers for the conclusion of international treaties and agreements of special significance, and the ratification and denunciation of these treaties and accords.[39]

In its ceremonial capacity, the Presidium confers all diplomatic ranks and titles of a plenipotentiary character, formally appoints and recalls diplomatic representatives of the U.S.S.R., and receives the letters of credence and recall from foreign envoys. Although foreign representatives almost always present their credentials to the Chairman of the Presidium, they are, in fact, accredited to the Presidium as a collective entity.

The Presidium's substantive powers are considerable. Article 49 of the Constitution authorizes it to interpret all Soviet laws, convene and dissolve the Supreme Soviet, annual decisions and orders of the Council of Ministers, appoint and remove the higher commands of the armed forces, and issue decrees in its own right, virtually without limits. Furthermore, the Presidium, during intervals between sessions of the Supreme Soviet, "proclaims a state of war in the event of armed attack . . . or whenever necessary to fulfill international treaty obligations concerning mutual defense against aggression," can order general or partial mobilization, and can proclaim martial law in separate localities or throughout the country. The exercise of many of these powers is not subject to later confirmation by the Supreme Soviet, although the Presidium remains technically accountable for all its activities to the Soviet legislature, which theoretically can replace its personnel.

Certain important powers vested in the Presidium are provisional and delegated. Thus, the Presidium, during periods when the Supreme Soviet is not in session, can appoint and dismiss ministers upon the recommendation of the chairman of the Council of Ministers, but this is subject to later confirmation. Similarly, if the Presidium promulgates decrees of a fundamental nature, outside its formal constitutional competence, they also are subject to confirmation, although this may be several years later.

Although the Constitution appears to give the Presidium a monopoly on the ratification and denunciation of treaties, a law of the Supreme Soviet, "On the Procedure for Ratification and Denunciation of International Treaties," passed on August 19, 1938, defines as treaties requiring its ratification: (1) treaties of peace; (2) mutual defense treaties; (3) treaties of nonaggression; and (4) treaties requiring mutual ratification for their implementation.[40] By implication, and in accordance with past practice, all treaties not specifically enumerated as requiring ratification by the Presidium are left to the discretion of the Council of Ministers. On the other hand, on rare occasions the Supreme Soviet has

---

[39] *Istoriya Diplomatii*, III, 765.

[40] *Second Session of the Supreme Soviet of the U.S.S.R.*, verbatim report (New York: International Publishers 1938), p. 678.

been asked to ratify or give preliminary approval to particularly important treaties, although there exists no constitutional imperative.

The Supreme Soviet. As the "highest organ of state authority in the U.S.S.R.," the power of the Supreme Soviet under the Constitution is coterminous with that of the Union.

Composed of two coordinate chambers—the Council of the Union and the Council of Nationalities—of approximately equal size, the constitutional competence of the Soviet legislature in foreign affairs surpasses that of any other organ. In practice, it has abdicated most of its powers to the Presidium and has been left only with the empty shell of ceremony, which may sometimes border on consultation. Both chambers are equally impotent, singly or together, and neither has specific functions or powers denied the other.

The formal authority of the Supreme Soviet in foreign policy falls into seven categories: (1) the enactment of basic legislation and constitutional amendments; (2) the confirmation of the decisions and decrees of the Presidium and the Council of Ministers; (3) ratification of selected treaties; (4) declaration of war and peace; (5) confirmation and authorization of territorial changes and of the creation, admission, promotion, demotion, and abolition of new republics; (6) hearing and approving of foreign policy reports delivered by the Premier or the Foreign Minister; and (7) the preliminary examination of treaties prior to ratification by the Presidium. Since Stalin's death, all of these activities have been accorded greater publicity.

All proposed laws, treaties, significant statements of policy, results of important conferences, or simply reviews of the international situation—with one or two alleged exceptions, however—were taken on the initiative of the government, under instructions from the Party.

The sessions of the Supreme Soviet are short. Between 1946 and 1954 the Supreme Soviet sat for a total of only 45 days, with the longest session lasting seven days (June 1950) and the shortest, 67 minutes (March 1953); its performance before and during the war was even less auspicious. By far the most significant function of the Supreme Soviet is to hear reports on the foreign policy of the government. It is customary, but by no means the invariable rule, that the Foreign Minister review the government's foreign policy before this body, usually to joint sessions. It listens attentively, with conditioned enthusiasm; if requested, it enacts legislation with rare precision and extraordinary dispatch, unencumbered with either debate or criticism. Fulsome panegyrics delivered by a dozen or more carefully selected deputies on the wisdom and correctness of the government's policies are euphemistically described as "discussion" in the official records, a close examination of which has failed to produce a single note of criticism, to say nothing of a negative vote, in all the deliberations of the Supreme Soviet.

In the words of *Kommunist,* "until recently its [*i.e.* the Supreme Soviet's] sessions concerned for the most part consideration of budget questions and approval of the decrees of the Presidium," [41] but with the replacement of Malenkov by Bulganin in February 1955, a calculated effort has been made to give it a more conspicuous role in foreign affairs. These changes have, so far, been more ornamental than substantive.

With the installation of Bulganin as

[41] *Kommunist* (No. 10), August 1956, pp. 3–15.

Premier in February 1955, the Supreme Soviet, with much fanfare, issued an appeal to other parliaments for a program of parliamentary exchanges in the form of visiting delegations addressing each other's legislatures; more than a dozen such exchanges have taken place. In July of the same year the Supreme Soviet adhered to the Inter-Parliamentary Union (ITU) and sent a delegation to its 44th annual conference in Helsinki.

Although the two Foreign Affairs Commissions of the two chambers of the Supreme Soviet are supposed to make "a preliminary examination of all matters connected with foreign affairs to be considered by the Supreme Soviet (and its Presidium)," this function had all but withered away and the existence of these bodies was virtually rendered superfluous; they were suddenly brought back to life when the Soviet-Iranian Agreement of 1954, the denunciation of the Anglo-Soviet and Anglo-French Treaties of Alliance, the Warsaw Pact, and the agreement to establish diplomatic relations with West Germany were all submitted, with considerable publicity, to joint sessions of the two Commissions (the Supreme Soviet was not in session) for their solemn consideration. After hearing reports by Molotov and his deputies, they dutifully recommended approval to the Soviet Presidium. At about the same time the two chairmen of the chambers, together with allegedly prominent members of the two Commissions, suddenly appeared at diplomatic receptions, received foreign dignitaries, and pompously pontificated on foreign policy in patent, but bogus, imitation of their counterparts in the American Congress.

The Supreme Soviet was awarded the honor of proclaiming an end to the state of war with Germany on January 25, 1955, and on August 4, 1955, it was called into special session to hear Bulganin's report on the Summit Conference at Geneva, a procedure not used since Molotov addressed a special session on the Nazi-Soviet Pact of 1939. On this same occasion the Supreme Soviet, after "debating" the policy of the government and "interpellating" the Foreign Minister, issued an appeal to the parliaments and governments of the world to "put an end to the arms race." The regular session of the Supreme Soviet was arranged to coincide with the return of Bulganin and Khrushchev from their tour of Southeast Asia, so that both might address the Supreme Soviet on the results of their trip.

Although the activities of the Supreme Soviet have been stepped up, there is little reason to believe that there has been a corresponding enhancement of its influence and power. It hears more reports on foreign policy, but it has also retained intact its undeviating characteristic of absolute unanimity, whether convened on the spur of the moment or after contrived deliberation. The invocation of the formal prerogatives of the Supreme Soviet, however, is no idle exercise, since it creates certain advantages for Soviet diplomacy. (1) It serves to infuse Soviet citizens with the notion that their representatives participate in the formulation of foreign policy decisions. (2) As a propagandistic maneuver it strives to create the illusion of evolving constitutionalism in the Soviet system. (3) As a purely diplomatic device, it permits the Kremlin to invoke constitutional procedures as a stumbling or delaying mechanism in negotiations and affords a basis for demanding reciprocal action in the ratification of treaties and other diplomatic instruments.

The possibility, no matter how slight, that ceremony may some day be replaced with substance cannot be ignored, but this expectation must yield to the realization that the flurry of activity we have noted can be arrested as abruptly as it began.

The Council of Ministers (Formerly the Council of People's Commissars, or *Sovnarkom*). As the "highest executive and administrative organ" of the government, the Council of Ministers "exercises general supervision" over the execution and administration of the country's foreign policy, and also directs the state's foreign trade monopoly. Constitutionally, since 1944 the central government no longer exercises a monopoly over foreign affairs but merely represents the Federal Union as a whole and establishes the "general procedure in mutual relations between the Union Republics and foreign states," and thus shares the conduct of diplomacy with its 15 constituent republics.

In actual practice, however, foreign policy in the Soviet Union is the most tightly centralized activity of the Soviet government.

The Council of Ministers has the following powers: (1) grant or withdraw recognition of new states or governments; (2) sever and restore diplomatic relations; (3) order acts of reprisal against other states; (4) appoint negotiators and supervise the negotiation of international treaties and agreements; (5) declare the adherence of the Soviet Union to international conventions not requiring formal ratification; (6) conclude agreements not requiring ratification with other heads of governments (similar to American executive and administrative agreements); (7) ratify all treaties and agreements not requiring ratification of the Presidium; (8) give preliminary examination of all treaties submitted to the Presidium for its ratification; (9) oversee "the current work of the

diplomatic organs, effectually direct that work and take the necessary measures in that field;" and (10) appoint and accredit all diplomats below plenipotentiary rank and foreign trade representatives.[42]

Actually there appears to be a great area of overlapping activity between the Presidium and the Council of Ministers in the conduct of diplomacy, and were it not that the one-party system makes all basic decisions, rivalries and jealousies would almost certainly develop between these two organs, rendering coordination of diplomatic activity virtually impossible.

a) The Chairman and his Cabinet. The most influential member of the Council of Ministers is its Chairman, referred to in the West as the Premier, who is always an important figure of the highest rank in the Party hierarchy. This office, including its predecessors under previous constitutions, has been filled by only seven men since the establishment of the Soviet state: Lenin (1917–1924); Rykov (1924–1930); Molotov (1930–1941); Stalin (1941–1953); Malenkov (1953–1955); Bulganin (1955–1958); Khrushchev (1958–   ). After Lenin's death, when Stalin refused to hold formal office, this post was reduced to a mere shadow of the secretary-general of the Party, but after Stalin assumed formal responsibility for the policies of the government in April 1941, and held it until his death in March 1953, the post retrieved its former prestige and power. Stalin's death, and the resultant power rivalries that were unleashed, temporarily revived the division of power between the Premier and First Secretary of the Party, and the two positions have once again been sepa-

[42] *Cf.* A. Y. Vyshinsky, *The Law of the Soviet State* (New York: Macmillan, 1948), p. 376; *Istoriya Diplomatii*, III, 767–768, 806–807; Towster, *op. cit.*, p. 279.

rated and re-united. Khrushchev's unexpected assumption of the office after Bulganin's resignation reflected the internal and external symbolic significance which it has acquired during Stalin's long tenure as well as the fact that as a position from which to challenge the power of the First Secretary, it was too risky to permit a continued separation of the two positions. The post of Premier serves to legitimize and legalize the power of the First Secretary, just as the latter imparts to the premiership the necessary ideological sanctity. It is likely that the post of Premier will continue to acquire authority and prestige at the expense of the first secretaryship as an institution, and any successor who wishes to stabilize his position must eventually occupy both positions in order to enjoy both the legal and ideological attributes of legitimacy and power. Malenkov's failure to use the premiership successfully as a stepping stone to full power is not precedential; it simply marks another stage in the shifting equilibrium between the Party and the State, in which the State will eventually win out unless it "withers away" in conformity with the ideological hope of the Party.

The Chairman has primary responsibility for the conduct of the country's foreign policy and, presumably, has the authority to appoint and remove the ministers concerned with its day-to-day execution. Immediately below the Chairman are his First Deputy Chairmen and Deputy Chairmen, who normally are in charge of a specific ministry, or may be without portfolio. The chairman, his First Deputies, and his Deputies constitute the Presidium (cabinet) of the Council of Ministers.

The size and composition of the Presidium have undergone serious transformations in recent years. Under Stalin, the Presidium became so large that a Bureau—or inner cabinet—of the Presidium was secretly organized, whose composition and membership have never been made public. After his death, the number of First Deputies was reduced to four and of Deputies to one, with only the Chairman and the first deputies admitted into the Presidium. The Bureau of the Presidium was technically abolished, but in fact the Presidium was reduced to the smaller size of the Bureau. The execution of First Deputy Beria and the replacement of Malenkov as premier resulted in enlargement of the Presidium until it reached its maximum post-Stalinist number of five First Deputies and eight Deputies. As a result of the reorganization of the economic ministries and the expulsion of Molotov, Kaganovich, Malenkov, Pervukhin, and Saburov from the Presidium, it was first reduced to four members, and then raised to six.

The Council of Ministers and its Presidium are subordinate in fact to the Party Presidium and in theory to the Supreme Soviet and its Presidium. If the current Premier of the Government loses a vote of confidence in the Party organ, the decision is reviewed by the Central Committee, whereupon, if it is upheld, he submits his resignation to the Presidium of the Supreme Soviet. The Central Committee, through its First Secretary, nominates the next Premier to the appropriate State organs and a new Government is thus formed.

Since the formation of the Bulganin Government, the Premier and other key members of the Presidium of the Council of Ministers have played an increasingly personal and active role in the country's diplomacy. This pattern was further accelerated after Khrushchev became Premier. Not only the Premier, but important ministers and the Chairman of the Presidium of the Supreme Soviet, have made state visits to many countries as a part of the Kremlin's new diplomatic offensive. While he was Foreign Minister, Molotov played an active personal role in the country's diplomacy, but he apparently objected to the interference of the other members of the Government in Soviet diplomatic activity. In particular he objected to the travels of Bulganin and Khrushchev and their meetings with the heads of various governments.

b) *The Foreign Minister.* In forty years of Soviet diplomacy there have been only seven Foreign Ministers: Leon Trotsky (November 1917–April 1918); Georgi Chicherin (1918–1929); Maxim Litvinov (1929–1939); Vyacheslav Molotov (1939–1949; 1953–1956); Andrei Vyshinsky (1949–1953); Dimitri Shepilov (during 1956); Andrei Gromyko (1957–   ). Until 1949, the typical tenure of a Soviet Foreign Minister was ten years, and nearly 35 years of Soviet diplomacy have been directed by only three individuals, thus giving Soviet diplomacy a measure of enviable continuity. Since Stalin's death the foreign ministry has changed hands almost as many times as it had up to the time of his passing, reflecting the bitter conflicts that have raged over foreign policy in the past few years.

The Foreign Minister's role and influence in Soviet diplomacy depend almost entirely upon his Party rank. When the Minister is of relatively low rank in the Party, he constitutes little more than a caretaker of the department. If he is of top Party rank, as Trotsky and Molotov were, he participates in the decisions he is asked to execute, and in at least two cases (Molotov and Shepilov), has actually flouted the will of the decision-makers in favor of executing a foreign policy of his own choosing. Even though Chicherin and Litvinov, like Gromyko, were relatively low-ranking members

in the Party hierarchy, this by no means indicates that they were less effective as diplomats. There is ample evidence to suggest that the Party leaders would prefer a low-ranking Party member as Foreign Minister rather than one of first rank, except under critical circumstances, since it enhances the flexibility of Soviet diplomacy while hampering that of other countries, who are forced to accommodate their diplomacy to the bureaucratic channels of the Soviet Foreign Office. Normally the Foreign Minister is at least a full member of the Central Committee, although both Chicherin and Litvinov achieved that status some time after they had become Foreign Commissars. Gromyko was elevated to full membership only at the 20th Party Congress. Trotsky and Molotov were the only Foreign Ministers who were full members of the Party's highest body; Vyshinsky and Shepilov were alternate members of the Presidium during their incumbency.

The Ministry of Foreign Affairs (formerly the People's Commissariat for Foreign Affairs, or Narkomindel)

Evolution of the Ministry. The government department directly charged with the day-to-day administration of Soviet diplomacy does not materially differ in its structure and organization from its counterparts in other Great Powers, although it betrays a pattern of historical evolution that is unique among foreign ministries. Since its establishment it has undergone a triple metamorphosis.

In the beginning, its primary purpose was to trigger a world revolution and thus create the conditions for its own extinction. It was thought that if the world revolution failed, a Soviet diplomacy would be impossible, and, if it succeeded, unnecessary. It was Leon Trotsky's boast, "I will issue a few revolutionary proclamations to the people of the world, and then close up shop." [43] On November 26, 1917, a decree from Trotsky's Foreign Affairs Commissariat virtually dis-established the diplomatic apparatus of the Russian state: all members of the Russian foreign service abroad were summarily dismissed unless they expressed loyalty to the Bolshevik regime. In their places, Bolshevik émigrés abroad were appointed as "unofficial" agents of the new government (Litvinov was such an appointee to Great Britain). Trotsky even neglected to establish a permanent home office; he appeared at his office only once—to dismiss all employees reluctant to pledge loyalty to the new regime and to set up a committee to publish the secret treaties in the archives of the Russian Foreign Office.

The Treaty of Brest-Litovsk imposed upon the new regime diplomatic relations with Germany and its allies, so the Council of People's Commissars was forced to recreate a provisional diplomatic service. With obvious petulance, in a decree of June 4, 1918, they attempted to rewrite unilaterally the principle of diplomatic ranks adopted by the Congress of Vienna in 1815, by abolishing all Soviet diplomatic titles in favor of a single designation, "plenipotentiary representative" (*Polpred*). In a naive attempt to impose Soviet egalitarian principles upon foreign envoys, the decree peremptorily announced that "all diplomatic agents of foreign states . . . shall be considered equal plenipotentiary representatives regardless of their rank." [44]

Pending the eventual liquidation of the Foreign Affairs Commissariat, the functions of Soviet diplomacy during this initial period fell into three principal categories: (1) the publication of "secret treaties" in order to expose the duplicity and hypocrisy of the Allies and compromise them in the eyes of their own people; (2) the conduct of necessary negotiations and diplomatic relations, on a temporary basis, with capitalist states in a position to impose them; and (3) the utilization of Soviet embassies and legations abroad as centers of revolutionary propaganda, conspiracy, and activity, in clear violation of treaty obligations. In this connection, the Soviet government announced that "The Council of People's Commissars considers it necessary to offer assistance by all possible means . . . to the left internationalist wing of the labor movement of all countries [and] . . . for this purpose . . . decides to allocate two million rubles for the needs of the revolutionary international movement and to put this sum at the disposal of the foreign representatives of the Commissariat for Foreign Affairs." [45]

The failure of the revolution to spread beyond Russia, the success of the seceding border states in maintaining their independence, and the failure of foreign intervention to subdue the Bolshevik regime, forced the expansion of diplomatic contact with the bourgeois world. By 1921 the Soviet foreign office was prepared to pass out of its initial phase into its second, as a quasi-permanent agency for "normalizing" relations with the capitalist powers on the basis of "mutual interests" during the prolonged period of "co-existence" which Lenin now recognized as the inevitable interval between the first and final stages of the world revolution.

[43] Cited in E. H. Carr, *The Bolshevik Revolution, 1917–1923,* III (London: Macmillan 1953), p. 16.

[44] Full text in T. A. Taracouzio, *The Soviet Union and International Law* (New York: Macmillan, 1935), p. 383.

[45] Jane Degras, ed., *Soviet Documents on Foreign Policy,* I (London: Royal Institute of International Affairs, 1951), 22.

From an instrument of world revolution the foreign office was converted into an instrument for furthering the interests of the Soviet state.

Since the revolutionary and conspiratorial activities of Soviet diplomats complicated the establishment of desirable trade and political connections with the bourgeois world, the new Commissar of Foreign Affairs, Georgi Chicherin (who succeeded Trotsky in April 1918), was instrumental in shifting the function of revolutionary agitation from the Foreign Office to the Party. A new diplomatic service was organized from scratch by Chicherin, and shortly after he assumed office, the Foreign Commissariat was organized into more than a dozen departments. The first Statute on the Commissariat for Foreign Affairs was issued by the Council of Ministers on July 6, 1921; it defined the sphere of competence of each of the departments. After the formation of the Union and the centralization of diplomacy in Moscow, the Commissariat on November 12, 1923, received its definite statute which still constitutes the juridical basis for the organization and structure of the Foreign Ministry. However, it was not until 1924 that Soviet diplomacy was juridically relieved of its revolutionary mission and it entered into its current phase. According to a decree issued November 21, 1924, and still effective:

It goes without saying that diplomatic missions abroad are appointed by each of the parties establishing diplomatic relations for purposes which exclude propaganda in the country to which they are accredited. The Soviet diplomatic missions follow and are to follow this principle with absolute strictness.[46]

Although technically the Soviet Foreign Office is supervised by the Council

of Ministers, it has always enjoyed a unique, direct relationship with the Party Presidium. Unlike the other departments of government in the new Bolshevik regime, the Foreign Commissariat was unencumbered with holdovers from the old bureaucracy, Chicherin being the only prominent figure who had previous diplomatic experience. Consequently, from the very beginning, it was cherished by Lenin:

The diplomatic apparatus . . . is quite exceptional in the governmental apparatus. We excluded everyone from the old Tsarist apparatus who formerly had even the slightest influence. Here, the whole apparatus, insofar as it possesses the slightest influence, has been made up of Communists. For this reason this apparatus has acquired for itself . . . the reputation of a Communist apparatus which has been tested and cleansed of the old Tsarist bourgeois and petty bourgeois apparatus to a degree incomparably higher than that attained in the apparatus with which we have to be satisfied in the other people's commissariats.[47]

This quality, in the words of a Soviet diplomat, "helped make it a peculiarly well-fitted apparatus for the expression of new policies." [48]

The Statute governing the Foreign Affairs Commissariat, decreed on November 12, 1923, which has been frequently amended, but never superseded, defined its principal duties as:

(a) The defence of the political and economic interests of the U.S.S.R. . . .
(b) The conclusion of treaties and agreements with foreign countries in accord-

---

[46] Full text in Taracouzio, op cit., 389–390.

[47] The New York Times, July 1, 1956. Extract is from suppressed Lenin documents distributed at the 20th Party Congress and later made public.
[48] Alexei F. Neymann, in S. N. Harper, ed., The Soviet Union and World Problems (Chicago: Chicago University Press, 1935), p. 229.

ance with the decisions of the government. (c) Supervision over the proper execution of treaties and agreements concluded with foreign states, and enabling the corresponding organs of the U.S.S.R. and the Union Republics to exercise rights conferred by these treaties. (d) Supervision over the execution by the competent organs of treaties, agreements, and accords concluded with foreign states.[49]

The Foreign Minister and his Collegium. The administration of the Foreign Commissariat was initially entrusted to a collegium in accordance with the Bolshevik principle of collective responsibility. The Foreign Commissar was forced to share authority and responsibility with a board of three or four other senior officials of the Commissariat.

With the promulgation of the first Constitution in March 1918, the germ of one-man management was implanted, when the Commissar was invested with the personal power of decision relating to matters within the competence of his department, but if this decision conflicted with the views of the collegium, the latter, without the power of stopping execution of the decision, could appeal its differences to the Council or to the Presidium. As a consequence, collective responsibility became a convenient evasion of concrete responsibility and the collegium frequently abused its powers by issuing orders in its own name, thus lowering the prestige and personal responsibility of the Foreign Commissar.

By 1934, defects of collective responsibility became so serious that Stalin condemned the collective principle as obsolete and subversive of efficient administration; the collegium was abolished and the Foreign Minister installed in complete charge of his department and, in turn, he assumed full personal responsibility for its work.

Four years later, in March 1938, the collegium was restored in modified form, but was clearly divested of its former tyrannical power over the Commissar. The Council, which was too large and unwieldy as a decision-making or even advisory body, was retained as a convenient institution for the diffusion of policy and administrative decision, and the collegium retained its character as the executive committee of the Commissariat. The Commissar retained his plenary authority and responsibility, but the formal prerogatives of the collegium remained considerable.[50]

The institutional relationship established in 1938 between the Foreign Minister and his collegium has survived, substantially unaltered, till now. Its size and composition appear to vary, depending upon the discretion of the Foreign Minister, except in unusual circumstances, although appointments to the collegium continue to be made by the Council of Ministers. The collegium is presided over by the Minister or one of his First Deputies. It includes not only the First Deputy and Deputy Ministers, but also about four to six senior officials in the department, one of whom frequently is the Chief of the Press and Information Division. The number of First Deputies has varied from one to three; their rank roughly corresponds to that of the undersecretary in the American State Department. Immediately below the First Deputies are the Deputies, whose rank corresponds to that of Assistant Secretaries in the American hierarchy; there may be up to six Deputies (in 1961 there were

---

[49] The full text of this statute, with amendments through 1927, is reprinted in *Yezhegodnik Narodnovo Komissariata Po Inostrannym Delam Na 1928 God* (Moscow, 1928), pp. 182–193. All subsequent references and extracts refer to this text. *Cf.* also *Istoriya Diplomatii*, III, 770–771.

[50] *Cf. Vyshinsky, op. cit.*, pp. 387–389.

six). The other members of the collegium are normally department heads. Thus the size of the collegium may vary up to more than a dozen members.

The institutional prerogatives of the collegium fall just short of the power of actual decision, but without weakening in any way the full responsibility of the Minister. It cannot overrule the Minister's decisions, nor issue orders in its own name, but it is mandatory for the Minister to report any disagreement with his collegium to the Council for disposition. The collegium retains the right, individually or collectively, to appeal to the Council and the Central Committee of the party.[51]

The organization and structure of the Foreign Ministry. The basic organization and structure of the Soviet Foreign Ministry remain governed by the Statute of 1923, which established a flexible system of administration, permitting a wide latitude for internal reorganization at the discretion of the Minister. The Ministry is organized into "divisions according to the main geographical divisions of the world and the main functions of the department and . . . this apparatus both in its offices in Moscow and its missions in foreign countries does not present any striking differences in structure compared with similar departments in other countries," as one former Soviet diplomat informs us.[52]

At the apex of the Ministry stands the Minister with his collegium, which is provided with a Central Secretariat —headed by a Secretary-General— performing routine secretarial and staff administrative work for the Minister, his deputies, and members of the collegium. The functional divisions, which have become increasingly differentiated with the expansion of Soviet diplomatic activity, are conventional: Protocol,

Political Archives, Courier and Liaison, Passport and Visa, Treaty and Legal, Economic, Consular Affairs, Administration, Personnel, Finance, Supplies, and Press and Information.[53] Several related functional divisions are grouped together and supervised by Deputy Ministers, and perhaps also by collegium members.

Since the 1923 Statute does not stipulate the precise number of geographical divisions, the number and composition of these departments vary considerably, and currently are in a phase of expansive reorganization. The Statute merely states that "the divisions of Western Affairs . . . are charged with securing diplomatic relations with the states of Europe and America, the observation and study of the political and economic and other relations between these states and other institutions of the U.S.S.R. which may also have relations with missions in the U.S.S.R." The divisions for "Eastern Affairs" assume identical responsibilities for the states of Asia and Africa.

The cataclysmic political changes of the past twenty years, the massive expansion of Soviet diplomatic relations, and the creation of many new states in Asia and Africa, have profoundly affected the internal organization of the Foreign Office. In the past few years the number of geographical divisions has been increased, while the number of functional divisions has remained fairly constant. As compiled from Soviet press accounts, there are now seven "Western" divisions and five "Eastern" divisions, plus two separate departments for International Organizations and International Economic Organizations. The geographical divisions, which closely resemble those of 1925, are as follows:

[51] *Ibid.*
[52] Neymann, *op. cit.,* pp. 226–227.

[53] *Cf. Yezhegodnik,* 1925, 1926, 1928, 1929.

1. Division for American Countries (North and South).
2. First European (France, Benelux, and Italy).
3. Second European (United Kingdom and white Commonwealth countries).
4. Third European (the two Germanies, Austria, Switzerland).
5. Fourth European (Czechoslovakia, Poland, Hungary).
6. Fifth European (Balkan states).
7. Sixth European (Scandinavian countries and Finland).
8. Division for Near Eastern Affairs.
9. Division for Middle Eastern Affairs.
10. Division for Southeast Asian Affairs (Pakistan, India, Burma, Northern Vietnam, Cambodia, Laos, Thailand, Ceylon, and Indonesia).
11. Division for Far Eastern Affairs (China, Outer Mongolia, North Korea, and Japan).
12. Division for African Affairs.

Normally, a deputy minister exercises general administrative supervision over the work of several contiguous geographical divisions, and usually he is a former ambassador with diplomatic experience in the geographical area in question.

The appearance of kindred Communist states in Eastern Europe and in the Far East has not modified the geographical divisions of the Ministry. Relations with Communist countries through the Foreign Ministry, however, have been reduced to the bare minimum required by international law and protocol, since substantive and policy questions are handled through corresponding Party organizations. Soviet envoys to important Communist countries are considered primarily as functionaries and emissaries from the Party and secondarily as government agents. Thus, when Tito complained that the

Soviet Ambassador was meddling in the affairs of the Yugoslav Party, Stalin replied:

Tito and Kardelj . . . identify the Soviet Ambassador, a responsible Communist . . . with an ordinary bourgeois ambassador, a simple official of a bourgeois state. . . . The Soviet Ambassador, a responsible Communist . . . not only has the right but is obliged, from time to time, to discuss with Communists in Yugoslavia all questions which interest them.[54]

This relationship has been confirmed and emphasized since Stalin's death with the adoption of the practice of dispatching high Party functionaries as ambassadors to important Communist states.

The Soviet diplomatic service. The decree of 1918 reducing all diplomatic ranks to the single and equal rank of plenipotentiary representative remained technically in force until 1941, although it was neither possible nor desirable to honor it in practice. The principle of diplomatic equality was based on the discarded theory that "the representatives of . . . the U.S.S.R. do not personify a quasi-mythical Leviathan state, but only . . . the plenipotentiary of the ruling class," and that diplomats from bourgeois countries were likewise emissaries of their ruling classes.[55] This view was condemned as unduly doctrinaire and subversive of Soviet prestige and diplomacy, since, in practice, it amounted to unilateral renunciation of all the privileges and prerogatives of seniority and rank under traditional norms of diplomatic intercourse.

[54] *The Soviet-Yugoslav Dispute* (London: Royal Institute of International Affairs, 1948), pp. 34–35.
[55] E. Korovin, *Mezhdunarodnoye Pravo Perekhodnovo Vremeni* (Moscow, 1924), p. 63.

Soviet diplomacy gradually accommodated itself to existing international practice through the extralegal exchange of supplementary protocols granting informal recognition of rank so that Soviet diplomats might avoid forfeiting recognized privileges accorded to rank and seniority. By 1941, the discrepancy between the law and practice of Soviet diplomatic ranks had reached the point of absurdity, so on May 9, the Presidium issued a decree establishing three diplomatic categories: (1) Ambassador Extraordinary and Plenipotentiary; (2) Minister Extraordinary and Plenipotentiary; and (3) *Chargé d'Affaires*. This decree gave legal sanction to existing *de facto* distinctions. Two years later, on May 28, 1943, the Presidium decreed the establishment of eleven grades in the diplomatic service and thus brought Soviet diplomatic ranking into complete focus with general diplomatic practice: (1) Ambassador Extraordinary and Plenipotentiary; (2) Minister Extraordinary and Plenipotentiary of the First Class; (3) Minister Extraordinary and Plenipotentiary of the Second Class; (4) Counselor, First Class; (5) Counselor, Second Class; (6) First Secretary, First Class; (7) First Secretary, Second Class; (8) Second Secretary, First Class; (9) Second Secretary, Second Class; (10) Third Secretary; and (11) Attaché.[56]

Until Stalin's death, one of the chief peculiarities of the Soviet diplomatic service was the relative permanence of the Foreign Minister as contrasted with the turnover of all ranks below. This is almost precisely the reverse of the situation found in other countries where kaleidoscopic changes occur at the ministerial level in contrast to the relative permanence of the diplomatic

bureaucracy as a whole. This frequent turnover of personnel has arrested more than once the orderly development of a career diplomatic service, if that is desirable, or even possible, in a one-party state. While scores of ambassadors and high Foreign Ministry officials have been arrested or executed on charges of treason, not a single Foreign Minister (Trotsky excepted) has ever been liquidated or charged with high treason. Ministers appointed to other departments have not been so lucky. The disgrace suffered by Molotov and Shepilov recently while the career service survived virtually unscathed indicates the possible existence of a career service that scrupulously avoids involvement in power intrigues and thus may gain immunity from the effects of factional rivalry.

Although it appears that a professional diplomatic service has been assuming shape during the past decade and a half, it is still fundamentally distinguishable from what is generally understood to be a career service. In Western countries, career officials are insulated from political partisanship (except under unusual circumstances) and manage to survive the changing fortunes of political parties or movements, serving as impersonal instruments of the party that happens to exercise political power. This was true even of Fascist totalitarian states. In contrast, since the Communist Party has a permanent monopoly on political power, all Soviet diplomats must be members of the Communist Party, and senior officials of the Ministry frequently are members of Party organs corresponding to their diplomatic importance.

As a rule, career Soviet diplomats do not rank very high in the Party hierarchy. The foreign minister is at least a full member of the Central Committee and frequently a member

---

[56] Cf. *Istoriya Diplomatii*, III, 778–780. Date of the decree is mistakenly given as June 14, 1943, in this work.

or alternate member of the Presidium. First deputies are normally full members of the Central Committee, while career diplomats rarely achieve higher status than candidate membership in the Central Committee. Foreign Minister Gromyko is the only career official with full membership in the Central Committee; only three other career officials (G. N. Zarubin, V. A. Zorin, and Y. A. Malik) were elected candidate members in 1956.

Since Stalin's death, the Soviet diplomatic service has been subjected to a unique infusion of new personnel. Alongside members of the career service, who serve as diplomatic technicians, there now exist numerous high-ranking Ministry officials and diplomats who are primarily State administrators and Party functionaries who appear to correspond to the political appointee in the American diplomatic hierarchy. The transfer of high Party officials and State administrators into the diplomatic service has gone through four distinct phases since Stalin's death, corresponding to the principal milestones in the struggle for power after 1953. Each time a major change in the power equilibrium took place in the Presidium, Party officials were shifted to diplomatic work. Consequently, the most obvious trend is that the Foreign Ministry is once again being used as a convenient post of exile from the centers of political power for Party bureaucrats wounded in the power struggles. A second trend is the assignment of career Party bureaucrats—not all of them in disgrace—to Communist capitals, which has resulted in the formation of a distinct parallel diplomatic pattern which serves to combine both Party and State relations in the Communist orbit. A third trend is that a Ministry long under the control of Molotov and exposed to the temptations of the outside world is being placed under quasi-surveillance and provided with Party ballast.

Since 1953, not counting Molotov and the late A. Y. Vyshinsky, no less than six full members and five alternate members of the Party Presidium elected in 1952 have been shifted to the diplomatic service, most of whom are still there. Many of these new Party diplomats enjoy higher Party rank than their technical superior, Foreign Minister Gromyko, and they constitute a distinct cluster of Party luminaries who outshine any combination of career diplomats. The year 1958 represented the high-water mark of Party infusion into the Foreign Ministry, when Gromyko's two First Deputy Ministers and at least six of his ambassadors appeared to outrank him in the Party galaxy, although in most cases their stars were in decline. Five of these new diplomats were admitted to the Party Central Committee in 1939, the same year in which Gromyko entered the diplomatic service as a junior official. In 1958, Gromyko's non-career subordinates included, aside from Molotov, eight former Presidium members, two former deputy premiers, several ex-Ministers, and a number of former First Secretaries of Republican and local Party organizations. The non-career diplomats accounted for a total of nine full members of the Central Committee in contrast to only one for the career diplomats (Gromyko himself, who was elected in 1956 after four years as an alternate), and five alternate members as opposed to only three for the professional diplomats (Malik, Zorin, and Zarubin). Two other non-career diplomats had recently been demoted from membership in the Central Committee.

Since 1958 some of the Party officials have worked themselves back into the Party Apparatus, others have died, and some have been appointed to quasi-diplomatic ministerial positions. None have fully recovered their former Party eminence, while additional Party and Government officials have been shifted to diplomatic careers. The decentralization of the economic establishment in 1957–1958 left many powerful economic administrators without positions of prestige and some were moved into the diplomatic service. The most recent and important shift from the Party to diplomacy was the appointment of A. A. Aristov as Ambassador to Poland in February 1961, while he was still formally a member of the Party Presidium, Secretariat and Party Bureau for the Russian Republic. Since he replaced a low-ranking functionary in the Warsaw post, this represents a considerable demotion in power and prestige. A partial list of career Party *apparatchiki* re-assigned to the Foreign Ministry follows:

V. V. Kuznetsov, First Deputy Foreign Minister: Full member of the Central Committee, former full member of Presidium, 1952–1953, and long-time Chairman of the Central Council of Trade Unions; Ambassador to China, 1953.

N. S. Patolichev, First Deputy Foreign Minister (1956–1958): Alternate and full member of the Central Committee since 1939; former First Secretary of the Byelorussian Party; ex-alternate member of the Presidium, 1952–1953; appointed Minister of Foreign Trade, 1958.

P. K. Ponomarenko, Ambassador to the Netherlands: Full member of the Central Committee since 1939; full member of Presidium, 1952–1953; alternate member, 1953–1954; former overlord of Soviet cultural affairs; former First Secretary of Byelorussian and Kazakhstan Parties; former Ambassador to Poland, 1955–1957; Ambassador to India, 1957–1959.

P. F. Yudin, Ambassador to China (1952–1959): Full member of the Central

Committee, alternate member, Presidium, 1952–1953; former director of the Cominform and prominent Party ideologist; replaced in Peking in late 1959 by low-ranking Party functionary.

N. M. Pegov, Ambassador to Iran: Full member of the Central Committee since 1939; alternate member of Stalin's expanded Presidium; former Secretary of the Party Central Committee and Secretary of the Presidium of the Supreme Soviet just prior to his appointment to Teheran.

I. F. Tevosyan, Ambassador to Japan (1957–1958): Full member of the Central Committee since 1939; former alternate member of Stalin's expanded Presidium; Deputy Premier in charge of metallurgical industries under Malenkov and Bulganin up to the time of his diplomatic appointment. Died in 1958.

N. A. Mikhailov, Ambassador to Indonesia: Full member of the Central Committee since 1939; full member, Party Presidium, 1952–1953; Ambassador to Poland, 1954. Left diplomatic service for succession of Party and State posts, the most recent being Minister of Culture. Returned to diplomacy in 1960.

A. A. Aristov, Ambassador to Poland: Full member of the Central Committee; elected to Presidium and Secretariat, 1952; dropped after Stalin's death, reappointed to Secretariat in 1955, to Presidium in 1957. Known Khrushchev supporter and trouble-shooter; member of Party Bureau for R.S.F.S.R. Shifted to diplomacy, February 1961.

M. G. Pervukhin, Ambassador to the German Democratic Republic: Full member of the Central Committee since 1939; full member, Presidium, 1952–1957; alternate, since 1957; former First Deputy Chairman, Council of Ministers and holder of other powerful economic Ministries. Exiled to diplomatic service for his part in the anti-Khrushchev plot of 1957.

A. M. Puzanov, Ambassador to North

Korea: Ex-full member of the Central Committee, now candidate member; former Premier of the Russian Republic, then Deputy Premier of the Russian Republic, and former alternate member of Stalin's expanded Presidium.

L. G. Melnikov, Ambassador to Rumania (1953): Full member, Presidium, 1952–53; reduced to alternate rank after Stalin's death and dropped soon after. Former First Secretary of Ukrainian Party. Left diplomatic service in 1954 to occupy series of low-ranking government positions; elected alternate member of Central Committee in 1956.

The channels of Soviet diplomacy. It is general practice for Soviet envoys to report to the Ministry through routine bureaucratic channels, that is, through the appropriate geographical divisions in the Ministry, but ambassadors in important posts frequently report directly to the Foreign Minister. Reports of an exceptionally important character are also sent directly to the Foreign Minister or his First Deputies, rather than through normal channels. The close supervision of the diplomatic service by the Party center cannot be overemphasized; and diplomatic channels remain deliberately flexible.

Not all Soviet representatives abroad report to the Foreign Ministry. Envoys to Communist states, particularly those holding high Party rank, probably report to the Central Committee or the Presidium, except for reports of essentially protocol or legalistic significance, which are funnelled through normal channels. The jurisdiction of the Foreign Ministry over envoys to Communist countries appears marginal at best.

Although the Ambassador, as the chief legal representative of the Soviet Union in foreign countries, is charged with general supervision over the activities of Soviet representatives and missions abroad to ensure that they are in accord with the general policy of the government, this responsibility is often of little more than formal or legal significance. According to defectors like Igor Gouzenko and Vladimir Petrov, Soviet missions abroad are organized into five separate divisions, each with separate and independent channels of communication: (1) the Ambassador and his staff, reporting directly to the Ministry of Foreign Affairs; (2) the Commercial Counsellor, reporting to the Ministry of Foreign Trade; (3) the Secret Police representative, disguised as a minor diplomat, reporting directly to the foreign section of the Security Ministry (now Committee); (4) the Attachés, reporting directly to the Director of Military Intelligence in Moscow; (5) the Party representative, also disguised as a minor diplomatic functionary, communicating directly with the foreign section of the Central Committee of the Party.

All of these representatives, with the exception of the Ambassador and the embassy staff proper, may be actively engaged in the overt or clandestine collection of intelligence information. In order to comply with the letter of their agreements with foreign countries, the Ambassador is scrupulously insulated from all knowledge of illegal espionage activities organized by the other sections, and although the Foreign Ministry Statute gives him the power to determine whether their activities are in accordance with government policy, in practice the Ambassador rarely sees the reports dispatched by the other sections through their respective channels.

In addition to espionage and intelligence activities, the Secret Police and Party sections maintain general surveillance over the other members of the mission and over each other. If the accounts of high-ranking defectors from the diplomatic and police service are accurate, Soviet missions abroad are often centers of intrigue, personal vendettas, and institutional rivalries and jealousies.

Information coming through various channels is screened, coordinated, and evaluated by a special agency of the Central Committee, which then submits its reports to the Presidium to be used as a factor in the formulation of foreign policy and in the making of decisions.

As instruments, rather than makers of policy, professional Soviet diplomats play a minor role in the formulation of foreign policy decisions. Their work is essentially technical and legalistic; the content of their reports is concerned primarily, if not exclusively, with observations and suggestions for more effective implementation of existing policy. Their area of initiative is carefully circumscribed and discouraged, and often they are themselves ignorant about the exact intentions of their superiors in the Kremlin. Their reports constitute but a minute fraction of the information upon which the Presidium takes action, and final disposition of all information from routine diplomatic channels and intelligence sources is made by the Presidium as it sees fit. As Merle Fainsod points out, accurate evaluation of information in the Soviet Union is often frustrated by special hazards:

But the mountains of material have to be reduced to manageable proportions before they are brought to the attention of the leadership. What the rulers read reflects the selection and emphasis of an editorial staff which may be guided by its own preconditioning as well as its sensitivity to the anticipated reactions of its readers. The tendency to embrace data that confirm established predilections while rejecting the unpalatable facts

that offend one's preconceptions is a weakness . . . [to] which . . . totalitarian societies appear to be particularly susceptible. . . . Every dictatorship has a tendency to breed sycophancy and discourage independence in its bureaucratic hierarchy. When the pronouncements of the dictator are sacred and unchallengeable, the words which subordinates must throw back at him tend to flatter his whims rather than challenge his analyses. . . . The ideological screen through which facts are received, filtered, and appraised constitutes an additional possibility of misrepresentation. . . . Not even the most pragmatically oriented member of the ruling group can wholly liberate himself from the frame of responses that represent the residue of a lifetime in Communist thought patterns.[57]

Khrushchev's explanation of why Stalin ignored repeated warnings from Churchill and from his own efficient espionage networks that the Nazis were planning to attack the Soviet Union appears to confirm Fainsod's perceptive appraisal when he revealed that "information of this sort concerning the threat of German armed invasion of Soviet territory was coming in also from our own military and diplomatic sources . . . [but] because the leadership was conditioned against such information, such data were dispatched with fear and assessed with reservation."

THE PARTICIPATION OF FOREIGN COMMUNIST PARTIES IN SOVIET FOREIGN POLICY DECISIONS

As rulers of the first country in which a Marxist revolutionary party had been elevated to power, the Bolsheviks early had to define their relationship with

[57] Fainsod, op. cit., p. 283.

kindred Marxist parties engaged in revolutionary activity in other countries.

Although the international Communist movement has been institutionalized only in two organizations, the Comintern and the Cominform, Moscow's relations with foreign Communist parties falls into three distinct, but closely interrelated, periods: (1) The Leninist period (1919–1928); (2) the Stalinist period (1928–1953), and (3) the post-Stalinist period (1953–   ). These distinctions are purely arbitrary, based neither on the programmatic nor the institutional metamorphosis of the world Communist movement, but exclusively on the degree to which foreign Communist parties participated in the formulation of decisions concerning revolutionary strategy or Soviet foreign policy.

The Leninist period: partners in world revolution

The Comintern, founded by Lenin in 1919, was invested with two basic and interdependent functions: (1) to coordinate the strategy and direction of the world revolutionary movement, and (2) to defend the Soviet state against counterrevolution and foreign capitalist intervention. These two purposes in turn rested upon two fundamental assumptions concerning the world revolutionary movement: (1) the Russian Revolution was merely the first phase of a general revolution, and had neither a justification nor a purpose independent of it; (2) the revolution in Western Europe, particularly in Germany, was imminent.

The entire history of the relationship between Moscow and foreign Communist parties has been determined by the two essentially contradictory purposes of world revolution and the defense of the Soviet Union.

The latter purpose in turn has rested upon the shifting assumptions concerning the fortune and direction of the revolutionary movement outside Russia.

When Lenin convened the first Congress of the Comintern in 1919, neither the concept of a world "Communist" movement, nor of foreign "Communist" parties, existed. Under Bolshevik sponsorship, radical or left-wing factions of the Social Democratic parties splintered off to form separate Communist parties affiliated with the new Third International. At the 2nd Congress in 1920, Statutes were drawn up defining "The Communist International [as] . . . a universal Communist party of which the parties operating in each country [including Russia] form individual sections," whose aim was "the establishment of . . . the international Soviet Republic." [58]

Although the Russian was the only ruling Party—except for the Hungarian during a brief period—and although a Russian, Grigori Zinoviev, was installed as president, the Soviet Party was not invested with a privileged and dominant status in the organization, but, like all other Parties, was subordinate to the decisions of the World Congress and its Executive Committee. The more imminent the revolution in Germany appeared, the more precarious was the "leading" role of the Russian Party. The facts, however, that it was the only Soviet state in the world and that the headquarters of the Comintern could be established only in Moscow made it inevitable that, as the prospects of the revolution faded, the position of the Soviet Party would correspondingly be enhanced.

Disagreements between Bolshevik leaders and foreign Communist parties,

[58] W. H. Chamberlin, ed., *Blueprint for World Conquest* (Chicago: Human Events, Inc., 1946), p. 36.

particularly the German, were frequent. Revolutionary doctrine and strategy and the role of Soviet diplomacy were discussed in the World Congress and in the meetings of its Executive Committee. The participation of foreign Communist parties was by no means a mere formality, and the Soviet state, which was conceived primarily as an instrument of the world revolution, frequently had to adjust its foreign policy to the views of foreign Communist parties, over which it did not exercise full control. The failure of revolution to take hold in Hungary and Germany, and the success of the Bolshevik regime to survive, forced a corresponding modification of the assumptions upon which the Comintern rested. The power struggle unleashed by Lenin's death in 1924 also found its reflection in the Comintern and within foreign Communist parties abroad. A re-examination of the previous estimates of the revolution in Germany, and the victory of Stalin's policy of "Socialism in One Country" in opposition to Trotsky's idea of "Permanent Revolution," forced leaders in the Comintern and in foreign Communist parties to choose sides. As Stalin squeezed out his rivals at home, his supporters in the Comintern and in foreign Communist parties carried out corresponding purges in their organizations. By 1930 Stalin had established his mastery over the Party Apparatus at home and this was immediately followed by a corresponding subjugation of the Comintern.

The Stalinist period: instruments of Soviet diplomacy

From 1928 to 1953 foreign Communist parties, even after they assumed power in their own countries, played little part in the formulation of Soviet foreign policy and were, on the contrary, completely subservient to it as pliable and expendable instruments.

The world Communist movement during the Stalinist period rested upon assumptions radically divergent from those upon which the Comintern was originally founded. These were: (1) the Soviet Union is the center and bulwark of the world revolution; (2) revolution independent of Moscow's support is impossible; and (3) the preservation of the Soviet as the indispensable base of the world revolution is the most important objective of all Communists, who must owe undeviating loyalty to Russia as the "proletarian fatherland." These new assumptions were incorporated into the 1928 *Program of the Comintern,* and the extension of world revolution became identified with the expansion of Soviet power:

The U.S.S.R. inevitably becomes the base of the world revolutionary movement. . . . In the U.S.S.R., the world proletariat for the first time acquires a country that is really its own. . . . In the event of the imperialist declaring war upon and attacking the U.S.S.R., the international proletariat must retaliate by organizing bold and determined mass action and struggle for the overthrow of the imperialist governments.[59]

The basic philosophy justifiying this submission to Moscow's control was euphemistically defined by Stalin himself as "proletarian internationalism":

A *revolutionary* is he who without evasions, unconditionally openly and honestly . . . is ready to uphold and defend the U.S.S.R. . . . An *internationalist* is he who unconditionally, without hesitation and without provisos is ready to defend

[59] *Ibid.,* pp. 220–223.

the U.S.S.R. because the U.S.S.R. is the base of the world revolutionary movement, and to defend and advance this movement is impossible without defending the U.S.S.R.[60]

Communist parties abroad were subordinated as expendable instruments manipulated in the interests of the Soviet state. Orders transmitted through the Comintern were followed with unquestioning obedience, even if they invited self-destruction (China, Germany) or conflicted with the fundamental interests of their own people (France). As Moscow changed its policies, foreign Communists followed suit, even if the new policies were diametrically opposed to the current line. The Kremlin functioned as a GHQ of the world Communist movement, sacrificing a division or corps here and there in the interest of the movement as a whole.

The dissolution of the Comintern in 1943 did not materially alter the relationship between Moscow and foreign parties, except, as noted by Andrei Zhdanov at the founding of the Cominform in 1947, that "some comrades understood the dissolution of the Comintern to imply the elimination of all ties, of all contact, between the fraternal Communist Parties [which] . . . is wrong, harmful and . . . unnatural." [61]

After World War II, when Communist parties were installed in power in the countries of Eastern Europe and the Soviet Union was deprived of its unique position as the only Communist state in the world, the theory of "proletarian internationalism" was transformed from a system justifying Moscow's control of parties into a system justifying her control of entire countries and subordinating their interests to those of Russia. Some satellite Communist leaders considered the Soviet theory of "proletarian internationalism" applicable only to parties in capitalist countries, otherwise it became a philosophical justification for Soviet colonialism.

As satellite leaders betrayed signs of uneasiness and independence in their new role as government leaders with the interests of their own countries and peoples to consider, Stalin organized the Cominform, ostensibly as an organ of mutual consultation based on the equality and independence of its members, but in reality to solidify his control over the satellites and to root out all tendencies towards independence. Unlike the Comintern, the new organization was carefully restricted to only the seven Communist states of Eastern Europe (Albania was denied membership) and to the two largest parties in the West, the Italian and the French. The refusal of Tito and other satellite leaders to place the interests of Russia above those of their own Communist countries and to act as Moscow's subservient agents of plunder and exploitation of their own people led to the expulsion of Yugoslavia from the Cominform and the wholesale slaughter of satellite leaders who showed signs of independence. "Loyalty to the Soviet Union," ran the Moscow line, "is the touchstone and criterion of proletarian internationalism." [62] This was echoed by satellite Communists and by Communist leaders in capitalist countries, who agreed with Dimitrov that "proletarian internationalism . . . means complete coordination of the activities of Communist Parties and of the lead-

[60] J. V. Stalin, *Sochineniya* (Moscow, 1949), Vol. X, p. 61.
[61] *Strategy and Tactics of World Communism*, p. 229.

[62] *For a Lasting Peace, For a People's Democracy*, June 30, 1950.

ing role of the Bolshevik [i.e. Soviet] Party." [63]

In rebuttal, Yugoslav leaders complained:

The leaders of the U.S.S.R. consider that Yugoslavia as a state should be subordinated . . . and its entire development in a general way should be made dependent upon the U.S.S.R. At the same time, they have forced other socialist states to act in a similar manner. . . . The political relations . . . are also based upon . . . the need to maintain in the various socialist countries the kind of regimes that will always be prepared to agree . . . to accept such unequal status and exploitation of their country. Thus—subservient and vassal governments and vassal states are actually being formed.[64]

The post-Stalinist period: developing polycentrism

Stalin's insistence that the Communist parties in Eastern Europe and in the Far East continue their subservience to Russia's interests introduced serious strains in the Communist orbit, of which Tito's defection was merely the most obvious manifestation. Moscow continued to interfere crudely in the internal development of the satellite states, while disclaiming interference; it plundered their economies and called it disinterested aid; and it rigidly dictated their "progress" to socialism, while paying lip-service to national peculiarities. On all these matters, satellite leaders were not consulted before decisions were taken in the Kremlin, but were simply commanded

to carry them out as efficiently as possible.

Whereas the small Communist states of Eastern Europe were at the mercy of Soviet power, the attempt to dictate to Peking involved considerable resistance. Satellite leaders elsewhere were slaughtered by the score, but no Stalinist purges took place in the Chinese Party. One measure of Stalin's patent contempt for Chinese interests or national sensitivities was his refusal to relinquish the Soviet stranglehold on Manchuria, dissolve "joint stock companies," or surrender the special extraterritorial interests in Port Arthur and Darien, although this refusal was clearly resented by the Chinese. According to Walter Ulbricht, Stalin's brazen attempts to treat China like an ordinary satellite almost forced Mao to desert the Soviet camp. Another clue to the deteriorated state of relations between Moscow and Peking during Stalin's lifetime was the enigmatic statement in the joint Sino-Soviet communiqué of January 19, 1957, that "since the conclusion of the Treaty of Friendship, Alliance and Mutual Assistance between the U.S.S.R. and China in 1950, the relations between the two countries have greatly developed. The events of the past few years demonstrate that the great alliance of the Soviet Union and China [is] . . . unbreakable." [65]

Stalin's successors were almost immediately confronted with the vexing problem of trying to perpetuate his system of vassalage or of modifying it. This re-examination unleashed a "great debate" within the Kremlin which divided the Soviet leadership into one faction insisting that the old system be retained with minor adjustments and another advocating a "liberalization" that bordered upon revolutionizing the

[63] G. Dimitrov, *Report to the 5th Congress of the Bulgarian Communist Party* (Sofia, 1948), p. 55.

[64] Milovan Djilas, *Lenin on Relations between Socialist States* (New York, 1949), pp. 16, 31.

[65] Full text in *The New York Times,* January 19, 1957.

entire relationship between Moscow and her allies. While Malenkov was Premier no radical departures from Stalin's satellite policies could be detected, but in retrospect it appears that the faction headed by Khrushchev and Bulganin was pressing for a complete rupture with the past. Its program included: (1) elimination of the dangerously developing schism with Peking; (2) rapprochement with Marshal Tito; (3) halting the outrageous economic exploitation of the satellites, and (4) permitting the gradual evolution of partial political autonomy. These proposals presupposed not only a break with the past, but also an actual repudiation of Stalin's policies, and consequently they were strongly resisted by Molotov and others as dangerous to the unity of the Communist movement.

The defeat of the Malenkov-Molotov policy was clearly apparent by July 1954. Neither Premier Malenkov nor Foreign Minister Molotov accompanied the Khrushchev-Bulganin mission to Peking in the autumn of 1954, whose purpose was to assuage Peking's resentments and inaugurate a new era in the relations between the two countries. The Soviet grip on Manchuria was relinquished, the joint stock companies liquidated, and full Chinese sovereignty restored over Darien and Port Arthur. Furthermore, Mao was apprised in advance of the impending changes in policy and government to be announced in February.

The most spectacular gesture of the Bulganin government was the decision to apologize to Marshal Tito, retract the accusations of treason and heresy, and make proper reparations for damages. As his price for a reconciliation Tito demanded, and apparently was granted, a consultative voice in the making of Soviet policy, which at one time virtually bordered on a veto privilege

in affairs affecting Eastern Europe. At Tito's insistence, the following measures were taken: (1) Stalin's satellite policies were openly condemned and repudiated; (2) Stalin's victims in Eastern Europe, like Rajk in Hungary and Koslov in Bulgaria, were posthumously rehabilitated, their trials pronounced a fraud, and Tito absolved of all implications of subversion and deviation; (3) "National Deviationists" or "Titoists" still alive, like Gomulka in Poland and Kadar in Hungary, were released from prison and restored to high rank in the Party; (4) satellite "Stalinists" were in turn dethroned and replaced with personalities more acceptable to Tito; (5) the Cominform was liquidated; (6) Molotov was ousted as foreign minister because he was *persona non grata* to Tito; and (7) Moscow accepted the Yugoslav theory "that the roads and conditions of socialist development are different in different countries . . . that any tendency of imposing one's views in determining the roads and forms of socialist development is alien." [66] Never before had a foreign Communist leader—and a heretic at that—exercised such a decisive role in the deliberations of the Kremlin.

The policy of de-Stalinization not only evoked resistance from the opposing faction in the Presidium but introduced new pressures upon its deliberations from other Communist parties who disapproved of the capitulation to Tito. The decision to denounce Stalin and Stalinism at the 20th Congress carried the day in the Kremlin; and aside from Mao Tse-tung and Marshal Tito, it is unlikely that other Communist leaders were consulted in advance. However, satellite leaders who had a vested interest in the Stalinist policies resisted the rupture, but the

[66] *The New York Times,* June 21, 1956.

pressures exerted by Tito upon the Khrushchev faction were sufficient to force many of them out of office. Reactions to the "de-Stalinization" program in Eastern Europe were far from uniform, and it was not entirely clear how far Moscow itself was ready to go. In Poland, Gomulka was catapulted to power; and in Hungary a national revolution threatened to sweep out the entire Communist system.

While Soviet troops succeeded in the resubjugation of Hungary, the "palace revolution" in Warsaw introduced another important and autonomous pressure upon the Soviet decision-makers— a quasi-independent Communist state of Poland which successfully defied Kremlin threats, purged Stalinists from high positions, and demanded and received a veto on the movement of Soviet troops in Poland. The Polish revolution was hailed in Peking and Belgrade, but it was generally condemned by the other satellite leaders.

Soviet intervention in Hungary also evoked divergent reactions in various Communist parties. Warsaw, Peking, and other influential centers privately were disturbed by the ferocity and brutality of the Soviet move, while Tito openly condemned the Soviet explanation of the revolution and deplored the use of troops. In his famous "Pula" speech,[67] Tito revealed the existence of "Stalinist" and "anti-Stalinist" factions in the Soviet hierarchy and in the Communist movement as a whole, and Yugoslavia was once again removed to the periphery of respectable communism. The situation over Hungary was so serious that Moscow asked Peking for support. A statement was issued condoning the Hungarian repression and repudiating the Yugoslav criticisms; Chou En-lai

[67] Full text of Tito's speech reprinted in *U.S. News and World Report,* November 30, 1956.

was dispatched on a fence-mending tour through Budapest, Warsaw, and Moscow. This clearly gave Peking a voice nearly equal to that of Moscow in the Communist orbit, while that of Marshal Tito appeared to dwindle.

Since Moscow's flirtation with Tito, the entire equilibrium of power in the Communist world has undergone fundamental redistribution. Moscow has been compelled to relinquish its dictatorial control over those Communist states having a power position sufficient to establish partial independence, but the pressure of events has forced her to yield more than she anticipated and less than enough to satisfy Tito. Indications are that the Kremlin, supported by Peking, decided to arrest further decentralization, convinced that any further concessions to Tito would unleash irreversible centrifugal forces that would disintegrate the Communist orbit.

Instead of a single dominant center of world Communism, there exist now two principal centers—Moscow and Peking—with one subsidiary center, Warsaw, and a peripheral one, Belgrade. The current aim of Moscow is to win for itself universal Communist recognition as *primus inter pares* in the Communist world as distinguished from its former autocratic position. Yugoslavia refuses to accord this recognition and will acknowledge only the chronological pre-eminence of the Soviet revolution. On the other hand, all other Communist parties, including the Chinese and the wavering Poles, have accepted the Soviet Union as the leading center of world Communism. The significant fact is, however, that Moscow must literally beg for this recognition and it no longer has the power to make decisions affecting other parties without consulting them in advance; thus it must share the power of decision. The split in the Kremlin was reflected throughout the entire Communist world, producing diverse pressures upon its deliberations which it can no longer conveniently ignore.

The basic statement governing Russia's new relationship with other Communist parties was the statement of October 30, 1956, issued during the Hungarian uprising. Admitting that "downright mistakes which infringed the principle of equality in relations between Socialist States" had taken place in the past, the statement pledged that "the Soviet Government is ready to discuss, together with the governments of other Socialist States, measures . . . to remove the possibilities of violating the principle of national sovereignty and . . . equality." In place of Stalin's monolithic hegemony, the new Soviet policy would subscribe a "Great Commonwealth of Socialist Nations" based on "the principles of proletarian internationalism."[68]

Although the Soviet statement serves as the basic document, a statement of the Chinese Communist Party has been accorded the dignity of an authoritative interpretation of the new policy:

Communist parties of all countries must be united, but at the same time must maintain their independence. . . . Solidarity among Communist parties . . . is strengthened when . . . they attain unanimity of views and action by means of real, and not formal, consultation. On the other hand, if in their mutual relations they forcibly impose their views on one another . . . then their solidarity will be harmed. . . . Stalin in his relations with fraternal parties . . . demonstrated a certain tendency toward great power chauvinism. . . . He sometimes interfered incorrectly in the internal affairs of . . . fraternal parties,

an interference that resulted in serious consequences. . . . It is also necessary to overcome nationalist tendencies in the smaller countries [*i.e.* Titoism]. . . . For the sake of interests . . . of the proletariat of different countries . . . we must continue to strengthen the solidarity of the international proletariat with the center in the Soviet Union.[69]

The discontinuation of the Cominform and the relaxation of the Stalinist system of controls raised the question of the future organizational forms of consultation and coordinated action. Moscow agreed that the institutional forms of consultation were not predetermined, but she frantically called them a matter of immediate urgency:

The establishment of businesslike contacts between Communist, Socialist, and Workers' Parties in order to eliminate the split in the international labor movement has become one of the most urgent problems of our time. . . . The forms and ties among Marxist parties are not predetermined and immutable. They arise from the requirements of the Communist movement at each stage . . . and are determined by the parties themselves in the interest of victory of the common cause and not of course to satisfy someone's whim.[70]

These new relationships have not yet crystallized into a new supranational Communist organ of consultation, since the very nature of these consultative organs and practices remains a matter of serious dispute. The Soviet Union favors the recreation of a multinational organization, similar to the Cominform in its structural outlines, but to be based on the principles

[68] Full text in *The New York Times,* October 31, 1956.

[69] *Pravda,* December 31, 1956.

[70] Mikoyan's speech to the 8th Congress of the Chinese Communist Party, *Pravda,* September 18, 1956.

of equality, full discussion, "proletarian internationalism," and unity of action. An alternative pattern of multilateral consultation reportedly suggested by Moscow was the exchange of permanent Party representatives. Both suggestions were frowned upon by Peking, Warsaw, and the Italian Communist Party, while Belgrade was not consulted.

The principal resistance to a new Cominform comes from Yugoslavia, although both Poland and China also oppose a revival of the organization in any form, which they fear may once again be employed by Moscow as an instrument of centralization and domination, since the Soviet Union can still muster the allegiance of more than a majority of the Communist parties in Europe. Opposed to the Soviet multilateral approach was the Yugoslav-Polish view that consultation be primarily a bipartisan affair:

Both parties recognized that the bilateral interparty relations in the present conditions constitute the most appropriate form of consultation between Communist and Workers' Parties. This does not exclude, however, a broader cooperation of Communist and Workers' Parties and progressive movements in connection with individual questions of common interest.[71]

Pending the formation of definitive institutions and methods of consultation, bilateralism and *ad hoc* multilateralism have been the general rule. This has followed three patterns: (1) mutual exchange of Party delegations to Party conferences and congresses; (2) bilateral discussions throughout the Communist world, followed by the issuance of joint communiqués, which have betrayed interesting deviations

from the crude uniformity of the past; (3) multiparty conferences, in the form of periodic gatherings of delegates from all Communist Parties and selective conferences restricted to Parties which exercise power in their respective states. The first of these post-Cominform conferences was a rump meeting held in Budapest in January 1957, which was attended only by delegates from Moscow, Budapest, Sofia, Prague and Bucharest, while the one held in Moscow the following November was universally attended, in that it also attracted delegates from Belgrade. The Yugoslav representatives, however, refused to accept the Declaration issued by the ruling Communist Parties, in which a common core of ideological principles and policy positions were hammered out after long and arduous negotiation. The purpose of the Declaration was to restore the unity among the various ruling Parties, which had been ruptured by the denunciation of Stalin and the events which followed, but it became impossible to reconcile the extreme positions of China and Yugoslavia, in spite of the wide latitude which the November Declaration afforded for individual variation within a common program.

The concessions made by Moscow, however, did earn the public support of Peking for the ideological innovations introduced at the 20th Party Congress and the denunciation of at least some aspects of Stalinism, but the Chinese could not accept positions which would be acceptable to Belgrade. Now that China supported the Soviet position, Warsaw had no alternative but to alter its heretical position and to support the Declaration. The main points at issue, which the Yugoslavs could not accept, were the questions of the leading role of the Soviet Union in the Communist World, the dogmatic insistence that all international ten-

71 *The New York Times,* January 1, 1957.

sions were generated by Western Imperialism and that peace was possible only after the liquidation of capitalism, but that "peaceful co-existence" would govern relations with the capitalist world pending its final liquidation, and finally that "revisionism" (*i.e.,* Titoism) constituted the chief threat to the unity of the Communist orbit. "Dogmatism" (*i.e.,* Stalinism) was condemned as a lesser deviationary evil and threat to Communist unity.

The net result was the elimination of Yugoslavia as a factor in making decisions for the Communist orbit and the elevation of Peking to a position of rivalry with Moscow for power and influence in the Communist world. The November 1957 meeting signalled China's independence in political and ideological matters from Moscow and underlined the voluntary character of her recognition of Soviet primacy, with the implication that she could withdraw this recognition at will. The auspicious inauguration of the People's Communes in 1958 in China and the bitter attacks levelled against them by Soviet leaders betrayed a bold attempt on the part of China to leap over, not only the stage of capitalism, but also socialism as well, into the phase of communism, in a clumsy effort to claim primacy for the Chinese State as the most advanced society in the world.

The 1957 Declaration also called for a new authoritative international journal of the Communist movement, presumably to replace the defunct paper issued by the Cominform, and a third multiparty conference held in Prague in March 1958, without benefit of the Yugoslavs, could only agree to issue a theoretical and informational monthly, the *World Marxist Review,* which has proven to be little more than a trivial journal of Communist scholastic opinion.

Beginning in late 1958 and continu-ing into the sixties was the gradual polarization of Peking and Moscow as the two ideological and power centers in the Communist camp. Warsaw gradually and grudgingly gave up its quasi-heretical position, while Belgrade remained isolated from the Communist world and drew closer to the Afro-Asian neutralist powers. A new Soviet policy began to emerge which sought to solidify Soviet control and influence over the Eastern European Communist States as a separate and distinct process from maintaining the unity of the Communist orbit as a whole. This has led to the existence of a European Communist bloc, led by the Soviet Union, within the camp as a whole. Only Albania, whose special fear is Yugoslavia—the main focus of attack by Peking—remains outside the Soviet bloc, playing a strange game of pitting Peking against Moscow. China has not yet organized a comparable regional Communist bloc, but indications are that Peking would like to organize such an intra-Communist regional grouping made up of the four Asian Communist states, China, North Korea, Mongolia and North Vietnam. Her geographical position *vis à vis* the smaller Asian countries, however, is not as decisive as the Soviet position with respect to Eastern Europe since three of the four Asian Communist countries border on the U.S.S.R. itself, and the fourth, North Vietnam, seems ready to play the Albanian game in reverse—using the Soviet Union as leverage against Chinese domination.

In forging a common policy towards the non-Communist world, the intra-bloc rivalries play a conspicuous role. The Soviet Union and China appear to be significantly divided over important matters of ideology and policy suffi-cient to prevent the development of a common outlook. Peking has not fully accepted Khrushchev's revision of the

Leninist-Stalinist formula on the in-inevitability of wars, for Chinese leaders continue to stress the inevitability of war with the Western Powers led by the United States. The formula of "peaceful co-existence" and the efforts to avoid the outbreak of nuclear war on the part of Moscow have been publicly criticized by Chinese spokesmen, while in the underdeveloped countries, China has taken Moscow to task for supporting local bourgeois-nationalist political movements and regimes at the expense of encouraging Communist revolutionary parties. These ideological and policy differences could not be concealed by the superficial unity of the November 1960 meeting of world Communist leaders. They reflect a basic conflict of national interests between a maturing social and industrial order (the Soviet Union and the European satellites), which has a greater vested stake in avoiding the risks of nuclear war, and a pre-industrial revolutionary society which feels that its political and economic goals can be achieved only by destroying the vestiges of the old social and economic order.

Irrespective of the detailed nature, causes, and underlying motivations of Sino-Soviet controversies or "dissimilarities" as Chou En-lai has quaintly captioned them—ranging from traditional historical and territorial questions to fundamental differences between the basically European character and culture of Moscow and the orientalism of China that transcend ideological matters—the significant point in that the world Communist movement has been divested of its single directing center and threatens to fragment into several centers. While this need not lead to immediate conflict, it does result in a lower level of ideological consensus. Red China is still not sufficiently powerful to chal-

lenge the Soviet Union for absolute leadership in the Communist orbit, nor is she prepared to conduct an independent foreign policy. Although still dependent upon the Soviet Union for military weapons and assistance, she is not so dependent that she becomes a pawn of Soviet foreign policy. Territorial claims against India, aid to Algerian rebels, and bellicose threats in the Formosa Straits are examples of Red China's independence from absolute Soviet control.

Regardless of what institutional forms are adopted for interparty cooperation, the Kremlin has abdicated its monopoly on making decisions for the entire Communist world and to some extent must coordinate its foreign policy with that of its allies rather than the other way around. What remains clear, however, as an aftermath of the Polish and Hungarian episodes, is that although Moscow is willing to allow considerable latitude in the internal evolution of the satellites, she has clearly laid down the outer limits beyond which the satellite states cannot go without inviting interference. These are: (1) acceptance of the basic irreconcilability of the capitalist and socialist camps; (2) recognition of the Soviet Union as the "leader" of the socialist camp; (3) intolerance of an independent or "neutralist" foreign policy for Communist states; and (4) retention of the dictatorship of the proletariat, *i.e.,* the communist one-party system.[72]

These limitations apparently represent what Moscow believes to be the minimum requirements for the preservation of Communist power and Soviet security interests. By implication, the violation of any of these conditions by satellite Communist leaders will invite

[72] Mikhail Suslov's speech on the 39th anniversary of the Bolshevik Revolution, *Pravda,* November 7, 1956.

Soviet armed intervention. Since Tito refuses to accept the first three conditions, he retains his heretical status in the Communist world.

These limitations, however, cannot be imposed upon China, and must be recognized simply as the indispensable minimum core of common ideological principles governing the European Communist states. The institutionalization of Communist regional associations remain reflected essentially on the State level, as demonstrated by the Warsaw Pact (military aspect), the Council of Economic Mutual Aid (CEMA), which is economic in character, and the periodic Communist Summit meetings, the most spectacular of which was the congregation of European Communist leaders at the meeting of the General Assembly in 1960, where representatives of Asian Communist states were conspicuous for their absence. The only missing link is a European Communist political organization—State or Party—whose creation will constitute a definitive stage in the development of relations among Communist states. The maneuvers and intrigues of Albania in supporting Peking, and receiving political and economic support in return, reflects not only Albania's anxiety that Moscow may eventually make sufficient concessions to bring Yugoslavia back into the Communist fraternity (perhaps after Tito's death), but also China's *de facto* recognition of a special Soviet sphere.

CONCLUSION

Since the death of Stalin the latent corrosive elements inherent in the Communist system have been activated. The centralized monopoly over decision-making in the Soviet Union has experienced a partial diffusion which is still continuing. First there was the transition from one-man decisions to collective rule and the tolerance of opposing opinions within the oligarchy. The Central Committee now exercises at least a consultative voice in decision-making which may eventually evolve into a form of participation. Informal recognition has been accorded special interest groups by co-opting their representatives into the highest councils of the Party.

The partial decentralization of the decision-making process then had its ramifications outside the Soviet Union, particularly on questions involving other Communist states. First China, then Yugoslavia, and finally Poland and other countries were accorded a greater or lesser degree of participation and consultation in foreign policy matters of general interest. The Parties of these countries, like their Soviet prototype, in turn are under diverse factional and internal pressures.

Privileged groups, not only in the Soviet Union but in other Communist states as well, are loath to embark upon adventures likely to endanger the system from which they benefit, and hence they all have an identical interest in the preservation of the Communist system. But each national elite is preeminently concerned with its own security and self-perpetuation. Just as the transcendental goal of world revolution was subordinated to the security and power interests of the Soviet state during Stalin's lifetime, it is natural to assume that each national Communist elite will tend to identify its own survival with the ideological imperative of world revolution, subordinating the latter to its own interests.

Although it was possible for a single Communist state to rationalize the subjugation of the movement to its own impulse for survival and to gain a wide acceptance for this identification, it is hardly likely that the interests of nearly a dozen Communist states can be so harmonious that each can utilize the world Communist movement in its own interests. Inevitably, the interests of the various national Communist elites will come into conflict (as in the case of Tito and Stalin)—particularly when the interests of one Communist state endanger the survival of an other—and the consequence may be either another schism (Poland), or armed intervention (Hungary).

If the interests of China and the Soviet Union ever diverge in a serious way, that may well be the end of the world Communist movement. This is recognized by both Peking and Moscow, but whether their intention to preserve solidarity can overcome the objective forces that drive them apart is questionable.

The rigidity of Soviet diplomacy has been replaced with a greater flexibility, but at the expense of abdicating its ineluctable advantage of instantaneous maneuverability. Multiple restraints have been introduced, although still in rudimentary form, in the Soviet decision-making process, and the diplomacy of Soviet Russia, like that of the United States, must now be attuned to diverse internal and external sensitivities. As a result, lapses into hesitation, vacillation, and compromise (as exhibited during the Hungarian crisis) will likely be more frequent now that a consensus must first be hammered out in the Presidium and then accommodated to similar consensuses reached by the ruling Communist elites of its coalition and ideological partners. "Collective rule" and "polycentrism" cannot but introduce serious strains into a system whose superstructure was erected upon the foundations of one-man dictatorship and imposed uniformity. Although this basis imparted to Soviet diplomacy its greatest immediate advantage, it also threatened eventually to shatter the very edifice it supported.

SELECTED BIBLIOGRAPHY

Armstrong, H. F., ed., *The Foreign Affairs Reader* (New York: Harper & Brothers, 1947). Articles by Bukharin, Radek, and "X" (George Kennan).

———, *Tito and Goliath* (New York: The Macmillan Company, 1951).

Barghoorn, F. C., *The Soviet Image of the United States* (New York: Harcourt, Brace & World, Inc., 1950).

———, *Soviet Russian Nationalism* (New York: Oxford University Press, 1956).

Barmine, A., *One Who Survived* (New York: G. P. Putnam's Sons, Inc., 1946).

Aspaturian, Vernon V., *The Union Republics in Soviet Diplomacy* (Paris: Libraire Droz, 1960).

Barghoorn, Frederick C., *The Soviet Cultural Offensive* (Princeton, N. J.: The Princeton University Press, 1960).

Beloff, Max, *The Foreign Policy of Soviet Russia, 1929–1941* (New York: Royal Institute of International Affairs, 1947).

———, *Soviet Policy in the Far East, 1944–1951* (London: Royal Institute of International Affairs, 1953).

Borkenau, F., *The Communist International* (London: Faber & Faber, Ltd., 1938).

———, *European Communism* (New York: Harper & Brothers, 1953).

Brzezinski, Zbigniew K., *The Soviet Bloc* (Cambridge, Mass.: Harvard University Press, 1960).

Carr, E. H., *The Bolshevik Revolution, 1917–1923*, III (London: Macmillan, 1953).

———, *German-Soviet Relations between the Two World Wars* (Baltimore: Johns Hopkins Press, 1951).

Chamberlin, W. H., ed., *Blueprint for World Conquest* (Chicago: Human Events, Inc., 1946).

Dallin, Alexander, ed., *Soviet Conduct in World Affairs* (New York: Columbia University Press, 1960).

———, *Soviet Foreign Policy After Stalin* (New York: J. P. Lippincott Company, 1961).

Dallin, D. J., *Soviet Espionage* (New Haven: Yale University Press, 1955).

Dedijer, V., *Tito* (New York: Simon and Schuster, Inc., 1953).

Degras, Jane, ed., *Soviet Documents on Foreign Policy* (New York: Oxford University Press, 1951–1953), 3 vols.

Dennet, R., and J. Johnson, eds., *Negotiating with*

the Russians (Boston: World Peace Foundation, 1951).

Deutscher, I., Stalin (New York: Oxford University Press, 1949).

Dinerstein, Herbert, War and the Soviet Union (New York: Praeger, 1959).

Fainsod, M., How Russia Is Ruled (Cambridge, Mass: Harvard University Press, 1953).

Falsifiers of History (Moscow: Soviet Information Bureau, 1948). Official Soviet explanation of the diplomacy of the Nazi-Soviet Pact and its aftermath.

Fischer, L., The Soviet in World Affairs (Princeton: Princeton University Press, 1951) 2 vols.

Fischer, R., Stalin and German Communism (Cambridge: Harvard University Press, 1948).

Garthoff, R., Soviet Military Doctrine (Glencoe, Illinois: Free Press, 1954).

Goodman, Elliot R., The Soviet Design for a World State (New York: Columbia University Press, 1960).

Gurian, Waldemar, ed., Soviet Imperialism: Its Origins and Tactics (Notre Dame: University of Notre Dame, 1953).

Haines, C. G., ed., The Threat of Soviet Imperialism (Baltimore: Johns Hopkins Press, 1954).

Hilger, G., and A. G. Meyer, The Incompatible Allies (New York: The Macmillan Company, 1953).

Kennan, George, Soviet Foreign Policy Under Lenin and Stalin (Boston: Little, Brown and Company, 1961).

Kulski, W. W., Peaceful Co-existence (Chicago: Henry Regnery Co., 1959).

Leites, Nathan, A Study of Bolshevism (Glencoe, Illinois: Free Press, 1953).

Lenczowski, George, Russia and the West in Iran, 1918–1948 (Ithaca, N. Y.: Cornell University Press, 1949).

Marx, K., and F. Engels, The Russian Menace to Europe (Glencoe, Illinois: Free Press, 1952).

Moore, Barrington, Soviet Politics: The Dilemma of Power (Cambridge, Mass.: Harvard University Press, 1950).

Moseley, Philip E., The Kremlin and World Politics (New York: Vintage Books, 1960).

———, et al., The Moscow-Peking Axis (New York: Harper & Brothers, 1957).

Nazi-Soviet Relations, 1937–1941 (Washington, D.C.: Government Printing Office, 1948). Selected documents from the German archives.

North, Robert C., Moscow and Chinese Communists (Stanford: Stanford University Press, 1953).

Reshetar, J. S., Jr., Problems of Analyzing and Predicting Soviet Behavior (Garden City: Doubleday & Company, Inc., 1955).

Roberts, H. L., Russia and America (New York: Harper & Brothers, 1956).

Rossi, A., The Russo-German Alliance, 1939–1941 (Boston: Beacon Press, 1951).

Rubinstein, Alvin Z., The Foreign Policy of the Soviet Union (New York: Random House, 1960).

Russian Institute (Columbia University), The Anti-Stalin Campaign and International Communism. A selection of documents (New York: Columbia University Press, 1956).

The Soviet-Yugoslav Dispute (London: Royal Institute of International Affairs, 1948).

Stalin, J. V., Problems of Leninism (Moscow: Universal Distributors, 1947).

———, The Great Patriotic War of the Soviet Union (New York: International Publishers Co., Inc., 1945).

———, Economic Problems of Socialism (New York: International Publishers, Inc., 1952).

Stettinius, E. R., Roosevelt and the Russians (Garden City: Doubleday & Company, Inc., 1949).

Taracouzio, T. A., The Soviet Union and International Law (New York: The Macmillan Company, 1936).

———, War and Peace in Soviet Diplomacy (New York: The Macmillan Company, 1940).

Towster, Julian, Political Power in the U.S.S.R. (New York: Oxford University Press, 1948).

Ulam, A. B., Titoism and the Cominform (Cambridge, Mass.: Harvard University Press, 1952).

Wolfe, B. D., Khrushchev and Stalin's Ghost (New York: Frederick A. Praeger, Inc., 1957). Khrushchev's secret report in full text, with commentary.

Zinner, P. E., ed., National Communism and Popular Revolt in Eastern Europe (New York: Columbia University Press, 1947). A selection of documents.

6

THE AMERICAN TRADITION IN FOREIGN POLICY

Throughout its history, the United States has pursued a consistent foreign policy. Beneath the clamour of contending philosophies, the controversies of factions, the contradictions and reversals of individual moves on the international scene, the foreign policy of the United States presents a simple and coherent pattern. This pattern results from the character of the interests which the United States has traditionally pursued on the international scene.

In the Western Hemisphere, the United States has always endeavored to preserve its unique position as the predominant, unrivalled power. The United States has recognized from the very beginning that its predominance could not be effectively threatened from within the hemisphere without support from outside it. This peculiar situation has made it imperative for the United States to isolate the Western Hemisphere from the political and military policies of non-American nations. The interference of these nations in the affairs of the Western Hemisphere, especially through the acquisition of territory, was the only way in which the pre-

HANS

J.

MORGENTHAU

dominance of the United States could have been challenged from within the hemisphere itself. The Monroe Doctrine and the policies implementing it express that permanent national interest of the United States in the Western Hemisphere.

Since the interests of the United States in the Western Hemisphere can be effectively threatened only from outside—historically, from Europe—the United States has always striven to prevent the development of conditions in Europe which would be conducive to interference in the affairs of the Western Hemisphere, or contemplation of a direct attack upon the United States. These conditions would be most likely to arise if a European nation having unchallenged predominance within Europe could look across the sea for conquest without fear of being threatened at the center of its power.

It is for this reason that the United States has consistently pursued policies aiming at the maintenance of the balance of power in Europe. The War of 1812 is the sole major exception to this tradition. It has opposed whatever

European nation was likely to gain ascendancy over its European competitors and jeopardize the hemispheric predominance and, eventually, the very existence of the United States as an independent nation. Conversely, it has supported whatever European nation appeared capable of restoring the balance of power by offering successful resistance to the would-be conqueror. While it is hard to imagine a greater contrast in political philosophy than that between Alexander Hamilton and Woodrow Wilson, they agree in their concern for the maintenance of the balance of power in Europe. It is with this in mind that the United States has intervened in both World Wars on the side of the initially weaker coalition, and has pursued European policies largely paralleling those of Great Britain; for from Henry VIII to this day Great Britain's single objective in Europe has been the maintenance of the balance of power.

Asia has vitally concerned the United States only since the turn of the century, and the meaning of Asia for American interests has never been obvious or clearly defined. In consequence, American policies in Asia have never as unequivocally expressed the permanent national interest as have the hemispheric and European policies. Yet beneath the confusions and incongruities which have sometimes marred American policy in Asia, one can detect a consistency that reflects, however vaguely, the permanent interest of the United States in Asia. And this interest is again the maintenance of the balance of power.

The principle of the "open door" in China expresses this interest. At the beginning, its meaning was purely commercial. But when other nations, especially Japan, threatened to close the door to China not only commercially but also militarily and politically, the United States sought to keep the door to China open in order to safeguard the latter's territorial integrity and political independence for political rather than commercial reasons. However unsure the United States may have been in the particular moves of its Asian policy, it has always assumed that the domination of China by another nation would create so great an accumulation of power as to threaten the security of the United States.

This extraordinary position of safety, which could be threatened only sporadically from afar, gave rise to a peculiarly American attitude toward foreign policy and war. All other politically active nations have been forced by their continuous exposure to danger from abroad to recognize the truth of Karl von Clausewitz's dictum that war is the continuation of policy by other means. The peaceful and warlike means by which a nation pursues its interests vis-à-vis other nations form a continuous process in which, though one means may replace the other, the end remains the same. Foreign policy itself is a continuum beginning with the birth of the nation and ending only with its death.

Yet under the impact of the extraordinary position in which the United States found itself vis-à-vis other nations from the beginning of its history to the end of the second World War, Americans came to embrace a different philosophy. According to this philosophy, it was "normal" for a nation to have no foreign policy at all. If a crisis should require a temporary departure from that normalcy in the form of an active foreign policy or of intervention in a foreign war, it was taken for granted that after the crisis was settled the nation ought to return to the normalcy of detachment. On this assumption that the nation had a choice between involvement in or detachment from world affairs, and that the latter was to be preferred, both the isolationists and internationalists of the interwar period agreed. They disagreed only in their assessment of the urgency of intervention in a particular crisis situation. Furthermore, the internationalists believed that in order to forestall the next crisis and meet it with the greatest chance for success, the United States should participate in the development and support of international organizations seeking to maintain international order and peace.

Foreign policy was thus regarded as something like a policeman's night stick, to be used only when necessary to bring a disturber of the peace to reason; war, in turn, was assigned the function of the policeman's gun, to be used only *in extremis* to rid the world of a criminal. But here the analogy ends: the policeman always carries his gun with him, but the United States threw its gun away twice, after it had done the job in two world wars.

The United States could see that war did have a necessary connection with the criminal aggression that preceded and provoked it, but it did not realize the organic relation that exists between war and what follows it. The purpose of war appeared to be the elimination of a disturbance by eliminating the disturber; once that was done, the world would presumably settle back into normalcy and order. War as prepared for and waged by the United States was a mere technical operation to be performed according to the rules of the military art—a feat of military engineering like building a dam or flattening a mountain. The organic relationship between foreign and military policy was lost, and, in consequence, foreign policy was with-

out strength, and military policy lacked purpose.

THE REVOLUTION IN AMERICAN FOREIGN POLICY

The aftermath of World War II witnessed a drastic change not in the traditional interests, but in the traditional policies and attitudes of the United States. This change was imposed by the conditions of unprecedented novelty under which the United States had to pursue its traditional interest in the preservation of the balance of power in Europe and Asia. What is the nature of the unusual threat with which the Soviet Union confronts the balance of power in Europe and with which China confronts the balance of power in Asia? When the United States was called upon in the two World Wars to redress the European balance of power, the German threat was being contained, however precariously, by a counterweight located in Europe itself. The Japanese threat, in turn, was contained on the Asian mainland by the power of China. The United States only needed to add its strength to these counterweights until victory was achieved, and then it expected to return to the normalcy of isolation. This is what it did after the first World War, and what it was prepared to do after the second. After some months of hesitation and confusion, the United States realized that the nations of Western Europe had become too weak to contain the Russian threat to the European balance of power and that the United States, in order to prevent the Russian conquest of all of Europe, had to commit itself in virtual permanence to the defense of Western Europe. When, in 1948, China fell to Communism and nothing stood in the way of its expansion except Chiang Kai-shek's forces, the United States took upon itself similar permanent obligations in Asia.

By 1947 the new pattern of American foreign policy was set. It manifested itself in four political innovations: the Truman doctrine, containment, the Marshall Plan, and the American alliance system. Foreign aid and liberation were added to them in the fifties. These policies have in common the permanent assumption, by the United States, of responsibilities beyond the limits of the Western Hemisphere.

The Truman doctrine is contained in President Truman's message to Congress of March 12, 1947. The President recommended the appropriation of four hundred million dollars for assistance to Greece and Turkey and the authorization to send civilian and military personnel as well as commodities, supplies, and equipment to these two countries. The immediate occasion for these requests was the inability of Great Britain to continue the historic function, which she had performed for almost a century and a half, of protecting the eastern shores of the Mediterranean from Russian penetration. Since the end of the Napoleonic Wars, one of the basic assumptions of British foreign policy had been that Russian control of Greece and of the Dardanelles constituted a threat to the European balance of power. Great Britain was no longer able to shoulder the over-all responsibility for the maintenance of the balance of power in Europe, and she had just notified the United States that she no longer possessed the military and economic resources to defend Greece against Communist attack.

The interest of the United States in the maintenance of the European balance of power had been historically identical with that of Great Britain, and by the beginning of 1947, the United States had already become— by the logic of the distribution of power, if not by design—the successor to Great Britain as the main counterweight against a threat to the independence of the nations of Europe. It was then almost inevitable that the United States take over the particular British burden for the protection of the independence of Greece and the territorial integrity of Turkey, an action justified both by traditional interest in the European balance of power, and by the particular conditions prevailing in the eastern Mediterranean at the beginning of 1947.

Yet the Truman doctrine went beyond the immediate occasion by committing the United States to the defense of democratic nations everywhere in the world against "direct or indirect aggression" and against "subjugation by armed minorities or by outside pressure." At this point, the Truman doctrine merges into the policy of containment.

The policy of containment was never officially formulated. It grew as an almost instinctive reaction to the threat of Russian imperialism. It called a halt to the territorial expansion of Russian power beyond the line of military demarcation drawn at the end of the second World War between the Soviet orbit and the Western world. It said in effect to the Soviet Union: "Thus far and no farther, else you will be at war with the United States." Or as the London *Economist* of December 2, 1950 put it: "The object of the endeavor in which the nations of the free world are now united is to contain Russian imperialism without having to fight another world war."

The United States recognized that the policy of containment could not succeed while the nations of Western Europe remained economically prostrate and politically unstable. Thus Secretary of State George Marshall declared in an address at Harvard on June 5, 1947 that the United States would welcome the initiative and co-operation of the European countries in the elaboration of an economic program of self-help combined with American assistance. The Western European nations quickly responded to this "Marshall Plan," forming as their vehicle of cooperation a Committee of European Economic Cooperation which laid the foundation for the establishment the following year of the Organization for European Economic Cooperation (OEEC). In April 1948, Congress approved the bill creating the Economic Cooperation Administration (ECA) as the instrument for channeling billions of dollars to the nations of Europe over a four-year program.

The American tradition limited to the Western Hemisphere the continuous presence of the United States on the stage of foreign policy. The great reversal of 1947 extended the permanent military commitments of the United States immediately beyond the Rhine and, potentially, to any region, anywhere, threatened by Communist aggression or subversion. It further committed the economic resources of the United States immediately to the support of the nations of Western Europe, of Greece and Turkey, and potentially of any nation anywhere which needed it to preserve its freedom. It had become the policy of the United States, in the words of the Truman Doctrine, "to support free peoples who are resisting attempted subjugation by armed minorities or by outside pressures." Since peoples throughout the world, in Europe, Africa, Asia, and Latin America, are resisting such subjugation, the commitments of the United States, by virtue of the Truman Doctrine, have become world-wide, unlimited geographically and limited only by the lack of need for support or a nation's unwillingness to accept it.

Of the traditional foreign policy of the United States, this revolution in America's relations to the outside world made short shrift. Nothing is left of it but a memory and, in some, a vain desire to return to an age when the United States was committed to defend only its own territory and the Western Hemisphere, not the nations of Western Europe, Berlin, Greece, Turkey, Australia, New Zealand, Pakistan, Thailand, South Vietnam, South Korea, Japan, and Taiwan, and when the United States endeavored to transform the world by its own example rather than by intervening, assisting, and advising.

America, once its policy of containment had met successfully the Russian military threat to Western Europe, had to achieve three difficult tasks. First of all, it had to create out of the makeshift arrangements aimed at meeting the Russian military threat a viable international order which would translate common interests into a common purpose, fuse the power of individual nations, and assign to them responsibilities commensurate with their interests and power. Second, it had to create a relationship with the uncommitted new nations of Africa and Asia which would be conducive to the development of domestic and international stability. Third, it had to establish a relationship conducive both to peace and freedom with those nations who were unwilling objects of Communist domination, such as the nations of Eastern Europe.

How did the United States endeavor to meet these tasks? It developed three policies to serve them: alliances, foreign aid, liberation.

The policy of alliances

Since the end of the second World War, the United States had concluded four collective alliances: The Inter-American Treaty of Mutual Assistance of 1947, also called the Rio Pact; the North Atlantic Treaty of 1949 under which the North Atlantic Treaty Organization (NATO) was established; the Security Treaty with Australia and New Zealand—called ANZUS—of 1951; and the Southeast Asia Treaty Organization of 1954, called SEATO. To these collective agreements must be added individual alliances the United States has concluded with Japan, the Philippines, South Korea, South Vietnam, and the Republic of China. The Baghdad Pact of 1955, concluded among Turkey, Iraq, Great Britain, Pakistan, and Iran, and succeeded after the defection of Iraq in 1958 by the Cento Pact, has been actively supported, but was not formally joined, by the United States.

The Rio Pact, of which the United States and all Latin American nations are members, serves the common defense of the Western Hemisphere by transforming the Monroe Doctrine from a unilateral American declaration into a collective arrangement. NATO, to which the United States and all nations of Western Europe—with the exception of Sweden, Switzerland and Spain—as well as Greece and Turkey, belong, serves the defense of Western Europe. The ANZUS Treaty serves the defense of the Pacific. SEATO, of which the United States, Great Britain, France, Australia, New Zealand, the Philippines, Thailand, and Pakistan are members, serves the defense of South and Southeast Asia.

The relationships within an alliance are determined by two fundamental factors—the interests and the power of its members. In this respect, the alliance between the United States and the nations of Western Europe must be distinguished from the other American alliances. The interests which tie the United States to its European allies are more profound, more comprehensive, and more stable than the interests upon which alliances have traditionally been based. Far from concerning nothing more than a limited territorial advantage against a temporary enemy, these interests enclose the national identity of all the members within a common civilization, threatened by an alien and oppressive social system. Thus this alliance was not formed through a process of bargaining among suspicious temporary associates, but rather sprang naturally and almost inevitably from a concern with a common heritage which had a chance to survive only through common support. The members of the alliance had to choose between the alliance and the loss of their national identity and cultural heritage; that is to say, they had no choice at all.

The cement that has maintained that alliance has been the paramount power of the United States. While in past alliances power had been unequally distributed, with one ally predominant, rarely had there been such a concentration of power, with all other allies in a subordinate position. The United States was not only paramount in the military and economic fields, but also in the intangible sphere of the values of Western civilization, and had become in every respect the predominant power of the alliance.

If the institutions and operations of the alliance had been as comprehensive and intense as its underlying interests, and if the influence of the United States had been commensurate with its power, the alliance might have amounted to a confederation of states merging their most vital activities in the fields of foreign policy, defense, finance, and economics. However, during the fifties, the United States did not play its required role in the Western alliance. Three inherited patterns of thought and action prevented this: the traditional limitation of the direct exercise of American power to the Western Hemisphere, the principle of equality, and the military approach to foreign policy.

On the two previous occasions when American power went beyond the limits of the Western Hemisphere, America retreated to its traditional confines after it had failed to establish itself firmly beyond them. The liquidation of the conquests of the Spanish-American War, in view of its accidental and peripheral connection with the American tradition of foreign policy, could begin as soon as the conquests had been made. The failure of Wilson's attempt to make the world safe for democracy rendered pointless the presence of American power in Europe. The nature of the Russian threat after the second World War left the United States no rational choice but to establish its power in virtual permanence at the circumference of the Russian empire. But should that power be established in terms of American supremacy, which would reduce America's allies to the status of satellites, or was it to be the equality of all members of the alliance, which would, ideally, result in the harmonious cooperation of like-minded nations? This dilemma had to be solved in a way that would not deny either of these essentials of American policy.

American power had to operate in the territory of friendly nations whose consent provided the only title for the American presence, the purpose of which was the defense of the freedom and territorial integrity of the allies. If the United States had reduced its allies to the status of satellites, the very purpose of the European alliance would have been defeated. On the other hand, the establishment of the alliance on the basis of complete equality was feasible only on the assumption that the identity of interests among the allies was so complete that they could pursue common ends with common measures through free and equal cooperation. If this cooperation fell short of the ideal expectation, the purpose of the alliance as a cooperative effort on behalf of the common interests would be defeated.

Of these alternatives, the United State chose the latter. It refused to bring its superior power to bear on the alliance on behalf of common interests which would compete with divergent ones. When the United States left the Western Hemisphere, it carried only its military and economic power, not its creative imagination and its constructive will. Significantly, this imagination and will came to play in that sphere closest to the American tradition in foreign affairs, the military sphere.

The United States emerged from the second World War as the most powerful nation on earth by chance and not by design, and it assumed the leadership of the coalition of free nations by virtue of necessity and not of choice. In consequence, its will and mind were not equal to its power, responsibility, and opportunity. Since America's responsibility was not the result of conscious choice, it approached the tasks incumbent upon the paramount power of the Western alliance with unbecoming humility and unwarranted self-restraint. The political predominance required by its power was incompatible with its anti-imperialist tradition, which is the manifestation abroad of the principle of equality. Confronted with the choice between assuming the position of leadership and treating its allies as equals, the United States chose the latter. Accustomed to expanding its rule into political empty spaces but not to imposing it upon existing political entities, it endeavored to establish a consensus within the Western alliance by the same methods of rational persuasion and economic inducements with which the American commonwealth had been created, maintained, and developed.

Yet the application of the equalitarian principle of democratic consensus to alliances resulted in disintegration and anarchy. The integrating effects of the domestic equalitarian consensus depend upon a pre-established hierarchical relationship in the form of a sovereign central government; any equality among allies drastically differing in power and responsibility must be subordinated to a hierarchical relationship between the paramount power and the rest. This relationship was lacking between the United States and its allies. As a result of this lack, the alliance was either incapable of pursuing new, positive policies in common, or else the most determined ally was able to impose its will upon the United States.

NATO is the outstanding example of the former consequence. The principle of equality among its fifteen members, applied to the political operations and over-all military planning of the alliance, put a virtually insurmountable obstacle in the way of new policies to be pursued in response to new opportunities or threats. The principle of equality would have been compatible with new departures in policy only on the unattainable conditions that all members of the alliance had an equal interest in such departures, were equally aware of these interests, and agreed completely on the means to be used in support of them. Short of an open threat of military conquest or revolution, such as confronted the members of NATO in the late 1940's, these conditions cannot be expected to be present at the same time. In the

absence of one of them, the best an alliance can achieve is to translate the lowest common denominator of agreed interests into common action. While the objective conditions under which the fifteen allies live require a degree of unity in purpose and action far transcending that of a traditional alliance, and while NATO was designed to be the instrument of that kind of unity, NATO has become more and more undistinguishable from a traditional, loosely knit alliance.

The other consequence of the equalitarian approach to alliances has been most marked in the bilateral relations between the United States and its allies. Governments which govern only because the United States maintains them or which have no alternative to the American association have been able to play a winning game in which the United States holds all the trumps. The United States has not been disposed to play these trumps for two reasons. Its commitment to the principle of equality made it impossible to bring its superior power to bear upon a weak ally on behalf of its interests. These interests were conceived in terms of what might be called the collector's approach to alliances. The United States in the fifties was primarily interested in the conclusion of alliances per se, regardless of the specific and concrete interests these alliances were supposed to serve. An alliance thus conceived is a standing invitation for a weak ally to make the alliance serve its specific and concrete interests. Thus the United States has paid for the willingness of weak and even unviable nations to become its allies by underwriting the interests of these nations, regardless of whether these interests coincide with, or even run counter to, its own.

This relationship, unhealthy even by the standards of traditional foreign policy, is a far cry from the new order through which the United States was called upon to realize the common purpose of the nations of Western civilization in the atomic age. The United States was not able to free itself from the pattern of thought and action established both by its tradition and its successful reaction to the threat of Russian power in the aftermath of the second World War—it continued to conceive of its relations to the outside world primarily in military terms. It saw itself surrounded by allies, by uncommitted nations which thus far had refused to become allies, and by satellites which Russian power had thus far prevented from becoming allies. From this picture of the world, three militarily oriented objectives ensued. The allies had to be kept in the American orbit, the uncommitted nations had to be drawn into it, and the satellites had to be liberated in order to enable them to join it. SEATO and the abortive Eisenhower Doctrine of March 1957 were open-ended—and largely unsuccessful—invitations to the uncommitted nations of Asia and the Middle East respectively to become allies of the United States, or at least to accept military assistance from it.

These policies were largely unsuccessful because the picture of the world from which they derived was at odds both with the facts of experience and the interests of the United States. What the United States had to cope with outside Europe was not the threat of Russian military power but the promise of the new order of Communism. A policy of military alliances was irrelevant to the problems raised by that promise. It was also counter-productive, for by strengthening the forces of the status quo and the military establishments in the allied nations, it tended to identify the United States with those forces and with preparations for war. This, in turn, gave Communism the opportunity to identify itself with the forces of progress and peace.

The policy of foreign aid

The policy of foreign aid, considered the main instrument for strengthening the uncommitted nations in their uncommitted position, has similarly suffered from this predominantly military orientation. But it has also suffered from two other handicaps.

The American theory and practice of foreign aid during the fifties was derived largely from certain unexamined asumptions which are part of the American folklore of politics. The popular mind has established a number of simple and highly doubtful correlations between foreign aid, on the one hand, and a rising standard of living, social and political stability, democratic institutions and practices, and a peaceful foreign policy on the other. The simplicity of these correlations is so reassuring that the assumption of a simple and direct relationship between foreign aid and economic, social, and political progress is rarely questioned.

Thus fundamental questions like the following were hardly ever asked explicitly: what are the social, political, and moral effects of foreign aid likely to be under different circumstances? Does successful foreign aid require a particular intellectual, political, and moral climate, or will the injection of capital and technological capability from the outside create this climate? To what extent and under what conditions is it possible for one nation to transform, through outside intervention, the economic and technological life of another nation? More specifically, in terms of the political objective of keeping the uncommitted nations uncommitted, how is one to create that positive relationship in the mind of the recipient between the aid and its beneficial results, and the political philosophy, system, and objectives of the giver? As long as the recipient disapproves of the politics of the giver, the political effects of the aid are lost. These effects are similarly lost as long as the recipient remains unconvinced that the aid received is but a natural manifestation of the politics of the giver. Foreign aid, then, remains politically ineffective as long as the recipient says either, "aid is good, but the politics of the giver are bad," or "aid is good, but the politics of the giver have nothing to do with it."

Questions such as these require policies of extraordinary subtlety and intricacy to answer them. The simple correlation between foreign aid and what the United States desires in the uncommitted nations could not provide the answers. That correlation is a projection of the domestic experience of America onto the international scene. Capital formation and investment and technological innovation created the wealth and prosperity of America, and, so it was assumed, the export of American capital and technology into the underdeveloped nations would bring forth similar results there. The similarity between this and the Wilsonian expectation is striking. Wilson wanted to bring the peace and order of America to the rest of the world by exporting its democratic institutions. His contemporary heirs wanted to bring the wealth and prosperity of America to the rest of the world through the export of American capital and technology. Yet while the failure of the Wilsonian experiment was quick and drastically revealed, the failure of foreign aid, simplistically conceived, has been less obvious, albeit no less drastic.

However, even if the United States had developed a well-planned philosophy of foreign aid, its application would have come up against the same equalitarian principle which has frustrated the alliance policy of the United States. While the application of this principle to the alliance policy was not warranted by the objective situation, foreign aid has confronted the United States with a real dilemma. If you apply the equalitarian principle, expressed in the slogan "no strings attached," to foreign aid, you put yourself at the mercy of unenlightened or corrupt governments which might misuse foreign aid through incompetence or by design. If, on the other hand, you assume responsibility for the way your aid is used, you feed the nationalistic suspicion of "imperialist" motives. By choosing the former method, the United States gave the recipient governments at least a potential leverage against itself, similar to that its allies enjoy. This leverage is increased by the competitive participation of the Soviet Union in foreign aid, which allows the recipient governments to play one super-power out against the other. Yet while the Soviet Union used foreign aid as an integral part of its political policy, seeking the expansion of its influence either directly or through Communist movements, the United States was at a disadvantage in trying to serve consistently either its own purpose or the purposes of the underdeveloped nations.

The policy of liberation

The weakness of the foreign policies of the United States, as conducted in the fifties, has come to a head in the total failure of its policies towards the satellites of the Soviet Union. The character of that failure suggests, as we shall see, the nature of the remedy. The inspiration from which the policies towards the satellites are derived is within the American tradition of seeking the expansion of the area of freedom. These policies continue the anti-imperialistic tradition of America, yet with one significant difference. The anti-imperialistic tradition has operated on two levels, the general one of revulsion against the normal practices of European power politics, and the specific one of revulsion against a particular case of oppression of one nation by another. The political consequences of the first type were the abstention and isolationism of the Farewell Address. The second type had almost no political consequence at all, but led to emotional commitment to what appeared to be the cause of freedom and humanitarian assistance to its suffering supporters. Thus the American anti-imperialism of the nineteenth century favored the national movements of Europe against monarchical enemies and opposed certain colonial ventures of European nations, and the American anti-imperialism of the early twentieth century took its stand against Imperial and Nazi Germany and against Tsarist and Soviet Russia, and both received the fighters in the lost causes of freedom as citizens.

The new anti-imperialism, aimed at the conquests of the Soviet Union, obviously partakes of these characteristics, but possesses a quality its predecessors lacked. It has become an integral and crucial part of the foreign policy of the United States. The traditional anti-imperialism of America was without a political objective either by virtue of its very nature or else because the radius of an active American foreign policy was limited to the Western Hemisphere. The new anti-imperialism can no longer afford to condemn the suppression of liberty from afar and limit its tribute to freedom to charitable deeds. Committed to the containment of Communism, to the preservation of national freedom wherever it is threatened by Soviet imperialism, the United States can reconcile itself to the loss of national freedom only if it altogether ceases being anti-imperialistic. If it wants to remain faithful to its anti-imperialist tradition, it must embark upon positive political and military policies on behalf of both the preservation and the expansion of national freedom. Yet at this point, when it came to adapting the traditional attitude of America to the opportunities and limitations of the contemporary world, American foreign policy failed.

The traditional American goal of expanding the area of freedom encountered a new opportunity and a new limitation in the foreign policy of the United States. It did not come to terms with either. Of this failure, the policy of liberation and the explicit inaction on the occasion of the Hungarian revolution of 1956 have been the outward manifestations. The policy of liberation manifested unconcern with the limitations; inaction on the occasion of the Hungarian revolution demonstrated unawareness of the opportunities.

The policy of liberation must be seen as a logical extension of the policy of containment and as the positive implementation of the American refusal to recognize the Soviet Union's European conquests. Stalin and his successors attempted to liquidate the Cold War by concluding an agreement with the United States dividing Europe into two spheres of influence, with the European conquests of the Soviet Union recognized as definite and legitimate. The United States has consistently refused to consider even the possibility of such an agreement. The United States could let it go at that, satisfied with containing Russian power within the limits reached in 1945, and that is essentially what it did up to the beginning of 1953. The impulse to go beyond this negative policy of containment and non-recognition, and to give that policy a positive implementation, stems from the traditional American purpose of expanding the area of freedom. But once America yielded to that impulse, it was up against the problem of what kind of positive policy should be pursued.

Consistent with its general conception of foreign policy, the United States conceived of liberation essentially in military terms, as the evacuation of Eastern Europe by the Red Army. Such evacuation could be brought about only through military pressure which carried the risk of war. As the London *Economist* put it on August 30, 1952, when the policy of liberation was first proclaimed: "Unhappily 'liberation' applied to Eastern Europe—and Asia—means either the risk of war or it means nothing. . . . 'Liberation' entails no risk of war only when it means nothing." Since liberation was to be achieved without resort to war, according to repeated official statements, it was, as conceived by American policy, incapable of achievement.

Thus what pretended to be a new dynamic policy turned out to be no policy at all, nothing more than a verbal commitment incapable of implementation by action. However, that commitment was taken as a threat by the Soviet Union and as a promise by the satellites. Instead of contributing anything to the liberation of the satellites, it served as a pretext for the Soviet Union to maintain its military rule of Eastern Europe, and as an incentive for the satellites to entertain illusions about what the United States might do, to be disillusioned with American policy, and reconciled to their fate when no action was forthcoming. The policy of liberation not only did not liberate, but actually strengthened the forces opposed and detrimental to liberty.

The Hungarian revolution of 1956 provided the ultimate test of this self-defeating unreality of the policy of liberation. For here the United States was faced, not with the impossible task of liberating without resort to war, but with the opportunity to support a liberation already achieved. By remaining inactive under these most favorable circumstances, it demonstrated that there was no such thing as a policy of liberation but only verbal pronouncements designed to give the appearance that there was one. The United States declared from the outset through its most authoritative spokesman, the President, that it would abstain from active interference. While it is a moot question as to how much the United States could have done, it is obvious in view of the since-revealed dissension within the Soviet government over the use of force, it could have done more than nothing.

THE REVOLUTION IN THE INTERNATIONAL ENVIRONMENT

These weaknesses, inherent in the foreign policy of the United States as it developed during the fifties, were aggravated by fundamental changes in the international environment to which American foreign policy did not adapt itself. At the end of the period, the international scene was different in four fundamental respects from what it had been at its beginning.

First of all, the balance of military power had changed radically. In the aftermath of the second World War, the United States was unquestionably the most powerful nation on earth. Under the umbrella of its atomic monopoly the United States formed the European alliance, implementing the policy of containment. The atomic monopoly of the United States provided a virtually absolute protection for the nations which felt themselves threatened by Communist aggression. This protection has disappeared. It has been replaced by an atomic stalemate or by what Sir Winston Churchill has called a "balance of terror"—the United States is able to destroy the Soviet Union and the Soviet Union is able to destroy the United States in an all-out nuclear war.

In view of this stark and simple situation, an alliance with the United States is no longer regarded as an un-mixed blessing. It still provides a certain protection, but it also implies a certain liability. Can the United States be relied upon to come to the aid of an ally if it might mean risking its own destruction? And wouldn't such aid, even if provided, seal the doom of the ally, since it would probably be in the nature of nuclear war to be countered in kind by the enemy? The allies of the United States are raising questions such as these, and they answer them by seeking safety in greater independence from the United States. Either they try to develop foreign and military policies of their own, especially in the nuclear field, or else they tend to move away from the United States into a neutral or at least a more detached position.

The second great transformation in the political world during the fifties is the restoration of the economic and, to a certain extent, the political health of most of the nations of Western Europe. At the beginning of the fifties, the alliance with the United States was for nations such as Italy, France, and Great Britain a matter not of choice but of life and death. Without the economic, political, and military support of the United States, those nations might not have survived as independent national entities and would have been in great danger of being subverted by Communism or swallowed up by the Soviet Union. Today, this dependence

upon the United States has to a great extent disappeared, especially in the economic field. It has become rather ineffective in the political field, and its ambivalence in the military field has become obvious.

Furthermore, and most importantly, the foreign policy of the Soviet Union has fundamentally changed. In the years immediately following the second World War, the greatest asset of United States foreign policy was the foreign policy of Stalin. Whenever there was a slackening in the Western effort or a weakening of the alliance system, Stalin would make a drastic move which demonstrated how necessary the American connection was for survival.

Khrushchev's foreign policy during the fifties was of an entirely different nature. His was not a policy of direct military aggression or of direct military threats. Even the threat against the Western presence in Berlin, uttered for the first time in November 1958, and repeated many times since, was quite different from the threats Stalin would have uttered or would have followed up by action, as in the case of the Berlin blockade in 1948. Khrushchev's policies aim not so much at the conquest of territories by diplomatic pressure or military threats as at the subversion of the whole non-Communist world through the impact of Soviet power and technological and economic accomplishments. This is a much more insidious, a much subtler way of undermining the position of the United States and of the Western world.

To these three fundamental changes must be added a fourth: the rise of the former colonial nations in Africa and Asia. These enormous masses of land and populations no longer belong to any of the power blocs. They are no longer under the control of any of the great powers. But they will in all likelihood have to seek the support of stronger nations and fashion their political, economic, and social lives in the image of one of the great political and social systems competing for their allegiance. Hence, they have become the great prize in the struggle between East and West. Whoever can attract the loyalties of these uncommitted nations and impress them with the excellence and superiority of his form of government, of his social and economic system, will in all probability win the struggle for the world. And Khrushchev has proclaimed that the Soviet Union, through the attractiveness and achievements of Communism, will conquer the minds of the uncommitted peoples and thereby inherit the earth.

These four fundamental changes in the international environment imposed upon the United States the task of rethinking and refashioning American foreign policy in five major areas: the relations with the allies, the relations with the uncommitted nations, the relation between domestic politics and foreign policy, the relations with the Communist bloc, and, finally, the supranational control of nuclear power.

The several alliances of which the United States is a member owe their existence, as we have seen, to two different factors: the need in which our European allies, as well as our former enemies, found themselves after the second World War to have American economic, military, and political support; and the objective of the United States to contain by military means the Soviet Union throughout the world and Communist China in the Middle East and Asia. During the fifties, the foundations for the first type of alliance changed radically, whereas the foundations for the second type were weak from the very outset.

The economic recovery of the nations of Western Europe and the former enemies made them less dependent upon American support than they once had been. As a consequence, they have at times been able to pursue their own narrower interests regardless of the common interests of the alliance. The United States must find a new foundation for these alliances, one which reflects more faithfully the present underlying community of interests of the major nations of the non-Communist world. These alliances were primarily conceived in military terms. They must now be given an economic, political, and cultural content as well.

The transformation of the Cold War into what is now called "competitive coexistence" has revealed the essential unsoundness of the policy of military containment as extended to Asia and the Middle East. The conflict between East and West has taken on the aspects of a struggle for the minds of men, especially in the uncommitted nations of Asia, Africa, and Latin America: a struggle to be fought with the weapons of prestige, subversion, political pressure, foreign aid, and foreign trade. Military alliances—in any contest for men's minds—are likely to be at best of minor importance, and at worst a political handicap.

If the United States is to wage this struggle for the minds of men with any chance of success, it must devise a new grand strategy. Two fundamental reforms are called for: the integration of all the factors involved in the struggle—military, political, economic —for the single purpose of maintaining and expanding the influence of the non-Communist world; and the adaptation of these various factors to the local conditions prevailing in any country. The United States must develop, and act upon, a coherent philosophy of foreign aid and foreign trade.

The uncommitted nations also confront the United States with a problem in political organization. Many of the new nations owe their existence to mere accidents of colonial history, and are therefore not likely to become viable political, economic, and military units within the boundaries they now occupy. They present a standing invitation for a new imperialism to establish a new order where the old colonial order has disappeared, or they are threatened with an anarchy which might well involve the rest of the world. This enormously complex problem will test the political creativity and determination of the United States.

It is obvious that the domestic policies pursued by the United States, especially in the field of race relations, are bound to have a direct influence upon its ability to wage the struggle for the minds of men. The United States needs to be fully aware of this influence in its conduct of domestic policies. Where it cannot entirely control these policies, it must at least give moral support to the positions which conform most closely to the best traditions of America. Throughout the better part of American history, the foreign policy of the United States drew strength and its attractiveness to other nations from the character of its domestic politics. The American experiment in government and social organization was intended from the very outset not only for America but for the world. It was meant as a model for other nations to emulate. The United States must restore that meaning.

The outcome of these new policies will depend upon the kind of relations the United States is able to establish with the Communist bloc. If these relations should deteriorate further, the very success of the new policies might turn out to be self-defeating, bringing closer the probability of a third World War fought with nuclear weapons. Thus the United States must achieve the supreme task of statesmanship by suc-cessfully waging the competitive struggle with the Communist bloc without at the same time increasing the risk of war.

The first pre-condition for minimizing that risk is the stabilization of the present territorial frontiers between the Western world and the Communist bloc. The second pre-condition is the maintenance of the Western nuclear deterrent. The risk of war will diminish only in the measure that the points of conflict which might ignite a war can be reduced, at the same time that deterrence against the starting of a war is strengthened.

Finally, even if the United States should be successful in the pursuit of all these policies, the United States and the world will still be confronted with the mortal danger of the spread of atomic weapons to an indefinite number of nations. This danger the United States can cope with only in cooperation with the other great nations of the world. The prospect of such a spread is bound to become a reality unless the present trend is reversed; if the trend continues, it is likely to cause unprecedented anarchy which will finally go beyond the control of the big powers. To bring nuclear weapons under supranational control is the overriding task of the age. History is likely to judge the United States by its approach to this task and its success in accomplishing it.

THE CONDUCT AND FORMATION OF AMERICAN FOREIGN POLICY

The character of a foreign policy conducted in a democracy is not determined by the requirements of sound foreign policy alone. It is also characterized by the willingness of the domestic political forces, whose approval is either required by the Constitution or necessary for political reasons, to support the foreign policies favored by the Executive Branch of the government. To secure that support becomes a prerequisite for the conduct of foreign policy. While it is certainly an exaggeration to say, as an eminent observer of American foreign policy has done, that 90 per cent of American foreign policy consists of domestic politics, it is no less certain that an American administration which fails to secure domestic political support for its foreign policies will find itself incapable of pursuing those policies effectively.

To secure support is bound to be a difficult task, for there exists an inevitable incompatibility between the requirements of good foreign policy and the preferences of a democratically controlled public opinion. "Foreign politics," says de Tocqueville with special reference to the United States, "demand scarcely any of those qualities which are peculiar to a democracy; they require, on the contrary, the perfect use of almost all those in which it is deficient . . . a democracy can only with great difficulties regulate the details of an important undertaking, persevere in a fixed design, and work out its execution in spite of serious obstacles. It cannot combine its measures with secrecy or await their consequences with patience." The history of foreign policy conducted under democratic conditions illustrates the truth of these observations. The conditions under which popular support can be obtained for a foreign policy are not necessarily identical with the conditions under which a foreign policy can be successfully pursued. Whenever these two sets of conditions diverge, those responsible for the conduct of foreign policy are confronted with a tragic choice. Either they must sacrifice what they consider good policy upon the altar of public opinion, or they must by devious means gain popular support

for policies whose true nature is concealed from the public.

Nations with a long experience in the conduct of foreign policy and a vivid awareness of its vital importance, such as Great Britain, have developed constitutional devices and political practices which tend to minimize the dangers to the vital interests of the nation inherent in the democratic conduct of foreign policy. Parliamentary democracy, especially under the conditions of the two-party system, provides in the Cabinet a mechanism which ensures the support, by the majority of the elected representatives of the people, of the foreign policies pursued. The collective parliamentary responsibility of the Cabinet compels the government to speak in foreign affairs with one voice, so that there can be no doubt, either at home or abroad, about the government's foreign policy at a particular moment.

It is the peculiar quality of the conduct of foreign policy in the United States that it maximizes the weaknesses inherent in the formulation and execution of foreign policy under democratic conditions, and that it aggravates these inherent weaknesses by unique constitutional devices and political practices.

On the constitutional level, the method of conducting foreign policy is determined by four general characteristics of the American Constitution: (1) its lack of definition in assigning functions to the different agencies of the Government; (2) the separation of powers, which allows the executive and legislative branches of the Government to hold office, and within certain limits to pursue policies, without regard to the other; (3) the system of checks and balances, which within certain limits makes it possible for one branch of the Government to prevent another branch from pursuing its policies; and (4) the requirement that under certain conditions measures can be taken by neither branch alone, but only through the concerted action of both.

The Constitution nowhere makes clear with whom the ultimate responsibility for the conduct of foreign policy rests. It assigns to the President alone certain specific functions, such as the reception of foreign diplomatic representatives; it assigns others, such as the regulation of foreign commerce and the declaration of war, to Congress alone; it provides for still others, such as the conclusion of treaties, which the President can discharge only in cooperation with the Senate. Apart from these specific grants, the Constitution limits itself to an over-all distribution of powers between the President and Congress by vesting in the former the executive power and making him Commander-in-Chief of the armed forces, and by vesting all legislative powers and the power of appropriations in Congress.

To locate, with the guidance of these "great generalities" and specific instances, the ultimate authority for the conduct of foreign policy is a task for constitutional theory and political practice. Jefferson's dictum that "The transaction of business with foreign nations is executive altogether" has claimed that ultimate authority for the President. On the other side of the argument, there is a chorus of voices which claim for the Senate, if not for both Houses of Congress, at least an equal share in the conduct of foreign policy. Constitutional theologies have covered these two positions with clusters of legalistic cobwebs, and have left the issue where the Constitution has left it—undecided. For in view of the affirmative powers granted by the Constitution to the President and Congress, the issue cannot be decided through constitutional interpretation. By giving some powers to the President, some to the Senate, some to Congress, and by remaining silent on the ultimate responsibility for the conduct of foreign policy, the Constitution, in the words of Professor Corwin, an eminent expounder of its law, "is an invitation to struggle for the privilege of directing American foreign policy." Just as the question of the location of sovereignty in the United States, an issue similarly held in abeyance by the Constitution, had to be answered by a civil war, so the issue of the ultimate responsibility for the conduct of American foreign policy is being decided individually each time it arises, in a series of running battles between the Senate or the two Houses of Congress on one side and the executive branch on the other. Each side uses the weapons provided by the Constitution as well as the extra-constitutional ones which have grown in its shadow.

The political relations between the President and Congress are determined by the fact that the President can hardly ever be certain of the support of a majority of both Houses of Congress for his policies. This is obviously so when the President and the majority of Congress belong to different parties, but even if the President is a member of the majority party, a minority of his own party will regularly vote against the policies with which he is identified. This defection is somewhat offset by a minority of the opposition party generally voting in favor of the President's policies. Yet the traditional jealousy with which any Congress guards its prerogatives against any President tends to give the edge to the hostile minority of the President's party. The President operates under the perpetual threat that his policies will be disavowed by a bipartisan majority of Congress.

To make such a threat come true Congress has at its command legislation, appropriations, and resolutions. To the same end, the Senate alone has power over treaties and over the appointment of diplomatic representatives and the high officials of the executive branch. This power of the Senate over appointments, by virtue of Article II, Section 2, of the Constitution, is a potential threat in the field of foreign policy rather than an active weapon. The Senate has sometimes refused to confirm individuals nominated by the President to ambassadorial positions or high positions in the Department of State, but it has not used that power for the purpose of making it impossible for the President to pursue a certain foreign policy.

The weapon of legislation can be used in two different ways. Whenever a foreign policy needs to be implemented by legislation, Congress can modify, emasculate, or negate the foreign policy pursued by the executive branch. Congress can also take the initiative and, as in the case of the neutrality legislation of the thirties and the successive immigration acts, limit the President's freedom of action through restrictive statutory provisions.

The weapon of appropriations can be wielded in two different ways. Congress can either withhold in part or in whole appropriations necessary to the execution of a certain foreign policy and thus cripple that policy or make its execution altogether impossible. The customary Congressional changes in appropriations for the Department of State, for foreign aid, and for information policies illustrate the potentialities of this weapon. The financial requirements of present American foreign policy make it the most potent of all the weapons at the disposal of Congress. Or Congress can attach a rider to an appropriation bill, providing expenditures for purposes not contemplated by the executive branch. In that case, the President must either reject the appropriation *in toto* and forego the policy for which the appropriation was to be used, or he must accept the appropriation *in toto* and against his better judgment execute a policy imposed upon him by Congress. Thus Congress in 1948 earmarked in the bill providing aid to Western Europe an appropriation for aid to China, a rider which the President had to accept since he did not want to jeopardize the European aid program.

Through resolutions, either joint or by one of the Houses, Congress expresses its preference for certain policies. While such expression of preference has no legally binding effect upon the executive branch, it indicates what kind of foreign policies Congress is likely to approve when called upon to act by way of legislation or appropriation. The Vandenberg Resolution of 11th June, 1948, for instance, calling for the conclusion of regional compacts for the purpose of mutual defense, influenced the form in which the North Atlantic Treaty was submitted to the Senate.

Public opinion has come to regard the constitutional provision which requires approval of two-thirds of the Senate for treaties negotiated by the President as the main weapon by which one-third of the Senate members plus one can veto the foreign policies of the executive branch which have taken the form of international treaties. In view of the relations between majority and minority party mentioned above, and given a politically controversial issue calling for a partisan stand, the chances of a treaty being approved by two-thirds of the Senate are slim. "A treaty entering the Senate," wrote Secretary of State Hay summing up his bitter experience, "is like a bull going into the arena. No one can say just how and when the final blow will fall. But one thing is certain —it will never leave the arena alive." The death-blows which the Senate dealt in the interwar years to Presidential policies of international co-operation are remembered, for whatever different reasons, by President and Senate. Their memory has exerted a powerful influence toward avoiding conflict situations and securing in advance bipartisan support for the foreign policies to be pursued by the executive branch.

The general power of Congress in the field of foreign affairs has been met by the President with the general weapon put at his disposal by his position as Chief Executive and Commander-in-Chief. The President has a natural eminence in the conduct of foreign affairs from which constitutional arrangements and political practices can detract, but which they cannot obliterate. His powers in this field are, in the words of the Supreme Court, "delicate, plenary, and exclusive." Short of the expenditure of money, the binding conclusion of treaties, and the declaration of war, the President can almost do as he pleases in formulating and executing foreign policies. He can, without reference to any other agency of government, make a public declaration of policy, such as the Monroe or Truman Doctrines. He can recognize or refuse to recognize a foreign government, as successive Presidents did with respect to the government of the Soviet Union. He can give advice, make promises, enter into informal commitments as he sees fit. He can send the armed forces of the United States anywhere in the world and can commit them to hostile acts short of war. In sum, he can narrow the freedom of choice which constitutionally lies with Congress to such an extent as to eliminate it for all practical purposes. If, for instance, the President had wanted to use armed force during the Berlin crisis of 1948 or in response to the military operations of Communist China in the Straits of Taiwan during the late fifties, he could have done so on his own responsibility and committed Congress to a declaration of war regardless of the latter's preferences. The course of American policy toward Germany and Japan during the initial phase of the second World War was determined primarily by Presidential action, and it was left to Congress to ratify or, at worst, to retard and weaken the consummation of that course.

The ascendancy of the President over Congress in the determination of American foreign policy is dramatically revealed by the extent to which the President has been able to circumvent Senate participation by substituting executive agreements, not requiring legislative approval, for formal treaties. The executive agreement has recently become the normal medium for international compacts. Most of the great political understandings of the war years, from the destroyer deal to Potsdam, were concluded by the President alone in the form of executive agreements. In 1939, ten treaties were concluded by the United States as opposed to 26 executive agreements. The corresponding figures for the following years are eloquent: 1940: 12—20, 1941: 15—39, 1942: 6—52, 1943: 4—71, 1944: 1—74, 1945: 6—54. They are even more eloquent for the decade starting in 1950: 1950: 12—59, 1951: 13—200, 1952: 20—356, 1953: 12—128, 1954: 9—251, 1955: 23—291, 1956: 10—241, 1957: 19—227, 1958: 6—178, 1959: 13—227.

The relations between President and Congress, however, cannot be conceived only in terms of actual or potential conflict, but also in terms of cooperation. For while the power of the President is pre-eminent in starting the course of American foreign policy, Congress's potential for obstruction remains, and the dependence of the Executive upon Congressional consent has increased with the expanding financial requirements of American foreign policy. Since the end of the second World War, successive Presidents and Secretaries of State have developed a system of cooperation with Congress in the formulation and execution of foreign policy. Its main purpose is the avoidance of the situation, which was the undoing of Wilson, in which the minority party opposes Presidential policies primarily because they are the President's and his party's policies. It has become the established practice of the executive branch to brief, and consult with, the foreign policy experts of the two parties, especially those of the Senate, in advance of major steps to be taken, to secure their consent, and to take their advice into account. This practice has worked with different results in different fields of American foreign policy. At times, the executive branch has not dared to take a step for fear of Congressional disapproval, and on other occasions, Congress has not dared to oppose certain policies proposed or initiated by the executive branch for fear it be accused of partisan obstruction. The over-all result, however, has been the formation of a coalition, composed of the majority of the two parties, in support of the President's foreign policy.

Bipartisanship, as originally conceived at the end of the second World War, carried the negative implication that a foreign policy ought not to be opposed by one party solely because the President and Secretary of State belonging to the other party were carrying it out. In positive terms, bipartisanship implied that the opposition party should support sound foreign policies and oppose unsound ones, regardless of the party affiliation of those carrying them out. Conceived in these terms, bipartisanship recognized the elementary fact that the consequences of foreign policy are not limited, as are those of many domestic ones, to a particular segment of the population identified with one or the other party, but affect the whole nation for generations to come. Bipartisanship drew from this fact the sound and indispensable conclusion that party strife for its own sake must stop at the point where the whole nation meets other nations in defense of its interests and its very existence.

Yet there is a point where the bipartisan policy of cooperation between Executive and Congress reverts to the traditional pattern of conflict and competition. The insistence by Congress upon full use of its inquisitorial powers becomes more jealous and bitter as the pre-eminence of the Executive in the conduct of foreign policy is unassailable, and Congressional frustration must find the semblance of relief in harassment and delay. Here is the crux of today's relations between the executive branch and Congress concerning the conduct of foreign policy. It can safely be said that, in a period of international relations dominated by the psychology and techniques of the Cold War, the executive branch of the Government of the United States must make a greater effort to maintain friendly relations with the United States Congress than with the Soviet Union. The constitutional separation of powers and the political practices growing from it, together with the stalemate in Russo-American diplomatic relations, have brought about the paradox of traditional diplomatic techniques of persuasion, pressure, and bargaining being applied by the executive branch of the American Government in its relations with Congress rather than with foreign powers.

Thus far we have referred to the President and the executive branch in their relations with Congress and foreign powers as though the President and the executive branch were one single entity pursuing one single policy. Nothing could be farther from the truth. It is true that the President, as Chief Executive and Commander-in-Chief, has the constitutional power to impose his own conception of most foreign affairs upon the executive and military departments. In reality, however, even so strong and astute a President as Franklin D. Roosevelt was unable to assume full control even of the State Department, the constitutional executor of his foreign policies.

The reason for this anomaly must be sought in two factors. One is the absence of a Cabinet which could integrate the policies of the different executive departments in the field of foreign policy—the American Cabinet is an informal advisory body. The other factor is the frequent inability of the President to definitely resolve major dissensions between executive departments or to meet head-on resistance to his policies on the part of an executive department, without risking inopportune conflicts with Congress. Congress is always ready to take advantage of open dissensions within that branch. President Roosevelt, rather than taking on a reluctant State Department, entrusted the execution of his more delicate and controversial foreign policies to special representatives, operating directly from the White House, or created special agencies for the performance of special functions. Some-

times Roosevelt pursued foreign policies of his own without even the knowledge of the State Department. The classic example is Roosevelt's approval in June 1944 of the division of the Balkans into British and Russian spheres of influence, while for almost three weeks afterwards the State Department continued to pursue a policy of opposition to the Anglo-Russian agreement. Sometimes, as with regard to certain phases of Middle Eastern policy, the State Department emerges victorious from the struggle with the President.

The problem of unity of action arises not only between the President and the executive departments, but also and especially when strong leadership from the White House is lacking, among the executive departments themselves, and even within them. Washington is the scene of continuous inter-office feuds, sometimes growing from real differences of policy, more often the result of a mere struggle for power. The Hoover Commission on Organization of the Executive Branch of the Government counted about 45 executive agencies, aside from the State Department, which are concerned with some phase of foreign policy. While most of them deal only with minor matters, some have exerted an important influence upon the conduct of American foreign policy. Among them, the military establishment is outstanding. The main vehicle for its influence is the National Security Council, composed of the President, the Vice President, the Secretaries of State and Defense, and the director of the Office of Civil and Defense Mobilization as statutory members. Its purpose is "to advise the President" in those fields of policy "relating to the national security." In a period of Cold War, the whole field of foreign policy becomes the proper object of the Council's advice. The National Security Council has become the key agency through which the views of the executive departments are filtered. Through the daily reports of its executive secretary it exerts a potent influence upon the President's mind.

The task of coordinating American foreign policy under the President's direction does not end with the settlement of disputes between executive departments. It extends to the executive departments themselves and their representation abroad. Certain ambassadors, such as Dodd in Berlin and Kennedy in London in the thirties, Hayes in Madrid during the second World War, were able for months to pursue foreign policies at variance with the policies of the State Department, if not the President. Generals Clay in Germany and MacArthur in Japan, during the period immediately following the second World War, in large measure formulated and executed their own policies which the executive departments concerned could do little else but ratify.

The success of the American way of conducting foreign affairs is due to that elusive factor which gives direction and unity to the American political system on all levels—public opinion. The Constitution makes public opinion the arbiter of American policy by calling upon the American voter to pass judgment upon the President and his party every four years, upon all members of the House of Representatives and one-third of the membership of the Senate every other year. The American people live perpetually in a state of pre-election or election campaigns. Presidential and Congressional policies are always fashioned in anticipation of what the voter seems likely to approve. The President, as the most exalted mouthpiece of the national will and the initiator of foreign policies, will test the state of public opinion by submitting new policies in the tentative form of public addresses and messages to Congress. These new policies will then be pursued or shelved, according to the reaction of public opinion. Democratic control of American foreign policy will depend largely upon the correctness of the President's estimate of the willingness of public opinion to support his policies, and upon his ability to marshal public opinion to that support. It is here that another, perhaps fundamental, weakness of the conduct of American foreign policy becomes apparent.

The state of American public opinion is ascertained by a special branch of the State Department and by the intuitive estimates of individuals through the media of press, radio, public opinion polls, Congress, and private communications. Yet the mass media of public opinion paint a distorted picture of the actual state of the American mind. While they may point with approximate accuracy to its lack of information, they give only a hint of its susceptibility to strong and wise leadership, derived from its native intelligence and moral reserves. The President and State Department seem to be taking at face value the discouraging picture conveyed by the mouth pieces of public opinion of the moral and intellectual qualities of the American people. In particular, fear of what Congress might do to their policies has become a veritable obsession with many members of the executive department, a fear derived from a misjudgment of the powers of Congress as an organ of public opinion.

That this fear is not justified by the actual control of Congress over the conduct of foreign affairs has already been pointed out. That the temper of Congress and especially of the Senate is not necessarily representative of public opinion is evident from a consideration of the four factors which limit the representative function of Congress: the disproportionate influence of rural over urban representatives by virtue of the approportionment of Congressional districts favoring the former; the disproportionate influence of the less populous states by virtue of the representation of all states, regardless of population, by two Senators; the disproportionate influence, upon members of Congress, of the spokesmen of special interest groups; finally, the limited representative character of members of Congress from a number of Southern states by virtue of the limitation of the franchise to a small fraction of the population.

The mistaken identification of press, radio, polls, and Congress with public opinion has had a distorting as well as paralyzing influence upon American foreign policy. It is here that the way American foreign policy is conducted has a direct bearing upon the kind of foreign policy pursued by the United States. By equating what Congress will approve with what the American people might be willing to support, President and State Department underrate the intellectual and moral resources of the American people and are demanding less of the American people than they could obtain. In consequence, the foreign policies they present to public opinion for approval often stop short of what they deem necessary in the national interest.

This fear of public opinion, especially in the form of Congressional opinion, together with the ever-present risk of conflict between the Executive and Congress and within the executive branch itself, constitutes a very serious handicap for any fresh departure in foreign policy. If one wants to win the next election, if one wants to advance in the bureaucratic hierarchy, if one wants to retain and increase the powers of one's office, it is well to

avoid conflict and to swim with the prevailing current. Yet any fresh departure in foreign policy, especially in a period of "cold war," means conflict—conflict with a half-informed and at times hysterical public opinion, conflict with a suspicious and reluctant Congress, conflict between and within executive departments. Thus the foreign policy of the Cold War, with its emphasis upon military preparations and its minimization of the traditional methods of diplomacy, is in a sense the foreign policy which the procedures of the American government are best fitted to conduct, although it is not the best fitted to preserve peace. The overriding concern for the preservation of peace makes imperative a change in the methods and, more importantly, in the spirit in which American foreign policy is conducted.

The factors which determine the conduct of American foreign policy cooperate as a brake upon executive initiative in foreign affairs. The evils which de Tocqueville finds in the democratic conduct of foreign affairs are compounded by the peculiarities of the American constitutional and political system. Not only does Congress act as a brake upon the executive branch, as it should, but so does public opinion, which ought to provide the fuel to carry American foreign policy forward. In that task of re-establishing public opinion as an independent positive force, the responsibility of the President is paramount.

The President must reassert his historic role as both the initiator of policy and the awakener of public opinion. Only a strong, wise, and shrewd President can marshall to the support of wise policies the strength and wisdom latent in that slumbering giant, American public opinion. Yet while it is true that great men have rarely been elected President of the

United States, it is upon that greatness, which is the greatness of its people personified, that the United States has had to rely in the conduct of its foreign affairs. It is upon that greatness that Western Civilization must rely for its survival.

SELECTED BIBLIOGRAPHY

Almond, Gabriel, *The American People and Foreign Policy* (New York: Harcourt, Brace & World, Inc., 1950).

Bemis, Samuel Flagg, *American Foreign Policy and Diplomacy* (New York: Holt, Rinehart & Winston, Inc., 1959).

Bloomfield, Lincoln P., *The United Nations and U.S. Foreign Policy* (Boston: Little, Brown & Co., 1960).

Goldwin, Robert A., ed., *Readings in American Foreign Policy* (New York: Oxford University Press, 1959).

Gordon, Morton and Kenneth N. Vines, *Theory Practice of American Foreign Policy* (New York: Thomas Y. Crowell Company, 1955).

Jacobson, Harold K., *America's Foreign Policy* (New York: Random House, 1960).

Kennan, George F., *American Diplomacy 1900–1950* (Chicago: University of Chicago Press, 1951).

——, *Realities of American Foreign Policy* (Princeton: Princeton University Press, 1954).

Kissinger, Henry A., *The Necessity for Choice* (New York: Harper & Brothers, 1960).

Lefever, Ernest, *Ethics and United States Foreign Policy* (New York: Meridian Books, 1957).

Morgenthau, Hans J., *In Defense of the National Interest* (New York: Alfred A. Knopf, Inc., 1951).

——, *The Purpose of American Politics* (New York: Alfred A. Knopf, Inc., 1960).

Osgood, Robert, *Ideals and Self-Interest in America's Foreign Relations* (Chicago: University of Chicago Press, 1953).

Perkins, Dexter, *The Evolution of American Foreign Policy* (New York: Oxford University Press, 1948).

——, *The American Approach to Foreign Policy* (Cambridge: Harvard University Press, 1952).

Rostow, W. W., *The United States in the World Arena* (New York: Harper & Brothers, 1960).

Spanier, John W., *American Foreign Policy Since World War II* (New York: Frederick A. Praeger, 1960).

Wolfers, Arnold, ed., *Alliance Policy in the Cold War* (Baltimore: Johns Hopkins Press, 1959).

7

THE FOREIGN POLICY OF MODERN JAPAN

THE BACKGROUND OF JAPANESE FOREIGN POLICY

In geopolitical terms, there are some obvious reasons for making a rough comparison between Japan and Great Britain. Both are island societies lying within the Temperate Zone and close to a great continental mass. From earliest times, cultural interaction with the continent has been vital in shaping the character of each society; each has definitely been a part of the larger cultural orbit centering upon the continent. The sea, however, has been both a lane and a barrier. It has prevented recent invasions, enabling the development of a relatively homogeneous people who despite many foreign adaptations have retained a strong quality of uniqueness. Thus the encircling sea has been important to culture as well as to livelihood and defense. It has also been central to the historic policy dilemma over isolation versus continental involvement. This has been the basic foreign policy issue of both societies throughout their existence. And in recent eras, the interaction between internal and external

ROBERT

A.

SCALAPINO

pressures has been such as to present essentially the same answer to this question in both Japan and Great Britain. The growth of foreign pressures and the needs flowing from modernization—the scarcity of certain domestic resources combined with the rise of unused power—these and other factors led to regional and then global commitment. There is the temptation to add that for both societies there now exists the need to adjust to a permanent decline in world power. This analysis, of course, stresses the similarities, not the differences. The latter will become apparent as we turn now to the Japanese scene.

The Tokugawa era

The diplomacy of modern Japan opened in the mid-nineteenth century on a decidedly reluctant and confused note. Prior to Perry's arrival in 1853, the Japanese government had pursued a rigorous policy of isolation toward the outside world for over two hundred years. It abandoned that policy only under strong pressure and with many misgivings. Isolation had first been imposed as a method of maintaining internal stability. When the Tokugawa family first came to power in Japan in 1606, the West had already been represented in the country for fifty years. Missionaries and traders had come in a steady stream, first from Portugal and Spain, then from the Netherlands and England. In the first years of the Tokugawa era, however, abuses were regularly reported to the government. Christian converts among the provincial nobility sought Western arms or alliances to fortify their position against the central regime. Western trade also became a means of augmenting local power, especially in the Kyushu area. Between 1616 and 1641, therefore, the Tokugawa government applied a series of anti-Christian and anti-trade edicts, leading up to a policy of almost total exclusion of the West. As is well known, only the Dutch were allowed to trade, very restrictedly, at Nagasaki. This, together with some limited relations with China and Korea, constituted Japanese foreign relations until the middle of the nineteenth century.

To draw up a balance sheet upon the isolation policy is not easy. It can be argued that had Western intercourse been allowed to continue, Japan might well have plunged into chaos and warfare, subsequently suffering the colonial fate of Southeast Asia. On the other hand, isolation clearly exacted its price. This is true not merely in terms of institutions and material developments, but also in the realm of emotions and attitudes. Isolation always breeds some of the symbols of the garrison state—exclusivism, ethnocentrism, and xenophobia, accompanied by mounting fears of the unknown, outside world. Most of these factors have been present in the Japanese scene, helping to shape the foreign policies and attitudes of that nation.

But in its time, Tokugawa isolation seemed to present only one major problem to Japan: how to maintain it? The expansion of the West toward Asia was building up an intense pressure upon Japan by the beginning of the nineteenth century. From the north, the Russians were moving forward on a broad front; Saghalien, the Kuriles, and even Hokkaido seemed threatened. Overtures for trade and coaling stations were made and rejected. At the same time, English intrusions began to take place in the southwest. These events were climaxed by news of the Opium War and repeated warnings from the Dutch. A debate began to shape up in Japan over fundamental policies.

This debate enabled Japanese nationalism to come forward, borne aloft by intellectuals from the agrarian-military class, and rooted in the primitive mythology of Shintoism. It was a movement with many facets: in part, dedicated to a restitution of Imperial prerogatives and their defense against Tokugawa usurpation; in part, an attack upon the long-standing intellectual subservience to China and an insistence upon the unique character and basic priorities of Japan; and finally, a fierce assault upon Western encroachment born out of an admixture of condescension and fear. All of these factors were implied in the chief slogan of the era, *sonno-joi,* "Revere the Emperor; oust the Barbarians."

In the precise form just described, this movement did not enjoy complete success, but within its evolution and adaptations was carried the destiny of modern Japan. That evolution followed in some measure the broad stages characteristic of the whole panorama of Asian-Western relations during this period, whether stated in policy or intellectual terms: an initial stage dominated by the total rejection of

Westernism as barbarian by definition, inferior to and completely incompatible with the Asian way of life; a second stage, in which Western science and technology—distilled into the unforgettable spectacle of Western power —were accorded a begrudging but nonetheless deeply felt respect, from which followed, after much soul-searching and confusion, a conscious majority decision to attain these sources of power while holding firmly to traditional values; and thence inevitably there developed that stage in which such a rigid and unrealistic dichotomy as that between technology and values had to be abandoned in favor of a more broadly based and integral synthesis, the exact ingredients and balance of which have depended upon the background and convictions of each individual or group. It is within this general trend—its various exceptions, time-lags, and all-important local distinctions not to be ignored—that the major elements of foreign policy in modern Asia have taken shape. Japan has been no exception.

Even before the arrival of Perry, a small group of Japanese intellectuals had begun to question the policy of rigid isolation. Out of "Dutch learning" had come exciting ideas; and there grew in some minds the desirability of leading the commercial revolution rather than fighting it, and of using foreign trade to develop power. How else could the intriguing slogan, "A rich country; a powerful soldiery," be effected; how else could Japan defend herself against Western imperialism? But this group was a small minority in the early period. Even the Tokugawa government supported the opening of the country only as a temporary expedient until force could be garnered to throw out the West. In accepting Perry's demands, it decided to accede rather than risk war, but it gave as little

ground as possible. With the initial step taken, however, it was impossible to retreat. Our first envoy, Townsend Harris, secured major liberalization of the Perry treaty in 1858, and similar rights were soon granted to other Western powers. From this date Japan was truly opened up to Western commerce, and shortly the Tokugawa regime was even to seek assistance in developing arsenals and shipyards. "Support the government" and "Open the country" seemed to be slogans indissolubly linked.

Yet basically, Tokugawa policy remained more a product of pressure than of purpose, and this fact worked against the effectiveness of the policy. Beset by many problems, the regime grew steadily weaker; its capacity to act vigorously in any direction diminished. It satisfied neither the West, which complained of its inability to control unruly elements, nor the provincial samurai, who regarded the central government as arch-appeasers. As so often happens in history, the regime in power found by tortuous means the only feasible policy for national survival—in this case, the policy of opening the country—but in the course of reaching that policy it was itself fatally weakened so that the actual execution and fulfillment of the policy had to pass to other hands.

Meiji foreign policy

In 1867, the Tokugawa regime was finally overthrown and the young Emperor Meiji was "restored" to the position of ruler, a position which the nationalists claimed the Tokugawa family had stolen. But real power in Meiji Japan gravitated into the hands of a small group of Court officials and young leaders of the former military class. Their first major objective in foreign policy became that of removing the blemish of the unequal treaties, thereby attaining "complete independence" and equity with the Western powers. This task proved more difficult than they had expected; to accomplish it took nearly three decades. The Western powers, and particularly Great Britain, saw no reason to revise the treaties until Japanese standards came close to Western norms. The Japanese discovered that treaty revision was closely connected with basic reform in such fields as law and commerce. Thus the Iwakura mission, which left for the West so hopefully in 1871 to persuade the powers to abandon the fixed tariffs and extraterritoriality, came home realizing that many internal developments had first to be undertaken.

Through the years, "modernization" progressed by means of German, French, British, and American models. Japanese economic and military power showed remarkable gains. Law and order prevailed despite occasional domestic crises. Finally, in 1894, after repeated failures, the first great objective of Japanese foreign policy was obtained: agreements with the West were concluded on basic treaty revisions, all of which went into effect by 1899. As the nineteenth century ended, Japan had become the first nation of Asia to attain nearly complete parity with the West in legal terms. She had done so in part by satisfying the West that she was prepared to abide by the general rules of Western conduct, in part by the obvious facts of her internal progress and stability, and in part by her persistence and by certain clear signs that inequity toward Japan had reached a point of diminishing returns.

In the long struggle for treaty revision, latent elements of anti-foreignism occasionally came to the surface in various forms. Officials deemed obsequious to foreign powers, too pro-Western in their own personal habits, or disrespectful of Japanese tradition ran grave risks. The history of these years is filled with records of assassination plots, some successful, against more moderate leaders. This was one price to be paid for cultivating a nationalist movement so assiduously while scarcely daring to admit its excesses. But quite apart from its extremists, Japanese society as a whole tended to react in pendulumlike fashion to the West. In many respects this was most natural. Periods of intensive borrowing and adaptation at both individual and group levels would be followed by noticeable retreats, with the primary targets being those excesses and absurdities most easily discernible, but with secondary attacks ranging over as broad a front as conditions would permit. On the one hand, Japan wanted to catch up with the West, be accepted as a "progressive" and "civilized" nation, and match the West in the areas of its own talents; in addition, a very genuine fondness for things Western was entertained by many Japanese, great and small. But on the other hand, in this period of intensive nationalist indoctrination, and when the old antiforeign traditions were not yet completely dead, the periodic cry of "excessive Europeanization!" or "un-Japanese practices!" could be rendered with telling effect. Moreover, if selected aspects of Westernism appealed to almost everyone, there was no widespread desire to abandon the main stream of Japanese culture or customs. These factors are not completely absent from contemporary Japan.

During the early Meiji era, there were strong overtones of defensiveness in Japanese policy and psychology. But the climate was also ripe for the rise of expansionism. Northeast Asia was largely a vacuum of power, tended haphazardly by the sick man of Asia, China, on the one hand, and the somewhat stronger but essentially unstable and overcommitted Czarist forces on the other. The Japanese mission seemed even clearer when it could be posed against the prospects of continuous Korean turmoil and the increasing threat of Western imperialism in this entire area. The theme of "Asia for the Asians" was first applied here, and sometimes by sincere men who had a vision of liberating other Asians from backwardness and Western domination, sharing with them the fruits of the new era in Japan. Private societies like the *Genyosha* (Black Current Society) and the *Kokuryukai* (Amur River Society) emerged to exercise a great influence on Japanese foreign policy as influential pressure groups on behalf of a forceful continental policy with some such objectives in mind.

The "ideology" of expansionism was complex, and it knew no single form of expression. From one perspective, groups like the Kokuryukai represented the past, holding firm to Japanese Confucianism, exalting the primitive mythology that surrounded the Emperor-centered state, ultranationalists of a peculiarly medieval type. Yet from another point of view these same men were radicals associated with the new era. Wherever Asian nationalism took root, they were willing to give it nourishment, even when its ideological bases were greatly different from their own. To movements as widely disparate as those of Aguinaldo and Sun Yat-sen their assistance was given freely, and in this they often went beyond what the Japanese government was willing or prepared to do. Moreover, there was an element of radicalism in their approach to internal affairs as well, though its source might be largely traditional. Decrying the corruption, materialism, and excessive wealth of the new order, they demanded stringent internal reforms, some of which could

be considered national socialist in character. Thus were connected the themes of internal reform and external expansion as twins that were to have recurrent echoes throughout modern Japanese history.

The goals of the expansionists received their first major advance in the extraordinary decade between 1895 and 1905. Prior to that time, Japan had already added the Ryukyu islands and the Bonins to her domain, and made more secure her northern outpost, Hokkaido, by extensive colonization, but these were not spectacular ventures. By 1894, however, Japanese leadership was ready to challenge China, the weakest of her rivals, for influence on the Korean peninsula. For Japan, the war was unexpectedly short and easy, the first of a series of wars that "paid." The Western-style training and the nationalist indoctrination of her conscript military forces stood the initial test with flying colors. For China, defeat at the hands of a foe long regarded with some contempt, and treated at best as a pupil, was a profound shock. Demands for fundamental reform were now renewed, especially by younger intellectuals, and against Manchu resistance China was pushed toward accelerated change and revolution.

In Japan the implications of victory were fourfold. The beginnings of the Japanese Empire were laid, and the first tentative steps as a modern continental power were taken; China ceded Formosa, the Pescadores, and, for a time, the Liaotung Peninsula until the intervention of Russia, France, and Germany forced its return. And China was eliminated as a serious competitor in the Korean contest. Second, the war served as a further stimulus to industrial growth and general economic development. In an atmosphere of patriotic fervor, industrial investment and expansion were undertaken, with an emphasis upon heavy industry. The war boom brought prosperity; and afterwards, Japan received both indemnities and new China markets. Third, Japan enjoyed a sharp rise in her world prestige; most of the West looked on approvingly as their most apt pupil demonstrated her progress and valor, and it was in the aftermath of this victory that Japan began to be received in Western circles with some semblance of equality. Finally, these factors naturally accrued to the credit of the nationalist movement and to the prestige of the military class. The professional soldier, his samurai traditions now supplemented by Western science and by a new sense of mission not present in the Tokugawa era, promised to play a vital role in determining the future of his society.

In the aftermath of the Sino-Japanese War a crucial decision had to be made. Japan was dedicated to increasing her ties with other Asian societies and providing leadership for them when possible. But to obtain these objectives and to have any basic security for herself, she needed a major alliance with a non-Asian power. This was still the world of the nineteenth century, when Europe collectively exercised a global influence, and when the unfolding of European power politics had a direct and immediate effect upon the non-European world. With the United States, Japan needed only to achieve some general agreement that would serve to neutralize potential conflict; indeed, she could expect no more, since American commitments toward the Pacific were still very limited even after the annexation of the Philippines. The major powers in Asia were Great Britain and Russia, and between these two, the choice had to be made.

Initially, top political circles in Japan were divided. Men like Ito and Inoue hoped for an agreement with Russia that would establish long-term peace in northeast Asia on the basis of satisfying mutual interests. Had such an agreement been reached, Japanese expansion might have been directed toward the south at a much earlier point. An alliance with Great Britain, on the other hand, was recognized as a step toward stabilization in the south and fluidity in the northeast. Not merely in this respect, however, but in every respect, Japanese foreign policy was affected for nearly two decades by the Anglo-Japanese Alliance of 1902. This pact was widely heralded as insuring the peace of Asia. Within certain limits, perhaps it did contribute to that end. England, now finished with isolation, needed global alliances to protect her global interests. In the Western hemisphere she cultivated the United States; in Asia she directed her attentions to Japan. Once established, the alliance not only supported the *status quo* in south and southeast Asia; it also provided within the limitations of British policy some protection for China. In exchange, Japanese "special interests" in northeast Asia were given recognition by the leading power of the world. Under such conditions Japan could scarcely afford not to advance those interests.

Thus the first fruit of the Anglo-Japanese Alliance was not peace but war. The question of Japanese or Russian hegemony over northeast Asia, having its antecedents back as far as the seventeenth century, was now given over to military decision. As is well known, Japanese victory against a weary and distracted foe was swift. From the Portsmouth Treaty Japan emerged in control of much of northeast Asia as the first Asian world power. The fruits of defeat and victory were similar to those of the Sino-Japanese War: to the defeated—soul-searching, unrest, and revolution; to the victor—a new gain of territory and fame. Clear title was obtained to the Kuriles, and southern Saghalien was added to the Empire; control over Korea could no longer be challenged, although outright annexation did not come until 1910; the Manchurian-Mongolian area also fell within the shadow of expanding Japanese power, a situation placing new pressure upon China. Again, Japanese industry had enjoyed great expansion as a part of the war effort, with some support from British and American loans. And once more Japanese nationalism had risen to the test. Only a handful of intellectual pacifists and radicals denounced the war; the great majority of the people had been deeply loyal to the cause of a greater Japan.

Some costs for the victory could be tabulated. One lay on the surface. Nationalist propaganda had been carried so far during the war that many patriots assumed that the peace would be dictated in Moscow, not realizing that a long war of attrition might be dangerous for a smaller country. Consequently, ugly riots broke out over the Portsmouth settlement and the government had difficulty in restoring order. There were also deeper costs to be tallied. At home, militarism had grown stronger; the non-conformist had little protection, either in law or by the customs of his society. Abroad, Japan was moving into a new orbit of power and influence, but as a result, she was now the object of new suspicions and fears, some of them coming from such traditional supporters as the United States and Great Britain. Already it seemed likely that the critical test might be China.

In partial recompense, immediately ahead lay an era of unprecedented influence for Japan throughout Asia. It was an influence, moreover, derived from much more than mere military prowess. There is no doubt that most of the Asian world experienced a thrill at the Japanese victory over Russia, because it gave hope that the West could be beaten at its own game. But in the broader sense, Japan had become the symbol of the new Asia, a society that had successfully made the transition toward modernization by a process of synthesizing new ideas with its indigenous culture. In the Japanese context Western science and progress had come alive, and from this experience the rest of Asia had much to learn. The success of Japanese nationalism was also a tremendous stimulus, even though its precise ideological forms might not be acceptable elsewhere. Thus as this era unfolded Japan embarked upon an extensive career as model, tutor, and leader to eager Asians everywhere. Thousands of students flocked to Tokyo and other Japanese centers of learning and industry. The majority came from China, but every section of Asia was represented in some degree. Likewise, Asian nationalist movements found in Japan a haven and source of support. Their leaders in exile wrote polemics, collected funds, and sometimes obtained official encouragement. Tokyo became a revolutionary center for the Far East. Japan was riding the crest-tide of the developing "Asia for the Asians" movement.

Already, however, the central problem of Japanese foreign policy was becoming that of distinguishing the thin line between acceptable leadership in Asia and unwelcome domination. This problem could be put in various forms. Would Japanese national interests in the long run be made compatible with the Asian march toward independence? Would Japanese technological, economic, and political assistance to Asia rest upon mutual benefit and truly cooperative bases, or were the methods and intentions such as to be readily labelled the underpinnings of Japanese imperialism? Did the Japanese have, or would they acquire a fitting psychology for world leadership, or would their actions and attitudes be marked by ethnocentrism, insecurity, and brutality, thereby producing the hatred of those whom they wished to persuade? From these, the universal questions of twentieth-century relations between advanced and lagging societies, Japanese foreign policy was by no means immune. The events of the first World War accentuated the issues.

The rise of Japan as a world power

The first World War was the third conflict within a generation to pay handsome and immediate dividends to the cause of Japanese prestige. It is not difficult to understand why later glorification of war by Japanese militarists produced such weak rebuttals from the society as a whole. Against the true desires of her ally, Japan entered the war "to fulfill her obligations under the Anglo-Japanese Alliance." She proceeded to capture without difficulty the German holdings on the Chinese Shantung Peninsula and in certain other parts of the Pacific. With this mission accomplished, she directed her energies to supplying the Asian markets cut off from their normal European contacts, and to providing her Western allies with the materials of war. These tasks required enormous industrial expansion. Indeed, it was at the close of this period that industrial productivity overtook agrarian productivity in yen value, and Japan could thereby claim to have moved into the ranks of industrial societies.

These trends and complemental factors elsewhere stimulated the drive for a more intensive China policy. The Manchu dynasty had fallen in the Revolution of 1911, but in its major objectives that revolution had failed. The Chinese scene was now marked by deep political cleavages, with rival factions striving desperately for both internal and external support. With Europe fully engaged in a bloody "civil war" and the United States prepared to go no further than a policy of moral suasion, Japan was soon heavily involved in Chinese politics. In 1915, the Japanese government demanded an extensive list of concessions from the Yuan Shihk'ai regime, known as the "Twenty-one Demands." These were bitterly resisted by China with some success. But Japanese influence moved steadily forward by means of loans, advisers, and technical assistance. Yet Japan soon acquired a new image in China: that of the chief enemy to Chinese nationalism. This era was climaxed by the historic May Fourth Movement, now widely heralded by the Chinese Communists as their point of origin, a fervent demonstration against Versailles and Japanese imperialism spearheaded by Peking students and spreading throughout China in May 1919.

At the close of the first World War, however, there could be no question that Japan had become a world power. She was the one major nation besides the United States to emerge from that war in a stronger position. Her preeminence in East Asia could not be doubted despite the uncertain new force of Bolshevism. What were the ingredients of this power as the third decade of the twentieth century began?

One source clearly derived from the evolving economic capacities of Japanese society. Perhaps the full secret of the Japanese industrial revolution still escapes us. However, in its essence, it seems to have involved the capacity of Japanese society to utilize effectively selected elements of Western technique and experience, adapting these to its own cultural and timing proclivities without duplicating either the historical context of Western development or the precise set of Western drives, impulses, and incentives. Toward this process were contributed both the conscious purposes of state and the remarkable talents of a people who could display creativeness through integration and discipline. By 1920, Japan was already becoming the workshop of Asia. Her large factories, equipped in many cases with the most modern machinery, contributed such basic products as textiles in great volume; at the same time, an infinite variety of cheap manufactured items flowed out of the thousands of small and medium plants that formed the base of the pyramidal Japanese industrial structure. Sharing with management the credit for such productivity was the new Japanese labor force, abundant in numbers, cheap in cost, malleable within limits to its new task, moving out of the paddy fields into the factories and acquiring sufficient know-how to give Japan an industrial character of which their fathers could not have dreamed.

But if manpower was a strength, it was also a problem—and one that now began to have an overt influence upon policy. Shortly after the first World War the Japanese population reached sixty million, more than double the figure at the beginning of the Meiji era. In many respects the facilities existing within Japan to accommodate this great mass already seemed seriously strained, yet no levelling-off was in sight. Increasing talk of *lebensraum* was inevitable. And if the population explosion had produced an abundance of cheap labor, by the same token, it had placed certain limits upon the consumption capacities of the domestic market, throwing increased emphasis upon foreign trade.

Other factors underlined Japanese dependence upon foreign lands. The four main islands of Japan were not richly blessed with those natural resources vital to the industrial development of this period. Coal was present in sufficient quantities except for high-grade coking coal, but iron ore was very limited, petroleum negligible, and most essential metals were either absent or available only in modest quantity. Moreover, because of her limited land space and her location, Japan had to import many of the agricultural resources to supply her industries; raw cotton and rubber were two prominent examples. The Japanese empire of this period was helpful; from Formosa, Saghalien, and particularly from Korea came important raw materials and food-stuffs. However, the larger needs lay outside these areas, and the Manchuria-Mongolian region could be depicted in impressive economic terms.

If we revert to our discussion of the ingredients of Japanese power, those in the military and political realm certainly cannot be overlooked. The Japanese navy had become the third largest in the world, and her army in size, equipment, and training dwarfed other forces readily available in this part of the world. There was no foreign force that seemed prepared to challenge successfully a Japanese force that was fully committed in its own territories or in any part of East Asia. The size and equipment of the Japanese military was a testament to the lavish yearly budgetary contributions of the people; the morale of that force was a tribute to intensive indoctrination, sustained by the realities of great political power and prestige within the society.

Politics in its broader reaches also fitted into the power quotient. For a society without totalitarian restraints (albeit one strongly paternal-authoritarian in character), Japan presented a picture of remarkable stability up to this point. Beside a handful of intellectual radicals there were few who would dare (or think) to question *Kokutai,* "the national polity," or more vaguely, the Japanese Way of Life. Thus state decisions, especially in the realm of foreign policy, could be taken on the assumption that they would be accepted with a maximum of conformity. The oracles of national interest could speak without fear of discordant responses, at least so long as they spoke within a consistently nationalist framework. What leadership group has not found some advantage in this?

Yet as the postwar era began, there were indications that Japanese politics might be drastically affected by the democratic tides. The influence of Western liberalism, crowned by the global idealism of Woodrow Wilson, was strongly felt in Japanese intellectual and urban circles. Party government had assumed new importance, the office of Premier was held for the first time by a commoner, and the movement for universal suffrage was receiving widespread support. Japan's "liberal era" was opening, bringing with it some serious efforts to establish parliamentary and civilian supremacy in Japanese politics. Temporarily at least, the long-entrenched bureaucrats and even the military had to move to the defensive. For the latter, the Siberian Expedition was the first clearly unrewarding venture abroad. And however strong the attempt to shift blame to political timidity and lack of resolution at home, the army could not prevent some questions from arising in the public mind.

Hence, moderation in foreign policy during this period was possible. At the Washington Conference, Japan accepted the famous 5-5-3 naval ratio with the United States and Great Britain, despite the bitter protests of her naval authorities. She agreed to the return of the Shantung concessions. Withdrawal from Siberia was slowly and cautiously undertaken. One cabinet even had the audacity to retrench sharply the military budget, and there were some discussions (although no action) on a permanent reduction in the institutional power of the military in Japanese government. During this era no figure symbolized moderation in foreign policy more than Kijuro Shidehara, Foreign Minister under the Minseito Cabinets. Shidehara was a conservative, a nationalist, and a loyal servant of the Emperor. He believed that Japan had "special interests" in northeast Asia and a special responsibility toward China. But he wanted to avoid a "get-tough" policy which would only provoke boycotts, anti-Japanese hostility, and possibly war. Rather he hoped Japanese influence could be exerted through trade, financial agreements, and political negotiation.

Militarism and defeat

The "liberal era" was short-lived. With its collapse went much of the hope for moderation either at home or abroad. This is not the place to spell out the story of democratic failure in prewar Japan, but its more immediate causes are familiar: economic crisis and depression; political confusion and corruption; and the consequent rise of opponents from left and right. Repercussions were felt almost immediately in terms of Japanese foreign policy. In 1928, under the Tanaka Cabinet, there was a sharp turn toward a more militant nationalism in both the economic and political fields. State support to home industry was combined with a more "positive" program of support for Japanese interests abroad, especially in China. Overtures from Chiang Kai-shek—who had just broken with the Communists—were rejected, partly because of fear that his successful northern expedition would jeopardize the future Japanese position in Manchuria and north China. Ironically, while the Tanaka China policy was provoking sharp Chinese reaction because of its "strengths," it was under simultaneous attack by Japanese military extremists because of its "weaknesses." Some of these elements working through the Kwantung Army in Manchuria engineered the murder of Chang Tso-lin in June 1928, hoping to force a decisive Japanese move in this area. The Japanese government was posed with the first of a series of direct military challenges to civilian control, challenges which went unmet.

Japanese foreign policy in the fifteen years between 1930 and 1945 represented the natural culmination of these new trends. To be sure, not all the old themes were reversed, particularly those that could be read with different inflections. Stress continued to be placed upon Sino-Japanese cooperation, and on the need for a stable, friendly China, purged of Communist and anti-Japanese elements. But actions continually interfered with words. As the Japanese militarists gained control of the strategic heights of policy, especially in the field, any cooperation had to be strained through the tightening net of aggression, fanatical "patriotism," and individual, sometimes mass, acts of brutality. Through these field actions, and as a result of a contrived "incident," war came to Manchuria in September 1931. Weaker Chinese

forces were quickly defeated, but Manchukuo remained to the great body of the Chinese an unacceptable symbol of Japanese aggression.

With the Manchurian region at last under complete Japanese control, the militarists could not avoid spreading outward toward Mongolia and north China. Thus the "Second China Incident" erupted in 1937 and led eventually to total war and defeat. Throughout this entire era, Japan could always find some Chinese allies, whether as a result of the acrid internal rivalries for power in China, sheer opportunism, or some genuine hopes that this route might lead to a new and better Asia, freed from Western control. Indeed, the allies garnered from all of these sources were not inconsiderable either in numbers or in influence. In a man like Wang Ch'ing-wei Japan finally found an able if embittered leader. But as against these facts, Japanese policy achieved what had always been feared most: a union of the dominant wing of the Kuomintang with the Communists and many independents into a nationalist popular front that was bitterly anti-Japanese. And having as one of its supreme goals the salvation of Asia from Communism, ironically, Japanese policy in the end contributed more than any other single factor to Communist success.

To concentrate solely upon China policy, however, would be to examine only the weakest link of a general Asian policy which for all its militant aggressive qualities had elements of real power and appeal. Building from the old "Asia for the Asians" theme, Japanese policy in the 1930's moved toward the concept of a Greater East Asia Co-Prosperity Sphere. The economic background for this policy lay in the rapid strides made by Japanese trade throughout Asia. By means of general deflation, changes in currency valuation, industrial rationalization, and extensive state support, Japanese trade came to enjoy highly favorable competitive conditions in East Asia by the mid-thirties. Western Europe complained vigorously about the practice of "social dumping" onto the colonial markets. Japan retorted with charges of economic discrimination and attempted monopoly. The fact remained, however, that Japanese penetration of the Asian market during this period was substantial. The basis was thus provided for later proposals of greater economic integration under an Asian regionalism led by Japan and divorced from Western control.

The center of the Japanese appeal to greater Asia, however, remained in the sphere of political nationalism. As Japan drifted toward the Fascist bloc, Western imperialism in Asia could be attacked with less inhibitions than in the past. These attacks were particularly effective in areas where nationalism was still treated as subversive by Western governors, and where Japanese policies could not yet be tested. Once again, an attempt was made to develop an expanded program of cultural relations and technical assistance. Students flocked to Japan from all parts of Asia; cultural missions were exchanged on an increasing scale; Japanese technicians went forth; and as the Pacific War approached, the Japanese government provided underground assistance to various Asian nationalist movements in the form of funds, political advice, and even the training and equipping of military forces.

Most of the present independent governments of south and southeast Asia owe an enormous debt to Japanese propaganda, military successes, and political concessions—even when the latter were self-serving, empty, or last-minute gestures. There can be no doubt that Japan both in victory and in defeat contributed mightily to the end of the old era and the emergence of a more independent, dynamic Asia. Yet her record was tarnished, and today she must combat a legacy of suspicion and even hatred in many of these countries. In part this can be attributed to such factors as the misconduct of her troops, but more importantly, it is the product of the great cultural barriers that separated her from the regions she occupied and of her inability—through lack of experience, insecurity, and because of her own traditions—to develop the type of flexibility and broad tolerance necessary in leadership. In considerable degree, Japanese hopes for cooperation and friendship were strangled by the very force of nationalism that pushed them forward.

As a corollary to her new Asian policy Japan naturally developed a new policy with respect to the West. Nearly a decade earlier, at the time of the Washington Conference of 1921, Japan had reluctantly given up the Anglo-Japanese Alliance, her shield and support for twenty years. In its place were substituted the more general agreements among the major powers. This concept of collective agreement (not, it should be emphasized, collective security) was especially attuned to the American position. The United States wanted an end to exclusive alliances, but it was prepared to undertake only the most limited of commitments, and it still wished to rely essentially upon moral suasion for policy enforcement. The great symbol of this hope and this era was the famous Kellogg-Briand Peace Pact, outlawing war.

Thus the decline of Japanese liberalism at home was complemented by the absence of effective external checks or controls. The old system of alliances and the type of checks they imposed upon unilateral action had been declared obsolete in the Pacific, but no effective international order had replaced them. Consequently, in the name of her national interests, Japan could successfully defy the Nine Power Agreement and the League of Nations, with no single nation or group making an effective stand against her. Inevitably as she challenged "the *status-quo* powers," Japan gravitated toward Germany and Italy, the dissidents of Europe. The Anti-Comintern Pact sealed an alliance of mutual interest, though not one of great intimacy.

But the real decision that confronted Japan as the Pacific War approached had a familiar ring: was she to seek a stabilization of her northern or her southern flanks; who was to be engaged, the Soviet Union or the Western allies? The decision was not an easy one. In the late 1930's, Japan had participated in large-scale clashes with Russian forces in the Mongolian region; her historic rivalry was augmented by her hatred of Communism. In the final analysis, however, she decided to count upon a German victory on the steppes of Russia, and she turned to the south whose resources had to be unlocked and whose Western masters had to be overthrown if the Japanese vision of the future were to be attained. Possibilities for agreement with the West to avoid this fateful step were explored, as all the moderates desired, but hopes were broken on the rock of China. Too much had been invested in blood and treasure to concede to Chiang Kai-shek, and so, infinitely more was to be invested—and all in vain.

THE FORMULATION OF FOREIGN POLICY IN PREWAR JAPAN

In the Tokyo trials of "major war criminals" that followed the Japanese surrender, the Allied prosecutors repeatedly sought the answer to one central question: "Who bears the responsibility for leading Japan toward aggression and war?" If they did not obtain a completely satisfactory answer, no blame should be assigned. Few questions involve greater difficulties. The problem has taken on universal dimensions as the modern state has grown in conscious complexity and as foreign policy has developed into the composite, uncertain product of a myriad of "technicians," men rigidly compartmentalized, skilled and jealous of these skills, but almost always frustrated by the limits of their power; an indeterminate number of free-roaming "generalists," yet not so free, being bound by the limits of the single mind, the niceties of group decision, and the pressures—subtle or direct—of subalterns; finally, the larger, vaguer "public," varying in size but never comprising the whole of its society nor the sum of its parts—alternately indifferent and excited, overwhelmed by the complexities and focusing directly upon some vital issue, ignored and watched with anxiety, molded and breaking out of molds.

Japan partook of this central problem to a high degree, and with some differences of kind. Here only its broader dimensions can be sketched. In the narrow sense, Japan appeared as a society of great personal absolutism. At both the familial and the national levels the head of the house (state) was invested with absolute powers. The injunction upon inferiors was complete and unswerving obedience. There seemed no measure of egalitarianism or individualism to alleviate the rigidities of a hierarchical system which through primogeniture and an Emperor-centered mythology found its apex in a single source. But in fact, the essence of power in Japanese society has not been that of personal absolutism. The vital center of decision-making has uniformly lain in its collective or group character, and in its extensive reliance upon consensus as the primary technique. It is critical to understand that despite all superficial signs to the contrary, the basic nature of Japanese society can only be approached by a thorough appreciation of the intricate refinements of group interaction, the high importance of induced voluntarism, and the generally eclectic quality of final agreements.

In all likelihood, only if these things were true could the outward signs of rigid hierarchy and absolutism have been so well maintained into the modern era. Elaborate methods had already been developed to integrate theory and appearance with the needs of a dynamic society. Just as the system of adopted sons had long preserved the necessary flexibility in the Japanese family, so the institutions of senior councillor, adviser, and go-between had each, in its own way, facilitated the making of group decisions. That process, giving extraordinary attention to form and status, was often wearisome and prolonged, but every care had to be taken to make concessions and consensus possible with minimal violence to the position and prestige of those involved. Necessarily, "equals" were wary of confronting each other in person until the formula for consensus seemed assured; and "inferiors" developed to a fine art all forms of subtle pressures and persuasive devices, with successful "superiors" paying silent homage to these in the course of final action.

Not all of these conditions sound strange to Western ears, although the aggregate process might seem foreign or extreme. In any case, how were such basic factors in Japanese social relations translated into politics and the making of foreign policy? In theory, the Meiji Constitution of 1889 paid its highest tribute to Imperial absolutism, but for successful practice it demanded a unity or consensus of its disparate working parts. The weakest of these, the two-house Diet, with its lower house elective, had at least the power to withhold its consent from basic policies. The administrative bureaucracy, culminating in such executive offices as the Prime Ministership, Cabinet, and Privy Council, had a vast range of powers and had legal responsibility only to the Emperor, but could not be effective alone. The military also drew their power from the Emperor, and had direct access to him; in practice, moreover, this branch acquired a potent weapon in that Ministers of War and Navy had to come from its ranks, which served to limit sharply the independent power of the Japanese Cabinet. The military, however, could operate effectively only in conjunction with the other major branches.

There was never any serious thought of having these forces coordinated by the Emperor personally, despite the awesome nature of his stipulated powers. Instead, that task was handled for some thirty years by a small oligarchy of Restoration leaders who acted in the name of the Emperor as his "chief advisers." Ultimately, this group came to be known as the *Genro* or Senior Councillors, an institution without a vestige of legal recognition or responsibility, but central to the process of Japanese politics. Every basic policy decision was placed before the Genro, and their approval was a prerequisite to action. Even the daily affairs of state frequently engaged their attention. With protégés in every branch of government and with their own vast accumulation of experience, these men were at once the source of integration, the court of final appeal, and the summit of power. To be sure, agreement among them was not always easy; there were deep personal and policy cleavages in this as in other Japanese groups. Timed withdrawals and temporary concessions, however, enabled the consensus process to operate with a minimum of crises. Until the close of the first World War, with rare exceptions, the fountainhead of Japanese foreign policy existed within this group.

With the postwar era, however, basic changes in government began to emerge, paralleling those in society. The Genro became old men, and their ranks were not refilled. No group came forth to undertake the integrative role. Instead, Japanese politics was marked by an increasing struggle for supremacy and control among the parties, the bureaucracy, and the military. It is interesting to note that at the outset of this era an attempt was made to establish a liaison council under the aegis of the Prime Minister for the development of a "unified" foreign policy. It was intended to include major party, official, and military representation, but it was never accepted by the major opposition party and ultimately faded away.

Without a supreme coordinator such as the Genro, Japanese constitutionalism, in both its written and unwritten aspects, revealed serious flaws. In the hectic party era, foreign policy decisions taken in Cabinet or government party circles were not only subject to legitimate attacks in the Diet, but also to extensive sabotage by the ranks of the subordinate bureaucracy and to angry challenges by the military groups. The parties never attained more than a quasi-supremacy, and as they faded, the military moved from verbal challenge to open defiance. Japanese society in the period after 1928 represented a classic example of a government divided against itself. Important segments of the military operated both in the field and at home in such a manner as to scorn the government. They received substantial support from within the bureaucracy, and from certain party figures as well. Every branch of government was riddled with dissension. Within the Ministry of Foreign Affairs various cliques maneuvered for position—the militarist clique, the Anglo-American clique, and numerous others. For a time, consensus was impossible, and conditions close to anarchy prevailed.

Gradually, however, greater stability was achieved. Making full use of traditional procedures, top court officials surrounding the Emperor involved themselves in unending conferences with representatives of all major groups; innumerable go-betweens explored the possible bases of compromise; certain voluntary withdrawals, strategic retreats, and silent acquiscences were effected. Slowly a new basis for interaction developed, one which gave due recognition to military superiority but still was broad enough to include essential elements of the civil bureaucracy, court officials, and important pressure groups. Once again the basic decisions were reached through the consensus process, but with somewhat greater cognizance than usual for the realities of power. In this period a new group of senior councilors, the *Jushin,* was organized. Although lacking the influence of the Genro, it was fashioned after its model, indicating the continuing search for an integrative center. That search was destined never to be completely successful. Another experiment was conducted in a liaison council, the purpose being to pool military and civilian policy with particular reference to the foreign scene. Ultimately, the Imperial Conference, with the Emperor himself presiding over a small group of top military and administrative officials, became the final decision-making body. Indeed, it was this group that determined the Japanese surrender, with the Emperor personally settling this great issue. Perhaps this was the only basis left for the organic unity envisaged by the Meiji Constitution.

The foregoing trends are not completely meaningful without some brief reference to other important socioeconomic groups. First, however, it should be noted that the type of consensus being developed during the militarist era was abetted by an increasing control over all communications media. As one of the most literate societies in the world, Japan had national newspapers and magazines with massive circulation. After the early thirties, prominent dissent from ultranationalism became increasingly dangerous, and after the "Second China Incident" all public organs were echoing the official line.

Meanwhile, a process of accommodation had been taking place between conservative militarists and the industrial-commercial world of Japan. In the initial stages of the military revolt against liberalism and a "weak-kneed" foreign policy, the strong notes of a radical, anti-capitalist theme were heard; the historic cry of "internal reform, external expansion" once again sounded forth. However, after the February 26th Incident of 1936, when army units in Tokyo under radical command rebelled, this type of revolutionary activity was suppressed. Although some "liberal" business elements were regarded with suspicion and certain onerous controls were sharply protested by entrepreneurs, still the necessary compromises were made, and Japanese industry at all levels rose to the war effort.

Japanese labor reacted in the same way. Its radical and liberal elements had long since been silenced, and the great masses worked with patriotic fervor. It was from the rural areas, however, that the bedrock of Japanese conservatism derived. The peasant-soldier alliance now held more meaning than at any time since the Restoration. As is so frequently the case, rural provincialism bred its own type of ultranationalism. The Japanese common man played a role in the formulation of foreign policy in his own way: he posed no obstacles to expansionism, his complete loyalty was assured, and no sacrifice would be too great if it contributed to the nationalist cause.

JAPAN SINCE 1945: OCCUPATION AND ITS AFTERMATH

When Japan surrendered in August 1945, both her leaders and her people were forced to reconcile themselves to the status of a vanquished nation. By the terms of the Yalta and Potsdam agreements, the Japanese Empire was to be dissipated and Japan reduced in size to the approximate boundaries of the Restoration era. The homeland was to be occupied for an indefinite period by foreign forces. For the first time in recorded history, Japanese sovereignty was to be superseded by foreign rule. Some of the broad objectives of this rule had already been stipulated: action was to be taken to insure that Japan never again would become a world menace (or world power). Total disarmament was to be carried out, and those responsible for past aggression were to be punished; even the fate of the Emperor was unclear, although Japanese leaders sought desperately to gain assurances on this point during the surrender negotiations. Along with these essentially negative tasks, the occupation was also to encourage Japanese democratic forces and movements, so that Japan could eventually take her place in a peaceful world. Thus was inaugurated in September 1945, a radically new era for Japan, one that might well be labelled "the era of the American Revolution."

If the contemporary processes and substance of Japanese foreign policy are to be discussed meaningfully, certain pertinent aspects of this period must be set forth. In the first place, the American occupation and its aftermath can easily be divided into three broad phases: (1) the early revolutionary era, when the emphasis was upon punishment and reform; (2) the era of reconstruction, when the stress was shifted to stabilization and economic recovery; and (3) the era of proffered alliance, which is continuing at present. Each of these eras, in its own way, has contributed to the current nature and problems of Japanese society.

The revolutionary era

The American Revolution in Japan was that of 1932, not that of 1776, although some of the spirit of the latter as it applied to basic democratic values was certainly present. The New Deal had new opportunities along the bombed-out Ginza and in the rice fields. But first, the old order had to be eradicated. Japanese military forces were totally disbanded in a remarkably short time; before the end of 1947, some six million Japanese troops and civilians had been returned from overseas, demobilized, and poured into the homeland. The military forces within Japan proper had also been completely dissolved. The Ministries of War and Navy were abolished. And in an effort to seal these actions with the stamp of permanency, the now-famous Article Nine was written into the new Japanese Constitution:

Aspiring sincerely to an international peace based on justice and order, the Japanese people forever renounce war as a sovereign right of the nation and the threat or use of force as means of settling international disputes.

In order to accomplish the aim of the preceding paragraph, land, sea, and air forces, as well as other war potential, will never be maintained. The right of belligerency of the state will not be recognized.

The American vision for Japan during this period became widely associated with the phrase, "The Switzerland of the Far East," although in this pacifism was added to neutralization. It was a vision that had a powerful appeal to many Japanese who lived amidst rubble, without adequate food or warmth, and with vivid memories of lost ones, fire raids, and the final atomic holocaust. There could be no question as to whether this war had paid, and the extraordinary vulnerability of the great Japanese cities had been fully demonstrated during the war's last terrible months. For most thoughtful Japanese, the early postwar era was a period of deep reflection. Its dominant theme was one of trenchant criticism of past leaders and institutions. Once more there was a Japanese surge toward new ideas and ways; MacArthur no less than Perry symbolized the end of an old order, and a war-weary people turned hopefully to "demokurashi," without being precisely sure of its contents. These sentiments, widespread as they were, aided the revolution that was getting under way.

Among the various SCAP [1] actions, none had more long-range implications than those which affected the nature

[1] SCAP is the commonly used abbreviation for the term, Supreme Commander of the Allied Powers. It is used to designate not only General MacArthur personally, but the Occupation Force collectively.

242 ROBERT A. SCALAPINO

and position of Japanese pressure groups. As we have noted, for more than a decade the most powerful group in Japanese society had been the military. Suddenly it was entirely liquidated, and in the early 1960's nearly two decades later it has not yet reappeared as a significant force. The process of liquidation was not merely in demobilization, but also in the purge that barred all professional military officers from future political activity, and in the war crimes trials, which saw the top military men of the nation executed or sentenced to prison. Although many of these actions were subsequently modified or rescinded, still their total effect, combined with other circumstances, has thus far been sufficient to render postwar militarism in Japan impotent.

Through the purge and other measures, SCAP ate still further into prewar conservative ranks. For the old guard it seemed like the reign of terror, though without violence or brutality. Most professional politicians of the old conservative parties had to step aside because they had belonged to some ultranationalist group or had been endorsed by the Tojo government in the elections of 1942. Conservative leadership was hastily thrust into the hands of the one group that could be cleared: the so-called Anglo-American group from within the Foreign Ministry. Kijuro Shidehara, Shigeru Yoshida, and Hisashi Ashida, all from this group, became the top conservative leaders of Japan for nearly a decade. Even the commercial-industrial world felt the shock of reform. In the midst of purges, a deconcentration program to break down the *zaibatsu* or big combines, and the general toll of wartime ravage and postwar inflation, most business elements sought merely to survive, as if seeking shelter during a gale.

Meanwhile, under American encouragement, the labor union movement attained a massive size; within a brief period it numbered some six million workers, whereas in the prewar period *bona fide* union membership had never exceeded one-half million. These postwar figures masked many divisions and weaknesses, but nonetheless there could be no doubt that Japanese organized labor was a new force with which to reckon on the economic and political scene. And in the rural areas the American Revolution was operating in the most forceful fashion. Under a far-reaching program of land reform, absentee landlordism was almost completely abolished, tenancy was reduced to less than 10 per cent of total agrarian families, and land holdings were equalized beyond the wildest imagination of prewar landreform advocates. Basically, this program was dedicated to the creation of a huge independent yeomanry. Socioeconomic repercussions in the rural areas over this upheaval, especially among younger age groups, are only now becoming measurable.

Certain reforms cut across economic class lines and into the broadest categories of society. Legal attempts were made to abandon primogeniture and also to emancipate women. The latter were given full equality before the law, including equal rights of inheritance, divorce, and suffrage. Sweeping reforms in education were inaugurated, dedicated to the development of freer, more independent students, unshackled from the old chauvinism and submissiveness. Even that very special category of men, the subordinate government officials, were given lectures on democracy, in the hope that some of the old attitude of *kanson mimpi*, "officials honored, people despised," could be removed.

To recite these various efforts in

such bald fashion may lead to the supposition that a total social revolution took place in Japan during the first years after 1945. Any such impression would be false. Conservatism both in the form of certain dominant classes and in the form of certain traditions that operated in every class was a sturdy force. Moreover, as might be surmised, not all SCAP experiments were successful, and by the end of 1947, in any case, the era emphasizing reform was drawing to a close. In its ripest forms, it had lasted only about two years, and the conservatives definitely survived.

It would be equally misleading, however, to underestimate the changes that took place during this era, whether because of SCAP reforms or as a result of the total complex of postwar circumstances. Some of these changes should be regarded as part of the continuum inherited from prewar days. Others were largely the product of foreign intervention or the new conditions prevailing as a result of military defeat. In any case, changes developing during this period have had a direct influence upon the processes and substance of Japanese foreign policy. Most important have been the altered composition of Japanese pressure groups and the accelerated movement toward a mass society.

The nature of Japanese conservatism has been strongly effected by the demise of the military, the levelling process that was applied to agriculture, and the combined impact of defeat and technological revolution that struck industry and commerce. The nature of Japanese "reformism" has been equally effected by the rise of organized labor and the total freedom accorded the intellectual-student elements. It is still too early to be certain about the political path that will be taken by a rapidly changing Japanese society. One

thing, however, seems apparent: the trend has been toward a closer balance of competing pressure groups within that society than there was in the prewar era. As a result of this and other factors, the Japanese common man has become the object of increasing political solicitation and concern. As we shall note, public opinion has become one important factor in the shaping of Japanese foreign policy.

The stabilization era

Before we turn to the current status of foreign policy formulation and substance, however, some brief consideration should be given to the second and third phases of the Occupation and the gradual emergence once again of an independent Japan. The shift of emphasis in Occupation policy from punishment and reform to economic stabilization and recovery began as early as 1947. The change was motivated by many problems. Certain earlier American premises about the postwar world now seemed unjustified: the prospects were dim for a China that would be friendly and democratic by any American definition; the honeymoon with the Soviet Union was clearly over and the Cold War was beginning; the threat of Communism throughout Europe and Asia as a result of postwar chaos and economic misery was a matter of profound concern. With respect to Japan itself, the close relation between economic recovery and the prospects for democratic success could no longer be slighted or ignored. In addition, as long as the Japanese economy was in the doldrums, occupational expenses and relief undertakings constituted a heavy burden for the American taxpayer; at its peak, the cost ran close to one-half billion dollars per year.

The new emphasis brought many

changes in policies and techniques. Increasingly, the supreme test to which any policy could be put was, "Does it advance productivity and economic stabilization?" An assessment was made of the primary obstacles—war damage, inflation, the lack of raw materials, and low morale owing to miserable conditions for workers and uncertainties for management. First, SCAP began to interest itself in problems of productive efficiency, and moved from merely keeping Japan alive to furnishing her with industrial raw materials and acquainting her entrepreneurs with the most advanced industrial machinery and techniques. The complex problem of inflation was finally faced. Under the Dodge Nine-Point Stabilization Program, stringent reforms were put into effect. These were unpopular in many quarters, but the inflationary tide was at last turned.

Meanwhile, other "disruptions" to production were dealt with. The deconcentration program was relaxed and gradually abandoned after successful initial attempts to reduce certain large *zaibatsu* families and cartels. The United States also progressively receded from its early severity on the issue of reparations. By the end of this era, the American government had indicated its acceptance of the thesis that the Japanese ability to repay war damages was strictly limited, that large reparations would indirectly become a responsibility to the United States, and that the basic heavy industrial complex upon which Japan was so dependent for her future could not be used for these purposes. Finally, SCAP took a sterner attitude toward radicalism in the labor movement, amending its earlier generous legislation on unionism so as to give the employer and especially the government a stronger position.

The net effect of these actions, ac-companied by certain broader trends at home and abroad, was to stimulate rapid economic recovery. Japanese society could build upon an industrial revolution already well advanced and a legacy of technical know-how. Deflation and internal readjustments were followed by new opportunities for industrial expansion. The Korean War and the great prosperity of the free world were of major assistance. Beginning in 1950, therefore, Japan entered a decade of amazing economic development. For the next ten years, the average annual rise in gross national product was approximately 9 per cent, constituting one of the most spectacular rates of growth in the world.

This second phase of the Occupation which triggered the economic surge was not without internal political reverberations. In the revolutionary era, American actions had been an anathema to the conservatives; now, the conservatives became the new allies. The liberal left, which had cheered in the early days, was filled with dismay and resentment at many actions of which it did not approve but from which it had no recourse. Japanese democracy was still under the tutelage of American military rule. Criticism and opposition were strictly limited by that fact. Inevitably, however, the United States and its policies became the central issue in Japanese politics, paving the way for the sharp divergencies that came into the open later. For every political group, moreover, this second era was one of reflection and reconsideration of Western values. There was an unmistakable tendency at all levels to emphasize synthesis and adjustment rather than uncritical acceptance of foreign concepts. The pendulum had begun to swing back.

As can be seen, the beginnings of

postwar Japanese foreign policy were established in this era, albeit under American direction. These beginnings followed a course that Japanese leadership itself might well have taken and labelled "in the national interest," had it been an independent agent. Indeed, on issues like reparations and trade, the United States was widely accused of being excessively "pro-Japanese." One policy emphasized was that of rehabilitating Japanese heavy industry and encouraging its orientation toward the needs and markets of the "late-developing" societies, particularly those of non-Communist Asia. Again, the concept of Japan as the workshop of Asia was advanced, but without certain former connotations. As a concomitant to this policy, the United States also took steps to adjust Japanese political and economic relations with erstwhile enemies whenever possible. Like a benevolent warden convinced of the successful rehabilitation of his charge, the United States now pressed for Japanese re-entry into the world community on terms of equality.

But the second phase of the Occupation also marked the origins of an intimate and largely new relationship between Japan and the United States. This relationship had its foundation in a rising tempo of economic interaction that became increasingly important to both societies. Japanese products began to flow into the United States in exchange for American raw materials, food stuffs, and machinery. Technical assistance from the United States smoothed the way for later foreign investment and patent sharing. The economic interaction was thus very broadly based. It was supported, moreover, by an expanding cultural interaction: appreciation and exchange in the fields of custom, ideas, and pattern of life.

The era of alliance

Within these trends lay the seeds of the third era, that of proffered alliance by the United States to Japan. By 1949, American authorities realized on the one hand that the Occupation was reaching a point of diminishing returns, and on the other, that continuing economic and political ties between the two countries were a mutual necessity. Explorations were begun which led to the San Francisco Peace Treaty of 1951. In the process, a series of decisions were reached between Japanese and American authorities that added further dimensions to the new Japanese foreign policy and provoked heated political debate.

The critical issue pertained to the question of Japanese defense. Two broad alternatives seemed to exist. One was to continue a reliance upon pacifism, seeking universal agreements guaranteeing the sanctity of Japanese territory and backing these with pledges of protection through the auspices of the United Nations, and possibly of the United States separately. The other alternative was to move away from pacifism and neutralization, acknowledging the Japanese need for, and right to, military defense forces, and underwriting Japanese rearmament efforts with American power until these could reach some degree of self-sufficiency. Obviously, the choice between these two broad courses would effect and shape most other aspects of Japanese foreign policy.

The Yoshida government did not hesitate to support the second alternative, that of political, military, and economic alliance with the United States. Its arguments were that this was the only course compatible with world conditions and Japanese needs. To adopt a policy of neutralism, the conservatives argued, would make Japan dependent upon the mercurial policies of the Communist world. It would provide neither security nor prosperity. They insisted that both the economic and the political interests of Japan were best served by alignment with the free world, particularly the United States.

These arguments prevailed. While making known its desire for an "over-all" peace treaty, the Japanese government agreed to sign a treaty with the non-Communist allies alone if necessary. The Cold War had become hot in Korea while preliminary treaty negotiations were getting underway. Because of this fact and the wide divergence between Soviet and American views on Japan, no serious attempt was made to obtain Communist approval for the treaty draft, as the Japanese socialists had wished. In exchange for their willingness to sign a separate treaty, the conservatives were given a treaty considered generous by all, "soft" by some. Reparations and certain territorial issues (the Kurile and Ryukyu islands) were left open, providing Japan with some bargaining power. The treaty contained no stipulations concerning SCAP reforms. Japan was left free to make any changes desired in her internal institutions. This included the right to rearm.

Official independence for Japan finally came on April 28, 1952, the day on which the Treaty of San Francisco came into effect. Accompanying the main treaty was a bilateral mutual security treaty with the United States providing for the continuance of American bases in Japan proper until adequate defenses were prepared by the Japanese government. At least as early as 1949, the creation of a Japanese defense force was being urged in some American and Japanese circles. Japanese rearmament was first started in the summer of 1950, shortly

after the outbreak of the Korean War. The National Police Reserve was activated in August of that year with an authorized component of 75,000 men. With the coming of Japanese independence, in May 1952, this number was increased to 110,000 and a small Maritime Safety Force was established. In August, these were brought together under the National Safety Agency. Two years later, on July 1, 1954, the name was changed to the Defense Agency, brought directly under the office of the Prime Minister, and authorized to have a small Air Self-Defense Force in addition to its other units. The slow build-up of Japanese defense forces continued. By the end of 1955, there were about 200,000 men in the total Defense Force. Six years later, in early 1961, the Force still numbered only some 230,000. Modernization of equipment and training had occurred, but in comparison to the Communist bloc, Japanese military power remained minuscule. For reasons we shall discuss later, the military aspect of the American-Japanese alliance has become an uncertain and uneasy one.

In economic terms, however, the alliance has flourished during the past decade. Between 1952 and 1960, Japanese-American trade doubled. Japan, obtaining nearly one-third of all her imports from the United States, became its second best customer, next to Canada. And Japanese exports to the United States skyrocketed to over one billion dollars yearly; in 1960, the United States took some 28 per cent of total Japanese exports. Underwriting these developments was the growth of an impressive network of private agreements between American and Japanese companies, whereby industrial techniques, patents, and skills were shared. Despite certain problems to be noted later, economic interaction between Japan and the United States has become the most powerful stimulus to continuing alliance.

If the alliance has been largely attuned to the business community and conservative circles, however, it has not been totally lacking in a larger cultural component. Heightening cultural exchange began during the Occupation. Seldom if ever in history have millions of people from two such diverse societies had an opportunity to see each other at work and play. The results were generally favorable. For various complex reasons, a certain rapport between Americans and Japanese was rather easily established. Attitude polls give indications of the reasons for this. On the Japanese side, there was a general appreciation of American humanism, friendliness, and energy. On the American side, the qualities of Japanese politeness and discipline, cultural achievements, and industriousness were respected. Favorable attitudes have facilitated the exchange of elements from the culture of each society to the other. And exchange at elite levels has probably been even more significant than mass interaction. In spite of serious language handicaps, the Japanese and American elite can communicate with each other on an increasingly meaningful basis as their two societies move closer together in the process of modernization. The development of a communication grid encompassing industrial techniques, social science methodology, and scientific theory is of profound importance.

Having thus survived the transition from Occupation to independence, the alliance between Japan and the United States continues. As was suggested earlier, however, this alliance is more applicable and more acceptable to some segments of Japanese society than to others. In political terms, it is supported by the conservatives, opposed by the socialists. Relations between socialists and American authorities rapidly deteriorated after 1948, due in part to a major shift in Occupation policy. Differences concerning foreign policy became especially pronounced. The Socialist Party favored an over-all peace treaty with non-Communist, Communist, and neutral states. To the argument that, given present circumstances, this was unrealistic, the socialists answered that no real attempt had been made due to American opposition. The socialists were also strongly antagonistic to Japanese rearmament; they bitterly denounced the new defense forces as illegal, and charged an American-conservative coalition with undermining the Constitution of 1947. They were equally opposed to the Mutual Security Pact that accompanied the Treaty of San Francisco, and to the post-independence American bases in Japan that it sanctioned.

Against the conservative policy of alignment with the United States, the socialists advanced a policy of neutralism. In part, this policy was a product of their own historic traditions. Both the pacifist and the Marxist streams in Japanese socialism have been strong, and each of these streams in its own way has contributed to the modern socialist proclivity for neutralism. The socialist movement in Japan emerged partly as a Christian humanist protest against social injustice, militarism, and war. Thus the socialist-pacifist bias long predates similar sentiments generated in the Japanese public after the disastrous second World War. In the second stage of its development, moreover, the Japanese socialist movement was strongly influenced by Marxism. On the one hand, this separated many Japanese socialists from the ideology and practice of Western-style parlia-mentarism. And yet, because of the particular academic and "deviationist" qualities of Marxism in its Japanese socialist setting, it did not connect them with Moscow. Rather, the social-ists took as their ideal the foreign policy of Nehru.

The socialist case for neutralism has encompassed many arguments: the danger of involvement in war via an alliance with the United States, and the extreme vulnerability of Japan; the importance of serving as a balance-wheel in a bipolar world, and identify-ing more closely with the aspirations of the Asian-African states; the internal threats to democracy implicit in a revitalized Japanese military force; and the need for Japan to free itself com-pletely from American influence and control. The conservatives have an-swered with counter-arguments: the lack of realism in seeking to meet Communism with a policy of pacifism and isolation; the moral and political rightness of associating with those who share a broadly common ideology, and the economic value in doing so; the diffi-culty in having great influence in the world without having some military potential and being connected with a world power; and the possibility of having an independent foreign policy while still being aligned with the West, especially the United States.

Not only have the conservatives maintained their political supremacy and hence their foreign policy views; issues of foreign policy have been in-volved in the various splits that have occurred in socialist ranks. The first of these took place shortly after the San Francisco peace conference. The right-wing socialists, who plainly leaned toward the West in an ideological sense, were willing to accept the peace treaty even though it did not constitute an over-all agreement. The left-wing

socialists, who sought to adhere closely to the neutralist position, remained sharply opposed to the treaty. Both groups rejected the Mutual Security Treaty. However, the arguments over the peace treaty both exacerbated and reflected a wide range of differences within socialist ranks. The party split into two wings and was not reunited until 1954.

Another division occurred in 1959 and continues to the present. The right-wing Nishio faction, joined by a few other moderates, left the party in revolt against the strongly Marxist orientation of the dominant left-wing. On foreign policy issues, the Demo-cratic Socialist Party recognized the importance of a balance of armed strength between the two major blocs, accepted the need for some military protection until a new international order could be attained, and supported the idea of friendly relations with neighboring states regardless of ideo-logical or political differences (includ-ing both Communist China and Taiwan). The Democratic Socialist Party, however, fared badly in the 1960 election, obtaining only 9 per cent of the vote and 17 Diet seats to 28 per cent and 145 seats for the Socialist Party. The left is still in decisive com-mand of Japanese socialism, although there are some indications of a moderate movement within the left it-self.

In conservative ranks also, the con-cept of alliance has its limits. It must be remembered that after more than a thousand years of relative isolation, Japan comes to any alliance with diffi-culty. Even her modern alliances with Great Britain and, later, with the Axis powers were essentially superficial de-spite their importance to Japan. They involved minimum policy coordination or bilateral ties. Actually, the alliance with the United States is the most far-reaching alliance in Japanese history. But the conservatives as well as other Japanese have been involved in the resurgence of nationalism that naturally followed the Occupation. They never approved of many American policies implanted during the Occupation era, and proceeded to overturn a number of these quickly. They did more than merely talk about "an independent foreign policy aligned with the West"; they proved to be tough bargainers on a number of issues effecting the alliance, including the revised security treaty of 1961. Some might say in this connection that they wanted equality of rights but not equality of responsibility. Notwithstanding these facts, however, the era of alliance continues.

THE FORMULATION OF FOREIGN POLICY IN POSTWAR JAPAN

To compare the decision-making and administrative processes in Japanese foreign policy before and after World War II is a very difficult undertaking. A vast amount of detailed research is still necessary before generalizations can be advanced with any certainty. In some respects—for example, in terms of the constitutional allocation of responsibility—greater clarity and simplicity have been realized in the postwar era. But against this fact, one must acknowledge the increasing complexity that is the product of a more even balance of pressure groups and the rising importance of public opinion.

The new Japanese Constitution of 1947 did much to clarify the ultimate responsibility for policy, domestic and foreign. Patterned almost wholly after Anglo-American institutions, it drastically altered the old system. Under its provisions, the Emperor was relegated to ceremonial and symbolic functions. Sovereignty was assigned to the people, to be exercised by their elected representatives. A parliamentary system modelled after that of Great Britain was established, with certain modifications of a distinctly American flavor.

The Diet, instead of being peripheral to the political process, is now its center. Both houses of the Diet are elective. The upper house, the House of Councillors, is constructed in a complicated fashion, with both nationwide and prefectural constituencies; the lower house, the House of Representatives, is based upon medium-sized election districts (three to five members chosen from each district depending upon its size, with each voter having one vote). Executive responsibility to the Diet is clearly stipulated. The Prime Minister must be approved by the Diet, and if the houses disagree, by the lower house. In case of a vote of no-confidence, the government must either dissolve the lower house and call for new elections, or resign.

A new Diet law was enacted to accompany the Constitution of 1947. Among other things, it provided for a system of standing committees, in contrast to the prewar system of British style *ad hoc* committees. Thus, Foreign Affairs Committees exist for both houses of the Diet. After agreement among the parties on the allocation of committee seats, members are selected by each party, on the basis of training, experience, and political connections. The standing committees exist to hold hearings upon government legislation or any policy matters within their general jurisdiction. Special, *ad hoc* committees, however, are still used extensively in the Japanese Diet, sometimes on issues involving foreign policy. The Japanese committee system as it currently operates does not give either to the Diet as a whole or to individual Diet members the degree of power possessed in the U.S. Congress. Of course, party, or more precisely, factional discipline interacts with the institutional framework of the Diet to make this true. In any case, initiative and power in the field of foreign policy lie strongly with the executive branch of government.

Thus the new legal framework and continuing political practices combine to place a high premium upon the cooperation of bureaucracy and party leadership in the formulation of Japanese foreign policy. Under a Western-style parliamentary system, major party leaders constitute the apex of authority. The Emperor no longer serves as an independent and legally omnipotent channel of power. The military branch of government no longer represents another separate and competitive source of influence. And even the civil bureaucracy is now clearly subordinated in law to a political administration that must be consonant with a majority of the popularly elected members of the House of Representatives.

In concrete terms, how do the bureaucracy and the parties cooperate in foreign policy formulation? Generally speaking, the party (that is to say, the dominant party, the Liberal Democratic Party) provides the broad policy framework and the Foreign Office drafts specific policy within this framework. The draft is then subject to scrutiny and approval by the party, after which the Foreign Office proceeds to execute policy in its final forms. To understand this process in terms of some of its current operations and complexities, however, one must have a general appreciation of the present Japanese party system and bureaucracy.

With respect to the party system, perhaps four general trends are significant for purposes of understanding the foreign policy process. First, the conservatives have continued up to this point to hold a commanding position in Japanese politics. They have consistently polled close to two-thirds of the total vote, and at all times—divided or united—they have held a large majority of the seats in both houses of the Diet. Perhaps the major reasons for regular conservative victories have been their prewar ties and strength at local levels, especially in rural areas; their prominent, "name" candidates; the funds at their disposal; the relative prosperity in Japan since 1950; the divisive, weak nature of the opposition; and last but by no means least, the capacity of the conservatives to adjust to new socio-political factors. For these reasons, the Liberal Democratic Party is the government, now and for the foreseeable future.

The rising importance of the postwar socialists, however, cannot be ignored. Although they are currently both weak and divided, they have moved a considerable distance from their pre-1945 position of total impotence. Socialists occupy roughly one-third of the Diet seats, and their percentage of the vote has generally increased since 1949. In the election of November 1960, the two socialist parties got a combined total of 36.4 per cent of the vote, with the Communists obtaining an additional 2.9 per cent. The conservatives, therefore, have to be aware of competition in a sense that was unnecessary before World War II. The Japanese "left" is not close to power, but it cannot be disregarded.

These facts lead to a second generalization about Japanese politics, namely, that the party system can be variously defined as "two-party," "one and one-half party," or "federation type." Despite the socialist split of 1959, there are only two significant parties in Japan at present: the massive Liberal Democratic Party which received nearly 58 per cent of the vote in 1960 and the Socialist Party which obtained over 27 per cent. The splinter Democratic Socialist Party, the moderate group, got only 9 per cent of the 1960 vote and the Communists less than 3 per cent. In one sense, therefore, Japan has a two-party system.

In functional terms, however, Japan can be said to have a one and one-half party system: one dominant party that knows only how to govern and a half party (or parties) that know only how to oppose. The Socialists' position creates some serious problems. It is not easy to acquire responsibility, whether in foreign or domestic policy matters, if one has never had power and hence never had the responsibility that goes with formulating and defending policy.

There is still another way in which the Japanese party system can be defined and explained: as a system of rival federations within which operate the real "parties," namely, the small factions that are based upon intimate personal ties and mutual interests. Each of the major parties is composed of such factions. Thus the Liberal Democratic Party has currently its Ikeda, Kishi, Sato, Ishii, Ono, Kono, Miki-Matsumura, and Fujiyama factions. The shifting alliances among these factions determine leadership of the "federation." Factional loyalty generally takes precedence over loyalty to the "federation"; hence in many respects, the real party is the faction.

Considering the circumstances noted above, it is not surprising that bipartisanship on foreign policy issues does not exist in Japan. Indeed, such issues are even used on occasion as weapons in the struggle for power among rival factions *within* a major party. Thus within the Liberal Democratic Party recently, such issues as China policy and even the revised Security Treaty with the United States were made intraparty issues against Kishi and his

supporters. Needless to say, socialist opposition is much more continuous and absolute. When we talk about Japanese foreign policy or government attitudes, therefore, it must be constantly borne in mind that there is a vigorous and adamant opposition with its own channels to the public.

Finally, the party system as a whole is still on trial with the Japanese people. It is not yet thoroughly ingrained either in institutional practice or in public behavior. Popular commitments to individual parties and the party concept may be growing, but they remain basically weak at this point. There is some danger that in an age of increasing mass participation in Japanese politics, the parties and the Diet will be circumvented. There is a tendency on the part of the "left" to protest via the streets, and the "ultraright" to protest via the knife.

The Japanese bureaucracy also merits special attention. Its policy role is a vital one, especially with respect to foreign affairs. Once again, a few broad trends need to be noted. First, the general prestige and power of the Japanese bureaucracy continues to be extremely high. To be sure, there are powerful, new challenges. Industry, commerce, and the higher professional fields have undoubtedly made steady advances as "prestige occupations." In relative terms, therefore, the prestige of the official in Japan has declined in recent decades. This is indicated by the degree of popular homage currently paid him, by his present emoluments, and by his own attitude toward his status. But these are changes relative to the Japanese past. In comparison with other democratic societies, the Japanese official still enjoys great prestige and power. Despite the efforts of the Occupation to encourage local autonomy, the forces of centralization ultimately triumphed. Today, the national government is as powerful as at any time in the past. Notwithstanding the new constitutional position of the Diet, the central bureaucracy wields enormous power, partly because of its legacy and partly as a natural result of its technical expertise. Under these conditions, it is not surprising that many young Japanese aspire to careers as officials. Indeed, competition for the available civil service positions is as intense as for top positions in industry or the leading professions.

In some respects, the bureaucracy has changed less in its basic character than most other facets of postwar Japan. In structure, it remains strongly hierarchical. Its modes of operation have also been slow to change. Yet in socio-economic composition and in basic training, the Japanese bureaucracy is undergoing significant evolution. No doubt young men from the upper and upper-middle classes still have sizeable advantages—the maximum educational opportunities and proper social connections. But other elements have been pushing their way into the civil service in increasing numbers. Tokyo University, moreover, does not have the training monopoly it possessed before 1945. A larger proportion of successful candidates come from other institutions. Above all, Japanese civil servants are now receiving a much broader college education on the one hand, and much more advanced technical training where it is desired, on the other hand. The premium upon specialized skills has grown steadily higher. Some observers believe that the Japanese civil service today is not only attracting top talent in such fields as economics, but giving it more opportunity than actually exists in the academic world of Japan.

Another vital fact cannot be ignored. As in the prewar period, an increasing bureaucratic "infiltration" of the conservative party has been taking place. The percentage of conservative Diet members who are ex-officials (from the national civil service) has steadily risen since 1946. Today, approximately one-fourth of the Liberal Democratic Diet members are in this category. And the percentage of party leaders and Cabinet members who are ex-officials is much higher. It is this fact that makes easy the close interaction between party leadership and higher bureaucracy in contemporary Japan.

The Japanese Foreign Office is small in size and organized in a simple fashion. It has less than 2000 men of civil service rank. Its major sub-divisions are Bureaus of two types, those covering geographic areas and those representing specialized functions. The latter include economic affairs, treaties, information and culture, and international cooperation. Within the Ministry, there is also a Secretariat which serves as a central coordinating and administrative unit. It includes a Policy Planning Staff charged wit. over-all evaluation and planning of basic policy positions. Official liaison with the Diet is maintained thro h a parliamentary vice-minister, no y appointed from the Diet membe ship.

Today, a fairly high degree of coordinati , efficiency, and continuity exists i he formulation of Japanese foreign olicy. In the prewar period, as we have seen, the struggle to control foreign policy was a complex one waged by may diverse forces. The ultimate c t to Japan was enormous. In the immediate post-surrender period, the Japanese Foreign Office could play only a minor role. Both foreign and domestic policy were first laid down by Occupation authorities. The Japanese function was essentially to discern what the policy was and then to exercise—with uncertain results—the right of suggestion. In any case, diplomacy had to be directed primarily toward the United States. As the Occupation drew to a close, Japanese initiative was gradually reasserted. Initially, diplomacy in the hands of Prime Minister Yoshida, himself an ex-Foreign Office man, was highly personalized. His opponents charged him with "one man diplomacy." General party participation in foreign policy decisions was very limited. And the Foreign Office itself still struggled to overcome its earlier weak and ineffectual position.

As Japan regained her independence, however, the conduct of foreign policy was gradually placed on a broader base. This base is the network of collaboration between conservative party and Foreign Office representatives. By the time of the Kishi era (Kishi became Prime Minister in February 1957), Foreign Office Bureau chiefs had begun to have close contacts with conservative party leaders. Many of these contacts were with the pertinent committees of the Liberal Democratic Party: the Research Committee on Foreign Relations, the Policy Research Committee, and the General Affairs Board. These committees, and particularly the General Affairs Board, determine the foreign policy position of the party.

Foreign Office-Liberal Democratic Party liaison has not always been smooth or uncomplicated. The factional character of Japanese parties on occasion can represent a major problem. The primacy of factionalism makes it relatively easy for foreign policy to become a weapon in intraparty strife, especially if this is encouraged by certain external pressure groups. Thus, at the time of negotiations between Japan and the Soviet Union for a treaty of peace, some leaders within the Liberal Democratic Party, supported by certain fishery and commercial groups, built up maximum pressure for a rapid settlement. This was resisted by top Foreign Office officials. For a time, Japan suffered once again from "dual diplomacy." In spite of the absence to date of an independent military element, the Foreign Office has faced jurisdictional and policy rivalries from other ministries on occasion. Japan, however, does not have the massive problem of reconciling and integrating a Pentagon-CIA-State Department triumvirate in the foreign policy field. And on the whole, coordination in the formulation and execution of foreign policy has been more satisfactory in recent years than at any other time in the history of Japan.

There is another side to the coin. Developments with respect to Japanese pressure groups, public opinion, and opposition parties have added many new complexities to the scene. As noted earlier, pressure groups of all types have been operative in postwar Japan. In comparison with the period before 1945, the number and diversity of pressure groups, and their impact upon Japanese foreign policy, has greatly increased. It is not appropriate here to attempt any detailed discussion; only a few salient points can be presented. As in the prewar era, the commercial-industrial groups have the greatest single influence upon the Liberal Democratic Party, especially in the field of foreign policy. Through the Japan Employers Association and many similar organizations, single and multi-purpose, their policy positions are made known. It would be a mistake to assume that the Japanese business-industrial world speaks with a single voice. On such an issue as the importance of trade with Communist China, for example, it is far from unanimous. Still, the broad outlines of Japanese foreign policy at present are deeply influenced by the interests and views of leading industrial-commercial pressure groups. They remain the chief sources of financial support for the Liberal Democratic Party, the most intimate confidants of conservative politicians, and hence, the most powerful unofficial influence upon public policy, domestic and foreign.

On certain issues, pressures emanating from rural Japan can also be important. Almost every Japanese farmer belongs to an Agricultural Cooperative Association today, and these Associations are vital to the fortunes of individual conservative politicians and the Liberal Democratic Party as a whole. Rural Japan still constitutes over 40 per cent of the electorate, a portion that votes overwhelmingly conservative. The greatest agrarian pressures are exercised on domestic issues, but standing agrarian interests and attitudes do not need to be articulated constantly to establish certain guidelines and limits in the foreign policy area.

The more serious complexities that have recently emerged in foreign policy formulation, however, refer less to traditional Japanese pressure groups than to certain new ones, and to the force of mass "public opinion" as it is revealed in countless polls. Among the opposition pressure groups, the most important is organized labor. The General Council of Trade Unions of Japan (Sohyo) has been especially vocal on foreign policy issues. It has hewed closely to (and helped to shape) the left socialist position on such subjects as neutralism, relations with the Communist world, opposition to "American imperialism," and many other issues. In addition, it has supported these position with political action: demonstrations, work stoppages, and quantities of political literature.

Sohyo, with its more than three million members, is probably the most formidable of the opposition pressure

groups (though it should not be implied that it can commit all its members on any issue). There are, however, a number of pressure groups that occupy similar positions vis-à-vis conservative foreign policy. Most of them represent intellectual-student-labor elements in Japanese society. This opposition, as was indicated earlier, cannot be ignored. It maintains a substantial forum by means of newspapers, magazines, and radio. Its message reaches the Japanese public, especially the urban public, regularly. And since 1950, foreign policy has become a vital part of the political battlefield in Japan, probably the most vital part. The conservatives have been forced to recognize a far more significant opposition than any experienced in the prewar era, and they have had to devise new methods of meeting that opposition. Suppression or indifference are no longer feasible. Thus the conservatives are also resorting to mass media and seeking public support more actively than in the past.

Under present circumstances, it is a most difficult task to assess the influence of Japanese public opinion upon the foreign policy formulation process. In recent years, polling has become very popular in Japan. It is carried out by a variety of organizations, and the most widely-regarded polls are conducted on the basis of techniques similar to those employed by leading American professional pollsters. The major Japanese newspapers in particular have thrown themselves into polling the public at regular intervals on a wide variety of subjects, including many issues of foreign policy. Opinions on rearmament, a security treaty with the United States, and relations with Communist China have been asked for frequently. And in a number of cases, the polls have indicated either a large minority or an actual majority of those polled differing with current government policy.

There is little doubt that public opinion, now being presented in these concrete, measured forms, has had a rising impact upon the decision making in Japan. Increasingly, it is a factor which Japanese leaders take seriously. Sometimes, to be sure, public opinion is used as an excuse to justify a decision based mainly on other grounds. But more frequently, when the polls indicate substantial public opposition to a given policy, conservative leaders respond with modifications, a shift in timing, and/or a more intensive public relations campaign. Thus the reluctance of recent conservative administrations to rearm rapidly or fully, the long and fairly firm Japanese bargaining in connection with the revised security treaty, and the cautious, ambivalent position on relations with Communist China are all indications of the new power of the Japanese common man.

Some important qualifications must be added to this picture, however. The Japanese conservatives are well aware of the fact that elections in Japan are not won primarily on the basis of issues, particularly issues of foreign policy. In recent elections, the Liberal Democrats have placed their main stress on domestic issues—notably on the theme of prosperity and progress. They also count heavily and correctly upon superiority of organization, funds, and local leadership. Thus they can afford to take chances, even when they know or suspect that there is strong public opposition to specific foreign policy positions. This is the more true because they believe (with reason) that a mere numerical count of opposition is misleading. Opposition of the intensity likely to be translated into political action is largely confined to urban centers, especially Tokyo. Thus when confronted with evidence of hostile public opinion, the government tactic quite naturally is to camouflage or alter slightly a policy so as to disarm some of the opposition, but rarely if ever to make changes. With respect to the socialists also, a *caveat* must be entered regarding the influence of public opinion. The record would indicate that often the Japanese socialists have ignored public opinion when it conflicted with their ideological "purity."

In sum, the process of formulating, executing, and defending Japanese foreign policy today is in the hands of a conservative elite. The formal and informal institutional processes have been greatly refined in the postwar era, and now operate at a fairly high level of efficiency. Foreign Office-Liberal Democratic Party liaison is close and continuous. Despite some problems, therefore, the old difficulties of coordination and rivalry have largely been eliminated. With the military clearly subordinated, and with party-official cooperation at a peak, Japanese foreign policy has achieved an unprecedented degree of coordination and continuity. The new Japanese Foreign Office men, moreover, as a group are more broadly recruited and trained than prior to World War II, and also have a higher level of technical proficiency.

In political terms, the conservative elite that directs Japanese foreign policy is sustained and influenced mainly by the industrial, commercial, and agrarian segments of Japanese society. Contradictory pressures, however, sometimes flow from these elements, and in any case, no simple economic analysis does justice to the realities of the situation. Among other things, Japan is becoming a mass society in which the conservative elite is forced to pay increasing attention to public opinion. In part, this is reflective of the fact that the public has a choice: the socialist opposition, while weak in many respects, is infinitely more important than at any time in the pre-1945 period, and it offers the Japanese people a dramatically different foreign policy. But the influence of public opinion in Japan today can easily be exaggerated. With respect to foreign policy, it would be most accurate to say that public opinion serves to effect certain modifications, both of substance and of timing, and causes the conservatives to give more attention to the image of their policies in the Japanese public mind.

CONTEMPORARY ISSUES IN JAPANESE FOREIGN POLICY

At present, three dominant considerations underlie the debates and decisions pertaining to foreign policy in Japan. First, there are the interrelated issues of nationalism and security, issues involving Japanese relations with the United States, the Communist bloc, and the world. Second, there is the high priority that must be accorded economic considerations in foreign policy—the extreme importance attached to such matters as trade, technical assistance opportunities, and equality of economic treatment by others. Finally, there exists within Japanese society an ardent search for some basic purpose or function, especially one that will relate Japan in a suitable manner to the Asian world, catering to her "special interests" there, while allowing her a place on the world stage in concert with other major societies. We must study these general considerations further in the context of specific policy issues, for they are likely to be the enduring as well as the underlying forces motivating Japanese society. Indeed, if the background that we have projected is examined closely, these

forces will be seen in different forms throughout the history of modern Japan.

Nationalism, security, and foreign policy

Given the years of defeat, occupation, and subordination to foreign authority, the recent resurgence of Japanese nationalism is completely understandable. But today, in contrast to the prewar situation, nationalism in Japan is based upon no narrow range of ideology or line of attack. It runs the entire political gamut. Old-line conservative and ultra-rightist doctrines and tactics are once more displayed openly. Some attempt is being made to preserve or revive the Emperor cult and assassination is again a factor in the political scene. But now the left also uses nationalism as a potent political weapon. American bases in Japan, the Okinawan occupation, and all issues revolving around the so-called "subordination to America" are brought under assault. On foreign policy issues particularly, socialist and Communist attacks upon the conservatives are generally spearheaded by nationalist slogans. Regarding domestic issues, the situation is sometimes reversed. When the Liberal-Democrats attack the new Constitution, they do so in nationalist terms, referring to it as "the translation" and unsuitable for Japan in some of its provisions. It is the socialists who defend this document as representing the true will of the Japanese people. And there are many other respects in which the nationalist mantle seems to be worn by the conservatives.

In some respects, nationalism in this period is reminiscent of the Meiji era. Once again, its dominant notes are defensive in character. Japan is an island of weakness surrounded by a sea of power. But this time the power is Asian as well as Western. The continent is no longer a vacuum; Communist China in itself is en route to becoming a major power, and behind it stands the Soviet Union. Under these conditions, it seems highly unlikely that Japanese nationalism will revert quickly or easily to its former themes of expansionism and a militant messianic mission. The burning issues are more likely to concern the best way in which to preserve the territorial integrity of Japan and her true independence. And these are the issues of the day. On the one hand, questions of extraterritoriality, foreign residency and bases, and equality of treatment—in short, questions of "true independence"—have come to the fore. But there is another way in which the basic question can be posed: under present conditions, how can Japan achieve security, lasting prosperity, and meaningful independence except in alliance with the United States?

Thus the great debate in Japan continues over neutralism versus alliance. It is clear that neutralism has substantial support, and not merely from the organized left. World War II left terrible scars that will not soon be eradicated. Two hundred and thirty thousand Japanese still suffer from radioactive diseases as a result of the atomic bombs dropped on Hiroshima and Nagasaki. There are additional thousands who bear the marks of the great fire raids on major Japanese cities or actual combat injuries. Thus both memories and the living symbols of the last war contribute strongly to a Japanese distaste for rearmament or involvement in the game of international power politics. And there is a widespread fear that alliance with the United States, particularly the presence of American bases on Japanese territory, will greatly increase the risk of Japanese involvement in some future war.

The question is also asked, will or can the United States actually provide security for Japan in the final analysis? Japan lies on the peripheries of Sino-Soviet power. (Should we join "Sino-Soviet" with a hyphen, or advance the historical process by separating them with a slash mark, "Sino/Soviet"?) In any case, many Japanese argue that in the face of these huge states, Japan should reconcile herself to the status of a minor power, that the days when she could take advantage of the weakness of giants are over. The Japanese population which is now approaching ninety-three million must depend upon imports for 80 per cent of its industrial raw materials and about 20 per cent of its foodstuffs. Its cities are massive, densely packed, and highly vulnerable. They lie minutes away from Communist bases. But the lines of supply and communication to continental United States centers are long, and in the event of war, uncertain. Perhaps all of these points add up to a feeling in some Japanese circles that the combination of developments in military technology and massive political change, especially in Asia, make warfare a form of certain suicide for modern Japan.

Some of these feelings lay behind the serious political crisis that developed in the spring of 1960 over the revised security treaty with the United States. This crisis produced the most substantial mass movement in Japanese political history. Millions of Japanese signed petitions asking for the Diet to be dissolved and new elections to be held so as to test public sentiment. Hundreds of thousands demonstrated in Tokyo and other major cities. The acute stage of the crisis lasted for nearly one month from mid-May to early June.

Naturally, the organized left-wing played an important part in this crisis, but to dismiss the episode as a Communist or even Socialist inspired riot is to misunderstand seriously the present climate of Japanese politics and public opinion. No one knows this better than the Japanese conservatives. The May-June Incident was the product of many complex factors: the ineptitude and increasing unpopularity of the Kishi government; the almost unanimous opposition of the metropolitan press to government actions, which helped to mobilize public sentiment; factionalism inside the Liberal Democratic Party which helped to weaken Kishi's internal base of support; and the tactics used in forcing the treaty through the House of Representatives which gave opponents a new slogan, "for the protection of democracy," an appeal that enlisted support even from some conservatives. Nor can the Socialists be exempted from responsibility; toward the concept of parliamentarism, there exists a considerable ambivalence in socialist circles. Certain socialists believe in parliamentarism—plus. They are willing to go beyond parliamentary procedures if necessary to attain their ends. They do not accept completely the right of the majority to govern. And they do not eschew violence if it offers a chance of success.

Actually, the May-June Incident revealed some of the continuing weaknesses of Japanese parties and parliamentarism. No party really gained as a result of the crisis. With the revised treaty safely enacted, Kishi resigned after playing a major role in selecting his successor, Hayato Ikeda. Ikeda took office with conciliatory offers to consult with the opposition and operate in democratic fashion, to pay attention to public opinion, and to build a prosperous, peaceful Japan. The opening months of the Ikeda government were marked by moderation and many pledges to the Japanese people. In November 1960, running on a platform of economic expansion, increased public welfare, and prosperity for all, the Liberal Democratic Party won another major victory, with 58 per cent of the vote and 296 Diet seats. However, the divided "left" (Democratic Socialists, Socialists, and Communists) received nearly 40 per cent of the vote, a new high for this combined group. Moreover, the moderate Democratic Socialists suffered a serious defeat, obtaining only 8.8 per cent of the vote and 17 Diet seats, whereas the Socialists got 27.6 per cent of the vote and 145 seats. The Communists remained powerless with only 2.9 per cent of the vote and 3 Diet seats.

Thus despite their sizeable electoral victories, the Japanese conservatives are well aware of the deep division in Japanese public opinion over security issues, and the hazards that this might present to them in view of opposition strength. They know that approximately one-third of the electorate have repeatedly registered their opposition to rearmament and military alliance, with another one-third being uncertain or uninterested. Consequently, they have been cautious in approaching these issues. In the budget for the fiscal year 1961, appropriations for the Japan Self-Defense Force totalled about 9 per cent, as compared with 10 per cent in fiscal 1960; but major increases were voted for social security, public works, and school expenditures, in harmony with the Ikeda promises.

There is every indication that Japan will retain a military tie with the United States, but will not become a major military ally in the foreseeable future. Japanese military policy will be predicated upon limited, conventional rearmament for defense purposes only. In all likelihood, public opposition will preclude the addition of atomic weapons to the arsenal of the Defense Force, or the storage of such weapons on Japanese soil for United States use. Numerical growth of the defense force will be very gradual and limited. As noted earlier, the present size is only about 230,000 men in all branches. There will be no attempt in the near future to commit these forces abroad, even for use by the United Nations. It is also unlikely that Article Nine of the Constitution will be repealed or altered, since the conservatives do not have the votes to accomplish this.

As long as the conservatives remain in power, however, Japanese foreign policy will continue on the pathway of gradual rearmament and alliance with the United States. Prime Minister Ikeda expressed the government position in a speech of October 25, 1960 to the Diet:

To build up and replenish our self-defense power on our own initiative is the proper responsibility of ours as an independent nation. Needless to say, this defense power will have to be such as is appropriate to our national resources and circumstances. This is why our country, while entrusting the fundamentals of our security guarantee to the United Nations and the Japanese-American Security Treaty, has pursued a policy of expanding gradually our self-defense power. With a small—relatively the smallest in the world—defense cost, Japan has been able to maintain peace and security and at the same time achieve a startling development of the national economy. This, I believe, is proof of the diplomatic success of the successive Conservative Governments in the past. On the other hand, there is a tendency among some Japanese to advocate neutralism as a means effective enough for ensuring our country's security. These are the people who neglect the concrete examinations of the international environment of our country, who ignore the fact that Japan's power has an enormous bearing upon the East-West balance, and who

lack insight into the position of our country, which considers its cooperation with free countries as the primary basis of the national prosperity and economic development. . . .

To make alliance more acceptable, however, and to advance Japanese national interests, the conservatives will continue to approach military-security issues with an admixture of caution and tough bargaining. For example, under the revised security treaty, the United States has the use of certain air and naval installations in Japan proper, but the Japanese government currently insists that under the terms of the new treaty, it must be consulted and give its approval prior to the use of these bases in connection with any hostility.

There are other respects in which the Japanese conservative leaders will seek to prove that this is an alliance of equal partners, and that theirs is "an independent foreign policy within the framework of cooperation with the West, and particularly the United States." In Okinawa where some 875,000 people live who culturally are Japanese, the United States has recognized the "residual sovereignty" of Japan, and at present, Japanese interaction with Okinawa is steadily increasing. Commercial investment, educational aid, and political counselling all give evidence of the mounting participation of the Japanese government in Okinawan life. Reversion on some basis is only a question of time.

Meanwhile, the Japanese government is committed to seeking friendly relations with the Communist bloc, and especially to improving relations with Communist China. Shortly after the Korean War ended, an attempt to attain a "normalization" of relations with the Communist bloc was begun. Negotiations with the Soviet Union culminating in the Treaty of 1956 constituted the opening and rather frustrating move. Russia made very few concessions, in keeping with the past. As yet, there are no indications that the future of Russo-Japanese relations will diverge greatly from those of the last few decades. Within Japan, antipathy to the U.S.S.R. is relatively strong, a product of historic rivalries, the last-minute attack in 1945, Russian treatment of Japanese prisoners, and its "get-tough" policy toward Japan on most postwar issues.

Conceivably, the Soviet Union could alter its position, and at a rather minimal price, woo the Japanese by trade offers, greater liberality on fishery and prisoner issues, and minor territorial concessions. Up to date, however, the relatively tough line has continued. The Russians have even refused to yield the two small islands of Habomai and Shikotan off Hokkaido unless the security treaty with the United States is abandoned. Thus the indications are that Russo-Japanese relations will not go far beyond the levels of correct formality and very minor, reciprocal concessions. Japanese policy will be marked by vigilance, determined bargaining, and the hope for some thaw in the Soviet attitude, possibly as a by-product of increasing Sino-Soviet difficulties.

Relations with Communist China are regarded as much more important and potentially different. With China, Japan has had a lengthy historic relationship and it remains inconceivable to most Japanese that the ties can long remain almost completely severed. Within Japan, pressures have mounted for a "realistic China policy." Various business interests continue to believe that the China trade could be meaningful under "normalized" relations, even if it were different in type and less in quantity than in the period before 1945. Certain conservative leaders are at odds with the present policy, which they regard as the result of deference to the United States. The socialists, of course, have sought to make a major political issue out of China policy. They have demanded full and unqualified recognition of the People's Republic, and have denounced the conservatives for preventing this by a policy of military alliance with the United States.

Conservative policy is to seek some readjustment of China policy that will accord with the realities of the situation without conceding on all points to the Chinese Communists and thereby jeopardizing relations with the United States and Taiwan. On January 30, 1961, Prime Minister Ikeda uttered the following carefully chosen words to the Diet:

Japan welcomes any improvement of relations, particularly expansion of trade, with Mainland China. In fact, how to approach this question is our task this year. But the question of Mainland China is not one that can be disposed of between Peking and Tokyo alone; it must be taken up from the viewpoint of a general adjustment of East-West relations. I think Japan and Communist China, on common recognition of this fact and through mutual respect for each other's position, should seek to establish friendly relations, on the basis of the existing conditions, for the sake of the peace and prosperity of the Far East.

In reality, the Japanese government would like to realize a "Two Chinas" policy, or more properly, a "One China-One Taiwan" policy. To this end, it can be expected to work and to put increasing pressure upon the United States. The Chinese Communists are aware of this, and determined to prevent it if possible. That is why they have been pursuing a tough policy, refusing any substantial trade unless they are accorded formal recognition and Taiwan is accepted as "an internal problem of China." Moreover, there can be no doubt that the Chinese Communists see the American-Japanese military alliance as a potential threat to them, and would like to break it up. Whether in the future they will attempt this by switching from a tough to a soft policy remains unclear.

Thus once again, Japan is faced with the problem of finding a workable China policy, and this time it must be based more upon the strength than the weakness of that nation. Her success cannot be predicted; the variables are too numerous and they go far beyond Japan. Even if improvements are scored, however, given the political realities of the present, it is very doubtful that Sino-Japanese relations will be marked by great intimacy in the near future. The chances are strong that China will remain Communist and Japan anti-Communist; that economic as well as political rivalries will build up in the Asian area; that both states will reflect their differences within Asia through alliances out of Asia. But even if this proves to be the case, Japan will seek to follow a flexible, realistic policy under conservative leadership, exploring all economic opportunities and moving toward a One China-One Taiwan policy if at all possible.

In summary, all forces in Japan today pay homage to the idea of an independent foreign policy, and the removal of those inequities remaining from the era of Occupation. The conservatives believe that that independence can only be truly achieved and maintained if Japan has her own military force, and is connected with the military power of the United States. Therefore they support alliance, emphasizing strongly its economic and political advantages, and cancelling its military risks against those of neutralism. If the internal

prosperity of Japan continues and no general war occurs, the conservatives will probably remain in power for the indefinite future, and they are not likely to undertake drastic shifts in this policy. At the same time, however, it is entirely possible that a combination of internal and external developments will heighten the appeal of neutralism to the Japanese public, making conservative policies in this field increasingly difficult. The great debate over neutralism versus alliance may well get hotter in the years ahead.

The economic basis of Japanese foreign policy

The high priority given to economic considerations in formulating Japanese foreign policy stems from many factors. In 1961, the Japanese population was approaching 93 million. This vast number of people now live in a country the size of California with approximately 16 per cent of the land arable. If present calculations are correct, population stability will probably be attained within the next twenty-five years, but the stabilization figure is not likely to be less than 110 to 120 million people. Meanwhile, for the next few years, the average yearly increase of workers on the labor market will be well over one million. This requires further industrialization. And Japanese industry cannot avoid a heavy dependence upon foreign trade. Over 80 per cent of all industrial raw materials must be imported at present.

In addition, there are some dynamic, new factors in the scene. For the past decade, the Japanese economic growth rate has been spectacular. In recent years, her gross national product has been increasing at an average annual rate of about 9 per cent. The major gains, of course, have been in industrial production, but agricultural production also has been making sizeable advances. The result has been an unprecedented degree of prosperity for Japan. While the per capita income is still very low compared with that of Western Europe, not to mention the United States, it has been moving upward at a rapid rate. The result is that Japan represents one of the very few countries of the Afro-Asian region where the revolution of rising expectations is really in progress. A consumer boom has been taking place. Even rural families have participated.

But once this pace is set, it becomes imperative from a political standpoint to retain and, if possible, advance it. The Japanese conservatives are well aware of the fact that their future depends heavily upon their capacity to meet the new desires and expectations. Thus the new long-range economic program has been named "The Plan for Doubling the People's Income," and it envisages this accomplishment in ten years. Furthermore, conservatives like Ikeda are frankly talking about the need for a welfare state. Indeed, they are doing more than talking; they are putting increasing sums of money into fields such as housing, road construction, and social security. To sustain these expenditures, and to increase them, general economic expansion—and particularly the expansion of trade—is vital.

Economic relations with the United States are likely to remain the single most important factor in determining the fate of the Japanese economy. Almost one-third of Japanese trade is presently with this country. In 1960, Japan exported over one billion, one hundred million dollars worth of goods to the United States and purchased over one billion, three hundred million dollars worth of goods from her. Trade with the United States has expanded so rapidly in the past decade that it has caused some serious problems for Japan. In certain industries, such as textiles, American producers have demanded protection against "low wage" Japanese goods, and unions have threatened a boycott. There has been some discriminatory state legislation and heightened pressure for more tariff protection.

Thus far, the issue has been kept within bounds by the strong desire of both governments to work out a compromise, and by Japan's acceptance of a quota system to limit the export to the United States of certain goods. The problem, however, is a serious one, and not susceptible to easy solution. The diversification of Japanese exports to the United States continues. There has also been improvement in market research and public relations. But American complaints of "dumping," patent infringement, and discrimination against American capital and goods in Japan are frequently made. The threat of higher tariffs is a nightmare to the Japanese. They too have complaints: unscrupulous American buyers who take advantage of the highly competitive nature of Japanese small and medium industry, pursuing cut-throat tactics and encouraging illegal or immoral practices; the penchant of American industry to exaggerate Japanese competition; and the problem of a trade deficit with the United States. Until some more rational, regularized method of planning United States-Japan economic relations and handling grievances is adopted, tensions are likely to continue. The newly announced United States-Japan Committee on Trade and Economic Affairs represents a positive step in the right direction, and may alleviate some of the current problems.

The remainder of Japanese trade is marked by great diversity, both of area and of product. Outside the United

States, no single country at present accounts for more than a small fraction of Japanese exports. In part, this pattern reflects the serious decline in Japanese trade with the northeast Asian area, including China-Manchuria and the former Japanese Empire. In the prewar period when Japan controlled Manchuria and used China as an area both for investment and markets, that trade was of great importance. Japan recognizes that the old trade pattern, which rested upon vastly different conditions, cannot be reestablished. As noted earlier, there is considerable doubt in some commercial circles whether trade with Communist China under any conditions can be very significant. There is also the knowledge that it may be used primarily as a political weapon by the Communists. That has been the case thus far. Many Japanese business interests, however, are anxious to explore this question fully. Even if the China trade does not reach prewar percentages, any improvement over the present negligible exchange would be welcomed. The Japanese government, beset with numerous pressures, will continue to explore methods of improving her economic relations with Communist China, subject to the political conditions outlined earlier.

Meanwhile, the quest for new markets and economic opportunities continues everywhere. With governmental encouragement, Japanese businessmen have canvassed possibilities on every continent. Currently, there is hope that the European market, which has been weak in the past, can be more effectively developed. However, Japan places her greatest faith in the Afro-Asian world. She expects to find her major export in goods and services to societies en route to modernization. She is continuing to shift her emphasis toward heavy industrial and chemical products, recognizing that in the light industrial field, new competition and increasing self-sufficiency are probable. And at the same time, she is anxious to explore every cooperative means whereby capital and technical assistance can be advanced to these countries, hoping to participate in all such programs.

In sum, the conservative leaders will continue to give very heavy weight to economic considerations in determining Japanese foreign policy, because this is required by the political and economic facts of life in contemporary Japan. They will count strongly upon favorable and expanding economic relations with the United States. At the same time, they will be anxious to lessen somewhat their dependency upon American trade, not by reducing it, but by expanding greatly their trade with all other regions of the world. Their emphasis will be upon the markets of Africa and Asia, especially the latter.

Basic Japanese goals

In many respects, Japan is still searching for a basic purpose, a role to play in the modern world. The fact that this purpose or role has not been easy to find in the shattering aftermath of total defeat helps to account for some of the unrest in Japanese society, especially among the youth. There has been a certain tendency in the postwar period to go from moods of black despair to quests for lofty, idealistic causes. Perhaps this accounts in part for the enthusiasm shown in Japan for the United Nations, and the eagerness with which Japanese participation was greeted.

The high degree of support accorded the United Nations may also reflect Japanese acceptance of a "minor state" status for their nation. But here, there is considerable ambivalence and unhappiness. Mindful of her meteoric rise in this century and possessed of a surplus of energy and creativeness, Japan has an inner need to utilize her talents on the world stage. Perhaps this need can be fulfilled if Japan is able to interact in technical-economic terms with those societies now embarking upon programs of rapid modernization. This is becoming the major Japanese goal.

Japan also hopes to play a considerable role in the United Nations and other international bodies, in part as a bridge between Asia and the West. She knows that she has numerous competitors for this role, and that she has some lost ground to regain. However, she has certain unique capacities, among them the fact that she is still the only advanced industrial society in the Asian area. This uniqueness is not an unmixed blessing, as we have noted earlier. It produces conflicting sentiments. In part, Japan sees herself as *sui generis* and on occasion displays a strong trait of ethnocentrism, finding it difficult to understand, communicate with, or adjust to others, including her fellow Asians. But Japan also sees herself as a synthesis of Asian and Western culture, an embodiment of the modern, non-Western society, and when this image predominates, she can display a highly sophisticated quality of universality, a capacity to understand, adjust, and lead.

For twenty years the Anglo-Japanese Alliance underwrote Japanese policy in Asia. Then through the disintegration of that alliance and the abuses of Japanese policy, Japanese plans and hopes came to nought. Now an American alliance has given Japan a second opportunity for an Asian policy which, if it is to be successful, must be marked by moderation, a cooperative spirit, and a predominance of the second image noted above. How long will this new

alliance last? To this question, there is no certain answer. For the past decade, it has been a logical alliance in terms of the needs and goals of both nations as viewed by their respective leaders. Needs, goals, and leaders sometimes change, however. And it is likely that the international climate that surrounds this alliance—particularly the climate in Asia—will become more stormy in the years ahead. Thus the premium will be upon flexibility, a capacity of both parties in the alliance to adjust to new conditions. The greatest hazards probably lie in the military aspects of the alliance. Still, if economic relations retain a vital meaning for both societies, and cultural ties continue to expand, such hazards may be surmounted. The Japanese-American alliance could have as long a life as the earlier alliance with Great Britain. One would hope that it also could serve as an even greater instrument of peace.

SELECTED BIBLIOGRAPHY

There is a wealth of primary and secondary source materials on Japanese foreign policy for the reader who can use the Japanese language. Memoirs of prominent statesmen are abundant; a number of documentary collections and good secondary works exist; and many of the Japanese Foreign Office Archives, having been microfilmed during the Occupation, are obtainable through the Library of Congress. To list even the most essential Japanese materials would be a lengthy task, and one not appropriate here. Fortunately, the reader of Japanese can refer to a number of sources for bibliographic assistance. We shall merely suggest some English-language materials, with emphasis upon more recent books.

Although English materials are still far too limited, the last ten years have seen an increasing number of worthy articles, monographs, and general studies, many of which deal in some fashion with Japanese foreign policy.

To start with the historical background of Japanese international relations, one might mention the older work of R. H. Akagi, *Japan's Foreign Relations: 1542–1936* (Argus, 1936), but the historical writings of Sir George Sansom provide an excellent introduction to this as to other facets of traditional

Japan: *Japan—A Short Cultural History* (Appleton, 1943), *A History of Japan to 1334* (Stanford, 1958), *A History of Japan, 1334–1615* (Stanford, 1960), and *The Western World and Japan* (Knopf, 1950). To these should be added C. R. Boxer's *Christian Century in Japan* (U. of Cal., 1951) for a careful exposition of initial Western contacts.

In the modern period, a few general works include materials on foreign policy. One might select Hugh Borton's *Japan's Modern Century* (Ronald, 1955) and Chitoshi Yanaga's *Japanese People and Politics* (Wiley, 1956) as recent works of this type.

For those particularly interested in the early Meiji period, we are fortunate in having the work of W. G. Beasley: *Great Britain and the Opening of Japan, 1834–1858* (Luzac, 1951) has been followed by *Select Documents on Japanese Foreign Policy, 1853–1868* (Oxford, 1955). These serve as an admirable introduction to the problems of the early Meiji era, which began in 1867.

The memoirs and accounts of Western diplomats and other residents are also of interest: E. M. Satow, *A diplomat in Japan* (Lippincott, 1921); Sir Rutherford Alcock, *The Capital of the Tycoon* 2 vols. (London, 1863); J. H. Gubbins, *The Progress of Japan, 1853–1871* (Oxford, 1911). There are also a few monographs of special interest, mainly pertaining to the later Meiji period. Two of these are Hilary Conroy, *The Japanese Seizure of Korea* (U. of Penn., 1960) and Marius B. Jansen, *The Japanese and the Chinese Revolutionary Movement, 1895–1915.*

The Taisho period (1912–1926) is rather sparsely covered as yet. Masamichi Royama has written one work in English entitled *The Foreign Policy of Japan, 1914–1939* (Tokyo, 1941); the older work by T. Takeuchi, *War and Diplomacy in the Japanese Empire* (Doubleday, 1935), may still have some utility.

The books by A. M. Young, especially his *Japan in Recent Times, 1912–1926* (Morrow, 1928), are of interest as contemporary accounts, and the Young newspaper, the *Kobe* (later *Japan*) *Chronicle*, is a most important source for many events of the entire period between the mid-Meiji and prewar Showa eras.

For most readers, the Showa period is likely to be of greatest interest. For the militarist era of the 1930's the most important materials are contained in two memoirs: the so-called *Harada-Saionji Memoirs* and the *Kido Diary*; neither of these has been published in English, but both are available at certain leading libraries in the United States in mimeographed form, in whole or in part.

Perhaps no single English source is as valuable as the voluminous War Crimes Trial Documents, running into thousands of pages, which were translated for purposes of the famous Tokyo trials.

These also can be obtained; a complete set exists, for instance, at the Berkeley library.

Among existing Western memoirs, special mention should be made of J. C. Grew, *Ten Years in Japan* (S. and S., 1944), and Sir R. Craigie, *Behind the Japanese Mask* (Hutchinson, 1946).

From the Japanese side, see Mamoru Shigemitsu, *Japan and Her Destiny* (Dutton, 1958).

We have a general account of this wartime period in F. C. Jones' *Japan's New Order in East Asia; Its Rise and Fall, 1937–1945* (Oxford, 1954).

A growing number of monographs dealing with this general period are available. Yale Maxon explores the problems involved in formulating Japanese foreign policy in his *Control of Japanese Foreign Policy: A Study of Civil-Military Rivalry, 1930–1945,* (U. of Cal., 1957).

For other worthy studies, see Harry J. Benda, *The Crescent and the Rising Sun* (Institute of Pacific Relations, 1958), Robert Butow, *Japan's Decision to Surrender* (Stanford, 1955), Willard H. Elsbree, *Japan's Role in Southeast Asian Nationalist Movements, 1940–1945* (Harvard, 1953), Ernst Preusseisen, *Germany and Japan: A Study in Totalitarian Diplomacy, 1933–1941* (The Hague, 1958), and Paul Schroeder, *The Axis Alliance and Japanese-American Relations, 1941* (Cornell, 1958).

Japanese accounts of the war can be obtained from T. Kase, *Journey to the Missouri* (Yale, 1950), M. Kato, *The Lost War* (Knopf, 1946), and Saburo Hayashi in collaboration with Alvin D. Coox, *Kogun: The Japanese Army in the Pacific War* (Marine Corps Association, 1959).

Various aspects of the postwar period are covered in certain general books: Ardath Burks, *Government in Japan* (Praeger, 1961), Allan B. Cole, *Japanese Society and Politics* (Boston, 1956), Esler Dening, *Japan* (Praeger, 1961), Nobutaka Ike, "Japan" in George Kahin (ed.), *Major Governments of Asia* (Cornell, 1958), Kazuo Kawai, *Japan's American Interlude* (U. of Chicago, 1960), Ivan Morris, *Nationalism and the Right Wing in Japan* (Oxford, 1960), and Harold Quigley and John Turner, *The New Japan: Government and Politics* (U. of Minnesota, 1956).

See also the forthcoming *Parties and Politics in Contemporary Japan* by this author and Junnosuke Masumi (U. of Cal., 1962).

In his forthcoming book, *The Japanese People and Foreign Policy,* Douglas Mendel, Jr. presents an important collection of public opinion polls pertaining to foreign policy issues (U. of Cal., 1962).

Naturally, the American reader will tend to have a special interest in American-Japanese relations. A substantial number of books has been written on this subject. Among the older works, those of Payson J. Treat are well known: *Japan and the United States* (rev. ed.; Stanford, 1928), and *Dip-*

lomatic Relations between the United States and Japan, 3 vols. (Stanford, 1932, 1938).

There is also Foster Rhea Dulles, *Forty Years of American-Japanese Relations* (Appleton, 1937).

A broad cultural account is to be found in T. Dennett, *Americans in Eastern Asia* (Macmillan, 1922).

More recently, such an approach has been effectively used by Robert Schwantes in his *Japanese and Americans; A Century of Cultural Relations* (Harper, 1955).

In terms of current political relations, the reader can refer to E. O. Reischauer, *The United States and Japan* (Revised edition, Harvard, 1957), a section entitled *The United States and Japan* by the present author in the American Assembly publication, *The United States and the Far East* revised edition, (Prentice-Hall, 1962), and *United States Foreign Policy—Asia,* a study prepared for the Committee on Foreign Relations, United States Senate (Washington, 1959).

Official publications from the State Department, such as the series on *Foreign Relations of the United States and Japan,* are useful for major documents.

In addition there are a number of more specialized accounts, limited in scope or time. Only three will be mentioned here: H. L. Stimson, *The Far Eastern Crisis* (Harper, 1936), Herbert Feis, *The Road to Pearl Harbor* (Princeton, 1950), and Ray W. Curry, *Woodrow Wilson and Far Eastern Policy* (Twayne, 1957).

No serious study of Japanese foreign policy should be undertaken, of course, without reference to the periodical literature. Among the English-language journals, those carrying articles of significance at rather regular intervals include *Contemporary Japan, The Japan Quarterly,* (formerly *The Far Eastern Quarterly),* *Foreign Affairs, Pacific Affairs,* and *Asian Survey* (formerly *Far Eastern Survey*).

Some reference should also be made to the increasing number of English-language materials being published by the Japanese government, including valuable items pertaining to foreign policy problems and policies from the Ministries of Finance, Trade and Commerce, and the Foreign Office. In reference to contemporary issues it will be helpful to consult the translations of the vernacular press and translations of selected articles from Japanese vernacular magazines, put out by the American Embassy, if one can obtain access to these.

Such newspapers as the *Japan Times* (formerly *Nippon Times*), the *Osaka Mainichi* English edition, and the *Asahi Evening News* should also be examined. Naturally, many of the above materials will contain further leads and much fuller bibliographies.

8

Foreign Policy of Communist China

SCOPE OF STUDY: 1949 TO PRESENT

China, like Japan, is a relative new-comer to orthodox conduct of foreign relations. For centuries relations between the imperial court at Peking and the outside world remained tributary in nature. No concept of sovereignty or equality interfered with domination by the Middle Kingdom over dependencies such as Tibet and Mongolia, or vassal states such as Korea and Annam. Beyond these peripheral areas the presence of "foreign barbarians" only occasionally interrupted the splendid isolation of the emperor.

Not until the nineteenth century did Western pressure forcefully break down this isolation. During the first decades demands for trade, backed with arms, won limited concessions from Peking, but negotiations were restricted to provincial officials immediately concerned with coastal areas. Even when British and French troops shot their way to Peking, forcing establishment of the Tsungli Yamen as an office to deal with foreign governments, Chinese

ALLEN

S.

WHITING

officialdom remained hostile to conventional Western practices of international law and comity.

Collapse of the Manchu Empire and birth of the Republic of China in 1912 offer a convenient point of demarcation in the foreign relations of modern China. Still, the resemblance with Western states is more apparent than real. To be sure the Waichiao Pu with its consular establishments abroad and its acceptance of international protocol at home functioned as did most ministries of foreign affairs. The difference lay in China's political fragmentation, which left nominal authority with a central government but permitted local warlords to conduct *de facto* if not *de jure* foreign relations.

Civil war rent China apart during the decade 1918–1928 as a northern government at Peking, dominated by shifting military factions, vied for power with a southern government at Canton, headed by Sun Yat-sen and his Kuomintang cohorts. Officially Peking enjoyed recognition as the legal voice of China until its final defeat by the Nationalist Army in 1928. Its actual power, however, extended through only a small section of the country. During the turbulent twenties most of South China, Tibet, Sinkiang, Mongolia, and Manchuria lay beyond control of the capital.

Thus, examination of foreign policy during this period would have to consider not only Waichiao Pu activities but also relations between Soviet advisers and the Canton government. These important clandestine relations continued even after recognition was established between Moscow and Peking in 1924. Similarly, Russian troops assisted a revolutionary regime in Outer Mongolia to oust Chinese control in 1921. Despite recognition in 1924 of Peking's sovereignty over the area, the Soviet Commissar for Foreign Affairs continued to describe its "autonomy" as permitting "independence in its foreign policy." [1] In like fashion Moscow ignored Chinese protests and concluded an agreement with Marshal Chang Tso-lin for operation of the Chinese Eastern Railway which ran through his bailiwick of Manchuria, although a similar agreement had been concluded with Peking only four months before.

In fact, the history of modern China until 1949 finds few years wherein a central government exercised sufficient authority throughout the legal limits of its declared competence to preclude local conduct of foreign affairs. Japan overran Manchuria in 1931 and set up the independent state of Manchukuo. Soviet authorities concluded extensive agreements with local governors in the border province of Sinkiang, covering loans, trading privileges, and mineral exploitation rights all without reference to the central government. Even the miniscule Chinese Communist Party took upon itself the power to declare

[1] Commissar for Foreign Affairs, Chicherin, to the Congress of Soviets, *Pravda*, No. 54 (2985), March 6, 1925, p. 5.

war against Japan in 1932, acting as a Chinese Soviet Republic.

We see that analysis of Chinese foreign policy requires a continual adjustment of scope depending upon the time-span considered, for it would be a fiction to ignore these side-currents, some of which proved rather critical in determining the fate of large sectors of China. Communist victory over the forces of Chiang Kai-shek in 1949, however, provides a partial solution to to the problem, albeit not a wholly successful one. Communist control over the mainland of China and its general acceptance by Asia, if not by the world, as the *de jure* as well as the *de facto* government, compels our studying the regime of Mao Tse-tung. Yet another claimant to China conducts foreign policy in its name—the regime of Chiang Kai-shek, which withdrew to Taiwan in 1949 and continued to function there as the Republic of China. In view of the relatively small domain under Nationalist control and the impossibility of this group reconquering the mainland, we shall focus solely on the Communist People's Republic of China (PRC).

PROBLEMS OF ANALYSIS

Obstacles to analysis of Chinese Communist foreign policy are several and severe. Our perspective of Chinese foreign policy in general is limited by the formidable language barrier, which restricts the number of Western scholars able to read original documents. Extensive translation of nineteenth-century materials on foreign policy occurred only during the past decade. Furthermore, the turbulence of recent Chinese politics and the authoritarian tendencies of most regimes concerned combined to place serious limitations on the availability of materials. Again it has been only in the past decade that volumes of documents on the important T'ai P'ing rebellion of a century ago were published by the Peking regime.

The present government of China is as secretive about its foreign policy process as is its mentor, the Soviet Union. A determined appearance of "monolithic unity" within the authoritarian elite masks whatever differences may exist. Complete control over all media of communication censors information made available to the West. Public discussion comes only after policy has been decided within the highest levels of the Chinese Party. Government spokesmen rationalize but need not defend policy in the absence of an organized opposition.

Compounding these physical obstacles to analysis is the interpretive debate among non-Communists as to the nature of policy-making in Peking. Is it principally Chinese and therefore comprehensible only within a continuous flow of policies preceding it from Nationalist or even Manchu days? Or is it principally Communist, necessitating close study of Marxist-Leninist-Stalinist precedents for clues and insights?

Our analysis admits elements of both arguments without supporting either side exclusively. The present rulers of China are Chinese. They have lived there, with few exceptions, during most of their past. The environment within which they operate is essentially the same as that which prevailed in China for the previous century. At the same time, they view that environment through Communist lenses. The elite possesses a highly articulated ideology which it consciously proclaims as the basis of behavior: the Marxist-Leninist creed of Communism.

Therefore, we must examine the Chinese component of policy in terms of the external environment within which it operates. Part of this may be termed objective—the physical factors such as territory, accessibility, and material development, which confront all elites with certain tangibles. Part of this environment is subjective in the way in which historical trends are experienced and perceived by decision-makers. Insofar as the subjective factor remains relatively constant in groups preceding the Communists, we may term it a Chinese component of policy.

Then we shall analyze the Communist component of policy. Its ideological content is defined by the canons of Marx, Lenin, Stalin, and Mao. Its institutional structure springs from ideological convictions about the role of the Party, the nature of government, and the function of authoritarian rule— or "democratic centralism" as it is termed by the ideology. By combining these varied factors we can discern more clearly not only the goals of Chinese Communist foreign policy, but the means available to and likely to be adapted by the elite in support of that policy.

EXTERNAL ENVIRONMENT: THE CHINESE COMPONENT

Physical factors

Although the days of the Chinese Empire are long past, contemporary elites continue to pay obeisance to the memory of vanished glory in their delineation of China's territorial sovereignty. Chiang Kai-shek, borrowing Adolf Hitler's concept of *lebensraum,* or "living-space," laid claim to past holdings on the basis of population pressure as well as of historical possession:

In regard to the living space essential for the nation's existence, the territory of the Chinese state is determined by the requirements for national survival and by the limits of Chinese cultural bonds. Thus, in the territory of China a hundred years ago [*circa* 1840], comprising more than ten million square kilometers, there was not a single district that was not essential to the survival of the Chinese nation, and none that was not permeated by our culture. The breaking up of this territory meant the undermining of the nation's security as well as the decline of the nation's culture. Thus, the people as a whole must regard this as a national humiliation, and not until all lost territories have been recovered can we relax our efforts to wipe out this humiliation and save ourselves from destruction.[2]

Although Chiang does not specify his "lost territories," a Chinese textbook published shortly after his statement contains a table listing them (see Table 1).

Table 1 ● CHINA'S "LOST TERRITORIES"[3]

Date	Area, in square kilometers	Location	New ownership
1689................	240,000	North side Khingan Mountains	Russia
1727................	100,000	Lower Selenga Valley	Russia
1842................	83	Hong Kong	United Kingdom
1858................	480,000	North of Heilungkiang	Russia
1858................	8	Kowloon	United Kingdom
1860................	344,000	East of Ussuri River	Russia
1864................	900,000	North of Lake Balkhash	Russia
1879................	2,386	Liuchiu Islands	Japan
1882–1883..........	21,000	Lower Ili Valley	Russia
1883................	20,000	Irtysh Valley east of Lake Zaysan	Russia
1884................	9,000	Upper Koksol Valley	Russia
1885–1889..........	738,000	Annam and all Indochina	France
1886................	574,000	Burma	United Kingdom
1890................	7,550	Sikkim	United Kingdom
1894................	122,400	West of the Upper Salween	United Kingdom
1894................	91,300	West of the Upper Yangtze	United Kingdom
1894................	100,000	Upper Burma, Savage Mountains	United Kingdom
1895................	220,334	Korea	Japan
1895................	35,845	Taiwan	Japan
1895................	127	Pescadores	Japan
1897................	760	The edge of Burma	United Kingdom
1897................	2,300	The edge of Burma	United Kingdom
Total............	4,009,093		

Nor do Communist leaders remain indifferent to China's past holdings, although they temper their immediate claims according to time and place. Thus Mao Tse-tung staked out his future realm in an interview more than twenty years ago:

It is the immediate task of China to regain all our lost territories. . . . We do not, however, include Korea, formerly a Chinese colony, but when we have re-established the independence of the lost territories of China, and if the Koreans wish to break away from the chains of

2 Chiang Kai-shek, *China's Destiny* (New York: Roy Publishers, 1947), p. 34.
3 Hou Ming-chiu, Chen Erh-shiu, and Lu Chen, *General Geography of China* (in Chinese), 1946, as cited in G. B. Cressey, *Land of the 500 Million* (New York: McGraw-Hill, 1955), p. 39.

Japanese imperialism, we will extend them our enthusiastic help in their struggle for independence. The same thing applies for Formosa. . . . The Outer Mongolian republic will automatically become a part of the Chinese federation, at their own will. The Mohammedan and Tibetan peoples, likewise, will form autonomous republics attached to the Chinese federation.[4]

True to his word, at least in part, Mao, despite Indian protests one year after establishment of the People's Republic of China in 1949, drove his Red Armies to the Tibetan heights. His implicit definition of Korea as within China's sphere of interest received implementation when Chinese armies hurled back United Nations troops from the Yalu River to the thirty-eighth parallel during 1950–51. Sinkiang, presumably referred to above as "the Mohammedan people" because of its predominantly Moslem population, became an autonomous region in 1955 after considerable "pacification" by the Red Army. Only Formosa, held by Chiang Kai-shek, and Outer Mongolia, recognized as independent by the Treaty of Friendship and Alliance concluded between the Nationalist Government and Moscow in 1945 and adhered to in this particular by Peking, remained beyond Mao's control in 1958.

Similarly, both Nationalist and Communist maps place China's borders far down in the South China Sea, off the shores of Borneo. Mao would subscribe to the statements of the official Nationalist handbook, "Both the southernmost and westernmost borders remain to be defined. The Pamirs in the west constitute a contested area among China, the U.S.S.R., and Afghanistan.

The sovereignty of the Tuansha Islands (the Coral Islands) in the south is sought by China, the Republic of the Philippines, and Indo-China. The boundary between China and Burma also remains to be demarcated."[5] Movement of Chinese Communist forces into this disputed area bordering India during 1959–60 aroused protests in New Delhi. Lengthy negotiations demonstrated Peking's unwillingness to renounce its territorial demands, even when they possess little economic or strategic value and when they bring unfavorable political repercussions.

This persistent pattern of behavior stems from the traditional Chinese definition of a government possessing the Mandate of Heaven as one capable of defending the frontiers against barbarian incursions while maintaining the peace against domestic insurrection. So remote an area as Outer Mongolia became the subject of political controversy in 1912 when young nationalists agitated against Peking's concessions to Mongolian demands for autonomy under Russian protection. These nationwide protests proved a useful political weapon against the regime of Yuan Shih-k'ai. Similarly in 1950 Nationalist propaganda sought to embarrass Communist Peking by charges of "selling out" Chinese soil to the Soviet Union through acceptance of Outer Mongolian independence.

The leaders may not believe in this expansive definition of China's territory, but its acceptance may be dictated by political expediency. Whatever the cause, the effect is to saddle the government with serious international problems. Vague territorial claims based on concepts of suzerainty and tributary relations or on disputed treaties give no objective basis for determining international boundaries.

[4] E. Snow, *Red Star over China* (Modern Library Edition, 1944), p. 96; interviews with Mao Tse-tung in 1936.

[5] *China Handbook, 1955–56* (Taipei, Taiwan, 1955), p. 15.

Thus, it is a moot question whether "aggression" in the conventional usage could be legally charged against Chinese Communist invasion of Tibet in 1950.

Where such boundaries are fixed with rough approximation, precise definition is impeded by the absence of natural lines of demarcation. Except for the coast and the relatively short Yalu and Amur rivers in the northeast, none of China's frontiers can be readily identified by natural phenomena. They twist tortuously through jungle, mountain, and desert according to the temporary dictates of local needs and the relative power available to interested parties. The absence of natural demarcation is paralleled by an absence of natural barriers against migration or invasion, complicating the responsibilities facing the central government responsible for its citizens' welfare and defense.

Few lines of communication traverse the great distances from China's traditional capitals to its remote border provinces. At the same time, these remote provinces are relatively close to rival centers of power. Not until Chinese Communist rule was a railroad constructed linking Outer Mongolia with North China. At this same time the first rough road joined Tibet with South China. Currently, Russian assistance enables Peking to lay a railroad through the desert wastes into Sinkiang where it will meet a trunk line from the Turk-Sib railroad in the Soviet Union. Even Manchuria's transport ties with China proper, although infinitely better than those to other areas, were weak considering the strategic importance of this region.

Beside these obstacles those responsible for China's security have been confronted with British pressure upon Tibet from India; Russian pressure upon Sinkiang from adjacent Kazakhstan, upon Mongolia from Siberia, and upon Manchuria from the Far Eastern territories; and Japanese pressure first upon Korea and from there upon Manchuria, as well as upon the Ryukyu Islands and Formosa. China's attraction for invaders traditionally was one of food and wealth, luring from the interior certain nomadic groups against whom the Great Wall was originally designed. Modern invaders came after markets (Great Britain), raw materials (Japan), or imperialist prestige (Germany).

Throughout the past 300 years these conditions have been magnified in their seriousness by the inferiority of China's economic development compared with that of predatory powers arraigned against her. Russia's piecemeal nibbling at Chinese territory was facilitated by the remoteness of Sinkiang and Outer Mongolia from the base of China's strength. Bringing the contest nearer this base, however, revealed that the strength was more apparent than real. Despite the striking disparity of populations, Japanese offensives took Korea, Manchuria, and finally much of China proper from the "land of the four hundred million." Only industrialization could remedy this material weakness which left China vulnerable to all comers.

Thus, Chinese foreign policy during the nineteenth and twentieth centuries grappled with problems of defense against outer pressures to a degree unique among the countries under survey. These pressures were varied, but alike in their threat to Chinese civilization. Military attack literally tore off chunks of territory. Economic concessions carved out sheltered spheres of influence, disrupting domestic economic development through artificial emphasis upon coastal points of foreign control. Finally, ideological pressures were exerted by foreign missionaries, who, protected with force when necessary, challenged the Confucian order with destructive vigor.

Virtually no point along the 12,600 miles of China's perimeter has been safe from one or another of these pressures during the last 300 years. So vulnerable were they at the turn of the century that many wondered whether China was not to be the "sick man" of Asia, to be carved up by other countries as was the Ottoman Empire. These physical factors pose an objective challenge for Chinese foreign policy, be it Manchu, Nationalist, or Communist. Taken in conjunction with the subjective factor of historical experience, they provide an important clue to the behavior of Mao Tse-tung and his followers.

Historical factors

More than objective concerns explain defensive attitudes in China, which intermittently explode into xenophobia. Subjective evaluation of events during the past century convinces Nationalist and Communist alike that many, if not all of China's ills stem from contact with the "foreign devil," now castigated as "Western imperialism." Two hundred years ago Li Shih-yao, viceroy of Kwangtung and Kwangsi, memorialized the throne on regulations for the control of foreigners, warning, "It is my most humble opinion that when uncultured barbarians, who live far beyond the borders of China, come to our country to trade, they should establish no contact with the population, except for business purposes." [6]

Events since Li Shih-yao's day show little break in continuity so far as interpretation of foreign relations is concerned. Chiang Kai-shek blamed the

chaotic years of interregnum following collapse of the Manchu Dynasty upon "secret activities of the Imperialists . . . the chief cause of civil wars among the warlords." [7] Indeed, he attributed the Empire's disintegration to the so-called "unequal treaties" which "completely destroyed our nationhood, and our sense of honor and shame was lost. . . . The traditional structure of the family, the village, and the community was disrupted. The virtue of mutual help was replaced by competition and jealousy. Public planning was neglected and no one took an interest in public affairs." [8]

This simplistic explanation errs in attributing cause and effect where coincidence is the phenomenon. Western pressures hastened collapse of the Empire with its Confucian traditions, but they came after the process of disintegration had begun. By contrast, the ability of Japanese society to adopt new forms with old content under the combined impact of feudal decline and Western influence demonstrates the distortion of history in Chiang's analysis.

However, it is not the facts of history that condition political behavior but the way in which men view those facts. Hence the similarity of the following Communist analysis with those mentioned above preceding it in time, is highly suggestive of xenophobia as a Chinese component of policy.

They [the imperialists] will not only send their running-dogs to bore inside China to carry out disruptive work and to cause trouble. They will not only use the Chiang Kai-shek bandit remnants to blockade our coastal ports, but they will send their totally hopeless adventurist elements and troops to raid and to

---

[6] Hu Sheng, *Imperialism and Chinese Politics* (Peking, 1955), p. 9.

[7] Chiang Kai-shek, *op. cit.,* p. 78.
[8] *Ibid.,* pp. 79 and 88.

cause trouble along our borders. They seek by every means and at all times to restore their position in China. They use every means to plot the destruction of China's independence, freedom, and territorial integrity and to restore their private interests in China. We must exercise the highest vigilance. . . . They cannot possibly be true friends of the Chinese people. They are the deadly enemies of the Chinese people's liberation movement.[9]

Thus, the Chinese Communist devil-theory of imperialism coincides with popular mythology of evil inherent in foreign contacts to produce attitudes of suspicion and hostility at various levels of action. This popular mythology derives from perceived experience, which generalized foreign behavior on the basis of rape and pillage by Western troops during the nineteenth century. Western insistence on extraterritorial privileges to try persons by foreign law for crimes committed on Chinese territory rubbed salt in the wound. Insult was added to injury. While Chinese viewed white behavior as "barbaric," whites viewed Chinese punishment as "brutal." The inevitable cultural gap, widened by racial prejudice, reinforced hostility on both sides.

Injustice was also encountered at higher levels of diplomatic relations. Chinese experience in the international arena gave good reason for bitter resentment at being cast in the role of "a melon to be carved up by the powers." Throughout the nineteenth century, gunboat diplomacy forced abdication of customary rights of sovereignty

without reciprocal privileges for China. Extraterritorial law, economic concessions, and the stationing of foreign troops in Chinese cities were sanctified by treaty but won by force. Punitive expeditions in 1860 and 1900 delivered the supreme insult of foreign military occupation in the venerated capital of Peking.

The twentieth century brought little relief. Japan fought Russia on Chinese soil for control of the rich provinces of Manchuria. China's own allies in World War I swept aside her protests at Versailles to award Japan concessions in China held by defeated Germany. World War II saw the Yalta Conference of 1945 reward Soviet Russia with important military, economic, and political privileges in China, all without consultation with Chiang Kai-shek. Although President Roosevelt reminded Premier Stalin that those inducements for Russian entry into the war against Japan would have to be affirmed by Chiang, it was a foregone conclusion that allied pressure left China no alternative but capitulation.

In sum, China was the object of international relations but seldom the subject. Acted upon by others, she was unable to act in her own right. Long the primary power in Asia, she has been cut deeply during the past century by this induced feeling of inferiority. Fear of Japan followed a defeat caused by material inferiority. Resentment against the West followed capitulation caused by military inferiority and humiliation caused by sensed cultural and ideological inferiority. Small wonder that today Peking's militant insistence upon being heard in regional and world councils strikes a responsive chord among wide sectors of the populace. At long last a determined elite is working to restore China's place in the sun.

[9] K'o Pai-nien, "Hsin min chu chu yi te wai chiao tse" (The Foreign Policy of the New People's Democracy), *Hsüeh Hsi* (Study), I, No. 2, October 1949, 13–15.

To be sure, irredentist claims to "lost territories," denunciation of "unequal treaties," and the playing off of power against power—"use barbarians against barbarians"—are all traditional techniques of foreign policy. The difference in their use by Chinese elites lies in the psychological convictions behind these techniques. Among Western states, exploitation of grievance occurs as an accepted stratagem among assumed equals, struggling for limited gains and for the coveted position of *primus inter pares*. Between China and the rest of the world, however, the bitter remembrance of things past heightens the defensive-offensive aspects of foreign policy.

Communist emphasis upon imperialist aggression fits well into the objective and subjective factors conditioning Chinese views of world politics. Resulting xenophobia, manifested in exaggerated attitudes of belligerence, may ultimately work to Russia's disadvantage. Thus far it has been exploited by Soviet leaders against the West. Study of the Chinese Communist press over the past decade, however, reveals evidence of mutterings against Soviet behavior in Manchuria, concern over continued dependence on Russian economic assistance, and open protests against Red Army suppression of the Hungarian uprising in 1956. Official affirmation of the "monolithic unity of Sino-Soviet Friendship" seeks to repress the hostility with which many Chinese apparently view the Sino-Soviet Alliance. Chinese historians describing nineteenth-century imperialism do not exempt Tsarist Russia from criticism, to the dismay of Soviet writers. A question for continual study, therefore, is the degree to which Russia, like other nations, will suffer the consequences of the dragon's teeth sown in the past in China.

THE PROCESS OF POLICY: THE COMMUNIST COMPONENT

Ideological content: Marxism-Leninism

Beside those aspects of continuity in policy which we ascribe to the Chinese component, differences in degree or substance stem from the dedication of this elite to Communism. As Mao Tse-tung declared in 1945, "From the very beginning, our Party has based itself on the theories of Marxism, because Marxism is the crystallization of the world proletariat's most impeccable revolutionary scientific thought." [10]

General protestations of fidelity to Christianity, international law, and justice appear throughout statements of Western political figures. Rarely do these protestations enable us to determine the ends and means of these elites, especially in foreign policy. Marxism-Leninism, however, carries with it a construct of goals and ways of seeking those goals that structures ideology and institution for Communist elites to a degree unknown in the non-Communist world.

Foremost in this ideology is its determination to advance communism throughout the world. Almost three decades ago the fugitive Chinese Communist Party, beleaguered by Nationalist armies in Kiangsi, proclaimed, "The Provisional Government of the Soviet Republic of China declares that it will, under no condition, remain content with the overthrow of imperialism in China, but, on the contrary, will aim

[10] Mao-Tze-Tung [Mao Tse-tung], *The Fight for a New China* (report of April 24, 1945, to the Seventh National Congress of the Chinese Communist Party) (New York, 1945), p. 76, as quoted in O. Edmund Clubb, "Chinese Communist Strategy in Foreign Relations," in "Report on China," *The Annals*, Vol. 277, September 1951, p. 156.

as its ultimate objective in waging a war against world imperialism until the latter is all blown up." [11]

In terms of "progress" and "revolutionary scientific thought" this goal is justified as a desirable one, the "good society" found in utopian drives common to world philosophies. An additional element, however, distinguishes this compulsion toward ideological expansion from counterparts in Islam, Christianity, Wilsonian democracy, and Nazism. For the Marxist, destruction of the imperialist is not only desirable but necessary. The maximum goal of world conquest is the only guarantee for achieving the minimum goal of Communist survival.

Basic to this argument is the assumption of conflict as omnipresent in human relations. The "contradictions of the dialectical process" exist in various forms; conflict need not be military in manifestation. Yet Marx posited all historical development as a process of struggle, whether between classes within a nation or between nations themselves. The highest and final conflict is to come between classes on the international plane, in the world revolution springing from the basic contradiction between international Communism and international capitalism.

This struggle is not one that is "created" by the Communists. According to their credo, it is the imperialists who are to blame, engaging in a death-struggle to stave off the "inevitable victory" of the Communist ideal. As expressed by Peking's official voice, the *Jen Min Jih Pao* (Peking People's Daily), "Although we have consistently held and still hold that the socialist and capitalist countries should co-exist in peace and carry out peaceful competition, the imperialists are bent on de-

stroying us. We must therefore never forget the stern struggle with the enemy, *i.e.,* the class struggle on a world scale." [12]

Thus defensive dictates for the minimum goal of survival require policies employing offensive means, which simultaneously serve the maximum goal of world Communist domination. One such means is that of applying the classic Chinese dictum of "using barbarian against barbarian" so as to take advantage of the conflict that assumedly exists among capitalists. Mao Tse-tung wrote in 1940, "Our tactical principle remains one of exploiting the contradictions among them [the imperialists] in order to win over the majority, oppose the minority, and crush the enemies separately." [13]

However, "the enemy" will not rest content and permit the socialist camp to develop peacefully. His efforts to split that camp apart compel a corollary defensive response of unity among Communist elites in general and support for the Soviet Union in particular. An important statement of this principle came after the Hungarian uprising of 1956 when Peking justified Moscow's armed suppression of the insurgents:

There are before us two types of contradictions which are different in nature. The first type consists of contradictions between our enemy and ourselves (contradictions between the camp of imperialism and that of socialism, contradictions

[11] *Central China Post* (Hankow), November 25, 1931, as quoted in O. E. Clubb, *op. cit.,* p. 157.

[12] "More on Historical Experience of Proletarian Dictatorship" (article prepared by the Editorial Department of the *Jen Min Jih Pao* on the basis of a discussion at an enlarged meeting of the Political Bureau of the Central Committee of the Communist Party of China), Peking: *Jen Min Jih Pao,* December 29, 1956.

[13] Mao Tse-tung, "On Policy," December 25, 1940, as translated in *Selected Works of Mao Tse-tung,* III (Bombay, India, 1954), 218.

between imperialism and the people and oppressed nations of the world, contradictions between the bourgeoisie and the proletariat in the imperialist countries, etc.). *This is the fundamental type of contradiction, based on the clash of interests between antagonistic classes.* The second type consists of contradictions within the ranks of the people (contradictions between different sections of the people, between comrades within the Communist Party, or in socialist countries, contradictions between the government and the people, contradictions between socialist countries, contradictions between Communist Parties, etc.). *This type of contradiction is not basic;* it is not the result of a fundamental clash of interests between classes, but of conflicts between right and wrong opinions or of a partial contradiction of interests. *It is a type of contradiction whose solution must, first and foremost, be subordinated to the over-all interests of the struggle against the enemy. . . .*[14]

These assumptions of conflict receive reinforcement from attitudes and actions of the non-Communist world. In part this results from Chinese Communist behavior, the phenomenon of the "self-fulfilling prophecy." When Mao Tse-tung proclaimed establishment of the People's Republic of China in October 1949, Great Britain extended recognition. Twisting the lion's tail, Peking rejected recognition with spurious protests against phraseology contained in the British note as well as against British consular relations with the Nationalist authorities on Taiwan. Maltreatment of British business concerns in China undermined economic arguments advanced in England for wooing Peking in contrast with American hostility to the Communists. Subsequent British refusal to vote for

[14] *Jen Min Jih Pao,* December 29, 1956, *op cit.,* italics added.

Peking's admission to United Nations chambers and British support for United States action in the Korean war aroused violent reaction in China against the "Anglo-American imperialist bloc." In one sense that bloc came about in spite of the "contradictions" within it, largely because of Chinese Communist predispositions to hostility.

To a lesser extent United States relations with the new regime were a product of its own actions. As early as 1948 American consular officials were put under house arrest in Communist-held Mukden, jailed, tried, and eventually expelled from China. The seizure of Economic Cooperation Administration stocks in 1949, the inflaming of public opinion against United States personnel, both official and unofficial, and the confiscation of American consular property, held through treaty agreement, in January 1950 all served to obstruct a *rapprochement* between Washington and Peking. Chinese intervention in the Korean war with its attendant defeat of American troops at the Yalu in November 1950 wiped out whatever possibility remained of normal relations between the two countries, at least for many years to come. Yet prior to this war the record shows a number of instances where normal adherence by Peking to international custom might have strengthened the hands of groups within the United States seeking to establish ties with the new regime.

It would be misleading to attribute all Chinese Communist fears and resentments against the United States to this "self-fulfilling prophecy." America's support of Chiang Kai-shek in the civil war, its obstruction of Chinese Communist representation in the United Nations, and its promulgation of an economic embargo against Peking exacerbated relations between the two countries during the 1950's. The combination of expectation and realization reinforced the ideological content of Chinese Communist policy which posits conflict, overt or covert, inherent in relations with the non-Communist world.

The most famous formulation of this principle came in Mao Tse-tung's "lean to one side" declaration on July 1, 1949:

"You lean to one side." Precisely so . . . Chinese people either lean to the side of imperialism or to the side of socialism. To sit on the fence is impossible; a third road does not exist. . . . Internationally we belong to the anti-imperialist front headed by the U.S.S.R. and we can look for genuine friendly aid only from that front, and not from the imperialist front.[15]

Implementation of the principle came quickly with the signing of the Treaty of Friendship, Alliance, and Mutual Aid of February 14, 1950, between the Chinese People's Republic and the Union of Soviet Socialist Republics. Mao and Stalin agreed that "in the event of one of the Contracting Parties being attacked by Japan or any state allied with her and thus being involved in a state of war, the other Contracting Party shall immediately render military and other assistance by all means at its disposal." A proliferation of subsequent agreements regulate Soviet economic assistance to China in the form of loans, technical assistance, military aid, and cultural exchange, as well as routine agreements on telecommunications and postal regulations.

[15] Mao Tse-tung, "On People's Democratic Dictatorship," July 1, 1949, as translated in C. Brandt, B. Schwartz, and J. K. Fairbank, *A Documentary History of Chinese Communism* (Cambridge, Mass.: Harvard University Press, 1952), pp. 449 ff.

This "lean to one side" policy, excluding assistance from, much less alliance with, non-Communist countries, is antithetical to traditional Chinese politics of playing off one country against another. It can only be explained in terms of the Communist component of policy.

Ideology: Maoism

So far we have been discussing aspects of Chinese Communist policy that stem from the Communist component as developed in Marxism-Leninism. Assumptions of conflict, antagonism against capitalism, and unity within the socialist camp are all compatible with ideological concepts dominant in Soviet policy, at least to the death of Stalin in 1953. Indeed, on these three points there is no evidence of major revision in post-Stalin developments despite attempts by Khrushchev to temper expectations of general thermonuclear war at the 20th Party Congress in 1956 with his disquisition on the "absence of fatal inevitability" of war between the two camps.

Within the Marxist-Leninist framework, however, divergent strategies appear to have developed as evidenced by the statements of the Soviet elite compared with those of the Chinese elite. Admittedly, proof of divergence is complicated by a number of factors. The proliferation and vagueness of Marxist-Leninist scriptures permit almost any action to be interpreted as being sanctioned, explicitly or implicitly. Furthermore, insistence upon ideological conformity at the surface masks sub-surface differences within the Communist bloc.

Yet the course of Chinese communism over the past decades suggests a number of points in domestic and foreign policy that conflict with the Soviet view. Although divergencies on conduct of the Chinese revolution appear as far back as the 1930's, foreign policy disagreements remained hidden until the mid-fifties. Isolated from the outside world during most of the civil war, the elite faced no need and experienced no contradicting evidence to challenge Soviet interpretations of foreign affairs. With victory came pressing reliance upon Soviet economic and military aid, precluding disagreement with Stalin's policies. Seconding Kremlin expulsion of Tito from the Cominform proved politically expedient for Peking even were it informed of the actual roots of the dispute, which is doubtful.

Involvement in the Korean war, combined with the United Nations embargo, furthered Peking's dependence upon Moscow. As the official *Handbook of World Knowledge, 1954* stated, "It is erroneous to think that we have no need for international assistance and can still succeed. . . . Who can help us? Only the camp of peace, democracy, and socialism under the leadership of the Soviet Union can give us genuine friendly assistance." [16]

Beneath the surface, however, relations were strained. One bone of contention within China was the establishment of joint Sino-Soviet stock companies in 1950 to exploit oil and nonferrous metals in Sinkiang, as well as to operate a civil airline.[17] It is significant that these companies, established in 1950 for a period of thirty years, were dissolved by joint agreement in 1954 when Khrushchev and Bulganin visited Peking after the death of Stalin.

In addition, Chinese participation in the Korean war, albeit aided by Soviet military deliveries, saddled Peking with debts compounded by large Russian deliveries in 1954–55. By 1957 China owed the Soviet Union more than U.S. $2.4 billion, and open criticism within China received no factual contradiction from the elite.[18] The belated revelation of past grievance merits quotation at length:

It was unreasonable for China to bear all the expenses of the Korean war. . . . During the First and Second World War, the United States lent funds to its allies. . . . Afterward some of the countries repudiated their debts while in some cases the United States waived its claim for repayment. The Soviet loan . . . is repayable in full in ten years. The time is too short and moreover interest has to be paid. I propose that repayment be extended to 20 or 30 years so as to ease the tense economic situation in our country. . . . When the Soviet Union liberated our Northeast [Manchuria], it dismantled some machinery equipment in our factories. Was there compensation for it? Will there be repayment? [19]

[16] *Shih chieh chih shih shou p'eng, 1954* (Handbook of World Knowledge) (Peking, 1954), p. 7.

[17] For a sampling of adverse comment reported by the Chinese Communist press, see A. S. Whiting, "Communist China and 'Big Brother,' " *Far Eastern Survey*, No. 10, October 1955.

[18] For China's indebtedness to the Soviet Union see Li Hsien-nien, "Final Accounts for 1956 and the 1957 State Budget," delivered to the fourth session of the First National People's Congress on June 29, 1957; NCNA, Peking, June 29, 1957. Calculation of loan receipts as revealed by Li's report of timing, compared with previously announced loans and related references to military assistance from Russia, compels the conclusion that almost U.S. $2 billion covered military, as distinguished from purely economic, aid.

[19] Lung Yün, "My Ideological Review," *Jen Min Jih Pao*, July 14, 1957, as translated in *Current Background*, No. 470, July 26, 1957. Lung here recapitulated his criticisms voiced before the Standing Committee of the National People's Congress of which he is a member. As vice-chairman of the National Defense Council and travelling companion of Politburo member P'eng Chen on a tour of Soviet Russia and East Europe in late 1956, Lung's words merit attention. He recanted in this article but only "subjectively," leaving intact his factual assertions as quoted. No official refutation of these facts occurred although he was criticized for his motives.

The dramatic events of 1956, commencing with Khrushchev's denunciation of Stalin at the 20th Congress in February and climaxed in the Hungarian revolt of November brought Sino-Soviet differences to the fore. Commenting on Stalin's "cult of personality" *Jen Min Jih Pao* saw his errors not merely as the result of personality but as a product of "contradictions" in the socialist system.[20] Reviving Mao Tse-tung's 1937 theory on the "universality of contradiction," the editorial stated, "It is naive to assume that contradictions can no longer exist in a socialist society. To deny the existence of contradictions is to deny dialectics." Yet *Pravda* implicitly denied this assertion by deleting all portions relating to it from its translation of the editorial. Although a fuller version was subsequently published in Russia, Khrushchev explicitly denied applicability of the formula to the Soviet Union in a television interview one year later.[21]

Soviet sensitivity to this analysis from Peking is understandable in view of its implications for relations within the bloc, since it postulated "contradictions" among socialist countries rather than Stalinism as basic to the cause of tension. Explicit attention to Yugoslavia's difficulties in this editorial signalled growing Chinese concern with East European developments, vital to

China's own economic development as well as to its strategic interests.

Despite Khrushchev's open hostility to Gomulka, reliable reports indicated encouragement for independence on the part of the Polish leader from Mao Tse-tung personally.[22] When Hungary erupted in revolt, Peking press coverage offered a fuller version of events and one different from that of Moscow. Recalling its ambassador to the Soviet Union for consultation, the Chinese elite formulated an analysis in the *Jen Min Jih Pao* editorial of December 29, 1956, which marked the fullest statement to date of disagreement with Soviet policy, albeit tempered by a desire to compromise for the sake of unity within the bloc:

. . . Contradictions between socialist countries, between Communist Parties . . . are not basic, not the result of a fundamental clash of interests but . . . of a *partial* contradiction of interests. . . . Recent controversies in the international Communist movement, for the most part, have had to do with one's appraisal of the Soviet Union. . . . The Communist Party of the Soviet Union has been taking measures to correct Stalin's mistakes and eliminate their consequences. *These measures are beginning to bear fruit.* . . . Since Stalin's mistakes were not of short duration, their thorough correction cannot be achieved overnight but demands fairly protracted efforts and thorough-going ideological education. . . . Only by adopting an objective and analytical attitude can we correctly appraise Stalin and *all those comrades who made similar mistakes under his influence.* . . . We need therefore to adopt a comradely attitude towards these people and *should not*

[20] *Jen Min Jih Pao,* "On Historical Experience Concerning the Dictatorship of the Proletariat," April 5, 1956, in *Current Background,* No. 403. Mao's original statement of this theory is in his essay *On Contradictions,* August 1937 (English edition—Peking, 1952).

[21] R. Schlesinger, "Soviet Historians Before and After the XX Congress," in *Soviet Studies,* VII, No. 2, October 1956, 165–66 and fn. 31. *Pravda* published the full text as a pamphlet that went to press on June 10, 1956. Khrushchev's denial was deleted in all Soviet and Chinese versions of the interview.

[22] *The New York Times* issues of October 16, 1956, and January 11, 1957, tell of two instances of intervention by Mao on behalf of Gomulka, both apparently related by authoritative sources.

treat them as enemies . . . should not blankly denounce everything they did. . . . Their mistakes have a social and historical background.[23] [*Italics added*]

The faint touch of condescension and paternalism is apparent. For Peking the case was far from closed on Stalin or on Soviet policy. As another comment on Soviet-Polish relations noted, "In future relations between socialist countries, if only the bigger nations pay more attention to avoiding the mistake of big-nation chauvinism (this is the main thing) and the smaller nations avoid the mistake of nationalism (this is also important), friendship and solidarity based upon equality will undoubtedly become consolidated." [24] The source of such "big-nation chauvinism" was explained by *Jen Min Jih Pao.* "The time-worn habits of big countries in their relations with small countries continue to make their influence felt in certain ways, while a series of victories achieved by a Party of a country in its revolutionary cause is apt to give rise to a certain sense of superiority." [25]

In keeping with its insistence upon "equality" and "independence" in relations among socialist countries, *Jen Min Jih Pao* in the December 29 editorial dealt relatively lightly with Tito's criticism of the Soviet Union. Expressing "amazement," the editorial termed his views "wrong" insofar as they could "only lead to a split in the Communist movement. . . . Clearly

the Yugoslav comrades are going too far. Even if some part of their criticism of brother parties is reasonable, the basic stand and method they adopt infringe the principles of comradely discussion." Thus Peking did not castigate Belgrade in the same severe terms of censure used by Moscow, but reproached "Comrade Tito" with "our brotherly advice" for washing dirty linen in public. As Chou En-lai observed after his sudden trip to Russia and Eastern Europe in January 1957, "Even if no unanimity can be reached for the time being, it would also be normal to reserve the differences while upholding our solidarity." [26]

So long as the Communist component compels Peking to view the outside world as a hostile camp headed by a United States possessing weapons of devastating destruction, "solidarity" within the socialist camp is mandatory for China. Lacking any prospect of overtaking America in missile and thermonuclear development, reliance upon Russian protection is the only guarantee of survival, given this view of the world. Yet short of dissolution of the alliance, the dynamics of inner tension and Chinese response to it argue for identifying Peking separately from the so-called satellites of East Europe. Nor is the independence of Peking from Moscow more apparent than real. A concatenation of military, economic, and political trends during the first decade of the Sino-Soviet alliance provides a continual and consistent altering of the relationship between Moscow and Peking. The net effect is to increase the ability of the Chinese Communist elite to differ with its Soviet counterpart, never going so far as to cause a "Titoist" break but opening

[23] *Jen Min Jih Pao,* December 29, 1956, *op. cit.* Although Ambassador Liu Hsiao's return to Peking went unreported in the press, his presence at a Moscow reception in November and his subsequent departure from Peking with Chou En-lai, for Moscow, January 7, 1957, give support for this analysis.
[24] NCNA, Peking, November 21, 1956, "International Significance of the Soviet-Polish Talks."
[25] *JMJP,* December 29, 1956.

[26] Chou En-lai to the third annual plenary session of the Second National Committee of the CPPC on March 5, 1957, in *Current Background,* No. 439.

areas of disagreement pertinent for interested third parties, whether Polish, Indian, or American.

In 1958–60, Sino-Soviet differences flared into open debate on a wide range of domestic and foreign policy issues. Thinly veiled by Peking's attacks against "modern revisionists" and Moscow's warnings against "dogmatism and leftist adventurism," the debate nonetheless spilled over into Communist parties inside and outside the bloc, as well as into various Communist-front international organizations. By November 1960, relations between the two allies had deteriorated to the point that rival Chinese and Russian policy statements circulated among eighty-one Communist delegations summoned to Moscow in a vain attempt to resolve the conflict.[27] Simultaneous reports of Soviet technicians withdrawing from China and sudden petroleum shortages on the Chinese mainland, long dependent on bloc oil shipments, suggested the degree of strain in the alliance.

The debate turned around a host of issues related with differing Chinese and Russian estimates on the degree to which war might be risked in the thermonuclear era during the time when Soviet intercontinental ballistic missile developments appeared to lead those of the United States. It is impossible to say with certainty whether this grew out of Chinese disappointment in Soviet support for China's nuclear bomb program, or out of disputes over Sino-Soviet strategy in the abortive bombardment in 1958 of the Chinese Nationalist offshore islands, Quemoy and Matsu.[28] By early 1960, however,

it emerged as a scathing Chinese attack against Russian policy vis-à-vis the West, specifically, Khrushchev's demands for summit conferences and disarmament negotiations.

More important differences arose in areas where Communist China could act independently, as it could not influence Soviet-American relations. Mao's emphasis upon "armed struggle" challenged Khrushchev's championing of "the parliamentary path to power" for Communist parties in newly independent countries. Chinese attacks against "the national bourgeoisie" in these countries contrasted with Russian vacillation on the domestic anti-Communism of Nasser and Kassim. Perhaps the most ominous aspect, at least from a non-Communist vantage point, was Peking's demand for bloc support to "national liberation struggles," whether in Laos or in Algiers, explicitly denying Moscow's warnings against encouraging local wars which might explode into general thermonuclear catastrophe.

In sum, the ideological ingredients that posit similar ends of policy for the two elites do not necessarily posit identical means or identical timing. The "partial contradiction of interests" seen by Peking as characterizing "relations among socialist countries" compels us to consider China's alliance with Soviet Russia one of voluntary partnership, subject to cohesive and divisive forces which keep that partnership in constant flux. The content of Chinese Communist foreign policy will remain related to, but not dictated by, that of the Soviet Union.

Institutional structure

Decision-making in the People's Republic of China is the exclusive prerogative of the CCP, within that Party being confined principally to the Political Bureau (Politburo) or more probably its Standing Committee. Teng

[27] Donald S. Zagoria "Strains in the Sino-Soviet Alliance," *Problems of Communism,* IX, No. 3 (May–June 1960); see also his "Sino-Soviet Friction in Underdeveloped Areas," *Problems of Communism,* X, No. 2 (March–April, 1961), 1–12.

[28] Alice Langley Hsieh, "Communist China and Nuclear Warfare," *The China Quarterly,* Vol. I, No. 2, April–June 1960.

Hsiao-p'ing analyzed the relationship between party and state in his report to the 8th National Congress of the CCP in September 1956 as follows:

The Party is the highest form of class organization. It is particularly important to point this out today when our Party has assumed the leading role in state affairs. . . . [This] means first, that Party members in state organs and particularly the leading Party members' groups formed by those in responsible positions in such departments should follow the unified leadership of the Party. Secondly, the Party must regularly discuss and decide on questions with regard to the guiding principles, policies, and important organizational matters in state affairs, and the leading Party members' groups in the state organs must see to it that these decisions are put into effect with the harmonious cooperation of non-Party personalities. Thirdly, the Party must . . . exercise constant supervision over the work of state organs.[29]

This frank analysis lends substance to analysis of Party control of state organs based upon interlocking direction by high-ranking Party members. The State Council, corresponding to the Council of Ministers in the Soviet Union or the Western cabinet, allocates controlling positions to Party members in the case of the premiership, all ten vice-premiers, and such key ministries as foreign affairs, defense, public security, finance, state planning agencies, machine industries, electric power, railways, and foreign trade. Non-Communists hold ministries concerned primarily with consumption, such as food, textiles, and aquatic products, or posts concerned with cultural affairs and health.

Similarly, the Standing Committee of the National People's Congress is studded both with Politburo personalities (in its chairman and secretary-general) and with Party members (in six of its fifteen vice-chairmen). Although this group is vested by the constitution of 1954 with powers akin to those of legislative bodies in the West, its membership seems politically impotent in view of the extreme range of decree power held by the State Council. Inclusion of such dignitaries as Madame Sun Yat-sen (Soong Ch'ingling); China's outstanding literary polemicist, Kuo Mo-jo; and Tibet's Panchen Lama among its vice-chairmen suggests the nature of this body as an honorific gathering to provide public sanction for decisions arrived at elsewhere.

The Party's constitution makes clear the absolute duty of all members to carry out policies and practices decreed by the Central Committee or, in its absence, by the Politburo:

Article 19. (6) The decisions of the Party must be carried out unconditionally. Individual Party members must yield to Party organizations, the minority to the majority, the lower organizations to the higher organizations, and all the organizations throughout the country must yield centrally to the National Congress and the Central Committee.[30]

That such decisions are seldom those of the Central Committee is evidenced by the infrequency of its sessions, the size of its membership, and the relatively short intervals during which

[29] Teng Hsiao-p'ing, "Report on Revision of Party Constitution," delivered to the CCP Eighth National Congress on September 16, 1956, as quoted by NCNA, Peking, September 18, 1956.

[30] "The Constitution of the Communist Party of China," adopted by the Eighth National Congress of the CCP on September 26, 1956, as translated by the United States Consulate General, Hong Kong, in *Current Background*, No. 417, October 10, 1956.

lengthy reports are read and accepted with little discussion. The Eighth Central Committee, elected in 1956, now has more than 190 regular and alternate members. Although it meets approximately twice yearly as stipulated by the Party constitution, CC plenums seldom last more than five days. Moreover in crises-ridden 1960, no CC plenum was reported, despite record-breaking famines, reorganization of the communes, and the growing differences with Soviet Russia.

Decisions are not basically made by the Central Committee, then, but by its inner elite. This elite is composed of 17 regular and six alternate members of the Politburo. Of its workings we know virtually nothing except that only once in the past two decades has its composition been shaken by purge, and then only two fell from power. Essentially the core, represented by the Politburo Standing Committee of Mao Tse-tung, Liu Shao-ch'i, Chou En-lai, Chu Teh, Lin Piao, Ch'en Yün, and Teng Hsiao-ping, is a united group whose internal differences have remained concealed through more than twenty years of civil war and ruling responsibilities.

Political institutions of the PRC resemble those of non-Communist countries in name only. To be sure, other "democratic parties" exist, as in the Soviet Union they do not, but they play no part in policy formation. These groupings, such as the China Democratic League and the Revolutionary Committee of Kuomintang, are small in membership and limited in function. Less than one-third of the government ministries and chairmen of commissions under the State Council are headed by representatives of these party and so-called "nonparty" persons.[31] Of

the 1,226 deputies in the National People's Congress, only 269 came from the "democratic parties" in 1956.

Basically these organizations communicate from the center to the periphery according to the nature of their membership, which may concentrate on intellectuals, businessmen, or overseas Chinese. Control of these "parties" is facilitated by double enrollment of some members in the CCP. In addition the CCP never neglects its role as political leader, even while stressing "long-term co-existence and mutual supervision" between the CCP and the "democratic parties." As a spokesman for one of these groups warned, "We must not one-sidedly emphasize the political freedom and organizational independence of the democratic parties."[32] Their passive role in implementing but not formulating policy is clear from an official explanation of their responsibility "following the victory of socialism . . . Important results might be obtained then in our task of ideological remoulding if education and transformation is conducted through the democratic parties."[33]

These groupings perform on a limited scale functions parallel to those carried out by mass organizations throughout large sectors of the Chinese populace. The Communist Youth League, the Sino-Soviet Friendship Association, the All-China Federation of Trade Unions, and the All-China Democratic Women's Federation enmesh millions in a closely coordinated network of communications media directed from the Department of Propaganda of the

[31] *Biographic Information*, No. 1, November 29, 1959 (Hong Kong: American Consulate General).

[32] Huang Ch'i-hsiang, "Two Problems in Work of Democratic Parties," Peking *Kuang Ming Jih Pao,* January 3, 1957.

[33] Shih Ch'i and Sun Nan, "How to Understand the Policy of Long-Term Coexistence between the Communist Party and the Democratic Parties," *Cheng Chih Hsüeh Hsi* (Political Study), No. 9, September 13, 1956.

CCP. Annual gatherings, such as the National Committee of the Chinese People's Political Consultative Conference, bring together representatives of "democratic parties and mass organizations" to receive reports from government leaders and to endorse the contemporary program of the CCP. Additional *ad hoc* meetings convene these groups for ritualized avowals of support for particular compaigns of domestic or international import.

Thus both parties and interest-group organizations exist in the PRC, but their function is basically one-way communication from the top downwards, as distinguished from their dual role of influencing policy and explaining policy in the West. In this sense public opinion exists to be mobilized by the Party but not to direct the Party. It may fail to respond to Party propaganda, thereby compelling some revision of policy. It may articulate grievances by indirection, thereby stimulating examination of policy at the top. As an external pressure upon the government, however, public opinion cannot be identified in China as an articulate force.

The relevance of parties, interest groups, and public opinion to foreign policy is realized by the elite primarily as a means of affecting the cohesion of the populace. Mass campaigns carried out for months at a time over all communications media and with thousands of "study groups" characterize this effort to reduce dissent and maximize support for policy. These means are useful in three different situations.

Mass campaigns may serve a contingency purpose, preparing the populace for possible action without committing the government to such action. In 1954–55 all China signed petitions in blood, applauded speeches, and endorsed resolutions calling for "immediate liberation of Taiwan." No in-

vasion of Taiwan followed nor were any decisive preparations for invasion evident. Similarly in 1956 a shorter, less intensive campaign pledged "volunteers for Egypt" during the Anglo-French attack upon that country. Again no action followed words. Such instances serve to confuse the outside world as to the intent of Chinese policy, in addition to whatever domestic stimuli they may provide for higher production, renewing bonds of allegiance, or promulgating symbols of unity for the regime.

Such campaigns may also serve a preparatory function of whipping up public support for a decided action. In 1950, attack upon Tibet was preceded by public rallies, exhortatory articles, and ringing declarations by prominent leaders. Undoubtedly the most extensive use of this technique came in the celebrated "Resist-American-Aid-Korea" movement which accompanied Chinese intervention in the Korean war. During the three years of that action a steady drum-fire of propaganda carried the movement to every corner of China.

Finally, these campaigns serve a purpose of "feedback" similar to the presumed role of public opinion in the non-Communist world. Study groups are not passive lecture-audience sessions but active discussion meetings. They seek to bring out all questions of doubt and opposition for the purpose of achieving final unity under the skilled leadership of prepared Party personnel, activists, and cadres. Following Soviet intervention in the abortive Hungarian revolt of 1956, meetings at Chinese universities, factories, and farms discussed Peking's support for Soviet action and attempted to quell what was reported by the Communist press as "shock and confusion."

The limits upon public participation in policy are extreme and explicit, however. An authoritative Chinese analysis warned against "practicing democracy merely for the sake of democracy." Specifically, it advised the youth:

Before the liberation the forms used by the people in demanding democracy from the Kuomintang consisted mainly of strikes (of workers and students), demonstrations, and parades, bringing loss to the Kuomintang and applying pressure on the enemy so that they had to accept our demands. Today, in dealing with the Anglo-French imperialists who carry out aggression against Egypt, we still adopt the form of demonstration and parade. However, in dealing with divergences of views within the internal ranks of the people, the defects and mistakes of the people, we must resort principally to argument . . . and not the form of applying pressure. . . . The country today belongs to us, and we ourselves will bear the losses, political and economic, arising out of such forms as strikes of workers, strikes of students, and demontrations and parades for the solution of questions.[34]

Another caveat cautioned against "exaggerating" defects, particularly in Chinese or Soviet policy:

Some people find certain inappropriate measures carried out by individual socialist countries, and begin to doubt the superiority of the socialist system, and lose confidence. . . . Those who begin to waver as soon as they see mistakes in socialist countries are even more susceptible to pessimism and despair, and lose their political direction. And if counter revolutionaries should be watching at the time, who can say but such

[34] Chiang Ming, "Democracy Is the Means, Not the End," *Chung Kuo Ching Nien* (China Youth), No. 23, December 1, 1956.

young people will be utilized by the counter revolutionaries? The experiences of some Hungarian youth these past few weeks should give us cause for vigilance.[35]

The interaction of institution and ideology produces a foreign policy, formulated by a small, authoritarian, continuously functioning elite, whose ends and means are basically those followed by the Soviet elite with such modifications as are affected by the Chinese component of policy. The process of policy as such remains veiled from observation, but the content of policy may be determined with a high degree of probability because of the explicit and detailed nature of the Communist ideology and the conscious dedication of this relatively stable elite to that ideology. Allowing for the modifications of time, then, we may now proceed to examine the most likely alternatives of policy to be anticipated from the People's Republic of China in the near future.

THE SUBSTANCE OF POLICY

Ends

The foreign policy of the People's Republic of China embraces a range of goals extending along a minimum-maximum continuum. Maintenance of internal security as a minimum goal is not peculiar to the elite in Peking. Intermediate-range goals, however, projecting what might be called "friendly domination" of Asian political and economic developments, stem from Chinese as well as Communist components of policy. They are not, for instance, evident to any comparable degree in the range of goals held by Burmese or Thai elites. Finally, the maximum goal

[35] Fang Chun, "Do Not Deny Everything," *ibid.*, No. 23, December 1, 1956.

of Peking, direct control of Asia through Communist regimes that are political and economic satellites of China, is a more ambitious aim than is evident in any other ruling group in the area.

These different goals may employ similar means. Wooing the uncommitted or neutral groups of Southeast Asia following the Korean armistice in 1953 not only served the minimum goal of security by offsetting United States negotiations for the Southeast Asian Treaty Organization. It also smoothed the way for the increase of Peking's prestige and influence as an intermediate-range goal in the move to dominate governments in the area.

Yet it is important to recognize that this priority of goals is dictated by the necessity of circumstance. The first decade of PRC foreign policy grappled with problems of uniting traditionally Chinese territory on the Asian mainland while reducing the external threat as perceived by the ruling elite. Chou En-lai's skillful diplomacy at Geneva and Bandung provided a peaceful counterpart to military intervention in Korea, but both aimed basically at the minimum goal of internal security.

The intermediate goal is capable of realization only with economic development hoped for in the Second and Third Five Year Plans, and with the achievement of a more flexible political atmosphere within China following elimination of counterrevolution and completion of collectivization. These domestic developments, accompanied by armistices in Korea and Indochina, are a prerequisite for extending Peking's leadership in Asian affairs. Not until this process is completed, perhaps several decades distant, can the maximum goal of a Chinese "bloc" of Communist regimes in Asia be realistically contemplated by Peking.

Thus, although both China and the Soviet Union may hold identical maximum goals of extending Communism throughout the world, they are not in the same stage of development toward attaining this goal. Moscow has long since disposed of its minimum concern for internal security and has advanced well along the path of attaining intermediate goals of influencing governments along its periphery in Europe and the Middle East. Its economic and military means of policy are far ahead of those available to China. This differentiation of ends attainable within a given time-period provides further justification for distinguishing between Moscow and Peking, not only in our present analysis but in formulating future policy.

This difference in development, carrying with it difference in goals, may provide conflict in specific policy between the two Communist capitals. Prolongation of the Korean war in 1952–53 may have served Soviet ends of increasing strains in the North Atlantic Treaty Organization and of weakening its available force in Europe. This would facilitate Soviet influence over its East European satellites and extend its influence, at least negatively, into West Europe. For China, however, internal security called for throwing back United Nations troops from the Yalu but not necessarily beyond the thirty-eighth parallel. Continuation of the war drained the Chinese economy, shaky at the start, and increased the danger of retaliation upon China proper by United States airpower. Not until the death of Stalin in March 1953 did Peking's negotiators at Panmunjom agree to armistice terms essentially similar to those they had rejected months previously. Although not conclusive, the timing of this move lends credibility to our analysis.

This example suggests a spatial difference in goals in addition to one derived from time differences of development. For the Soviet Union, Europe remains its primary sphere of interest and concern, offensively and defensively. For China, the Asian periphery extending from Tokyo to Kabul demands prior attention. Both countries share interests as well as concern with Japan, but basically they are oriented in opposite directions. This increases the possibility of conflict of goals between Peking and Moscow, at least with respect to specific points of policy. It also suggests differences in the degree of conflict anticipated with United States interests aligned against those of Peking as compared with those of Moscow.

Means

Any construct of probable means to be adopted must take into consideration the availability of means as well as the likelihood of their being adopted. The latter consideration assumes rationality of decision-making insofar as a decision is logically consistent with the ideology of the elite. For reasons stated earlier, we cannot assume such rationality to be uniformly present in Chinese foreign policy. Compulsive belligerency, for instance, during the early years of the People's Republic of China was irrational even from the point of view of Peking's perceived interests, much more so in terms of objective appraisal of its assets and liabilities. However, such behavior seems less evident with the elite's maturing responsibility and its growing experience with international affairs. Therefore the likelihood of rash or essentially irrational action lessens with time, although it by no means disappears entirely.

The means least likely to be employed by Peking in pursuit of goals

in Asia are those of open military force. In the northeast, only South Korea and Japan might be targets of aggression from China. The former is definitely under United States protection; the latter is less vulnerable given the relative air and sea weakness of Chinese military forces. In South Asia, transportation media are few and primitive. The only rail lines venture from China into North Vietnam. Air bases are scattered and isolated from supply sources. Terrain along the frontier is predominantly thick jungle or rugged mountains. Although this favors border incursions, it argues against mass invasion directed at the distant capitals of Delhi, Rangoon, Bangkok, or Phnom Penh.

In addition, the base strength of China, presently located along the coast and northeastern sectors, is moving gradually toward the north and northwest. This is more secure from United States bases of attack and closer to the Soviet hinterland, safeguarded by alliance. It leaves China's south and southwestern areas extremely deficient in the manpower and economic strength necessary for supporting large-scale military action.

Finally, open use of force would risk the loss of influence and prestige that might otherwise be won through less costly alternative political and economic means. It might drive presently uncommitted countries to the side of the United States. If Soviet precedent serves as example, such use of military force enters only as an exceptional means of strategy when all other alternatives are exhausted. The Russian attack upon Finland in 1939 provides this precedent, but the singularity of such an occurrence argues against assuming high probability of military means being used in support of policy.

More likely is the use of Chinese

military assistance to local insurrections or civil wars that advance Peking's interests. Strengthening North Vietnam, bolstering insurgent Pathet Laos forces, and aiding guerilla groups in Malaya served China well during 1950–1954. Increased emphasis on the so-called "Bandung Spirit," however, brought abandonment of this strategy, for several years. Resumption in 1958–60 of a bellicose posture endangered the positive influence won by Peking in circles sensitive to armed insurrection, led by Nehru of India.

The least expensive and the least dangerous means of advancing intermediate-range goals would appear to be those employing economic and political techniques. Dramatic announcements of economic assistance, as in the case of food and factories to Cuba in 1960, or token teams of technical experts accompanied by loans or grants, as with Nepal, also in 1960, reap rewards far out of proportion to their expense. Chinese experience is closer than that of Western countries to the experience of underdeveloped countries. The cultural gap is easier to bridge, given the absence of racial or religious barriers between China and her neighbors. Finally, accomplishments by Chinese Communists appear more striking in contrast with recent conditions in their country than does continued industrial expansion by the United States.

Political channels available for exporting influence are several. Much of Asia is opposed to private capital and foreign investment. Communist credo supports this prejudice. Key groups in India, Burma, Indonesia, and Japan support varying degrees of Marxist or socialist ideology and are responsive to Peking's planned economy. Official "support" for Buddhism and Islam lessens the antipathy of Burmese and Indonesians, while Communist strictures against corruption, nepotism, and sloth provide a positive appeal throughout Asia.

Local agents for communicating Chinese messages may be found in various cultural groups organized ostensibly to promote Sino-Nepali or Sino-Burmese friendship. They may be assisted by local Communist parties of some strength, as in Indonesia. In these interpersonal contacts at the popular level Peking enjoys an advantage in political warfare generally denied Western capitals.

Furthermore, personal contact at the elite level plays a major role in Chinese Communist diplomacy which exploits shared attitudes of anticolonialism and bonds of so-called "Afro-Asian unity." In addition to a common sense of economic deprivation attributed to Western usurpations, this appeal masks an attempt at solidarity based on a negative "color line," *i.e.,* anti-white sentiments. The success of this approach is reflected in the fact that of 38 states recognizing the People's Republic of China in January 1961, 11 belonged to the Soviet bloc while 18 came from the so-called Afro-Asian areas.

Exploiting these contacts to the fullest, Chinese Communist leaders conclude pacts of "non-aggression and friendship" with weaker neighbors and exchange support for their grievances, whether in West Irian (Indonesia) or Goa (India), receiving support in turn for Chinese Communist claims to Taiwan and representation in the United Nations. In addition, growing technical assistance programs place a proliferation of efficient Chinese Communist experts throughout Africa and Asia. Their exemplary behavior and contribution to local felt needs mitigate the negative impact of Peking's brutal suppression of the Tibet revolt, or its

290 ALLEN S. WHITING

bellicose posture on various international problems.

Finally, suave and sophisticated Chou En-lai has played a signal role, lingering for days in little Cambodia or sipping long cups of tea in Rangoon, assuring his audiences of China's "need for peace," of its exclusive concern with domestic problems, and its common interest in assisting fellow Asians. This approach pays dividends in countries where personal figures play an important role in policy, unimpeded by opposition parties or by rival leaders in the bureaucracy.

These various tactics serve the familiar united-front strategy employed by Communists throughout the world intermittently since the days of Lenin. They either may act from above, joining forces at the elite level or they may act from below, infiltrating mass organizations to undermine present leadership. Either strategy is a temporary one designed to facilitate ultimate overthrow of the government.

In view of China's power compared with that confronting it, both from local sources and from the United States, this strategy maximizes Peking's assets while minimizing its liabilities. So long as societies in South and Southeast Asia continue to suffer from political and economic instability, and so long as the United States places primary emphasis upon military development within the area, we may expect increased economic and political action from the People's Republic of China.

The 1960's will see new dimensions, both geographic and strategic, in Communist China's foreign policies. Its activities in Africa and Latin America are certain to increase as Peking's economic capacity for trade and aid

strengthens its political appeals to newly independent regimes and local Communist parties. Moreover, in the likely event of a Chinese Communist nuclear weapons capability, Peking's prestige is certain to expand among the weaker, less developed countries, especially in Asia. Whether this is accompanied by more militant behavior on the part of the Chinese Communists depends upon many unknown factors, including the composition of the regime after Mao Tse-tung passes from the scene, the alternative means of advancing its goals, and the counterforce available to non-Communist countries. As final determinants of Chinese Communist policy, of course, the actions of Moscow and Washington are of prime importance. In this sense no analysis can predict the future course of China by focusing solely upon the decision-makers in Peking. Only a continuous correlation of their views with the changing environment within which they must operate can enable us to outline the likely alternatives which lie before the People's Republic of China as the most powerful country of Asia.

SELECTED BIBLIOGRAPHY

Barnett, A. Doak, Communist China and Asia, Challenge to American Policy (New York: Harper & Brothers, 1960, published for the Council on Foreign Relations).

Boormann, H., A. Eckstein, P. E. Mosely, B. Schwartz, Moscow-Peking Axis (New York: Harper & Brothers, 1957, published for the Council on Foreign Relations).

Levi, Werner, Modern China's Foreign Policy (Minneapolis: University of Minnesota Press, 1953).

North, Robert C., Moscow and Chinese Communists (Stanford: Stanford University Press, 1953).

In addition, the reader should consult the bibliographies published each August in The Far Eastern Quarterly, renamed The Journal of Asian Studies in 1957.

9

INDIA'S FOREIGN POLICY

RICHARD

L.

PARK

India's policy of non-alignment and the conciliatory diplomacy advocated by Prime Minister Jawaharlal Nehru have combined to elevate the Republic of India to a central role in the conduct of world affairs, despite its relatively low rank on the ladder of great world powers. This remarkable achievement of international eminence involved skillful strategy and a shrewd reading of current events. History also helped to shape the circumstances.

The emergence of India as an independent state in 1947, and the coming to power of the Chinese Communists two years later, represent the consequences of two major forces in the social and political revolutions that have been waged in Asia throughout the present century. The results of the competition between a liberal, democratic Republic of India and a communist People's Republic of China are recognized as being of critical importance to the ultimate success or failure in the spread of the communist movement throughout the world. More than half of the people on earth are encompassed in the great arc of nations that swings from Japan and Korea in East Asia to Pakistan and the Middle East in the west. What happens in India and in China, and between them, will affect the whole of Asia. For the non-communist as well as for the communist worlds, what comes of the Indian experiment with democratic government will not be of immediate significance only; it may well have repercussions in every other part of the globe. From this point of view, the stability of India's domestic politics, effectiveness in developing its internal economy, and skillful leadership for essential social change would seem to outweigh by far India's external influence on contemporary world affairs.

The leaders of India view their role in international politics from a different perspective. They place special emphasis upon the fact that the whole of Asia, and increasingly the Middle East and Africa as well, at last are escaping from the dominance and imposed tutelage of western imperial power. With freedom attained, the next objective is to raise living standards appreciably and to revitalize old civilizations with the best of modern technology and the most far-

291

reaching of social reforms. The communist issue, according to Jawaharlal Nehru and others close to him in the highest political circles in India, cannot be allowed to obscure the fact that internal national development must take priority over external involvement, and for reasons of domestic rather than ideological or international concern. Whereas it may be unfortunate that world communism and Asian nationalism have grown up together and have come to critical junctures calling for commitment and decision at about the same time, for India, at least, foreign policy must be exercised in the immediate interests of India, and not in accordance with the wishes and interests of other world powers. India believes that its own national interests would best be served by creating conditions of peace, encouraging cultural and economic cooperation on an unrestricted international scale, and fostering the acceptance of favorable conditions for political coexistence between competing forms of government. Under these circumstances India might enjoy an atmosphere conducive to the development of its own material and human resources. In this view, domestic and foreign policies necessarily interlink; foreign policy is a safeguard for the national interest.

To understand the dynamics of India's foreign policy it is advisable to look with care at the historical factors that have influenced its outlook on the world community, and to examine India's pattern of domestic problems, and its plans for their solution, out of which stem policies for external affairs.

THE NATIONAL BACKGROUND

Political history

Any full-scale inquiry into Indian foreign policy would lead one to range widely through history to identify the infinite variety of influences to and from India and its neighbors that characterized the early relations between the peoples of Asia. The relative isolation of segments of the region during the past few centuries was in large part the result of the parceling out of spheres of influence between the several western imperial powers. But cultural memories are lasting. Although India is a young nation, its civilization is ancient. Contemporary leaders are mindful of past greatness, at home and abroad, and are unwilling to build toward anything less than a new image of greatness.

The cultural vehicles of the Hindu and Buddhist ways of life carried Indian philosophy, artistic expression, and an epic literary tradition throughout Asia. No major part of that continent was left untouched by Buddhism, which arose in India but flourished on its borders and beyond. Pilgrims from the Buddhist world were drawn back to the birthplace of Gautama Buddha, bringing new ideas to India and taking back diaries of their observations in the "holy land." Through this interchange of culture and faith, ties were made that centuries of neglect could not entirely break.

From the north and west came Islamic invasions culminating in the Moghul Empire, splendidly exemplified by the rule of the Emperor Akbar. Akbar, like the Hindu-Buddhist Asoka long before him, is an Indian hero, remembered for combining compassion with strength, honor with efficiency—terms now reserved for modern leaders such as Mahatma Gandhi and Jawaharlal Nehru. Akbar represents Islam and the tie of India to the cultural traditions of the Middle East.

Much later, particularly from the seventeenth century onwards when European powers battled for trading rights in the Indian subcontinent, western and Indian ideas and institutions met, clashed, and in part coalesced in the creation of a pattern of political and social doctrine and forms of social organization that have persisted to a remarkable extent, and are clearly represented in the Constitution of the Republic of India.

Our concern must be directed towards more recent history, to the direct line of development of independent India's foreign policy. In concentrating on these latter years, however, it would be well to remember that India's leaders keep at least one eye reserved for five thousand years of history, and not a few of their contemporary decisions are made with due regard for this background of experience.

By the middle of the nineteenth century, India had become an administrative and political unity. Between 1600, when Elizabeth I chartered the East India Company for trading rights in the East, and about 1858 most of the lands of the Indian subcontinent were brought under British administration and control. The rapid decline of the Moghul Empire in the eighteenth century, plus the skill of the British in administration and in warfare had led to the gradual absorption and political control of local Indian rulers' lands. This process involved first revenue-collecting and imposition of law and order to assure trading rights, and then possession itself for the ultimate assurance of commercial security that such political control allows.

India had never before had an opportunity to draw together the many cultural strands that formed the basis of its unique community. In the Sanskritic tradition and in Indian philosophy there were ties that for millennia had given a sense of unity to the many Hindu peoples who inhabited the larger part of the subcontinent. But diversity of expression—in language, art, literature, religious belief, and intensity of loyalty—was the rule rather than the exception before the 19th century and the age of British dominance. The institutions of caste and the joint family, cemented by local symbols of loyalty and social custom, added to the patchwork-quilt cultural nature of the subcontinent—a condition, incidentally, which continues to divide the Indian people into competing regional groups.

British administration, to be effective and efficient, had to be tightly organized and centralized. Thus the country was divided and subdivided, not always rationally or in accordance with an integrated plan, but in any event in line with considerations that would bolster imperial British control. The objective was to organize an administrative state: one where revenues could be collected regularly and sufficiently; where a few top British political officers, and a small corps of Indian Civil Service members, could funnel orders from the top of the hierarchy to action at the grass roots, and conversely, where local sentiments could be channeled upwards; one where law and order—and proximate justice—could be enforced; and where British ideas about the ultimate destiny of the Indian people could be carried forward by means of education, imitation of colonial behavior, and experience over time in the use of western social and political institutions.

In 1858 a turning point came in Indian history. The year before, a mutiny, now often called the First War of Indian Independence, had broken out in several parts of northern India. The ostensible objective of the mutiny was to restore the Moghul Emperor to his throne in Delhi. Underneath, however, were a number of grievances against the Company's rule that focussed upon their failure to give adequate attention to the social and economic needs of the people. Agreements with local rulers had been set aside, often without consultation, and in general the social well-being of the population was subordinated to the personal and economic interests of the rulers themselves. Often ignorant of local customs, and sometimes oblivious of the social consequences of enforced rules and regulations, crises on many fronts led to outright revolt against Company power. London's response to the situation was to give control of India to the Crown, and for Parliament to assume the supervisory responsibilities for the conduct of state affairs.

Nationalism

From 1858 to 1947, authoritarian British rule in India conceded gradually to the liberal British view that a people should be trained to govern themselves, at least in local affairs. Indian nationalist opinion developed with the view that a people *must* be allowed to govern themselves. It was perhaps inevitable that the growth of an Indian nationalism would be encouraged by the liberal British tradition that dominated the Indian educational system from the middle of the 19th century.

Indian nationalism commenced more as a social and religious reform endeavor than as a political and economic movement. Faced with the facts of an earlier Muslim domination of a basically Hindu society, and then with the rapid takeover of Moghul reins by the British, 19th century Indian leaders were led to question the inherent strength of Hindu social institutions. Men such as Raja Rammohan Roy, often called the "Father of Indian Nationalism," vigorously fought in the early 19th century for a liberalization of Hindu social institutions, and for English education so that the new ideas

of Europe might be drawn to the reform of Indian life. Rammohan Roy founded the Brahmo Samaj in 1828 as an institutionalized means for giving opportunities to liberal Indians to make over Hindu society along more enlightened lines. Other reformers such as Dayananda Saraswati, founder of the Arya Samaj, urged a return to the purer—less historically and socially overladen—philosophy of the ancient Vedic age, unhindered by caste divisions, as his more indigenous response to the impact of the west. Late 19th century developments along the same general lines included the work of Annie Besant of the Theosophical Society and Swami Vivekananda of the Ramakrishna Mission.

But poverty, illiteracy, and disease, deep-rooted and widespread, were facts of Indian life that served as the mainsprings for a vigorous nationalism and, later, of the insistent demand for freedom from British rule. Centralized imperial administration provided the means for improving transportation and communication, broadening markets for industry and agriculture, and encouraging modern finance and commerce. In the process, British capital, more than Indian, reaped the profits, and British industry and commerce benefited most by the construction of a colonial economy with India providing the raw materials for a profitable European industry. And in the Indian backwaters the relatively self-sufficient village economy broke down as middle-scale industrialization came to India. No longer could village craftsmen hope to compete with the factories of the towns and cities. The tightly woven fabric of Indian village society, with its ancient system of interrelated economic functions and social services, was struck a heavy blow. The economy and related aspects of the society grew in a lop-sided manner. The tiny fraction that was urban India grew further apart from the four-fifths that was village India. Education, better health, and the benefits of modern technology hardly touched the countryside, and indeed even in the towns and cities cleavages between the well-off and the down-and-out were all too evident.

Indian National Congress

It was under these conditions of dominance by British power, of internal division between the several layers of Indian society, of separatist tendencies between Hindu and Muslim and between linguistic regions, plus a pervasive stagnation in the culture and in the general economy, that the Indian National Congress was founded in 1885. The Congress, destined to be the vehicle of the Indian nationalist movement and the organization in which the main lines of independent India's foreign policy would be tested and formed, was a moderate body with modest objectives in the years up to World War I. Congress leaders of those days, such as Pherozeshah Mehta, Surendranath Banerjea, or G. K. Gokhale, were mainly concerned with increasing Indian membership in the Indian Civil Service, extending the benefits of higher education, and arguing a persuasive case to the Parliament and people of Great Britain for a greater measure of Indian participation in running the affairs of India. In this effort, the Congress was encouraged by liberal British leaders in both Great Britain and India. It was the belief of those concerned with this early phase of nationalist expression that with experience and time the good sense of the British would capitulate to the obvious need for a loosening of British control over Indian affairs. Such optimism proved unwarranted, and a vigorous but uniquely non-violent nation-

alist movement, led by Mohandas K. Gandhi from 1919 onwards, was the result. The Congress-backed nationalist movement expanded its program of action to the masses of the Indian people, pressing harder and harder for the concessions from their rulers that ultimately led to an independent India in 1947.

As freedom came near, however, bitter feelings between the Hindu and Muslim communities grew more intense. The common nationalist cause against an alien ruler broke down, and from 1940 a large proportion of the Muslims demanded a separate state, Pakistan, in which to develop a nation based on Islamic brotherhood. Pakistan was founded in 1947 after widespread rioting, terrible bloodshed, and the transfer under fear of populations in the millions had forced the issue to a solution by partition. Needless to say, the circumstances of partition contributed much to the mutual sense of fear and enmity that has colored the international relations and foreign policies of Pakistan and India ever since.

This brief survey of the Indian nationalist movement and of the general conditions of 19th and 20th century India is intended to convey one important lesson in the better understanding of India's view of world affairs. Indians have been concerned—one might almost say obsessed—during the past half century with the imperial or colonial question. Almost everything else in world history has been read in terms of the colonial theme, including the communal rivalry between Muslims and Hindus which is felt to be the product of a British policy of divide and rule. It is understandable that contemporary leaders, like Nehru, who fought for independence for over a quarter of a century, would not forget easily their experiences in earlier years. In colonial status, India considered itself to be isolated from active participation in world affairs, and yet subject to the forces of world politics because tied to the decisions of Great Britain as the imperial power. In particular, India resented its involuntary, if legal, involvement in two World Wars. This condition of involuntary alignment with Great Britain and its allies in times of war and peace undoubtedly contributed to independent India's decision to develop its foreign policy among lines of non-alignment with other blocs of power, especially the western or free-world alignment with which India was most familiar.

Economic geography

However internationally isolated, in a formal sense, the Indian National Congress may have been in the years before independence, Indian leaders certainly were alert to the geographical, economic, and political facts of Indian life which formed the conditions of any Indian foreign policy, even as interpreted by Great Britain.

First, India was recognized as being strategically located in the west of Asia, with its peninsula stretching across the main lines of sea and air communications from west to east, and with its northern, mountainous boundaries touching upon important centers of the Middle East, Central Asia, and the Far East. India's near neighbors include several among the most powerful nations in the world, particularly Russia and China, but also, Burma, Indonesia, and the other countries of Southeast Asia with which India feels it has much in common. Relatively isolated, historically, by mountains to the north, and seas on its peninsular sides, nevertheless it has been recognized that India's geographic location in the modern air age is one involving a natural intercourse with the many economic, political, and cultural forces that cross or abut on its territory. Not only is protection from invasion the crucial question; also of importance is the skill with which India may take advantage of interrelations with the many who come its way.

Economically India has been and remains a country poor in the level of its exploited natural resources, in the rate of its industrial and agricultural development, and in the prospect for rapid rises in its standards of living. These facts were early recognized by the Indian National Congress. One of the great urges of the nationalist movement was the hope that with greater freedom to plan and legislate, adequate steps might be taken to improve the economic lot of the Indian people. Nationalist thinking on foreign affairs was never far removed from the economic implications of whatever steps might be taken abroad. And the first major step towards sound economic development, at least as seen by the 1930's, was the attainment of political freedom to permit national economic planning.

Competing ideologies

However, the geographic and economic facts affecting India's international position are of relatively minor significance to Congress leaders when these facts are compared with the influence of political ideas. The first major ideological influence was that of liberalism; the second, closely following on the first in historical sequence, was socialism.

The most far-reaching legacy of the period of British rule in India was the infusion of a liberal philosophy of government in the mental frame of India's educated hierarchy of leadership. The process by which this intermixture of ideas and institutions took place over the past 150 years is in large part the total social history of the period. Education in English from the mid-19th century, both at the secondary and higher educational levels, brought to Indian students the story of western European achievement in assuring that law, politics, and civil and military administration would be subject to the responsible control of the people. The connection between a vital liberal democracy and rapid economic and social development was not lost to those Indians who examined European experience. Moreover, significant numbers of Indian students took their higher degrees in London, or at Oxford and Cambridge, and a few on the continent, thus pouring back into Indian society leaders fully on a par, intellectually, with their European classmates.

As British Indian administrators faced novel problems for which no ready indigenous solution seemed present, it was only natural that they look to British experience for ideas and institutions applicable in India. Indian judges and lawyers, accountants and teachers, agricultural economists and engineers, editors and reporters, and of course politicians as well grew up in an institutionalized atmosphere that was reflective of the British liberal view of society's proper organization. Although this process of macrocosmic acculturation through time was largely an urban phenomenon, and affected only a small segment of India's society, the influence nevertheless was great, for it touched upon the lives of the greater part of India's educated ruling classes. By the 1920's, when the Indian National Congress under Gandhi opened its mass campaign for political freedom, liberalism was well established as the common core of political agreement concerning the kind of government and the kind of society that India's leaders wished to develop under

their own guidance. In fact, one of the most powerful of the weapons that leaders of the Congress used against the British was the assertion that Great Britain was denying to the Indian people the goals of liberal democracy extolled so vociferously in London.

The second major ideological influence in 20th century India has been socialism. For many, socialism was seen as a combination of utopian propositions and Fabian interpretations of social democracy. These ideas equated rather easily with the main tenets of liberalism as they had been developed in India. For others, Marxism and Marxian socialism were more influential, although organized political parties favoring Marxian socialism did not gain in prominence until the 1930's. Most Indian intellectuals and many politicians were convinced that India's economic and social conditions required active, regularized legislative and administrative direction by government to bring about needed social and economic changes. In the case of Marxism, the Russian revolution was closely followed by Indian leaders, since it was felt that here was an experiment in radical socialism operating in a social and economic situation not unlike that of India. The fact that the Soviet Union, and spokesmen for the Comintern, endorsed India's aspirations for independence and condemned British imperial power at a time when others were silent has not been forgotten. At least a portion of the sympathetic hearing now given to Soviet views on world affairs may be traced to the Communists' early support of Indian nationalism.

Ideologically, then, India's leaders had grown accustomed by the mid-1920's to the liberal democracy of western Europe, combined with an infusion of socialist solutions to economic problems, and they were fully committed to the perpetuation of such a mixed form of government in an independent India. This was true even though it was well understood by these leaders that some of the principles of liberal democracy, when applied in India, would conflict with the localized, group social behavior of village India which relied more on caste or class, than upon the individual, for the exercise of political responsibilities.

Foreign policy in the making

The Congress, of course, did not have a "foreign policy," in any formal sense, until it was the party conducting the government of the Republic of India. But as a strategy in the nationalist movement, the Congress adopted a policy of expressing itself by resolutions on foreign affairs at its annual sessions, or through statements by its officers at other times. The same policy was adopted for matters of domestic concern. This process was called "parallel government": the Congress, in this case, speaking for the Indian people who were unable to speak effectively through British Indian organs of government.

By the mid-1920's the Congress turned its attention more regularly to international politics. The new emphasis arose partially as a consequence of India's failure to secure a greater measure of freedom following the end of World War I, but perhaps more so because of the insistence of a young Congressman from the United Provinces, son of a then prominent Congress leader, Motilal Nehru.

Jawaharlal Nehru, a London-trained lawyer educated at Harrow and Cambridge, began to make his influence felt in circles of the Congress by the mid-1920's. Although he was interested in domestic politics, his special contribution to the nationalist movement was the education of several generations of Indians in the facts of international life. Nehru believed that India was inevitably to play an important role in international affairs, and that the Indian National Congress had a responsibility in preparing the people for the years ahead. An examination of the resolutions of the Congress from 1926 to 1947 reveals an acute awareness of the dangers in the growth of fascism, a sympathetic approach to the aspirations of the Soviet Union, a consistent criticism of the continuation or expansion of western imperial power anywhere in the world, and a sensitive exposure of all forms of racial, social, or economic discrimination. Such an examination of the record reveals the growth of the view that international disputes require peaceful means of solution, and that peaceful means for resolving disputes would be encouraged by a world organized to enforce the exclusive use of such means. The influence of Gandhi in the growth of this policy of non-violent methods in international affairs is obvious. Jawaharlal Nehru, as General Secretary of the Indian National Congress, re-established in 1936 a Foreign Department (originally formed in 1925) to study world affairs and to disseminate literature on the subject throughout India. Although it is unfair to credit Prime Minister Nehru for the whole construction of India's foreign policy, it can be said that he was the architect and the guide who prepared the way from 1926 for policies that by 1947 were acceptable and taken for granted by the vast bulk of the citizens of India.

THE POLICY-MAKING PROCESS

For the personal and historical reasons outlined above, Prime Minister Jawaharlal Nehru has impressed his personal stamp on the foreign policy of

India to a greater degree than any contemporary statesman has been able to achieve elsewhere. As a politically powerful, highly intelligent nationalist leader with a deep concern for world affairs, Mr. Nehru has articulated a policy based on his view of the present and future, bearing in mind the strengths and weaknesses of his country and people, that finds broad affirmation in India with all but rather small sectors of Indian political opinion. Since the Sino-Indian dispute over the Himalayan border was made public knowledge in 1959, there has been a sharp increase in public criticism of Nehru that has brought into focus the bureaucratic and legislative apparatus that supports the voice of the Prime Minister on matters of foreign policy.

Governmental agencies

The executive authority. India's Constitution places formal executive responsibility with the President of the Republic. But, as in Great Britain with the Queen, the President in India acts on the advice of his council of ministers. The cabinet, which in India does not necessarily include all ministers, is composed of senior ministers nominated by the Prime Minister and appointed by the President, who then act with collective responsibility to Parliament.

Since 1947 India has had one Prime Minister, Jawaharlal Nehru, who has continuously held the portfolio for external affairs as well. Since the Prime Minister's Congress Party has enjoyed a substantial majority in every session of Parliament since 1947, continuity in foreign policy has been sustained to the degree that the Prime Minister wished to sustain it. Although as Minister of External Affairs Mr. Nehru can take and has taken counsel with his cabinet colleagues on foreign policy, as Prime Minister he holds such broad responsibility for the domestic and external well-being of his country that explanations rather than questions appear to have been his normal presentations to the cabinet on foreign matters. The holding of the two portfolios by a man of such experience, who in turn is held almost in reverence by the bulk of his people, plus party-disciplined control over a substantive majority in Parliament, have given Mr. Nehru what amounts to a free hand in constructing and executing India's foreign policy.

The Ministry of External Affairs is a large and professionally staffed organization. A Deputy Minister, at present Mrs. Lakshmi Menon, assists Mr. Nehru both in the Ministry and in Parliament. A Secretary-General presides over much of the general administration, and a bank of senior secretaries and their many assistants compose the working staff of the Ministry. It is from the "country desks," from the research branches, and from the technical staffs that analytical materials flow to the Prime Minister to give him the raw materials and statements of alternative policies from which foreign policy ultimately is made.

The Ministry of External Affairs, as organized since 1949, has responsibility for the following functions: [1]

1. Foreign affairs
2. Diplomatic and consular representation; Indian Foreign Service; Indian foreign publicity
3. United Nations Organization; international conferences, associations and other bodies
4. Treaties and agreements with foreign countries

[1] Information on the functions and organization of the Ministry of External Affairs is taken from *The Organisation of the Government of India,* prepared by the Indian Institute of Public Administration (Bombay: Asia Publishing House, 1958), pp. 37–44.

5. Foreign jurisdiction and extradition
6. Emigration from India; passports and visas and pilgrimage to places outside India
7. The administration of the North East Frontier Agency and the Naga Hills-Tuensang area
8. The administration of Pondicherry and other former French possessions in India
9. The administration of certain laws, such as the Indian Emigration Act of 1922, the Reciprocity Act of 1943, etc.

In structure, the Secretary-General presides over the administration of the Ministry, aided by a Commonwealth Secretary for Commonwealth matters, a Special Secretary for managing the establishment, finance, personnel, communications, supplies, and records, and a Foreign Secretary to cover the world other than the Commonwealth, plus protocol, historical research, and related subjects.

The 85 Sections in the Ministry as of 1957 were arranged into 11 Divisions as follows:

1. American (including foreign aid)
2. Western (including the United Nations and excluding Great Britain)
3. Eastern (including the NEFA and the Naga Hills)
4. Southern
5. African (including Great Britain and its African colonies)
6. Pakistan
7. Protocol
8. Administration
9. External publicity
10. Foreign service inspectorate
11. Historical

Something of the extent of India's commitment to representation abroad may be gained by noting the number of missions established up to December of 1957:

36 Embassies
8 High Commissions
18 Legations
3 Special Missions (Bhutan, Sikkim, and United Nations)
8 Commissions
17 Consulates-General or Consulates
4 Vice-Consulates
3 Agencies (Gyantse, Gartok, and Yatung)
Permanent Representative at the Headquarters of the United Nations

Almost seven thousand staff members man the Ministry and its offices abroad.

Mr. V. K. Krishna Menon, at present Minister of Defense, also represents India on important matters of international concern, at the United Nations or elsewhere, when so requested by the Prime Minister. Although Mr. Menon is only loosely associated with the Ministry of External Affairs, in fact his influence is great because of the confidence in which he is held by Mr. Nehru.

The foreign service. Personnel recruited to the foreign service, now scattered throughout the world in the High Commissions and Commissions within the Commonwealth of Nations, and in the Embassies, Legations, Consulates-General, Consulates, United Nations and International missions elsewhere, are carefully selected by competitive examination and are thoroughly trained for their positions. At the highest levels—Ambassadors and High Commissioners—what might be called "political appointments" sometimes occur. But the tradition is to use the professional service to the maximum.

The foreign service, somewhat similar to its counterpart in Great Britain, is an elite service, admission to which is much sought after by India's most able graduates. Pressures after 1947 were very great to expand India's external representation rapidly, but trained personnel were in short supply.

Now the service is nearly stabilized and its standards have increased year by year. Protected from personal criticism by the restraints of responsible ministers, the foreign service has been able to give an even greater maturity to India's assessment of the facts of international affairs. More adequate linguistic skills, an improvement in foreign intelligence analysis, and a much greater bulk of collated information on world situations provide the Ministry of External Affairs with substantial resources to use in pursuing the global implications of India's foreign policy.

Parliament. Parliament is not concerned with day-to-day making or execution of foreign policy. But debates in the Lok Sabha (House of the People) or the Rajya Sabha (Council of State) initiated by the Prime Minister, or on questions raised during the Question Period, or following the President's addresses opening Parliament, or on the budget, give several opportunities for Members to participate in influencing policy. Since Mr. Nehru is concerned daily with foreign affairs, he tends to report regularly, often, and in detail to Parliament. Seldom is Parliament in doubt about the Government's views. But Parliament has not constituted a standing committee on foreign affairs. This prerogative remains with another organ of Parliament, the cabinet, and of course with the Prime Minister.

It should not be assumed, however, that Members of Parliament are not an integral part of the policy-making process on foreign affairs. To the contrary, articulate members of the opposition, such as Acharya J. B. Kripalani, Asoka Mehta, Minoo Masani, and several members of the Communist Party of India, as well as Congress Party members who disagree with accepted policy, often are heard, their words recorded, and the debate disseminated widely throughout the country in official records and in the press. Spokesmen in Parliament help to identify the controversial issues for the media of public opinion. Public opinion, in turn, acts as a restraint upon the Congress Party's Parliamentary majority.

Nongovernmental agencies

Political parties. The Congress Party, through its Annual Sessions usually held in December, through its policy-suggesting organ, the Working Committee, and through the party's administrative secretariat, the All-India Congress Committee, regularly discusses foreign policy and proposes policy changes to the Parliamentary Congress Party. The Prime Minister, as the actual leader of the party, remains in close communication with party headquarters and party leaders on foreign as well as on domestic matters. The considered opinion of the Congress Party today is likely to be official policy tomorrow.

As has been mentioned earlier, certain respected leaders from other parties, or from among the independents, can be influential from Parliament or the public platform on matters relating to foreign affairs, but only to the extent that their personal standing is high in the country. For example, the Praja [Peoples'] Socialist Party has not, as a party, been an effective critic of foreign policy. But a socialist leader, like Asoka Mehta, can personally make a significant impact, as can an ex-socialist like Jayaprakash Narayan who holds no political office at all. The communists, too, are not backward in voicing opposition to given policies. In this case, party rather than personal weight is applicable because of the monolithic character of the Communist Party of India.

But since the Congress Party rules

India more or less as if India were, in fact, a one-party state, debate *within* the Congress Party is the most critical locus of political controversy on matters of world and domestic affairs. The Congress Party is not inclined, substantively and for good political reasons, to deny Mr. Nehru his conlusions if he takes a positive stand and asks for support.

Interest groups. For the most part, interest groups do not have much influence in shaping India's foreign policy. Tradition excludes them from indirect involvement as informal advisers, and the law bars them from direct pressures. Such groups do, of course, have spokesmen in Parliament; they publish their views; they influence individuals. But groups such as the trade unions, professional societies, commercial, financial, and industrial organizations, and caste lobbies have a most limited range for influence. To the extent that these groups find a congenial home in a political party, interest can be more effectively passed on through recognized political channels.

The Indian Council of World Affairs, at its Sapru House headquarters in New Delhi and in its many branches throughout the country, as well as in its publications, can be (or could be) influential. But, for the most part, Council members and staff do not defy or analyze critically established Government policy.

Mass media and public opinion. World news is given extended and generally fair treatment in the English-language newspapers, the best of the Indian-language newspapers, and in the thousands of weeklies, fortnightlies, and monthlies published in all parts of the country. Indian newspapers are inclined to carry very long articles and informative editorials that may run two full columns on crucial concerns in foreign affairs. These publications in turn reflect in their editorials suggestions intended to influence foreign policy. Newspapers of the quality of *The Hindu* (Madras), The *Times of India* (Bombay and New Delhi), *The Hindustan Times* (New Delhi), or *The Statesman* (Calcutta and New Delhi) are read meticulously by officers in the Ministry of External Affairs. Party organs such as *Vigil* and the *Organiser,* or papers of opinion like *Thought* (Delhi) and *The Economic Weekly* (Bombay), the Congress for Cultural Freedom's *Quest* (Calcutta), and the late M. N. Roy's paper, *The Radical Humanist* (Calcutta), to name a few of the special publications, do help to shape opinion indirectly.

Television is not a communications factor in India, and All-India Radio is nationalized and without editorial influence on foreign policy.

These stimulants for public opinion, plus books and pamphlets, do appear to have made an impact on the urban intelligentsia. But India is over 70 per cent illiterate, and the bulk of the country is out of the range of radios that function. Thus public opinion, even at best, is expressed only by relatively few people and these largely in urban centers.

On the whole, the Indian press supports Mr. Nehru's conclusions on foreign affairs, and thus such criticisms as do appear normally are on minor issues. The exceptions have been the new Sino-Indian border dispute and the old Kashmir case. In these two cases, India's territorial integrity is at stake, and critics of government, including many journalists and editors, have been outspokenly critical—and perhaps thereby somewhat influential.

India is not a country of opinion pollers. However, the Indian Institute of Public Opinion (New Delhi) has produced two serial publications, one on public issues and one on economic matters, that (using George Gallup's methods) do give one useful resource for opinion study.

THE SUBSTANCE OF FOREIGN POLICY

The remarkable consistency in public expressions of India's foreign policy can be traced to the continuity of leadership held by Jawaharlal Nehru and the Congress Party since 1947. The trying circumstances of India's political and economic life have induced wide public support for the Government of India's stand on world affairs, particularly since this stand has resulted in the growth of India's prestige in the eyes of much of the world. Although the cases of Kashmir, Korea, Suez, Hungary, and China have produced bends and kinks on the main lines of foreign policy, India's principal international objectives and its strategy of diplomacy have not been changed fundamentally since independence.

On September 26, 1946, Mr. Nehru as the leader of the Interim Government issued the following statement on foreign policy—a statement that would be applicable today:

In the sphere of foreign affairs India will follow an independent policy, keeping away from the power politics of groups aligned one against another. She will uphold the principles of freedom for dependent peoples and will oppose racial discrimination wherever it may occur. She will work with other peace-loving nations for international cooperation and goodwill without exploitation of one nation by another.

It is necessary that with the attainment of her full international status, India should establish contact with all the great nations of the world and that her relations with neighboring countries in Asia should become still closer. . . .

Towards the United Nations Organiza-

tion India's attitude is that of wholehearted cooperation and unreserved adherence, in both spirit and letter, to the Charter governing it. To that end, India will participate fully in its varied activities and endeavor to play that role in its Councils to which her geographical position, population and contribution toward peaceful progress entitle her. In particular, the Indian delegate will make it clear that India stands for the independence of all colonial and dependent people and their full right to self-determination.[2]

One finds in this statement a number of principles that highlight the main strands of India's foreign policy:

1. The "independence" in outlook of a people who had been dominated for too long.
2. The fear that involvement in the affairs of others would restrict India's ability to construct a new and better social and economic order for itself.
3. The determination to assist others to attain the political freedom for which India fought for so many years.
4. The hatred of second and third class citizenship, particularly of an inferior status awarded because of race.
5. The confidence in cooperation and mutual goodwill, exemplified by the United Nations.
6. The urge for international contacts throughout the world, but with special attention given to neighboring countries in Asia.

Theory in practice

In practice, these principles have made it relatively easy to anticipate the Government of India's response to issues as they have arisen in world politics.

Non-alignment. The policy of

[2] Statement issued at a press conference in New Delhi, India, on September 26, 1946, and published in *Indian Information* (New Delhi: Government of India Information Bureau, October 15, 1946).

non-alignment (or of "neutralism" as some prefer to put it in a broader context) assured the fact that India would not participate in the South East Asia Treaty Organization or the Baghdad Pact (later CENTO). What was (and is) less well known is that India, in order to help create "conditions of peace," would exercise its influence to lessen the scope of effectiveness and range of membership in such mutual defense arrangements, particularly those pacts like SEATO and CENTO that impinge on the region of South Asia. To the extent possible, it appears that India has advised its diplomats to endorse non-military, peaceful solutions, and to bring into question military solutions. The exceptions, perhaps, are those military agreements (e.g., the North Atlantic Treaty Organization or the Warsaw Pact) that do not relate directly to Asian concerns and are distant from India geographically.

During the period of negotiations leading to the signing of the "Mutual Defense Assistance Agreement between the Government of the United States of America and the Government of Pakistan" on May 19, 1954, India pushed its non-alignment policy one step further; in this case arguing that a military agreement entered into by Pakistan—a country whose eastern and western sectors enclose India like bookends—inevitably involved India in dangerous military consequences not of India's choosing and without mutual consent. In Parliament Mr. Nehru explained why he felt it necessary to object to Pakistan's decision to sign such an agreement, even though Pakistan, a sovereign state, claimed that the matter was none of India's business:

. . . Of course, they are a free country; I cannot prevent them. But if something affects Asia, India especially, and if some-

thing, in our opinion, is a reversal of history after hundreds of years, are we to remain silent? We have thought in terms of freeing our countries, and one of the symbols of freedom has been the withdrawal of foreign armed forces. I say the return of any armed forces from any European or American country is a reversal of the history of the countries of Asia, whatever the motive. . . .

I am not prepared to express my opinion except in the most philosophic manner about the distant problems of Europe. India has not the slightest desire to impose its views or wishes on any other country. But because in Asia we have passed through similar processes of history in the last two hundred years or so, and thus can understand each other a little better, it is likely that I am in tune with some of my neighbor countries when I speak. If the great powers think that the problems of Asia can be solved minus Asia or minus the views of Asian countries, then it does seem to be rather odd.[3]

Pakistan did sign the agreement, of course, and the differences that separated Pakistan and India earlier, especially concentrated on Kashmir, were hardened in India's opinion. Whether the defense agreement was wise or not, depends upon one's point of view. But from the perspective of India's foreign policy and India's sense of the situation in Asia, an American offer of a similar defense arrangement with India to parallel the Pakistan arrangement, intended to offset the charge of upsetting the power balance in South Asia, was both ill-advised and impertinent. Leaders in India could read the United States' offer only as a

[3] This extract is taken from a speech by Jawaharlal Nehru given in Parliament on February 22, 1954, and is given in full in *Jawaharlal Nehru's Speeches,* Vol. 3, March 1953–August 1957 (New Delhi: Ministry of Information and Broadcasting, 1958), pp. 344–46.

total misunderstanding, or worse, an indifference to India's policy of non-alignment and its diplomatic strategy which India felt helped to create "conditions of peace." In this case, although India's foreign policy gave a clear indication of its probable response to a proposal for a defense agreement with the United States, the signs were ignored. This case provides a useful lesson in the dilemmas of international politics. Assuming mutual understanding of the issues involved in a dispute, agreement for resolution need not necessarily follow. Indeed, a sharp identification of the issues may well make agreement less likely, particularly if the probable ramifications of alternative solutions are rendered explicit.

Nationalist movements. India's policy has led in the past to a consistent support given to groups aspiring for national independence from western imperial control. On the subcontinent itself, French Indian territory was claimed by India and won (*de facto*) after some struggle; France has yet to turn over the territories *de jure*. Similarly, the dispute with Portugal over Goa and the rest of Portuguese India continues, based on the principle that Portugal improperly holds thousands of aspiring Indians in imperial political bondage. For the neighboring country of Nepal, whenever influence could be exercised, it has been in the direction of maintaining Nepal's independence and in encouraging internal change that would transfer political power to responsible hands from authoritarian control.

Further afield, nationalists in Algeria, in Kenya, in Malaya, in the Congo, in Angola, in Egypt and in many other areas have enjoyed the public support of India. On the more recent cases, especially after the tempering years of experience in the United Nations, India has been somewhat more cautious in supporting nationalist movements in Africa prematurely. But the principles of self-determination and the national right to independence remain firm.

India has been unwilling, however, to apply the "independence" principle to the communist world, except in the case of Yugoslavia—a solution that was determined by means other than internal national revolt. The uprisings in Poland and the notorious case of Hungary tested India's intentions. India was not in these cases willing to stretch its policy to help sustain national strivings behind the communist shield. The contrast between the reluctant and basically neutral response of India to the Soviet Union's behavior in Hungary, and the immediately hostile reaction to British, French, and Israeli behavior over Suez in 1956 underscore an inconsistency in India's foreign policy that would appear to be difficult to explain except in ideological or opportunistic terms. India's official reactions to the recent revolts in Tibet and to the escape of the Dalai Lama from Chinese communist hands also were cautious and non-committal, until the Sino-Indian border dispute involving Tibet elevated the national interests of India after 1959 to a point above the previous general strategy for peace relying on a recognition of the monolithic character of the communist world system. Under the pressures of the struggle with Communist China over Sino-Indian boundaries in the Himalayan region, India has recognized more clearly the nature and substance of Tibetan resistance to Chinese cultural and political absorption. The implications supporting the view that a communist form of imperialism exists—in Asia from China and in Europe from the Soviet Union—have been made more explicit in public and private forums over the past two years.

But the legend of imperialism's being uniquely the final stage of capitalism, grounded on Lenin's analysis and known to every schoolboy in India, dies hard.

Racial discrimination. For many years before independence, Indian leaders objected to discriminations based upon race or creed. Mahatma Gandhi established his world reputation before World War I by organizing effective non-violent resistance to such discrimination in South Africa. The continuation in South Africa of racial policies, and the enactment of permanent and legal discrimination in the form of *apartheid,* have led to India's boycott of South Africa and to a break in diplomatic relations. The withdrawal of South Africa from the Commonwealth of Nations is in no small part due to the adamant stand against *apartheid* taken by India, Pakistan, Ghana, and other Afro-Asian Commonwealth members, powerfully supported by Canada.

South Africa is only the most dramatic of the cases of India's involvement in international anti-discriminatory policies. Australia's "white" policy, the plight of the negro in the United States, the Sinhalese-Buddhist attacks upon the rights of the minority of Tamil-speaking Hindus in Ceylon are three among many other cases upon which India more cautiously speaks its piece on behalf of equality.

The United Nations and the Afro-Asian group. India's record in the United Nations is far too extensive to review here. But the record reveals the high importance given to the United Nations as an international forum for the resolution of conflicts, for the prevention of possible conflicts, and for the spreading of mutual understanding and cooperation, especially through the work of the specialized agencies. The Kashmir case, first brought to the attention of the United Nations by India in late December of 1947, resulted in some disillusionment for India, since Security Council actions did not coincide with India's wishes. For India, the handling of the Kashmir case by the United Nations gave a lucid lesson in the political operations of the Security Council. It is not likely that India will again bring a case of the Kashmir sort to the United Nations except after the most careful of pre-considerations.

The Afro-Asian consultative conference within the United Nations has become a significant force in the General Assembly since its formation in 1950, especially as the number of Afro-Asian member countries increases year by year. India and Egypt have played leading roles in this group. Although several shades of political outlook are encompassed in the bloc, the "neutralist" shade is dominant. Partially by means of this informal organization of states, India has been able to advance its "conditions of peace" formula in the limiting of military defense arrangements in the Afro-Asian region, and in gaining United Nations membership for potential members of the bloc. The power of this grouping has been shown in the steady rise in the proportion of states willing to vote for the admission of Communist China to the United Nations.

Circles of interest

Pakistan. India's foreign policy begins and ends with neighboring Pakistan. Partition was the consequence of bloodshed, arson, rape, abduction, tremendous losses of property, the transfer of populations to the extent of twelve millions, plus general ill will of a virulent and lasting variety. India's conciliatory and generous approach to more distant problems has not been applied to Pakistan, perhaps for understandable reasons.

Now that a decade and a half has passed since partition, functional ties between the two countries in transportation, communications, exchange of persons, commerce, and culture have been restored to a large degree. Piecemeal, many of the thorny differences over trade, boundary disputes, and the like have been settled. Even the refugee problem is much reduced in both countries. With the help of the International Bank, a spectacular technological achievement has been made in settling the Indus Valley (canal waters) dispute for the mutual benefit of both countries.

The Kashmir case, however, remains as the stark symbol of past differences and deep antagonisms. The case is too complex to detail in this accounting. In sum, each country presents its view from different premises: Pakistan—that possession of the territory, 77 per cent Muslim in 1941, should be settled by a plebiscite, as recommended by the United Nations; India—that the State of Jammu and Kashmir is an integral part of India by reason of the accession agreement of 1947, and that referral to the people already has taken place during elections conducted legally in the State.

The case has not advanced a step towards solution over the years, except that time has tended to stabilize India's possession of the larger part of the area, which in turn has resulted in authoritarian techniques of rule in Jammu and Kashmir to squash opinions favoring either Pakistan's stand or a desire for Kashmiri independence from India and Pakistan. Azad (Free) Kashmir on Pakistan's side is equally disturbed and ruled with a hard hand.

Solutions are feasible: (1) ceding the territory in whole to one party or the other; (2) agreement on the *status quo;* (3) repartitioning by agreement; (4) partition plus a plebiscite in the Vale of Kashmir; (5) condominium status, supported by India and Pakistan; (6) independence; or variations on these themes. But solutions have been barred to date because India sees in Kashmir not only an important link to its national security line and its economy, but also a majority-Muslim area that tends to justify India's secular political philosophy; Pakistan, in turn, sees the security advantages of Kashmir, plus a majority-Muslim area of some economic value contiguous to Pakistan that should, under the principles of partition, have come to Islamic Pakistan. Security, political, and economic issues here intertwine with religious and prestige considerations: a deadly combination. Only initiative from India can resolve the deadlock, since India controls the richest, largest, most populous core of the territory. Such initiative has not been forthcoming. This reluctance to move undoubtedly has reduced the effectiveness of India's general policies on world affairs. In fairness it should be said that India's reluctance to take initiative in part stems from the inability or unwillingness exhibited by many world powers to try to understand the enormous complexities of the case, and to comprehend the position of India. The basically communal argument of Pakistan has convinced the majority of impatient ears, since that case is much easier to present. Only one willing to dig deeply will ever understand the Indian case. And even when one understands, it is possible to disagree with India's solutions.

China. India was one of the first to recognize the People's Republic of China in 1949, and has worked for its recognition elsewhere and for Communist China's membership in the United Nations from the start. Under the Ambassadorship of K. M. Panikkar, India developed a policy of friendship towards the "New China" based upon a large nation's shrewd respect for a more powerful neighbor. India's was a strategy of functional and cultural involvement. Rather than allow China to become isolated and thus be ever more closely tied to power interrelationships with the Soviet Union, India hoped to see a China that would be at least as Asian as it was Communist; the more of the former the better.

In the process of building these relationships, India withstood many an affront: first over Tibet; then over trading rights; and finally over Indian territory itself.

Since at least 1957, China has laid positive claim to over 50,000 square miles of India-claimed lands in Ladakh, in the North East Frontier Agency, and elsewhere along the Himalayan frontier. China moreover actually has occupied some of this territory, including large segments in the Ladakhi sector of Kashmir. When these maneuvers were announced in Parliament in 1959, an uproar unprecedented on matters of foreign affairs, other than disputes involving Pakistan, arose in India. The fact that Parliament was kept in the dark for so long on a matter of national concern also led to an unusually heated and extended debate, the end of which is not yet in sight.

Others.   Beyond Pakistan and China, India's interests intersect with the safeguarding of Nepal, Sikkim, and Bhutan as integral parts of the subcontinental security line. To the northwest, Afghanistan is given special attention because of the proximity of the Soviet Union; to the south with Ceylon, and to the southeast with Burma, Malaya, Singapore, and Indonesia, relations are mutually supportive of nonalignment and "neutralist" policies. Members of SEATO are less cordially viewed, and Taiwan, officially, is ignored. Japan increasingly is of special interest to India as more detailed knowledge of Japan is accumulated, but the cultures clash, as do policies in international relations. The Philippines remains a curiosity and largely a mystery to most of India, even to those well informed.

India's relations with the Soviet Union and with the United States have been cordial and testy alternately, in both cases in terms of "Cold War" pressures that have tended to make India suspicious of any proposal coming from either side. Recently, as economic aid and technical assistance have predominated over ideological wooing, and as evidence of the United States' massive aid and general goodwill has shown it to be genuine, some shift of the balance to the United States' favor has occurred. The main lines of India's relations with the Soviet Union and the United States are well-known to newspaper readers, and will not be repeated here.

The Commonwealth of Nations is another of India's links around the world. Especially as an easy means for maintaining close relations with Great Britain, but also as a comfortable and noncommittal way for keeping informed on the affairs of old Commonwealth friends and new members from Asia and Africa, the Commonwealth is useful to India. At first the sterling balances held in London to India's credit, and the consultative facilities in London, were the most valuable assets of Commonwealth membership. Now India, rapidly taking on the status of an old constituent, is in a position to lead in discussions and to use the Commonwealth as a closed forum in the interests of the Indian outlook on world affairs. But one should not overemphasize the Commonwealth tie. For India, the Commonwealth is *a* connection, not *the* connection above all others. The Commonwealth nevertheless does provide exclusive and club-like contacts with Canada, with New Zealand and Australia, and with the many members in Afro-Asia.

Relations with western Europe, especially France, West Germany, Italy, and the Scandinavian countries, tend to be commercial and cultural, except as colonial issues arise. Latin America, to all but a few in India, constitutes a distant mystery of no great significance, except when votes are taken in the United Nations.

Panch Shila

Panch Shila, or the "Five Principles" of India's diplomacy, were first incorporated in the "Communiqué on the Trade and Intercourse Agreement between India and China" issued in Peking on April 29, 1954.[4] This communiqué put forward the principles as follows:

Both parties agreed to negotiate on the basis of the principles of [1] mutual respect for each other's territorial integrity and sovereignty, [2] mutual non-aggression, [3] mutual non-interference in each other's internal affairs, [4] equality and mutual benefit, and [5] peaceful co-existence.

Since the signing of the 1954 agreement, India has signed similar agreements with a good many of the countries of Asia. The hope was that promises to respect one another's territory and national aspirations would tend to strengthen over time the likelihood of peace. The outbreak of conflicts between "Panch Shila" nations, especially when the scope is broadened to include the seven-point adaptation affirmed during the Bandung Conference in

[4] The full text will be found in *Foreign Policy of India: Texts of Documents, 1947–1958* (New Delhi: Lok Sabha Secretariat, 1958), pp. 87–93.

1955, were disappointing to India. The demand of China in 1957 for substantial segments of territory occupied and claimed by India seems to have dealt a devastating blow to the Panch Shila ideal. One hears little of it today.

International trade and economic aid

India's economic problem is to raise the living standards of India substantially in as short a time as possible, with limited material and excessive human resources. Customs, tariff, taxation, and import-export rules are closely calculated to encourage industrialization at home, to discourage or prohibit imports, to extend the exploitation of natural resources domestically and to decrease their import, and at the same time to increase exports of all kinds. Here a favorable balance of trade is the object.

But the fact is that India can go only so far in "bootstrap" economic growth. Savings are relatively modest, and in any event are inadequate for needed investment; goods and services in large amounts are needed from hard currency countries, especially the United States; food is needed to fill needs in the transition to self-sufficiency. For the Third Five Year Plan (1961–1966), for example, six billion dollars in external aid is needed to meet the minimum goals.

Thus India's international economic policy is directed not so much at the regulation of home markets, in and out, as at the gaining of economic aid from abroad in massive amounts.

The United States has been the greatest subscriber to India's economic needs since 1947. Aid, as loans and grants, so far exceeds four billion dollars, whereas the Soviet Union has loaned less than a quarter of this amount. The United States is expected to guarantee more in the future, as is the Soviet Union. In addition, Great Britain, Canada, West Germany, and Japan, to name a few, have contributed a good deal as well.[5]

SUMMARY

The foreign policy of India has developed three main themes which interrelate:

1. The policy of non-alignment, to obviate involvement in military or political commitments, thus permitting the deciding of each issue on its intrinsic merits as it arises.

2. The policy of positive neutralism, as a technique for unrestricted cultural and personal interrelationships on a global basis, thus opening opportunities for extending the "area of peace" by all legitimate means.

3. The policy of national self-interest, to assure the security of the country and the social and economic well-being of its citizens.

Non-alignment provides the independent status that in turn makes positive neutralism possible; the first two policies seem best calculated, in an interdependent world, to satisfy the national goals of the third and crucial policy.

The political aspirations of India rest firmly upon the democratic base of Parliamentary and party government, on adult suffrage, on the rule of law, on responsible administrative and military services, and on the posi-

[5] For an analytical treatment of economic aid to India and to the rest of Southern Asia, see Charles Wolf, Jr., *Foreign Aid: Theory and Practice in Southern Asia* (Princeton: Princeton University Press, 1960).

tive search for individual liberty and national freedom. India's foreign policy, as its leaders see it, is devised to serve these ideals of national life.

SELECTED BIBLIOGRAPHY

Alexandrowicz, C. H., ed., *The Indian Yearbook of International Affairs* (Madras: University of Madras, 1952 and annually thereafter).

Berkes, Ross N. and Mohinder S. Bedi, *The Diplomacy of India* (Stanford: Stanford University Press, 1958).

Bowles, Chester, *Ambassador's Report* (New York: Harper & Brothers, 1954).

Brecher, Michael, *Nehru: A Political Biography* (New York: Oxford University Press, 1959).

———, *The Struggle for Kashmir* (New York: Oxford University Press, 1953).

India Quarterly, published from New Delhi by the Indian Council of World Affairs.

Jennings, Sir William Ivor, *The Commonwealth in Asia* (New York: Oxford University Press, 1951).

Karunakaran, K. P., *India in World Affairs: 1947–1950* (Calcutta: Oxford University Press, 1952).

———, *India in World Affairs: 1950–1953* (Calcutta: Oxford University Press, 1958).

Korbel, Joseph, *Danger in Kashmir* (Princeton: Princeton University Press, 1954).

Kundra, J. C., *Indian Foreign Policy, 1947–1954* (Bombay: Vora and Co., 1955).

Levi, Werner, *Free India in Asia* (Minneapolis: University of Minnesota Press, 1952).

Nehru, Jawaharlal, *Independence and After: A Collection of Speeches, 1946–1949* (New York: The John Day Company, Inc., 1950).

———, *Speeches: 1949–1953* [and annual volumes after 1953] (New Delhi: Government of India, 1954; and annual volumes after 1953).

Poplai, S. L., ed., *India: 1947–1950*, 2 vols., Vol. I. Internal Affairs [including Kashmir] and Vol. II. External Affairs (Bombay: Oxford University Press, 1959; issued under the auspices of the Indian Council of World Affairs).

Talbot, Phillips and S. L. Poplai, *India and America: A Story of Their Relations* (New York: Harper & Brothers, 1958 published for the Council on Foreign Relations).

Wolf, Charles, Jr., *Foreign Aid: Theory and Practice in Southern Asia* (Princeton: Princeton University Press, 1960).

10

Foreign Policy of Mexico

Two fundamental forces have come to be central to both the domestic politics and the foreign policy of Mexico during the twentieth century. The first of these forces is the Mexican Revolution, which began in 1910. The second is the rapid, even spectacular, economic development which has been afoot in the country since World War II. Together these forces have given course and character not only to the country's internal politics, but also to its relations with the rest of Latin America, with Western Europe, with the Union of Soviet Socialist Republics, and with the United States.

GEORGE

I.

BLANKSTEN

THE REVOLUTION

In 1910 Francisco Ignacio Madero, a curiously quixotic lawyer, launched a rebellion that in the following year brought down the government of General Porfirio Díaz, who had ruled Mexico since the 1870's. Madero's action inaugurated a generation of turmoil and reconstruction. This Revolution— the celebrated "wind that swept Mexico"—has flavored most things Mexican during the twentieth century.

So-called "revolutions" are, of course, frequent in Latin America. The bulk of these, however, are not genuine revolutions in the sense of bringing with them profound and thoroughgoing changes in the social and political structure of the states affected. But the Mexican Revolution stands apart. It has been as genuine a revolution as that which struck France in the eighteenth century or Russia less than a decade after the fall of Díaz. Although its initial goals were more limited, the Mexican Revolution came to constitute a frontal attack upon fundamental problems—such as land tenure, the temporal position of the Roman Catholic Church, the situation of the lower classes, and foreign economic influence in the country— that have historically troubled not only Mexico but also much of the rest of Latin America.

The Revolution's approach to the land question finds its antecedents in a century-long history of domestic struggle in Mexico. The Spaniards who conquered and colonized the country brought with them the quasi-feudal pattern of land tenure they had known at home. Throughout most of Mexico's subsequent history the country's economy was characterized by huge landed estates held by a small landowning aristocracy, with much of the rural population living and working on these estates in conditions reminiscent of the serfdom of medieval Europe. Some attempts at land reform had been made in Mexico before the Revolution, to be sure; the most notable of these occurred in the middle of the nineteenth century, when the "War of Reform" brought the remarkable Benito Juárez to power. With the passing of Juárez and the "War of Reform," however, the small landowning aristocracy resumed its role in the pattern of land tenure. Indeed, it has been estimated that in 1910, on the eve of the Revolution, about 1 per cent of the population owned approximately 70 per cent of the land surface of Mexico.

The Revolution was committed to, and has achieved, a basic change in the pattern of land ownership. Dedicated to the proposition that the large landed estates must be reduced, the Revolution has introduced two other land systems which are held to be mutually compatible. The first of these is designed to create a large group of individual owners of small parcels of land. The second is the *ejido* system, intended to deliver collectively owned lands to rural communities. Particularly in the early years of the Revolution, Mexico sought a solution to its historic land problem through these devices, notably the *ejido* system.

The place of the Roman Catholic Church in the temporal life of Mexico was a second historic problem challenged by the Revolution. Traditionally, the Church had played a dominant role in the affairs of this overwhelmingly Catholic country. The Church had at first brought formal education to Mexico, then stayed to monopolize its administration. Closely associated with the state in colonial days, the Church remained an arm of government after the achievement of Mexico's national independence in the 1820's. Against an historic background of frequent unions of Church and State, the Church had come, in the years before the Revolution, to be one of the major landowners in Mexico.

In the wake of the Revolution, the Church has been disestablished and placed in a weakened position. It has been deprived of much of the land it had acquired before the Revolution, and Church officials are forbidden to vote or to present themselves as candidates for public office. In short, much of the Revolution is distinctively anticlerical in nature.

The Revolution has, further, sought a redefinition of the place of the lower classes in the national life of the country. Historically, Mexico's class system has been made up of three rigidly separated groups, with interaction among them being held to a minimum. The small upper class, variously known as creoles or "whites," had long dominated the political and economic life of the nation, excluding from effective participation the two lower groups, the *mestizos* and the Indians. The Revolution has sought a new national role for these classes. A part of the answer is to be found in the *ejido* system, but the land issue is only a part of Revolutionary Mexico's handling of the Indians and *mestizos*. Illiteracy is fought by the Revolution, which has likewise endeavored to preside over a somewhat engineered *renaissance* of Indian culture. An attempt has been made with some success to destroy the older class system with a view to multiplying the opportunities available to the lower classes of the country.

And then there was the "foreign imperialist," another historic problem for Mexico. Particularly during the regime of Porfirio Díaz (1876–1911), foreign capital, especially from the United States, was encouraged to enter Mexico on a large scale and to develop and exploit its natural resources. Oil was the most important and the most dramatic of the sectors of Mexico's economy thus affected, but there were others, notably transportation, communication, and electrical energy. In rejecting the Díaz approach to foreign capital, the Revolution has endeavored to reduce outside economic influences in the affairs of Mexico. Restrictions and limitations have been placed upon the ability of foreigners to acquire most types of property in the country, with United States interests being primarily affected by these measures. Expropriation and other steps of the Revolution have deprived foreigners of their holdings in such areas of the Mexican economy as oil, land, and transportation. Foreigners attempting to do business in Revolutionary Mexico frequently find themselves discriminated against by the pattern of the laws.

Students of the process of revolution have advanced the hypothesis that all major revolutions experience a common set of steps or stages. Attempts to test this hypothesis have thus far been largely restricted to research on the French and Russian revolutions.[1] The terminology of the French Revolution has given a name—"Thermidor" —to what is held to be one of the later stages experienced by all profound revolutions.

Insofar as this hypothesis is valid, the Mexican Revolution may well have entered the stage of Thermidor in the early 1940's. Thermidor is the time of the cooling off of revolutionary ardor, the stage in which the ideals of the revolution become impure, the phase in which its ideology accepts compromises. In this sense, the last "pure" President of Revolutionary Mexico was Lazaro Cárdenas (1934– 1940). During subsequent administrations the Revolution has tended to cool down, its ardor has subsided, its programs have tapered off, its leaders have become more willing to make compromises of its principles. With Revolutionary Mexico at the stage of Thermidor, land reform has lost its fire and *ejidal* programs are pushed less vigorously than previously; the Revolutionary party's presidential candidate [2] can be elected after telling an anticlerical Revolution that he is a Catholic; it becomes easier to look down one's nose at the Indian once more; and a man who collaborated with the foreign invaders, the "Yankees," may head the Revolutionary party and be elected President.[3]

Thermidor is, no doubt, a subtle and sensitive proposition. It means a species of compromise on the principles of the Revolution, but it does not signify their rejection. Mexico in Thermidor has compromised on, but cannot reject, the Revolution. And it is this Revolution—Thermidor and all—that underlies contemporary Mexican national life. This condition lies central to Mexico's foreign policy, whether the

---

[1] See Crane Brinton, *The Anatomy of Revolution* (New York: W. W. Norton, 1938), and Lyford P. Edwards, *The Natural History of Revolution* (Chicago: University of Chicago Press, 1927).

[2] Miguel Alemán, who was President of Mexico from 1946 to 1952.

[3] President Adolfo Ruíz Cortines (1952– 58) aided the United States forces during their occupation of Vera Cruz.

issue at hand be relations with other Latin-American states, with western Europe, with the Soviet Union, or with the United States.

ECONOMIC DEVELOPMENT

Moreover, Thermidor has coincided with a remarkable stage in the economic development of Mexico. Economists are by no means in agreement on the question of whether the economic growth of underdeveloped areas can validly be charted in terms of steps and stages. Among those who believe such a formulation to be possible is W. W. Rostow, who has traced at least five stages in the economic growth of a given society. These are the traditional stage, the period of preconditions, the "take-off," the stage of self-sustained growth, and the period of the mature economy.[4]

Since the late 1940's, Mexico's economic growth has been in the stage referred to as "take-off." This is the phase in which economic change is particularly rapid. With the coming of "take-off," change appears to be irresistible. Indeed, change at this point seems to be the chief characteristic and the main preoccupation of the society. The "take-off" has been defined as "the interval during which the rate of investment increases in such a way that the real output *per capita* rises and this initial increase carries with it radical changes in production techniques and the disposition of income flows which perpetuate the new scale of investment and perpetuate thereby the rising trend in *per capita* output." [5] This is not the place for an examination of the technical economics of "take-off." Suffice it to say that it is a phase, largely economic in character, of decisive transformation, and that change is more rapid during this stage than during other phases of economic growth. Mid-twentieth-century Mexico is in "take-off."

It is a curious characteristic of the politics of "take-off" that countries in this stage tend to have what have been called "dominant non-dictatorial" political parties. These, frequently comprehensive and nationalist, resemble one-party systems in that the dominant parties are not seriously challenged by rival political organizations, but differ from dictatorial systems in that other political parties may and do exist legally in addition to the "dominant" ones.[6] Mexico's governing Party of Revolutionary Institutions (PRI [7]), formed in the 1920's, is such a "dominant non-dictatorial" party. Although other Mexican parties exist, only the PRI wins most elections and controls the overwhelming majority of the officials of the executive, and of the members of the legislative branches of the country's national government.

The "dominant non-dictatorial" party is, of course, a governing elite. Conventional elite analysis typically holds that governing groups normally

---

[4] W. W. Rostow's leading writings on these stages are *The Process of Economic Growth* (London: Oxford University Press, 1953); "Trends in the Allocation of Resources in Secular Growth," in Léon H. Dupriez (ed.), *Economic Progress* (Louvain: Institut de Recherches Economiques et Sociales, 1955); "The Take-off into Self-Sustained Growth," *The Economic Journal* (March, 1956), pp. 25–48; and *The Stages of Economic Growth* (New York: Cambridge University Press, 1960).

[5] Rostow, "The Take-off into Self-Sustained Growth," p. 25.

[6] See G. A. Almond and J. S. Coleman (eds.), *The Politics of the Developing Areas* (Princeton: Princeton University Press, 1960), pp. 40–41, 114, 188, 286–94, 295, 397–98, 479–81.

[7] After the initial letters of *Partido Revolucionario Institucional*. The literal translation of this is "Institutional Revolutionary Party," but the freer rendition used in the above text is more meaningful in English.

resist change likely to displace them from their ruling positions. Yet the controlling elite of "take-off" is dedicated to change and encourages it. The clear and sometimes passionate devotion of the PRI leadership to change is inescapable. The traditional conception of a ruling elite struggling to preserve the status quo is curiously irrelevant to the governing groups of Revolutionary Mexico. Born of revolution, the PRI in Thermidor remains committed to change. Deeply and even intolerantly devoted to economic development and political modernization, the PRI is dedicated to an impressive drive toward the industrialization of Mexico.[8] Thus oriented, this "dominant non-dictatorial" party has come to represent those political groups which gain in strength as the country's economic development proceeds. Especially important among these interest groups are the Confederation of Mexican Workers (CTM[9]), the urbanized "middle sectors"—identified as "politically ambitious middle groups" active in commerce and developing industry [10]—and other newly emerging industrializing and entrepreneurial groups. Revolutionary Mexico thus remains committed to change, but in Thermidor this commitment has acquired a heavy stake in sufficiently orderly change to promote Mexico's continued rapid economic development.

ORGANIZATION FOR THE CONDUCT OF FOREIGN AFFAIRS

In examining the institutional context in which Mexican foreign policy is

conducted it should be noted that, as in the cases of most of the other countries of Latin America, the constitutional system of Mexico has been strongly influenced by that of the United States. Many of the arrangements, agencies, and practices of her northern neighbor have their counterparts in the Mexican system.

The national history of Mexico is characterized by, among other things, frequent periods of domestic turbulence and political instability. Constitutions are occasionally among the casualties of these disturbances. Mexico's present Revolutionary Constitution of 1917 is a product of the Revolution. Thus, as compared with that of the United States, the Mexican Constitution is of quite recent vintage. Compared, however, with the basic laws of the other Latin-American states, where political instability is also a severe problem, the Mexican document enjoys considerable seniority. Of those 19 other countries, only Argentina and Colombia currently maintain constitutions antedating Mexico's.

Like most of its predecessors, the Revolutionary Constitution of 1917 provides for a presidential system somewhat resembling that of its United States model, characterized by a separation of powers on the national level among executive, legislative, and judicial branches of government.[11] The chief responsibility for the conduct of Mexican foreign affairs is the executive's under the Constitution; the legislative branch plays a more limited role in this field, while the international function of the Mexican judiciary is quite small.

The President of Mexico, who is elected for a six-year term, is normally the most powerful single individual in

[8] See Robert E. Scott, *Mexican Government in Transition* (Urbana: University of Illinois, 1959).
[9] After the initial letters of *Confederación de Trabajadores Mexicanos.*
[10] John J. Johnson, *Political Change in Latin America: The Emergence of the Middle Sectors* (Stanford: Stanford University Press, 1958), p. vii and *passim.*

[11] Mexico has twice—once in 1822–23 and again in 1864–67—experimented with monarchy. Both episodes are generally considered to have been failures.

the determination of the country's foreign policy. Two chief considerations —one constitutional and the other political—underlie this condition. Constitutionally, the major powers relating to foreign affairs are the President's. He is responsible for the country's diplomatic negotiations with other states, and he is empowered to suspend the Constitution in the event of invasion. He is authorized to banish from Mexico, without previous trial, any foreign nationals whose presence he considers dangerous to the country. The President appoints his Secretary of Foreign Affairs and all members of Mexico's diplomatic and consular corps. Further, the President is Commander in Chief of the nation's armed services, and appoints their higher-ranking officers.

Politically, the President is usually a stronger figure than even these constitutional provisions suggest. The Mexican political tradition has historically involved a strong executive, and many areas of national life have long been conditioned to seek his favor and do his bidding. The country's history is replete with instances of dictatorship; Mexicans have become accustomed to expect their presidents to be strong men. Further—and this is also true elsewhere in Latin America —militarism has long been a key feature of Mexican political life. The armed services are among the more powerful political groups in the country, and—with only four exceptions [12]—all of Mexico's presidents have been army officers who found their way to office through their influence in, or over, the military. Organizational behavior in the Mexican executive branch frequently resembles military command patterns despite the constitutional proposition

[12] Francisco Ignacio Madero (1911–13); Miguel Alemán (1946–52); Adolfo Ruíz Cortines (1952–1958), and Adolfo López Mateos (1958–   ).

that government is theoretically a civilian function.

Some ramifications of this are obvious. Thus, although the Mexican resembles the United States constitutional stipulation that the President is Commander in Chief of the armed forces, in Mexico this is normally much more literally and directly true than in the case of the northern republic. Again, the Mexican President's power to appoint the higher-ranking officers of the military is more than a constitutional formality. Finally, any discussion of the power of the President of Mexico is unrealistic if it fails to take the PRI into account. This governing party wins most elections and controls the overwhelming majority of the officials of the executive, and of the members of the legislative branches of the national government of Mexico. The role of the President in the leadership of the PRI varies somewhat from administration to administration. Sometimes he is recognized as the leader of the party. When this is not the case, he is at least a part of the PRI leadership. Thus the President of Mexico, for both constitutional and political reasons, emerges as a powerful political figure; foreign relations is but one of the areas of public affairs reflecting this condition.

Again resembling the prototype in the United States, the Mexican President is assisted by a Cabinet. In the southern republic this institution is composed of eleven members, all of whom are appointed by the President to administer executive departments, called "secretariats" in Mexico. One of these is the Secretariat of Foreign Affairs, the chief of which acts as the President's agent and lieutenant in the conduct of foreign policy. The Secretary of Foreign Affairs directs the secretariat, administers the country's diplomatic and consular corps, and advises the President on international matters.

Normally, the Secretary of Foreign Affairs is a major political figure in his own right. In terms of the pattern of domestic Mexican politics, two—Foreign Affairs and Interior—of the eleven Cabinet posts are normally more crucial than the rest. These two secretaries are frequently influential in the PRI leadership. Often, to be Secretary of Interior or Foreign Affairs is to be groomed for the presidency of the republic. Thus the Secretary of Foreign Affairs is often popularly regarded—albeit sometimes inaccurately—as the next President of Mexico.

Politically, then, the executive branch—particularly the President and his Secretary of Foreign Affairs—is even more critically important in the determination of Mexican foreign policy than the provisions of the Revolutionary Constitution of 1917 would suggest. This is in sharp contrast to the situation in the case of the legislative branch. Here the political pattern operates to reduce the foreign-relations powers of Congress to a measurably lesser role than a literal reading of the Constitution would seem to indicate.

The Mexican Congress—here again the constitutional influence of the United States is striking—is bicameral. The lower house is known as the Chamber of Deputies, and the second chamber as the Senate. The major constitutional functions of Congress relating to international affairs appear on their face to be impressive. The Mexican national legislature, for example, has the sole authority to declare war. Also, the power to admit new states and territories to the Mexican union is the legislators'. Further, Congress is empowered to create and maintain the armed forces, to establish rules for the regulation of the diplomatic and consular corps, to contribute to the definition of the legal status of foreign nationals in the country, and to establish the terms under which the President may negotiate loans on the credit of Mexico. Congress, of course, enacts tariff legislation. In addition, the Senate ratifies treaties and approves presidential appointments of the Secretary of Foreign Affairs and of members of the diplomatic and consular corps. Senatorial authorization is required to send Mexican troops outside the country, and the Senate's approval is also a prerequisite to the peaceful passage of foreign troops through Mexican territory. Foreign-relations and military-affairs committees are maintained by both the Chamber of Deputies and the Senate.

If it be assumed that the above, or some of them, might be crucial powers in certain types of international situations in which Mexico might become involved, a question still remains as to the extent to which Congress actually possesses independent discretion in the exercise of its constitutional functions. This question leads down two paths. The first is that of tradition: Mexican legislatures have historically been weak vis-à-vis the executive and the military. The second path stops at the door of the PRI. The two houses of Congress have a combined membership of 215 Deputies and Senators. Situations, of course, differ from election to election, but it rarely happens that fewer than 200 of the national legislators are members of the PRI. Little is as yet known by political scientists of the nature of party discipline within the PRI. It can be said, however, that since the establishment of the party in 1929 there have been no major instances of legislative revolt against the PRI leadership.

A further word may be in order with respect to the direction of the party. Founded by President Plutarco

Elías Calles, the PRI [13] in its early years was essentially under the one-man leadership of the President of the Republic. This was especially true during the administrations of Presidents Calles (1924–1928) and Lázaro Cárdenas (1934–1940). Although the Revolutionary Constitution of 1917 prohibits the re-election of the President, both Calles and Cárdenas remained politically powerful after the expiration of their terms of office. In a real sense, ex-President Calles dominated the government party until 1934. Cárdenas was the central leader of the party not only during his presidency but also for some years after. Although he never became the powerful "boss" that Calles had been, Cárdenas remained a strong figure for more than 20 years after relinquishing the presidency.

Thus, none of the presidents since Cárdenas [14] have held as much power in the PRI as had he or Calles; indeed, post-1940 Mexican presidents have been characterized as relatively weak executives. During this period, basic power within the PRI has moved progressively into the hands of a central executive committee, composed in significant part of military men, some of whom had seen action in the Revolution. Ex-President Cárdenas sits with this group as a species of elder statesman. His party role since 1940 is somewhat reminiscent of, but not so powerful as, that played by Ex-President Calles from 1928 to 1934. Where Calles had been an active policy-deter-mining leader, Cárdenas has preferred to perform more of what might be characterized as a veto function. PRI policies are initiated and, for the most part, decided by the central committee on a collective basis. Cárdenas is frequently consulted by the committee, which rarely makes a decision it believes him to oppose. Thus the role of Cárdenas is the largely passive one of veto-wielder rather than that of active leader, as in the earlier case of Calles.

In view of the traditionally strong place of the executive in Mexican political life, and the fact that it was that branch of government around which the PRI was originally formed and through which men like Calles and Cárdenas rose to power, the PRI has tended to focus its attention upon the presidency. Thus, whether or not the President at any given time is an influential PRI leader, party control of his office is a "must" in Mexican politics. With the executive and the legislative branches of government sensitively responsive to the PRI, decision-making in many fields, including foreign policy, is concentrated upon the presidency, with the Congress exercising little independent discretion, constitutional permission to the contrary notwithstanding.

The Mexican judiciary has at best a minor part in foreign policy. This is, for the most part, jurisdiction over those cases in international law which happen, for one reason or another, to fall to Mexican courts. Where this occurs, it is worth bearing in mind that Mexico is a Roman or code-law country, where the chief function of the judiciary is the application of relatively comprehensive legal codes laid down by the legislature.

Thus, the structure and operation of the Mexican government is such that the major policy-determining powers in the field of foreign affairs lie with

[13] Initially known as the National Revolutionary Party (PNR), the name was changed to Mexican Revolutionary Party (PRM) before the PRI acquired its present designation in a party reorganization of 1945.

[14] The subsequent Presidents have been Manuel Avila Camacho (1940–46), Miguel Alemán (1946–52), Adolf Ruíz Cortines (1952–58), and Adolfo López Mateos since 1958.

the executive branch, the primary responsibility falling upon the President and his Secretary of Foreign Affairs, provided normally that their actions have the approval of the leadership of the PRI.

MEXICO AND LATIN AMERICA

A cardinal feature of contemporary Mexico's foreign policy is the circumstance that in a real sense the country functions as a diplomatic leader in a large part of the Latin-American community. Five major considerations are involved in Mexico's position as an inter-American diplomatic leader, and each of these is worth exploring.

First, there is the ever-present Revolution, which has markedly increased Mexico's stature in the Latin-American community. Emilio Portes Gil, who was President of Mexico in the late 1920's, and subsequently Foreign Minister in the cabinet of President Cárdenas, has described the Revolution as a phenomenon that "Mexico regards with pride, because she holds that [it has] been made, not for her own benefit, but also for that of the interests dearest to humanity." [15] This is no idle nationalistic boast. The fundamental problems with which the Revolution grappled were not peculiarly Mexican problems. All of them—land tenure, Church-State relations, class privilege, and the riddle of the "foreign imperialist"—recur in one form or another, and in various combinations, throughout the Western Hemisphere. The belief is widespread in the Americas that the Mexican Revolution provides a formula for the solution of basic problems common to most of Latin America, and that Mexico points

the way. Through revolution, Mexico has acquired a distinguished position of leadership in the hemisphere, and this is recognized in an ever-increasing number of American nations. This writer was impressed, when he was in Ecuador, with attitudes in that country toward the Mexican venture. When Ecuador inaugurated a new President, the various governments with which Quito maintained diplomatic relations sent special delegations to attend the inauguration ceremonies. When the Mexican delegation, headed by Portes Gil, arrived, the Ecuadoran press assiduously interviewed the Mexicans on the progress of the Revolution. These interviews were given such publicity that they displaced even the inauguration of a new President of Ecuador from the front pages of the Ecuadoran press!

A second factor in Mexico's leadership in Latin America is the country's size. It is not the custom in the United States to regard Mexico as a significantly large country, but these matters are, of course, relative. "When Mexico is statistically assessed relative to the United States it is overwhelmed, as are its individual companions in the Latin-American community," Howard Cline has pointed out. "But when measured against other Latin-American countries and areas in the group as a whole, the outcome is quite different.[16] With a population of over 30,000,000 Mexico stands among the major states of Latin America. In the area only Brazil is more populous than Mexico; and, with the exception of Argentina, the remaining states of Latin America have individual populations under 12,-000,000.

A third consideration is Mexico's geographical proximity to the United

[15] Quoted in José Angel Ceniceros, *Mexico's Attitude in Its International Relations* (Mexico City: Ministry of Foreign Relations, 1935), p. 11.

[16] Howard F. Cline, *The United States and Mexico* (Cambridge, Mass.: Harvard University Press, 1953), p. 7.

States. "Poor Mexico!" Porfirio Díaz is said to have exclaimed. "So far from God—so close to the United States!" In the Latin-American world, Mexico is frequently viewed as a dyke obstructing various kinds of overflow from the United States. Mexico has suffered many difficulties arising from her northern neighbor and has, for the most part, withstood these hardships with what Latin Americans generally regard as dignity. Thus, in a sense, Mexico defends Latin America's northwestern frontier, often regarded as the Hispanic-American community's most vulnerable extremity.

Fourthly, Mexico's spectacular rate of economic development since World War II has been widely admired throughout Latin America, where the desire to emulate this rapid economic growth is widespread. Although Mexico's standard of living, computed on the basis of *per capita* gross national product, is only the tenth highest in Latin America, the speed of Mexico's economic development and its "takeoff" are surpassed in Latin America only by Brazil. The desire for a rapid rise in standards of living is widespread throughout the Western Hemisphere, and Mexico's economic growth, like her Revolution, is seen in many American republics as a goal toward which they might likewise aspire.[17]

Finally, consider the situations of Mexico's rivals for the diplomatic leadership of Latin America. These are, for most purposes, Brazil and Argentina. Neither can stand as an unchallenged standard-bearer for the area. Portuguese rather than Spanish in its European origins, Brazil is a part of Latin America, to be sure, but it is not a member of the *Hispanic*-American community. In the United States, it may be difficult to see why this should make much difference. Nevertheless, Portugal and Brazil are indeed foreign to many of the concerns of the Hispanic world. Since the early years of the eighteenth century, for example, Portugal has been involved diplomatically in the British orbit; Portuguese and Brazilians view international problems from a different historical background than do Spaniards and Hispanic Americans. During centuries of international politics, Portugal was often aligned with Britain against Spain. Contemporary Brazil, with a population of over 50,-000,000 and an area larger even that that of the United States, is a species of subcontinent in itself. Its life, its culture, its historical and diplomatic orientations differ from those of Spanish America. These perhaps subtle but nevertheless real considerations render Brazilians outsiders to a significant part of the world of which Mexicans are insiders. Argentina, with a population of over 18,000,000, was for many years a more serious bidder than Brazil. Argentina, however, has pursued a foreign policy opposed to inter-American cooperation. This policy reached its peak, and failed, during World War II. The events of the 1940's dealt severe blows to Argentina's diplomatic prestige in the Americas, and have detracted from that country's position of leadership.

Revolutionary Mexico, then, emerges as a diplomatic leader in the Latin-American community. To what uses has Mexican foreign policy put this prestigious position?

The Mexican Foreign Office is fond of describing its international policy as "traditionally peace-loving." [18] Most governments have come to advertise

[17] See George I. Blanksten, "The Aspiration for Economic Development," in *The Annals of the American Academy of Political and Social Science* (March, 1961), pp. 10–19, especially p. 11.

[18] Ceniceros, *op. cit.*, p. 29.

themselves as "peace-loving," especially since this has become a condition of membership in the United Nations. Again in the Mexican case, however, this is no idle boast. Consider the historical record. For more than a century, Mexico's dealings with the other states of Latin America have been almost uniformly peaceful. Where Mexico's foreign relations have been strained, the conflicts and difficulties have been not with other countries of Latin America but rather with the United States and also with Europe. Throughout her entire national history, Mexico has been involved in only two international wars. The first of these (1846–48) was fought against the United States; the second was World War II, with Mexico joining the anti-Axis cause in June of 1942. These were separated by almost a century in which the country suffered intervention on the part of France (1862–67) and was involved in renewed difficulties with the United States, particularly during the administrations of the "Yankee" President Woodrow Wilson, when Mexico was in the throes of the early stages of the Revolution. On the other hand, the record of Mexico's relations with the other states of Latin America has been one of virtually unbroken peace.

Stretched on a Latin-American rack, this background neatly divides Mexico's historic enemies from her friends. The enemies have been states larger and more powerful than Mexico, which has suffered invasion and intervention at their hands. The friends, on the other hand, have been the other states of Latin America, most of which—particularly Mexico's immediate neighbors—have been smaller and weaker than she. On this record, Mexico stands as a force for peace in Latin America. She has rarely threatened or attacked her neighbors, and she has uniformly

stood ready to participate in arrangements for arbitration and in other projects designed to achieve peaceful settlement of such international disputes as have arisen within the Latin-American community.

The question of whether a Latin-American "bloc" exists in international affairs is both subtle and intriguing. Some types of problems divide the states of the area among themselves; other international questions tend to draw the Latin-American countries together in a bloc or united front. In situations conducive to bloc behavior, Mexico normally participates in these coalitions, frequently taking the lead in forming them. In general, there are two types of international situations in which Mexico plays a leading role in Latin-American blocs.

The first of these involves situations in which the Latin-American governments are in general agreement among themselves as to some international objective sought by all of them. In such cases Mexico normally leads—and where she does not lead, she usually joins—the bloc in pursuit of the common cause. Two illustrations of this type of Mexican international role may be cited. The first has to do with what international lawyers refer to as the "law of local remedies." Recognition of this "law" has long been sought by the governments of Latin America in bloc fashion, and Mexico has led the bloc. Briefly, the "law of local remedies" provides that foreigners doing business or otherwise being present in a country would have the same legal rights as the nationals or citizens of that country, and, in case of difficulty, would have recourse to the same courts or other remedies as they, but no recourse to remedies not available to them. Thus, a United States citizen doing business in, say, Guatemala and in legal difficulties there, would, were this principle acted upon, have recourse only to the remedies available to Guatemalan citizens, and would be denied the intervention of the United States Department of State or other forms of diplomatic protection. Latin America, led by Mexico, has sought recognition of the "law of local remedies"; the United States has in many cases been reluctant to accept it. A second illustration of this type of bloc behavior involves the thorny question of extending diplomatic recognition to revolutionary governments in the Americas. The problem of whether or not to recognize a given regime that has come to power in Latin America by non-constitutional means is a difficult one. Latin America, led by Mexico, has sought the adoption of policies recognizing the right of revolution and permitting diplomatic relations with governments of questionable constitutional antecedents. Mexico's chief creative contribution in this field is the celebrated "Estrada Doctrine," advanced in 1930 by Foreign Minister Genaro Estrada, and supported by much of Latin America. Under this, Mexico would continue the practice of recognizing new states, but would discontinue the custom of recognizing new governments in states already recognized. Rather, Mexico's diplomatic mission in the affected state would do business with whomever the business was relevant.[19]

[19] The Estrada Doctrine, a remarkable instrument, is worth quoting in full: "Mexico does not make any announcement as to granting recognition, because she holds that this is an offensive practice which, besides wounding the sovereignty of other nations, lays them open to having their domestic affairs judged in one sense or another by other governments, which assume a *de facto* critical attitude when they decide, whether favorably or unfavorably, on the legal status of foreign regimes. Consequently, the Mexican Government confines itself to keeping or withdrawing, whenever it shall deem it ad-

The second type of international situation in which Mexico plays a leading role in Latin-American bloc behavior involves the position of the inter-American community in the creation of new patterns of relationships among the Great Powers. Thus, when the United States launched its "Good Neighbor Policy" in the 1930's, Mexico, one of the first Latin-American states to respond positively, did much to forge a bloc pattern of response to Washington's new approach. Again some years later, on the eve of World War II, Mexico took the lead in aligning the inter-American coalition in the anti-Axis camp. Later, at the Inter-American Conference on Problems of War and Peace (popularly known as the "Chapultepec Conference") held at Mexico City in 1945, Mexico, under the skilful leadership of Foreign Minister Ezequiel Padilla, performed the remarkable feat of separating the inter-American community from Argentina, which was then pursuing a pro-Axis foreign policy. A few months later at the San Francisco Conference, also held in 1945, Mexico, still under the foreign-policy leadership of Padilla, assisted in the reincorporation of Argentina in the inter-American fold and the admission of that country into the United Nations.

MEXICO AND EUROPE

The pattern of Mexico's relations with the various states of Europe is complex. For purposes of simplification, it would be well to single out only

visable, its diplomatic agents, and to continuing to accept, also when it shall deem it advisable, similar diplomatic agents accredited by such countries to Mexico, without judging, either hurriedly or *a posteriori,* the right of any foreign nations to accept, preserve, or change their governments or authorities." Quoted in Ceniceros, *op. cit.,* p. 25.

three European states, France, Spain, and the Soviet Union, and to examine Mexico's relations with them.

Mexico and France

France has long been regarded as a political and cultural leader of the Latin world, and Mexico normally falls into its orbit. French political, constitutional, and administrative ideas are aped throughout Latin America, with Mexico being no exception. Paris is looked to by Mexicans as the home of European culture and civilization, and most ideas or departures acquiring appreciable vogue in France soon find their repercussions and counterparts in Mexico, as well as elsewhere in Latin America.

The history of Franco-Mexican relations is, for the most part, a record of cordial dealings. One noteworthy exception is worth mentioning. During the Second French Empire, Napoleon III pursued the ambition of extending his holdings and influence to include Mexico. Under the pretext of forcing the collection of debts owed by Mexico, French troops landed in Mexico in the closing weeks of 1861. Mexico remained subject to the French intervention until 1867. This period marks the most strained relations that have occurred between France and Mexico. During the occupation, the French established a puppet monarchy, proclaiming Maximilian Hapsburg and his wife Carlotta Emperor and Empress of Mexico. Assuming this tottering throne in 1864, Maximilian remained in Mexico for three tragic years. The French troops were withdrawn in 1867, and the monarchy collapsed at that time. Throughout the intervention, Mexicans resisted the French and Maximilian, who was executed in 1867 by forces loyal to President Benito Juárez.

Mexico and Spain

Relations with Spain, the former mother country, have been cool and strained throughout most of Mexico's independent national existence. Difficult relations with Spain were, perhaps, to be expected in the period immediately following the achievement of Mexican independence in 1822. These, however, persisted throughout the nineteenth century. Plagued by controversy over succession to the throne at Madrid, Spain fell into the Carlist Wars in the 1830's, and civil war, instability, and near anarchy characterized Spanish political life for more than a generation. During this period Mexico exhibited little sympathy for any of the contending factions in the mother country. This remained the dominant Mexican attitude toward Spain until the closing years of the nineteenth century.

The Mexican position was altered somewhat, although not fundamentally, by the Spanish-American War. Mexicans, closely watching the controversy developing in Cuba in the 1870's, in general sympathized with the cause of the Cuban colonists against their Spanish rulers, and maintained this attitude when hostilities broke out in the island. With the entry of the United States into the fighting in 1898, Mexican bitterness toward Spain was mitigated somewhat by fear and resentment of the role of the "Colossus of the North" in the Cuban crisis.

After 1910, of course, the Revolution operated as a governing factor in defining Mexican policy toward Spain. Largely on revolutionary ideological grounds, Mexicans opposed the Primo de Rivera dictatorship which seized power in Spain in 1923 and paralleled developments in Fascist Italy until the fall of Primo de Rivera in 1930. Mexico was cheered by the abdication of

King Alfonso XIII and the establishment of the Spanish Republic in the following year.

In all of Mexico's national history, the country experienced no more cordial relations with the former mother country than was the case during the period of the Spanish Republic (1931–1936). The doctrinal bases of the Madrid Republic struck responsive ideological chords in Revolutionary Mexico, and the period is remarkable for its rebirth of cultural and political intercourse between the two countries. In that epoch, trade and communication increased, tourists and students were exchanged, and the Spanish-Mexican *rapprochement* reached an unprecedented peak.

The Spanish Civil War, breaking out in 1936, exercised a dramatically divisive effect on Latin America. Some of the countries of the Western Hemisphere hailed the rise of General Francisco Franco. Mexico, however, took a leading position among the Latin-American states supporting the Loyalist cause of the Spanish Republic. When the Republic fell before Franco's onslaughts in 1939, Mexico opened her doors to political refugees from Spain; indeed, a Spanish Republican Government-in-exile was headquartered in Mexico for many years after Franco's assumption of power at Madrid.

With the outbreak of World War II the Spanish *Falange,* under Franco, became one of the major outlets for Axis propaganda and influence reaching the Western Hemisphere. Again largely on ideological grounds stemming from the Revolution, Mexico resisted these pressures. Two Mexican political parties—the National Action Party (PAN [20]) and the National Sinarquist Union—were receptive to wartime *Falange* influences. The government of Revolutionary Mexico, then under the presidency of General Manuel Avila Camacho (1940–1946), stoutly resisted these influences; indeed, the Sinarquist party was outlawed during the war. In the years since the end of World War II, relations between Revolutionary Mexico and Franco Spain have become somewhat less strained, although remaining cool.

Mexico and the Soviet Union

Relations with the Soviet Union constitute one of the most intriguing chapters in Mexican foreign policy. Here again, the Mexican Revolution operates as a controlling consideration. More precisely, the central issue is the relationship between the Mexican and Russian revolutions. Three aspects are of high significance—the time differential between the two revolutions, the similarity in their ideological content, and the general developmental process of revolution.

Consider the time differential. The Mexican Revolution began in 1910, a full seven years before revolution came to Russia. These seven years were crucial. During that hectic period between the rise of Madero and the fall of Kerensky, the Mexican Revolution acquired its own course, character, and definition—its own identity as a major social and political movement. If anyone entertained the ambition, when the Bolsheviks came to power in Russia in the closing months of 1917, of joining the Mexican and Russian revolutions together into one unified over-all international movement, he was doomed to failure. By the end of 1917 it was too late. The Mexican Revolution, with its own course, character, and identity already defined, was

[20] After the initials of *Partido Acción Nacional.*

separate and distinct from the Russian upheaval; and separate and independent of each other the two have remained.

Nevertheless, a certain similarity between the ideological contents of the Mexican and Russian revolutions is inescapable. The similarity is largely coincidental, that is, there is little organizational relationship between them; but the similarity stands as a hard and present fact. The Mexican Revolution sought land reform, disestablishment of the Church, a change in the class structure, and the ejection of foreign capital.

So did the Russian Revolution.

Finally, there is the matter of the general process of revolution. It will be remembered that students of this process have advanced the hypothesis that all major revolutions experience a common set of steps or stages. One of these stages is variously known as the accession of the extremists, the reign of terror, the era of virtue, or the period of revolutionary dictatorship. Whatever the designation, this is the time when power is held by those revolutionists who are dedicated, often fanatically, to the social myth or the political philosophy of the revolution. They are, by their lights, rigidly honest men. They accept no compromise in the social myth, for they believe it immoral to compromise on political principles. Those who question these principles are ruthlessly dealt with; in the reign of terror the philosophical purity of the revolution cannot be attacked with impunity.

Thus the significance of the time differential between the Mexican and Russian revolutions is enhanced. In Mexico, the reign of terror began in 1913, and drew to a close in the 1930's. For a brief period the Mexican and Russian reigns of terror overlapped in time. This was the period when many observers saw similarities not only in ideological contents but also in process between the two revolutions, the period when books with titles such as *Soviet Mexico* were published in the United States. But, though the two reigns of terror overlapped briefly, they were essentially out of gear with each other, as was evidenced when Mexico entered Thermidor under Avila Camacho.

The two ships passed in the night. It was a close brush, but the essential point is that they *did* pass each other, to go in different directions. The seven years were crucial.

Perhaps because of this passing in the night, Mexicans maintained a more sympathetic interest in the progress of affairs in the Soviet Union than was to be found in most of the other states of Latin America. Mexico was among the first in the Western Hemisphere to extend diplomatic recognition to the Soviet Government. Mexicans watched Lenin come and go; and, upon his death in 1924, they witnessed the power struggle between Joseph Stalin and Leon Trotsky with a fascinated neutrality. When Stalin's triumph drove Trotsky into exile, Mexico welcomed the distinguished political refugee. He lived among the Mexicans until his assassination in 1940.

When World War II began in 1939, only four of the twenty states of Latin America maintained diplomatic relations with the Soviet Union. Mexico, of course, was one of these.[21] In the years before the war spread to the Western Hemisphere, Latin America was divided in its attitudes toward the conflict, especially after the Soviet Union joined the anti-Axis cause. Some American governments, notably that of Argentina, sympathized with

[21] The other three: Chile, Cuba, and Uruguay.

the Axis; and during the early phases of the war Mexico—under President Avila Camacho and his Foreign Minister, Ezequiel Padilla—played a leading role in aligning Latin America against the Axis. The success with which this endeavor was crowned was attested to by the fact that by the end of the war all of Latin America, including even Argentina, had declared war against the Axis, to become allies of Britain, France, the United States—and the Soviet Union.

The break between the Russians and their Western allies was in its early stages when the San Francisco conference met in April of 1945 to produce the Charter of the United Nations. As Mexico had been among the first in Latin America to enter into friendly relations with the Soviets, so—quite unexpectedly—she became, at San Francisco, one of the pioneers in the "cold war." Padilla, leading the Mexican delegation, clashed bitterly with Vyacheslav M. Molotov, who headed the Russians at San Francisco, originally on questions relating to the organization of the conference, and later on more fundamental issues. The ensuing Cold War found Mexico aligned with the West. This remained the country's position in the early years of the 1960's, although Mexico still maintained diplomatic relations with Moscow.

Mention should be made of the Mexican Communist Party, known since the late 1940's as the Popular Party. In the years since the Madero Revolution this group has played a curious role. Its influence in Mexican domestic politics has, in general, been small, especially since the administration of President Avila Camacho (1940–1946). Nevertheless, the Mexican Communists have included among their numbers such outstanding figures as Diego Rivera, the great artist,

and Vicente Lombardo Toledano, leader of the Confederation of Latin-American Workers (CTAL).[22] Perhaps more significant than its internal role in Mexico is the Popular Party's international function. Especially since the close of World War II, it has served as a point of liaison between Moscow and the Communist parties of other Latin-American countries, particularly those in Central America and the Caribbean islands. Although the evidence of this is not as complete as the careful student might wish, there is considerable indication that communications and information from Moscow have passed from the Communists of Mexico to those of neighboring states, notably Guatemala and Cuba. Since the end of World War II, meetings of the Communist leaders of these countries have on occasion been held in Mexico.

MEXICO AND THE UNITED STATES

There is no country in the international community with which Mexico has had more difficult relations than with the United States. In a sense, this was perhaps inevitable. "Mexico and the United States are constantly aware of each other's presence because they share an unfortified transcontinental boundary of 1,500 miles," it has been pointed out. "In the broadest sense, international relations are constantly occurring." [23]

Moreover, a sizeable chapter in the territorial expansion of the United States has been written at the expense of Mexico. Texas was a part of Mexico when that country achieved its independence in 1822. Under the leadership of "North Americans" who had settled there, Texas seceded from Mex-

22 After the initials of *Confederación de Trabajadores de América Latina.*
23 Cline, *op. cit.,* p. 10.

ico in 1836. The secession was bloody, and the Texan War ended with the independence of Texas recognized by Mexico, but with the precise location of the boundary between the two still in dispute. Following its annexation of Texas in 1845, the United States inherited this dispute. It was resolved through additional bloodshed. The United States won a decisive military victory in the Mexican war (1846–48), and, in the ensuing Treaty of Guadeloupe Hidalgo, relieved Mexico of approximately half its territory, constituting the later states of Arizona, California, Nevada, New Mexico, and Utah. The present frontier between the United States and Mexico was rounded out through the Gadsden Purchase of 1853, when the "Colossus of the North" acquired additional land from Mexico.

This episode has long colored Mexicans' attitudes toward the United States. The bitterness, however, was mitigated by events of the 1860's. The Civil War left the United States temporarily unable to enforce the Monroe Doctrine, and France embarked upon her military occupation of Mexico in the closing months of 1861. The French intervention revolutionized Mexican policy toward the United States. The change was best expressed by Matias Romero, Mexican Minister at Washington:

Before the Civil War commenced in the United States it appeared that they were the only enemies which Mexico had, because their ideas and usurping policy had deprived us of half our territory and were a constant menace against the integrity of what we had left. Nothing therefore was more natural than to see with pleasure a division which by a fortunate continuation of circumstances would render almost impotent against us each of the parts which remained. . . . But unfortunately the sedition from

which we expected such favorable results had hardly begun when we discovered another danger from which the power of this country had freed us and against which its present unity would be the surest guaranty. . . . We therefore find ourselves in the presence of the hard alternative of sacrificing our territory and our nationality at the hands of this country or our liberty and our independence before the despotic thrones of Europe. The second danger is immediate and more imminent; in evading the first we may count upon the future and the lessons of experience.[24]

Six figures stand out as the major architects of Mexican-United States friendship, as born in the 1860's: Romero; his chief, President Benito Juárez; Porfirio Díaz, then Juárez' key military commander; Abraham Lincoln; Andrew Johnson; and their Secretary of State, William H. Seward. Together they struggled against the French and their puppet Emperor, Maximilian I. United States assistance to the Juárez government was, of necessity, limited for the duration of the Civil War. After 1865, however, Washington gave impressive military, financial, and diplomatic aid to the Mexicans. The withdrawal of the French and the collapse of Maximilian in 1867 was a victory for Lincoln, Johnson, and Seward as much as for Juárez, Díaz, and Romero.

The "Big Stick" era of President Theodore Roosevelt (1901–09) damaged Mexican-United States relations somewhat. But a far more severe blow was dealt them by Washington's policies toward the early stages of the Mexican Revolution. After 1910, the Revolution became controlling in the

[24] Quoted in J. Fred Rippy, *Historical Evolution of Hispanic America* (New York: Appleton-Century-Crofts, 1940), pp. 492–93.

business the two states conducted with each other.

The Revolution has not only governed Mexican attitudes and policies toward the United States, but it has also exercised an impressive influence upon Washington's view of Mexico and, indeed, of revolutionary movements in general. "From its genesis to the present," Cline has said, "the Mexican Revolution has affected the United States, its attitudes toward Mexico, and toward social change in general." [25]

In the view of the Revolution, there were two terrible *gringo* villains. Both were named Wilson.

The first was Henry Lane Wilson. He was named United States Ambassador to Mexico by President William H. Taft (1909–13), and he remained at that post for some time after Woodrow Wilson assumed office at Washington.

Ambassador Wilson was in Mexico when the Revolution began. He developed a penchant for acting on his own initiative, frequently disregarding instructions from the State Department. He acquired a strong personal antipathy for Madero shortly after the fall of Díaz in 1911, and the feud between H. L. Wilson and Madero, today regarded by Mexicans as the leading hero of the Revolution, assumed the proportions of a personal vendetta. Ambassador Wilson supported the political ambitions of General Victoriano Huerta, a revolutionary rival of Madero. H. L. Wilson signed a general agreement, known as the "Pact of the Embassy," with Huerta. Subsequently in 1913, President Madero was assassinated. Most students of the affair place the primary responsibility for the murder of Madero at Huerta's door. Such satisfaction as Ambassador Wilson drew from the assassination of Madero

and the rise of Huerta was short-lived: Huerta fell in 1914.

Meanwhile, the second Wilson had arrived upon the scene. Assuming office in 1913, President Woodrow Wilson pursued an anti-Huerta policy. Following the fall of Huerta, the Mexican Revolution entered a phase of general civil war and near-anarchy which endured for almost two years, that is, until the rise of President Venustiano Carranza in 1915. Mexico's became the first of Latin-American "revolutionary" regimes to taste a new departure in Washington's recognition policy inaugurated by President Wilson. Whereas previously the United States had pursued a generally *de facto* recognition policy, accepting the right of revolution and maintaining diplomatic relations with Latin-American governments that had come to power by force, President Wilson replaced this with a *de jure* policy. Much interested in constitutionalism, Wilson was reluctant to recognize a government of questionable constitutional antecedents, and withheld recognition from regimes that had not come to power through a pattern of "constitutional legitimacy." Mexican revolutionary administrations, of course, could not meet this test; and, under President Wilson's leadership, the United States entered a period of suspended diplomatic relations with Mexico. An immediate result of this was the recall of Ambassador H. L. Wilson to Washington. Thereafter, the first Wilson did not plague Mexicans.

But the second was still with them. During the course of Mexico's general civil war and near-anarchy of 1914–1915, the Tampico area became a theater of hostilities among revolutionary factions. A number of oil installations, operated for the most part by United States companies, were located there, and the companies became fear-

25 Cline, *op. cit.,* p. 5.

ful of the safety of their property. To save the installations, the United States Navy occupied Vera Cruz in April of 1914. Thus occurred President Wilson's first "intervention" in the Mexican Revolution.

Despite his views on constitutionalism and recognition, W. Wilson was persuaded to establish diplomatic relations with the government of President Carranza (1915–20). However, this did not help the situation much, and President Wilson soon found himself feuding not only with Carranza but also with other Mexican revolutionary leaders. One of these was General Francisco ("Pancho") Villa, who had initially supported Madero and later came to be counted among Carranza's chief enemies. Villa led a guerilla army of considerable size, which warred against Carranza and, at times, against President Wilson. In March of 1916, Villa's guerillas crossed the United States border to raid the city of Columbus, New Mexico. W. Wilson, quite naturally, was incensed, and sent a detachment of the United States Army, under the command of General John J. Pershing, into Mexico on a punitive expedition. Pershing and his troops spent much of 1916 and the early months of 1917 wandering around in northern Mexico looking for Villa. Thus the second "intervention."

Then came the sensational Zimmerman Note, which, thanks to the British Government, was brilliantly timed. World War I, of course, had been in progress since 1914. Mexico remained neutral throughout the war, and in 1917 the United States, concerned with the submarine menace, was forced to choose between continuing in neutrality or entering the war against Germany and the Central Powers. The Zimmerman Note had been sent by the Germans to the Mexican government. It

had been intercepted by the British, and released by them in time to help the United States in making its decision on war or peace. In the celebrated note, Berlin offered Carranza what the German Foreign Office said it regarded as an opportunity for Mexico to escape from its difficulties with the "Colossus of the North." If Mexico were to enter the war on the side of Germany, Berlin would see to it in the peace settlement —assuming, of course, that the Central Powers would be the victors—that Mexico would regain from the United States the territory lost to it during the middle years of the nineteenth century. Carranza told the Germans that he regarded the imaginative project as inopportune; and the United States went to war. Pershing, withdrawn from Mexico, was sent to Europe to chase other villains.

The era of the two Wilsons has left its mark on the relations between Mexico and the United States. It has colored "North Americans'" views of Mexico, of revolution, and of social change; it has affected Mexicans' understanding of their northern neighbor. Nevertheless, relations between the two countries have improved measurably since the end of World War I.

The United States "Good Neighbor Policy," coinciding generally with the administration of President Franklin D. Roosevelt (1933–45), signalized a marked and probably long-lasting improvement in relations between the two countries. Mexico led among the states of Latin America in responding positively to these new and friendly overtures. This general trend toward more cordial dealings between the two countries was disturbed somewhat by the expropriation of the oil fields in Mexico. Responding primarily to the continuing process of the Revolution, the Mexican government in 1938 nationalized the oil industry, which had previously been worked by foreign companies, principally headquartered in the United States. This gave rise to renewed bitterness in some quarters in the United States. Relations with Mexico did not deteriorate over this issue as much as could have been expected in other times and in other contexts: the "North Americans" were beginning to learn to live with the Mexican Revolution, and the "Good Neighbor Policy" and a more understanding United States Ambassador in Mexico held the damaging consequences of the incident to a minimum.

This increased cordiality between the United States and Mexico was reflected by the latter's role in World War II as an ally in the anti-Axis cause. Since that period, Mexico has in general co-operated with her northern neighbor. A few minor difficulties between the two states remain, to be sure. There is, for example, the so-called "Chamizal" question. This is a small piece of land which the United States claims to be a part of El Paso, Texas, and the Mexicans claim to belong to Ciudad Juárez on the Mexican side of the frontier. Again, questions occasionally arise over matters of irrigation and flood control affecting the two countries. And then there is the problem of the so-called "Wetbacks," Mexican workers who, on a largely seasonal basis, illegally cross the border to take employment in the southwestern part of the United States. These issues are occasionally cause for friction, but in general they are minor problems in the over-all pattern of relations between the two countries. As of the dawn of the 1960's, the United States and Mexico are essentially firm friends. As the Revolution in its Thermidor phase has become more respectable in the northern republic, so the *gringos* since the "Good Neighbor Policy" have, in Mex-

ican eyes, gone a long way toward graduating from the role of threatening bully to that of understanding comrade in facing the increasingly complex and difficult problems of the international community. Each has grown, each has matured; and in maturation each not only finds the other easier to live with but also relies more heavily on mutual cooperation and friendship in resolving the remaining problems common to the two countries.

MEXICO AND INTERNATIONAL ORGANIZATION

A major point serves as the focus of contrast between Mexico's policies toward international organization and other aspects of her foreign affairs. In much of the latter, surveyed in the foregoing pages, the Revolution has been controlling during much of the twentieth century. In the case of international organization, however, Mexican policy finds its roots not so much in the Revolution as in other factors.

Like many another Latin-American state, Mexico presents what appears superficially to be a curious paradox. The record of Mexican internal politics has been one of violence, of turbulence and revolution. Disorder has been the rule rather than the exception. In international affairs, however, Mexico and other members of the inter-American community have long campaigned for order and the rule of law, have long condemned violence as an instrument of international policy.

Thus Mexico—and this was equally true before as it has been since the Revolution—has traditionally been counted among those states advocating and participating in international organization and other devices designed for the resolution of international difficulties by peaceful and orderly means. In assessing Mexico's policies in this area, a distinction should be drawn between two types of international organization—regional and universal.

The Western Hemisphere has enjoyed an impressive record of successful experience in regional international organization, a record not equalled in any other area of the world. The Second International Conference of American States, which met at Mexico City in 1901 and 1902, provided for the establishment of the Union of American Republics. This became the nucleus for the later Pan American Union, the transformation being formalized by the Fourth International Conference of American States, held at Buenos Aires, Argentina, in 1910. In the ensuing thirty-eight years, the Pan American Union functioned as a major instrument of inter-American cooperation. Through this regional international organization, cultural, economic, and political mutual understanding was promoted among the states of the Western Hemisphere.[26] By the close of World War II it could be said—thanks in appreciable measure to the Pan American Union—that regional international cooperation was more advanced among the American Republics than within any similar area of the international community. The inter-American system was again revamped by the Ninth Conference of American States, which met at Bogotá, Colombia, in 1948. Since then, the regional organization has been known as the Organization of American States, conceived primarily as the regional agent in the Western Hemisphere of the overall United Nations.

Historically, Mexico has played a central and frequently leading role in the affairs of the Union of American Republics, the Pan American Union, and the Organization of American States. Mexican policies toward the other American nations have normally been channeled through these organizations, and Mexico has supported their proposals directed toward peaceful cooperation within the hemisphere, introducing many of them herself.

A similar Mexican record is to be found in the field of global international organization. A member of the League of Nations, created at the close of World War I, Mexico contributed to the attempts of that institution to deal with world problems through the machinery of international organization. Likewise, Mexico has participated since World War II in the work of the United Nations, occasionally leading Latin-American bloc action in that organization.

Although it is true that this phase of Mexican policy antedates the Revolution, and responds not so much to it as to other factors of longer historical standing, it would be an error to conclude that the Revolution has not affected Mexico's role in international organization at all. Much of what Mexico has done in that context, and many of the policies pursued by her in the League of Nations and the United Nations have been colored by the Revolution. Thus, the effect of the Revolution could be found, for example, in Mexico's contribution to the work of the International Labor Office, affiliated at first with the League of Nations and later with the United Nations. Again, especially in the latter organization, Mexico has supported much international work designed to raise standards of living in underdeveloped areas of the world, and other programs whose objectives have been, at least in part, in conformity with the values emerging from the Revolution. However, historically considered, these values have

[26] Although repeatedly invited to join, Canada has refused to become a member of the Pan American Union or, later, of the Organization of American States.

not been so controlling in Mexico's role in international organization as in other areas of the country's foreign policy.

CONCLUSION

In summary, during much of the twentieth century the Madero Revolution has underlain, and given course and character to, many of Mexico's policies in the international field. That upheaval, combined with the country's economic growth, which reached "take-off" proportions after World War II, developed an integral relationship to Mexico's position as a diplomatic leader of Latin America, with many of the country's American neighbors believing that through revolution and orderly economic development Mexico has resolved many of the fundamental social, economic, and political problems common to most of them. These considerations have been crucial in Mexico's relations with many of the states of Europe, especially Spain and the Soviet Union. So far as the United States is concerned, the Revolution and subsequent economic growth of Mexico have significantly affected not only Mexican policy toward the northern republic, but also United States policies toward Mexico and toward revolution and social change in general. Similar forces affect Mexican policies toward, and participation in, international organization. These have given a somewhat selective coloration to the types of projects and measures Mexico has supported in the Pan American Union, the Organization of American States, the League of Nations, and the United Nations.

Two final points should be made with respect to Mexico's role in international affairs, particularly as it affects the United States. First, Mexico has been the leading Latin-American state with which Washington has had to deal. In this context, United States policies toward Mexico are basic in Washington's attitude not only toward Latin America but toward other areas of the world as well, particularly the underdeveloped regions where revolution looms as an active ingredient of the political scene. "The states of Europe and Asia within the United States' sphere of influence are going to be as touchy as the Latin-American states," the distinguished historian, Arnold J. Toynbee, has said; "and the United States is likely to handle them by a diplomatic technique that she has learned from her Latin-American experience." [27] Evidence already abounds of the tendency of the United States to apply to other areas of the world policies and techniques first tested in Latin America, particularly in Mexico.

Second, although much of the history of United States-Mexican relations has been a record of difficulty, of war and intervention, both the United States and Mexico have matured. They have not only learned to live with each other, but have also—especially since the "Good Neighbor Policy"—developed a relationship of solid and sound mutual respect and cooperation. As of the closing years of the 1950's, Mexico and the United States were genuinely firm friends. "The points of contention that might lead to serious friction have been largely eliminated in recent years. Mexico is not a major pawn in the struggle between Russia and the United States. . . . Recent United States dealings with Mexico have proved amazingly successful. In the international field we are discussing success, not failure.[28]

It is a human characteristic that success commands less attention than fail-

27 Cline, *op. cit.,* p. 6.
28 *Ibid.,* p. 1.

ure. There is no major crisis in the contemporary relations of Mexico with any state of the world. Mexican foreign policy, therefore, today rarely merits a front-page headline in the reporting of the progress of world politics. Nevertheless, success stands, at least as much as failure, as a significant lesson in foreign policy.

SELECTED BIBLIOGRAPHY

Adams, Richard N., et al., *Social Change in Latin America Today: Its Implications for United States Policy* (New York: Harper & Brothers, 1960).

Almond, Gabriel A., and Coleman, James S. (eds.), *The Politics of the Developing Areas* (Princeton: Princeton University Press, 1960).

Castañeda, Jorge, *Mexico and the United Nations* (New York: Carnegie Endowment for International Peace, 1958).

Ceniceros, José Angel, *Mexico's Attitude in Its International Relations* (Mexico City: Ministry of Foreign Relations, 1935).

Cline, Howard F., *The United States and Mexico* (Cambridge: Harvard University Press, 1953).

Gregg, R. D., *The Influence of Border Troubles on Relations between the United States and Mexico* (Baltimore: Johns Hopkins Press, 1937).

Johnson, John J., *Political Change in Latin America: The Emergence of the Middle Sectors* (Stanford: Stanford University Press, 1958).

Lieuwen, Edwin, *Arms and Politics in Latin America* (New York: Frederick A. Praeger, Inc., 1960).

Parkes, Henry Bamford, *A History of Mexico* (Boston: Houghton Mifflin Co., 1938).

Rostow, W. W., *The Stages of Economic Growth* (New York: Cambridge University Press, 1960).

Scott, Robert E., *Mexican Government in Transition* (Urbana: University of Illinois Press, 1959).

Tannenbaum, Frank, *Mexico: The Struggle for Peace and Bread* (New York: Alfred A. Knopf, 1950).

11

Foreign Policy of Egypt

On February 1, 1958, a joint communiqué signed by Presidents Nasser of Egypt and Shukri Kuwatli of Syria formally announced the formation of the United Arab Republic, which represented a union between Egypt, an Arabic-speaking country in Africa, and Syria, a part of the traditional Fertile Crescent in Asia Minor. The merger was legalized by a plebiscite held in both Egypt and Syria on February 21, 1958, followed by the promulgation of a provisional constitution in March 1958. Legislative assemblies in both regions of the new Republic were dissolved and political parties in Syria were declared disbanded by Executive Order of the new President of the UAR, Gamal Abdel Nasser. Although each region continued with its own laws, currency, and special regulations, the merger was immediately followed by the unification of defense, foreign affairs, and over-all executive authority. A Central Cabinet consisting of both Egyptians and Syrians was appointed by the latter, while executive cabinets were appointed for each region. Later, in October 1958, President Nasser announced by

P. J.

VATIKIOTIS

official decree the reorganization of the UAR's government, rendering more permanent the executive arrangements for both regions of the Republic, providing for the organization of a National Union organization to replace disbanded political parties, and for the future election-selection of a National Assembly. Yet, in September, 1961, Syrian officers revolted and proclaimed Syria's independence. Thus, two basic forces in contemporary Middle East history are evident: Arab nationalism and local national loyalties. Syria's successful revolt is a victory for the national states, but it is premature to say that efforts to forge a larger Arab union have failed.

THE EMERGENCE OF NASSERISM

So long as British troops occupied parts of Egypt, and particularly the Suez Base, the paramount foreign policy objective of all Egyptian governments since independence in 1923 and until 1954 was the expulsion of the British from Egypt. Governments foundered or flourished depending upon their suc-

335

cess or failure in coming closer to the attainment of this national goal. In fact, until 1954 Egypt was an object of international politics. It was not until 1955 that Egypt became a serious participant in international relations, scoring a tremendous and, until now, unassessable impact upon the Arab world. This impact and the international politics of the Middle East area as a whole have been inexorably connected with the coming of the Free Officers to power in Egypt in July 1952 and the so-called Free Arab Movement they inaugurated under the leadership of Gamal Abdel Nasser.

Popularly referred to as "Nasserism," the Egyptian Free Officers regime's involvement in inter-Arab and international politics came to symbolize the aspirations for independence from foreign control and/or domination of new Arab groups that had emerged in all Arab countries during the interwar period. Social and economic ferment in the Arab countries during the last 50 years gave rise to politically frustrated groups, such as middle class intelligentsia, a small urban proletariat, professional managers, and a few entrepreneurs. These groups associated their aspiration for independence with a resentment of existing social and political systems. Their political objectives, moreover, encompassed an impassioned sense of Arab unity superseding existing political frontiers among the various Arab states. These groups were further committed to a nationalist revolutionary goal, namely, the alteration of the *status quo* in the Arab countries by social and political revolution, to be followed by the unification of separate Arab states. Implied in this commitment was the destruction of imperialist (foreign and specifically Western) influence in the Arab world.

Nasserism in 1955 typified this Arab feeling of revolution against the *status quo* by subsuming in its specifically Nasserite-Egyptian aims the aspirations of emergent groups everywhere in the Arab world. Between 1955 and 1958 every Arab revolutionary came to regard himself as a Nasserite irrespective of his willingness to relinquish his sovereign independent status in favor of Egyptian domination. The idea of Arab unity became a potent revolutionary one under the banner of Nasserism.

To the Egyptian, Nasserism has come to mean the extension of Egypt's domination over the Arab world, the bid for leadership in Black Africa, and the strengthening of a military establishment that will ultimately eliminate the last outpost of imperialism in the Middle East: Israel. Indeed, closer scrutiny of these aims of Nasserism show that they are inexorably connected with domestic economic and political problems of Egypt that are practically insoluble without extension of Egyptian authority in the Arab world, the Middle East, or Africa.

It should be pointed out, however, that Nasserism as described above is not the singular creation of President Nasser. Many of the things Nasserism stands for have been elements of nationalist agitation in the Arab world long before Gamal Abdel Nasser appeared on the scene. He is simply the Arab leader best able to articulate and serve as a symbol for these aspirations.

While the July 1952 military coup by Nasser-led Free Officers did not usher in a totally novel understanding of the basic interests and objectives of Egypt's foreign policy, it did generate enough of a revolutionary momentum to activate certain objectives over others. President Nasser, in his personal statement (credo), *Egypt's Liberation; the Philosophy of the Revolution,* wrote:

Can we fail to see that there is an Arab circle surrounding us—that this circle is a part of us, and we are part of it, our history being inextricably part of its history. These are facts and no mere idle talk. Can we possibly ignore the fact that there is an African continent which Fate decreed us to be a part of, and that it is also decreed that a terrible struggle exists for its future . . . whose results will either be for us or against us, with or without our will? Can we further ignore the existence of an Islamic world, with which we are united by bonds created not only by religious belief, but also reinforced by historic realities? [1]

Although this cannot be considered a statement of policy, it cannot be ignored or underestimated as a reflection of Egyptian revolutionary sentiment and an expression of Egyptian aspiration to leadership in at least the Arab world. It is also a forceful depiction of the feeling of affinity between Egypt and a contiguous Islamic world to the east.

The fact that Egypt has identified herself culturally and spiritually with Arab Islam since the seventh century does not mean that Egypt has had an Arab policy as such for a very long time. But as recently as February 23, 1961, President Nasser said: "The United Arab Republic is the base for the Arab struggle, and the people of the UAR are the vanguard of the Arab struggle. The call for unity is a call for might, freedom and life." [2] This statement reveals Egypt's continued efforts to pre-empt Arab leadership, and

her self-proclaimed sponsorship of Arab nationalism as fundamental objectives of foreign policy. The nationalist revolutionary leaders of Egypt are motivated in this by the necessities of domestic political and economic problems. They are also committed to an ideological facet of Arab political awakening with which the military regime in Egypt is solidly identified in the minds of the members of the wider Arab political community: the leadership of revolutionary liberating movements against foreign domination, and the latter's "agents" represented by the older "corrupt" governments that were overthrown or that must be overthrown. [3]

Arabism as a general slogan for the emancipation of Arabs from foreign influence and subservient dynasts or rulers has thus been appended by Nasserism to two expectations of the Arab peoples: the political regeneration of the Arab national community, and the strengthening of that community through modernization so it can catch up with and defy the old "masters." This is the core of Nasserism's appeal to many Arabs today.

Nasserism's appeal derives also from traditional sources. The feeling of Islamic brotherhood—community—strengthens the image of a political future characterized by military strength, economic prosperity, and unity. Thus, Egyptian foreign policy-

[1] (Washington, D.C.: Public Affairs Press, 1955), pp. 85–86.
[2] *Speeches Delivered by President Gamal Abdel Nasser in the Northern Region of the United Arab Republic,* February-March 1961 (hereinafter referred to as *Nasser Speeches, 1961*) (Cairo: Information Department, 1961), p. 59.

[3] By 1958 and 1959 new terms in Arab nationalist vocabulary were being coined by the Egyptian press, such as *"umala"* (agents), *raj'iyya* (reactionaries), and *shuubiyya* (dissidents, separatists), to refer to the enemies of Arab nationalism, regardless whether or not these were identified as Imperialists or Communists. See *Collected Speeches of President Nasser, 1959* (Cairo: Information Department, 1960). See also editorial in weekly *Rose el-Youssef,* January 10, 1959, "Split in Communist Camp," p. 10.

makers cannot be satisfied with the *status quo* in the Arab world, because it would undermine the revolutionary momentum and appeal of Nasserism itself.

In order to maintain its collective strength, the Arab political community must adopt the Nasserist doctrine of positive neutrality and non-alignment in the East-West struggle as the only guarantee against the entry of big power influence into the area, and as the only means available for the linking of the Middle East with the Afro-Asian peoples. Positive neutrality, however, must also be used as a tactical device for the advancement of national aims and interests.

The Cold War, according to Nasserism, is not an Arab concern. Indeed, the involvement of any Arab state in its vagaries must be avoided because it would inevitably spell foreign influence. The Arab states must actively and consciously seek to establish themselves through unity as a possible Third Force in the world. The chances for this development, according to Nasserist thinking, are good, for the revolutionary impact of the Arab states since 1952, at least upon Africa, has been beneficent and great.[4]

Nasserism contends that the Egyptian model of political liberation established by the Free Officers in July 1952 has introduced into that part of the world a new *revolutionary style (uslub)* to be emulated by others and implemented elsewhere in the Arab world and the African continent. Emanating from Cairo, since 1956 Nasserism has indeed accelerated the movement among African peoples for self-determination and political freedom.[5]

Implied in Nasserism, or the Egyptain *revolutionary style,* today—for the Arab political community at least—are two important elements. First is the question of designating the boundaries of the Arab Nation (*al-umma al-arabiyya*). Being synonymous with revolutionary nationalism, Nasserism would by definition expand the Arab political community until the Arab Nation is embodied in one Arab State. Second is the question of tolerating political groups and leaders within the emerging Arab Nation that are not attuned to the new *style,* Nasserism.

ORGANIZATION FOR POLICY MAKING

In Egypt, or the UAR, today, sectional and other groupings within the political system are not tolerated. Leaders of the military regime have rejected partisan politics, with their institutional vehicles and devices of expression (parliaments, constitutions, political parties, interest groups), as the basis for a "socialist, cooperative, democratic" system. Representative institutions, they claim,

[4] In an address at one of the largest textile factories in Egypt, President Nasser declared: "We want to be outside all spheres of influence. We want to be outside the Cold War. Of course, the Cold War affects us. We consider that we, the small countries, are the battlefield of the Cold War. . . . We also welcome any rapprochement between the Western and Eastern camps, provided such rapprochement is not at the expense of small powers." Text of Speech at Mehalla al-Kubra, in *al-Ahram,* August 9, 1959.

[5] See *Rose el-Youssef,* especially Nos. 1680 and 1684 (August-September 1960) for feature articles and cartoons developing this view. Moreover, President Nasser in a speech at Rosetta on September 19, 1959, said: "We can make ourselves felt by examples such as the example we gave during the battle of the Canal. That battle was the torch which lit the road of the struggle for freedom all over Africa." *al-Ahram,* September 20, 1959.

were mere forms concealing the exploiting elements of capitalism, feudalism, and foreign intrigue.[6] They argue that the mobilization of national endeavor cannot be achieved through representative institutions which are importations from alien political systems, superimposed on a different social structure and culture that is not ready to adopt them meaningfully. Lacking the proper infrastructure for an elaborate democratic political process, the "national interest" might be dissipated by the opportunists who have always been ready to use such devices for the furtherance of their own ends.

Instead, the military regime in Egypt today speaks of the "planning of national interests" under the state-organized and supervised National Union. Citizens can participate in the political life of the state only through this national organization. It is the only vehicle through which the aims of the Revolution can be attained. At the same time, the National Union protects the Revolution from its enemies and detractors. One might suggest in this instance that an elite is forcibly mobilizing the masses toward specified aims by prohibiting the proliferation of associations for differentiated interests. Simultaneously, it can forego the delicate processes of constitutionalism and representative government and still claim to represent the national interest without permitting the public genuine participation in the political process.

The present political elite in Egypt can nevertheless claim to represent the national interest in contrast to the openly sectional and often personal and

incompetent nature of the previous civilian regime.[7] All the same, the present power structure in Egypt does not permit or afford the consideration of privately organized interests in the making and conduct of foreign policy.[8]

There is in Egypt, today, direct military rule, insofar as the decision-making elite is composed of a few ex-army officers, members of the Nasser-led Free Officers conspiracy that effected the successful coup against the Farouq regime in July 1952. The original constituency of this Executive of the Free Officers comprised between 200 and 300 officers in the Egyptian Armed Forces sympathetic to the Free Officers' cause, plus another 1700 or 1800 officers in all categories and some 75,000 troops who were uncommitted.

The Free Officers acted as a policy-making body in the early days of the revolution with cohesiveness, discipline, and despatch. Internal communications, chains of command, and a high degree of centralization were features of the military establishment advantageous for the control of a rather disintegrating political community. When the new ruling group of army officers established themselves firmly in power and legitimized their authority by a combination of traditional and modern techniques,[9] they were in a position to expand the operations of what appear to be civilian

[6] See Anwar Sadat, *Maana al-ittihad al-qawmi* (The Meaning of the National Union) (Cairo: 1959).

[7] See Abder Rahman Rafii, *Muqaddamat thawrat thalatha wa ishrin yulio 1952 (Prelude to the Revolution of July 1952)* (Cairo: 1957).

[8] See P. J. Vatikiotis, *The Egyptian Army in Politics, Pattern for New Nations?* (Bloomington, Ind.: Indiana University Press, 1961), especially Chapter VIII.

[9] See P. J. Vatikiotis, "Dilemmas of Political Leadership in the Arab Middle East: the Case of the UAR," *American Political Science Review,* Vol. LV, No. 1 (March 1961), pp. 103–111.

institutions—the cabinet, the bureaucracy, and a national assembly.

The fact that Egypt appears now as a quasi-civilianized political system does not contradict the idea that a fundamentally military core of power holders makes decisions. At best, the new executive structure decreed by President Nasser in 1958, featuring a cabinet, and the subsequent formation of a National Assembly to perform the legislative function in the state, merely assuage the persistent dependence of the President upon a viceregal system for the formulation and execution of policy.[10] Such a system of viceroys permits the rulers of Egypt to bypass the institutional delegation of authority or the need to expand civilian participation and responsibility in the making of policy.

This highly centralized view of policy-making is related to the notion held by the revolutionary officers that the military establishment is the defender of the nation, and therefore the most able and representative formulator of its interests. The image propagated by the Free Officers of the Officers Corps as the most advanced, modern, and organized group in Egyptian society allocates to this group the exclusive role and function of leading the nation in its search for national power, dignity, and world influence. Nor is this self-image of the Officers Corps at great variance with the tradi-

tional concept of leadership in both Islam and Egyptian history.

In the Egyptian-Islamic tradition, the emphasis on the personal qualifications of the ruler was the sole important proposition of constitutional theory. Most Islamic constitutional lawyers, in speaking of political leadership, emphasized specific personal qualifications. This emphasis was closely connected throughout Islamic history with military ability and prominence. There was rarely any serious discussion of checks to be placed upon the ruler, so he came to be accepted as law-maker, dispenser of justice, and chief executive. When he combined military leadership with these qualities, his position was still stronger. President Nasser appeared, in 1954 and 1961, to satisfy both these requirements in the eyes of his public.

A charismatic leader is more important in Egyptian politics than the mechanisms, checks, and balances that loom large in Western political practice, because the type of leadership has always been more important in Arab-Islamic societies than the type of political institutions. The old concepts of *Rayyis* (Chief) and *Zaim* (popular leader) in tribal and other institutions still command a great deal of status and respect. The tradition of centralized authority in Egypt facilitates the emergence of charismatic leaders.

When Egypt's President can be depicted as the *Zaim al-uruba,* popular hero of Arabism, the impact of this depiction on Egyptian foreign policy is tremendous. In a presently fragmented Arab world the views of the masses, such as their desire—romantic as it may seem—to achieve some form of unity that will lead to strength, are often at variance with those of their rulers. Under these circumstances a forceful "hero" who preaches the same desire in a most articulate manner con-

---

[10] The viceregal system has been used by President Nasser most effectively in Syria in 1959, when he appointed Vice-President Abdel Hakim Amer (Commander-in-Chief UAR Armed Forces) governor of Syria to supersede all other arrangements in the northern region of the Republic. The same system has been used by the President in the internal political organization and control of Egypt, especially the National Union, when he appointed Kamal al-Din Husein, a Free Officer, Supervisor-General of the National Union.

stitutes a significant ideological factor in inter- and intra-Arab politics.

It is difficult to elicit any kind of machinery for the formulation of Egyptian foreign policy under the present regime as described above. While a cabinet assists the President of the Republic in governing, and a National Assembly records its approval of policies already decreed by the executive,[11] the President continues to make policy in consultation with a core of Free Officers closest and most loyal to him, and presently in executive positions, but not necessarily with their real participation. Although he must tread a narrow path in keeping a volatile mass public opinion at an even keel and attuned to the requirements of his decisions, the President is not constitutionally responsible to any institutional checks upon his authority.

Considering the present commitment of the Egyptian ruling group to their bid for Arab leadership and future pre-eminence in African affairs, the councils and politics of bodies such as the League of Arab States, the various African and Afro-Asian Congresses, solidarity conferences, and youth rallies in Egypt are important instruments in the making and implementation of foreign policy.[12] Similarly, the Islamic Congress discussed below serves as an arm of Egyptian foreign policy, especially among the Muslim communities in Africa, regardless of the measure of its success or failure at present. Given a nationalized press (since May 1960) in Egypt, the ruling institution can preclude any divergent views of policy,

since these cannot be publicly expressed. Thus the responsibility for foreign policy-making in Egypt today rests with the President, in consultation with his loyal Free Officer colleagues, assisted by a Foreign Office, and centrally devised and rigidly controlled mass organizations and media. The fact that President Nasser is responsible for defining Egyptian foreign policy and that he is singularly responsible for the over-all conduct of Egyptian diplomacy became clear as early as February 1953, when Egypt and England were preparing for talks that led to the July 1954 Agreement on the British departure from the Canal Base.[13]

EGYPT AND THE ARAB WORLD

"For some reason," said Gamal Abdel Nasser very early in his political career,

it seems to me that within the Arab circle there is a role, wandering aimlessly in search of a hero. And I do not know why it seems to me that this role exhausted by its wanderings, has at last settled down, tired and weary, near the borders of our country and is beckoning to us to move, to take up its lines, to put on its costume, since no one else is qualified to play it.[14]

It is significant that this statement was made in 1955, for that year was the watershed of Egyptian foreign policy. It marked the resolution of the Egyptian military regime to export Nasser-

[11] The record and proceedings of the First National Assembly (1957) in Egypt indicate that this body did not exercise any legislative function, but merely approved decisions already made by the executive-in-council.

[12] These congresses and rallies have so far served as platforms for President Nasser's statements on Arab Nationalism. See *Nasser Speeches, 1959, 1960.*

[13] See statements to the press by Gamal Abdel Nasser quoted in *Hadhihi al-thawra* (This Revolution), First Anniversary of the Revolution Volume, (Cairo: 1953).

[14] *Egypt's Liberation, Philosophy of the Revolution* (Washington, D.C.: 1955), pp. 87–88.

ism to the Arab world as the most potent formula of Arab political salvation.
Having settled the Anglo-Egyptian
problem in July–October 1954, the
revolutionary officers were now ready
to link their revolution at home with
the solution of Arab problems elsewhere. The President's first excursion
outside Egypt, to attend the Afro-
Asian Conference at Bandung in April
1955, left an indelible mark upon his
personality and his view of international politics. He returned home fortified by newly acquired prestige, status,
and a slightly over-confident attitude
regarding Egypt's role and destiny in
Arab and Afro-Asian politics. Possibly
Anwar Sadat's description of the President's role in this connection is apt:
"he [Nasser] does not seek personal
leadership *(zaama);* he is a missionary
(sahib dawa)." This mission of the
President was no less than the "liberation of the Middle East from foreign
influence and domination." [15]

British responsibility for the defence
of the Middle East really ended with
the Suez Agreement. This left the question of defense arrangements in the
area unsettled. The first Egyptian attempts in the summer of 1954 to explore the prospects of defense with
Iraq were fruitless. When in February
1955, the Israelis carried out a successful large-scale attack on the Egyptian-
held Gaza strip, and Iraq signed the
Baghdad Pact with Turkey, President
Nasser felt dangerously exposed militarily. He thought Britain was trying,
through Iraq, to isolate him politically
from the rest of the Arab world. While
he may not have been consciously aspiring to replace British by Egyptian
hegemony, President Nasser was not
willing to forfeit the chance of future
hegemony by default to Iraq. Thus, one
of the most fundamental variables in

Egypt's Arab policy emerged in the rift
between Cairo and Baghdad. The revolutionary officers in Cairo could not
countenance a strong Iraq led by a sea-
soned politician, Nuri el-Said, in the
service of a Hashemite monarch.

Throughout 1955 three basic facets
of Egyptian policy began to emerge.
First, the revolutionary officers adopted
the political principles of their predecessors by reviving the classic rivalry
between the Euphrates and the Nile
for the control of lands lying in between, namely, the Fertile Crescent and
the Arabian Peninsula. The major tactic to be used in this strategy was the
idea that the best defense of the Middle
East lay in an Arab Collective Security
Pact (actually entered upon by the
Arab League states in 1950). Alliances
such as the Baghdad Pact were anti-
Arab because the expulsion of foreign
influence from the area was the common objective uniting all Arabs. The
containment of Iraq, therefore, whether
under the monarchy or under the subsequent republican regime (1958), became a cardinal principle of Egyptian
foreign policy.

Obstruction of Western-sponsored
defense schemes of any kind became a
second major objective of Egypt's Arab
policy, as was witnessed in the opposition of the revolutionary officers to
both the Baghdad Pact and the Eisenhower Doctrine later in 1957. The
"Armed Front," which would free the
Arab world from subservience to any
foreign power, could not be one that
included foreign partners in its ranks.
Indeed, there was an allusion here to
an Islamic-Arab bond, in the formula
of *Allahu akbar* (Allah is Greatest),
the "God of the Arabs." [16]

These two concerns of Egyptian policy-makers were followed by the only
logical derivative of such thinking: the
remaking of the Arab world "in the

[15] *Al-wahda al-arabiyya* (Arab Unity)
(Cairo: 1957), pp. 74–75.

[16] Ibid., p. 112–15.

Egyptian image" by a concerted drive for Arab hegemony, using the revolutionary prestige and popularity of the Egyptian regime among the Arab masses. In trying to capture the imagination and support of the Arab masses everywhere, President Nasser used to advantage the almost proverbial ambivalence of the Arabs' attitude to the outside world, and especially the West. His defiance of the West in 1955 by purchasing arms from the Soviet Bloc immediately raised his popularity and prestige with all Arabs. That was a relatively easy accomplishment when one considers the great preoccupation of the Arabs with Western imperialist plots against them. They were usually ready to attribute failure and deficiencies on their part to an outside source. Thus, their military defeat in Palestine in 1948–1949 was not due to any incompetence on their part but to the military disability imposed upon them by the West. President Nasser was also greatly admired, for he appeared as the first Arab ruler to be accorded some prestige and respect in international councils, such as the one at Bandung. It was therefore only logical, given the receptivity and favorable inclination of Arab communities, for the Egyptian rulers in their bid for leadership to develop a policy of revolutionary content for Arab nationalism, centered at first on a struggle for power against Iraq and Jordan, the remaining allies of the West in the Middle East.[17]

[17] In 1943–1944, for example, the Wafd government of Nahhas Pasha was anxious to assume leadership in the negotiations for the formation of the Arab League in order to obstruct any independent schemes of unity by the Hashemites in Jordan and Iraq in the Fertile Crescent. Again, in 1948, the decision of the Egyptian government to commit the army to battle in the Palestine War was, to a great extent, motivated by its aim of frustrating any independent designs the late King Abdullah of Jordan may have had regarding Palestine.

The major shortcoming of this overall Arab policy centering on a struggle for power in the Arab world was Egypt's lack of sufficient military strength to effect any change in the territorial *status quo*. At the same time the more pronounced rivalry among the Great Powers in the Middle East in 1955 tended to favor the maintenance of that *status quo*.

Between 1955 and 1957 it was not too clear whether the Egyptian decision to champion Arab nationalism had any serious dimensions other than the containment of Iraq, the control of the Arab League, and the campaign of villification against Israel. It was not until the merger with Syria in February 1958 that Egypt's Arab policy presented the dynamic notion of the Arab Nation based on a relatively new connotation of the term *qawmiyya,* the consciousness of being an Arab. It marked the beginning of a determined ideological push by the Egyptian rulers to convert (some would claim to subvert) all other Arab states to the idea that Arab nationalism would be meaningless and impotent without unity. "The aim of the Revolutionary government is to make the Arabs a united nation. The problems of the Arabs are also the problems of Egypt." [18]

Unfortunately, the idea of Arab unity was not an original contribution of the Egyptian junta. More accurately it constituted the basic platform of the Baath Party in Syria, which was most instrumental in bringing about union with Egypt. In Syria, on the other hand, Arab unity during the period 1928–54 was thought of in terms of union, federal or otherwise, between some of the Fertile Crescent countries, such as Iraq, Jordan, and Syria. The political prominence in Syrian politics of the socialist, anti-Iraq, Baath Party

[18] Excerpt from Nasser's speech reported in *al-Ahram,* July 23, 1954.

after 1956 precluded such plans. Instead, Egypt was now able to achieve at least one of its foreign policy objectives—securing a foothold in the Fertile Crescent. The merger constituted a victory over Iraq by giving her arch-rival, Egypt, a base in the "lands lying in between." By the same token, the Egyptian rulers found themselves in a proximate enough location from which to pursue their Arab policy toward Jordan and the Lebanon.[19]

The effect of the Syrian-Egyptian merger on the Arab public was tremendous. To the masses, this spelled the beginning of Arab unity, the cherished dream of all Arab nationalists. On the other hand, the union seemed to stiffen the confrontation between ruling institutions in other Arab states and Cairo, for to many of these the formation of the UAR implied the extension of Egyptian control in the north. The Egyptians nimbly sought rationalizations and justifications for the union dating back in history to Saladin. The theme of the traditional affinity and unity between Syria and Egypt in their defensive wars against common foes (Crusaders and Tartars), was emphasized. From a mere politician's slogan Arab unity had, it seemed, for the first time become a reality.

Syria thus became the Egyptian base in the north from which attempts were made to extend Egyptian hegemony over the rest of the Arab world. The crisis in Lebanon in May–September 1958, and the abortive anti-Kassem uprising in Iraq in March 1959 indicated that Egypt was temporarily successful in fanning the flames of Cairo-sponsored Arab nationalism. The Baath Party organization and its activities supplemented the Cairo Voice of the Arabs in inciting Arabs everywhere to join the bandwagon of Arab unity. Obviously, at that time, all Arabs who believed in the centripetal force of Arab unity identified Arab nationalism with Nasser's leadership, especially when other Arab rulers were jealously trying to guard their own political establishments against that leadership's incursions. The failure of the bandwagon for Arab unity to materialize ultimately caused the downfall of the supreme architects and theorists of Arab unity, the Baath Party in Syria.

Undoubtedly the effect of the Baghdad Pact and the subsequent Arms Deal between Egypt and the Soviet Bloc in 1955 enhanced Egyptian influence in the Arab world to the point where it exceeded the influence of any other Arab state. This latecomer in Arab nationalism displaced the traditional leaders of that nationalism—Iraq, Jordan, and Syria. President Nasser immediately capitalized on this development, especially after surviving the Suez War, with a campaign calculated to establish Egypt's primacy in the Arab world. There were four central themes in this offensive: Arab unity, Arab regeneration and leadership in world affairs, rejection of the West as a source of inspiration for Arab national endeavor, and the projection of Egypt's struggle against imperialism as representative of the struggle of all Arabs.

"Our nation is one even if imperialism tried to break it up," cried President Nasser early in 1957.[20] The Egyptian Revolution imbued renewed and stronger belief in this maxim among Arabs by providing a model for po-

[19] Speaking at a National Union rally in Hama, Syria, on February 20, 1960, Nasser said, "They [the imperialists] attempted to crush Arab nationalism in Palestine, and imagined that by so doing, they could separate the Arabs in Asia from the Arabs in Africa." *Nasser Speeches, 1960,* p. 65.

[20] See Gamal Abdel Nasser, "One Nation", *Al-Hilal,* Special Issue, January 1957, "Our Arab Nation."

litical liberation. Only through this oneness of the Nation can the Arabs recapture their past glory in the form of present leadership in world affairs. Arab nationalism cannot derive its principles or inspiration from the West. Such basis for Arab nationalism must be rejected by all Arabs, because the use of its imported liberalism in the past has brought about Arab political failure and led to the tragedy in Palestine.

Nasser, in effect, was trying to construct a new national myth for the Arabs which would also serve as an instrument of Egyptian policy. This myth would include as basic principles the concept of an Arab nationhood, unity, historical and spiritual power deriving mainly from the Islamic heritage of the Arabs, antagonism to the imperialist West, and the identification of the enemy—in this instance, Israel. Cleverly, the struggle of Egypt against aggression in 1956 was no less than the struggle of Arab nationalism against its enemies. As the aggressor was from the West, Egyptian policymakers for the Arab world were better able to impress upon other Arabs the idea that the enemy did indeed always come from the West.

The "blut und erde" aspect of Egypt's Arab policy, described by an eminent student of Arab politics,[21] was calculated to inspire neo-Arab movements of the Egyptian variety in other Arab states. Egypt was interested in becoming the Prussia of the Arab world. Thus, Anwar Sadat, often spokesman of the junta, asserted in March 1957: "and there was nothing behind our coup [in July 1952]

other than Arab nationalism . . . which awakened a new historical development. . . . We must nurture this link between

the peoples of the Arab nation . . . for when the revolution occurred in Egypt *it rendered the Arab Nation one nation,* sharing one history and claiming one destiny." [22]

On another occasion, President Nasser emphasized the Arabness of Egypt and its importance in the struggle against Israel as the major political and social weapon in the hands of the Arabs. "Nationalism," he said, "is the arm which protects the Arab Nation from imperialist plots. It is the nation's weapon for securing the future. Nationalism is the means by which we can retrieve the rights of independence and freedom." [23]

While the concept of the Arab Nation implies the essential unity of all Arabic-speaking peoples, in Egyptian usage Arabism implies more traditional aspects of Egyptian policy. The Egyptian Free Officers no doubt view their movement as the model for the emancipation of all the Arab countries. Their interest—part of their foreign policy—in universalizing or implementing the model elsewhere has frequently brought against them and their leader, Nasser, the charge of expansionism. The brief success of the Nabulsi-led government in Jordan during 1956–1957, and the early stand of the pan-Arabist opposition led by Saab Slam in the Lebanon during the May–September 1958 crisis, prompted other Arab rulers to guardedly interpret the Arabism espoused by the Egyptian military rulers as a convenient tool for the extension of Egyptian hegemony over the neighboring Arab countries. Iraq, the youngest republic among the Arabs, and also the creation of a native Free Officers group conspiracy, was soon alienated from Cairo in the

[21] See George Kirk, *Contemporary Arab Politics* (New York: 1961).

[22] Reported in *al-Ahram*, March 10, 1957. Italics added.
[23] Reported in *al-Ahram*, November 7, 1956.

early spring of 1959 by a similar interpretation of events and Egyptian intensions. Tunisia, having joined the Arab League in October 1958, proceeded to withdraw its membership a year later on the grounds that the League had become an instrument for the imposition of Egypt's control over sister Arab states. Arabs were reacting with mixed feelings towards the purported Nasserite leadership. Nor were all Arabs ready to subscribe to the theory advanced from Cairo since 1956 that the "struggle of the Egyptian people is the struggle of the Arab world." [24]

Unrivalled leadership of Arab nationalism or Arabism depends on the ability of the leader to solve Arab national problems. Many of these problems are essentially related to the struggle for independence in Algeria, the undermining and weakening of Israel as one of the purported obstacles to Arab unity, the achievement of a satisfactory solution to the plight of Palestinian Arab refugees (according to most Arabs such solution means their return to Palestine), and the extrication of Britain and British influence from the Gulf States and southwest Arabia. The appearance of rival political elites, forcefully motivated towards modernization and conscious of their interests within the Arab world—such as Kassem in Iraq and Bourguiba in Tunisia—activates the struggle for power within the community of Arab leaders. This is especially in terms of "solving Arab national problems," making it at present almost impossible for one to triumph over the other short of the use of military force or subversion from within.

It is the magnitude of these requirements for unchallenged leadership and hegemony over the Arab world that caused Egypt's Arab policy to lose its momentum by 1959, and blatantly fail in 1960. These requirements tend to impose a certain immobilism upon any Arab ruler who seeks to extend his authority over the Arab states. While one can justifiably claim that there is an intrinsic unity among Arabs on the basis of their common language, Islamic and other heritage, and political experience, one cannot at the same time overlook the disparate levels of development among the various Arab communities, the antagonism between their rulers, the uneven distribution of land and resources in the Arab world, the hardening of national boundaries, and the coalescence of interests occurring from the organization of most Arab communities as independent nation-states. On this basis alone the ebullience of the forceful Egyptian military elite in its attempt to spill over the entire Arab world was apt to produce defection, distrust, and opposition on the part of existing elites in positions of power elsewhere.

The failure of Egypt's Arab policy was branded above as rather temporary. It appears so at the present time because it is doubtful whether Egypt had much to offer to other Arabs besides a revolutionary "momentum." Neither its resources nor its standard of living appeared attractive enough for other Arabs to desire the benefits therefrom. Political freedom, which might conceivably have appealed to the Arab intelligentsia outside Egypt, has not been the trademark of the Egyptian regime. For the latter group, therefore, there was no good reason to exchange a native ruler for an outside one. If at any time in the future the Egyptian leadership is able to offer any of these desirable appurtenances of modern existence, Egypt may stand a

---

[24] On "Nasserite leadership" (*al-zaama al-nasiriyya*), expounded from Cairo, see editorial on Nasser's Fifth Anniversary Speech in *al-Ahram*, July 30, 1957.

good chance of achieving the end of her Arab policy.

Despite the temporary loss of her primacy among Arab leaders, Egypt continues to be committed to a policy of providing Arabism with some practical content. So far, however, the major characteristic of the Egyptian contribution has been a negative one: the discrediting of the revolutionary military regime in Iraq, the branding of Jordan as an imperialist base, and, more recently, the branding of certain Lebanese groups such as the *Kataeb* (Phalanges) and the Syrian Popular Party, as enemies of the UAR and, therefore, Arabism.[25] While Western imperialism continues to be the main deterrent to Egypt's bid for Arab leadership Communism has recently been linked with separatist movements among the so-called anti-Arab nationalism Arabs.[26]

There are perhaps two other serious causes for the current failure of Egypt's Arab policy. First, one must consider the inability of Egypt until now to solve the Palestine problem—in effect, to liquidate Israel for her own ends. Second, lacking access to the most profitable source of revenue and therefore wealth—Middle East oil—the Egyptian rulers are not presently in a position to use economic pressure and influence in pursuing their political ends.

EGYPT, THE SUDAN, AND AFRICA

As early as March 1953 the strictly censored press in Egypt was entertaining theories of an Egyptian destiny in Africa. On the heels of the Anglo-Egyptian agreement over the Sudan in

February 1953, one paper editorialized, "We look for a power which will protect Africa. . . . We see no one but Egypt. It is the nearest African power with a personality that the world recognizes. It is necessary for Egypt to pursue one African policy aiming at the enfranchisement of the Continent." [27] Cairo's broadcasts on the Sudan program elaborated on the effects of the Sudan's liberation upon the neighboring African peoples: The Congo, Kenya, and Uganda. Since the theory of an Egyptian destiny in Africa appeared of greater concern to Egypt's policy makers in 1960 than the destiny of Egypt in the Arab world, it is important to analyze briefly Egypt's African policy, if such policy indeed exists.

Reference was made earlier to the fact that Egyptian policy-makers have traditionally looked northeastwards. Since the seventh century Egypt came to identify her cultural and political fortunes with Arab Muslim Asia; apart from her interest in the Sudan immediately south of the border, there was no real tradition of an Egyptian policy toward Africa. It is proposed that the mounting interest of Egyptian policymakers in Africa since 1957 and the evolution of a Nasserite African policy are conditioned by at least three major factors, although this enumeration should not rule out other interpretations.

First, the failure of Egyptian attempts since 1951 to effect an "anschluss" with the Sudan under the slogan "Unity of the Nile Valley," has prompted the present military rulers of Egypt to "leap-frog" into Africa south of the Sahara. Second, the rapid withdrawal of the colonial powers from the African continent seemed to encourage Egyptian irredentist tendencies on the assumption that, being the first country among those African countries that

[25] See *Nasser Speeches*, 1961, p. 65.

[26] See especially Nasser's Port Said Speech of December 23, 1958, attacking the Communist parties in Syria and Iraq as *separatists* and anti-Arab nationalists. Text of speech in *al-Ahram*, December 24, 1958.

[27] Reported in *Al-Akhbar*, March 24, 1953.

had experienced colonial control to free itself from European rule, Egypt could seek a certain primacy among the emerging African states. Third, the acceptance of Israel's technical aid and trade by some of the newly independent African states (Ghana, Mali, Nigeria) as well as those not so new (Ethiopia), made it imperative for Nasser to contain Israel in Africa by seeking the support of African leaders in censuring Israeli presence as an intrusion into the Afro-Asian world.

There is also the recent awareness of Egyptian rulers that Egypt is very much in Africa. Egypt can claim Cairo as the largest city in Africa, and a population second only to Nigeria. The revolutionary Free Officers can point to their record of having led the first political-social revolution in the African Continent as well as having given asylum to revolutionary African leaders in the 1950's, especially from Arab North Africa.

As regards the Sudan, one writer has likened Egypt's ambitions to those of Japan in Asia fifty years ago. "Like Japan," argues this writer,

Egypt now needs an outlet for her dense population. . . . She is trying to evolve from an agrarian to an industrial economy. Beside the Union of South Africa (not any longer after Apartheid) Egypt possesses effective power and status perhaps more than any of the other free states in Africa at present. . . . In the past it appeared characteristic of the Egyptian to consider himself at best a European and at worst a Caucasoid African. When not accepted as a European, he sought consolation as a leader among Arab nations. But as the Arab League was not so effective against the European powers as it desired the Egyptian now looked for a place in the African sun and a position of leadership

as a liberating big brother among the suppressed colonial Africans.[28]

It should be noted, however, that apart from the long interest of Egypt in the Sudan since 1820, and the preoccupation of Egyptian governments with the distribution and availability of Nile waters, Egyptians feel a certain justifiable affinity with the Arabized ruling minority in the Sudan. This Arab link with the potentially independent Sudanese political elite could not be capitalized upon during the Anglo-Egyptian Condominium, 1889–1953. Any opportunity Egyptian troops stationed in the Sudan in 1923 might have had to act as a propaganda vehicle for Sudanese Egyptianization was lost in November 1924, when Egyptian nationalist extremists murdered Sir Lee Stack Pasha, Sirdar of the Egyptian Army. Not only were the Egyptians shaken by the realization that another controlling power (in this instance Britain) in the Sudan could tamper with their access to Nile Waters (the British ultimatum to the Egyptian Government in 1924 included a threat to that effect), but they also lost any direct influence they may have had in the Sudan itself.

When it became apparent, at the end of the second World War, that the British were contemplating the nurturing of an independent Sudan, Egypt's leaders realized that the establishment of a pro-Egyptian Sudanese political element was imperative. Thus, Egypt supported the Ashigga group in the Sudan once Sudan appeared to move towards an independent status. The unilateral abrogation of the 1936 Anglo-Egyptian Treaty in October 1951, which also

[28] See L. Fabunmi, *The Sudan in Anglo-Egyptian Relations,* (London: Longmans, Green & Co., Inc., 1960), p. 167. Parantheses added by the writer.

declared the unity of the Nile Valley under the Egyptian Crown, was a move towards that end. There was now, moreover, greater freedom of action on the part of the Egyptians, and they embarked upon a "Big Brother" policy to protect the Sudan from the trap of imperialist influence even after independence.

The coming to power of the Free Officers junta in July 1952 seemed to freeze Egyptian activity in the Sudan. Some have contended that whereas ex-President Naguib, part-Sudanese himself, was interested in a closer relationship between Egypt and the Sudan, Gamel Abdel Nasser was at first not interested. The latter's preoccupation with resolving outstanding issues with Britain helped to arrive at the Agreement of February 1953 over the Sudan as well as the Suez Agreement of July 1954.

Significantly, these two agreements heightened President Nasser's interest in the Sudan, but not in terms of the Unity of the Nile Valley slogan. Instead, the military rulers of Egypt now accepted the self-determination formula for the Sudanese. But they hoped to influence an independent Sudan in accepting an Egyptian-conceived ideology and policy toward the Arab world as well as toward world politics. In 1954, the activity of the Salem brothers, members of the Free Officers Executive born in Khartoum, reflected a deliberate step on the part of the Egyptian rulers to "make friends and influence people" there. The subsequent entry of the Sudan to full membership in the Arab League in January 1956 was welcomed by Egypt, for now it appeared possible to line up a pro-Egyptian Sudan with her own political interests.

The economic and strategic interests of Egypt in the Sudan cannot be under-

estimated. The military rulers of Egypt by 1954 viewed the Sudan as a possible place for the settling of surplus Egyptian population, a market for their exports and investments, and a potential absorptive area for their unemployed labor at home. More important was the potential use of a foothold in the Sudan as a stepping stone to Egyptian influence over other African areas.

But as in Egypt's bid for hegemony over the Arab states in Western Asia, the independent Sudanese political groups were hesitant to relinquish their newly acquired power. Agricultural potential through irrigation schemes for expanding cotton acreage presented an attractive base for competition with Egypt in the European and British markets. There was also the feeling among even the pro-Egyptian parties in the Sudan that an Egyptian-sponsored commonwealth of a united Nile Valley would invariably imply Egyptian predominance. Sudanese suspicion of Egypt's intentions is not without historical precedent. They have not yet forgotten the relative domination of the country by Muhammad Ali and the subsequent oppressive rule of an Egyptian-Turkish administration in the nineteenth century. Regardless of its Arab-Islamic orientation, the Sudanese ruling minority has a vague, yet significant, recollection of Arab slave-traders in its African land.

During the period from 1956 to 1958, however, the Egyptian policymakers were intensely interested in using the Sudan to advantage in their intra-Arab squabbles in the Arab League, and establishing a base from which to advance their African program. Although the Egyptian argument that the Nile imposes a natural unity between Egypt and the Sudan was a cogent one, the way the military regime in Egypt conducted their "love the Sudan" campaign was too neat. On the liabilities column of the balance sheet, the Sudanese felt uncomfortable by the fact that Egyptians were not ready to make concrete proposals regarding such issues as the distribution of Nile waters. More pronounced was the displeasure of the Sudanese at the way in which President Nasser contemplated the construction of the Aswan Dam, which would dislocate some 500,000 Sudanese from their homes and lands.

When the military took over the government in the Sudan under General Abboud in November 1958, the Egyptians misinterpreted this move as the acceptance by the Sudanese of Egyptian-brand militarist nationalism. Even though Egypt and the Sudan reached an agreement over Nile waters in 1960, it is now clear that there are serious limitations to Egypt's original plans for the Sudan. Some of these limitations are similar to those operative in Egypt's policy toward the other Arab states. There is for example the bitter fact that Egypt did not have much to offer to the Sudanese, or at least enough in terms of economic and political gains, to make the proposal of Nile Valley unity attractive. The new Sudanese political elite furthermore appears just as desirous to retain its sovereignty as other Arab political elites. There is also the influence that an ex-colonial power like Britain can still exert over the Sudanese political establishment, a factor which counteracts Egypt's advances. Finally, the fact that Egypt's Arab policy between 1955 and 1959 did not have an unqualified success elsewhere in the Arab world may have encouraged the present military regime in the Sudan to stay clear of any Egyptian-sponsored schemes of unity. Needless to say, internal pressure from political groups in the Sudan in favor of an independent Sudan, es-

pecially the *Ansar,* successors to the Mahdist movement, could spell political suicide for any ruler who is too anxious to join the country with Egypt.

For the time being, Egyptian plans for the Nile Valley are in abeyance; some would argue that they cannot succeed at all. But this rebuff in the Sudan did not particularly dampen the spirits of the military regime regarding its renewed efforts in the rest of the African continent, north and south of the Sahara. It would be unrealistic to attribute Irredentist aspects to Egypt's interests in the latter direction. One must look for the set of motives and considerations which gave impetus to Nasser's African policy in 1957. In welcoming President Nkruma of Ghana to Egypt in July 1958, President Nasser said

Today, when we meet as two African countries, representing free Africa, we look to the future so that Africa may attain this strong independent personality. We pledge you . . . that the UAR and the people of the UAR shall strive . . . with all determination and firmness for the sake of the liberation of Africa, and for the cause of support for liberty and the peoples who struggle for the liberation of Africa, and for the freedom of their countries.[29]

The military regime in Egypt was committing itself to a policy of helping the creation of strong centralized independent governments in Africa through the use of at least two devices: an ideological phase to be led by Egypt and expressed through the press media and The Voice of Free Africa, and the sponsorship of Afro-Asian solidarity Conferences in Cairo to strengthen the ties between Egypt and other

[29] *Nasser Speeches, 1958,* p. 208.

African states, as well as to provide the basis for new economic and trade relations between them.

Although not all the aims of this policy are clear, three objectives of Egyptian policy-makers are discernible. First, Egypt is interested in the future leadership of a bloc of independent African states in world politics. Whether the corollary of an African unity is a consideration at this time is not certain, for that would involve determining what type of unity, the question of who would lead such unity. The second objective is the concern of Egyptian policy-makers in using their privileged African position as a lever in their struggle for Arab leadership. Third, and perhaps of most practical and immediate importance to the Egyptian leaders, is the containment of Israel in the African continent, preferably her expulsion from there, and the achievement of a united African Front against Israel in the Middle East.

On the ideological front, independence, neutralism, economic development, and unity were put forward by Egypt to Africans aspiring to political emancipation as the essential requisites for a brighter future, and as sources of strength for defying the once-dominant West. Confident as a result of the prestige boost afforded their President by Bandung in 1955, Egypt's leaders daringly mused about the fact that their July 1952 coup gave new courage to the struggling African peoples. In 1960 and 1961 President Nasser's publicists were claiming that the revolutionary ideology of Africa was emanating (the Arabic term used here, literally rendered, was "radiating") from Cairo. The UAR became, according to its advocates abroad, "the center of freedom" for all Africans seeking independence. The Congo in fact, was the second major battle of Africa against

imperialists (the first was Suez in 1956). Economic development in the UAR in terms of industrialization, and especially the Aswan Dam Project, was becoming the model for the fulfillment of African aspirations.[30]

Part of this ideological drive or phase in Egypt's African policy is the elaborate program of scholarships to African students who wish to study in the state's universities. It is reported, for instance, that several thousand African students are currently in Egypt under this program. Also significant is the use of the oldest Islamic university, Al-Azhar in Cairo, for the religious training of African Muslims. The latter program is probably administered and supervised by the Islamic Congress (al-mu'tamar al-islami) established in November 1954 to serve Egypt's Islamic interests. Publicly, the Egyptian authorities expressed the hope that the Congress would afford an opportunity for wider participation of Muslim states in the advancement of the welfare of Muslims everywhere.

Other activities of the Islamic Congress have consisted of medical, educational, and other aid to backward Islamic communities in Africa, especially Somaliland. When one considers the concentration of numerous Muslim communities in Northern Nigeria, parts of West Africa, Somaliland, Tanganyika, and Zanzibar, the idea of such a Congress is quite formidable at first sight. It is not certain, however, that these African Muslim communities exposed to the activities of the Congress respond favorably to its Egyptian over-

[30] In a speech on January 9, 1960, President Nasser said: "The High Dam project which we have inaugurated today, is a constant incentive to all the nations of Africa and Asia." Text of speech reported in *al-Ahram*, January 10, 1960. See also, Ihsan Abdel Quddus, "Arab Leaders in Africa," *Rose el-Youssef*, January 3, 1961, p. 3.

tones. It is more likely that the Congress is a subtle device to link Egypt's purported leadership of the overwhelming Muslim Arab community to the north with Africa, and to impress Muslim Africans with the traditional dimension of Islamic Brotherhood.[31]

The attempt by President Nasser to link the Arab world to Africa was apparent in the first Afro-Asian Solidarity Conference that met in Cairo in December 1957–January 1958, the Afro-Asian Youth Conference that met in Cairo in February 1959, the Afro-Asian Economic Conference in Cairo in April 1960, and the latest Afro-Asian Conference that met in Cairo in March 1961. While an Egyptian Free Officer (Yusuf al-Sibai) became the Secretary-General of the Permanent Secretariat of the Afro-Asian Solidarity Council in Cairo, President Nasser announced that Egypt was entering the field of leadership not only in the Arab World, but also in Africa and Asia, on the grounds that there existed a common bond between Arabs and Africans: the struggle against Western imperialism.[32]

The interest and participation of the Egyptian military regime in Afro-Asian Economic Conferences, on the other hand, should be viewed in some respects as the arena in which Egypt seeks to improve its economic and trade relations with emerging African states, and to counteract, or better still evict from the continent, Israeli economic and technical aid. The latter object became quite clear during the Casablanca Conference in early January 1961, where President Nasser sought to extract from the heads of African states attending that conference a reso-

lution denouncing Israel as an "imperialist base." At the second Afro-Asian Economic Conference held in Cairo on April 30, 1960, this aim of President Nasser was made very clear. He said on this occasion

. . . when the Bandung Conference was held all the States that took part in it were keen to see it succeed, so they eliminated all the factors which would impair Afro-Asian solidarity. The Afro-Asian Conference met and all the Afro-Asian states attended with the exception of Israel. The dominant feeling was that Israel was not an Afro-Asian state. Israel had destroyed an Asian people, the people of Palestine, and could not be trusted to work for Afro-Asian solidarity.

Events have proved how true this perception was, for Israel stood at the UN against the aspirations of the Afro-Asian peoples. . . . Israel stood against the independence of Algeria. . . . Israel voted against granting independence to the Cameroons.[33]

With this statement, President Nasser proceeded to cast doubts on the ability of a state that lives on borrowed money, such as Israel, to give technical assistance to Afro-Asian states. His conclusion was that Israel could be nothing more than the spearhead of the imperialists who wish to continue their domination over Africa. He called it "a new form of economic imperialism."

This suggests that Egypt's African policy is an adjunct of President Nasser's nationalism campaign in the Arab world. The points President Nasser may have scored against Israel at Casablanca in January 1961 give added strength to his claim vis-à-vis other Arab rulers to lead the Arab national struggle. It is not reasonable to expect

[31] On the Islamic Congress and its role, see Vatikiotis, *Op cit., American Political Science Review* (Vol. LV, No. 1), March 1961, pp. 103–111.

[32] See *Nasser Speeches, 1959,* pp. 9–13.

[33] See *Nasser Speeches, 1961,* pp. 71–80.

that Egypt aspires to lead a united Africa, especially one based on its "blackness." Her association with such an arrangement would definitely undermine her claims in the Arab world. The more logical hypothesis is that Egypt at present hopes to be recognized as one of the leaders of an African, or Afro-Asian, bloc, by serving as the liaison with the Arab Middle East.

Generally speaking, the Egyptian rulers are faced with serious obstacles to even the latter modest aspirations. One of these is the readiness of rapidly multiplying independent African leaders to accept the allocation of such a status and position to Egypt. The Casablanca Conference has shown that there is no such readiness. Neither have North African leaders, especially Bourguiba, been too anxious to defer to Egypt's primacy in Africa or in the Arab world. It would take more than the promise of a strong and prestigious position in world affairs to convince Nigerians, Ethiopians, and Ghanians to abandon the technical assistance they are receiving from the Arabs' archenemy, Israel, in terms of water works, transport, and communications. Even Somaliland, an Egyptian favorite, has been reported recently to be grumbling about the inadequate economic aid she has received so far from Egypt. Again, the military regime in Egypt is faced with the very practical problem of concrete offerings to buttress its policy of leadership.

It is not unreasonable to argue, therefore, that whereas Egypt may have had an opening advantage in her bid for African leadership, new African leaders are catching up, and the circle of competitors for that leadership is expanding. At the same time, there is no sure way of ascertaining at this time the effectiveness of Egypt's African policy, nor the receptivity of African communities to that policy. The

more independent governments that emerge in Africa in the future, the more limited will be the ability of Egypt's rulers to deal with African "peoples" as such. If one observes the disparity between the aspirations of Egyptian leadership and the national capacity of their subjects to perform, the future does not look very bright.

EGYPT BETWEEN EAST AND WEST

Most writings on international politics use the term "East-West struggle." When these writings refer to the position of states and nations in relation to this struggle, however, they speak of "pro-Western" and "pro-Soviet" states. It is not our purpose here to determine Egypt's political sympathies or allegiance in this struggle. Moreover, the details of Egypt's recent apparently anti-Western attitude and its consequences regarding the further penetration of the Soviet Union into the Middle East have been amply and adequately presented.[34] Here we shall be concerned with certain generalizations and propositions about (1) the reaction of Egypt to the West both as a political force and influence as well as in terms of a cultural-civilizational confrontation, (2) the evolution of an *Egyptian* image regarding Egypt's role and position between East and West as developed through Egyptian writings, and (3) the total effect of the preceding two factors on Egypt's foreign policy.

Egyptian reaction to Western encroachments and impact is not a de-

[34] See especially, Walter Z. Laqueur, *Communism and Nationalism in the Middle East* (New York: Frederick A. Praeger, Inc., 1956) and *The Soviet Union and the Middle East* (New York: Frederick A. Praeger, Inc., 1959); Keith Weelock, *Nasser's New Egypt* (New York: Frederick A. Praeger, Inc., 1960); George Kirk, *Op. cit.;* and Tom Little, *Egypt* (New York: Frederick A. Praeger, Inc., 1958).

354   P. J. VATIKIOTIS

velopment of the last ten years. It has been going on for at least a century and a half. In the late nineteenth century, for instance, Egyptians reacted to the West's imminent domination in rather Islamic terms. The Islamic Community (the *umma*), they argued, had been stagnant, weakened, and made unable to withstand the European onslaught, armed as the latter was with superior knowledge and technical ability. A first requirement was the reform of the Islamic Community from within with a view to uniting it in one strong front against Europe. This, in essence, was the message of the Islamic reformer and agitator, Jamal al-Din al-Afghani, subsequently refined by his Egyptian disciple Muhammad Abdouh.[35] In the twentieth century, Western superiority became synonymous with political domination. With this, the nationalist movement and its ultimate goal of independence from European control gathered momentum.

The argument was presented earlier that the Islamization and Arabization of Egypt committed the Egyptian nation to a basically Asian heritage. There was thus a fairly continuous and consistent identification of Egypt with the East. The fact that modern nationalist ideas in the past hundred years were acquired from a mainly Western or European source never constituted clear proof that Egypt had subscribed to any kind of Western heritage. Mixed rather vaguely in this dichotomy between East and West is also the Egyptian's recollection of the sharpened cultural-religious antagonism between Muslim Arabs and the West, especially during the time of the Crusades. Some Egyptians have identified—perhaps without just cause—this antagonism

with a historical European dislike for the "Saracens." On this basis, they tend to equate European colonialism with racial hatred.[36]

Where contemporary Egyptians (mobilized as they now are by a forceful military regime) are concerned, the enemy has always come from the West. "The Middle East, Mr. Dulles, knows his enemies. They are not from the Eastern Bloc, but from Britain, France, and Israel—all allies of the United States in the West and the Atlantic—the knights of the October 1956 plot [against Egypt]." The same writer, a member of the original Free Officers conspiracy in Egypt, emphasized the Western origin of Egypt's enemies when he quoted the verses from "On the Banks of the Canal":

O brother in the East
In India, China, Malay, Ceylon, Afghanistan, Iran, and Pakistan
I write you these words while sitting on the Banks of the Canal
We have known them O Brother, and you have known them in your hallowed land . . .
Thieves of land and wealth . . .
We have known them in Egypt . . .
And expelled them . . .
We shall teach them to behave in order to render safe the road to you, My Brother. . . .[37]

This appeal by Egypt to the presumably universal experience of European colonialism in Asia was appended to the theory that now that Western imperialism is at bay and retreating, a battle is raging between Eastern culture (*hadara*) and Western civilization (*madaniya*). This battle will continue until the former triumphs over

[35] See Charles C. Adams, *Islam and Modernism in Egypt* (London, 1933) and J. M. Ahmed, *The Intellectual Origins of Egyptian Nationalism* (London, 1960).

[36] See Ahmad Zaki, "Why the West Fears the Arabs," *al-Hilal* (Cairo, January 1957), pp. 41–46.

[37] See Sadat, *Op. cit.,* pp. 224–225.

the latter. In the view of the Egyptian manipulators of mass media for the orientation of their followers at home as well as for securing the allegiance of the Arab world and Africa, the concept of East versus West is not one of geographical but of cultural division. In their political experience, moreover, it entails the recollection of a subjection-domination relationship that must never recur.

To prevent such relationship from recurring, two safeguard devices are required. Egypt and the ex-colonial nations of the East must build up enough strength to defy their old masters. But in order to achieve this capacity for defiance, Egypt must become adept at the techniques which made the West strong. Here is where the proverbial ambivalent attitude of the Egyptian and any other Arab regarding the East-West conflict appears. Before 1955, the Egyptians had to seek these means of strength from the West itself. Soon, however, they became available from the Soviet Bloc, inimical to their traditional enemy. In fact, a leading modern Egyptian historian has asserted that the division in the ranks of the West and the challenge to them from the rising power of the USSR helped Egypt rise in stature in the Middle East and Africa.[38]

It will be recalled that immediately after the Suez Agreement in 1954, commentators on Egypt forecast the smooth sailing of that state towards Western political shores. Very few, however, appreciated the effect of an agreement made by the revolutionary military regime with the "traditional enemy" (Britain) upon a public that had been geared for at least three generations to equate England with the Devil. The unpopularity of the agree-

[38] See Abder Rahman Rafii, "The Future is that of the Arab East," al-Hilal (Cairo, February 1957   ), pp. 6–9.

ment—in spite of the fact that it clearly meant the departure of the last vestiges of British occupation from Egypt—was reflected in the hesitation of the junta to even discuss Western-sponsored defense arrangements for the Middle East. At this juncture, there was still no clear alienation of the Egyptian military regime from its long relationship with the West, especially now that there was a possibility of a relationship between "equals." When the West, however, pressed as it was by the requirements of its containment policy against Communist expansion, sponsored the Baghdad Pact, the alienation of Egypt was to a great extent a reflex action. The devastating effect of the Israeli raid on Gaza in February 1955, so soon after the formation of the Baghdad Pact, upon the Egyptian military establishment, placed the revolutionary regime in a precarious political situation.

In the winter of 1955, the Nasser-led faction of the Free Officers had just emerged victorious from the famous Naguib-Nasser controversy; it had just managed to crush dangerous opposition from the Muslim Brotherhood, but was by no means firmly established in power. Major support for the ruling junta at that time was still confined to the Officer Corps and its army constituency. The Gaza raid reflected the weakness of the Egyptian Army and was apt to cause disaffection and division among its ranks. It was therefore imperative for the junta to seek strengthening of the military establishment, as well as a way to counteract the Iraqi "defection" to the West via the Baghdad Pact.

President Nasser's participation in the Bandung Conference in April 1955 was his first major diplomatic experience, as well as his first time outside the Middle East. His recent frustration with the West was assuaged by the discovery in Bandung that it was possible, with the help of other "Easterners," to extricate Egypt from the Western bond. Nasser's meeting with Chou En Lai, Nehru, and other Asian leaders had a great effect upon him, surpassed only by the popular exuberance of Egypt's masses over their leader's newly-acquired international stature. The chance of holding the Chinese, Soviet, or Indian models of economic development and international conduct as a lever against the West constituted an attractive tactic the Egyptian rulers could use in advancing their position. That President Nasser was willing to take his chances at this game was amply proved by the September 1955 Arms Deal with the Soviet Bloc. To the public this was interpreted as a national victory: it reflected Egypt's freedom to direct its destinies in world affairs. This, indeed, was the "dignity" President Nasser was promising Egyptians all along. ". . . Look, I am not a professional Premier. I am a Premier of a revolution," Nasser is reported to have told an American official. ". . . I shall proclaim to the Egyptian people that you wanted to disparage their grandeur and dignity. We shall all fight until the last drop of our blood. I shall myself fight for the grandeur and dignity of Egypt to the last drop of my blood. . . ." [39]

In its alienation from the West and gravitation towards the Eastern Bloc, the Egyptian junta was encouraged by the famous Soviet Note published on the same day of the opening of the Bandung Conference (April 16, 1955), giving formal notice of the entry of the USSR into the Middle East power conflict. Officially, the Note protested Western defense arrangements in the Middle East, particularly the Baghdad Pact. It also served notice to the West that any future accomodations in the Middle East must take into consideration the interests of the Soviet Union. Insofar as Egypt was concerned, the Note jarred the door slightly open to the subsequent Arms Deal negotiations.

The gradual alienation of Egypt from the West was also motivated by certain considerations that no ruler, especially a virtually dictatorial regime, could afford to ignore. There was pressure on the Egyptian rulers to seek economic and military aid from a major power. Public antagonism to the West was further exacerbated by a leftist-orientated Cairo press as well as by members of the junta itself. Security in such antagonism was anticipated by the realization that Egypt could be in a relatively impressive company—India, China and Indonesia—and by the willingness of the Soviet Union to respond, for obvious reasons, to Egypt's economic and military needs. Total defiance of the West by Egypt held attractive possibilities for her Arab policy. Yet all of these were not mere considerations for successful policy; they were necessary for the success of the Free Officers' bid for leadership.

"My visit to India proved a turning point in my political understanding," explained President Nasser. "I learned and realized that the only wise policy for us would be one of positive neutrality and nonalignment. Coming back home, I found out from the response it had that it is the only possible policy which would get the broadest support from the Arab people." [40] Recognizing

[39] Excerpts of Nasser's famous Alexandria speech on July 26, 1956, reported in *al-Ahram,* 27 July 1956; also quoted in Kirk, *Op. cit.,* pp. 39–40. On the general concern of Egypt's military leaders with their country's "dignity," see Wilton Wynn, *Nasser of Egypt, The Search for Dignity* (Cambridge, Mass.: Arlington Books, 1959).

[40] See R. K. Karanjia, *Arab Dawn* (Bombay, 1958), p. 187.

the beginnings of Big Power rivalry in the Middle East—a result of the weakened British position there and the anticipation that the United States would try to forestall further Soviet penetration into the area—President Nasser's neutralism initially implied a tactic whereby Egypt could disengage itself from the East-West struggle and still further its national interests. It meant another tactic in Egypt's bid for predominance in the Arab world, as well as for domestic political gain.

Neutralism as a national attitude of Egypt was not necessarily invented by the present military regime. It is reasonable to argue that traditionally Egypt has been neutralist, for it is doubtful whether Egyptians viewed the struggles of the powers involved in the first or second World War as their struggles. The Wafd's unilateral abrogation of the 1936 Anglo-Egyptian Treaty in 1951 was somewhat of a precedent, since Egyptian representatives at that time also sought Soviet backing in the United Nations. Nasser's positive neutrality concept, however, does imply significant national aims and desires. Foremost among these are freedom from the superior West, and building up a neutralist collection of Afro-Asian states that would constitute a Third World Force. Coupled with military strength, neutralism can facilitate Egypt's Arab aims in the Middle East. On the international scene, a united front of smaller neutralist states will not permit Big Power summitry to ignore them in problems of war and peace.

Beginning with President Nasser's visit to the United Nations in September 1960, Egyptians have been applauding the fruits of positive neutralism insofar as they contend that their leader now represents the majority of the world: the galaxy of ever-increasing smaller neutralist states. Referring to this group one writer asserted, "The Third Force has actually come to being . . . and it is the strongest of Blocs in the world . . . because it is a Bloc of People that wishes to free itself from imperialism." They contend further that, since they are neutralist, these states are interested in peace, so that peace can be maintained only through neutralism.[41]

One of the ablest students of Egyptian politics has suggested that neutralism in Egypt is not a doctrine as it may be in India, but merely a tactic for the achievement of national aims.[42] Whether or not this view is correct, there is no doubt that Egypt must shut out possible Big Power influence in the Middle East if she is seeking Arab leadership. It is the only way Nasser feels he can pre-empt the Arab world for Egyptian hegemony. "The axis of our Arab struggle is positive neutralism, for East is East and West is West—Kipling was right!" Positive neutralism, Egyptian style, would lead to military strength and ultimately Arab unity.[43]

It does seem that positive neutralism has brought the Egyptian rulers face to face with the issue of Communism in the Middle East. Here one must distinguish between the gradual infiltration of Soviet influence (through economic and military aid as well as trade) into Egypt's international political orientation, and the activity or influence of Communists in Egypt. By coming to the aid of Egypt, the Soviet Union has undoubtedly encouraged as well as justified all types of left-wing

[41] See Ihsan Abdel Quddus, "Abdel Nasser Represents the Majority of the People in the World," *Rose el-Youssef,* September 19, 1960, pp. 3–4.

[42] See Regis Agostini, "Egypte et Inde: deux conception du neutralisme," *Orient* (Vol. 2, No. 6), pp. 73–88.

[43] Sadat, *Op. cit.,* p. 208.

tendencies among Egyptians. This was especially noticeable during 1957 and 1958, when the influx of Soviet and other Communist publications, and cultural and educational missions and programs into Egypt were appealing to the Egyptian public on a grand scale. By the end of 1958 it became apparent, however, that the Free Officers ruling elite in Egypt was loath to permit the emergence of Communist groups in their country with any political potential. Consequently, strong government measures were taken against Communist groups and individuals in Egypt and Syria. The Communist parties in Egypt and Syria are outlawed despite continuing relations between the UAR and such leading communist states as the Soviet Union, China, and Yugoslavia. When communists appeared to be active in Syria and Iraq, President Nasser was forced to declare them enemies of Arab nationalism and unity, i.e., allies of imperialism.[44]

CONCLUSION

President Nasser declared recently

We say that we are in an Arab revolution which established . . . Arab unity and raised the flag of Arab Nationalism. So any person attempting to side-track this revolution must be corrected and any person who steps out of this revolution is an outsider, since he has turned his back on the principles and doctrines for which this nation fought. . . . However, we will realize our goals and we will trample on anybody who stands in our

[44] See Ihsan Abdel Quddus, "ayna yaqif al-hizb al-shuyui" (Where Does the Communist Party Stand), Rose el-Youssef, December 29, 1958, pp. 3 ff. See also a justification of UAR-USSR continued relations in spite of the attacks by President Nasser on Arab Communist parties by Ihsan Abdel Quddus in Rose el-Youssef, January 5, 1959, pp. 6–7.

way in this respect. This is our policy, fellow citizens, and neither Imperialism nor the imperialist stooges, American dollars, English Sterling pounds, nor the stooges of Imperialism throughout the Arab world will be able to defeat us. This is true due to the fact that we represent a nation which knows its path and a people which is aware that this strenuous path is the one which will lead to liberty, dignity, and glory.[45]

Egypt's ambitions for power are reflected in the preceding statement. Although she may have lost the first round in her bid for Arab leadership, Egypt continues to consider this possibility a basic aim and objective of her foreign policy. The advantages of this achievement would be immense; suffice it to mention among them the control of oil deposits and oil transport facilities in the area. Political Egyptianization of the Arab world would also mean a more or less immediate solution of Egypt's domestic human and economic problems.

Egypt's freedom of action in foreign policy since 1955 was strengthened by President Nasser and his Free Officers firmly establishing themselves in power with only token checks upon their authority and power. Since 1952, Army Officers in the Arab countries, and especially the Free Officers of Egypt, have become the repository of political power in the Arab world. When the traditional ruling classes were in decline, other emerging forces within the Arab political communities were not developed or organized enough to succeed them in power. The availability and ability of the Army Officer Corps to play this role and perform the function of governing elicited a favorable response from the masses. The latter

[45] See Nasser Speeches, February–March 1961, pp. 13, 27.

in the Arab world came to view this new class of rulers not only as the vanguard of Arab national consciousness, but as the saviors and regenerators of the Arab world.

When one considers the fact that Egypt lies at the meeting point of two continents colonized for a long time by the industrialized West, it is rather natural that Cairo should try to become the vociferous leader of these demands. Lacking anything more concrete to offer to the peoples of these areas, the Free Officers of Egypt would probably lose any of their present influence were they to slacken their foreign policy tactics of promising a New Jerusalem to the Arabs. As representatives of the revolutionary nationalist elite in areas previously dominated by European powers, the Egyptian Free Officers are keenly aware of the political frustrations of other Arabs and other Africans. It is only shrewd, if not feasible in the long run, to see all of these communities as potential allies, if not satellites. Pre-empting the representation of all struggling Africans and Arabs on the basis of a common future is a strategy pregnant with possibilities for the Egyptian military regime.

It is difficult for the Free Officers in Egypt to identify themselves with Black Africa. It is equally difficult for them to identify themselves with white Europe. But it is supremely practical for them to identify themselves with an Arab world, an Afro-Asian world struggling against a common foe: imperialism. The positive content of this struggle is presently vague and its main features uncertain. Its content, perhaps, cannot be known until the outcome—success or failure—of Egypt's bid for leadership and, therefore, its ability to shape this content, is clear.

As we pointed out in the beginning of this essay, Syria's defection is a bad omen for Nasser's efforts to assume the leadership of the Arab world. It raises legitimate doubts about Egypt's ability to forge and lead Arab unity. The forces in the Middle East continue to be explosive and fluid. Nasser's role and his chances of success in the future remain extremely uncertain.

SELECTED BIBLIOGRAPHY

Fabunmi, L. A., *The Sudan in Anglo-Egyptian Relations* (London: Longmans, Green & Co., 1961).

Kirk, George E., *Contemporary Arab Politics* (New York: Frederick A. Praeger, Inc., 1961).

Lacouture, Jean and Simonne, *Egypt in Transition* (London: Methuen & Co., 1958).

Little, Tom, *Egypt* (New York: Frederick A. Praeger, Inc., 1958).

Marlowe, John, *Arab Nationalism and British Imperialism* (New York: Frederick A. Praeger, Inc., 1961).

Nasser, Gamal Abdel, *Egypt's Liberation, Philosophy of the Revolution* (Washington, D.C.: Public Affairs Press, 1955).

St. John, Robert, *The Boss, The Story of Gamal Abdel Nasser* (New York: McGraw-Hill Book Company, Inc., 1960).

Wynn, Wilton C., *Nasser of Egypt: The Search for Dignity* (Cambridge, Mass.: Arlington Books, 1959).

Index